THESAURUS OF
ORCHESTRAL DEVICES

LE SACRIFICE: INTRODUCTION

STRAVINSKY. LE SACRE DU PRINTEMPS

THESAURUS OF ORCHESTRAL DEVICES

By

GARDNER READ

GREENWOOD PRESS, PUBLISHERS
NEW YORK

Reprinted by permission
of the Pitman Publishing Corporation

First Greenwood Reprinting 1969

Library of Congress Catalogue Card Number 69-14045

SBN 8371-1884-0

PRINTED IN UNITED STATES OF AMERICA

TO

ARTHUR COHN and NICOLAS SLONIMSKY

peripatetic encyclopedists and
indefatigable begetters of pandects,
lexicons, and thesauri

FOREWORD

THIS BOOK represents that rare thing in musical scholarship—a "first time anywhere." Musical literature is signally lacking in up-to-date manuals of orchestral practice. Texts that describe the individual instruments are plentiful, of course, but only a few consider in any detail the subtle art of combining instruments. The present volume is unique in that it summarizes and lists illustrations of hundreds of orchestral devices, thereby making it possible as never before for the student to survey the whole field of orchestration. It was a man-sized job, and it took Gardner Read's meticulous and persistent mind, and his composer's intimate knowledge of the orchestra and its potentialities, to carry it out successfully.

No one composer has ever exploited all the possibilities of the modern orchestra. More than any other phase of music, the art of orchestration has depended upon the combined imagination of practising composers everywhere. This *Thesaurus* is a compendium and storehouse of orchestral experience, especially of contemporary writers, as deduced from actual works. With a minimum of text and a maximum of example the author makes it possible for the music student and all others interested in orchestral craft to examine devices, from the most common to the most recondite, that may be found in the published scores of a wide variety of composers. No composer will ever want to use all the effects listed in this book. On the other hand, no composer is so universally adept as not to be able to profit from a perusal of the many illustrations exhibiting the ingenuity and coloristic imaginings of his colleagues.

It is a comment upon the present state of musical achievement in our country that this *Thesaurus of Orchestral Devices* should have been conceived and executed by an American composer and teacher. Both Gardner Read and his publisher deserve our thanks.

AARON COPLAND

NEW YORK,
January, 1953.

vii

PREFACE

ORCHESTRATING IS NOT just arranging music for the orchestra: it is *composing for the instruments*. It is thinking first and foremost in terms of instrumental color, balance, and sonority—inventing a melodic line that finds expression *only*, for example, in the English horn, and in no other instrument; writing a sonority that can be achieved by *no other combination* than muted brass; or weaving an insistent rhythmic *ostinato* that reaches full expressiveness *only* by the muffled tenor drum. Perhaps this is the reason why there are so many merely "good" instrumentators and so few outstanding masters of orchestration.

It must, however, be constantly borne in mind by the orchestrator—the experienced craftsman as well as the novice—that the employment *per se* of such devices as flutter-tonguing in the brass, *glissandi* in the harp, and *col legno* and *sul ponticello* in the strings does not necessarily guarantee colorful, or even effective, orchestration. And certainly the musical value of an orchestral work does not depend primarily on even the most skilful and imaginative use of these or other instrumental devices. Haydn, Mozart, Beethoven, and Brahms—four giants who find comparatively slight representation in this volume—created many fine works for the orchestra without so much as a hint of "effect" or the employment of colorful and unusual instrumental devices.

During the past hundred and fifty years or more, nevertheless, the conception of color, density, clarity, timbre—whatever one chooses to call it—has asserted a persuasive and cumulative influence on the creative orchestrator. All of the instrumental devices catalogued here are therefore perfectly legitimate, and by now even indispensable, ingredients in the orchestrator's tonal palette. Some of them, of course, have been in use for hundreds of years, such as the bow *tremolo* and *pizzicato*, first introduced by Monteverdi about 1624. Others, including most of the harp and percussion effects, are comparatively recent, and still newer devices are yet in the experimental stage—for example, the microphone techniques of radio and film music. It did not lie within the scope of the present volume to include movie, radio, and jazz effects other than those found in serious symphonic scores, nor to delve into the vast literature of chamber music and opera. In compiling any kind of thesaurus one must of necessity draw the line somewhere, and so it seemed advisable to concentrate on symphonic works readily available to the music student and professional musician. Numerous exceptions have been made, however, in the case of well-known operatic excerpts which have become part of the standard orchestral repertoire.

The perceptive orchestrator will observe that the overwhelming majority of the scores referred to in the *Thesaurus* are impressionistic or programmatic in content and style, for most of the orchestral devices listed herein are products of essentially harmonic music, dramatic and romantic in concept—descriptive in effect. The works of the linear composers, Bach to Hindemith, find small representation because the very nature of the music precludes thinking primarily in terms of exotic color and unusual sonority. This is perhaps the best answer possible to those who will look in vain—and with amazement—for extensive quotations from the scores of Hindemith, admittedly one of the creative giants of the twentieth century and an orchestrator without peer.

This *Thesaurus of Orchestral Devices* is intended to be a lexicon of instrumentation which will serve the student and/or professional orchestrator in the same manner and to the same degree that Bartlett's *Familiar Quotations*, Roget's *Thesaurus of English Words*, or Webster's *New International Dictionary* aid both the student of literature and the established writer. As far as is known, no such thesaurus of orchestration has ever before been compiled. It is hoped that the book will meet a very real need among embryo orchestrators and seasoned composers alike, especially since nearly every work quoted is available in a study score edition, generally at an agreeably modest price, and a great many are, of course, commercially recorded. In the interests of practicability, only works published in miniature or study score format (up to January 1, 1951, and made available to the author) are included in the *Thesaurus*. Certain exceptions have been made where a large score is the only one printed, but no manuscript works of any kind have been referred to. The detailed plan used for the presentation of the material quoted in the *Thesaurus* may be found on page 41.

It is regretted that the present scope of the *Thesaurus* did not allow for examples of the instrumental devices found in modern chamber music works, other than those from two notable exceptions: Stravinsky's *Histoire du Soldat* and Schönberg's *Pierrot Lunaire*. The six string quartets of Bartók as well as the complete chamber works of Schönberg and Stravinsky are veritable gold mines for the device-prospecting musician; in fact, they might almost be considered a basic text of modern string technique, at least so far as the various uses of *sul ponticello*, *sul tasto*, *col legno*, *glissandi*, and *pizzicati* effects are concerned. The adventurous and ambitious student of orchestration is strongly urged to make these works as integral a part of his score library as *Symphonie Fantastique*, *La Mer*, and *Le Sacre du Printemps*.

No one is more aware of the limitations and unavoidable omissions in the *Thesaurus* than the author himself. When nearly one thousand study scores had to be examined page by page, it was perhaps inevitable that some significant or interesting uses of any of the modern orchestral devices catalogued should be overlooked. Some examples, moreover, were deliberately not listed when it was felt that the device in question had been amply illustrated on certain other pages of the work in hand. If, for instance, every example of the use of bow *tremolo* in the strings had been given, there would literally have been room for nothing else in the book; and all the instances of the use of *détaché* bowing found in scores from Haydn's time to the present would fill a volume twice the size of this one!

Finally, it must be strongly emphasized that the number of times a work is, or is not, quoted from is absolutely no indication of the composition's artistic worth. Many extremely worthwhile scores are sparsely represented in the *Thesaurus* and some obviously meretricious works are quoted from quite extensively; it is entirely a matter of how much each makes use of and clearly illustrates the *technical* devices with which this book is primarily concerned. It is no part of the purpose of the *Thesaurus* to make an aesthetic or purely musical evaluation of the devices used in scores from the past to the present. Every musician would do well to remember

PREFACE

that the art of orchestration, like all Art, does not depend upon technique alone, no matter how brilliant this may be. But when technique and expression and musical content are inextricably joined and interwoven, musical creation, of which instrumentation is but one important facet, becomes valid and enduring.

G. R.

BOSTON, MASSACHUSETTS,
   January, 1953

ACKNOWLEDGMENTS

W ITHOUT THE SUPPORT and generous cooperation of the music publishers the compilation of such a volume as the *Thesaurus of Orchestral Devices* could not have been accomplished. The following publishers are deserving of much more than the conventional word of thanks and have, as they know, the author's deepest gratitude and appreciation—

Karl F. Bauer of Associated Music Publishers, Inc.; Maurice Baron of M. Baron Co.; Betty Randolph Bean and the late Ralph Hawkes of Boosey and Hawkes, Inc.; Alexander Broude of Broude Brothers; Ralph Satz of Chappell and Co., Inc.; Quinto Maganini of Edition Musicus —New York; Henri Elkan of Elkan-Vogel Co.; Joseph Fischer of J. Fischer & Bro.; Edwin F. Kalmus; Guy Freeman of Leeds Music Corp.; Felix Greissle of E. B. Marks Music Corp.; Milton Feist of Mercury Music Corp.; Lyle Dowling of Oxford University Press, Inc.; Walter Hinrichsen of C. F. Peters Corp.; Arthur Paffrath of Salabert, Inc.; Benjamin Grasso of G. Schirmer, Inc.; and Ray Green, who as executive secretary of the American Music Center made available the New Music and Arrow Music Press editions. The following publishing houses also generously donated their score publications to the author: C. C. Birchard Co.; Bomart Publishing Co.; Composers Press, Inc.; Carl Fischer, Inc.; Mills Music, Inc.; Novello and Co., Ltd.; Pro Art Publications; Robbins Music Corp.; Southern Music Publishing Co., Inc.; and Weintraub Music Co.

Kindest thanks are likewise due to Karl and Irene Geiringer, Dika Newlin, and Klaus G. Roy for their invaluable aid in compiling the extensive lists of foreign terminology; to Carlton Gamer, Richard Mann, and Vincent Trunfio for long hours spent double-checking spellings and page and measure numberings; to my wife for patiently helping to correct proofs, and to Nicolas Slonimsky, who scrutinized the book with an eagle's eye for errors and omissions.

Finally, very special appreciation must be extended to Dr. Philip James, head of the department of music in the Graduate School of New York University, who as Advisory Editor for the Pitman Books on Music brought the present volume to the publisher's attention, and who has at all times given to his editorial work on the *Thesaurus* unfailing conviction and infectious enthusiasm.

CONTENTS

FOREWORD by Aaron Copland vii

PREFACE ix

ACKNOWLEDGMENTS xiii

PART I

THE INSTRUMENTS OF THE ORCHESTRA

Introduction 4

Chapter 1 Nomenclature of Instruments 6

Chapter 2 Comparative Table of Ranges 11

Chapter 3 Evolution of the Modern Symphony Orchestra 29

PART II

WOODWINDS

Introduction 40

Chapter 4 Extreme or Extended Ranges 43
      (1) Piccolo (2) Flute (3) Oboe (4) English Horn (5) Clarinet (6) Bass Clarinet (7) Bassoon
      (8) Contrabassoon

Chapter 5 Double-tonguing 56

Chapter 6 Triple-tonguing 60

Chapter 7 Flutter-tonguing 63

Chapter 8 Glissandi and Portamenti 68

Chapter 9 Bells Up 72

Chapter 10 Harmonics 74

Chapter 11 Off-stage 75

Chapter 12 Echo-tone 76

Chapter 13 Vibrato 77

Chapter 14 Slap-tongue 78

Chapter 15 Muted 79

Chapter 16 Miscellaneous Effects 80

Chapter 17 Woodwind Terminology 83

CONTENTS

PART III

BRASSES

Introduction 90

Chapter 18 Extreme or Extended Ranges 92
    (1) Horn (2) Trumpet (3) Trombone (4) Tuba

Chapter 19 Mutes 104
    (1) Mute Types (2) Echo Sounds (3) Hand in bell (4) Hat over bell (5) In stand (6) Other indications

Chapter 20 Stopped or Brassy Tones. 112
    (1) Stopped (2) + (3) Stopped — + (4) Muted—brassy (5) Muted — + (6) Open—brassy (7) Open — + (8) Hand in bell (9) Half-stopped (10) Other indications (11) Stopped and Open Combined

Chapter 21 Stopped-Open (+ — o) 122

Chapter 22 Open-Stopped (o — +) 125

Chapter 23 Triple-tonguing 128

Chapter 24 Flutter-tonguing 130

Chapter 25 Trills and Tremoli 133

Chapter 26 Glissandi 137

Chapter 27 Bells Up 141

Chapter 28 Off-stage 144

Chapter 29 Jazz Effects 146
    (1) Flare (2) Growl (3) Lip slur (4) Rip (5) Smear (6) Vibrato (7) Wah-wah (8) Wow

Chapter 30 Miscellaneous Effects 149

Chapter 31 Brass Terminology 152

PART IV

PERCUSSION

Introduction 158

Chapter 32 Timpani 159
    (1) Extended Range (2) Chords [Intervals] (3) Dampened (4) Methods of Striking (5) Muffled (6) Pedal Glissandi (7) Stick Types (8) 2-Timpani Roll (9) With 2 Sticks (10) Other Effects

Chapter 33 Bells, Glockenspiel, Marimba, Vibraphone, and Xylophone . . 173
    (1) Glissandi (2) Muffled (3) Off-stage (4) Stick Types (5) Tremolandi (6) Other Effects

CONTENTS

Chapter 34 Cymbals (Pair and Suspended) 180
    (1) Dampened (2) Methods of Striking (3) Stick Types (4) Other Effects

Chapter 35 Bass, Snare, and Tenor Drums 196
    (1) Dampened (2) Methods of Striking (3) Muffled (4) Off-stage (5) Stick Types (6) Without snares (7) Other Effects

Chapter 36 Gong, Tambourine, and Triangle 213
    (1) Dampened (2) Methods of Striking (3) Muffled [Muted] (4) Off-stage (5) Stick Types (6) Other Effects

Chapter 37 Other Percussion Instruments 221
    (1) Methods of Playing or Striking (2)) Muffled [Muted] (3) Off-stage (4) Stick Types (5) Other Effects (6) Other Keyed Percussion Instruments (7) Other Pitched Percussion Instruments (8) Other Unpitched Percussion Instruments

Chapter 38 Percussion Terminology 232

PART V

KEYBOARD INSTRUMENTS

Introduction 237

Chapter 39 Celesta, Organ, and Piano 238
    (1) Glissandi (2) Tone-clusters (3) Tremolandi (4) Other Effects

PART VI

HARP

Introduction 250

Chapter 40 Glissandi 251
    (1) In one hand (2) In two hands (3) Chord—one hand (4) Chord—two hands (5) Combinations

Chapter 41 Harmonics 257
    (1) Single—either hand (2) Double (3) Triple (4) Quadruple (5) Combinations—two hands

Chapter 42 Homonyms (Enharmonics) 262
    (1) In one hand (2) In two hands

Chapter 43 Non-arpeggiato 264

Chapter 44 "Près de la table" 266

Chapter 45 "Sons étouffés" 268

Chapter 46 Tremolandi and Trills 269

Chapter 47 Miscellaneous Effects 271

Chapter 48 Harp Terminology 273

xvii

CONTENTS

PART VII
STRINGS

Introduction 278

Chapter 49 Bowing 283
(1) Détaché (2) Legato (3) Marcato and Martelé (4) Spiccato and Staccato (5) Saltando
(6) Strike with bow (7) Au talon (8) Punta d'arco (9) Full bow (10) Middle of the bow
(11) Reverse Bowing (12) Successive Down-bows (13) Successive Up-bows

Chapter 50 Pizzicati 322
(1) Arpeggiato (2) Chords (3) Glissando (4) Left-hand (5) Nail (6) On Harmonics
(7) "Slap" (8) "Snap" (9) Thumb (10) Tremolando (11) Vibrato (12) With 2 fingers
(13) Pizzicati and Non-pizzicati Combined

Chapter 51 Tremoli 347
(1) Bow (2) Finger (3) Bow-Finger (détaché trill or interval) (4) Glissando (5) Measured
(6) On Harmonics (7) Bow and Finger Combined (8) Tremoli and Non-tremoli Combined

Chapter 52 Col Legno 372
(1) Glissando (2) On Harmonics (3) Tremolo (4) Non-tremolo (5) Col Legno and Pizzicato
Combined (6) Col Legno and Modo Ordinario (arco) Combined

Chapter 53 Sul Ponticello 381
(1) Back of bridge (2) Glissando (3) On Harmonics (4) Pizzicato (5) Tremolo (6) Non-
tremolo (7) Sul Ponticello and Col Legno Combined (8) Sul Ponticello and Modo Ordinario
Combined

Chapter 54 Sul Tasto 394
(1) Glissando (2) On Harmonics (3) Pizzicato (4) Tremolo (5) Non-tremolo (6) Sul Tasto
and Sul Ponticello Combined

Chapter 55 Mutes 403
(1) Muted and Open Combined (2) Mutes on gradually (3) Mutes off gradually

Chapter 56 Natural Harmonics. 408

Chapter 57 Artificial Harmonics 441

Chapter 58 Multiple Divisi 455
(1) Divisi a 3 (2) Divisi a 4 (3) Divisi a 5 (4) Divisi a 6 (5) Divisi a 7 (6) Divisi a 8 (7) Divisi
a 9 (8) Divisi a 10 (9) Divisi a 11 (10) Divisi a 12

Chapter 59 Solo Parts 477

Chapter 60 Soli Parts 491

Chapter 61 Chord Notation 532

Chapter 62 Double-stopped Unisons 537

Chapter 63 Glissandi and Portamenti. 542
(1) Ordinary Glissando (2) Slow or Measured Glissando (3) In Harmonics (4) To a Harmonic
(5) Other Indications

Chapter 64 Off-stage 554

CONTENTS

Chapter 65 Open Strings 555

Chapter 66 Specific Strings 559

Chapter 67 Reverse Arpeggio 572

Chapter 68 Scordatura (Unusual Tuning) 573
    (1) Violin—I or II (2) Viola (3) Violoncello (4) Bass—Classical and Early Romantic Orchestra (5) Bass—Modern Orchestra

Chapter 69 Senza Vibrato 576

Chapter 70 Miscellaneous Effects 578

Chapter 71 String Terminology 581

LIST OF PUBLISHERS 583

LIST OF COMPOSERS AND WORKS 587

INDEX OF ABBREVIATIONS 601

INDEX OF NOTATION 605

INDEX OF NUMERALS 609

INDEX OF NOMENCLATURE AND TERMINOLOGY 611

ILLUSTRATIONS OF SCORES

STRAVINSKY: *Le Sacre du Printemps* . . . . *Frontispiece*

RIMSKY-KORSAKOFF: *Scheherazade* 2

MAHLER: *Symphony No. 4* 36

BRITTEN: *Sinfonia da Requiem* 38

STRAUSS: *Don Quixote* 86

SCHÖNBERG: *Fünf Orchesterstücke* 88

BARTÓK: *Violin Concerto* 154

MILHAUD: *Les Choéphores (IV. Présages)* 156

DEBUSSY: *La Mer* 246

RAVEL: *Rapsodie Espagnole* 248

BARTÓK: *Dance Suite* 276

PART I

The Instruments of the Orchestra

RIMSKY-KORSAKOFF. SCHEHERAZADE

2

3

INTRODUCTION

NOTHING SEEMS TO DATE more quickly than an orchestration text-book. New instruments are added to the symphony orchestra, others become obsolete, ranges are extended, techniques improved and expanded—and one more tome on instrumentation becomes itself outmoded. It is a regrettable fact that at this time there is not in existence a single completely thorough, reliable, or up-to-date text on even the basic technique of orchestration, including the correct ranges for the standard instruments. Such volumes as the Berlioz-Strauss *Treatise on Instrumentation* and Rimsky-Korsakoff's *Principles of Orchestration* have historical interest and significance, but are assuredly not adequate as methods of scoring for the modern orchestra. And certain more recent books, such as that of Schillinger, are not only full of popular (but erroneous) clichés and such informative gems as [sic] "There is an unwritten international code of ethics by which composers limit themselves to the written 'g' of the second octave [for clarinet]," but they also still largely indicate the restricted ranges of the eighteenth-nineteenth-century orchestra. We must await with patience the appearance of Arthur Cohn's monumental *Art and Science of Orchestration*, which gives promise of being the *ne plus ultra* in instrumentation treatises.

To show the orchestration student in particular how much standard texts on the subject disagree in the simple matter of ranges alone, a Comparative Table of Ranges has been compiled from sixteen well-known orchestration books, new and old. These are arranged not alphabetically but in order of date of first publication, so that the chronological expansion of the instrumental ranges may be better observed. The Table is completed with what is hoped is the final word (as of 1951) on ranges for the standard orchestral instruments: first, for the professional, major symphonic orchestra; and second, for the non-professional or semi-amateur group. After all, it is one thing to score a work for possible performance by the Boston Symphony Orchestra or the New York Philharmonic-Symphony, and quite another for a high school or college orchestra. The sooner the young orchestrator learns this simple and incontrovertible fact the sooner is his work likely to be performed.

Preceding the Table of Ranges will be found the customary Nomenclature of the orchestral instruments. For the sake of completeness all the names commonly used for each instrument have been given in the four basic score languages—English, Italian, French, and German. Beneath most of the instrumental names are the conventional abbreviations as used in printed scores. It will be seen, however, that apparently composers and publishers do not always agree with each other as to the proper abbreviations, and that as yet there exists no standardized procedure in this respect.

Finally, there is given a chart showing the evolution of the modern symphonic orchestra so far as general balance, number, and make-up of the instruments are concerned. Beginning with the *Festmesse* of the early Venetian composer, Benevoli, composed in 1621, and ending

4

INTRODUCTION

with Béla Bartók's *Concerto for Orchestra* of 1943, one can observe how the gradual trend during some three hundred years to the immense, often unwieldy orchestral apparatus of Mahler, Strauss, and early Schönberg has in the past few decades taken the opposite direction. Brought about by economic necessity, the tendency today is to score a work for a more modest and practicable instrumental aggregation, and to achieve maximum orchestral effect with minimum means—not altogether an undesirable goal or achievement! The works quoted in this chart were chosen as being the most representative both of the composer and of his time. They do *not* illustrate the first time certain instruments or combinations were added to the make-up of the orchestra. One may easily quarrel, of course, with the present selection—as with any such illustrative plan—but it is believed that the point is made with the chosen works, and that should be sufficient.

Chapter I

NOMENCLATURE OF INSTRUMENTS

(in order of appearance in the score)

English	Italian Partitura	French Partition	German Partitur

I. WOODWINDS

English	Italian Partitura	French Partition	German Partitur
Winds [Wind instruments]	Strumenti a fiato [Strumenti di vento]	Instruments à vent	Bläser [Blasinstrumente]
Woodwinds	Strumenti di legno	Bois	Holzbläser
Piccolo *Pic., Picc.*	Flauto piccolo *Fl. picc., Fl. p., Picc.*	Petite Flûte *P^{te} Fl., P.F.*	Kleine Flöte *kl. Fl.*
Small Flute *Sm. Fl.*	Ottavino *Otta., Ott.*		
Flute(s) *Fls., Fl.*	Flauto(i) *Fl.*	Grande(s) Flûte(s) *G^{des} Fl., Fl.*	Grosse Flöte(n) *gr. Fl., Fl.*
Alto Flute *Alto Fl.*	Flauto contralto *Fl. c'alto.*	Flûte Alto *Fl. Alto*	Altflöte *Altfl.*
Flute in G *Fl. in G, G Fl.*	Flauto in Sol *Fl. in Sol* Flautone *Fltne.*	Flûte en Sol *Fl. en Sol*	
Bass Flute *Bs. Fl.*	Flauto basso *Fl. basso; Fl.b.*	Flûte Basse *Fl. Basse, Fl. b.*	Bassflöte *Bassfl.*
Oboe(s) *Obs., Ob.*	Oboe(i) *Ob.*	Hautbois *Hautb., H^{th}, Hb.*	Hoboe(n) *Hob., Hb.* Oboe(n) *Ob.*
English Horn *Engl. Horn, Eng. Hn., Engl. H.,* *E. Hrn., E.H.*	Corno inglese *Cor. ingl., Cor igl., C. ingl.,* *C. Ing., C.I.* Oboe contralto *Ob. c'alto*	Cor Anglais *Cor Ang., C. Angl., Cor A.,* *C. An., Cg.*	Englisch(es) Horn *Engl. Hr., Englh.* Althoboe *Ahb.*
Oboe d'amore *Ob. d'amore*	Oboe d'amore *Ob. d'amore*	Hautbois d'amour *Htb. d'amour*	Oboe d'amore *Ob. d'amore*
Bass Oboe *Bs. Ob.*			Heckelphon *Heckelph., Heck*
E♭ [D] Clarinet *E♭ [D]Cl., Cl. in E♭ [D]*	Clarinetto piccolo in Mi♭ [Re] *Cl. picc., Cl. pc.. Cl. p., Cl. in* *Mi♭ [Re], Cl. (Mi♭, Re)*	Petite Clarinette en Mi♭ [Ré] *P^{te} Cl.*	K[C]larinette in Es [D] *Kl. in Es[D], Es-Kl., D-Klar.*
Clarinet(s) *Clarts., Clars., Clts., Cls., Cl.*	Clarinetto(i) *Clar., Cl.*	Clarinette(s) *Clar., Cl.*	K[C]larinette(n) *Klar., Kl.*
Bass Clarinet *Bass Clar., Bass Cl., Bs. Clar.,* *Bs. Cl., B. Clt.*	Clarinetto basso *Clar. basso, Clar. B., Cl. b'o.,* *Cl. b.* Clarone	Clarinette Basse *Cl. Basse, Clar. B., Cl. B.*	Bassk[c]larinette *Bassklar., B.-Kl.*
Saxophone(s) *Sax.*	Sassofone(i) *Sassaf.*	Saxophone(s) *Sax.*	Saxophon(e) *Sax.*
Bassoon(s) *Bssns., B'ss'n., Bsns., Bns., Bn.*	Fagotto(i) *Fag., Fg.*	Basson(s) *B^{ons}, Bns.*	Fagott(e) *Fag., Fg.*

6

NOMENCLATURE OF INSTRUMENTS

English	Italian	French	German
Contrabassoon *Con. Bssn., Cbssn., C.-Bsn.,* *C. B'ss'n., C. B'ssoon., C.* *Bn.* Double Bassoon *D. Bssn., D. Bn., Dbn.*	Contrafagotto *Cont. F., C.-Fag., C. Fg., Cfg.,* *C. F.*	Contrebasson *C^{tre} B^{on}, C. B^{on}, Cbn.*	K[C]ontrafagott *Kontrafag., K.-Fag., Kfg.*
Sarrusophone *Sarr.*	Sarrusofone *Sarr.*	Sarrusophone *Sarr.*	Sarrusophon *Sarr.*

II. BRASSES

English	Italian	French	German
Brasses [Brass]	Ottoni [Strumente d'ottone; strum- enti di metallo]	Cuivres	Blechbläser [Blechinstrumente]
Horn(s) *Hrns., Hns., Hn., Hs.*	Corno(i) *Cor., Cr.*	Cor(s)	Horn (Hörner) *Hrn., Hr., H.*
Trumpet(s) *Trpts., Tpts., Trp., Tps., Tpt.*	Tromba(e) *Trb., Tbe., Tr., Tb.* Clarino	Trompette(s) *Tpttes., Tromp., Trp.*	Trompete(n) *Tromp., Trmp., Trpt., Trp., Tr*
Cornet(s) *Cors., Cnts.*	Cornetto(i) a pistoni *Cnti., C. a p., Cor. a p.*	Cornet(s)-à-pistons *C. à p.* Piston(s) *Pns.*	Cornett(e) *Cor.* Pistons *Pist.*
Bass Trumpet *Bs. Trpt.*	Tromba bassa *Trb. bassa*	Trompette Basse *Tr. Basse, Tr. b.*	Basstrompete *Basstrp.*
(Tenor) Trombone *T.-bones., Trombs., Trbns.,* *T.Trb., Tbe.*	Trombone(i) tenore (i) *Tmboni., Trbni., Trbn., Tbni.,* *Trni., Trb., T.-ni., Tr.*	Trombone(s) *Tromb., Tbnes., Trb.*	(Tenor)posaune(n) *T.-Pos., Tenp., Pos.*
Bass Trombone *Bs. Trbn., Bs. Tbn., B. Trb.*	Trombone basso *Trbn. b.*	Trombone Basse *Trb. b.*	Bassposaune *Bassp., B.-Pos.*
Tenor Tuba *Ten. Tb.*	Tuba tenore *Tb. ten.*	Ténor Tuba *Tén. Tb.*	Tenortuba *Tentb.*
(Bass) Tuba *Bs. Tb., Tb.*	Tuba (bassa) *Tb. B., Tba., Tb.*	Tuba (Basse) *Tb.*	(Bass)tuba *Btb., BT.*

III. PERCUSSION

English	Italian	French	German
Percussion [Battery]	Percussione [Batteria; Strumenti a percossa]	Batterie	Schlagzeug [Schlaginstrumente]
Timpani *Timp., Tp.* Timpany[1] Tympany[1] *Tymp.* Kettle Drums *K. Drum, K. Drs., K.D.*	Timpani *Timp., Tp.*	Timbales *Timb., Tbles.*	Pauken *Pauke., Pk.*
Bass Drum *Bs. dr., B. Dr., B. D.*	Gran cassa *Gr. C., G. C., Ca.* Tamburo grosso Tamburo grande *Tamb. gr., Tmb. gr.*	Grosse Caisse *Gr., C^{se}, Gr. C., G.C.*	Grosse Trommel *gr. Tr., G. Tr.*
Military Drum *Mil. dr.* Snare Drum *Sn. dr., S. D.* Side Drum *Side dr., S. D.*	Tamburo (militare) *T'buro mil., Tamb., Tmb.,* *T. M.*	Tambour (militaire) *Tamb.* Caisse claire *Caisse, C^{sse}. cl., C. C^{lre}, C. cl.*	Kleine Militärtrommel *kl. Mtr.* Kleine Trommel *kl. Tr.*

[1] Erroneous spelling

THE INSTRUMENTS OF THE ORCHESTRA

English	Italian	French	German
Small Side Drum	Tamburo piccolo	Petite caisse claire	
Small S. D.	*Tamb. picc.*	*P^te c^sse cl.*	
Trap Drum		Petit tambour	
		P^te tamb.	
		Tarolle	
Tenor Drum	Tamburo rullante	Caisse roulante	Rührtrommel
Ten. dr., T. D.	*Tamb. r., Tmb. r.*	*Caisse R., C^se roul., C. r.*	*R. Tr.*
Parade Drum	Cassa rullante		
Par. dr.	*C. r.*		
Tabor	Tamburo	Tambourin de Provence	Tambourin
Tab.	*Tamb.*	*T. de P., T. p.*	*Tamb.*
Field Drum		Tambourin Provençal	
Field dr.		*Tamb. P.*	
Long Drum			
Cymbals	Piatti (a due; a 2)	Cymbales (libres)	Becken
Cymbs., Cym., Cy.	*Piat., Ptti., Pi., P.*	*Cymb.*	*Beck., Bck.*
	Cinelli		Cinellen
	Cin.		*Cin.*
			Zymbel
			Zymb.
Suspended Cymbal	Piatto (sospeso)	Cymbale (suspendue)	Becken (frei)
S. Cymb., Spd. Cym., S. C.	Piatto oscillante	*Cymb. s.*	Becken freihängend
Hanging Cymbal			Becken freischwingend
Hung Cymbal			
Cymbal, free			
Turkish crash			
Crash Cymbal	Piatto chinoso	Cymbale Chinoise	Chinesische Zimbel
Chinese Cymbal			
Antique Cymbals	Cimbali antichi	Cymbales antiques	Antike Zimbeln
Ant. Cymbs.	*Cimb. ant.*	*Cymb. ant.*	*Ant. Zimb.*
Finger Cymbals		Crotales	
Fing. cymbs.		*Crot.*	
Gong	Tam-tam	Tam-tam	Tam-tam
G.	*Tamt., Tam., T.-t.*	*T. T.*	*T.-t.*
Tam-tam			
Tam-t., T. T.			
Tambourine	Tamburino	Tambour de Basque	Tamburin
Tamb.	*Tmbrno., Tamb.*	*Tamb. de Basq., Tamb. de B.,*	*Tamb.*
Hand Drum	Tamburello Basco	*T. de B., T.b.*	Schellentrommel
	Tamburo Basco		*Schtr.*
	Tamb. B., Tbr. b.		
Triangle	Triangolo	Triangle	Triangel
Trgl.	*Triang., Trgl.*	*Trg.*	*Trgl.*
Castanets	Castagnette	Castagnettes	Kastagnetten
Casts.	*Cast.*	*Cast.*	*Kast.*
(Tubular) Chimes	Campane	Cloches	Glocken
Bells	*Camp.*	Tubes	*Glock.*
	Campanelle		Glockengeläute
	Cample.		*Glockengl.*
Glockenspiel	Campanelli	Carillon	Glockenspiel
Glock., Glsp., Gl.	*Cmplli.*	*Car.*	*Glocksp., Glsp.*
Chime-Bells	Campanetta	Clochettes	
	Camptta.	Jeu de Timbres	
		J. de T.	
		Timbres	
		Tbres.	
Xylophone	Xy[i]lofono	Xylophone	Xylophon
Xylph., Xyl.	*Xil., Xyl., Xf.*	*Xyloph.*	*Xylph., Xyl.*
	Silofono		Holzharmonika
	Sf.		
	Zilafono		
	Zilf.		

NOMENCLATURE OF INSTRUMENTS

English	*Italian*	*French*	*German*
Vibraphone *Vibraph.* Vibraharp *Vibrahp.*	Vibrafono *Vibraf.*	Vibraphone *Vibraph.*	Vibraphon *Vibraph.*
Marimba	Marimba	Marimba	Marimba
Harp(s) *Hrps., Hps., Hrp., Hp.*	Arpa(e) *Arp., A.*	Harpe(s) *Hrp.*	Harfe(n) *Hrf., Hfe.*

SUPPLEMENTARY LIST OF PERCUSSION INSTRUMENTS

Anvil [Steel Bar, Pipe]	Incudine	Enclume	Amboss
Auto [Taxi] Horn	Corno di automobile	Cor d'auto	Autohorn
Bongos	Bongos	Bongos	Bongos
Chains	Catene	Chaînes	Ketten
Chinese Blocks [Drums]	Ceppi chinosi	Blocs chinois	Chinesische Blocke
Claves	Claves	Claves	Claves
Cowbells	Campanelle di vacca	Grelots	Heerdenglocken
Cowhorn	Corno di vacca	Ranz de [à] vaches	Stierhorn
Dulcimer	Cembalon [Cimbalom]		
Guitar	Chitarra [Guitarre]	Guitare	Gitarre
Harmonica [Mouth Organ]	Armonica	Harmonica	Harmonika [Mundharmonika]
Jew's Harp	Scacciapensieri	Guimbarde	Brummeisen
Jingles	Bubbolo	Timbres	Schelle
Mandoline	Mandolino	Mandoline	Mandoline
Maracas	Marache	Maracas [Boîte à clous]	Maracas
Metal Block	Cassa di metallo	Bloc de métal	Metallkasten
Rasper [Güiro]	Raspe	Râpe	Raspel
Rattle [Ratchet]	Raganella [Sistrum]	Crécelle	Klapper [Knarre; Ratsche]
Sandpaper (blocks)	Ceppi di carta vetro	Blocs à papier de verre	Sandpapierblocke
Siren	Sirena	Sirène	Sirene
Slapstick [Whip]	Frusta	Fouet	Peitsche
Sleighbells	Sonagli	Grelots	Schelle
String Drum [Lion roar]	Rugghio di leone	Tambour à corde	Löwengebrüll
Switches	Verghe(i)	Verges	Rute (Ruthe)
Temple Blocks	—	—	—
Thunder-machine	Macchina di tuono	Machine à tonnerre	Donnermaschine
Thunder-sheet	—	—	—
Wind-machine	Macchina a venti	Machine à vent [Eoliphone]	Windmaschine
Wood Blocks	Casse di legno [Legno]	Blocs de bois [Wood-blocs]	Holzkasten [Holzton; Holztrommel]
Zither	Cytharra	Cithare	Zither

IV. KEYBOARD INSTRUMENTS

Keyboard instruments	Strumenti di tasto	Instruments à clavier	Tasteninstrumente
Celesta *Celes., Cel.*	Celeste *Cel.*	Celesta *Cel.* Glockenspiel à clavier	Celeste *Cel.*

THE INSTRUMENTS OF THE ORCHESTRA

English	*Italian*	*French*	*German*
Harmonium	Harmonium	Harmonium	Harmonium
Harm.	*Harm.*	*Harm.*	*Harm.*
Harpsichord	Clavicembalo [Cembalo]	Clavecin	Kielflügel
Hpsichd.	*Cemb.*	*Clav.*	*Kielfl.*
Organ	Organo	Orgue	Orgel
Org.	*Org.*		
Piano	Pianoforte	Piano	Klavier
Pno., Pn., P.	*Pfte., P.-no., Pf.*		*Klav.*

V. CHORUS—VOICES

Chorus	Coro	Chœur	Chor
Soprano(s)	Soprano(i)	Soprano(i)	Sopran(e)
Sop., S.	*Sop., S.*	*Sop., S.*	*Sopr., Sop., S.*
Alto(s)	Alto(i)	Mezzo-soprano(i)	Alt(e)
Alt., A.	*Alt., A.*	*M.-Sop.*	*A.*
		Contralto(es)	
		Cont., C.	
Tenor(s)	Tenore(i)	Ténor(es)	Tenor (Tenöre)
Ten., T.	*Ten., T.*	*Tén., T.*	*Ten., T.*
Baritone(s)	Baritono(i)	Baritone(s)	Baryton(e)
Bar.	*Bar.*	*Bar.*	*Bar.*
Bass(es)	Basso(i)	Basse(s)	Bass (Bässe)
Bs., B.	*Bs., B.*	*Bs., B.*	*Bs., B.*

VI. STRINGS

Strings	Archi [Strumenti a corde]	Cordes [Instruments à cordes]	Streicher [Saiteninstrumente]
Violin(s) I	Violino(i) I	1ers Violon(s)	I [1.] Violine(n)
Vlns., Vln., Vns., Vls., Vl., V. I.	*Viol., Vni., Vl., V. I*	1ers V^{ons}	*I, 1. Viol., Viol. 1, Vl. 1, 1. Vl.*
1st Violin(s)			Erste Violine(n)
1*st Vln.*			*Erste Viol.*
			1. Geigen
			Geig. I.
Violin(s) II	Violino(i) II	2^{ds} Violon(s)	II [2.] Violine(n)
2nd Violin(s)			Zweite Violine(n)
			2. Geigen
Viola(s)	Viola(e)	Alto(s)	Bratsche(n)
Vlas., Vla., Vas.	*Vle., Vla., Va.*	*Alt.*	*Br.*
Violoncello(s)	Violoncello(i)	Violoncelle(s)	Violoncell(e)
Vcellos., Vcell., Vlos., Vlc., Vcl., Vc.	*V.-Celli, Vcello., Vcllo., Vclli., Vlc., Vcl., Vc.*	*V^{elles}, Vc.*	*Violonc., Vcll., Vlc., Vlc., Vc.*
Cello(s)	'Cello(i)		
C.			
Bass(es)	Contrabasso(i)	Contrebasse(s)	K[C]ontrabass(bässe)
Bs., B.	*C.-bassi, Ctrb., Ctb., Cbi., Cb., C.-B., Bassi*	*C. B.*	*Kontrab., Kbass., Ktb., K.-B., Kb.*
Contra Bass(es)			
Con. Bs., Ctrb., C. B., Cb.	Violone		
Double-bass(es)			
D.-B., Db.			

Chapter 2

COMPARATIVE TABLE OF RANGES

1. BERLIOZ–STRAUSS	*Treatise on Instrumentation* (1882, 1904)	E. F. Kalmus, Inc., New York
2. GEVAERT, FRANÇOIS A.	*A New Treatise on Instrumentation* (1885, 192?)	Lemoine and Co., Paris
3. RIMSKY-KORSAKOFF, NICOLAS	*Principles of Orchestration* (1891)	E. F. Kalmus, Inc., New York
4. HOFFMANN, RICHARD	*Practical Instrumentation* (1893)	Augener and Co., London
5. PROUT, EBENEZER	*The Orchestra: Vol. I, Technique of the Instruments* (1899)	Augener and Co., London
6. KLING, HENRI	*Modern Orchestration and Instrumentation* (1905)	Carl Fischer, Inc., New York
7. WIDOR, CHARLES-MARIE	*The Technique of the Modern Orchestra* (1906)	Joseph Williams, Ltd., London
8. FORSYTH, CECIL	*Orchestration* (1914)	Macmillan Co., New York
9. CARSE, ADAM	*Practical Hints on Orchestration* (1916)	Augener and Co., London
10. JOHNSTONE, ARTHUR EDWARD	*Instruments of the Modern Symphony Orchestra and Band* (1917)	Carl Fischer, Inc., New York
11. HEACOX, ARTHUR E.	*Project Lessons in Orchestration* (1928)	Oliver Ditson Co., Philadelphia
12. ANDERSEN, ARTHUR OLAF	*Practical Orchestration* (1929)	C. C. Birchard Co., Boston
13. JACOB, GORDON	*Orchestral Technique* (1931)	Oxford University Press, London
14. HIND, HAROLD C.	*The Orchestra and its Instruments* (1936)	Hawkes and Son, London
15. SCHILLINGER, JOSEPH	*The Schillinger System of Musical Composition: Book XII, Theory of Orchestration* (1941)	Carl Fischer, Inc., New York
16. GARDNER, MAURICE	*The Orchestrator's Handbook* (1948)	Staff Music Pub. Co., New York

17. DEFINITIVE RANGES:

(*a*) For professional orchestras   (*b*) For non-professional orchestras

11

THE INSTRUMENTS OF THE ORCHESTRA

WOODWINDS

1. Piccolo

No. 1   Nos. 8, 9, 12, 16

Nos. 2, 3   Nos. 6, 7, 10, 11, 13, 14, 15

Nos. 4, 5

No. 17 (*a*)   No. 17 (*b*)

N.B. The *written* range for all instruments is indicated in white notes, i.e.

In the case of transposing instruments, the *sounding* range is given in black notes, i.e.

COMPARATIVE TABLE OF RANGES

2. Flute

Nos. 8, 15

Nos. 3, 4, 6, 16

Nos. 1, 2, 5, 7, 9, 10, 11, 12, 13, 14

No. 17 (a)

No. 17 (b)

3. Alto Flute

Nos. 8, 12

No. 3

Nos. 1, 16

No. 15

Nos. 2, 4, 5, 6, 7, 9, 10, 11, 13, 14. No range given

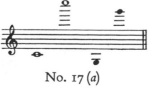

No. 17 (a)

No. 17 (b). Not used

4. Oboe

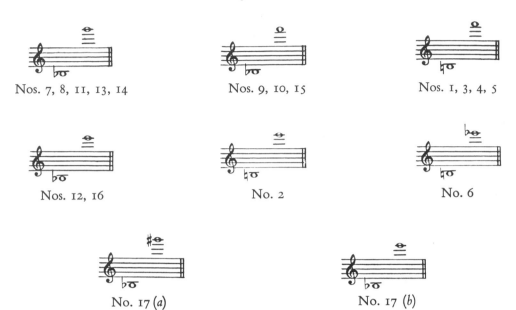

Nos. 7, 8, 11, 13, 14   Nos. 9, 10, 15   Nos. 1, 3, 4, 5

Nos. 12, 16   No. 2   No. 6

No. 17 (a)   No. 17 (b)

5. English Horn

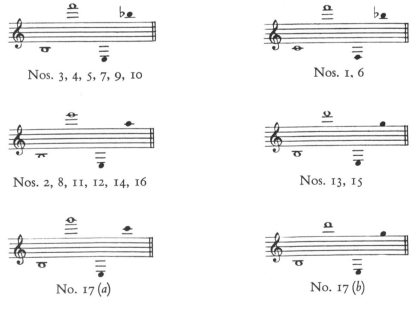

Nos. 3, 4, 5, 7, 9, 10   Nos. 1, 6

Nos. 2, 8, 11, 12, 14, 16   Nos. 13, 15

No. 17 (a)   No. 17 (b)

COMPARATIVE TABLE OF RANGES

6. E-Flat Clarinet

Nos. 1, 2, 4, 8, 12, 16

Nos. 3, 5, 6, 7, 9, 10, 11, 13, 14, 15. No range given

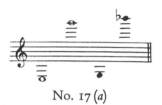

No. 17 (*a*)

No. 17 (*b*). Not used

7. B-Flat and A Clarinet

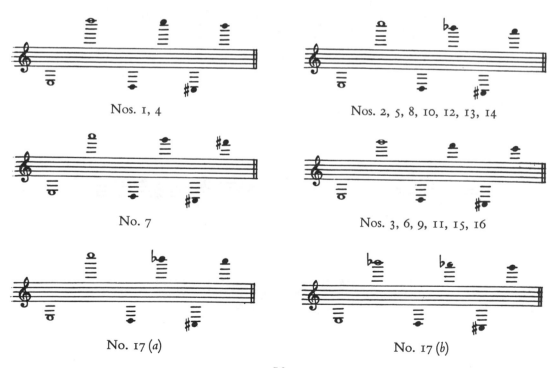

Nos. 1, 4   Nos. 2, 5, 8, 10, 12, 13, 14

No. 7   Nos. 3, 6, 9, 11, 15, 16

No. 17 (*a*)   No. 17 (*b*)

8. Bass Clarinet (B-Flat and A)

Nos. 10, 13

Nos. 1, 2, 4, 5, 6, 8, 9, 11, 12, 14

No. 3

Nos. 7, 16

No. 15. No range given

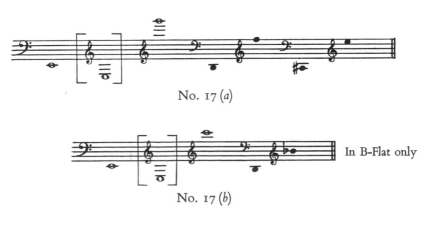

No. 17 (*a*)

In B-Flat only

No. 17 (*b*)

16

COMPARATIVE TABLE OF RANGES

9. Bassoon

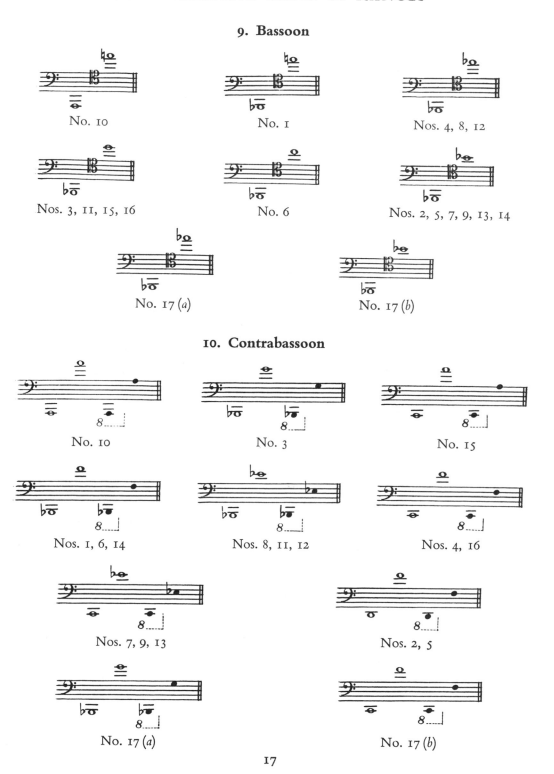

No. 10

No. 1

Nos. 4, 8, 12

Nos. 3, 11, 15, 16

No. 6

Nos. 2, 5, 7, 9, 13, 14

No. 17 (*a*)

No. 17 (*b*)

10. Contrabassoon

No. 10

No. 3

No. 15

Nos. 1, 6, 14

Nos. 8, 11, 12

Nos. 4, 16

Nos. 7, 9, 13

Nos. 2, 5

No. 17 (*a*)

No. 17 (*b*)

17

11. Saxophone

Nos. 7, 9, 10, 11, 12, 16

No. 14

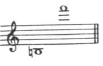

No. 15

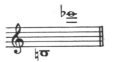

Nos. 2, 5, 6, 8

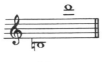

No. 1

No. 4

Nos. 3, 13. No range given

No. 17 (a)

No. 17 (b)

COMPARATIVE TABLE OF RANGES

BRASSES

1. Horn (F)

Nos. 3, 4, 8, 9, 10, 11, 13, 14

Nos. 1, 12

No. 2

Nos. 15, 16

No. 7

No. 5

No. 6

No. 17 (a)

No. 17 (b)

2. Trumpet (C and B-Flat)

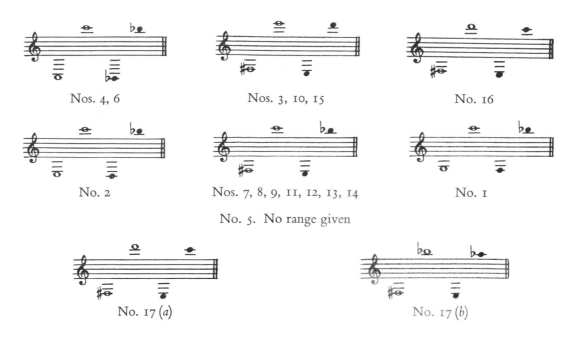

Nos. 4, 6   Nos. 3, 10, 15   No. 16

No. 2   Nos. 7, 8, 9, 11, 12, 13, 14   No. 1

No. 5. No range given

No. 17 (a)   No. 17 (b)

3. Tenor Trombone

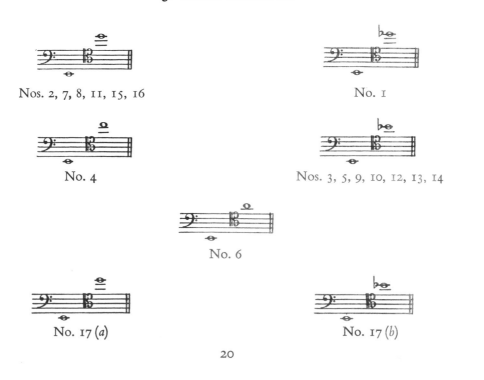

Nos. 2, 7, 8, 11, 15, 16   No. 1

No. 4   Nos. 3, 5, 9, 10, 12, 13, 14

No. 6

No. 17 (a)   No. 17 (b)

COMPARATIVE TABLE OF RANGES

4. Bass Trombone

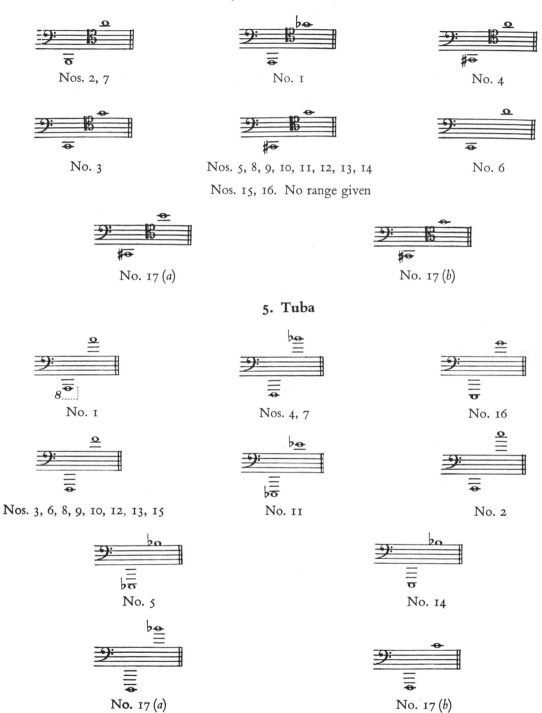

Nos. 2, 7

No. 1

No. 4

No. 3

Nos. 5, 8, 9, 10, 11, 12, 13, 14

Nos. 15, 16. No range given

No. 6

No. 17 (a)

No. 17 (b)

5. Tuba

No. 1

Nos. 4, 7

No. 16

Nos. 3, 6, 8, 9, 10, 12, 13, 15

No. 11

No. 2

No. 5

No. 14

No. 17 (a)

No. 17 (b)

THE INSTRUMENTS OF THE ORCHESTRA

PERCUSSION

1. Timpani

Nos. 12, 14

Nos. 3, 15

Nos. 4, 6, 8

No. 16

Nos. 1, 2, 5, 7, 9, 10, 11, 13

No. 17 (*a*)

No. 17 (*b*)

2. Glockenspiel

No. 15

No. 16

No. 3

Nos. 2, 4, 7, 8, 11, 13, 14

No. 5

No. 12

No. 6

Nos. 1, 9, 10. No range given

No. 17 (*a*)

No. 17 (*b*)

COMPARATIVE TABLE OF RANGES

3. Xylophone

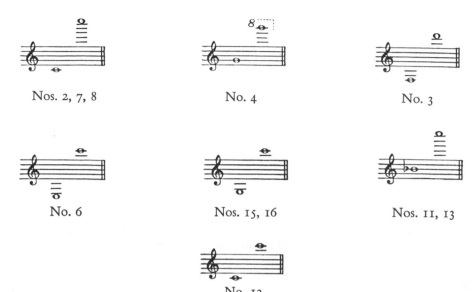

Nos. 2, 7, 8   No. 4   No. 3

No. 6   Nos. 15, 16   Nos. 11, 13

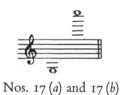

No. 12

Nos. 1, 5, 9, 10, 14. No range given

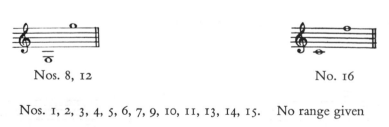

Nos. 17 (*a*) and 17 (*b*)

4. Chimes—Bells

Nos. 8, 12   No. 16

Nos. 1, 2, 3, 4, 5, 6, 7, 9, 10, 11, 13, 14, 15. No range given

No. 17 (*a*)   No. 17 (*b*)

5. Vibraharp

No. 15   No. 16

Nos. 1, 2, 3, 4, 5, 6, 7, 8, 9, 10, 11, 12, 13, 14.   No range given

Nos. 17 (*a*) and 17 (*b*)

6. Celesta

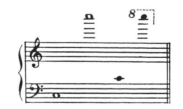

Nos. 2, 3, 7, 8, 10, 12, 13, 14, 15, 16

Nos. 1, 4, 5, 6, 9, 11. No range given

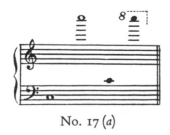

No. 17 (*a*)

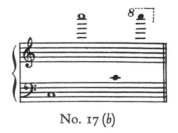

No. 17 (*b*)

7. Harp

No. 8

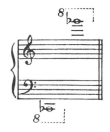

Nos. 4, 7, 9, 10, 11, 12, 13, 14

Nos. 3, 16

Nos. 2, 5

No. 6

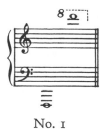

No. 1

No. 15. No range given

No. 17 (a)

No. 17 (b)

STRINGS

1. Violin

No. 9

Nos. 2, 3, 10, 15

No. 8

No. 12

Nos. 4, 5, 11, 14

No. 7

Nos. 1, 6, 13

No. 16

No. 17 (a)

No. 17 (b)

2. Viola

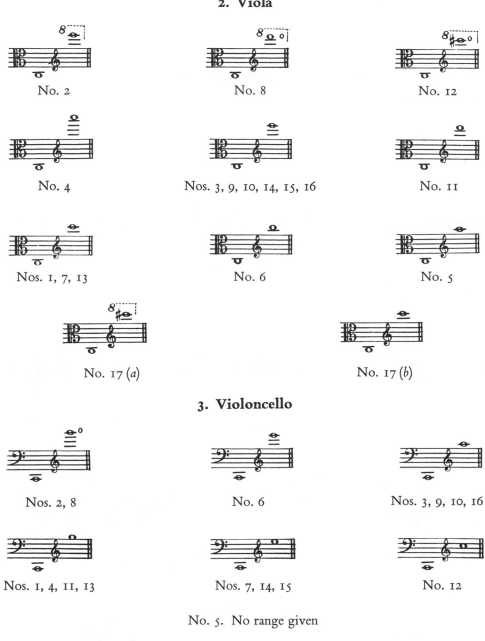

No. 2   No. 8   No. 12

No. 4   Nos. 3, 9, 10, 14, 15, 16   No. 11

Nos. 1, 7, 13   No. 6   No. 5

No. 17 (*a*)   No. 17 (*b*)

3. Violoncello

Nos. 2, 8   No. 6   Nos. 3, 9, 10, 16

Nos. 1, 4, 11, 13   Nos. 7, 14, 15   No. 12

No. 5. No range given

No. 17 (*a*)   No. 17 (*b*)

4. Bass

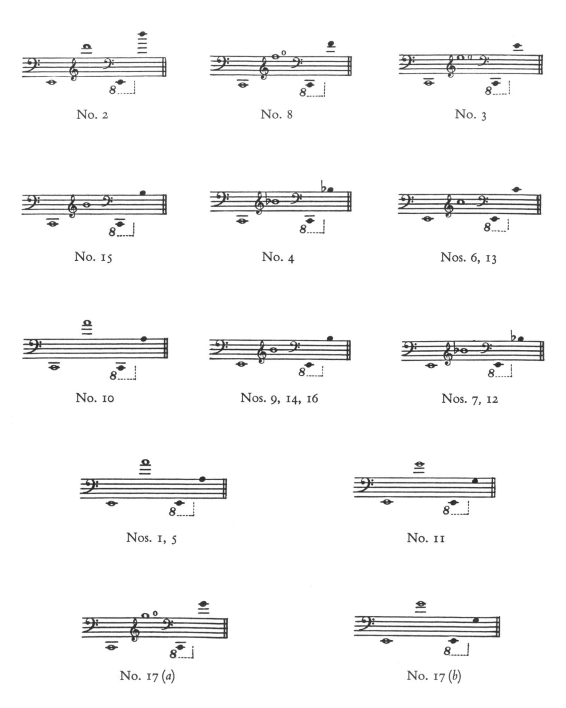

No. 2   No. 8   No. 3

No. 15   No. 4   Nos. 6, 13

No. 10   Nos. 9, 14, 16   Nos. 7, 12

Nos. 1, 5   No. 11

No. 17 (a)   No. 17 (b)

Chapter 3

EVOLUTION OF THE MODERN SYMPHONY ORCHESTRA

	BENEVOLI *Festmesse* (1628)	J. S. BACH *Suite (Overture) No. 4* *in D major* (1729-?)	MOZART *Symphony No. 41 in* *C major, "Jupiter"* (1788)	HAYDN *Symphony No. 2 in* *D major, "London"* (1795)
Woodwind	4 Flutes 2 Oboes	3 Oboes 1 Bassoon	1 Flute 2 Oboes 2 Bassoons	2 Flutes 2 Oboes 2 Clarinets 2 Bassoons
Brass	2 Clarini (high trumpets) 2 Cornetti 8 Trumpets 3 Trombones	3 Trumpets	2 Horns 2 Trumpets	2 Horns 2 Trumpets
Percussion	2 Timpani 2 Organs	2 Timpani	2 Timpani	2 Timpani
Strings	4 Violins 8 Violas	Violin I, II Viola Bass	Violin I, II Viola Violoncello Bass	Violin I, II Viola Violoncello Bass
Extra	Basso continuo Two 8-Part Choruses	Continuo (Cembalo)		

THE INSTRUMENTS OF THE ORCHESTRA

	BEETHOVEN *Symphony No. 9 in D minor* (1823)	SCHUBERT *Symphony No. 7 in C major* (1828)	BERLIOZ *Symphonie Fantastique* (1830)	LISZT *Eine Faust-Symphonie* (1857)
Woodwind	1 Piccolo 2 Flutes 2 Oboes 2 Clarinets 2 Bassoons 1 Contrabassoon	2 Flutes 2 Oboes 2 Clarinets 2 Bassoons	2 Flutes (2nd Fl. alt. Piccolo) 2 Oboes (2nd Ob. alt. English horn) 2 Clarinets 4 Bassoons	3 Flutes (3rd Fl. alt. Piccolo) 2 Oboes 2 Clarinets 2 Bassoons
Brass	4 Horns 2 Trumpets 3 Trombones	2 Horns 2 Trumpets 3 Trombones	4 Horns 2 Cornets 2 Trumpets 3 Trombones 2 Tubas	4 Horns 3 Trumpets 3 Trombones 1 Tuba
Percussion	2 Timpani Bass drum Cymbals Triangle	2 Timpani	4 Timpani (2 players) Bass drum Cymbals 2 Harps	2 Timpani Cymbals Triangle Harp
Strings	Violin I, II Viola Violoncello Bass	Violin I, II Viola Violoncello Bass	Violin I (15) Violin II (15) Viola (10) Violoncello (11) Bass (9)	Violin I, II Viola Violoncello Bass
Extra	Chorus: S.A.T.B. Solo Quartet			Male Chorus Tenor solo

EVOLUTION OF THE MODERN SYMPHONY ORCHESTRA

	WAGNER *"Götterdämmerung"* (1872)	BRAHMS *Symphony No. 4 in E minor* (1885)	RIMSKY-KORSAKOFF *Scheherazade* (1888)	BRUCKNER *Symphony No. 9 in D minor* (1894)
Woodwind	1 Piccolo 3 Flutes 3 Oboes 1 English horn 3 Clarinets 1 Bass clarinet 3 Bassoons	2 Flutes (2nd Fl. alt. Piccolo) 2 Oboes 2 Clarinets 2 Bassoons 1 Contrabassoon	1 Piccolo 2 Flutes 2 Oboes (2nd Ob. alt. English horn) 2 Clarinets 2 Bassoons	3 Flutes (3rd Fl. alt. Piccolo) 3 Oboes 3 Clarinets 2 Bassoons 1 Contrabassoon
Brass	8 Horns 3 Trumpets 1 Bass trumpet 3 Trombones 1 Contrabass trombone 2 Tenor tubas 2 Bass tubas 1 Contrabass tuba	4 Horns 2 Trumpets 3 Trombones	4 Horns 2 Trumpets 3 Trombones 1 Tuba	8 Horns (5th–8th Hns. alt. 4 Tubas) 3 Trumpets 3 Trombones 1 Tuba
Percussion	4 Timpani Cymbals Tenor drum Triangle Bells 6 Harps	3 Timpani Triangle	2 Timpani Bass drum Snare drum Cymbals Triangle Tambourine Gong Harp	3 Timpani
Strings	Violin I (16) Violin II (16) Viola (12) Violoncello (12) Bass (8)	Violin I, II Viola Violoncello Bass	Violin I, II Viola Violoncello Bass	Violin I, II Viola Violoncello Bass
Extra	13 Solo Voices			

THE INSTRUMENTS OF THE ORCHESTRA

	SCHÖNBERG *Gurre-Lieder* (1901)	DEBUSSY *La Mer* (1905)	MAHLER *Symphony No. 8 in E♭ major* (1906)	RAVEL *Daphnis et Chloé, Suites Nos. 1, 2* (1911)
Woodwind	4 Piccolos 4 Flutes 3 Oboes 2 English horns 2 E♭ Clarinets 3 Clarinets 2 Bass clarinets 3 Bassoons 2 Contrabassoons	1 Piccolo 2 Flutes 2 Oboes 1 English horn 2 Clarinets 3 Bassoons 1 Contrabassoon	2 Piccolos 4 Flutes 4 Oboes 1 English horn 2 E♭ Clarinets 3 Clarinets 1 Bass clarinet 4 Bassoons 1 Contrabassoon	1 Piccolo 2 Flutes 1 Alto flute 2 Oboes 1 English horn 1 E♭ Clarinet 2 Clarinets 1 Bass clarinet 3 Bassoons 1 Contrabassoon
Brass	10 Horns 6 Trumpets 1 Bass trumpet 6 Trombones 1 Contrabass trombone 1 Tuba 4 Bayreuth tubas	4 Horns 2 Cornets 3 Trumpets 3 Trombones 1 Tuba	8 Horns 4 Trumpets 3 Trombones 1 Tuba	4 Horns 4 Trumpets 3 Trombones 1 Tuba
Percussion	6 Timpani Bass drum Cymbals Triangle Snare drum Tenor drum Xylophone Gong Celesta 4 Harps	3 Timpani Bass drum Cymbals Triangle Gong Glockenspiel 2 Harps	3 Timpani Bells Mandoline Harmonium Celesta Piano Organ	4 Timpani Bass Drum Cymbals Snare drum Tenor drum Triangle Tambourine Castanets Antique cymbals Gong Eoliphone Glockenspiel Celesta 2 Harps
Strings	Violin I, II Viola Violoncello Bass	Violin I, II Viola Violoncello Bass	Violin I, II Viola Violoncello Bass	Violin I, II Viola Violoncello Bass
Extra	8-Part Chorus 3 4-Part Male Choruses 5 Solo Voices		4 Trumpets, 3 Trombones off-stage 2 8-Part Choruses Boys' Choir 8 Solo Voices	Chorus: S.A.T.B., off-stage

EVOLUTION OF THE MODERN SYMPHONY ORCHESTRA

	STRAVINSKY *Le Sacre du Printemps* (1913)	HOLST *The Planets* (1916)	STRAUSS, R. *Eine Alpensinfonie* (1918)	RESPIGHI *The Pines of Rome* (1924)
Woodwind	2 Piccolos 2 Flutes 1 Alto flute 4 Oboes (4th Ob. alt.2nd English horn) 1 English horn 1 E♭ Clarinet 3 Clarinets 2 Bass clarinets (2nd Bs. cl. alt. 3rd Cl.) 3 Bassoons 2 Contrabassoons (2nd alt. 4th Bssn.)	2 Piccolos (2nd Picc. alt. 3rd Fl.) 2 Flutes (2nd Fl. alt. Alto flute) 2 Oboes 1 English horn 1 Bass oboe 3 Clarinets 1 Bass clarinet 3 Bassoons 1 Contrabassoon	2 Piccolos 2 Flutes 3 Oboes (3rd Ob. alt. English horn) 1 Heckelphone 3 Clarinets 1 Bass clarinet 3 Bassoons 1 Contrabassoon	1 Piccolo 2 Flutes 2 Oboes 1 English horn 2 Clarinets 1 Bass clarinet 2 Bassoons 1 Contrabassoon
Brass	8 Horns (7th–8th Hns. alt. 2 Tubas) 1 D Trumpet 4 Trumpets (4th Trpt. alt. Bass trumpet) 3 Trombones 2 Tubas	6 Horns 4 Trumpets 3 Trombones 1 Tenor tuba 1 Bass tuba	8 Horns (5th–8th Hns. alt. 4 Tenor tubas) 4 Trumpets 4 Trombones 2 Tubas	4 Horns 3 Trumpets 3 Trombones 1 Tuba
Percussion	1 Small Timpani 4 Timpani (2 players) Bass drum Cymbals Triangle Tambourine Gong Antique cymbals Güiro	6 Timpani (2 players) Bass drum Snare drum Cymbals Triangle Tambourine Gong Bells Glockenspiel Xylophone Celesta Organ 2 Harps	4 Timpani Bass drum Snare drum Cymbals Triangle Gong Cowbells Wind-machine Thunder-machine Glockenspiel Celesta Organ 2 Harps	3 Timpani Bass drum Cymbals Small cymbals Triangle Tambourine Gong Rattle Gramophone record Glockenspiel Celesta Piano Organ Harp
Strings	Violin I, II Viola Violoncello Bass	Violin I, II Viola Violoncello Bass	Violin I, II Viola Violoncello Bass	Violin I, II Viola Violoncello Bass
Extra		6-Part Female Chorus, off-stage	12 Horns, 2 Trumpets, 2 Trombones off-stage	6 Roman Trumpets (Buccine), 1 Trumpet off-stage

THE INSTRUMENTS OF THE ORCHESTRA

	HINDEMITH *Mathis der Maler (Symphony)* (1934)	STRAVINSKY *Symphony in C* (1940)	SHOSTAKOVICH *Symphony No. 7,"Leningrad"* (1941)	BARTÓK *Concerto for Orchestra* (1943)

Woodwind	2 Flutes (2nd Fl. alt.
	  Piccolo)
	2 Oboes
	2 Clarinets
	2 Bassoons
		1 Piccolo (alt. 3rd Flute)
		2 Flutes
		2 Oboes
		2 Clarinets
		2 Bassoons
			3 Flutes (3rd Fl. alt.
			  Piccolo; 2nd Fl. alt.
			  Alto flute)
			2 Oboes
			1 English horn
			1 Eb Clarinet (Alt. 3rd
			  Clarinet)
			2 Clarinets
			1 Bass clarinet
			2 Bassoons
			1 Contrabassoon
				1 Piccolo
				2 Flutes
				2 Oboes
				1 English horn
				2 Clarinets
				1 Bass clarinet
				2 Bassoons
				1 Contrabassoon

Brass	4 Horns 2 Trumpets 3 Trombones 1 Tuba	4 Horns 2 Trumpets 3 Trombones 1 Tuba	4 Horns 3 Trumpets 3 Trombones 1 Tuba	4 Horns 3 Trumpets 3 Trombones 1 Tuba
Percussion	2 Timpani Bass drum Snare drum 1 Large cymbal 1 Small cymbal Triangle Glockenspiel	3 Timpani	5 Timpani Bass drum Snare drum Cymbals Triangle Tambourine Gong Xylophone Piano 2 Harps	3 Timpani Bass drum Snare drum Cymbals Triangle Gong 2 Harps
Strings	Violin I, II Viola Violoncello Bass	Violin I, II Viola Violoncello Bass	Violin I, II Viola Violoncello Bass	Violin I, II Viola Violoncello Bass
Extra			4 Horns, 3 Trumpets, 3 Trombones, 2nd Snare drum *ad libitum*	

PART II

Woodwinds

MAHLER. SYMPHONY No. 4

BRITTEN. SINFONIA DA REQUIEM

INTRODUCTION

THE MOST CASUAL COMPARISON of the woodwind parts of any Haydn or Mozart symphony with those of a work, let us say, by Bartók or Stravinsky, will illustrate better than any words the amazing development and expansion of technique made by these instruments in the last 200 years or so. This is particularly true in the basic matter of range, for the modern instrumentator's exploitation of extreme ranges is a characteristic feature of his craft.

Including only the so-called "standard" symphonic instruments, Chapter 4 lists instances where the most extreme ranges of each are to be found. In the case of the piccolo this means the highest C♯ to E, and the lowest D, D♭, and C[1]. For the flute these take in the highest C♯ to G♯ (*sic!*), and the added low B and B♭, found mainly in German and Russian scores. In the oboe the examples consist only of the top F to A♭, as the lowest notes are so commonly used—even if somewhat difficult and uncertain of intonation. For the English horn they include the highest A♯ and B, and the bottom E and optional E♭. In the clarinet they are the highest sounding G♯ to B♭ only, as the lowest tones of the instrument are so extremely common—excepting, of course, the rare instance of a low C♮, produced by inserting a cardboard extension in the bell. For the bass clarinet the examples include low C♮ down to F♮ (*sic!*), used by composers for the European instrument. In the bassoon they take in the highest C to E, and the added A, A♭, and G, produced—if at all—by means of a special extension on the instrument. Finally, in the contrabassoon, the instances of extreme range take in the bottom B and B♭, and added A, which are not, of course, comparable in ease of execution and effect to those of the bassoon. The student orchestrator is warned that whereas these instances of extreme and extended range certainly do exist, their use by inexperienced instrumentators is most assuredly not recommended, primarily because the novice is not very likely to have his work played at first by those major, professional orchestras capable of producing such extreme notes. Moreover, it is not at all improbable that some of the extreme examples quoted are actually quite impossible of execution, for even the best of composers and orchestrators have at times called for effects or devices theoretically possible but so difficult as to be impracticable. As in all technical matters of instrumentation, moderation and caution are required until one's orchestral technique has achieved maturity and sureness through actual experience.

The methods of articulation known as double- and triple-tonguing occupy Chapters 5 and 6, as well as the peculiar effect, listed in Chapter 7, of "flutter-tonguing," a device apparently first used by Mahler and Richard Strauss. Examples of woodwind *glissandi* and *portamenti* are catalogued in Chapter 8, and in Chapter 9 the direction, first extensively called for by Mahler, of raising the instrument's bell high in the air—for maximum volume. Instances of the use of harmonics in the flute, piccolo, oboe, and English horn—the only woodwind instruments capable of producing them, by means of over-blowing—are given in Chapter 10. There are a

---

[1] *N.B.* All examples are referred to *at pitch*; enharmonic spellings are given for most pitches.

40

few examples of a woodwind directed to play off-stage—the effect of which can be readily imagined—listed in Chapter 11, and Chapters 12-16 are devoted to miscellaneous indications, such as the " echo-tone" (a soft, sub-tonguing sound); the *vibrato*—done, of course, with the tongue; a jazz trick or two ("slap-tongue," "whip"); and muting the instrument by means of a cloth or small plug inserted in the bell. The section is completed with a chapter of miscellaneous terminology for the woodwind instruments—directions fairly common to the instruments but not coming conveniently under the various headings and sub-heads of the previous chapters. These terms, of course, refer only to devices, effects, or methods of playing and producing sound—never to tempo indications or directions as to mood or style.

The following plan has been adopted for presentation of the *Thesaurus* material.

At the head of each chapter will be found the terminology commonly employed for the device to be catalogued in the four basic score languages—English, Italian, French, and German, and/or the notation used for the effect in question; for example—

HARMONICS

English	*Italian*	*French*	*German*
Harmonic(s)	Armonico(i)	Harmonique(s)	Flageolett
harms.	*arm.*	*harm.*	*Flag.*
In harmonics	Suono(i) flautato(i)	En harmoniques	Mit Flageolett
		Sons harmoniques	

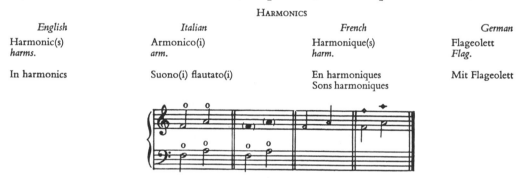

Plural endings are given in ( ) immediately following each term, and conventional abbreviations are indicated with italics below the term in question. The examples of notation are not necessarily taken from any one specific score but are more or less composite illustrations, designed to show the most commonly used forms of notation for the various effects. Grouped according to instrument and combinations of instruments in order of appearance in the score, there follow alphabetical listings by composer and work of the specific page and measure number where the device quoted may be located in available study scores, for example—

COMPOSER	WORK	PAGE	MEASURE
Bartók	*Dance Suite*	**14**	123
Ravel	*La Valse*	**77**	1b [57]
Stravinsky	*Fire-Bird Suite* (1919)	**65**	[39] 2f

All measure numbers, whether or not actually printed on the score page, are indicated without brackets. Some score editions conveniently number every 5, 10, or 25 measures throughout a work, but where these indications are not found the measure number is always counted from the first of the page being quoted. Thus, after the Bartók work listed above, measure 123 refers to the 123rd bar of the score, which is on page 14. And 1b [57]—following the Ravel score—refers to the first measure *before* rehearsal number [57]; [39] 2f indicates that the second measure *following* rehearsal number [39] is being quoted.

To find out the publisher or edition of each work listed in the *Thesaurus* the reader must turn to the "List of Composers and Works," pages 587-99. After the title of each work listed alphabetically beneath the composer's name will be found a number in ( ), which corresponds to that of the publisher, given in the "List of Publishers" on pages 583-85. As most of the standard orchestral literature exists in several varying editions, it is evident that only one edition could be used for quotation in the *Thesaurus*. The corresponding numbers of the publishers of other available imprints of such scores (the Haydn, Mozart, and Beethoven symphonies, to cite a few obvious examples) are given in [ ] following the quoted edition number. Thus—

RIMSKY-KORSAKOFF, Nicolas

Scheherazade (49); [7, 11, 32]

indicates that E. F. Kalmus, number 49 in the "List of Publishers," was the edition used for direct quotation of page and measure number, but that Belaïeff, Boosey and Hawkes, and Eulenburg also publish the same work. In most cases the rehearsal or measure numbers agree in the several different available editions of such works, but even though the page numbers may occasionally vary slightly, it should still be possible to find with little difficulty the quoted effect in other editions than the one used by the author.

To save space certain small liberties were taken in the listings of the devices. If, for example, on a certain page of the score being quoted the flutes play "flutter-tonguing" at measure 8, but the clarinets join in *simile* at measure 10, the effect was listed for both as of measure 8. And if in the strings the violins begin at [10], let us say, playing *détaché*, violas enter two bars later, and 'cellos four bars after [10], all *détaché*, again the effect would be catalogued as Violin I, II, Viola, and Violoncello at [10]. Also, if a device was well-illustrated on page 20 of a certain score and repeated on page 21 or page 22, only the first such page will be listed.

The enterprising orchestrator will find all the *Thesaurus* listings merely stepping-stones to the discovery of other equally fascinating uses of instrumental color devices in the immense literature for the symphonic orchestra.

Chapter 4

EXTREME OR EXTENDED RANGES

(1) PICCOLO

N.B. All notes are given at *actual pitch*.

(musical notation: 15va)

COMPOSER	WORK	PAGE	MEASURE
Harsanyi	Suite pour Orchestre	46	[155]

(musical notation: 15va)

COMPOSER	WORK	PAGE	MEASURE
Harsanyi	Suite pour Orchestre	46	1b [155]
Siegmeister	Ozark Set	11	[45] 2f

(musical notation: 15va)

COMPOSER	WORK	PAGE	MEASURE
Mahler	Symphony No. 2	172	[20] 1f

(musical notation)

COMPOSER	WORK	PAGE	MEASURE
Bartók	Hungarian Peasant Songs	6	3b [4]
Casella	Paganiniana	61	2
Copland	First Symphony	61	3b [44]
Dukas	La Péri	74	1
		116	2
Dukas	L'Apprenti Sorcier	1	3
Harsanyi	Suite pour Orchestre	4	1b [15]
Hindemith	Kammermusik No. 4	113	[R]
Inghelbrecht	El Greco	56	2b [47]
Mahler	Songs of a Wayfarer	47	50
Mahler	Symphony No. 1	134	[33] 1f
Mahler	Symphony No. 2	56	[27] 1f
Mahler	Symphony No. 3	104	[76] 3f
Milhaud	Le Carnaval de Londres	31	[240] 1f
Moeran	Sinfonietta	39	[54] 4f

COMPOSER	WORK	PAGE	MEASURE
Mozart	Overture to "Il Seraglio"	5	34
		20	186
Poulenc	Concerto pour deux Pianos et Orchestre	35	[28]
Respighi	Antiche Danze ed Arie, 2ª Suite	62	5
Schönberg	Kammersymphonie, Op. 9	73	[68]
Schreker	The Birthday of the Infanta, Suite	74	1b [405]
Schuman, W.	Symphony No. III	56	181
		69	352
Scriabin	Prométhée, Le Poème du Feu	34	2
Skilton	Suite Primeval, Part 1	28	6
Smetana	Overture to "The Bartered Bride"	22	227
Stravinsky	Petrouchka Suite	109	2b [96]
Stravinsky	Renard	23	[13] 4f
Tchaikovsky	Symphony No. 2	27	[G] 3f
		39	4
Tchaikovsky	Symphony No. 3	14	1
		31	[O]
		123	[R]
Thomson	Tango Lullaby	4	45
Thomson	The Seine at Night	28	[14] 3f
Varèse	Intégrales	29	3
Verdi	Messa da Requiem	141	699
		213	68

(musical notation)

COMPOSER	WORK	PAGE	MEASURE
Dukas	La Péri	74	1
Inghelbrecht	El Greco	54	[45] 1f
Mahler	Symphony No. 2	56	[27] 1f
Mahler	Symphony No. 3	182	2
Respighi	Antiche Danze ed Arie, 2ª Suite	63	3
Verdi	Messa da Requiem	213	68

WOODWINDS

(1) PICCOLO (contd.)

COMPOSER	WORK	PAGE	MEASURE
Dukas	La Péri	74	I
Harsanyi	Suite pour Orchestre	4	Ib [15]
Mahler	Songs of a Wayfarer	47	51
Mahler	Symphony No. I	134	[33] If

COMPOSER	WORK	PAGE	MEASURE
Mahler	Symphony No. 2	127	3
Mozart	Overture to	5	34
	"Il Seraglio"	20	186
Respighi	The Fountains of Rome	16	[5] If
Stravinsky	Quatre Études pour		
	Orchestre	18	3b [8]
Verdi	Messa da Requiem	213	69

(2) FLUTE

		PAGE	MEASURE
Milhaud	IIᵉ Symphonie	91	Ib [85]

		PAGE	MEASURE
Milhaud	IIᵉ Symphonie	89	[75]

		PAGE	MEASURE
Gould	Latin-American		
	Symphonette	93	3
Harsanyi	Suite pour Orchestre	46	[155]

		PAGE	MEASURE
Cesana	Second American	60	2
	Symphony	65	I
Kabalevsky	Suite from "Colas	105	3
	Breugnon"	110	[35]
Miaskovsky	Symphony No. 6	33	4
Milhaud	IIᵉ Symphonie	28	[C] 3f

		PAGE	MEASURE
Bach-Respighi	Prelude and Fugue in		
	D major	46	2b [15]

COMPOSER	WORK	PAGE	MEASURE
Britten	The Young Person's		
	Guide to the Orchestra	64	5
Cesana	Second American		
	Symphony	65	4
Coppola	Suite Intima	79	I
Gould	Latin-American		
	Symphonette	93	3
Harsanyi	Suite pour Orchestre	46	Ib [155]
Kabalevsky	Suite from "Colas	29	[21]
	Breugnon"	65	[57]
		110	[35] If
Kodály	Galanta Dances	19	[165]
Kodály	Háry János Suite	93	114
Mahler	Symphony No. 2	172	[20] If
Mahler	Symphony No. 8	47	[53] 4f
Milhaud	IIᵉ Symphonie	89	[75]
Milhaud	Quatrième Symphonie	103	[125] 2f
Prokofieff	Ala et Lolly (Scythian	100	[69] If
	Suite)	107	[72]
Prokofieff	Alexander Nevsky	70	[43]
		80	[47]
Prokofieff	Classical Symphony	34	[29]
		51	3
		61	[48] 2f
		83	[65] 2f
		96	[76]
Prokofieff	March and Scherzo		
	from "The Love of		
	the Three Oranges"	30	[13]
Prokofieff	Piano Concerto No. 3	108	2b [83]
		127	3
Prokofieff	Violin Concerto No. 2	41	Ib [37]
Respighi	The Pines of Rome	44	2
Shostakovich	Symphony No. 9	72	[56] If
Siegmeister	From my Window	52	2
Siegmeister	Ozark Set	11	[45] 2f
		42	Ib [75]
		58	I
Siegmeister	Western Suite	87	2b [105]
		108	[120] If

44

(2) FLUTE (contd.)

COMPOSER	WORK	PAGE	MEASURE
Strauss, R.	Also Sprach Zara-thustra	202	8
Strauss, R.	Ein Heldenleben	108	1b [56]
Strauss, R.	Symphonia Domestica	18	[23] 1f
Stravinsky	Renard	52	[33]
Villa-Lobos	Amazonas	14	1b [5]
Villa-Lobos	Danses Africaines	78	1b [15]
Walton	Façade, Suite No. 2	3	2

(musical notation example)

COMPOSER	WORK	PAGE	MEASURE
Albéniz–Arbós	El Albaicín	27	2b [Q]
Bartók	Second Suite	19	[17]
Bax	Second Symphony	51	[29] 1f
Bax	Tintagel	31	[N] 2f
Becker	Concerto for Horn and Orchestra	12	1
Britten	Sinfonia da Requiem	15	[11] 7f
Britten	The Young Person's Guide to the Orchestra	64	4
Cesana	Second American Symphony	59	[2]
Coppola	Suite Intima	79	2
Debussy–Ansermet	Six Épigraphes Antiques	33	[D] 1f
Elgar	Symphony No. 1	53	[46] 3f
Elgar	Symphony No. 2	36	[40] 1f
Fitelberg	Symphony No. 1	120	3b [352]
Gould	Latin-American Symphonette	93	3
Harrison	Alleluia for Orchestra	18	[N] 3f
Harsanyi	Suite pour Orchestre	43	1b [130]
Hindemith	Mathis der Maler	8	[4] 5f
		18	[15] 1f
Ireland	Symphonic Rhapsody, "Mai-Dun"	15	2
		21	3
Janssen	New Year's Eve in New York	17	[7]
Kabalevsky	Suite from "Colas Breugnon"	16	[11]
		24	[18]
		29	1b [21]
		55	[41]
		104	[31]
Khachaturian	Concerto for Piano and Orchestra	130	[348]
Kodály	Háry János Suite	9	2
		16	2
Mahler	Symphony No. 2	172	[20] 1f

COMPOSER	WORK	PAGE	MEASURE
Mahler	Symphony No. 3	170	[25] 4f
Mahler	Symphony No. 7	49	[41] 2f
Mahler	Symphony No. 8	33	[37] 1f
		246	[286] 2f
Miaskovsky	Symphony No. 6	33	4
		140	98
		190	390
		264	[21]
Miaskovsky	Symphony No. 21	7	[3] 1f
		46	[45] 1f
Milhaud	IIe Symphonie	28	[C] 3f
		91	1b [85]
Milhaud	Quatrième Symphonie	103	[125] 2f
Prokofieff	Ala et Lolly (Scythian Suite)	106	2
Prokofieff	March and Scherzo from "The Love of the Three Oranges"	23	[8] 1f
		30	[13]
Prokofieff	Piano Concerto No. 3	76	3
		85	[65] 1f
Read	Symphony No. I	7	1
		80	5
		126	[45]
Reger	Variations on a Theme of Mozart	146	2
Ruggles	Sun-Treader	12	[49]
Schönberg	Fünf Orchesterstücke	57	1b [11]
Shepherd	Horizons	54	[D] 2f
Shostakovich	Symphony No. 9	72	[56] 1f
Siegmeister	From my Window	52	2
Siegmeister	Ozark Set	43	3
Siegmeister	Sunday in Brooklyn	47	[30] 2f
		62	1b [15]
Strauss, R.	Also Sprach Zara-thustra	68	1
Strauss, R.	Don Quixote	118	1
Strauss, R.	Eine Alpensinfonie	16	1
		141	[124]
Strauss, R.	Ein Heldenleben	101	1
Wagner, R.	Magic Fire Music from "Die Walküre"	25	1
Walton	Façade, Suite No. 2	3	2

(musical notation example)

COMPOSER	WORK	PAGE	MEASURE
Bartók	Concerto for Orchestra	69	[20]
Bartók	Concerto No. 3 for Piano and Orchestra	9	48
Bartók	Dance Suite	16	138
Bax	Second Symphony	50	6

WOODWINDS

(2) FLUTE (contd.)

COMPOSER	WORK	PAGE	MEASURE	COMPOSER	WORK	PAGE	MEASURE
Berg	Three Excerpts from "Wozzeck"	6	[330]	Miaskovsky	Symphony No. 6	259	1b [18]
Berg	Violin Concerto	42	2b [205]	Prokofieff	Ala et Lolly (Scythian Suite)	25	1b [13]
		60	1			61	[38]
Bernstein	"Jeremiah" Symphony	61	[20] 5f	Prokofieff	Classical Symphony	8	[5]
Bloch	Schelomo	62	3b [38]			51	2
Delius	Eventyr, Once Upon a Time	5	[1] 3f	Prokofieff	Romeo and Juliet, Suite No. 2	65	2b [43]
Hindemith	Konzert für Orchester	2	5	Respighi	Feste Romane	63	3
		11	4	Respighi	The Fountains of Rome	9	3
Mahler	Das Lied von der Erde	43	[9] 2f	Respighi	The Pines of Rome	50	1
		136	[60] 5f			56	3
Mahler	Songs of a Wayfarer	45	[22]	Schönberg	Pierrot Lunaire	72	[10] 1f
		55	1	Shostakovich	Symphony No. 7	70	1b [59]
Mahler	Symphony No. 2	131	[4] 6f	Sibelius	Tapiola	55	569
Mahler	Symphony No. 3	48	4b [32]	Smetana	Vysehrad	54	3
		222	1	Strauss, R.	Don Quixote	71	2
Mahler	Symphony No. 4	113	349	Stravinsky	Le Sacre du Printemps	60	[70]
		123	[4]	Tchaikovsky	Manfred-Symphonie	49	292
		163	55			283	397
		180	128	Tchaikovsky	Symphony No. 6, "Pathétique"	206	147
		187	171	Weinberger	Polka and Fugue from "Schwanda, the Bagpiper"	4	[15]
Mahler	Symphony No. 5	34	1				
		62	[8] 4f				
		86	2				
		205	8				
		245	4				
Mahler	Symphony No. 6	40	[25]				
		95	4				
Mahler	Symphony No. 7	104	[95] 2f	Mahler	Symphony No. 4	111	334
Mahler	Symphony No. 8	61	5b [74]	Mahler	Symphony No. 6	47	3
		128	[87] 2f			95	3
		141	3b [109]	Mahler	Symphony No. 8	185	4b [174]
Mahler	Symphony No. 9	181	5	Mussorgsky– Ravel	Pictures at an Exhibition	139	[112] 5f
McKay	Sinfonietta No. 4	42	3				

(3) OBOE

COMPOSER	WORK	PAGE	MEASURE	COMPOSER	WORK	PAGE	MEASURE
				Casella	La Donna Serpente, I. Serie	15	4
Cesana	Second American Symphony	56	[40] 1f	Cesana	Second American Symphony	93	1b [23]
Revueltas	Sensemayá	31	[31]			151	[35] 3f
Scriabin	Prométhée, Le Poème du Feu	69	5	Copland	First Symphony	78	[55]
				Honegger	Chant de Joie	6	5
				Ravel	La Valse	39	2b [27]
				Ravel	Rapsodie Espagnole	55	2
						75	[23]
				Ravel	Tzigane	25	6b [25]
				Rivier	Chant Funèbre	7	4
				Rudhyar	Sinfonietta	7	1
				Schuman, W.	Symphony No. IV	5	35
Bax	Fourth Symphony	57	5b [45]	Stravinsky	Concerto en Ré pour Violon et Orchestre	60	[121] 2f

EXTREME OR EXTENDED RANGES

(3) OBOE (contd.)

COMPOSER	WORK	PAGE	MEASURE
Stravinsky	Le Sacre du Printemps	28	2b [38]
		74	[82] 5f

[musical staff example]

COMPOSER	WORK	PAGE	MEASURE
Bax	Fourth Symphony	55	[43]
Berg	Three Excerpts from "Wozzeck"	34	[65]
Britten	Sinfonia da Requiem	43	6
Bruckner	Symphony No. 5	49	2b [Y]
Cesana	Second American Symphony	19	6
		55	5
		91	2
Chávez	Sinfonia de Antigona	19	2
Diamond	Timon of Athens	32	228
Ferroud	Au Parc Monceau	40	[14] 1f
		43	3
Honegger	Chant de Joie	6	5
Honegger	Horace Victorieux	68	1
Honegger	Pacific 231	39	[15] 1f
Honegger	Symphonie Liturgique	15	2b [7]
		43	2
Mahler	Symphony No. 6	197	[130] 2f
Mihalovici	Toccata pour Piano et Orchestre	87	1b [305]
		117	[440]
Milhaud	2me Suite Symphonique	161	4
Piket	Curtain Raiser to an American Play	5	3b [20]
Piston	Concerto for Orchestra	14	4
Piston	Prelude and Fugue	32	1
Piston	Suite for Orchestra	66	1
Poulenc	Concerto pour deux Pianos et Orchestre	91	2
		105	[67]
Prokofieff	March and Scherzo from "The Love of the Three Oranges"	17	1b [3]
		27	1b [11]
Prokofieff	Piano Concerto No. 3	49	[38] 2f
Ravel	Le Tombeau de Couperin	32	[16] 1f
Ravel	Tzigane	16	1
		25	6b [25]
Revueltas	Sensemayá	31	[31]
Rivier	Chant Funèbre	7	3
Rosenthal	Les Petits Métiers	63	1
Roussel	4me Symphonie	43	4
Rudhyar	Sinfonietta	23	7
		27	2
		38	3

COMPOSER	WORK	PAGE	MEASURE
Schmitt	Mirages pour Orchestre, No. 2	61	2
Schönberg	A Survivor from Warsaw	23	96
Schönberg	Fünf Orchesterstücke	58	4b [12]
Schreker	The Birthday of the Infanta, Suite	62	1
Scriabin	Prométhée, Le Poème du Feu	69	3
Sessions	Suite from "The Black Maskers"	72	3b [69]
Sessions	Symphony No. II	16	[J]
Strang	Intermezzo	10	61
Stravinsky	Chant du Rossignol	16	[16] 5f
Stravinsky	Le Sacre du Printemps	28	2b [38]
		49	[60] 1f
		75	1b [84]
		112	[144] 1f
		139	[201] 1f
Stravinsky	Quatre Études pour Orchestre	27	1
Trapp	Symphonie No. 4	93	2b [39]
Weiss	American Life	11	[E] 3f

[musical staff example]

COMPOSER	WORK	PAGE	MEASURE
Antheil	Symphony No. 5	56	[38] 1f
Bax	Fourth Symphony	56	[44] 4f
Bloch	America	114	1
Bruckner	Symphony No. 5	27	6
Cesana	Second American Symphony	92	2
Copland	Concerto for Piano and Orchestra	53	3
Copland	First Symphony	72	4
Copland	Music for the Theatre	16	[11]
		65	[54]
Copland	Third Symphony	44	1b [33]
Coppola	Suite Intima	25	4
Diamond	Fourth Symphony	41	1b [60]
Ferroud	Au Parc Monceau	10	2
		30	2
Gillis	Symphony No. 5½	74	[A] 5f
Gould	Latin-American Symphonette	65	5
Honegger	Pacific 231	38	179
Honegger	Rugby	16	5
Honegger	Symphonie Liturgique	14	3

WOODWINDS

(3) OBOE (contd.)

COMPOSER	WORK	PAGE	MEASURE	COMPOSER	WORK	PAGE	MEASURE
Ibert	La Ballade de la Geôle			Rosenthal	Les Petits Métiers	123	[A] 3f
	de Reading	21	[13] 2f	Roussel	4me Symphonie	55	1
Khrennikov	Symphony No. 1	67	[35]	Rudhyar	Sinfonietta	12	3
		99	2b [260]			31	3
		104	[295]	Schmitt	Mirages pour Orchestre,		
Mahler	Symphony No. 3	101	2		No. 2	7	3
		166	6	Schönberg	A Survivor from		
Mahler	Symphony No. 5	106	[30] 2f		Warsaw	23	96
Mahler	Symphony No. 6	53	1	Schönberg	Fünf Orchesterstücke	42	[5] 2f
Mahler	Symphony No. 8	5	3b [3]	Schuman, W.	American Festival	6	[35] 2f
Martinet	Orphée	29	[6]		Overture	9	[55] 4f
McDonald	Bataan	22	[65] 2f			16	2b [170]
Milhaud	2me Suite Symphonique	40	[18] 1f			30	[320]
		143	2	Schuman, W.	Prayer in Time of War	21	289
Milhaud	Two Marches	7	1	Schuman, W.	Symphony No. III	42	351
Piston	Suite for Orchestra	22	2b [J]	Schuman, W.	Symphony No. IV	5	34
Poot	Symphonie	96	4	Scriabin	Le Divin Poème	22	4
Poulenc	Concerto pour deux			Sessions	Suite from "The Black	30	2b [34]
	Pianos et Orchestre	83	[52]		Maskers"	71	[68]
Prokofieff	Ala et Lolly (Scythian	90	[59]	Strang	Intermezzo	10	60
	Suite)	107	[72]	Strauss, R.	Eine Alpensinfonie	55	[47] 1f
Prokofieff	March and Scherzo			Stravinsky	Concerto en Ré pour		
	from "The Love of				Violon et Orchestre	60	[121] 2f
	the Three Oranges"	23	[8]	Stravinsky	Jeu de Cartes	43	[82] 1f
Prokofieff	Piano Concerto No. 3	21	[15] 2f	Stravinsky	Le Sacre du Printemps	55	2
Ravel	Concerto pour la main					138	2b [198]
	gauche	85	1	Stravinsky	Oedipus Rex	77	[104] 1f
Ravel	Le Tombeau de			Stravinsky	Scherzo à la Russe	22	[18]
	Couperin	32	[16] 1f	Stravinsky	Symphony in Three		
Rieti	Sinfonia Tripartita	37	2b [32]		Movements	14	[16]
Rivier	Chant Funèbre	7	2	Villa-Lobos	Uirapurú	67	[17] 1f

(4) ENGLISH HORN

COMPOSER	WORK	PAGE	MEASURE	COMPOSER	WORK	PAGE	MEASURE
Milhaud	2me Suite Symphonique	30	1	Copland	Concerto for Piano and		
Piston	Suite for Orchestra	14	1		Orchestra	25	3
		31	3	Delius	Brigg Fair	41	[35] 6f
				Piston	Suite for Orchestra	33	6
				Ruggles	Sun-Treader	29	[142]
				Schmitt	Mirages pour Orchestre,		
					No. 1	24	2
				Stravinsky	Le Sacre du Printemps	132	[184]
Britten	Sinfonia da Requiem	43	3				
Casella	La Donna Serpente,						
	I. Serie	25	[25] 3f	Antheil	Symphony No. 5	69	[49] 1f

48

EXTREME OR EXTENDED RANGES

(4) ENGLISH HORN (contd.)

COMPOSER	WORK	PAGE	MEASURE	COMPOSER	WORK	PAGE	MEASURE
Barber	Second Symphony	33	[23] 2f	Prokofieff	Romeo and Juliet, Suite		
Bax	First Symphony	31	1		No. 1	83	2
Berg	Violin Concerto	17	[90] 4f	Prokofieff	Romeo and Juliet, Suite	14	[6]
		86	[175] 3f		No. 2	91	8
Britten	Sinfonia da Requiem	62	[43] 3f	Read	Symphony No. I	12	4
Casella	Paganiniana	155	4b [30]	Respighi	Ballata delle Gnomidi	84	3
Caturla	Trois Danses Cubaines	50	[5] 2f	Rivier	Chant Funèbre	8	5
Chávez	Sinfonia de Antigona	22	[33]	Schelling	A Victory Ball	29	[6]
Copland	Concerto for Piano and			Schönberg	Theme and Variations	35	162
	Orchestra	67	[50] 2f	Schuman, W.	Symphony No. III	71	369
Copland	First Symphony	77	2	Sessions	Symphony for Orchestra		
Delius	Appalachia	128	559		(No. 1)	37	5b [56]
Delius	Brigg Fair	24	5	Sessions	Symphony No. II	96	[P]
Diamond	Fourth Symphony	91	1b [195]	Siegmeister	From my Window	56	2b [40]
Dukas	La Péri	8	2	Strauss, R.	Don Quixote	72	1
		67	[10]	Stravinsky	Mass	27	[55] 1f
		90	1	Stravinsky	Quatre Études pour		
Ferguson	Partita for Orchestra	66	1		Orchestre	21	4
Ferroud	Au Parc Monceau	11	[4]	Tchaikovsky	Manfred-Symphonie	229	III
Franck	Symphony in D minor	76	72	Vaughan	Job, A Masque for		
Gershwin	Concerto in F for Piano			Williams	Dancing	7	5b [C]
	and Orchestra	65	[10] 2f	Vaughan			
Golestan	Concerto Roumain pour			Williams	Pastoral Symphony	8	3
	Violon et Orchestre	74	1	Vaughan	Symphony in F minor		
Harris	When Johnny Comes			Williams	(No. 4)	81	1b [6]
	Marching Home	34	5	Vaughan	Symphony in D major	74	[3] 1f
Honegger	Concertino pour Piano			Williams	(No. 5)	77	6
	et Orchestre	26	4b [17]	Vaughan	Symphony in E minor		
Honegger	Horace Victorieux	60	3	Williams	(No. 6)	112	1
Honegger	Le Roi David	193	5	Villa-Lobos	Amazonas	7	2
Honegger	Pacific 231	13	[7] 3f				
Honegger	Prélude pour "La						
	Tempête"	20	[7]				
d'Indy	Istar, Variations						
	Symphoniques	11	7				
Inghelbrecht	El Greco	2	1b [1]	Elgar	Symphony No. 2	6	[6]
Mahler	Symphony No. 1	3	5			75	4
Mahler	Symphony No. 7	17	6b [13]			169	[160]
		196	5	Harris	When Johnny Comes	39	4
Mahler	Symphony No. 8	119	4b [77]		Marching Home	41	1
Mahler	Symphony No. 9	41	4	Honegger	Concertino pour Piano		
Milhaud	Ière Symphonie	54	2b [150]		et Orchestre	26	4b [17]
Milhaud	IIe Symphonie	95	1b [115]	Mahler	Das Lied von der Erde	27	[32] 7f
Pierné	Viennoise	13	3	Mahler	Symphony No. 1	88	[13] 3f
Piston	Concerto for Orchestra	30	2	Mahler	Symphony No. 2	31	[15]
Piston	Prelude and Fugue	17	3b [1]	Read	Symphony No. I	110	1
		29	4	Strauss, R.	Eine Alpensinfonie	29	[24] 6f
Piston	Suite for Orchestra	36	1				

49

WOODWINDS

(5) CLARINET

COMPOSER	WORK	PAGE	MEASURE
Elgar	*Falstaff*	132	8
Rudhyar	*Sinfonietta*	32	2

COMPOSER	WORK	PAGE	MEASURE
Berg	*Three Excerpts from "Wozzeck"*	45	[335]
Casella	*Pupazzetti*	48	[5]
Diamond	*Fourth Symphony*	41	[60]
Diamond	*Music for Shakespeare's "Romeo and Juliet"*	3	2
		14	[90] 2f
Elgar	*Falstaff*	132	7
Respighi	*Feste Romane*	106	6
Rudhyar	*Sinfonietta*	32	1
Schuman, W.	*Symphony No. IV*	29	244

COMPOSER	WORK	PAGE	MEASURE
Siegmeister	*Sunday in Brooklyn*	77	3
Strauss, R.	*Eine Alpensinfonie*	12	[7]

COMPOSER	WORK	PAGE	MEASURE
Berg	*Three Excerpts from "Wozzeck"*	35	1
Casella	*Pupazzetti*	46	[4] 5f
Ferroud	*Au Parc Monceau*	40	[14]
Hanson	*Symphony No. 2, "Romantic"*	49	2
Harsanyi	*Suite pour Orchestre*	72	2b [150]
Moeran	*Symphony in G minor*	99	1
Read	*First Overture*	55	2

COMPOSER	WORK	PAGE	MEASURE
Stravinsky	*Chant du Rossignol*	79	[92] 2f

(6) BASS CLARINET

COMPOSER	WORK	PAGE	MEASURE
Chávez	*Sinfonia de Antigona*	19	4
Khachaturian	*Concerto for Piano and Orchestra*	52	[398]
		88	[233]
Miaskovsky	*Fragment Lyrique*	8	5
Piston	*Symphony No. 2*	77	3
Prokofieff	*Alexander Nevsky*	5	1
		9	[4] 6f
Prokofieff	*Cinderella Suite No. 1*	7	[2]
Prokofieff	*Romeo and Juliet, Suite No. 1*	65	2
		83	2
		91	3
Prokofieff	*Romeo and Juliet, Suite No. 2*	65	[42]
		90	1b [56]
		110	3
Prokofieff	*Suite from the Ballet "Chout"*	50	[70] 2f
Revueltas	*Cuauhnahuac*	3	8b [4]
Shostakovich	*Symphony No. 6*	27	1b [33]
		45	4b [51]
		73	4

COMPOSER	WORK	PAGE	MEASURE
Shostakovich	*Symphony No. 7*	11	[8] 6f
		29	[37] 3f
		150	5

COMPOSER	WORK	PAGE	MEASURE
Janáček	*Sinfonietta*	61	9
		70	[5]
Khachaturian	*Concerto for Piano and Orchestra*	88	[233]
Khachaturian	*Gayne Ballet Suite No. 1-A*	4	4
Piston	*Symphony No. 2*	77	3
Prokofieff	*Romeo and Juliet, Suite No. 1*	68	46
Prokofieff	*Romeo and Juliet, Suite No. 2*	30	5b [16]
		36	[34]
Revueltas	*Sensemayá*	36	[34]
Shostakovich	*Symphony No. 6*	27	1b [33]
Shostakovich	*Symphony No. 7*	82	[80] 2f
		99	[97] 1f
		161	3b [186]
		164	[198]

EXTREME OR EXTENDED RANGES

(6) BASS CLARINET (contd.)

COMPOSER	WORK	PAGE	MEASURE
Janáček	Sinfonietta	70	[5] 2f
Khachaturian	Concerto for Piano and Orchestra	88	[233]
Khachaturian	Gayne Ballet Suite No. 1-A	4	4

COMPOSER	WORK	PAGE	MEASURE
Piston	Symphony No. 2	77	3

COMPOSER	WORK	PAGE	MEASURE
Janáček	Sinfonietta	70	[5] 2f
Piston	Symphony No. 2	77	3

COMPOSER	WORK	PAGE	MEASURE
Janáček	Sinfonietta	70	[5] 4f
		72	2

COMPOSER	WORK	PAGE	MEASURE
Janáček	Sinfonietta	70	[5] 4f

(7) BASSOON

COMPOSER	WORK	PAGE	MEASURE
Engel	The Creation	15	[7]
Moross	Biguine	10	[B] 1f
		15	2
Ravel	Concerto pour Piano et Orchestre	14	1
Stravinsky	Le Sacre du Printemps	71	5
Trapp	Symphonie No. 4	67	[24]

COMPOSER	WORK	PAGE	MEASURE
Casella	Pupazzetti	27	5
		42	[2] 4f
Mahler	Symphony No. 5	21	7
Mahler	Symphony No. 6	48	1
Schönberg	A Survivor from Warsaw	7	30
Schuman, W.	Prayer in Time of War	20	280
Schuman, W.	Symphony No. III	37	325
		42	349
Schuman, W.	Undertow	43	4b [530]
Sessions	Suite from "The Black Maskers"	13	[9]
Shostakovich	Symphony No. 6	4	[1] 2f
Stravinsky	Chant du Rossignol	9	1b [6]
		29	3
		62	[65] 1f

COMPOSER	WORK	PAGE	MEASURE
Thomson	Orchestra Suite from "The Plow that Broke the Plains"	58	1b [53]

COMPOSER	WORK	PAGE	MEASURE
Bartók	Second Rhapsody for Violin and Orchestra	48	[38] 3f
Bax	In the Faery Hills	29	[M] 3f
Bloch	Trois Poèmes Juifs	74	6
Casella	Pupazzetti	27	5
Copland	Third Symphony	24	2
		122	2
Engel	The Creation	14	3
Johnson	Imagery	14	2
Kodály	Marosszék Dances	75	[340]
Kodály	Summer Evening	50	313
Mahler	Symphony No. 3	15	[11]
		51	[35]
		95	[71] 3f
		168	3b [24]
Mahler	Symphony No. 5	49	[1] 4f
		213	[20] 3f
Mahler	Symphony No. 6	184	[122] 6f
Mahler	Symphony No. 7	135	[141] 2f
Mahler	Symphony No. 9	55	2
		69	6
Milhaud	Deuxième Concerto pour Violoncelle et Orchestre	62	1

(7) BASSOON (contd.)

COMPOSER	WORK	PAGE	MEASURE
Milhaud	Suite Provençale	40	1b [35]
Moross	Biguine	10	[B] 1f
		15	1
Rivier	Ouverture pour un don Quichotte	31	[13] 1f
Rosenthal	Les Petits Métiers	26	1
Roussel	Rapsodie Flamande	45	3
Schmitt	Mirages pour Orchestre, No. 2	59	3
		69	1
Schönberg	A Survivor from Warsaw	8	36
Schuman, W.	Symphony No. III	42	350
Schuman, W.	Undertow	5	2b [30]
		44	5
Shostakovich	Symphony No. 6	4	[1] 2f
Siegmeister	Ozark Set	48	3b [10]
Stravinsky	Fire-Bird Suite (1919)	39	3b [14]
Stravinsky	Le Sacre du Printemps	3	2b [1]
		71	5
Stravinsky	Oedipus Rex	79	1b [108]
Stravinsky	Pulcinella Suite	49	[76] 2f
Thomson	Orchestra Suite from "The Plow that Broke the Plains"	21	6
Tippett	Symphony No. 1	18	[11] 1f
Trapp	Symphonie No. 4	68	1
		122	2
Villa-Lobos	Chôros No. 8	32	[13] 1f
Villa-Lobos	Uirapurú	67	[17]
Walton	Symphony	136	[103] 3f

COMPOSER	WORK	PAGE	MEASURE
Bartók	Second Rhapsody for Violin and Orchestra	39	[27] 4f
Bax	In the Faery Hills	29	7
Berg	Violin Concerto	62	1
Bloch	Trois Poèmes Juifs	63	[2]
		67	2
Carter	Holiday Overture	22	3
Casella	La Donna Serpente, I. Serie	10	[15] 2f
Casella	La Donna Serpente, II. Serie	38	1b [49]
Casella	Paganiniana	64	[33] 1f
Casella	Pupazzetti	9	[4] 3f
		27	4
Copland	Third Symphony	122	3
Debussy	Rondes de Printemps	50	1b [26]
Delius	A Dance Rhapsody (No. 1)	27	3

COMPOSER	WORK	PAGE	MEASURE
Delius	Appalachia	132	588
Delius	A Song of Summer	18	[135] 1f
Dukelsky	Symphony No. 3	35	1
Elgar	Symphony No. 1	26	3
		54	4b [47]
Levant	Nocturne	18	65
		45	209
Mahler	Symphony No. 3	63	4
Mahler	Symphony No. 5	21	3
		35	[13] 5f
		49	[1] 4f
		213	[20] 3f
Mahler	Symphony No. 6	48	1
		185	6b [123]
Mahler	Symphony No. 8	143	[111] 5f
Milhaud	IIe Symphonie	42	[155]
Moross	Biguine	29	3
Mussorgsky–Ravel	Pictures at an Exhibition	64	3
Pierné	Viennoise	6	[C] 5f
Prokofieff	Suite from the Ballet "Chout"	121	[154] 2f
Ravel	Boléro	5	4
Respighi	Metamorphoseon, XII Modi	29	[I]
Respighi	Vetrate di Chiesa	60	2
Rosenthal	Les Petits Métiers	46	4
Roussel	Rapsodie Flamande	45	3
Schelling	A Victory Ball	117	2b [37]
Schmitt	Mirages pour Orchestre, No. 2	59	2
Schönberg	A Survivor from Warsaw	3	12
		8	36
Schönberg	Theme and Variations	26	102
Schuman, W.	Symphony No. III	37	324
		41	346
Sessions	Suite from "The Black Maskers"	11	6b [8]
Siegmeister	Ozark Set	48	1b [10]
Strauss, R.	Eine Alpensinfonie	14	[9]
Strauss, R.	Ein Heldenleben	73	[37]
Stravinsky	Chant du Rossignol	9	2b [6]
		29	2
		62	[65]
Stravinsky	Le Sacre du Printemps	11	9b [13]
Stravinsky	Oedipus Rex	79	1b [108]
Thomson	Orchestra Suite from "The Plow that Broke the Plains"	57	6
Tippett	Symphony No. 1	18	[11]
		43	1b [28]

(7) BASSOON (contd.)

COMPOSER	WORK	PAGE	MEASURE
Trapp	Symphonie No. 4	5	1
		67	[24]
		119	4
Vaughan Williams	Job, A Masque for Dancing	39	[W]
Villa-Lobos	Uirapurú	46	[10]
		67	1b [17]
Walton	Symphony	136	[103] 2f
Weiss	American Life	14	3

COMPOSER	WORK	PAGE	MEASURE
Bach–Respighi	Passacaglia and Fugue in C minor	16	[11]
Barber	Medea	25	1
		82	2
Barber	Second Symphony	33	[23] 3f
		58	3
		87	5
Bartók	Second Rhapsody for Violin and Orchestra	35	[21] 2f
		48	[38] 3f
Bartók	Second Suite	98	[5] 3f
Bax	In the Faery Hills	29	[M] 2f
Berg	Three Excerpts from "Wozzeck"	44	[330] 2f
Bloch	America	169	1
Bloch	Trois Poèmes Juifs	6	1
		34	3
		55	1
		63	[2]
		76	1b [11]
Casella	La Donna Serpente, II. Serie	38	1b [49]
Casella	Pupazzetti	9	[4] 3f
Chávez	Sinfonia India	26	[33]
Copland	Lincoln Portrait	2	1b [10]
Copland	Statements	1	1
Debussy	Gigues	15	[9]
Debussy	Rondes de Printemps	35	[19]
Delius	Appalachia	116	496
Delius	A Song of Summer	18	[135] 1f
Diamond	Fourth Symphony	26	1
Dukas	La Péri	5	[1]
		52	1
Egge	Symphony No. 1	33	[36] 5f
Engel	The Creation	14	3
Ferroud	Au Parc Monceau	11	[4]
Honegger	Horace Victorieux	9	3

COMPOSER	WORK	PAGE	MEASURE
Honegger	Le Chant de Nigamon	9	3
Honegger	Symphonie Liturgique	10	[5] 3f
Inghelbrecht	La Métamorphose d'Ève	18	[16] 4f
Johnson	Imagery	14	2
Levant	Nocturne	6	20
		18	65
		45	209
Mahler	Symphony No. 3	9	2b [5]
		150	1b [11]
		180	8
Mahler	Symphony No. 4	97	182
Mahler	Symphony No. 5	21	3
		68	[11] 2f
		156	[23] 3f
Mahler	Symphony No. 6	35	[21]
Mahler	Symphony No. 7	206	1b [246]
Mahler	Symphony No. 8	30	2b [32]
		74	2b [92]
		148	[116] 6f
Mahler	Symphony No. 9	27	1
		103	[27] 8f
		121	5
Martinet	Orphée	48	5
McKay	Sinfonietta No. 4	13	4
Milhaud	Opus Americanum No. 2	91	1b [650]
Milhaud	Ière Symphonie	41	[70] 4f
Milhaud	Quatrième Symphonie	29	[110] 1f
Milhaud	Suite Provençale	40	1b [35]
Moeran	Sinfonietta	42	[57] 2f
Moross	Biguine	29	3
Pierné	Divertissements sur un Thème Pastorale	8	[6] 2f
Piston	Symphony No. 2	87	3
Poulenc	Concerto pour deux Pianos et Orchestre	39	[30] 2f
Ravel	Boléro	5	1
Respighi	Vetrate di Chiesa	44	4
Rosenthal	Les Petits Métiers	26	1
		35	4
Roussel	Rapsodie Flamande	45	2
Schelling	A Victory Ball	116	6
Schmitt	Ronde burlesque	55	2
Schönberg	A Survivor from Warsaw	7	30
Schönberg	Fünf Orchesterstücke	55	1b [8]
Schuman, W.	Symphony No. III	38	328
		40	338
		42	349
Schuman, W.	Symphony No. IV	47	147

WOODWINDS

(7) BASSOON (contd.)

COMPOSER	WORK	PAGE	MEASURE
Schuman, W.	*Undertow*	5	2b [30]
		44	5
Sessions	*Suite from "The Black Maskers"*	13	[9]
Sessions	*Symphony No. II*	141	[X]
Slonimsky	*My Toy Balloon*	24	4
Strauss, R.	*Eine Alpensinfonie*	38	[35] 5f
Strauss, R.	*Symphonia Domestica*	63	[81] 1f
Strauss, R.	*Till Eulenspiegel's Merry Pranks*	8	2b [4]
		23	6b [17]
		59	11
Stravinsky	*Feuerwerk*	17	2
Stravinsky	*Fire-Bird Suite* (1919)	37	[12] 5f
Stravinsky	*Le Sacre du Printemps*	3	1
		71	5
Stravinsky	*Petrouchka Suite*	117	2
Stravinsky	*Suite No. 1 for Small Orchestra*	21	3b [1]
Thomson	*Orchestra Suite from "The Plow that Broke the Plains"*	21	5
Trapp	*Symphonie No. 4*	5	1
		67	[24]
Walton	*Symphony*	33	[19] 4f
Whithorne	*Fata Morgana*	42	[45] 1f
Whithorne	*The Dream Pedlar*	49	4
Vaughan Williams	*Symphony in E minor (No. 6)*	109	[20] 1f
Verdi	*I Vespri Siciliani Overture*	7	28

COMPOSER	WORK	PAGE	MEASURE
Mahler	*Das Lied von der Erde*	4	2
		6	1
		32	[40] 2f
		38	[49] 5f
Mahler	*Symphony No. 4*	104	262
Mahler	*Symphony No. 6*	178	[119]
Mahler	*Symphony No. 7*	77	[65]
		186	[225]
Mahler	*Symphony No. 9*	9	4b [4]
		14	2
		98	8
		129	5
		165	7
Prokofieff	*Piano Concerto No. 3*	32	[24]
Stravinsky	*Mass*	24	[50]
Shostakovitch	*Symphony No. 3*	57	[72]
Stravinsky	*Symphony in C*	21	[34] 4f

(8) CONTRABASSOON

COMPOSER	WORK	PAGE	MEASURE
Antheil	*McKonkey's Ferry*	1	6
Bach–Stokowski	*Komm Süsser Tod*	4	[3] 4f
Barber	*First Symphony*	94	1b [49]
Debussy	*Le Martyre de Saint Sébastien*	43	1
Delius	*Sea Drift*	90	4b [24]
Honegger	*Chant de Joie*	9	[4] 2f
Honegger	*Le Roi David*	55	1
Honegger	*Prélude pour "La Tempête"*	9	1
Mahler	*Symphony No. 3*	4	[1] 1f
		49	2
		224	[24] 1f

COMPOSER	WORK	PAGE	MEASURE
Milhaud	*Quatrième Symphonie*	100	[115] 2f
Piston	*Suite for Orchestra*	51	4
Read	*Sketches of the City*	22	2b [1]
		36	[9] 2f
Read	*Symphony No. I*	57	2
Schuman, W.	*Symphony No. III*	19	177
		22	188
Vaughan Williams	*Symphony in E minor (No. 6)*	5	[1]
		40	3
		51	1
Whithorne	*The Dream Pedlar*	19	3
Bach–Stokowski	*Fugue in G minor— The Shorter*	20	[13]

54

EXTREME OR EXTENDED RANGES

(8) CONTRABASSOON (contd.)

COMPOSER	WORK	PAGE	MEASURE	COMPOSER	WORK	PAGE	MEASURE
Bach–Stokowski	Komm Süsser Tod	5	[4] 3f	Schuman, W.	Symphony No. III	22	189
						51	103
Bloch	Trois Poèmes Juifs	41	1	Shostakovich–Stokowski	Prelude in E-Flat minor	2	2
		47	4	Strauss, R.	Eine Alpensinfonie	4	2b [2]
Brahms	Song of the Fates	8	3			162	14
Brahms	Symphony No. 1	154	374	Taylor	Through the Looking	45	[2] 1f
Elgar	Falstaff	109	8		Glass	52	8
Honegger	Mouvement	30	3	Tippett	Symphony No. 1	45	7
	Symphonique No. 3	34	2b [12]	Vaughan Williams	Symphony in F minor (No. 4)	58	[15] 4f
Honegger	Pacific 231	6	46	Vaughan Williams	Symphony in E minor (No. 6)	20	[6] 2f
Honegger	Prélude pour "La Tempête"	9	1			40	3
Inghelbrecht	El Greco	32	[29] 2f			71	[11] 3f
Mahler	Symphony No. 2	31	[15] 2f			115	2b [24]
		153	[13] 2f				
Mussorgsky–Ravel	Pictures at an Exhibition	9	7				
		132	3				
Prokofieff	Alexander Nevsky	155	6				
Ravel	La Valse	38	[26]				
Read	First Overture	56	2				
Read	Symphony No. I	59	4b [24]	Trapp	Symphonie No. 4	68	3

8 bassa

55

Chapter 5

DOUBLE-TONGUING

Piccolo

COMPOSER	WORK	PAGE	MEASURE	COMPOSER	WORK	PAGE	MEASURE
Maganini	*South Wind*	24	[T]	**Stravinsky**	*Chant du Rossignol*	36	[36]
Ravel	*Tzigane*	24	[24]			43	[44]
Schönberg	*Pierrot Lunaire*	12	2b [5]	**Verdi**	*Messa da Requiem*	210	54

Flute

COMPOSER	WORK	PAGE	MEASURE	COMPOSER	WORK	PAGE	MEASURE
Albéniz–Arbós	*Fête-Dieu à Séville*	7	1	**Ravel**	*Menuet Antique*	8	[5]
		11	3			24	[20]
Bartók	*Dance Suite*	28	84	**Ravel**	*Shéhérazade*	2	2b [1]
Casella	*Paganiniana*	99	1			29	[14]
Debussy–Ansermet	*Six Épigraphes Antiques*	69	1	**Ravel**	*Tzigane*	14	[12]
		86	[D]	**Ravel**	*Valses Nobles et*		
Honegger	*Le Chant de Nigamon*	17	[66]		*Sentimentales*	54	1b [53]
d'Indy	*Jour d' été à la Montagne*	99	[47] 4f	**Read**	*Symphony No. I*	23	[11]
Liadov	*Eight Russian Popular*			**Respighi**	*The Fountains of Rome*	55	3
	Songs	17	[2]	**Rimsky-Korsakoff**	*Russian Easter Overture*	3	[A] 1f
Liadov	*The Enchanted Lake*	7	1b [4]			7	[C] 1f
		16	2	**Rimsky-Korsakoff**	*Symphony No. 2,*	13	9
Maganini	*South Wind*	14	[M]		*"Antar"*	129	4
Miaskovsky	*Symphony No. 6*	63	[41]	**Rogers**	*Once Upon a Time,*		
Mussorgsky–Ravel	*Pictures at an Exhibition*	40	2		*Five Fairy Tales*	20	[14] 1f
		87	[71]	**Rossini**	*Semiramide Overture*	20	122
Parodi	*Preludio ad una*			**Roussel**	*Évocations, I*	37	[10]
	Commedia	15	[H]	**Schreker**	*The Birthday of the*		
Poot	*Symphonie*	19	5		*Infanta, Suite*	15	1
Poulenc	*Deux Marches et un*			**Sibelius**	*Symphony No. I*	134	1
	Intermède	11	2b [17]	**Stravinsky**	*Chant du Rossignol*	7	[4]
Prokofieff	*Ala et Lolly (Scythian*					75	3b [83]
	Suite)	71	[48]	**Stravinsky**	*Petrouchka Suite*	88	1
Prokofieff	*Romeo and Juliet, Suite No. 1*	98	[61]	**Stravinsky**	*Quatre Études pour Orchestre*	37	2b [10]
Prokofieff	*Summer Day Suite*	62	1b [30]	**Taylor**	*Through the Looking Glass*	120	[9]
		69	[34] 7f	**Walton**	*Concerto for Violin and*		
Rachmaninoff	*The Bells*	4	[3] 1f		*Orchestra*	17	1
Ravel	*Daphnis et Chloé, Suite No. 2*	51	[180]	**Zimbalist**	*American Rhapsody*	28	[20]

DOUBLE-TONGUING

Clarinet

COMPOSER	WORK	PAGE	MEASURE	COMPOSER	WORK	PAGE	MEASURE
Ferroud	*Au Parc Monceau*	11	2b [4]	Strauss, R.	*Eine Alpensinfonie*	139	[123]
Rachmaninoff	*The Bells*	46	[53]				

Bass Clarinet

COMPOSER	WORK	PAGE	MEASURE
Gould	*Spirituals*	15	5

Bassoon

COMPOSER	WORK	PAGE	MEASURE	COMPOSER	WORK	PAGE	MEASURE
Schreker	*The Birthday of the Infanta, Suite*	41	2b [220]	Vaughan Williams	*Pastoral Symphony*	90	5b [F]

Piccolo and Flute

COMPOSER	WORK	PAGE	MEASURE	COMPOSER	WORK	PAGE	MEASURE
Britten	*Four Sea Interludes from "Peter Grimes"*	11	6	Respighi	*Feste Romane*	72	[20] 4f
Cadman	*Dark Dancers of the Mardi Gras*	33	2	Rimsky-Korsakoff	*Russian Easter Overture*	32	**4**
Diamond	*Timon of Athens*	13	84	Rimsky-Korsakoff	*Scheherazade*	218	484
Harsanyi	*Suite pour Orchestre*	10	3	Rosenthal	*Les Petits Métiers*	5	[A]
d'Indy	*Istar, Variations Symphoniques*	18	[H] 2f			39	3
Janssen	*New Year's Eve in New York*	59	[23]	Roussel	*Évocations, II*	12	[6] 4f
		76	4	Strauss, R.	*Don Quixote*	47	5
Mahler	*Symphony No. 8*	110	[62] 2f	Stravinsky	*Feuerwerk*	18	[17] 1f
Prokofieff	*Suite from the Ballet "Chout"*	32	[41]			27	4b [27]
				Stravinsky	*Fire-Bird Suite* (1919)	10	3
Ravel	*Rapsodie Espagnole*	19	2b [9]	Stravinsky	*Scherzo Fantastique*	46	[67]
		77	[24]	Walton	*Façade, Suite No. 1*	69	1b [J]
		88	[31]				

Flute and Alto Flute

COMPOSER	WORK	PAGE	MEASURE
Shostakovich	*Symphony No. 7*	99	[97]

Flute and Oboe

COMPOSER	WORK	PAGE	MEASURE	COMPOSER	WORK	PAGE	MEASURE
Kerr	*Symphony No. 1*	58	2b [325]	Tansman	*Deux Moments Symphoniques*	15	1
Pierné	*Viennoise*	6	[C]				
Roussel	*Symphonie en Sol mineur*	57	1b [34]				

Flute and Clarinet

COMPOSER	WORK	PAGE	MEASURE	COMPOSER	WORK	PAGE	MEASURE
· **Bartók**	*Second Rhapsody for Violin and Orchestra*	19	[12]	Berlioz	*Benvenuto Cellini Overture*	37	2
Bax	*In the Faery Hills*	54	4	Casella	*Elegia Eroica*	13	2

WOODWINDS

Flute and Clarinet (contd.)

COMPOSER	WORK	PAGE	MEASURE	COMPOSER	WORK	PAGE	MEASURE
Honegger	Le Chant de Nigamon	46	2	Ravel	Introduction et Allegro	2	[1]
d'Indy	Deuxième Symphonie					12	8b [7]
	en Si♭	37	4			26	[19]
Mahler	Symphony No. 8	111	[63] 4f	Tchaikovsky	Manfred-Symphonie	69	1
		160	[136]	Tchaikovsky	Nutcracker Suite	35	[E]

Flute and Bassoon

COMPOSER	WORK	PAGE	MEASURE
Tansman	Deux Moments Symphoniques	33	1

Oboe and Clarinet

COMPOSER	WORK	PAGE	MEASURE
Schelling	A Victory Ball	34	1

Clarinet and Bassoon

COMPOSER	WORK	PAGE	MEASURE	COMPOSER	WORK	PAGE	MEASURE
de Falla	Three Dances from "The Three-Cornered Hat"	7	[6]	Mendelssohn	Symphony No. 3, "Scotch"	74	176
				Stravinsky	Histoire du Soldat	28	3b [18]

Piccolo, Flute, and Oboe

COMPOSER	WORK	PAGE	MEASURE	COMPOSER	WORK	PAGE	MEASURE
Knipper	Symphony No. 4	98	[15]	Read	Prelude and Toccata	29	5

Piccolo, Flute, and Clarinet

COMPOSER	WORK	PAGE	MEASURE	COMPOSER	WORK	PAGE	MEASURE
Read	Prelude and Toccata	28	[10] 2f	Roussel	Évocations, II	57	[25]

Flute, Oboe, and Clarinet

COMPOSER	WORK	PAGE	MEASURE	COMPOSER	WORK	PAGE	MEASURE
Balakirev– Casella	Islamey	29	[27] 1f	Chabrier	Joyeuse Marche	27	7
Berlioz	Benvenuto Cellini Overture	30	3	Dello Joio	Variations, Chaconne, and Finale	6	3b [30]
Cadman	Dark Dancers of the Mardi Gras	5	4	Kabalevsky	Suite from "Colas Breugnon"	137	3b [8]
				Tchaikovsky	Francesca da Rimini	86	1

Flute, Clarinet, and Bassoon

COMPOSER	WORK	PAGE	MEASURE	COMPOSER	WORK	PAGE	MEASURE
Borodin	Symphony No. 2	136	[D]	Rimsky-Korsakoff	Symphony No. 2, "Antar"	149	[L]

Oboe, English Horn, and Clarinet

COMPOSER	WORK	PAGE	MEASURE
Strauss, R.	Eine Alpensinfonie	127	2

DOUBLE-TONGUING

Piccolo, Flute, Oboe, and Clarinet

COMPOSER	WORK	PAGE	MEASURE
Hindemith	*Mathis der Maler*	**72**	[21]

Flute, Oboe, Clarinet, and Bassoon

Tchaikovsky	*Symphony No. 2*	**71**	[G]

Piccolo, Flute, Oboe, English Horn, and Clarinet

COMPOSER	WORK	PAGE	MEASURE	COMPOSER	WORK	PAGE	MEASURE
Honegger	*Pacific 231*	**41**	190	**Inghelbrecht**	*Rapsodie de Printemps*	**44**	1

Piccolo, Flute, Oboe, Clarinet, and Bassoon

Bliss	*Concerto for Piano and Orchestra*	**51**	2b [29]

Flute, Oboe, English Horn, Clarinet, Bass Clarinet, and Bassoon

Glière	*Russian Sailors' Dance*	**30**	[195] 1f

Chapter 6

TRIPLE-TONGUING

(t k t   t k t)

Piccolo

COMPOSER	WORK	PAGE	MEASURE	COMPOSER	WORK	PAGE	MEASURE
Charpentier	*Impressions d'Italie*	4	[8]	**Strauss, R.**	*Also Sprach Zara-thustra*	99	1

Flute

COMPOSER	WORK	PAGE	MEASURE	COMPOSER	WORK	PAGE	MEASURE
Barber	*Second Symphony*	74	5b [11]	**Ravel**	*La Valse*	86	5
Becker	*Concerto for Horn and Orchestra*	13	7	**Rimsky-Korsakoff**	*Scheherazade*	119	[E]
Elgar	*Symphony No. 1*	108	[96]	**Schelling**	*A Victory Ball*	34	1
Golestan	*Concerto Roumain pour Violon et Orchestre*	55	6b [T]	**Stillman-Kelley**	*New England Symphony*	63	[L]
Prokofieff	*Ala et Lolly (Scythian Suite)*	64	[41]	**Strauss, R.**	*Ein Heldenleben*	60	[32]
				Stravinsky	*Le Sacre du Printemps*	106	[134]
Prokofieff	*Violin Concerto No. 2*	35	[34]	**Szymanowski**	*Symphonie Concertante pour Piano et Orchestre*	16	[9]
Ravel	*Alborada del Gracioso*	10	[6]				
		33	[27]				

Clarinet

COMPOSER	WORK	PAGE	MEASURE	COMPOSER	WORK	PAGE	MEASURE
Kabalevsky	*Symphony No. 2*	97	[1]	**Schönberg**	*Pierrot Lunaire*	75	3b [25]
Ravel	*Shéhérazade*	2	2b [1]				

Bassoon

COMPOSER	WORK	PAGE	MEASURE
Rimsky-Korsakoff	*Scheherazade*	170	[F]

Piccolo and Flute

COMPOSER	WORK	PAGE	MEASURE	COMPOSER	WORK	PAGE	MEASURE
Dukas	*La Péri*	98	[14 bis]	**Ravel**	*Rapsodie Espagnole*	55	2
Ferroud	*Au Parc Monceau*	11	2b [4]			75	[23]
Grofé	*Grand Canyon Suite*	131	[10]	**Roussel**	*Symphonie en Sol mineur*	56	2
Ibert	*Escales*	79	[68] 3f	**Stravinsky**	*Fire-Bird Suite (1919)*	15	[18]

60

TRIPLE-TONGUING

Piccolo and Oboe

COMPOSER	WORK	PAGE	MEASURE
Gould	*Philharmonic Waltzes*	**32**	[411]

Flute and Oboe

COMPOSER	WORK	PAGE	MEASURE	COMPOSER	WORK	PAGE	MEASURE
Debussy	*La Mer*	**53**	[27]	**Mihalovici**	*Divertissement pour Petit Orchestre*	**33**	[M] 4f
Goldmark	*Overture, In Spring-time*	**25**	[51]				

Flute and Clarinet

COMPOSER	WORK	PAGE	MEASURE	COMPOSER	WORK	PAGE	MEASURE
Barber	*Second Essay or Orchestra*	**5**	4	**Debussy**	*La Mer*	**41**	[21]
Bax	*Sixth Symphony*	**28**	2b [24]	**Ravel**	*Introduction et Allegro*	**37**	7
Bruckner	*Symphony No. 2*	**18**	[200] 3f	**Schelling**	*A Victory Ball*	**30**	I

Clarinet and Bassoon

COMPOSER	WORK	PAGE	MEASURE	COMPOSER	WORK	PAGE	MEASURE
Chabrier	*Ouverture de "Gwendoline"*	**28**	[10]	**Taylor**	*Ballet Music from "Casanova"*	**I**	2
Debussy	*La Mer*	**47**	3				

Piccolo, Flute, and Alto Flute

COMPOSER	WORK	PAGE	MEASURE
Stravinsky	*Le Sacre du Printemps*	**32**	[42]

Piccolo, Flute, and Clarinet

COMPOSER	WORK	PAGE	MEASURE	COMPOSER	WORK	PAGE	MEASURE
Bax	*First Symphony*	**119**	1b [N]	**Ibert**	*Escales*	**83**	[72] 3f
Grofé	*Grand Canyon Suite*	**152**	[15] 1f				

Flute, Oboe, and Clarinet

COMPOSER	WORK	PAGE	MEASURE
Fauré	*Pénélope Prélude*	6	2

Flute, Clarinet, and Bassoon

COMPOSER	WORK	PAGE	MEASURE
Mendelssohn	*Symphony No. 4, "Italian"*	I	I

Flute, Oboe, English Horn, and Clarinet

COMPOSER	WORK	PAGE	MEASURE
Tchaikovsky	*Romeo and Juliet*	**53**	388

Flute, Oboe, Clarinet, and Bassoon

COMPOSER	WORK	PAGE	MEASURE
Lalo	*Le Roi d'Ys Ouverture*	**18**	[F]

WOODWINDS

Piccolo, Flute, Oboe, English Horn, and Clarinet

COMPOSER	WORK	PAGE	MEASURE	COMPOSER	WORK	PAGE	MEASURE
Enesco	Ière Rhapsodie Roumaine	88	[41]	Stravinsky	Le Sacre du Printemps	34	[45]

Piccolo, Flute, Oboe, Clarinet, and Bassoon

COMPOSER	WORK	PAGE	MEASURE
Strauss, R.	Don Juan	4	4

Flute, Oboe, English Horn, Clarinet, Bass Clarinet, and Bassoon

COMPOSER	WORK	PAGE	MEASURE
Pierné	Divertissements sur un Thème Pastoral	58	3b [38]

Chapter 7

FLUTTER-TONGUING

English	Italian	French	German
Flutter	Colpo(i) di lingua	Trémolo	Alle in den Bläsern als 
Flutter-tongue	Frulato	*Trém.*	notierten Stellen sind
Tremolo	Rullato	Trémolo avec la langue	mit Zugenschlag aus-
Trem.	Tremolo	Trémolo dental	zuführen
Trill with tongue	*Trem.*	Trémolo en roulant la langue	Flatterzunge
while playing	Vibrando	Trémolo roulé	*Flatterz.*
	Vib.		Tremolo
	Vibrato linguale		*Trem.*

Piccolo

COMPOSER	WORK	PAGE	MEASURE	COMPOSER	WORK	PAGE	MEASURE
Dukas	La Péri	64	[9]	**Siegmeister**	Ozark Set	10	3
Maganini	South Wind	22	[R]			79	[75] 1f
Milhaud	La Mort d'un Tyran	39	169	**Stravinsky**	Chant du Rossignol	72	[80]
Milhaud	Le Bal Martiniquais	29	3b [65]	**Szymanowski**	Symphonie Concertante		
Moross	Paeans	5	[E]		pour Piano et Orchestre	110	[40]
		11	[K]	**Taylor**	Through the Looking		
Ravel	Ma Mère l'Oye	7	[5] 1f		Glass	99	[15] 4f
Rogers	Once Upon a Time,	7	1b [5]	**Villa-Lobos**	Amazonas	64	[27]
	Five Fairy Tales	30	[19] 5f	**Villa-Lobos**	Chôros No. 8	51	2
Schönberg	Pierrot Lunaire	14	[15]				

Flute

COMPOSER	WORK	PAGE	MEASURE	COMPOSER	WORK	PAGE	MEASURE
Atterberg	The Wise and the			**de Falla**	El Retablo de Maese		
	Foolish Virgins	38	1		Pedro	31	1
Bartók	Concerto for Piano and			**Fitelberg**	Symphony No. 1	54	[31]
	Orchestra	59	6b [13]	**Golestan**	Concerto Roumain pour		
Bartók	Dance Suite	75	25		Violon et Orchestre	35	1b [200]
Bartók	Vier Orchesterstücke	11	4b [7]	**Graener**	Comedietta	7	30
Berg	Three Excerpts from			**Honegger**	Le Roi David	62	[3]
	"Wozzeck"	14	[370]	**Honegger**	Pacific 231	2	10
Bernstein	"Jeremiah" Symphony	18	[7]			9	[5]
Britten	Sinfonia da Requiem	13	1b [10]	**Honegger**	Suite d'Orchestre,		
Diamond	Timon of Athens	17	107		"L'Impératrice aux		
Engel	The Creation	56	[32]		Rochers"	50	1

WOODWINDS

Flute (contd.)

COMPOSER	WORK	PAGE	MEASURE	COMPOSER	WORK	PAGE	MEASURE
Janssen	New Year's Eve in New	16	2	**Ravel**	Daphnis et Chloé, Suite		
	York	22	[9]		No. 2	7	1
		36	[14]	**Ravel**	La Valse	8	1
		54	[21] 3f			45	[32]
Mahler	Das Lied von der Erde	3	3			79	[58] 2f
		9	[7] 4f	**Read**	Sketches of the City	6	[3]
		13	[12] 2f	**Rogers**	Once Upon a Time,	40	3
		16	[17]		Five Fairy Tales	57	1b [33]
		19	[20] 4f	**Rosenthal**	Les Petits Métiers	26	1
		24	[28]	**Schelling**	A Victory Ball	31	1
		73	1	**Schönberg**	A Survivor from		
Mahler	Symphony No. 7	227	2b [265]		Warsaw	1	3
Mahler	Symphony No. 9	115	[31]	**Schönberg**	Fünf Orchesterstücke	53	[6]
		141	[39] 4f	**Schönberg**	Pierrot Lunaire	45	[10] 2f
Mihalovici	Divertissement pour					72	[10] 1f
	Petit Orchestre	47	11	**Schönberg**	Theme and Variations	33	156
Mihalovici	Toccata pour Piano et			**Siegmeister**	Ozark Set	35	[50]
	Orchestre	102	[390] 2f			84	1
Milhaud	Concerto pour Piano et			**Siegmeister**	Western Suite	88	2
	Orchestre	44	[45]	**Strauss, R.**	Don Quixote	111	1
Milhaud	Deuxième Concerto pour			**Strauss, R.**	Eine Alpensinfonie	114	3b [110]
	Violon et Orchestre	71	1b [100]	**Stravinsky**	Chant du Rossignol	15	[13]
Milhaud	La Création du Monde	23	[25]	**Stravinsky**	Scherzo Fantastique	31	[47]
Moross	Biguine	10	[B]			55	[77]
Mussorgsky–	Pictures at an Exhibition	59	[55]	**Stravinsky**	Suite No. 1 for Small		
Ravel					Orchestra	18	3b [7]
Poot	Symphonie	15	[7] 5f	**Szymanowski**	Symphonie Concertante		
		45	[24] 1f		pour Piano et	10	3
		70	2		Orchestre	35	[19]
Poulenc	Aubade	33	[23] 6f	**Taylor**	Through the Looking	79	[2]
Poulenc	Deux Marches et un				Glass	87	[9] 2f
	Intermède	7	[12] 2f			91	[11]
Rachmaninoff	The Bells	41	[45]	**Thomson**	The Seine at Night	13	2b [8]
Ravel	Concerto pour la main					18	[10]
	gauche	40	[20]				

Oboe

COMPOSER	WORK	PAGE	MEASURE
Stravinsky	La Sacre du Printemps	29	39

English Horn

Schönberg	Kammersymphonie, Op. 9	31	[29]

Clarinet

COMPOSER	WORK	PAGE	MEASURE	COMPOSER	WORK	PAGE	MEASURE
Gould	Latin-American			**Strauss, R.**	Suite from "Le		
	Symphonette	86	8		Bourgeois Gentil-	123	1
Honegger	Pacific 231	6	46		homme"	127	2
Sessions	Symphony No. II	39	3b [Y]	**Varèse**	Intégrales	19	[8] 2f
Strauss, R.	Don Quixote	52	4				

64

FLUTTER-TONGUING

Bass Clarinet

COMPOSER	WORK	PAGE	MEASURE
Schönberg	*Pierrot Lunaire*	27	2b [15]

Saxophone

COMPOSER	WORK	PAGE	MEASURE
Thomson	*Orchestra Suite from "The Plow that Broke the Plains"*	35	[32]

Piccolo and Flute

COMPOSER	WORK	PAGE	MEASURE	COMPOSER	WORK	PAGE	MEASURE
Bartók	*Dance Suite*	92	152	**Ravel**	*Concerto pour Piano et Orchestre*	53	3
Britten	*Sinfonia da Requiem*	24	1	**Sessions**	*Symphony No. II*	38	[X]
Copland	*Third Symphony*	135	[117]	**Siegmeister**	*From my Window*	7	1b [35]
Diamond	*Timon of Athens*	23	152			22	3b [20]
Fitelberg	*Nocturne for Orchestra*	63	1	**Siegmeister**	*Sunday in Brooklyn*	24	[20]
Honegger	*Le Roi David*	51	1b [4]			76	[65] 1f
Honegger	*Prélude pour "La Tempête"*	18	2			94	[120]
Honegger	*Suite d'Orchestre, "L'Impératrice aux Rochers"*	32	[4]	**Siegmeister**	*Western Suite*	10	[35] 1f
		36	[5] 1f	**Stravinsky**	*Chant du Rossignol*	54	[58] 2f
Ibert	*La Ballade de la Geôle de Reading*	13	[9]	**Stravinsky**	*Le Sacre du Printemps*	6	6b [8]
Milhaud	*IIe Symphonie*	21	1	**Stravinsky**	*Petrouchka Suite*	114	3
		39	[135] 1f	**Szymanowski**	*Symphonie Concertante pour Piano et Orchestre*	76	[13]
Prokofieff	*Symphony No. 5*	126	3				

Piccolo and Clarinet

COMPOSER	WORK	PAGE	MEASURE	COMPOSER	WORK	PAGE	MEASURE
Britten	*Sinfonia da Requiem*	25	[18]	**Ravel**	*Concerto pour Piano et Orchestre*	30	[24]
Milhaud	*La Mort d'un Tyran*	40	2	**Villa-Lobos**	*Chôros No. 10*	4	[B]

Flute and Alto Flute

COMPOSER	WORK	PAGE	MEASURE
Stravinsky	*Le Sacre du Printemps*	54	7

Flute and Oboe

COMPOSER	WORK	PAGE	MEASURE	COMPOSER	WORK	PAGE	MEASURE
Britten	*Sinfonia da Requiem*	26	5b [19]	**Maganini**	*An Ornithological Suite*	5	[A] 4f
Honegger	*Le Roi David*	27	1			17	[G]

Flute and Clarinet

COMPOSER	WORK	PAGE	MEASURE	COMPOSER	WORK	PAGE	MEASURE
Berg	*Violin Concerto*	11	2b [60]	**Milhaud**	*La Création du Monde*	56	2b [54]
		70	[100]	**Sessions**	*Suite from "The Black Maskers"*	96	[91]
Golestan	*Concerto Roumain pour Violon et Orchestre*	12	2b [D]			106	1b [96]
Honegger	*Symphonie Liturgique*	99	1	**Strauss, R.**	*Symphonia Domestica*	5	4b [4]

WOODWINDS

Oboe and Clarinet

COMPOSER	WORK	PAGE	MEASURE
Strauss, R.	*Eine Alpensinfonie*	**58**	3b [51]

Clarinet and Bass Clarinet

Strauss, R.	*Don Quixote*	**56**	2

Flute, Alto Flute, and Clarinet

Stravinsky	*Le Sacre du Printemps*	**13**	[17]
		25	[34]
		88	[107]
		119	[161]

Flute, Oboe, and Clarinet

COMPOSER	WORK	PAGE	MEASURE	COMPOSER	WORK	PAGE	MEASURE
Mahler	*Symphony No. 2*	**181**	[26] 7f	**Stravinsky**	*Le Sacre du Printemps*	**8**	3

Piccolo, Flute, Alto Flute, and Clarinet

Stravinsky	*Le Sacre du Printemps*	**85**	[103]

Piccolo, Flute, Oboe, and Clarinet

COMPOSER	WORK	PAGE	MEASURE	COMPOSER	WORK	PAGE	MEASURE
Britten	*Sinfonia da Requiem*	**28**	[20]	**Ravel**	*Alborada del Gracioso*	**31**	2

Flute, Alto Flute, English Horn, and Clarinet

Stravinsky	*Le Sacre du Printemps*	**89**	2b [109]

Flute, Alto Flute, Clarinet, and Bass Clarinet

Stravinsky	*Le Sacre du Printemps*	**24**	2b [33]

Oboe, English Horn, Clarinet, and Bass Clarinet

Grofé	*Grand Canyon Suite*	**33**	4

Piccolo, Flute, Oboe, Clarinet, and Bassoon

Shostakovich	*Symphony No. 1*	**68**	[14]

Piccolo, Flute, Oboe, Clarinet, and Saxophone

Britten	*Sinfonia da Requiem*	**48**	[32]

FLUTTER-TONGUING

Piccolo, Flute, Alto Flute, Oboe, English Horn, and Clarinet

COMPOSER	WORK	PAGE	MEASURE
Stravinsky	*Le Sacre du Printemps*	**87**	[106]

Piccolo, Flute, Oboe, English Horn, Clarinet, and Bass Clarinet

Grofé	*Grand Canyon Suite*	**152**	[15]

Piccolo, Flute, Oboe, English Horn, Clarinet, Bassoon, and Saxophone

Britten	*Sinfonia da Requiem*	**51**	[34]

Chapter 8

GLISSANDI AND PORTAMENTI

English	Italian	French	German
English	*Italian*	*French*	*German*
Glissando	Glissando	En glissant	Glissando
gliss.	*gliss., gl.*	Glissando	*Gliss., Gl.*
Slide	Portamento	*gliss.*	Hinaufziehn
	Portando	Glissé	Hinunterziehn
	Portare	Glissez	Starkes Portamento
	port.	Les portamenti indiquées	
	Strisciando	par le signe:→	
	Striscia(ta)	Traînez	

Flute

COMPOSER	WORK	PAGE	MEASURE
Maganini	*Tuolumne*	**22**	4

Oboe

COMPOSER	WORK	PAGE	MEASURE	COMPOSER	WORK	PAGE	MEASURE
Mahler	*Symphony No. 9*	**42**	3b [14]	**Varèse**	*Intégrales*	**39**	[19]

English Horn

COMPOSER	WORK	PAGE	MEASURE
Villa-Lobos	*Uirapurú*	**46**	[10]

Clarinet

COMPOSER	WORK	PAGE	MEASURE	COMPOSER	WORK	PAGE	MEASURE
Copland	*Dance Symphony*	**87**	[52] 4f	**Honegger**	*Concertino pour Piano et Orchestre*	**20**	1b [12]
Copland	*El Salón México*	**28**	2b [28]	**Mahler**	*Symphony No. 5*	**124**	1b [5]
Gershwin	*Rhapsody in Blue*	**2**	1	**Mahler**	*Symphony No. 7*	**120**	[114] 2f
		11	[9] 3f	**Stravinsky**	*Chant du Rossignol*	**24**	[25] 2f
Grofé	*Grand Canyon Suite*	**61**	[C]				

Bass Clarinet

COMPOSER	WORK	PAGE	MEASURE	COMPOSER	WORK	PAGE	MEASURE
Gould	*Latin-American Symphonette*	**39**	[2] 3f	**Schönberg**	*Pierrot Lunaire*	**42**	[20]

GLISSANDI AND PORTAMENTI

Bassoon

COMPOSER	WORK	PAGE	MEASURE
Schönberg	*Fünf Orchesterstücke*	**55**	[8]

Contrabassoon

Strauss, R.	*Don Quixote*	**99**	8

Saxophone

COMPOSER	WORK	PAGE	MEASURE	COMPOSER	WORK	PAGE	MEASURE
Delannoy	*Figures Sonores*	**74**	6	**Poot**	*Jazz-Music*	**10**	1b [5]
Janssen	*New Year's Eve in New York*	**65**	[26]	**Poot**	*Symphonie*	**49**	1
				Villa-Lobos	*Chôros No. 8*	**72**	1

Piccolo and Flute

COMPOSER	WORK	PAGE	MEASURE	COMPOSER	WORK	PAGE	MEASURE
Chávez	*Sinfonia India*	**76**	4b [103]	**Rosenthal**	*Les Petits Métiers*	**12**	2

Piccolo and Clarinet

Moross	*Paeans*	**2**	[A]

Flute and Oboe

COMPOSER	WORK	PAGE	MEASURE	COMPOSER	WORK	PAGE	MEASURE
Berlioz	*Symphonie Fantastique*	**163**	2	**Mahler**	*Symphony No. 9*	**144**	[40] 3f
		166	3				

Flute and Clarinet

COMPOSER	WORK	PAGE	MEASURE	COMPOSER	WORK	PAGE	MEASURE
Berg	*Violin Concerto*	**35**	1b [170]	**Strauss, R.**	*Till Eulenspiegel's Merry Pranks*	**22**	3
Honegger	*Le Roi David*	**184**	1b [3]				
Ives	*"The Fourth of July" from Symphony, "Holidays"*	**33**	[X]				

Flute and Bass Clarinet

Still	*Dismal Swamp*	**12**	1

Oboe and Bassoon

Ives	*Three Places in New England*	**46**	2

English Horn and Bassoon

Mahler	*Symphony No. 4*	**158**	42

Clarinet and Saxophone

Britten	*Sinfonia da Requiem*	**51**	[34] 6f

WOODWINDS

Bass Clarinet and Bassoon

COMPOSER	WORK	PAGE	MEASURE
Read	*First Overture*	**57**	[20]

Bassoon and Contrabassoon

Mahler	*Symphony No. 3*	**11**	[7]

Piccolo, Flute, and Clarinet

Parodi	*Preludio ad una Commedia*	**36**	1b [R]

Piccolo, Oboe, and Clarinet

Gould	*Philharmonic Waltzes*	**43**	[500]

Flute, Oboe, and Clarinet

COMPOSER	WORK	PAGE	MEASURE	COMPOSER	WORK	PAGE	MEASURE
Cesana	*Second American Symphony*	**70**	[2] 1f	**Read**	*Symphony No. I*	**18**	2

Flute, English Horn, and Clarinet

Strauss, R.	*Ein Heldenleben*	**66**	[34]

Oboe, English Horn, and Clarinet

Inghelbrecht	*El Greco*	**2**	1b [1]

Oboe, Clarinet, and Bass Clarinet

Chávez	*Sinfonia India*	**70**	4b [97]

Oboe, Clarinet, and Bassoon

Cesana	*Second American Symphony*	**155**	[38] 1f

Piccolo, Flute, Oboe, and Clarinet

Gillis	*Symphony No. 5½*	**72**	1

Piccolo, Oboe, Clarinet, and Bassoon

Cesana	*Second American Symphony*	**73**	[4] 1f

GLISSANDI AND PORTAMENTI

Flute, Oboe, English Horn, and Clarinet

COMPOSER	WORK	PAGE	MEASURE	COMPOSER	WORK	PAGE	MEASURE
Honegger	*Symphonie Liturgique*	86	I	**Janssen**	*New Year's Eve in New York*	7	3
Inghelbrecht	*El Greco*	10	[7]				

Flute, Clarinet, Bass Clarinet, and Bassoon

COMPOSER	WORK	PAGE	MEASURE
Piket	*Curtain Raiser to an American Play*	38	3

Piccolo, Flute, Oboe, English Horn, and Clarinet

Grofé	*Grand Canyon Suite*	53	I

Piccolo, Flute, Oboe, Clarinet, and Bass Clarinet

Chávez	*Sinfonia India*	79	4b [106]

Piccolo, Flute, Oboe, Clarinet, and Saxophone

Gould	*Latin-American Symphonette*	123	I

Flute, Oboe, English Horn, Clarinet, Bass Clarinet, and Bassoon

Honegger	*Symphonie Liturgique*	94	1b [10]

Chapter 9

BELLS UP

English	Italian	French	German
Bell(s) in the air	Campane in alto	Les pavillons en l'air	Mit aufgehobenem Schall-trichter
Bells up	Campana in aria [su]	*Pav^on en l'air*	
Hold high	Campane nell'aria	Pavillon(s) en haut	Mit aufwärts gerichteten Schalltrichter
Raise the bell(s)	Levato	Pavillon en l'air	
	Paviglione(i) in alto [su]		Schalltrichter auf! [hoch]
	Sopra		Schalltrichter in die Höhe
			Stürze hoch
			Stürze in die Höhe

NATURAL POSITION

English	Italian	French	German
Bell(s) down	Al ordinario	Naturel	Gewöhnlich
In usual manner	(In) modo ordinario	*nat.*	*gwöhn.*
Lower the bell(s)	*modo ord.*	Ordinaire(ment)	Natürlich
Natural (position)	Loco	*ord.*	Normal
nat.	Ordinario	Position naturelle	
Ordinary	*ord.*	*pos. nat.*	
ord.	Posizione ordinaria	Position ordinaire	
	pos. ord.	*pos. ord.*	

Oboe

COMPOSER	WORK	PAGE	MEASURE	COMPOSER	WORK	PAGE	MEASURE
Mahler	*Symphony No. 4*	**26**	146	**Mahler**	*Symphony No. 6*	**122**	[83] 1f

Clarinet

COMPOSER	WORK	PAGE	MEASURE	COMPOSER	WORK	PAGE	MEASURE
Mahler	*Das Lied von der Erde*	**24**	[26] 9f	**Mahler**	*Symphony No. 4*	**22**	120
Mahler	*Symphony No. 3*	**16**	[12]			**30**	161
		150	[11] 1f			**83**	90
						167	78
				Mahler	*Symphony No. 5*	**119**	[2] 3f
				Schönberg	*Pierrot Lunaire*	**47**	2b [20]

Saxophone

COMPOSER	WORK	PAGE	MEASURE
Gershwin	*An American in Paris*	**76**	[63]

Piccolo and Clarinet

COMPOSER	WORK	PAGE	MEASURE
Varèse	*Hyperprism*	**17**	7

BELLS UP

Oboe and Clarinet

COMPOSER	WORK	PAGE	MEASURE	COMPOSER	WORK	PAGE	MEASURE
Mahler	*Das Lied von der Erde*	35	[44]	**Mahler**	*Symphony No. 5*	22	1b [8]
Mahler	*Symphony No. 1*	51	[5] 1f			43	[18]
Mahler	*Symphony No. 2*	7	[2]			64	7
		25	6			90	[22]
		114	[49] 3f			101	[28] 1f
		160	[16]			149	[19]
Mahler	*Symphony No. 3*	100	[74]			172	3
		168	1b [24]			184	[3]
		229	[30]	**Mahler**	*Symphony No. 6*	18	[11]
Mahler	*Symphony No. 4*	31	164			44	1b [27]
		44	[16]			169	1b [115]
		121	89	**Mahler**	*Symphony No. 7*	28	1b [22]
		130	195			184	4
						253	[293] 1f
				Mahler	*Symphony No. 8*	4	3b [2]
						36	1b [40]
						55	[64]

Clarinet and Saxophone

COMPOSER	WORK	PAGE	MEASURE
Gould	*Latin–American Symphonette*	85	[5] 1f

Oboe, English Horn, and Clarinet

COMPOSER	WORK	PAGE	MEASURE	COMPOSER	WORK	PAGE	MEASURE
Mahler	*Symphony No. 2*	46	3	**Mahler**	*Symphony No. 6*	202	2
Mahler	*Symphony No. 4*	133	210				

Chapter 10

HARMONICS

English	Italian	French	German
Harmonic(s)	Armonico(i)	Harmonique(s)	Flageolett
harm.	arm.	Harm.	Flag.
		En harmonique en se servant du doigté du Fa grave	

Flute

COMPOSER	WORK	PAGE	MEASURE	COMPOSER	WORK	PAGE	MEASURE
Casella	*Elegia Eroica*	34	[51] 1f	**Ravel**	*Rapsodie Espagnole*	70	[20] 2f
Diamond	*Music for Shakespeare's*			**Ravel**	*Shéhérazade*	38	[19]
	"Romeo and Juliet"	66	[120] 2f	**Read**	*Symphony No. I*	4	[3]
Ibert	*Escales*	46	[41]	**Stravinsky**	*Concerto en Ré pour*		
Ibert	*La Ballade de la Geôle*				*Violon et Orchestre*	62	[125] 2f
	de Reading	62	[44] 2f	**Stravinsky**	*Le Sacre du Printemps*	77	[87]
Mussorgsky–	*Pictures at an*					84	[101]
Ravel	*Exhibition*	96	[78] 5f	**Stravinsky**	*Pulcinella Suite*	11	[10]
Pizzetti	*Concerto dell'Estate*	71	7			31	[42]
Ravel	*La Valse*	48	[35]			33	[50]
Ravel	*Menuet Antique*	13	4b [10]	**Varèse**	*Hyperprism*	5	3b [2]

Oboe

COMPOSER	WORK	PAGE	MEASURE	COMPOSER	WORK	PAGE	MEASURE
Ferroud	*Au Parc Monceau*	18	[4] 9f	**Taylor**	*Through the Looking*	79	[3]
					Glass	92	[12]

English Horn

COMPOSER	WORK	PAGE	MEASURE
Prokofieff	*Romeo and Juliet, Suite No. I*	32	[17] 5f

Piccolo and Flute

COMPOSER	WORK	PAGE	MEASURE
Ravel	*Tzigane*	9	[8]

Chapter II

OFF-STAGE

English	*Italian*	*French*	*German*
Behind the scene [stage]	A calotta	Dans la coulisse	Auf dem Theater
In the distance	Dietro la scena	Derrière la scène	Auf der Bühne
Off-stage	In distanza	Lointain	Aus der Ferne
	In lontananza ed invisibili		Hinter dem Orchester
	Interna		Hinter der Bühne [Scene]
	Lontano		In der Entfernung [Ferne]
	Nella scena lontano		In Entfernung aufgesteilt
			In weiter Entfernung
			Isoliert postiert

Flute

COMPOSER	WORK	PAGE	MEASURE
Skilton	*Suite Primeval, Part II*	3	1

Oboe

COMPOSER	WORK	PAGE	MEASURE	COMPOSER	WORK	PAGE	MEASURE
Berlioz	*Symphonie Fantastique*	100	3	**Prokofieff**	*Alexander Nevsky*	6	[1] 1f

English Horn

COMPOSER	WORK	PAGE	MEASURE	COMPOSER	WORK	PAGE	MEASURE
Prokofieff	*Alexander Nevsky*	53	4b [34]	**Wagner, R.**	*Introduction to Act III, "Tristan und Isolde"*	6	[2] 10f

75

Chapter 12

ECHO-TONE

English	Italian	French	German
Echo-tone	Come un eco	Écho	Echoton
	Eco		

Clarinet

COMPOSER	WORK	PAGE	MEASURE	COMPOSER	WORK	PAGE	MEASURE
Berlioz	*Three Pieces from "The Damnation of Faust"*	**36**	18	**Mahler**	*Symphony No. 2*	**8**	1b [3]
						17	3
Debussy–						**183**	[27] 14f
Ansermet	*Six Épigraphes Antiques*	**14**	1b [B]	**Mahler**	*Symphony No. 3*	**15**	[11] 4f
Mahler	*Symphony No. 1*	**23**	[17] 2f			**51**	[35]
		142	[39]			**54**	[38] 6f
				Mahler	*Symphony No. 4*	**11**	69

Chapter 13

VIBRATO

English	*Italian*	*French*	*German*
Vibrant	Fa vibrare il suono	Faire vibrer le son	Vibrato
Vibrate (the sound)	Vibrando	Vibrant	Vibrierend
Vibrato	Vibrato	*vib.*	*vib.*
vib.	*vib.*	Vibrer	
		Vibrez	

Flute

COMPOSER	WORK	PAGE	MEASURE
Mahler	*Symphony No.* 3	**215**	[14]

Clarinet

COMPOSER	WORK	PAGE	MEASURE
Dello Joio	*Variations, Chaconne, and Finale*	**25**	[205] 1f

Bassoon

COMPOSER	WORK	PAGE	MEASURE	COMPOSER	WORK	PAGE	MEASURE
Khachaturian	*Gayne Ballet Suite No.* 1	**49**	[6]	**Ravel**	*Concerto pour Piano et Orchestre*	**13**	[9]

Saxophone

COMPOSER	WORK	PAGE	MEASURE
Delannoy	*Figures Sonores*	**74**	6

Chapter 14

SLAP-TONGUE

English	*Italian*	*French*	*German*
Slap-tongue	—	—	—

Clarinet

COMPOSER	WORK	PAGE	MEASURE
Moross	*Paeans*	**13**	[L]

Bassoon

Copland	*Music for Radio*	**27**	[18]

Saxophone

COMPOSER	WORK	PAGE	MEASURE	COMPOSER	WORK	PAGE	MEASURE
Copland	*Music for Radio*	**29**	[19]	**Walton**	*Façade, Suite No. 2*	**34**	[A] 2f

Oboe and Saxophone

Gershwin	*Rhapsody in Blue*	**12**	[10]

Chapter 15

MUTED

English	*Italian*	*French*	*German*
Muted	Con sordino(i)	Avec sourdine(s)	Mit Dämpfer
	con sord., c.s.	*avec sourd.*	*m.D.*

(for complete terminology see Chapter 19, page 104)

Oboe

COMPOSER	WORK	PAGE	MEASURE
Stravinsky	*Petrouchka Suite*	155	[131]

Oboe and Bassoon

Liadov	*The Enchanted Lake*	1	1

79

Chapter 16

MISCELLANEOUS EFFECTS

Flute

English	*Italian*	*French*	*German*
Like a bird-call	Come richiamo	Comme une voix d'oiseau	Wie eine Vogelstimme

COMPOSER	WORK	PAGE	MEASURE	COMPOSER	WORK	PAGE	MEASURE
Mahler	*Symphony No. 2*	**185**	[29] 6f	**Toch**	*The Chinese Flute*	**10**	12
Mahler	*Symphony No. 7*	**116**	[108] 1f				

English	*Italian*	*French*	*German*
No vibrato	Non-vibrato	Non-vibrant	Nicht vibrierend
Without vibrato	Senza vibrato	Sans vibrer	

COMPOSER	WORK	PAGE	MEASURE
Kay	*Suite for Orchestra*	**57**	[64]

Oboe

English	*Italian*	*French*	*German*
As if muted	Quasi con sordino	Comme avec sourdine	Wie gedämpft
Tippett	*Symphony No. 1*	**71**	1b [6]

English	*Italian*	*French*	*German*
Like a trumpet	Come tromba	Comme une trompette	Wie eine Trompete
	Quasi trombe		
Rogers	*Once Upon a Time, Five Fairy Tales*	**31**	1

English	*Italian*	*French*	*German*
Shrill, pinched tone	Tono squillante e pizzicotto	Sonorité aigre, pincée	Schriller, scharfer Ton
Varèse	*Intégrales*	**37**	2

Clarinet

English	*Italian*	*French*	*German*
Coarsely blown	Suonare ruvido	Sonorité grossière	Grob geblasen
Bax	*Second Symphony*	**116**	1

MISCELLANEOUS EFFECTS

Clarinet (contd.)

English	Italian	French	German
Hollow sounding, cracked, without tone (color)	Tono cavernoso, senza colore	Sonorité creuse, fêlée, sans timbre	Hohl klingend, tonlos

COMPOSER	WORK	PAGE	MEASURE
Varèse	Intégrales	**17**	[7] 1f
		36	3b [18]

English	Italian	French	German
Like a trumpet	Come tromba	Comme une trompette	Wie eine Trompete

Mahler	Symphony No. 7	**44**	[38] 3f
		101	[92] 3f

English	Italian	French	German
"White" tone	Non-vibrato	Sans vibrer	Nicht vibrierend

Copland	Appalachian Spring	**1**	2
		82	1b [73]

Bassoon

English	Italian	French	German
As nasal as possible	Anche nasale che possibile	Aussi nasillard que possible	Möglichst nasal

Roger-Ducasse	Le Joli Jeu de Furet	**29**	[8]

English	Italian	French	German
Like pizzicato	Quasi pizzicato	Comme pizzicato	Wie pizzicato

Walton	Façade, Suite No. 2	**27**	1b [A]

Saxophone

English	Italian	French	German
Like a guitar	Quasi guitarra	Comme guitare	Wie eine Gitarre

Albéniz–Arbós	El Albaicín	**3**	1

English	Italian	French	German
"Whip"	—	—	—

Janssen	New Year's Eve in New York	**57**	2
		74	[30] 2f

WOODWINDS

Oboe, English Horn, and Bassoon

English	*Italian*	*French*	*German*
Dry	Secco	Sec	Trocken

COMPOSER	WORK	PAGE	MEASURE	COMPOSER	WORK	PAGE	MEASURE
Albéniz–Arbós	El Albaicín	18	[I] 7f	**Gershwin**	An American in Paris	8	[7] 4f

Piccolo, Flute, Oboe, and Clarinet

English	*Italian*	*French*	*German*
Tongued	Non-tremolo	Non-tremolo	Zungenstosse

COMPOSER	WORK	PAGE	MEASURE
Mahler	Symphony No. 2	181	[26] 7f

Chapter 17

WOODWIND TERMINOLOGY

English	Italian	French	German
Change to A	Mutano in A	Changez en La	Wechseln in A
Change to B♭	Mutano in B♭	Changez en Si♭	Wechseln in B
Take A [B♭] Clar.	Prendero Clar. in A [B♭]	Prenez la Clar. in La [Si♭]	Nehmen Klar. in A [B]
Change Eng. Hn. to 2nd Ob. [Ob. II]	Cor. ing. muta in Ob. 2 [Ob. II]	Le Cor Ang. prendra le 2ᵈ Hᵗᵇ	Engl. Hn. nimmt Ob. 2 [Ob. II]
Change to Fl.	Muta in Fl.	Reprendre la Grande Flûte Reprenez la Gᵈᵉ Fl.	Nimmt grosse Fl.
Contrabassoon change to 3rd Bssn.	Cfg. muta in Fag. 3 [Fg. III]	Le Cᵇᵒⁿ prend le 3 Bᵒⁿ	Kontrafag. nimmt ein drittes Fagott
Piccolo takes Fl.	Picc. cambia in Fl. gr.	La Pᵗᵉ Fl. reprend la Gᵈᵉ Fl.	Picc. nehmen gr. Fl.
Picc. takes 2nd Fl. [Fl. II]	Picc. muta in Fl. 2 [Fl. II]	Picc. change en 2ᵉ Fl.	Picc. nimmt zweite Fl.
2nd Fl. takes Picc. Fl. 2 [II] take Picc.	Fl. IIᵒ muta in Picc. Fl. 2 riprenda l'Ottavino	La 2ᵉ prend la Pᵗᵉ	Kleine Fl. vorbereiten
2nd Ob. takes Eng. Hn. II Ob. to E.H.	2. prende Cor. ing.	La 2ᵉ prend le Cor Ang.	Zweite Ob. nimmt Engl. Hn.
Take Fl.	Mutano in Fl. Cambia in Fl. gr.	Prenez la Gᵈᵉ Fl. Change en Gᵈᵉ Fl.	Grosse Flöte vorbereiten
Take Oboe	Cambia in Ob.	Prenez le Hᵗᵇ	[H]Oboe nehmen
Take Picc.	Mutano in Picc. Prende I Picc. Prendono Picc.	Prenez la Pᵗᵉ Fl.	Nimmt kl. Flöte
The 2 Fls. change to Piccs.	I 2 Fl. muta in Picc.	Les 2 Gᵈᵉˢ Fls. prennent la Pᵗᵉ Fl.	Die 2 Fl. nehmen kl. Fl.
3rd Cl. change to Bs. Cl.	Cl. 3 mutano in Cl. basso	La 3ᵉ change en Cl. basse	Kl. 3 nimmt B.–Kl.
3rd Cl. in B♭ change to E♭ Cl.	Cl. 3ᵒ in B♭ muta in Cl. Picc. in E♭	La 3ᵉ Cl. en Si♭ prend la Pᵗᵉ Cl. en Mi♭	Die dritte Kl. in B nimmt Es-Klar.
3rd Fl. alternates with Picc.	Il 3 Fl. alterna con un Picc.	La 3ᵉ change avec la Pᵗᵉ	Die dritte Fl. wechselt mit einer kleinen Flöte
Unison	A due [2]	A deux [2]	Zu 2
Together			Zusammen
2-fold			*zus.*

PART III

Brasses

langsam *)

*) alle in den Bläsern als ◆ notierte Stellen sind mit Zungenschlag auszuführen.

STRAUSS. DON QUIXOTE

86

Schönberg. FÜNF ORCHESTERSTÜCKE

INTRODUCTION

SWEEPING GENERALITIES are usually best avoided, yet it is difficult to resist the temptation to point out here the interesting development of the choirs of the orchestra in relation to convenient time-spans. In the eighteenth-century orchestra, that of Haydn, Mozart, and Beethoven, the strings were the predominating body of instrumentalists, woodwinds were of secondary importance, and brasses considerably less than that. In the nineteenth-century orchestra the winds were improved to such an extent that they assumed an equal role with the strings in symphonic orchestration, as is evidenced by the scores of Berlioz, Franck, Brahms, and Wagner. And in the twentieth-century orchestra it is clearly the brasses that have come to the fore, as the most superficial glance at the scores of Stravinsky, Hindemith, or Bartók will show. Even the many new percussion instruments do not exhibit such amazing technical resources and diversity of effect as do the orchestral brasses. For better or for worse, we have the jazz, movie, and radio performers and arrangers to thank for this prodigious expansion of brass technique. Unfortunately for the serious composer and orchestrator, however, not all symphonic brass players have developed their own individual techniques to the same extent as the popular dance orchestra men. Jazz trumpet players, for instance, are quite accustomed to ascending to dizzy heights on their instruments, but the serious composer does well to reflect before writing a high C♯!

The examples in Chapter 18 of extreme ranges for the standard orchestral brasses—horns, trumpets, trombones, and tuba—may not, to the jazz arranger at least, seem out of the ordinary. But, just as with the woodwinds, it must again be emphasized to the inexperienced composer that the use of these extended registers should be essayed with caution and considerable restraint. As far as intonation and lip control are concerned, these extreme notes are not produced easily and with certainty, even by top-notch players. Dynamics are the controlling factor, plus the multiple complications of tempo, doubling and reinforcement, and spacing. The examples include: in the horn, the highest E up to A[1], and the bottom C down to A; for the trumpet top C to E♭, and the lowest F♯ down to C; in the trombones, high C to D (tenor and bass trombones only), and the so-called "pedal notes"—C down to F; and in the bass tuba, the use of the highest notes, middle C up to B♭, and the bottom E down to A.

The important subject of mutes for the various brass instruments seems to be almost unknown where the average orchestrator is concerned. Apparently very few composers for the symphony orchestra take the trouble to indicate just what *kind* of a mute they had in mind, possibly because most of them seemingly are unaware of the amazing number and types of mutes now generally available—or else they are just lazy! But there is certainly no excuse for any composer or orchestrator to continue to indicate merely *con sordino;* one should indicate specifically that he wishes cup mute, fibre mute, Harmon mute, wah-wah mute—or any other one of the many

[1] *N.B. All examples are given at pitch.*

90

types now at his disposal. That each has its own peculiar and individual tone color should be, of course, perfectly obvious. In this respect, at least, the jazz arranger has the advantage over his "long-hair" colleagues, for not only does he thoroughly know and appreciate the difference between the various mute types, but he uses them most effectively. Chapter 19 lists the kinds of brass mutes generally available to the symphonic orchestrator, with instances of their use in published study scores. Other muted effects are also catalogued here, including "echo sounds"; muting (but not stopping) the instrument by inserting the hand in the bell; muting by placing a hat over the bell, and by playing directly into the music-stand.

Closely allied to the general subject of mutes is the device, largely used in the horns, of hand-stopping, or so-called "brassy sounds." The student will no doubt be surprised at the number of different ways this effect has been notated, for there seems to exist a considerable amount of confusion among composers as to the clear and proper notation to employ for such stopped notes. The word "brassy," for example, is used both as an indication for an overblown —but open—sound, and for a hand-stopped, rather snarling metallic tone. As the terms "brassy," "closed," "overblown," and their foreign equivalents are used both with and without the small cross: + (a sign invented by Wagner), it is obvious that no standardized notation has as yet been established to differentiate between the two similar, yet dissimilar, effects in question. At the head of Chapter 20 will be found all the terminology employed for these effects, and the examples of stopping (or brassy sounds) have been grouped according to the specific direction and notation in the scores. Chapters 21 and 22 are devoted to the correlative effect of immediately following a stopped note by an open one, and the reverse—these are practical mainly for the horn, because of the awkwardness in hand-stopping the trumpet and trombone.

As double-tonguing is so fundamental and common to brass instruments no attempt has been made to include such examples, as in the woodwinds, but illustrations of both triple-tonguing and "flutter-tonguing" are catalogued in Chapters 23 and 24.

Whereas trills and *tremoli* in the woodwind instruments are generally easy of execution and characteristic of the instruments' technique, they are less common in the brasses. Owing to the mechanical improvements of the modern brass instruments, and to the players' development of technique, the effect is now more widely called for, and numerous examples are listed in Chapter 25. The same is true of the *glissando*, first employed almost exclusively by the trombones; illustrations of this now overworked device are given in Chapter 26. But the device of raising the instrument's bell high in the air is assuredly not so unusual in the brasses as in the woodwind section, as is evidenced by the number of such examples quoted in Chapter 27. There are numerous instances, also, of the off-stage use of brass instruments, either solo or in groups, catalogued in Chapter 28, and Chapter 29 lists a few of the common jazz effects, such as the "flare," "growl," and "smear." No attempt has been made to include other radio, film, or dance orchestra "tricks" not found in published symphonic study scores. The newer, still largely experimental, radio and movie orchestral devices must for the present be omitted from the *Thesaurus*, as well as the other jazz effects not yet commonly utilized by the serious composer.

Chapter 30 lists a few miscellaneous effects, such as the use of the natural notes of the horn, and Chapter 31, the final one of the present section, gives various brass terminology not included under the previous chapter headings.

Chapter 18

EXTREME OR EXTENDED RANGES

(1) HORN

N.B. All notes are given at *actual pitch*.

COMPOSER	WORK	PAGE	MEASURE
Strauss, R.	Symphonia Domestica	III	[145]

COMPOSER	WORK	PAGE	MEASURE
Strauss, R.	Symphonia Domestica	III	1b [145]

COMPOSER	WORK	PAGE	MEASURE
Coppola	Symphonie en La mineur	18	2
Ives	"The Fourth of July" from Symphony, "Holidays"	17	[M] 1f
Rudhyar	Sinfonietta	12	5
		35	1
Ruggles	Sun-Treader	2	[4]
Schönberg	Fünf Orchesterstücke	45	3

COMPOSER	WORK	PAGE	MEASURE
Albéniz–Arbós	El Albaicín	17	7
Bax	First Symphony	119	[N]
Bernstein	"Jeremiah" Symphony	26	2
Blancafort	Mati de Festa a Puig-Gracios	56	1
Britten	Passacaglia from "Peter Grimes"	24	1
Britten	Serenade for Tenor, Horn and Strings	14	[10] 4f
Britten	Sinfonia da Requiem	34	5

COMPOSER	WORK	PAGE	MEASURE
Casella	La Donna Serpente, II. Serie	39	[50]
Copland	Appalachian Spring	17	[13] 3f
Copland	First Symphony	39	1b [26]
Copland	Third Symphony	70	7
		109	2b [99]
Coppola	Symphonie en La mineur	18	2
		98	2b [17]
Dukas	La Péri	55	[8]
Fuleihan	Mediterranean	31	4
Grofé	Grand Canyon Suite	152	[15]
Gruenberg	The Enchanted Isle	32	1
Hanson	Symphony No. 2, "Romantic"	39	1b [O]
Honegger	Le Roi David	127	6
Honegger	Suite d'Orchestre, "L'Impératrice aux Rochers"	32	1b [4]
Honegger	Symphonie pour Orchestre	106	[20] 1f
Inghelbrecht	El Greco	53	2
Inghelbrecht	La Valse Retrouvée	42	3
Ives	"The Fourth of July" from Symphony, "Holidays"	17	[M] 2f
Knipper	Symphony No. 4	18	[15]
Mahler	Symphony No. 1	107	8
Mahler	Symphony No. 2	144	7
Mahler	Symphony No. 5	24	6
Milhaud	Les Choéphores	157	1b [L]
Milhaud	2me Suite Symphonique	150	2
Prokofieff	Romeo and Juliet, Suite No. 2	9	[4] 4f
Prokofieff	Suite from the Ballet "Chout"	93	1b [122]
Ravel	Concerto pour Piano et Orchestre	32	[25] 2f
Rosenthal	Les Petits Métiers	126	[B] 2f
Rudhyar	Sinfonietta	23	7

92

(1) HORN (contd.)

COMPOSER	WORK	PAGE	MEASURE	COMPOSER	WORK	PAGE	MEASURE
Schönberg	Fünf Orchesterstücke	45	3	Britten	Passacaglia from "Peter	22	3
Schönberg	Theme and Variations	25	101		Grimes"	24	1
Sessions	Symphony No. II	137	[U]	Britten	Serenade for Tenor,	4	8b [3]
Shostakovich	The Golden Age, Ballet				Horn and Strings	14	[10] 5f
	Suite	61	1b [70]	Britten	Sinfonia da Requiem	35	4
Siegmeister	Ozark Set	93	1	Casella	La Donna Serpente,	54	3
Strauss, R.	Also Sprach Zara-				II. Serie	61	[73]
	thustra	90	2	Casella	Paganiniana	47	1b [25]
Strauss, R.	Don Quixote	148	3			64	[33] 1f
Strauss, R.	Eine Alpensinfonie	10	1	Copland	Appalachian Spring	17	[13] 3f
		87	2b [86]			79	4b [67]
		119	[113] 1f	Copland	El Salón México	19	1b [19]
Strauss, R.	Ein Heldenleben	121	2	Copland	First Symphony	39	1b [26]
Strauss, R.	Symphonia Domestica	105	[138] 3f	Copland	Lincoln Portrait	21	4
		123	[160] 2f			44	1b [270]
Strauss, R.	Till Eulenspiegel's			Copland	Third Symphony	50	[36] 7f
	Merry Pranks	41	3b [30]			95	[86] 4f
Stravinsky	Chant du Rossignol	3	1			109	2b [99]
Stravinsky	Feuerwerk	18	[18]	Copland	Statements	11	[6] 3f
Stravinsky	Fire-Bird Suite (1919)	36	1b [11]			48	[6] 4f
Stravinsky	Le Sacre du Printemps	91	[111] 3f	Coppola	Interlude Dramatique	11	3
Stravinsky	Oedipus Rex	66	2			47	[24] 3f
		125	[180] 4f	Coppola	Symphonie en La	18	2
Stravinsky	Quatre Études pour				mineur	24	3
	Orchestre	33	4	Debussy	Rondes de Printemps	56	4
Stravinsky	Symphony in Three			Dukas	La Péri	121	3
	Movements	14	1b [17]	Dvořák	Symphony No. 5,		
Villa-Lobos	Amazonas	41	5		"From the New		
Wagner, R.	Siegfried's Rhine				World"	148	1
	Journey from			Ferroud	Au Parc Monceau	8	1b [3]
	"Götterdämmerung"	10	[7]			17	1
Walton	Symphony	83	[59] 8f	Fuleihan	Mediterranean	31	5
				Gretchaninoff	Troisième Symphonie	225	[31] 3f
				Grofé	Grand Canyon Suite	130	1
						158	[17] 2f
				Gruenberg	The Enchanted Isle	31	1b [80]
						100	[495]
				Hanson	Symphony No. 1,		
Albéniz–					"Nordic"	94	2
Arbós	Navarra	24	4	Hanson	Symphony No. 2,		
Antheil	Symphony No. 5	57	3		"Romantic"	39	1b [O]
Atterberg	Ballade und Passacaglia	38	3	Harsanyi	Suite pour Orchestre	78	[210] 2f
Barber	Medea	63	3	Hindemith	Konzertmusik für		
Bartók	Second Suite	45	[16]		Streichorchester und		
Beethoven	Symphony No. 7	16	[B]		Blechbläser	25	1
		49	324	Honegger	Le Roi David	7	1
		67	441	Honegger	Mouvement	18	2b [7]
		153	237		Symphonique No. 3	48	3
		177	447	Honegger	Symphonie pour		
Berg	Three Excerpts from				Orchestre	106	[20] 1f
	"Wozzeck"	52	[365]	Inghelbrecht	La Valse Retrouvée	41	2b [61]
Bernstein	"Jeremiah" Symphony	26	1	Ireland	A London Overture	33	4

93

(1) HORN (contd.)

COMPOSER	WORK	PAGE	MEASURE	COMPOSER	WORK	PAGE	MEASURE
Khrennikov	*Symphony No. 1*	55	1b [105]	**Rudhyar**	*Sinfonietta*	18	4
Levant	*Nocturne*	4	12			23	6
		45	209	**Ruggles**	*Sun-Treader*	18	[86]
Mahler	*Symphony No. 1*	63	[15] 3f			47	[224]
Mahler	*Symphony No. 2*	94	[37] 6f	**Schelling**	*A Victory Ball*	59	3
		114	[49] 6f			80	1
Mahler	*Symphony No. 5*	102	2	**Schönberg**	*Fünf Orchesterstücke*	43	1b [7]
Mahler	*Symphony No. 8*	18	[17] 1f			58	[12] 1f
		39	[43] 6f	**Schönberg**	*Theme and Variations*	25	101
Mason	*Chanticleer—Festival*			**Schuman, W.**	*Symphony No. III*	19	176
	Overture	50	[30] 1f	**Scriabin**	*Le Poème de l'Extase*	140	1b [29]
Milhaud	*2me Suite Symphonique*	148	2			192	1
Milhaud	*Ière Symphonie*	52	1b [140]	**Sessions**	*Symphony No. II*	3	3
		94	[95]			11	2
Milhaud	*Quatrième Symphonie*	58	[130] 2f			36	[W]
Milhaud	*Suite Provençale*	5	[25] 1f			100	2
		8	[45] 1f			141	[X]
Moeran	*Symphony in G minor*	22	2b [11]	**Shostakovich**	*The Golden Age, Ballet*		
		175	3b [118]		*Suite*	59	6
Moross	*Biguine*	6	[A]	**Sibelius**	*Symphony No. 6*	72	[G]
		15	2	**Sibelius**	*Symphony No. 7*	73	[Z]
Parodi	*Preludio ad una*			**Siegmeister**	*Ozark Set*	46	3
	Commedia	36	1b [R]	**Siegmeister**	*Western Suite*	15	[50]
Pierné	*Viennoise*	54	4	**Slonimsky**	*My Toy Balloon*	16	4
Piket	*Curtain Raiser to an*	11	1b [60]	**Strauss, R.**	*Dance Suite after*		
	American Play	40	3		*François Couperin*	65	2
Poulenc	*Concert Champêtre pour*			**Strauss, R.**	*Eine Alpensinfonie*	72	3
	Clavecin et Orchestre	12	[9]			86	5b [84]
Prokofieff	*Ala et Lolly (Scythian*	38	[20] 1f	**Strauss, R.**	*Ein Heldenleben*	131	[68] 3f
	Suite)	56	2b [33]			195	2
Prokofieff	*Romeo and Juliet,*	9	[4] 4f	**Strauss, R.**	*Symphonia Domestica*	26	6
	Suite No. 2	78	[48] 1f			77	1b [100]
		95	[59] 2f			83	6b [108]
		100	4			120	[157] 4f
Prokofieff	*Symphony No. 6*	81	[51] 2f	**Stravinsky**	*Chant du Rossignol*	5	3b [2]
Ravel	*Concerto pour la main*					47	[48] 1f
	gauche	16	2	**Stravinsky**	*Feuerwerk*	18	2b [18]
Read	*First Overture*	57	[20]			23	1b [23]
Read	*Symphony No. I*	60	5	**Stravinsky**	*Fire-Bird Suite (1919)*	24	1
		72	2			55	[28]
		85	5	**Stravinsky**	*Le Sacre du Printemps*	91	[111] 1f
		100	6	**Stravinsky**	*Oedipus Rex*	48	[67] 3f
Respighi	*The Fountains of Rome*	34	3			64	4
Respighi	*The Pines of Rome*	78	1b [22]	**Stravinsky**	*Petrouchka Suite*	127	9
Respighi	*Vetrate di Chiesa*	45	2	**Stravinsky**	*Scènes de Ballet*	79	[127]
Rieti	*Sinfonia Tripartita*	36	[31] 1f	**Stravinsky**	*Scherzo à la Russe*	6	[5] 2f
Roussel	*Suite en Fa*	39	4			21	[17]
		46	4	**Stravinsky**	*Symphonie de Psaumes*	37	3b [8]
Roussel	*Symphonie en Sol*	13	4			43	6
	mineur	87	2			54	2
				Stravinsky	*Symphony in C*	18	2b [30]

EXTREME OR EXTENDED RANGES

(1) HORN (contd.)

COMPOSER	WORK	PAGE	MEASURE	COMPOSER	WORK	PAGE	MEASURE
Stravinsky	Symphony in Three	16	[19] 1f	Respighi	Ballata delle Gnomidi	15	1
	Movements	41	[69]	Respighi	Concerto Gregoriano per		
		79	[142] 2f		Violino e Orchestra	17	[8] 5f
		97	[163]	Respighi	The Birds	37	1
Trapp	Symphonie No. 4	66	4	Rivier	Danse	46	[36]
		83	2	Strauss, R.	Also Sprach Zara-		
Walton	Façade, Suite No. 1	53	6		thustra	84	5
		63	1	Strauss, R.	Eine Alpensinfonie	80	[74] 6f
Walton	Symphony	127	[96] 2f				

				Mahler	Symphony No. 3	4	[1] 1f
Albéniz–						187	[7] 2f
Arbós	El Puerto	20	[G]				
Bax	Third Symphony	113	1b [32]				
Brahms	Ein deutsches Requiem	183	72				
		202	184				

Brahms	Symphony No. 1	144	294				
Debussy	Gigues	23	5	Beethoven	Symphony No. 4	1	1
Dukas	La Péri	90	1	Britten	Serenade for Tenor,		
Mahler	Symphony No. 2	127	9		Horn and Strings	33	[28] 8f
Mahler	Symphony No. 3	5	8b [2]	Mahler	Symphony No. 2	31	[15] 2f
		24	[19]	Mahler	Symphony No. 3	13	2b [9]
Mahler	Symphony No. 4	39	[15]			77	6b [54]
		76	[1]	Mahler	Symphony No. 4	176	[10]
		98	[8]	Strauss, R.	Eine Alpensinfonie	3	1
		110	332	Stravinsky	Le Sacre du Printemps	48	4b [59]
		142	299	Vaughan	Symphony in E minor	55	5
		176	[10]	Williams	(No. 6)	78	3
Mahler	Symphony No. 5	62	[8] 5f				
		231	[30] 4f				

Mahler	Symphony No. 6	149	1				
		155	[106]				
Mahler	Symphony No. 7	118	[111] 4f	Mahler	Symphony No. 3	5	8b [2]
Mahler	Symphony No. 9	103	[27] 10f	Mahler	Symphony No. 6	123	[84]
Ravel	Concerto pour Piano et			Mahler	Symphony No. 8	20	1
	Orchestre	41	[32] 1f	Mahler	Symphony No. 9	140	4
Ravel	Daphnis et Chloé,			Shostakovich	Symphony No. 5	146	[121] 3f
	Suite No. 2	39	[170] 2f				
Ravel	Rapsodie Espagnole	7	[5] 3f				

(2) TRUMPET

Mahler	Symphony No. 8	18	[17] 4f	Britten	Four Sea Interludes		
Ruggles	Sun-Treader	26	[126]		from "Peter Grimes"	28	[4] 1f
		51	[237]				

(2) TRUMPET (contd.)

COMPOSER	WORK	PAGE	MEASURE
Handel	Royal Fireworks Music	15	67
		20	4
		32	147
		36	167
		44	3
Parodi	Preludio ad una Commedia	11	[E] 1f
Respighi	Feste Romane	44	2
Respighi	Metamorphoseon, XII Modi	82	2
Respighi	Vetrate di Chiesa	23	4
Ruggles	Sun-Treader	26	[126]
		51	[237]
Strauss, R.	Eine Alpensinfonie	74	[68] 1f
		100	[96] 4f
		120	[113] 1f

COMPOSER	WORK	PAGE	MEASURE
Bartók	Violin Concerto	135	[603] 1f
Casella	Paganiniana	63	2
Gillis	Symphony No. 5½	21	1b [J]
Kabalevsky	Suite from "Colas Breugnon"	117	3
Levant	Nocturne	15	51
Mahler	Symphony No. 8	37	[41]
Read	Prelude and Toccata	4	[2]
Read	Symphony No. I	32	2
		129	4
Respighi	Feste Romane	141	6
Rudhyar	Sinfonietta	29	2
		32	1
Ruggles	Sun-Treader	2	[7]
		26	[126]
Schönberg	A Survivor from Warsaw	10	45
Sessions	Suite from "The Black Maskers"	72	[69] 2f
Sessions	Symphony No. II	29	[R]
Strauss, R.	Eine Alpensinfonie	91	6b [89]
		98	[94]
		115	3

COMPOSER	WORK	PAGE	MEASURE
Albéniz–Arbós	Fête-Dieu à Séville	10	2

COMPOSER	WORK	PAGE	MEASURE
Antheil	Symphony No. 5	56	[38]
Bach–Respighi	Passacaglia and Fugue in C minor	10	[8] 3f
		28	1
Bartók	Concerto for Orchestra	18	[364]
		141	[570]
Bax	First Symphony	70	[F]
Bernstein	"Jeremiah" Symphony	32	5b [22]
		44	[37] 1f
Casella	La Donna Serpente, II. Serie	25	[32]
		82	[87]
Cesana	Second American Symphony	30	2b [23]
Copland	Dance Symphony	87	[52] 1f
Copland	First Symphony	37	[24] 4f
		59	4
Copland	Lincoln Portrait	44	3b [270]
Copland	Music for the Theatre	26	[19] 3f
Copland	Statements	11	1b [6]
Copland	Third Symphony	48	3
		109	[99]
		148	3
Coppola	Symphonie en La mineur	9	[6]
Cowell	Short Symphony (No. 4)	73	[P]
Dohnányi	Variations on a Nursery Song	6	2
Dukas	La Péri	48	1
Elgar	Symphony No. 1	170	8
Gershwin	An American in Paris	23	7
Gillis	Symphony No. 5½	95	[O] 2f
Hanson	"Merry Mount" Suite	21	1
Hanson	Symphony No. 2, "Romantic"	44	3
Hindemith	Konzertmusik für Streichorchester und Blechbläser	29	1
Honegger	Concertino pour Piano et Orchestre	12	3
Honegger	Horace Victorieux	68	1
Inghelbrecht	Sinfonia Breve No. 1	9	2
Ireland	Symphonic Rhapsody, "Mai-Dun"	6	[4]
Khachaturian	Gayne Ballet Suite No. 1-A	49	[8]
Lambert	The Rio Grande	13	[7] 4f
		37	4
Levant	Nocturne	15	52
McDonald	Rhumba from 2nd Symphony	36	[210] 1f
Milhaud	Opus Americanum No. 2	82	2b [590]
Milhaud	Ière Symphonie	40	3

(2) TRUMPET (contd.)

COMPOSER	WORK	PAGE	MEASURE	COMPOSER	WORK	PAGE	MEASURE
Milhaud	Quatrième Symphonie	10	[35] 1f	**Shostakovich**	The Golden Age, Ballet	36	3
		21	3		Suite	65	1
		68	3b [215]	**Strauss, R.**	Eine Alpensinfonie	75	[69] 2f
		85	[50] 1f			83	[80] 2f
Moeran	Symphony in G minor	39	[19]			92	3
Mohaupt	Town Piper Music	57	3b [60]	**Strauss, R.**	Ein Heldenleben	133	[69]
		67	[68] 2f			139	[73]
Poulenc	Concert Champêtre pour			**Stravinsky**	Feuerwerk	19	[19] 1f
	Clavecin et Orchestre	107	[28]	**Stravinsky**	Jeu de Cartes	43	[82]
Prokofieff	March and Scherzo from			**Stravinsky**	Oedipus Rex	2	[1]
	"The Love of the					139	[197]
	Three Oranges"	12	[7] 3f	**Stravinsky**	Petrouchka Suite	156	[132] 2f
Prokofieff	Piano Concerto No. 3	70	2	**Stravinsky**	Quatre Études pour		
Prokofieff	Suite from the Ballet	147	[191] 1f		Orchestre	47	4b [16]
	"Chout"	155	[202] 1f	**Stravinsky**	Scènes de Ballet	79	[127]
Prokofieff	Symphony No. 5	200	[111] 1f	**Stravinsky**	Scherzo Fantastique	10	[10] 1f
Read	Prelude and Toccata	8	1	**Stravinsky**	Symphonie de Psaumes	12	[12]
Read	Symphony No. I	87	5b [33]	**Wagenaar**	Sinfonietta for Small		
Respighi	Feste Romane	9	1		Orchestra	5	[3]
		20	1	**Walton**	Façade, Suite No. 2	2	10
		44	2	**Weiss**	American Life	27	[O] 1f
Respighi	Metamorphoseon,						
	XII Modi	80	1b [40]				
Respighi	The Pines of Rome	15	2				
		20	4	**Bartók**	Second Suite	39	2b [10]
		79	4	**Copland**	Music for the Theatre	20	1
Respighi	Vetrate di Chiesa	45	[13]			36	[28] 4f
Rieti	L'Arca di Noè	8	1b [7]	**Hanson**	Symphony No. 2,		
Rieti	Serenata	1	1		"Romantic"	90	4
Rudhyar	Sinfonietta	23	7	**Hindemith**	Konzertmusik für		
Ruggles	Sun-Treader	26	[126]		Streichorchester und		
		37	[177]		Blechbläser	39	[P]
		51	[237]	**Honegger**	Symphonie Liturgique	30	4
Schönberg	Fünf Orchesterstücke	45	3	**Janáček**	Sinfonietta	29	2
Schreker	The Birthday of the			**Kodály**	Háry János Suite	60	99
	Infanta, Suite	82	2	**Mahler**	Symphony No. 3	48	5b [32]
Schuman, W.	American Festival	20	[230] 1f	**Piston**	Suite for Orchestra	66	2
	Overture	38	[355]	**Prokofieff**	Ala et Lolly (Scythian		
Schuman, W.	Symphony No. III	82	426		Suite)	48	[27]
Schuman, W.	Symphony No. IV	21	192	**Prokofieff**	Alexander Nevsky	64	[40]
Scriabin	Le Poème de l'Extase	184	3			89	1
		192	1	**Prokofieff**	Cinderella Suite No. 1	156	[131]
Scriabin	Prométhée, Le Poème du			**Prokofieff**	Suite from the Ballet	28	[34] 1f
	Feu	71	5		"Chout"	82	[114]
Sessions	Suite from "The Black					125	[161]
	Maskers"	74	1b [71]	**Prokofieff**	Symphony No. 5	117	[66] 3f
Sessions	Symphony No. II	43	3	**Prokofieff**	Symphony No. 6	4	2
Shepherd	Horizons	87	[H]			123	3b [90]
Shostakovich	Symphony No. 3	72	[85] 4f	**Rivier**	Danse	28	[23
		76	2b [93]	**Rudhyar**	Sinfonietta	8	3
Shostakovich	Symphony No. 5	163	1				
Shostakovich	Symphony No. 7	115	3				

BRASSES

(2) TRUMPET (contd.)

COMPOSER	WORK	PAGE	MEASURE
Schönberg	*Fünf Orchesterstücke*	18	1
Schönberg	*Theme and Variations*	29	127
		43	207
Schumann, R.	*Symphony No. 4*	23	[E] 4f
		101	2b [Y]
Stravinsky	*Chant du Rossignol*	22	1
Wagner, R.	*Overture to "Tannhäuser"*	81	424
Weinberger	*Polka and Fugue from "Schwanda, the Bagpiper"*	9	1b [35]
		19	[85] 1f

COMPOSER	WORK	PAGE	MEASURE
Brahms	*Symphony No. 3*	1	1
		121	223
		130	268
Copland	*Music for the Theatre*	20	2
Honegger	*Le Dit des Jeux du Monde*	32	[4] 3f
Honegger	*Prélude, Fugue, Postlude*	37	[16] 4f
Kodály	*Háry János Suite*	60	99
Mahler	*Symphony No. 4*	159	44
Mahler	*Symphony No. 5*	63	4b [9]
Mahler	*Symphony No. 6*	96	[64] 2f
Prokofieff	*Cinderella Suite No. 1*	155	1
Prokofieff	*Suite from the Ballet "Chout"*	9	3b [9]
		28	[34] 1f
		119	2b [150]
		135	[173]
Prokofieff	*Symphony No. 5*	98	2
Prokofieff	*Symphony No. 6*	39	[27]
		83	[52] 5f
Rivier	*Danse*	28	[23]
Schönberg	*Fünf Orchesterstücke*	18	2
Schönberg	*Theme and Variations*	29	127
Schumann, R.	*Symphony No. 3*	34	303
		123	93
Stravinsky	*Orpheus*	56	[141] 4f
Varèse	*Intégrales*	36	3b [18]
Wellesz	*Symphony in C*	10	[50] 1f
		40	[295]

COMPOSER	WORK	PAGE	MEASURE
Chávez	*Sinfonia de Antigona*	7	[5] 3f

COMPOSER	WORK	PAGE	MEASURE
Honegger	*Le Dit des Jeux du Monde*	32	[4] 3f
Janáček	*Sinfonietta*	27	3
Mahler	*Symphony No. 3*	12	[8]
Prokofieff	*Ala et Lolly (Scythian Suite)*	49	[28]
Prokofieff	*Cinderella Suite No. 1*	155	1
Prokofieff	*Suite from the Ballet "Chout"*	18	[22]
		43	[60]
		135	[173]
Riegger	*Symphony No. 3*	46	[245] 1f
Rivier	*Danse*	28	[23]
Schumann, R.	*Symphony No. 3*	33	292
Wagner, R.	*Overture to "Tannhäuser"*	82	427

COMPOSER	WORK	PAGE	MEASURE
Prokofieff	*Suite from the Ballet "Chout"*	21	[26]
		44	3b [61]
		126	3b [162]
		135	[173] 1f
Ravel	*Daphnis et Chloé, Suite No. 1*	31	3
Strauss, R.	*Ein Heldenleben*	113	1
		210	2

COMPOSER	WORK	PAGE	MEASURE
Prokofieff	*Suite from the Ballet "Chout"*	40	6b [55]
		49	[69] 1f
		135	[173]

COMPOSER	WORK	PAGE	MEASURE
Prokofieff	*Suite from the Ballet "Chout"*	125	[161] 1f

EXTREME OR EXTENDED RANGES

(3) TROMBONE

COMPOSER	WORK	PAGE	MEASURE
Brahms	Symphony No. 2	25	246
		144	401
Casella	Paganiniana	83	[11]
Ferroud	Au Parc Monceau	10	3
Prokofieff	Suite from the Ballet "Chout"	78	1b [109]
Starokadomsky	Concerto for Orchestra	29	1b [28]
Stravinsky	Le Sacre du Printemps	25	[34]

COMPOSER	WORK	PAGE	MEASURE
Brahms	Academic Festival Overture	29	245
Brahms	Symphony No. 2	144	401
Brahms	Symphony No. 4	148	165
Casella	La Donna Serpente, II. Serie	19	6
Casella	Paganiniana	64	[33] 1f
Delius	Eventyr, Once Upon a Time	22	2
Egge	Symphony No. 1	104	[13]
Ferroud	Au Parc Monceau	10	3
Prokofieff	Ala et Lolly (Scythian Suite)	41	1b [22]
		69	[47] 1f
Prokofieff	Piano Concerto No. 3	70	2
Prokofieff	Suite from the Ballet "Chout"	79	1b [110]
Ravel	Boléro	28	4
		51	2
		60	2
Ruggles	Sun-Treader	3	[10]
Schumann, R.	Symphony No. 3	102	31
Starokadomsky	Concerto for Orchestra	29	1b [28]
Strauss, R.	Eine Alpensinfonie	92	1
		141	[124] 2f
Stravinsky	Le Sacre du Printemps	106	[134]
		132	2b [184]

COMPOSER	WORK	PAGE	MEASURE
Brahms	Ein deutsches Requiem	58	202
		188	102
		229	312
Brahms	Symphony No. 3	93	69
Brahms	Symphony No. 4	150	174

COMPOSER	WORK	PAGE	MEASURE
Casella	La Donna Serpente, II. Serie	19	5
		83	[88] 2f
Chávez	Sinfonia India	30	[39]
Copland	First Symphony	59	4
Cowell	Short Symphony (No. 4)	5	1b [B]
Elgar	Symphony No. 1	170	8
Ferroud	Au Parc Monceau	10	3
Golestan	Concerto Roumain pour Violon et Orchestre	97	[L] 2f
Honegger	Horace Victorieux	53	2
Honegger	Le Chant de Nigamon	57	[195]
Knipper	Symphony No. 4	10	[7] 1f
Kodály	Háry János Suite	113	[7] 2f
Mahler	Symphony No. 5	24	5
Martinet	Orphée	78	3
Milhaud	Ière Symphonie	59	1b [180]
Milhaud	Suite Française	35	[35]
Milhaud	Suite Provençale	20	[15] 2f
Piket	Curtain Raiser to an American Play	15	1
Prokofieff	Ala et Lolly (Scythian Suite)	41	1b [22]
Prokofieff	March and Scherzo from "The Love of the Three Oranges"	5	[3] 2f
Prokofieff	Romeo and Juliet, Suite No. 1	131	4
Prokofieff	Suite from the Ballet "Chout"	79	1b [110]
		155	[202] 1f
Ravel	Boléro	28	1
		51	2
		60	2
Ravel	Concerto pour la main gauche	86	[49]
Revueltas	Sensemayá	46	[42] 1f
Rosenthal	Les Petits Métiers	94	[F]
Roussel	Évocations, I	21	3
Ruggles	Sun-Treader	16	[75]
		23	[111]
Schelling	A Victory Ball	119	1b [38]
Schmitt	Mirages pour Orchestre, No. 2	62	[34] 3f
Schönberg	Fünf Orchesterstücke	42	[5]
Schumann, R.	Symphony No. 3	104	[C] 2f
		153	292
Shostakovich	Symphony No. 3	75	3b [91]
		78	4b [98]
Strauss, R.	Eine Alpensinfonie	137	[122]
Stravinsky	Le Sacre du Printemps	25	[34]
Stravinsky	Petrouchka Suite	66	3
		76	3
Trapp	Symphonie No. 4	51	2

BRASSES

(3) TROMBONE (contd.)

English	Italian	French	German
Pedal tone [note]	Tono di pedale	Ton de pédale	Pedalton

COMPOSER	WORK	PAGE	MEASURE
Bach–Respighi	Passacaglia and Fugue in C minor	1	[1]
Bach–Respighi	Prelude and Fugue in D major	18	4
Bartók	Concerto for Piano and Orchestra	49	8b [51]
Berg	Three Excerpts from "Wozzeck"	9	1
Berg	Violin Concerto	9	2
		91	3
Britten	Sinfonia da Requiem	46	[31] 5f
Egge	Symphony No. 1	85	3
Janáček	Sinfonietta	92	6
Mahler	Das Lied von der Erde	6	1
		33	[41] 4f
		125	[46] 4f
Mahler	Symphony No. 9	83	6
Piket	Curtain Raiser to an American Play	34	3
Rimsky-Korsakoff	Le Coq d'Or Suite	74	[49] 4f
Schönberg	Fünf Orchesterstücke	51	9
Scriabin	Le Divin Poème	273	2
Sessions	Symphony No. II	11	2
		25	[O] 1f
Strauss, R.	Eine Alpensinfonie	21	[16]
		65	1b [60]
		81	[76] 5f
		83	2b [80]
		86	[84]
Stravinsky	Le Sacre du Printemps	46	[57]
Stravinsky	Mass	2	1b [3]
		10	[23] 1f
		19	[38]
Stravinsky	Orpheus	5	[7] 2f
Tippett	Symphony No. 1	32	2b [21]
Varèse	Intégrales	9	1
		18	3
		47	[22] 2f
Wellesz	Symphony in C	67	[115]

COMPOSER	WORK	PAGE	MEASURE
Bartók	Concerto for Orchestra	73	[90]

COMPOSER	WORK	PAGE	MEASURE
Berg	Three Excerpts from "Wozzeck"	9	1
Berg	Violin Concerto	9	1
		91	3
Britten	Passacaglia from "Peter Grimes"	28	1
Britten	Sinfonia da Requiem	46	[31] 5f
Janáček	Sinfonietta	76	3b [8]
		95	1
Rudhyar	Sinfonietta	13	5
Schönberg	Fünf Orchesterstücke	19	2b [1]
Scriabin	Le Divin Poème	273	2
Siegmeister	Western Suite	64	[30]
Stravinsky	Mass	4	[9] 4f
		10	[23] 1f
		16	2b [34]
		25	2b [52]
Stravinsky	Orpheus	5	[7] 2f
Varèse	Hyperprism	17	4

COMPOSER	WORK	PAGE	MEASURE
Bartók	Concerto for Piano and Orchestra	4	[2]
Berg	Three Excerpts from "Wozzeck"	8	1b [340]
Britten	Sinfonia da Requiem	46	[31] 6f
Copland	Dance Symphony	87	[52] 5f
Elgar	Cockaigne, Concert Overture	19	3b [10]
Janáček	Sinfonietta	92	[6] 2f
		96	2
Loeffler	Evocation	32	1b [30]
Mahler	Symphony No. 2	31	[15] 2f
Ravel	Daphnis et Chloé, Suite No. 1	12	[82] 1f
Ravel	Rapsodie Espagnole	63	1
		66	17
Schönberg	Fünf Orchesterstücke	4	1b [2]
Schmitt	Rapsodie Viennoise	41	[19]
Sibelius	Tapiola	45	456
Siegmeister	From my Window	27	[40]
Sessions	Suite from "The Black Maskers"	61	[60] 5f
Strauss, R.	Eine Alpensinfonie	8	1b [6]
		15	[10]
		138	2

(3) TROMBONE (contd.)

COMPOSER	WORK	PAGE	MEASURE
Varèse	Intégrales	18	2
Verdi	Messa da Requiem	141	699
		218	96

COMPOSER	WORK	PAGE	MEASURE
Bartók	Concerto for Piano and Orchestra	3	3
Bax	Second Symphony	72	[41] 2f
Bax	Third Symphony	16	1b [15]
Bax	Sixth Symphony	109	[29]
Berg	Three Excerpts from "Wozzeck"	8	2b [340]
		13	[363]
Janáček	Sinfonietta	76	2b [8]
		93	[7] 2f
Loeffler	Evocation	32	1b [30]
Mahler	Das Lied von der Erde	6	1
Prokofieff	Cinderella Suite No. 1	148	3
Rudhyar	Sinfonietta	13	5
Schönberg	Fünf Orchesterstücke	4	[2]
		42	[5] 1f
Scriabin	Le Divin Poème	273	1
Trapp	Symphonie No. 4	68	3
Vaughan Williams	Job, A Masque for Dancing	33	1

COMPOSER	WORK	PAGE	MEASURE
Bax	First Symphony	59	1
Berg	Three Excerpts from "Wozzeck"	13	1b [363]

COMPOSER	WORK	PAGE	MEASURE
Elgar	Cockaigne, Concert Overture	11	3
Elgar	Symphony No. 1	123	[110]
Janáček	Sinfonietta	92	[6] 2f
		104	1
Piket	Curtain Raiser to an American Play	33	[240] 1f
Rudhyar	Sinfonietta	13	6
Strauss, R.	Eine Alpensinfonie	137	[122]

COMPOSER	WORK	PAGE	MEASURE
Berg	Three Excerpts from "Wozzeck"	10	[345]
Janáček	Sinfonietta	76	1b [8]
		93	2b [7]
Rudhyar	Sinfonietta	14	1
Strauss, R.	Eine Alpensinfonie	83	3b [80]
		86	[84] 4f

COMPOSER	WORK	PAGE	MEASURE
Janáček	Sinfonietta	108	[12]

COMPOSER	WORK	PAGE	MEASURE
Varèse	Hyperprism	5	[2]
		13	1

(4) TUBA (BASS)

COMPOSER	WORK	PAGE	MEASURE
Bax	Fifth Symphony	88	1
Brahms	Ein deutsches Requiem	222	284
Britten	Sinfonia da Requiem	36	[25] 1f
Chávez	Sinfonia de Antigona	13	1b [15]
Elgar	Symphony No. 2	135	1
Honegger	Chant de Joie	26	4
Honegger	Mouvement Symphonique No. 3	47	3
Honegger	Pacific 231	33	165

COMPOSER	WORK	PAGE	MEASURE
Honegger	Symphonie Liturgique	35	4
Inghelbrecht	La Valse Retrouvée	47	6
Lambert	The Rio Grande	17	2
Martinet	Orphée	78	2
Milhaud	Quatrième Symphonie	15	1
		42	[105] 3f
Mussorgsky-Ravel	Pictures at an Exhibition	45	5
Parodi	Preludio ad una Commedia	32	3
Pierné	Viennoise	54	4
Read	Symphony No. 1	135	[47] 2f

BRASSES

(4) TUBA (BASS) (contd.)

COMPOSER	WORK	PAGE	MEASURE
Schönberg	Fünf Orchesterstücke	42	[5]
		45	2
Schuman, W.	Symphony No. III	18	170
Shostakovich	Symphony No. 3	74	[88] 3f
Stravinsky	Le Sacre du Printemps	24	[33]
		57	1b [65]
		71	1
		92	3b [113]
		119	[161] 1f
Stravinsky	Petrouchka Suite	115	[100] 3f
Vaughan Williams	Job, A Masque for Dancing	34	[U]
Vaughan Williams	Symphony in F minor (No. 4)	58	[14] 6f
Wagner, R.	Prelude to "Die Meistersinger"	43	2

8 bassa

COMPOSER	WORK	PAGE	MEASURE
Bach–Respighi	Prelude and Fugue in D major	16	[6] 3f
		45	4
Bax	Second Symphony	56	3
Bax	Fourth Symphony	142	[27] 1f
Bax	Sixth Symphony	35	4b [34]
Berg	Violin Concerto	48	[240]
Britten	Sinfonia da Requiem	29	1
		62	1b [43]
Caturla	Trois Danses Cubaines	40	2b [17]
Copland	Billy the Kid Ballet Suite	46	[27] 1f
Copland	Four Dance Episodes from "Rodeo"	39	1
Copland	Lincoln Portrait	28	4b [160]
Copland	Statements	10	1b [4]
Delius	Eventyr, Once Upon a Time	24	5
Dohnányi	Variations on a Nursery Song	125	2b [79]
Dukelsky	Symphony No. 3	100	[41]
		109	3
Dunn	Overture on Negro Themes	10	2
		34	7
Egge	Symphony No. 1	147	3
Hindemith	Konzert für Orchester	33	3
Inghelbrecht	Rapsodie de Printemps	46	1b [24]
Janáček	Sinfonietta	49	3
Kay	Suite for Orchestra	59	[65] 1f
Martinet	Orphée	76	2
		86	17

COMPOSER	WORK	PAGE	MEASURE
Milhaud	Deuxième Concerto pour Violoncelle et Orchestre	31 / 100	2b [90] / [90]
Milhaud	2me Suite Symphonique	115	[57] 2f
Milhaud	IIe Symphonie	5	[45]
		80	[5] 1f
Milhaud	Quatrième Symphonie	79	2
		85	[50] 3f
Piket	Curtain Raiser to an American Play	41	[270] 1f
Prokofieff	Romeo and Juliet, Suite No. 2	5	[2]
		23	3
		97	2
Prokofieff	Suite from the Ballet "Chout"	18	[22]
		78	[108]
Prokofieff	Symphony No. 5	4	1b [1]
Prokofieff	Symphony No. 6	48	5
		90	3
Respighi	Ballata delle Gnomidi	86	3
Respighi	Metamorphoseon, XII Modi	69	1
Respighi	Vetrate di Chiesa	20	3
Ruggles	Sun-Treader	37	[177]
Schönberg	Fünf Orchesterstücke	49	[3] 3f
Scriabin	Prométhée, Le Poème du Feu	67	[50] 3f
Sessions	Suite from "The Black Maskers"	55	4b [54]
Sessions	Symphony for Orchestra (No. 1)	66	[104] 1f
Shostakovich	Symphony No. 3	21	[25] 1f
		62	[75] 1f
		72	3b [85]
Starokadomsky	Concerto for Orchestra	33	[32] 2f
Stravinsky	Jeu de Cartes	87	1b [171]
Stravinsky	Scherzo à la Russe	21	[17]
		30	[25]
Tippett	Symphony No. 1	15	4b [9]

8 bassa

COMPOSER	WORK	PAGE	MEASURE
Antheil	McKonkey's Ferry	5	3b [4]
Bax	First Symphony	13	4
		56	4
Bax	November Woods	21	1
		63	1
Dohnányi	Variations on a Nursery Song	16	4
Dunn	Overture on Negro Themes	10	1
		34	6

EXTREME OR EXTENDED RANGES

(4) TUBA (BASS) (contd.)

COMPOSER	WORK	PAGE	MEASURE
Elgar	Falstaff	75	5b [75]
Hindemith	Konzert für Orchester	23	1b [50]
		45	1
Inghelbrecht	El Greco	10	[7]
Ireland	Symphonic Rhapsody, "Mai-Dun"	11	4
Kabalevsky	Symphony No. 2	87	2
		171	[66] 2f
Mahler	Symphony No. 5	10	2
Martinet	Orphée	76	3
Milhaud	Deuxième Concerto pour Violoncelle et Orchestre	41	1
Milhaud	Les Choéphores	18	2
Milhaud	Ière Symphonie	59	[180]
Milhaud	Quatrième Symphonie	90	2
Milhaud	Suite Provençale	26	[10] 1f
Prokofieff	Lieutenant Kijé	20	[21]
Prokofieff	Romeo and Juliet, Suite No. 1	56	4
		60	1b [39]
Prokofieff	Romeo and Juliet, Suite No. 2	4	[1] 3f
		103	3
Prokofieff	Symphony No. 5	33	2
Prokofieff	Symphony No. 6	60	7
Respighi	Metamorphoseon, XII Modi	69	1
Respighi	Vetrate di Chiesa	79	3
		94	[28]
Ruggles	Sun-Treader	3	9
Schelling	A Victory Ball	85	[26] 1f
Scriabin	Prométhée, Le Poème du Feu	56	6b [38]
Sessions	Symphony No. II	149	1
Shostakovich	Symphony No. 3	70	[83] 4f
Shostakovich	Symphony No. 6	47	[54]
Shostakovich	Symphony No. 7	111	[123]
Stravinsky	Le Sacre du Printemps	41	[53]
		95	[116] 2f
Stravinsky	Petrouchka Suite	81	[67] 3f
Vaughan Williams	A London Symphony	150	[A]
		177	2
Vaughan Williams	Pastoral Symphony	53	[B] 2f
Trapp	Symphonie No. 4	15	[5]
		41	[14]

(musical staff, bass clef, 8 bassa)

COMPOSER	WORK	PAGE	MEASURE
Bach–Respighi	Prelude and Fugue in D major	13	2b [5]
		45	4

COMPOSER	WORK	PAGE	MEASURE
Bach–Stokowski	Chorale-Prelude, "Wir Glauben All' An Einem Gott"	18	[10] 4f
Bax	First Symphony	45	[N] 3f
Britten	Sinfonia da Requiem	1	1
		52	2b [35]
Kabalevsky	Suite from "Colas Breugnon"	152	4b [20]
Kabalevsky	Symphony No. 2	87	2
Prokofieff	Ala et Lolly (Scythian Suite)	24	2
Prokofieff	Cinderella Suite No. 1	160	4
Prokofieff	Symphony No. 6	66	1b [43]
Respighi	Metamorphoseon, XII Modi	69	2
Respighi	Vetrate di Chiesa	79	3
Schönberg	Fünf Orchesterstücke	8	[7]
		17	[16] 2f
Shostakovich	Symphony No. 3	62	[75] 1f
		72	3b [85]
Stravinsky	Le Sacre du Printemps	73	[80]
Trapp	Symphonie No. 4	68	1
		105	[43]
Vaughan Williams	A London Symphony	67	3b [RR]
		177	2
Vaughan Williams	Pastoral Symphony	53	[B] 3f

(musical staff, bass clef, 8 bassa)

COMPOSER	WORK	PAGE	MEASURE
Kabalevsky	Symphony No. 2	87	3
Prokofieff	Symphony No. 6	66	[43]
Respighi	Vetrate di Chiesa	94	[28] 3f
Trapp	Symphonie No. 4	67	[24]
		105	[43] 1f

(musical staff, bass clef, 8 bassa)

COMPOSER	WORK	PAGE	MEASURE
Berg	Violin Concerto	29	1
Trapp	Symphonie No. 4	15	[5] 1f

(musical staff, bass clef, 8 bassa)

COMPOSER	WORK	PAGE	MEASURE
Trapp	Symphonie No. 4	68	3

Chapter 19

MUTES

English	Italian	French	German
Add mute(s)	Colle sordine	Avec sourdine(s)	Dämpfer ansetzen [aufsetzen]
Muted	Con sordina(e)	*avec sourd.*	Dämpfer nehmen
Mute(s) on	Con sordino(i)	Mettent la sourdine	Dämpfer vorbereiten
Place mute(s)	*con sord., c.s.*	Mettez la sourdine	Gedämpft
Prepare mute(s)	Mette il sordino	Mettez les sourdines	Mit Dämpfer
Put on mute(s)	Mette la sordina	Mettre sourdine(s)	*Mit Dmpf., m. Dpf., m. D.*
Take mute(s)	Mettere sordino	Prenez la sourdine	Mit Sordinen
With mute(s)	Mettete i sordini	Prenez les sourdines	*mit Sord., m. Sord.*
	Mettono le sordine	Préparez la sourdine	Nehmen Dämpfer
	Preparare la sordina	Préparez les sourdines	Nimmt (auch) Dämpfer
	Riprende la sordina	Remettez [remettre]	Sordinen
	Sordina(e)	les sourdines	*sord.*
	Sordino(i)	Sourdine(s)	
	sord.	*sourd.*	
	Sordino mettere		

Mutes Off

English	Italian	French	German
Mute(s) off [out]	Alzate sordini	Enlevez la sourdine	Dämpfer ab! [auf!]
No mute(s)	Aperta(e)	Enlevez les sourdines	Dämpfer absetzen
Not muted	Aperto(i)	Levare la sourdine	Dämpfer weg
Off mute(s)	In modo ordinario	Ôtent la sourd.	Keine Dämpfer
Open	Levare la sordina	Ôter la sourdine	Nicht mit Dämpfer
Remove mute(s)	Non sordina(e)	Ôtez la sourdine	Nicht sordinirt
Take off mute(s)	Non sordino(i)	Ôtez les sourdines	Offen
Unmuted	Ordinario	Ouvert(s)	Ohne Dämpfer
Without mute(s)	*ord.*	Ouvrez	*ohne Dmpf., o. Dpf., o. D.*
	Senza sordina(e)	Retire la sourdine	Ohne Sordinen
	Senza sordino(i)	Sans sourdine(s)	Setz den Dämpfer ab
	senza sord.	*sans sourd.*	Sordinen ab! [auf]
	Si levano i sordini	Son(s) naturale(s)	*Sord. ab!*
	Sine sordino(i)	Son(s) ordinaire(s)	Surdinen **weg**
	Sordino levare	Son(s) ouvert(s)	
	Toglie la sordina		
	Togliere sordino(i)		
	Tolgono le sordine		
	Via sordina(e)		
	Via sordino(i)		

(1) MUTE TYPES

English	Italian	French	German
Cardboard	Sordino di cartone	Sourdine en carton	Kartondämpfer
Cup	—		
Double	Doppio sordino	Double sourdine	Doppeltdämpfer
Fibre	Sordino di capoc	Sourdine de capoc	Fiberdämpfer
Harmon	—	—	—
Hat			
Jazz	Il sordino "Jazz"	La sourdine "Jazz"	"Jazz"-dämpfer
Metal	Sordino di metallo	Sourdine de métal	Metalldämpfer
		[Sourdine en cuivre]	
Non-transposing	—	—	—

MUTES

(1) MUTE TYPES (contd.)

English	*Italian*	*French*	*German*
Ordinary	Sordina(e)	Sourdine(s)	Dämpfer
Regular	Sordino(i)		Sordinen
Straight			
Plunger	—	—	—
"Ray Robison"	—	—	
Soft cardboard	Sordino di cartone molle	Sourdine en carton doux	Weicher Kartondämpfer
Solo tone	—	—	—
Wa-wa [Wah-wah; Wha-wha]	—	Sourdine oua-oua [Sourdine Woo-woo]	
With felt crown	—	—	—
With rubber bushing	—	—	—

CARDBOARD MUTE

Trombone

COMPOSER	WORK	PAGE	MEASURE
Bartók	*Violin Concerto*	114	[446] 2f

Trumpet and Trombone

COMPOSER	WORK	PAGE	MEASURE
Bartók	*Violin Concerto*	91	[199] 3f

CUP MUTE

Trumpet

COMPOSER	WORK	PAGE	MEASURE	COMPOSER	WORK	PAGE	MEASURE
Copland	*Music for Radio*	23	[15]	**Siegmeister**	*Ozark Set*	13	[55]
		30	[20]			75	1b [60]
Gillis	*Symphony No. 5½*	67	[J]	**Siegmeister**	*Sunday in Brooklyn*	7	1b [20]
		85	[I]	**Siegmeister**	*Western Suite*	10	[35]
Moore	*Symphony in A major*	69	[51]			50	[10] 2f
Siegmeister	*From my Window*	9	[45]	**Still**	*In Memoriam*	5	5
		22	3b [20]				

Trombone

COMPOSER	WORK	PAGE	MEASURE	COMPOSER	WORK	PAGE	MEASURE
Gillis	*Symphony No. 5½*	87	[K]	**Siegmeister**	*Western Suite*	3	1b [15]
Siegmeister	*From my Window*	17	4b [35]			23	1b [95]
Siegmeister	*Ozark Set*	14	4			66	2
Siegmeister	*Sunday in Brooklyn*	8	[25] 2f	**Still**	*Bells*	3	[3]
		16	2b [55]				
		27	1				

Trumpet and Trombone

COMPOSER	WORK	PAGE	MEASURE	COMPOSER	WORK	PAGE	MEASURE
Siegmeister	*Ozark Set*	52	3b [30]	**Still**	*Poem for Orchestra*	7	4
Siegmeister	*Sunday in Brooklyn*	70	[45] 1f				

DOUBLE MUTE

Trumpet

COMPOSER	WORK	PAGE	MEASURE
Bartók	*Violin Concerto*	119	[500]

BRASSES

(1) MUTE TYPES (contd.)

FIBRE MUTE

Trumpet

COMPOSER	WORK	PAGE	MEASURE
Rogers	Characters from Hans	9	[5]
	Christian Andersen	26	2b [13]

HARMON MUTE

Trumpet

COMPOSER	WORK	PAGE	MEASURE	COMPOSER	WORK	PAGE	MEASURE
Copland	Music for Radio	30	[20]	Stravinsky	Ebony Concerto	23	1b [6]
Gillis	Symphony No. 5½	4	[A] 1f	Turner	Fanfare, Chorale and	10	1b [70]
		81	3		Finale	21	[150] 1f
Rogers	Once Upon a Time,	14	1				
	Five Fairy Tales	25	6				

Trombone

COMPOSER	WORK	PAGE	MEASURE	COMPOSER	WORK	PAGE	MEASURE
Gillis	Symphony No. 5½	17	5	Stravinsky	Ebony Concerto	7	[8] 3f

Trumpet and Trombone

COMPOSER	WORK	PAGE	MEASURE	COMPOSER	WORK	PAGE	MEASURE
Gillis	Symphony No. 5½	30	[N] 6f	Stravinsky	Ebony Concerto	13	[9a]
Still	Dismal Swamp	12	1				
		20	[13]				

Horn, Trumpet, and Trombone

COMPOSER	WORK	PAGE	MEASURE
Stravinsky	Ebony Concerto	39	[33]

JAZZ MUTE

Trumpet

COMPOSER	WORK	PAGE	MEASURE	COMPOSER	WORK	PAGE	MEASURE
Copland	Concerto for Piano and	36	1b [25]	Copland	Music for the Theatre	26	[19] 2f
	Orchestra	59	[45]			47	1
				Moross	Biguine	2	4

METAL MUTE

Cornet

COMPOSER	WORK	PAGE	MEASURE
Villa-Lobos	Uirapurú	46	[10]

Trombone

COMPOSER	WORK	PAGE	MEASURE
Villa-Lobos	Chôros No. 8	30	3

NON-TRANSPOSING MUTE

Horn

COMPOSER	WORK	PAGE	MEASURE
Still	Bells	4	[4]

(1) MUTE TYPES (contd.)
ORDINARY [REGULAR, STRAIGHT] MUTE

Trumpet

COMPOSER	WORK	PAGE	MEASURE	COMPOSER	WORK	PAGE	MEASURE
Copland	*Music for Radio*	24	5	Siegmeister	*Ozark Set*	15	[60] 2f
Gillis	*Symphony No. 5½*	53	4	Siegmeister	*Western Suite*	15	[50] 1f
Kay	*Suite for Orchestra*	4	1			53	[40] 1f
		29	[30]	Still	*In Memoriam*	2	1
		57	[64] 1f	Thomson	*Louisiana Story Suite*	20	114
Rogers	*Once Upon a Time,*	14	[11]			45	11
	Five Fairy Tales	57	1b [33]	Thomson	*The Seine at Night*	2	[1] 1f
Rosenthal	*Les Petits Métiers*	52	3			12	4
Siegmeister	*From my Window*	10	1b [50]	Turner	*Fanfare, Chorale and Finale*	1	6

Tuba

COMPOSER	WORK	PAGE	MEASURE	COMPOSER	WORK	PAGE	MEASURE
Bach–Stokowski	*Komm Süsser Tod*	4	[3]	Milhaud	*Deuxième Concerto pour Violon et Orchestre*	50	[5] 3f
Bartók	*Dance Suite*	2	9	Milhaud	*IIᵉ Symphonie*	12	2b [95]
		56	[40]	Milhaud	*Quatrième Symphonie*	37	[35]
		63	[44]	Mussorgsky–Ravel	*Pictures at an Exhibition*	8	[8]
Bax	*First Symphony*	11	[C]			19	[17] 4f
Bax	*Third Symphony*	9	4b [9]	Ravel	*Daphnis et Chloé, Suite No. 1*	43	[112]
Bax	*Fourth Symphony*	61	[48] 2f				
Bax	*Fifth Symphony*	87	1	Schönberg	*A Survivor from Warsaw*	8	34
Berg	*Three Excerpts from "Wozzeck"*	23	2b [15]	Schönberg	*Fünf Orchesterstücke*	8	[7]
		55	[375]			30	4
Berg	*Violin Concerto*	8	[45] 1f			43	[7] 1f
		41	[200]	Schuman, W.	*Undertow*	13	[150]
		80	1b [135]	Siegmeister	*Sunday in Brooklyn*	10	[35]
Britten	*Sinfonia da Requiem*	28	2b [20]			23	3
Casella	*Elegia Eroica*	26	[34]	Siegmeister	*Western Suite*	52	[25]
Copland	*Billy the Kid Ballet Suite*	15	[11]	Strauss, R.	*Don Quixote*	8	8
				Strauss, R.	*Ein Heldenleben*	112	[58]
Copland	*Statements*	14	[2]	Stravinsky	*Le Sacre du Printemps*	73	[80]
Gillis	*Symphony No. 5½*	20	6	Thomson	*The Seine at Night*	18	1b [10]
Inghelbrecht	*Rapsodie de Printemps*	38	[19]				
Levant	*Nocturne*	35	154				

Horn and Trombone

COMPOSER	WORK	PAGE	MEASURE
Stravinsky	*Ebony Concerto*	25	1b [10]

Trumpet and Trombone

Walton	*Façade, Suite No. 2*	41	4

PLUNGER MUTE

Trumpet

Stravinsky	*Ebony Concerto*	22	[2] 1f
		34	2b [28]

BRASSES

(1) MUTE TYPES (contd.)

Trombone

COMPOSER	WORK	PAGE	MEASURE
Stravinsky	*Ebony Concerto*	**19**	[3] 2f

"RAY ROBISON" MUTE

Trumpet

COMPOSER	WORK	PAGE	MEASURE
Still	*Dismal Swamp*	**9**	1b [6]
		19	4

SOFT CARDBOARD MUTE

Trombone

COMPOSER	WORK	PAGE	MEASURE
Bartók	*Concerto for Orchestra*	**11**	5b [220]

SOLO TONE MUTE

Trumpet

COMPOSER	WORK	PAGE	MEASURE	COMPOSER	WORK	PAGE	MEASURE
Copland	*Music for Radio*	**35**	[24]	**Turner**	*Fanfare, Chorale and Finale*	**9**	[60] 5f

Trombone

COMPOSER	WORK	PAGE	MEASURE
Turner	*Fanfare, Chorale and Finale*	**14**	1

Trumpet and Trombone

COMPOSER	WORK	PAGE	MEASURE
Copland	*Music for Radio*	**13**	[8]

WA-WA [WAH-WAH, WHA-WHA] MUTE

Trumpet

COMPOSER	WORK	PAGE	MEASURE	COMPOSER	WORK	PAGE	MEASURE
Gershwin	*Rhapsody in Blue*	**4**	[2]	**Thomson**	*Orchestra Suite from "The Plow that Broke the Plains"*	**31**	[26]
		17	[13] 2f				
Inghelbrecht	*La Valse Retrouvée*	**6**	[38] 4f	**Zimbalist**	*American Rhapsody*	**1**	4
Rosenthal	*Les Petits Métiers*	**53**	4				
Siegmeister	*Western Suite*	**73**	2				

Trombone

COMPOSER	WORK	PAGE	MEASURE	COMPOSER	WORK	PAGE	MEASURE
Gershwin	*Rhapsody in Blue*	**18**	4b [14]	**Rosenthal**	*Les Petits Métiers*	**63**	3
						80	3

Trumpet and Trombone

COMPOSER	WORK	PAGE	MEASURE
Walton	*Façade, Suite No. 2*	**38**	[C] 1f

MUTES

(1) MUTE TYPES (contd.)

MUTE WITH FELT CROWN

Trumpet

COMPOSER	WORK	PAGE	MEASURE	COMPOSER	WORK	PAGE	MEASURE
Gershwin	*An American in Paris*	51	2	**Gershwin**	*Concerto in F for Piano*	53	5
		57	4b [51]		*and Orchestra*	64	[8]

MUTE WITH RUBBER BUSHING

Trumpet

COMPOSER	WORK	PAGE	MEASURE
Thomson	*Louisiana Story Suite*	35	5

(2) ECHO SOUNDS

English	Italian	French	German
Echo	Come un eco	En écho	Echoton
Echo sound(s)	Eco	Son(s) d'écho	Echotonartig
Echo tone(s)		(Prenez le doigté $\frac{1}{4}$ ton au-dessous de la note réelle)	
		Son(s) voilé(s)	
		Voilé(s)	

Horn

COMPOSER	WORK	PAGE	MEASURE	COMPOSER	WORK	PAGE	MEASURE
Charpentier	*Impressions d'Italie*	16	7	**Elgar**	*In the South, Concert Overture*	80	5
		22	1	**Inghelbrecht**	*Sinfonia Breve No. 1*	50	[28] 10f
		70	[18] 2f			74	[41]
Debussy	*Gigues*	34	[20] 2f	**Milhaud**	*Cinq Symphonies pour Petit Orchestre*	68	[25]
Debussy	*Jeux*	1	1				
Debussy	*Rondes de Printemps*	10	[5] 2f	**Milhaud**	*2me Suite Symphonique*	10	4
Delius	*Appalachia*	1	5			65	2
Delius	*The Song of the High Hills*	12	[8] 1f			110	2
Dukas	*L'Apprenti Sorcier*	3	[3]	**Milhaud**	*Les Choéphores*	27	3
Dukas	*Symphonie en Ut majeur*	129	4			141	5
				Milhaud	*Saudades do Brazil*	22	5
						39	8

Trumpet and Trombone

COMPOSER	WORK	PAGE	MEASURE
Schönberg	*Fünf Orchesterstücke*	47	[1] 5f

(3) HAND IN BELL

English	Italian	French	German
Hand in bell	Colla mano	Avec la main	Hand im Schalltrichter
Hand over bell	La mano nella campana	La main dans le pavillon	Mit der Hand
Mute with hand			
With the hand			

BRASSES

(3) HAND IN BELL (contd.)

Horn

COMPOSER	WORK	PAGE	MEASURE
Schuman, W.	*Prayer in Time of War*	**27**	377

Trumpet

COMPOSER	WORK	PAGE	MEASURE	COMPOSER	WORK	PAGE	MEASURE
Gillis	*Symphony No. 5½*	**38**	6	**Thomson**	*The Seine at Night*	**5**	3b [3]
Thomson	*Louisiana Story Suite*	**37**	42			**35**	[18] 2f
		54	109				

Trombone

COMPOSER	WORK	PAGE	MEASURE	COMPOSER	WORK	PAGE	MEASURE
Gillis	*Symphony No. 5½*	**28**	[M]	**Gillis**	*The Alamo*	**53**	4
		73	4				

(4) HAT OVER BELL

English	Italian	French	German
Felt hat(s) over bell(s)	Cappello sopra campana	Chapeau sur le pavillon	Hut über den Schalltrichter
Hats(s) over bell(s)	Coperto con un cappello	Dans un chapeau	In einem Hut
In hat(s)	In uno cappello		
In felt [soft] hat(s)			
Soft hat(s) over bell(s)			

Horn

Copland	*Music for Radio*	**14**	[9] 1f

Trumpet

COMPOSER	WORK	PAGE	MEASURE	COMPOSER	WORK	PAGE	MEASURE
Cesana	*Second American*	**11**	[9]	**Still**	*Bells*	**2**	[2] 5f
	Symphony	**45**	[32]	**Still**	*Dismal Swamp*	**7**	1b [5]
		65	3			**24**	4
		111	1b [9]	**Stravinsky**	*Ebony Concerto*	**3**	[2]
Copland	*Music for Radio*	**51**	[34] 4f			**25**	2b [10]
Siegmeister	*From my Window*	**13**	3b [15]				

Trombone

COMPOSER	WORK	PAGE	MEASURE	COMPOSER	WORK	PAGE	MEASURE
Cesana	*Second American*	**11**	[9]	**Still**	*Bells*	**2**	[2] 5f
	Symphony	**45**	[32] 1f	**Still**	*Dismal Swamp*	**7**	[5]
		65	3			**24**	2
		111	[9]	**Still**	*In Memoriam*	**12**	[9] 3f
Copland	*Music for Radio*	**51**	[34] 4f	**Stravinsky**	*Ebony Concerto*	**33**	[26]

(5) IN STAND

English	Italian	French	German
In stand	Contro il leggio	Contre le pupitre	Gegen das Pult
Mute in stand			

Trombone

Moore	*Symphony in A major*	**112**	4

MUTES

(5) IN STAND (contd.)

Trumpet and Trombone

COMPOSER	WORK	PAGE	MEASURE
Thomson	*Louisiana Story Suite*	**52**	93
		54	109

(6) OTHER INDICATIONS

English	*Italian*	*French*	*German*
Open little by little	Apri poco a poco	Ouvrez peu à peu	Allmählich öffnen

Horn

Charpentier	*Impressions d'Italie*	**45**	[10] 3f

English	*Italian*	*French*	*German*
Muted, without stopping	Con sordino, non-chiuso	Avec sourdine, non-cuivrer	Mit Dämpfer, nicht gestopft

Horn

Debussy– Ansermet	*Six Épigraphes Antiques*	**94**	2

English	*Italian*	*French*	*German*
Half-mute(d)	Mezzo-sordino	Demi-sourdine	Halb gedämpft

Horn

Schuman, W.	*Symphony No. IV*	**31**	25

Chapter 20

STOPPED OR BRASSY TONES

English	*Italian*	*French*	*German*
Brassy (sounds, tones)	Chiuse	Bouché	Blechern
Closed (tones)	Chiuso(i)	Bouchez	Gestopft
Overblown	Coperto(i)	Bouché et cuivré	*gest.*
Stopped (tones)	Suono(i) chiuso(i)	Bouchez et cuivrez	Gestopfter Ton
		Cuivré	Schmetternd
		Cuivrez (le son)	Stark anblasen
		En cuivrant	
		Sons bouchés	
		Sons cuivrés	

+ = sign for stopped tones	+ = segno per il suono chiuso	+ = signe pour les sons bouchés	+ = Zeichen für einzelne gestopfte Töne
			Einzelne gestopfte Töne sind mit + bezeichnet

OPEN TONES

Natural (sounds, tones)	Aperto(i)	Naturel(s)	Natürlich
nat.	Loco	*nat.*	*nat.*
Open	Modo ordinario	Ouvert(s)	Normal
	modo. ord.	*ouv.*	Offen
	Naturale	Son(s) naturel(s)	
	nat.	Son(s) ordinaire(s)	
		Son(s) ouvert(s)	

(I) STOPPED

(Chiuso, Cuivré, Gestopft)

Horn

COMPOSER	WORK	PAGE	MEASURE	COMPOSER	WORK	PAGE	MEASURE
Albéniz–Arbós	El Puerto	3 11	2 [D] 2f	Bizet	L'Arlésienne Suite No. 1	39	1
				Bloch	Schelomo	68	[43]
Alfvén	A Legend of the Skerries	62	3b [25]	Bruckner	Symphony No. 9	51	356
				Caturla	Trois Danses Cubaines	6	[5]
Barber	Second Essay for Orchestra	15	[7] 2f	Charpentier	Impressions d'Italie	79	[5]
				Converse	American Sketches	41	[23]
Bax	Mediterranean	8	2	Debussy	Fêtes	21	[1] 2f
Bax	Tintagel	24	2			37	4
Benjamin	Overture to an Italian Comedy	26	[M]			69	2
Berg	Three Excerpts from "Wozzeck"	17 51	[385] 3f 1b [360]	Debussy	La Mer	31 57 120	[15] 2f [29] 3
Bernstein	"Jeremiah" Symphony	12	[13] 2f			126	[60]

STOPPED OR BRASSY TONES

Horn (contd.)

COMPOSER	WORK	PAGE	MEASURE	COMPOSER	WORK	PAGE	MEASURE
Debussy	Le Martyre de Saint Sébastien	47	2	Mahler	Symphony No. 4	33	173
						158	[3]
Debussy	Prélude à l'après-midi d'un Faune	26	2			167	[7]
				Mahler	Symphony No. 6	24	[14] 3f
Debussy	Rondes de Printemps	14	1			62	[38]
		49	[25]			86	[53]
Debussy	Sirènes	101	1			222	[143] 1f
		104	2	Mahler	Symphony No. 7	8	4
Delannoy	Figures Sonores	6	7b [3]	Mahler	Symphony No. 8	36	1b [40]
Dello Joio	Variations, Chaconne and Finale	18	1b [150]	Mahler	Symphony No. 9	35	2
		62	[110] 1f			140	10
Dukas	L'Apprenti Sorcier	3	[3] 3f	Milhaud	Cinq Symphonies pour Petit Orchestre	78	[25]
		58	[49] 2f	Milhaud	Deuxième Concerto pour Violon et Orchestre	50	[5]
Enesco	Ière Rhapsodie Roumaine	59	6	Milhaud	Introduction et Marche Funèbre	4	[15] 1f
Fauré	Pelléas et Mélisande	43	4	Milhaud	Ière Symphonie	41	[70] 1f
Gershwin	An American in Paris	49	1b [44]			92	2
Gershwin	Concerto in F for Piano and Orchestra	55	5b [3]	Milhaud	Quatrième Symphonie	22	[80] 1f
		78	2b [1]			85	1b [50]
Golestan	Concerto Roumain pour Violon et Orchestre	69	[D]	Milhaud	Saudades do Brazil	34	5
Hill	Lilacs	4	1b [2]			48	5
Ibert	Divertissement	52	4	Moross	Biguine	4	5
Ibert	Escales	18	[12]	Piston	Concertino for Piano-forte and Chamber Orchestra	8	3b [40]
		23	[17]				
		55	[48]	Piston	Prelude and Fugue	14	[G]
		66	2b [61]	Piston	Symphony No. 1	42	254
Ibert	Féerique	17	[12]			50	6
d'Indy	Deuxième Symphonie en Sib	102	[50]			59	[95]
d'Indy	Istar, Variations Symphoniques	1	1	Piston	Symphony No. 2	13	2
						115	1
d'Indy	Jour d'été à la Montagne	41	[17] 6f	Poulenc	Aubade	7	2
Inghelbrecht	El Greco	23	[19]	Poulenc	Concert Champêtre pour Clavecin et Orchestre	13	4
Inghelbrecht	La Métamorphose d'Ève	41	[27] 1f	Rachmaninoff	Die Toteninsel	10	9
Janssen	New Year's Eve in New York	55	[22]	Rachmaninoff	The Bells	96	6b [100]
Johnson	Imagery	15	[5]	Ravel	Rapsodie Espagnole	17	[7] 2f
Liszt	Eine Faust-Symphonie	3	[A] 5f			69	[19] 2f
		72	[W] 4f	Respighi	Ballata delle Gnomidi	25	[6] 3f
		77	1b [Z]			43	6
		208	3	Respighi	The Pines of Rome	13	6
		262	1			25	1
Mahler	Das Lied von der Erde	33	[42]	Rimsky-Korsakoff	Symphony No. 2, "Antar"	11	4b [G]
		65	[7] 2f	Rosenthal	Les Petits Métiers	56	2
		71	1	Roussel	Évocations, I	14	2
Mahler	Symphony No. 1	47	4			42	3
		100	[5] 1f	Roussel	Évocations, II	20	5b [10]
Mahler	Symphony No. 2	4	13			53	7
		106	9	Roussel	Évocations, III	2	[1]

BRASSES

Horn (contd.)

COMPOSER	WORK	PAGE	MEASURE	COMPOSER	WORK	PAGE	MEASURE
Roussel	Suite en Fa	2	[1]	Strauss, R.	Death and Transfigura-		
Satie–					tion	57	2
Debussy	Gymnopédies	4	9	Strauss, R.	Don Juan	73	[V] 6f
Schelling	A Victory Ball	67	[19]	Strauss, R.	Ein Heldenleben	218	[109] 1f
		87	[27]	Strauss, R.	Salomé's Dance	9	[L]
Schmitt	Mirages pour			Strauss, R.	Symphonia Domestica	82	[106] 1f
	Orchestre, No. 1	35	[16]	Stravinsky	Chant du Rossignol	66	2b [72]
Schmitt	Ronde burlesque	3	1	Stravinsky	Fire-Bird Suite (1919)	36	[11] 2f
Schreker	The Birthday of the			Stravinsky	Le Sacre du Printemps	95	[116] 2f
	Infanta, Suite	12	[45] 1f	Stravinsky	Petrouchka Suite	65	[51]
Schuman, W.	American Festival					75	[60]
	Overture	7	[45] 1f	Stravinsky	Renard	112	[72]
Schuman, W.	Symphony No. III	30	285	Stravinsky	Scherzo Fantastique	7	[7]
Schuman, W.	Symphony No. IV	35	65	Stringfield	A Negro Parade	2	6b [1]
		45	95	Tansman	Deux Moments		
Sessions	Symphony No. II	4	1b [B]		Symphoniques	29	6b [9]
		12	[F]	Tchaikovsky	Hamlet	17	55
		55	1b [Kk]			110	5
		89	1b [J]	Tchaikovsky	Suite from the Ballet,		
Sibelius	Karelia Suite	2	12b [A]		"The Sleeping		
Sibelius	Pelleas and Melisande				Beauty"	25	2
	Suite	22	1	Tchaikovsky	Symphony No. 5	103	1
Sibelius	Pohjola's Daughter	3	1	Tchaikovsky	Symphony No. 6,		
Sibelius	Symphony No. 4	4	[C] 3f		"Pathétique"	202	126
		37	1	Thomson	Louisiana Story Suite	14	78
		58	14			39	62
Sibelius	Violin Concerto	88	[4]			67	35
Siegmeister	From my Window	26	[35] 3f	Wagner, R.	Eine Faust-Overture	17	102
Siegmeister	Ozark Set	45	[85] 1f	Wagner, R.	Funeral Music from		
Siegmeister	Sunday in Brooklyn	27	1		"Götterdämmerung"	22	71
Skilton	Suite Primeval, Part 1	17	[C]	Walton	Concerto for Viola and		
Strauss, R.	Also Sprach Zarathustra	23	3		Orchestra	59	[52]
		44	4	Wolf	Der Feuerreiter	29	82
		194	4				

Trumpet

COMPOSER	WORK	PAGE	MEASURE	COMPOSER	WORK	PAGE	MEASURE
Bruckner	Symphony No. 9	102	150	Milhaud	Les Choéphores	21	[J] 2f
		140	660			76	3b [V]
Graener	Comedietta	15	75	Milhaud	Saudades do Brazil	48	3
Hindemith	Kammermusik No. 1	32	[70] 2f	Milhaud	Sérénade pour Orchestre	24	1b [2]
Honegger	Le Chant de Nigamon	36	[125]			32	3
d'Indy	Deuxième Symphonie					38	[2]
	en Sib	129	1	Roussel	Évocations, II	17	5
Mahler	Symphony No. 1	93	3b [18]	Stravinsky	Feuerwerk	6	1
Mahler	Symphony No. 2	7	2	Stravinsky	Le Sacre du Printemps	127	[176] 1f
Milhaud	2me Suite Symphonique	80	3	Zimbalist	American Rhapsody	35	1b [28]
		127	2				
		159	4b [74]				

STOPPED OR BRASSY TONES

Horn and Trumpet

COMPOSER	WORK	PAGE	MEASURE	COMPOSER	WORK	PAGE	MEASURE
Debussy	*Gigues*	16	1	Strauss, R.	*Till Eulenspiegel's*		
Elgar	*Variations, "Enigma"*	117	[76]		*Merry Pranks*	35	7
Graener	*Comedietta*	42	193	Stravinsky	*Feuerwerk*	30	[29]
Mahler	*Symphony No. 3*	92	10	Zimbalist	*American Rhapsody*	37	1b [29]

Horn, Trumpet, and Trombone

Mahler	*Symphony No. 3*	11	2	Milhaud	*Saudades do Brazil*	63	2

$$(2) \quad \overset{+}{\rho}$$

Horn

COMPOSER	WORK	PAGE	MEASURE	COMPOSER	WORK	PAGE	MEASURE
Alfvén	*A Legend of the Skerries*	15	[4] 1f	de Falla	*Nuits dans les Jardins*		
		53	[21] 1f		*d'Espagne*	15	3
Bartók	*Dance Suite*	84	86	de Falla	*Three Dances from*		
Bartók	*Vier Orchesterstücke*	54	⌈21⌉ 2f		*"The Three-*		
Bartók	*Violin Concerto*	83	[111]		*Cornered Hat"*	43	3
Bax	*In the Faery Hills*	11	[C]	Gershwin	*Rhapsody in Blue*	27	[23]
Bax	*November Woods*	70	2	Glière	*Russian Sailors' Dance*	8	[62]
Bax	*Second Symphony*	36	1b [20]	Grieg	*Peer Gynt Suite No. 1*	22	1
Bloch	*America*	115	1	Grofé	*Grand Canyon Suite*	35	[1] 1f
		155	[88]			57	[A]
Brahms	*Academic Festival*					107	5
	Overture	31	258	Holst	*The Planets*	3	3b [I]
Britten	*Passacaglia from "Peter*			Ibert	*Divertissement*	52	4
	Grimes"	21	[9]	Ibert	*Escales*	14	[9] 3f
Britten	*Sinfonietta*	32	[8]	Ibert	*La Ballade de la Geôle*		
Carse	*A Romantic Legend*	14	[F] 5f		*de Reading*	94	[69]
Casella	*La Donna Serpente,*			Janssen	*New Year's Eve in*		
	II. Serie	15	1b [22]		*New York*	62	[24]
Casella	*Paganiniana*	72	[5]	Kabalevsky	*Suite from "Colas*	59	[47]
Copland	*An Outdoor Overture*	43	1b [255]		*Breugnon"*	77	1
Copland	*Appalachian Spring*	45	3			123	[4]
Copland	*Billy the Kid Ballet*					167	[29]
	Suite	58	[36] 4f	Kabalevsky	*Symphony No. 2*	13	3b [9]
Copland	*Statements*	14	[2]			23	[18]
Cowell	*Short Symphony*					100	6b [7]
	(No. 4)	53	4			148	1b [53]
Debussy	*Iberia*	84	2	Kabalevsky	*The Comedians*	15	[7]
Debussy	*La Mer*	77	5	Khachaturian	*Concerto for Piano and*	30	[240]
		95	2b [48]		*Orchestra*	74	[126]
		119	6	Khachaturian	*Gayne Ballet Suite*	6	1b [4]
Diamond	*Timon of Athens*	11	72		*No. 2*	29	[21]
Dukas	*L'Apprenti Sorcier*	11	[14] 2f			66	5
de Falla	*El Amor Brujo*	7	[1] 11f	Knipper	*Symphony No. 4*	7	[4]
		60	[34]			30	4b [24]
de Falla	*El Retablo de Maese*					57	2b [10]
	Pedro	79	[76] 3f	Kodály	*Psalmus Hungaricus*	18	[11] 1f

BRASSES

Horn (contd.)

COMPOSER	WORK	PAGE	MEASURE	COMPOSER	WORK	PAGE	MEASURE
Liadov	Baba-Yaga	1	1	Rimsky-Korsakoff	Le Coq d'Or Suite	19	[12]
Liadov	Eight Russian Popular Songs	21	[2]			25	3
						79	1
Liadov	Kikimora	2	[3]	Rimsky-Korsakoff	Russian Easter Overture	9	1
Maganini	An Ancient Greek Melody	6	[C]	Ropartz	Soir sur les Chaumes	40	[12]
Mahler	Das Lied von der Erde	17	5	Roussel	Suite en Fa	67	[32]
		29	[35] 2f			93	3b [51]
Mahler	Songs of a Wayfarer	37	11	Roussel	Symphonie en Sol mineur	22	[13]
Mahler	Symphony No. 6	5	[2] 5f			41	3
Mahler	Symphony No. 7	84	[73] 1f	Schlein	Dance Overture	14	7b [G]
Mahler	Symphony No. 8	38	[42] 2f	Schönberg	Kammersymphonie, Op. 9	49	[47]
		82	2b [18]				
Milhaud	Les Choéphores	17	[H] 1f	Scriabin	Deuxième Symphonie	12	3b [7]
Moore	Symphony in A major	91	[62]	Scriabin	Le Divin Poème	56	4
Moross	Biguine	2	1	Sessions	Suite from "The Black Maskers"	5	1
Mussorgsky	Night on the Bald Mountain	21	[E]	Sessions	Symphony No. II	40	4
		80	393			63	[Pp]
Mussorgsky–Ravel	Pictures at an Exhibition	11	3b [10]	Shepherd	Horizons	7	1
		19	[17] 4f			13	[D] 3f
		90	1b [73]			52	3b [C]
Pescara	Tibet	22	[7]			79	3
		32	1b [11]			150	[P]
Prokofieff	Ala et Lolly (Scythian Suite)	69	[47]	Shostakovich	Symphony No. 1	51	3b [7]
Prokofieff	Cinderella Suite No. 1	73	2b [55]	Siegmeister	Western Suite	37	2
Prokofieff	Romeo and Juliet, Suite No. 1	117	[74]	Strauss, R.	Also Sprach Zarathustra	17	3
Rachmaninoff	Piano Concerto No. 3	20	7	Stravinsky	Chant du Rossignol	64	2b [68]
Rachmaninoff	Symphony No. 2	22	1	Stravinsky	Le Sacre du Printemps	84	1b [101]
		57	[1]	Szymanowski	Symphonie Concertante pour Piano et Orchestre	30	[17]
		81	3			112	1
		113	3	Taylor	Through the Looking Glass	17	[10] 6f
		144	2			32	5
		157	[59]			87	[9]
Rachmaninoff	The Bells	20	6b [18]	Tchaikovsky	Symphony No. 5	121	169
Ravel	Alborada del Gracioso	8	[5] 1f	Tchaikovsky	Symphony No. 6, "Pathétique"	202	126
Ravel	Concerto pour la main gauche	44	[23] 2f	Thomson	Orchestra Suite from "The Plow that Broke the Plains"	29	[23]
Ravel	Daphnis et Chloé, Suite No. 1	39	1				
Ravel	Daphnis et Chloé, Suite No. 2	45	[176]	Vaughan Williams	A London Symphony	9	[D] 1f
		70	[195] 1f	Vaughan Williams	Overture to "The Wasps"	34	246
Ravel	La Valse	63	[46] 4f				
		79	[58]	Wagner, R.	Prelude and Love Death from "Tristan und Isolde"	31	26
Ravel	Ma Mère l'Oye	14	[4]				
		36	[2] 4f				
Ravel	Menuet Antique	14	[12] 3f				
Ravel	Rapsodie Espagnole	61	1b [13]	Whithorne	Fata Morgana	8	[9] 4f
Read	Sketches of the City	4	3b [1]	Whithorne	The Dream Pedlar	65	4
Respighi	The Pines of Rome	19	[5] 5f				

STOPPED OR BRASSY TONES

Trumpet

COMPOSER	WORK	PAGE	MEASURE	COMPOSER	WORK	PAGE	MEASURE
Bloch	*America*	114	2	**Enesco**	*Ière Rhapsodie Roumaine*	70	1

Horn and Trumpet

COMPOSER	WORK	PAGE	MEASURE	COMPOSER	WORK	PAGE	MEASURE
Shostakovich	*The Golden Age, Ballet Suite*	53	[62]	**Stravinsky**	*Danses Concertantes*	8	1b [11]

(3) STOPPED — +

(Chiuso — + , Cuivré — + , Gestopft — +)

Horn

COMPOSER	WORK	PAGE	MEASURE	COMPOSER	WORK	PAGE	MEASURE
Balakirev–Casella	*Islamey*	7 / 18	3 / [15]	**Copland**	*Dance Symphony*	12 / 48	[7] / 4b [28]
Bax	*First Symphony*	11 / 93	2b [C] / [D] 1f	**Copland**	*Four Dance Episodes from "Rodeo"*	13 / 40 / 96	[13] / [37] / 1
Bax	*Second Symphony*	54	5				
Bax	*Third Symphony*	55	[57]	**Copland**	*Music for Radio*	27	4b [18]
Bax	*Sixth Symphony*	76	3	**Copland**	*Statements*	31	[6] 4f
Bax	*In the Faery Hills*	69	[EE]	**Copland**	*Third Symphony*	20	4
Bax	*November Woods*	89	1			30	1
Bax	*The Garden of Fand*	70	2			135	[117] 2f
Bax	*Tintagel*	39	2				
Benjamin	*Jamaican Rhumba*	8	5	**Coppola**	*Suite Intima*	57	2
Benjamin	*Overture to an Italian Comedy*	5	1	**Diamond**	*Timon of Athens*	11 / 26	67 / 174
Berg	*Violin Concerto*	68 / 99	[95] 1f / 2b [230]	**Dukas**	*La Péri*	43	3
				Dukas	*Polyeucte, Ouverture*	10	[D] 1f
Bloch	*Schelomo*	42 / 49	[25] / 3	**Dunn**	*Overture on Negro Themes*	4 / 45	3 / [U] 6f
Bloch	*Trois Poèmes Juifs*	6	2b [2]	**Enesco**	*Ière Rhapsodie Roumaine*	70	1
Casella	*Elegia Eroica*	28	4b [37]	**Enesco**	*2e Rhapsodie Roumaine*	22	2
Casella	*La Donna Serpente, I. Serie*	25	[25] 2f	**Gershwin**	*An American in Paris*	6 / 29 / 38 / 66 / 84	[5] / [26] / [36] 2f / 5 / 1
Casella	*La Donna Serpente, II. Serie*	71	[80]				
Casella	*Paganiniana*	86 / 116	1 / [3] 1f	**Glazounov**	*Violin Concerto in A minor*	50	[30]
Chabrier	*Joyeuse Marche*	23	6	**Honegger**	*Horace Victorieux*	38	[15]
Chabrier	*Suite Pastorale*	56	7	**Honegger**	*Le Chant de Nigamon*	2 / 52	1b [7] / [178]
Chávez	*Sinfonia India*	1 / 15 / 58	1 / 1b [14] / [81]	**Honegger**	*Le Roi David*	22 / 49	1 / [3]
Copland	*Appalachian Spring*	4 / 22 / 28	[6] 2f / [19] / [26]	**Honegger**	*Mouvement Symphonique No. 3*	39	5

BRASSES

Horn (contd.)

COMPOSER	WORK	PAGE	MEASURE	COMPOSER	WORK	PAGE	MEASURE
Honegger	Musique pour la "Phaedre" de G. D'Annunzio	1	1	**Read**	Symphony No. 1	2	1b [1]
						38	1
						88	11
Honegger	Pacific 231	3	[1] 3f			114	3
d'Indy	Jour d'été à la Montagne	42	4b [18]			130	[46]
		58	[28] 3f	**Rimsky-Korsakoff**	Capriccio Espagnol	14	1
Ireland	A London Overture	35	1b [21]	**Rogers**	Characters from Hans Christian Andersen	27	1
		76	2b [52]				
Janssen	New Year's Eve in New York	41	[16]	**Schlein**	Dance Overture	18	[285]
Maganini	An Ancient Greek Melody	3	[A]	**Schmitt**	Étude pour le "Palais Hanté" d'Edgar Poe	3	3
						26	[18] 3f
Mahler	Das Lied von der Erde	108	1b [20]	**Schönberg**	Fünf Orchesterstücke	45	4
Mahler	Symphony No. 5	20	[7] 4f	**Schönberg**	Kammersymphonie, Op. 9	103	1
		43	[18]				
Mahler	Symphony No. 7	103	2b [94]	**Sessions**	Symphony No. II	14	2
		129	2b [130]			106	2
		238	6	**Stravinsky**	Petrouchka Suite	78	[63]
Mahler	Symphony No. 8	127	[85] 3f			92	1b [79]
Mahler	Symphony No. 9	36	6b [13]	**Thomson**	Louisiana Story Suite	23	138
Malipiero	Impressioni dal Vero, 1ᵃ Parte	32	167	**Thomson**	Orchestra Suite from "The Plow that Broke the Plains"	34	[30]
Malipiero	Impressioni dal Vero, 3ᵃ Parte	16	4	**Tippett**	Symphony No. 1	157	[14] 2f
Miaskovsky	Symphony No. 8	85	3	**Turner**	Fanfare, Chorale and Finale	1	6
Milhaud	Cinq Symphonies pour Petite Orchestre	68	3b [25]	**Varèse**	Hyperprism	5	[2] 1f
Milhaud	2ᵐᵉ Suite Symphonique	53	7	**Varèse**	Intégrales	45	2
		84	[43] 2f	**Vaughan Williams**	Job, A Masque for Dancing	47	1
Milhaud	Les Choéphores	65	3b [R]			67	4
Milhaud	Saudades do Brazil	10	5	**Vaughan Williams**	Overture to "The Wasps"	62	6
		35	9	**Wagner, R.**	Good Friday Spell from "Parsifal"	15	122
Morris	Prospice Symphony	12	[125] 2f	**Walton**	Symphony	25	2
Poot	Symphonie	9	8			74	4
		39	[22] 6f			103	[76] 4f
Ravel	Rapsodie Espagnole	8	[6] 1f			158	3
		30	[2]				
		47	[5]				
Read	First Overture	34	5				

Horn and Trumpet

COMPOSER	WORK	PAGE	MEASURE
Enesco	Iᵉʳᵉ Rhapsodie Roumaine	67	[33]

(4) MUTED—BRASSY

(Con sordino—chiuso, Avec sourdine—cuivré, Mit Dämpfer—Gestopft)

Horn

COMPOSER	WORK	PAGE	MEASURE	COMPOSER	WORK	PAGE	MEASURE
Debussy	Fêtes	68	21	**Inghelbrecht**	Pour le jour de la première neige au vieux Japon	35	[21]
Debussy	Sirènes	99	[9]				

STOPPED OR BRASSY TONES

Horn (contd.)

COMPOSER	WORK	PAGE	MEASURE	COMPOSER	WORK	PAGE	MEASURE
Rogers	Characters from Hans Christian Andersen	9	[5]	Villa-Lobos	Chôros No. 8	35	[15]
				Villa-Lobos	Danses Africaines	62	[9]

(5) MUTED — +

(Con sordino — +, Avec sourdine — +, Mit Dämpfer — +)

Horn

COMPOSER	WORK	PAGE	MEASURE	COMPOSER	WORK	PAGE	MEASURE
Bartók	Concerto for Orchestra	58	[54]	Read	Prelude and Toccata	4	[2] 4f
Bartók	Violin Concerto	45	2b [304]			17	[6] 4f
Bernstein	"Jeremiah" Symphony	48	[2] 4f			25	[9] 2f
Copland	Appalachian Spring	46	2b [38]	Saminsky	Litanies des Femmes	1	[1]
Copland	Billy the Kid Ballet Suite	28	1	Walton	Concerto for Violin and Orchestra	4	2b [2]
Pick-Mangiagalli	Notturno e Rondo Fantastico	2 16	1 1				

Trumpet

COMPOSER	WORK	PAGE	MEASURE	COMPOSER	WORK	PAGE	MEASURE
Diamond	Timon of Athens	19	125	Stravinsky	Petrouchka Suite	125	[107]

(6) OPEN—BRASSY

(Senza sordino—chiuso, Sans sourdine—cuivré, Ohne Dämpfer—Gestopft)

Horn

COMPOSER	WORK	PAGE	MEASURE	COMPOSER	WORK	PAGE	MEASURE
Rivier	Rapsodie pour Violoncelle et Orchestre	47	[30]	Stravinsky	Renard	69	[46] 1f
Schönberg	Kammersymphonie, Op. 9	55	[52] 1f	Thomson	Louisiana Story Suite	68	39

(7) OPEN — +

(Senza sordino — +, Sans sourdine — +, Ohne Dämpfer — +)

Horn

COMPOSER	WORK	PAGE	MEASURE	COMPOSER	WORK	PAGE	MEASURE
Debussy	Iberia	86	[55] 1f	Ravel	Rapsodie Espagnole	4	[3]
Ravel	Daphnis et Chloé, Suite No. 1	7 44	2 [113]	Roussel	Suite en Fa	58	4b [26]

BRASSES

(8) HAND IN BELL

English	Italian	French	German
Hand in bell	Colla mano	Avec la main	Hand im Schalltrichter
Hand-notes	La mano nella campana	La main dans le pavillon	Mit der Hand
Hand-stopped			
Stopped with hand			

Horn

COMPOSER	WORK	PAGE	MEASURE	COMPOSER	WORK	PAGE	MEASURE
Loeffler	*A Pagan Poem*	**17**	2	**Schuman, W.**	*American Festival*		
Loeffler	*Evocation*	**15**	[2] 2f		*Overture*	**11**	1b [80]
		16	[4]	**Schuman, W.**	*Symphony No. III*	**52**	110
Loeffler	*Poem, La Bonne*	**47**	[19]				
	Chanson	**54**	[25]				

Trumpet

COMPOSER	WORK	PAGE	MEASURE	COMPOSER	WORK	PAGE	MEASURE
Bloch	*Trois Poèmes Juifs*	**6**	3	**Thomson**	*Orchestra Suite from*		
Rogers	*Characters from Hans*				*"The Plow that*		
	Christian Andersen	**18**	1		*Broke the Plains"*	**23**	[18] 2f

(9) HALF-STOPPED

($\frac{1}{2}$ chiuso, $\frac{1}{2}$ bouché, $\frac{1}{2}$ gestopft)

Horn

COMPOSER	WORK	PAGE	MEASURE	COMPOSER	WORK	PAGE	MEASURE
Ibert	*Féerique*	**29**	[19] 2f	**Varèse**	*Intégrales*	**18**	2

(10) OTHER INDICATIONS

English	Italian	French	German
Muted—brassy — +	Con sordino—chiuso — +	Avec sourdine—cuivré — +	Mit Dämpfer—Gestopft — +

Horn

COMPOSER	WORK	PAGE	MEASURE	COMPOSER	WORK	PAGE	MEASURE
Copland	*Concerto for Piano and*	**56**	[42]	**Copland**	*Lincoln Portrait*	**36**	4b [220]
	Orchestra	**61**	[47]				

English	Italian	French	German
Open—brassy — +	Senza sordino—chiuso — +	Sans sourdine—cuivré — +	Ohne Dämpfer — Gestopft — +

COMPOSER	WORK	PAGE	MEASURE
Debussy– Ansermet	*Six Épigraphes Antiques*	**17**	3

STOPPED OR BRASSY TONES

English	*Italian*	*French*	*German*	
Stopped, imitating a horn	Chiuse, imitando il Corno	Cuivré, imitant un Cor	Gestopft, ein Horn nach-ahmend	

Trumpet

COMPOSER	WORK	PAGE	MEASURE
Respighi	*Feste Romane*	57	1b [16]

(II) STOPPED AND OPEN COMBINED

Horn

COMPOSER	WORK	PAGE	MEASURE	COMPOSER	WORK	PAGE	MEASURE
Bax	*First Symphony*	24	2	**Read**	*Symphony No. I*	69	2
Bax	*Fifth Symphony*	53	4			121	2
Bloch	*America*	131	3b [75]	**Schmitt**	*Étude pour le "Palais*	33	4
Casella	*Paganiniana*	4	1		*Hanté" d'Edgar Poe*	51	4b [38]
Debussy	*Iberia*	86	[55] 1f	**Schmitt**	*Mirages pour Orchestre,*		
de Falla	*El Amor Brujo*	60	[34]		*No. 2*	44	3
Guarnieri	*Brazilian Dance*	1	1	**Schönberg**	*Fünf Orchesterstücke*	57	1b [11]
Honegger	*Chant de Joie*	18	3	**Schreker**	*The Birthday of the*		
Honegger	*Le Chant de Nigamon*	41	2b [142]		*Infanta, Suite*	5	[15] 1f
MacDowell	*2nd Suite (Indian)*	99	4b [I]	**Sessions**	*Symphony (No. 1)*	9	[12]
Mahler	*Symphony No. 3*	9	[5]			53	[82]
		12	[8] 5f			72	[112]
		223	[23] 9f	**Shepherd**	*Horizons*	150	1b [P]
Mahler	*Symphony No. 5*	52	3b [3]	**Stravinsky**	*Le Sacre du Printemps*	30	[40]
		226	6			34	[44]
Mahler	*Symphony No. 6*	160	2b [109]	**Szymanowski**	*Symphonie Concertante*		
Mahler	*Symphony No. 9*	36	4b [13]		*pour Piano et*		
McKay	*Sinfonietta No. 4*	66	3		*Orchestre*	93	[27]
Read	*First Overture*	21	[7]	**Walton**	*Concerto for Violin and*		
					Orchestra	36	[19] 2f

Trumpet

COMPOSER	WORK	PAGE	MEASURE	COMPOSER	WORK	PAGE	MEASURE
Honegger	*Le Chant de Nigamon*	44	1	**Mahler**	*Symphony No. 5*	95	6

121

Chapter 21

STOPPED-OPEN (+ − o)

English	*Italian*	*French*	*German*
Brassy—Open	Chiuso(i)—Aperto(i)	Avec sourdine(s)—Ouvert(s)	Gedämpft—Offen
Muted—Open	Con sordino—Naturale	Bouché(s)—Ouvert(s)	Gestopft—Offen
Stopped—Open		Bouchez—Ouvert	
		Cuivré(s)—Ouvert(s)	
		Cuivrez—Ouvert	

Horn

COMPOSER	WORK	PAGE	MEASURE	COMPOSER	WORK	PAGE	MEASURE
Albéniz–Arbós	*El Puerto*	25	3	**Converse**	*American Sketches*	41	[23] 4f
Albéniz–Arbós	*Fête-Dieu à Séville*	21	3	**Copland**	*Dance Symphony*	83	1b [50]
Balakirev–				**Copland**	*Lincoln Portrait*	9	[60] 1f
Casella	*Islamey*	22	[19] 3f	**Coppola**	*Scherzo Fantasque*	40	3b [20]
Barber	*Medea*	53	3b [42]	**Coppola**	*Symphonie en La*		
		63	5		*mineur*	4	[2] 2f
Barber	*Second Essay for*			**Debussy**	*La Mer*	72	5
	Orchestra	31	2	**Debussy**	*Prélude à l'après-midi*		
Bartók	*Concerto for Orchestra*	83	[41]		*d'un Faune*	27	1b [10]
Bartók	*Dance Suite*	28	83	**Debussy**	*Première Rhapsodie*	38	1
		81	60	**Debussy**	*Rondes de Printemps*	52	[27] 2f
		85	90	**Delannoy**	*Figures Sonores*	7	1
Bartók	*Concerto No. 3 for*					48	[22]
	Piano and Orchestra	77	3b [560]	**Delius**	*A Dance Rhapsody,*		
Bartók	*First Rhapsody for*				*No. 2*	33	6
	Violin and Orchestra	11	[12] 1f	**Diamond**	*Timon of Athens*	11	68
Bax	*First Symphony*	11	[C]	**Dukas**	*La Péri*	44	2
		33	4			130	1
Bax	*Second Symphony*	36	[20]			137	2
Benjamin	*Overture to an Italian*	6	[C]	**Dukas**	*Polyeucte, Ouverture*	11	2
	Comedy	14	[G] 2f			15	5
Berg	*Violin Concerto*	99	1b [230]	**Elgar**	*Concerto for Violoncello*		
Bloch	*Trois Poèmes Juifs*	20	1		*and Orchestra*	88	1
		35	[22] 4f	**Elgar**	*Falstaff*	48	[49] 5f
Borodin	*Polovetzian Dances from*	47	75	**Elgar**	*Symphony No. 1*	59	[52] 4f
	"Prince Igor"	50	[N]	**Gershwin**	*An American in Paris*	34	[32] 4f
Britten	*Serenade for Tenor,*			**Honegger**	*Symphonie Liturgique*	53	[4]
	Horn and Strings	17	[13] 8f	**Ibert**	*Escales*	88	5
Chabrier	*Ouverture de*			**Ibert**	*La Ballade de la Geôle*		
	"Gwendoline"	7	[2] 2f		*de Reading*	97	3
Charpentier	*Impressions d'Italie*	70	[18] 3f				

Horn (contd.)

COMPOSER	WORK	PAGE	MEASURE	COMPOSER	WORK	PAGE	MEASURE
d'Indy	*Deuxième Symphonie*	5	[2] 7f	Rachmaninoff	*Symphony No. 2*	58	2b [24]
	en Si♭	25	4b [13]			188	72
		132	3	Ravel	*Daphnis et Chloé,*		
d'Indy	*Symphony on a French*				*Suite No. 2*	47	1
	Mountain Air	10	4	Ravel	*Ma Mère l'Oye*	25	7
d'Indy	*Tableaux de Voyage*	46	7b [E]	Ravel	*Rapsodie Espagnole*	71	3
Janssen	*New Year's Eve in*			Read	*Sketches of the City*	9	1b [5]
	New York	52	2			33	1
Khachaturian	*Concerto for Piano and*	30	[244]	Rimsky-			
	Orchestra	138	[388]	Korsakoff	*Le Coq d'Or Suite*	29	4
Khachaturian	*Gayne Ballet Suite*	38	5	Rimsky-	*Symphony No. 2,*		
	No. 2	70	[6]	Korsakoff	*"Antar"*	87	9
Khachaturian	*Masquerade Suite*	65	1	Rosenthal	*Les Petits Métiers*	68	[B]
		70	[6] 1f	Roussel	*Évocations, III*	62	2
Knipper	*Symphony No. 4*	29	[23]	Roussel	*Suite en Fa*	104	4
		49	1	Roussel	*Symphonie en Sol*	22	[13] 3f
Lekeu	*Fantaisie sur Deux Airs*				*mineur*	42	1b [27]
	Populaires Angevins	34	[M] 1f	Sessions	*Symphony for Orchestra*		
Liadov	*Kikimora*	9	2b [13]		*(No. 1)*	15	22
		13	[17]	Sessions	*Symphony No. II*	15	1b [H]
		42	[43] 1f			92	[L]
Loeffler	*Evocation*	29	2b [26]			122	1
Loeffler	*Poem, La Bonne*					153	[Ee]
	Chanson	55	1	Shepherd	*Horizons*	45	[P]
Mahler	*Das Lied von der Erde*	84	[3] 1f	Shostakovich	*The Golden Age,*		
Mahler	*Symphony No. 1*	109	4		*Ballet Suite*	53	[62] 2f
Mahler	*Symphony No. 3*	224	[24] 1f	Sibelius	*En Saga*	22	6
Mahler	*Symphony No. 4*	21	3b [9]	Siegmeister	*Western Suite*	20	1b [75]
		177	116			25	5
Mahler	*Symphony No. 5*	18	3	Strauss, R.	*Also Sprach Zarathustra*	196	7
		24	4	Strauss, R.	*Death and Transfigura-*		
		81	[18] 4f		*tion*	58	[S] 2f
Mahler	*Symphony No. 6*	122	[83] 4f	Stravinsky	*Feuerwerk*	20	[20]
Mahler	*Symphony No. 7*	9	[5]			30	[29] 2f
		83	2	Stravinsky	*Fire-Bird Suite (1919)*	39	[14]
		129	[130] 2f	Stravinsky	*Le Sacre du Printemps*	96	[117] 1f
Mahler	*Symphony No. 9*	163	4	Stillman-	*Gulliver—His Voyage*		
Miaskovsky	*Symphony No. 6*	161	[24]	Kelley	*to Lilliput*	49	[O]
		269	[25] 2f	Wagner, R.	*Siegfried's Rhine Journey*		
Miaskovsky	*Symphony No. 8*	151	[25]		*from "Götter-*		
Moore	*Symphony in A major*	10	[9] 2f		*dämmerung"*	18	3
Mussorgsky	*Night on the Bald*	39	204	Walton	*Façade, Suite No. 1*	45	[B]
	Mountain	59	297	Walton	*Symphony*	4	3
Poot	*Jazz-Music*	10	[5]			27	5
Poot	*Symphonie*	9	9			104	[77] 4f

Trumpet

COMPOSER	WORK	PAGE	MEASURE	COMPOSER	WORK	PAGE	MEASURE
Barber	*Medea*	33	6	Mahler	*Symphony No. 2*	7	2b [2]
Bloch	*Trois Poèmes Juifs*	8	4			24	6
Hanson	*Symphony No. 2,*			Siegmeister	*Western Suite*	31	[30] 1f
	"Romantic"	4	[A] 3f	Stravinsky	*Ebony Concerto*	15	[14a] 2f
						22	[2] 1f

BRASSES

Horn and Trumpet

COMPOSER	WORK	PAGE	MEASURE	COMPOSER	WORK	PAGE	MEASURE
Bloch	*Trois Poèmes Juifs*	7	[2]	**Mussorgsky**	*Night on the Bald Mountain*	57	288

Trumpet and Trombone

COMPOSER	WORK	PAGE	MEASURE	COMPOSER	WORK	PAGE	MEASURE
Gould	*American Salute*	20	1b [J]	**Ward**	*Jubilation—An Overture*	15	1
Gould	*Latin-American Symphonette*	29	1				

Chapter 22

OPEN-STOPPED (o – +)

English	Italian	French	German
English	*Italian*	*French*	*German*
Open—Brassy	Aperto(i)—Chiuso(i)	Ouvert(s)—Avec sourdine(s)	Offen—Gedämpft
Open—Muted	Naturale—Con sordino	Ouvert(s)—Bouché(s)	Offen—Gestopft
Open—Stopped		Ouvert—Bouchez	
		Ouvert(s)—Cuivré(s)	
		Ouvert—Cuivrez	

Horn

COMPOSER	WORK	PAGE	MEASURE	COMPOSER	WORK	PAGE	MEASURE
Albéniz–Arbós	*El Puerto*	25	3	**Chávez**	*Sinfonia de Antigona*	17	[25]
Albéniz–Arbós	*Fête-Dieu à Séville*	21	2	**Chávez**	*Sinfonia India*	58	[81]
Balakirev–				**Copland**	*Billy the Kid Ballet*		
Casella	*Islamey*	45	[43] 3f		*Suite*	48	[27A]
Barber	*First Symphony*	10	3	**Copland**	*Concerto for Piano and*		
Barber	*Medea*	53	5b [42]		*Orchestra*	16	1b [11]
		81	[58]	**Copland**	*Dance Symphony*	16	[9]
Barber	*Second Essay for*					45	4
	Orchestra	39	1b [22]	**Copland**	*El Salón México*	3	2
Bartók	*Concerto for Orchestra*	61	[74]	**Copland**	*First Symphony*	78	[55] 2f
Bartók	*Concerto No. 3 for*	76	[550] 3f	**Copland**	*Four Dance Episodes*		
	Piano and Orchestra	80	[600] 7f		*from "Rodeo"*	23	3b [23]
Bartók	*Dance Suite*	26	71	**Copland**	*Statements*	44	[2] 2f
		49	[36]	**Copland**	*Third Symphony*	62	1b [48]
		86	[56]	**Coppola**	*Scherzo Fantasque*	40	2b [20]
Bartók	*Second Suite*	79	1	**Coppola**	*Symphonie en La*		
Bartók	*Vier Orchesterstücke*	86	7		*mineur*	48	4b [25]
Bax	*The Garden of Fand*	29	[G]	**Debussy**	*Gigues*	16	1
Benjamin	*Jamaican Rhumba*	8	5	**Debussy**	*Iberia*	26	[17] 2f
Benjamin	*Overture to an Italian*			**Debussy**	*La Mer*	73	1
	Comedy	35	[P]	**Debussy**	*Première Rhapsodie*	37	3
Berg	*Three Excerpts from*			**Debussy**	*Rondes de Printemps*	16	4b [9]
	"Wozzeck"	24	1			49	[25]
Berg	*Violin Concerto*	45	[220] 1f			53	1
		99	2b [230]	**Debussy–**	*Six Epigraphes*		
Bloch	*Trois Poèmes Juifs*	31	2b [20]	**Ansermet**	*Antiques*	33	[D]
Britten	*Serenade for Tenor,*	17	[13] 7f	**Delius**	*A Dance Rhapsody,*		
	Horn and Strings	29	[24] 6f		*No. 2*	31	[250] 4f
Busoni	*Rondo Arlecchinesco*	20	[20]	**Diamond**	*Fourth Symphony*	4	3b [25]
Charpentier	*Impressions d'Italie*	70	[18] 2f	**Diamond**	*Timon of Athens*	30	211

125

BRASSES

Horn (contd.)

COMPOSER	WORK	PAGE	MEASURE	COMPOSER	WORK	PAGE	MEASURE
Dukas	La Péri	130	1	Mahler	Symphony No. 8	84	3b [21]
Egge	Symphony No. 1	27	2b [31]	Mahler	Symphony No. 9	12	9
		71	1			24	5
Elgar	Concerto for Violoncello					49	2
	and Orchestra	19	3b [17]			101	2b [26]
de Falla	Nuits dans les Jardins			McDonald	Three Poems for		
	d'Espagne	48	4b [13]		Orchestra	17	[29]
Ferroud	Au Parc Monceau	9	2	McPhee	Four Iroquois Dances	12	1b [3]
Gershwin	An American in Paris	34	[33]	Miaskovsky	Symphony No. 8	151	2b [25]
Gershwin	Concerto in F for Piano			Milhaud	Les Choéphores	2	1
	and Orchestra	78	2b [1]	Moeran	Symphony in G minor	13	[6] 3f
Goossens	Sinfonietta	66	[2] 2f	Moore	Symphony in A major	10	[9]
Griffes	The Pleasure Dome of			Moross	Paeans	6	[F] 2f
	Kubla Khan	7	2	Mussorgsky	Night on the Bald		
Honegger	Musique pour la				Mountain	35	[H] 1f
	"Phaedre" de			Pescara	Tibet	22	[7]
	G. D'Annunzio	2	[1] 2f	Poot	Symphonie	27	3
Ibert	Escales	68	1b [62]	Poulenc	Aubade	69	[56]
		75	[65] 2f	Rachmaninoff	Piano Concerto No. 1	56	[37] 2f
		91	[80] 1f	Rachmaninoff	Symphony No. 2	31	[14]
Ibert	La Ballade de la Geôle			Rachmaninoff	The Bells	36	[39] 1f
	de Reading	94	[69]	Ravel	Alborada del Gracioso	10	2b [6]
d'Indy	Deuxième Symphonie en			Ravel	Daphnis et Chloé,		
	Si♭	5	[2] 4f		Suite No. 2	47	1
Ireland	A London Overture	35	1b [21]	Ravel	Rapsodie Espagnole	32	[4] 3f
Janssen	New Year's Eve in	8	1	Read	Sketches of the City	32	[7] 2f
	New York	51	[20] 1f	Read	Symphony No. I	31	[13]
Kabalevsky	Symphony No. 2	128	[35]			36	[15]
Khachaturian	Gayne Ballet Suite					121	2
	No. 1	30	8	Respighi	Antiche Danze ed Arie,		
Khachaturian	Gayne Ballet Suite				2ª Suite	12	[4] 11f
	No. 2	38	3	Rimsky-			
Knipper	Symphony No. 4	7	[4]	Korsakoff	Capriccio Espagnol	14	1
		32	[27]	Roger-Ducasse	Poème Symphonique sur		
Lekeu	Fantaisie sur Deux Airs				le nom de Gabriel		
	Populaires Angevins	35	1		Fauré	11	2
Mahler	Symphony No. 2	92	11	Rosenthal	Les Petits Métiers	55	1b [A]
Mahler	Symphony No. 3	47	[31]			68	[B]
		171	4b [26]			102	3
		183	[2]	Saint-Saëns	Danse Macabre	51	19
		224	[24] 2f	Saint-Saëns	La Jeunesse d'Hercule	13	4
Mahler	Symphony No. 4	21	3b [9]	Schmitt	Mirages pour Orchestre,		
		37	185		No. 2	9	[4] 3f
		77	43	Schönberg	Theme and Variations	14	55
Mahler	Symphony No. 5	43	[18]	Schreker	The Birthday of the		
		55	7		Infanta, Suite	54	2b [335]
		95	6	Sessions	Symphony for Orchestra		
		106	[30]		(No. 1)	10	3b [14]
		226	6	Sessions	Symphony No. II	14	2
Mahler	Symphony No. 6	46	1b [29]	Shepherd	Horizons	24	[I]
		122	[83]			44	3b [P]
Mahler	Symphony No. 7	84	[73]			54	[D]

OPEN-STOPPED (O — +)

Horn (contd.)

COMPOSER	WORK	PAGE	MEASURE	COMPOSER	WORK	PAGE	MEASURE
Sibelius	*En Saga*	22	3	**Vaughan**	*Symphony in E minor*		
Siegmeister	*Western Suite*	54	[50]	**Williams**	*(No. 6)*	16	3
Strauss, R.	*Also Sprach Zarathustra*	196	3	**Wagner, R.**	*Siegfried's Rhine Journey*		
Stravinsky	*Le Sacre du Printemps*	108	[135]		*from "Götter-*		
Stravinsky	*Petrouchka Suite*	87	6		*dämmerung"*	18	3
Szymanowski	*Symphonie Concertante*			**Walton**	*Concerto for Viola and*		
	pour Piano et				*Orchestra*	30	[28]
	Orchestre	43	[23]	**Walton**	*Concerto for Violin and*		
Taylor	*Through the Looking*				*Orchestra*	35	2
	Glass	91	4b [11]	**Walton**	*Symphony*	1	14
Varèse	*Hyperprism*	10	1b [6]			28	[16]
Varèse	*Intégrales*	28	4b [13]			74	4
		34	[17] 1f	**Whithorne**	*The Dream Pedlar*	9	[4]
Vaughan	*Overture to "The*	20	170				
Williams	*Wasps"*	29	212				

Trumpet

COMPOSER	WORK	PAGE	MEASURE	COMPOSER	WORK	PAGE	MEASURE
Ravel	*Rapsodie Espagnole*	38	2	**Stravinsky**	*Symphonie de Psaumes*	26	[17]
Stravinsky	*Ebony Concerto*	15	[14a] 2f				

Horn and Trumpet

COMPOSER	WORK	PAGE	MEASURE
Bloch	*America*	114	1

Trumpet and Trombone

COMPOSER	WORK	PAGE	MEASURE
Gould	*American Salute*	20	1b [J]

Chapter 23

TRIPLE-TONGUING

(for notation see Chapter 6, page 60)

Horn

COMPOSER	WORK	PAGE	MEASURE	COMPOSER	WORK	PAGE	MEASURE
Ibert	La Ballade de la Geôle de Reading	28	[18]	Ravel	Daphnis et Chloé, Suite No. 2	119 123	[218] 3
Mahler	Symphony No. 2	179	[25]	Rimsky-Korsakoff	Scheherazade	143	[O]
Mendelssohn	Symphony No. 4, "Italian"	1	1	Rosenthal	Les Petits Métiers	89	3
Ravel	Alborada del Gracioso	10	2b [6]	Sessions	Suite from "The Black Maskers"	92	[89]
		33	1b [27]				

Trumpet

COMPOSER	WORK	PAGE	MEASURE	COMPOSER	WORK	PAGE	MEASURE
Elgar	Symphony No. 2	50	[56]	Ravel	Alborada del Gracioso	8	[5]
Gould	Philharmonic Waltzes	4	4b [47]			32	[26]
		14	[140]	Rimsky-Korsakoff	Scheherazade	127	[G]
Hindemith	Mathis der Maler	60	[12] 3f	Sessions	Suite from "The Black Maskers"	93	2
Honegger	Concertino pour Piano et Orchestre	20	[12]	Sibelius	Karelia Suite	26	[B] 3f
Mahler	Das Lied von der Erde	71	2	Stravinsky	Le Sacre du Printemps	107	1

Cornet

COMPOSER	WORK	PAGE	MEASURE
Villa-Lobos	Chôros No. 10	73	1

Horn and Trumpet

COMPOSER	WORK	PAGE	MEASURE	COMPOSER	WORK	PAGE	MEASURE
Bax	Fifth Symphony	103	2b [5]	Ravel	La Valse	86	5
Debussy	La Mer	51	[26]	Ravel	Rapsodie Espagnole	77	1
d'Indy	Istar, Variations Symphoniques	26	[L]	Rimsky-Korsakoff	Scheherazade	162	[C]
Ravel	Alborada del Gracioso	9	4	Trapp	Symphonie No. 4	51	3

TRIPLE-TONGUING

Trumpet and Cornet

COMPOSER	WORK	PAGE	MEASURE
Lambert	*The Rio Grande*	**5**	I

Horn, Trumpet, and Cornet

Enesco	*Ière Rhapsodie Roumaine*	**88**	[41]

Horn, Trumpet, Cornet, and Trombone

Mohaupt	*Town Piper Music*	**51**	4

Chapter 24

FLUTTER-TONGUING

(for terminology and notation see Chapter 7, page 63)

Horn

COMPOSER	WORK	PAGE	MEASURE	COMPOSER	WORK	PAGE	MEASURE
Antheil	*Symphony No. 5*	57	3	**Knipper**	*Symphony No. 4*	52	4b [3]
Britten	*Sinfonia da Requiem*	30	[21]			88	2b [8]
Carter	*Holiday Overture*	62	3b [30]			97	[14]
Debussy	*Le Martyre de Saint*			**Maganini**	*An Ornithological Suite*	33	2b [B]
	Sébastien	31	[13] 1f	**Milhaud**	*Quatrième Symphonie*	67	[205] 2f
Honegger	*Le Chant de Nigamon*	57	2b [195]	**Milhaud**	*Two Marches*	29	1b [70]
Honegger	*Musique pour la*			**Sessions**	*Symphony No. II*	41	[Z] 2f
	"Phaedre" de					111	[G] 3f
	G. D'Annunzio	36	[1] 1f			151	1b [Dd]
Honegger	*Suite d'Orchestre,*			**Strauss, R.**	*Eine Alpensinfonie*	138	3
	"L'Impératrice aux	27	[2] 2f	**Stravinsky**	*Ebony Concerto*	18	2
	Rochers"	33	[2]			25	[10]
Honegger	*Symphonie Liturgique*	16	4	**Stravinsky**	*Oedipus Rex*	112	[162]
		24	2b [11]	**Stravinsky**	*Symphony in Three*	102	1
		30	[14]		*Movements*	118	[194] 1f
		48	[21]	**Tansman**	*Sonatine Trans-*		
Honegger	*Symphonie pour*	2	2		*atlantique, I*	19	[7] 1f
	Orchestre	27	3	**Varèse**	*Hyperprism*	3	6
		55	3				

Trumpet

COMPOSER	WORK	PAGE	MEASURE	COMPOSER	WORK	PAGE	MEASURE
Bernstein	*"Jeremiah" Symphony*	18	[7]	**Honegger**	*Musique pour la*		
		44	[37] 7f		*"Phaedre" de*		
Bloch	*America*	36	1		*G. D'Annunzio*	38	5
Borodin	*Polovetzian Dances from*	21	9	**Honegger**	*Symphonie Liturgique*	99	1
	"Prince Igor"	24	33	**Johnson**	*Imagery*	66	[8] 2f
Copland	*Music for the Theatre*	3	6	**Khachaturian**	*Masquerade Suite*	62	1
Diamond	*Timon of Athens*	7	38	**Miaskovsky**	*Symphony No. 22*	85	4
Dukas	*La Péri*	65	1	**Mihalovici**	*Divertissement pour*		
Fitelberg	*Nocturne for Orchestra*	60	[374]		*Petit Orchestre*	39	4
Gershwin	*Concerto in F for Piano*			**Milhaud**	*La Création du Monde*	24	2b [26]
	and Orchestra	52	3			56	1b [54]
Gershwin	*Rhapsody in Blue*	10	[8] 4f	**Milhaud**	*Le Bal Martiniquais*	29	3b [65]
Grofé	*Grand Canyon Suite*	134	3	**Milhaud**	*Ière Symphonie*	5	2b [20]
		142	1			47	[105] 2f
Hindemith	*Kammermusik No. 1*	9	2	**Milhaud**	*IIe Symphonie*	21	1
		105	1			39	[135] 1f

130

FLUTTER-TONGUING

Trumpet (contd.)

COMPOSER	WORK	PAGE	MEASURE	COMPOSER	WORK	PAGE	MEASURE
Milhaud	*Quatrième Symphonie*	16	2b [60]	Sessions	*Suite from "The Black*		
Milhaud	*Saudades do Brazil*	75	6		*Maskers"*	76	[72]
Moross	*Paeans*	15	[N]	Sessions	*Symphony No. II*	38	[X]
Poulenc	*Concerto pour deux*					150	6
	Pianos et Orchestre	21	4b [16]	Shostakovich	*Symphony No. 7*	54	[49]
Ravel	*Concerto pour Piano et*			Siegmeister	*From my Window*	22	3b [20]
	Orchestre	31	3	Siegmeister	*Ozark Set*	84	2
Respighi	*Feste Romane*	88	[27] 6f	Siegmeister	*Sunday in Brooklyn*	22	2b [15]
Respighi	*The Pines of Rome*	5	[2] 6f	Siegmeister	*Western Suite*	49	1
		10	[3]			64	2b [30]
Riegger	*Dichotomy*	16	1b [5]	Stravinsky	*Le Sacre du Printemps*	30	[40]
		54	3			55	1
Riisager	*Torgot Dance*	6	[20] 1f			87	[106]
Rogers	*Once Upon a Time,*					121	[165] 2f
	Five Fairy Tales	14	1	Stravinsky	*Scènes de Ballet*	69	[120]
Rosenthal	*Les Petits Métiers*	34	3	Stravinsky	*Scherzo Fantastique*	55	[77] 2f
		146	[B]	Thomson	*Louisiana Story Suite*	18	104
Schönberg	*A Survivor from Warsaw*	2	5	Varèse	*Hyperprism*	7	[3] 6f
		14	68	Villa-Lobos	*Chôros No. 8*	36	3
Schönberg	*Fünf Orchesterstücke*	26	[9]	Walton	*Façade, Suite No. 2*	39	4b [D]

Trombone

COMPOSER	WORK	PAGE	MEASURE	COMPOSER	WORK	PAGE	MEASURE
Bartók	*Violin Concerto*	18	[III] 2f	Milhaud	*Concerto pour Violon-*		
Diamond	*Timon of Athens*	14	91		*celle et Orchestre*	21	1
Honegger	*Mouvement*			Milhaud	*Ière Symphonie*	35	[35] 3f
	Symphonique No. 3	49	1			51	4b [135]
Mihalovici	*Divertissement pour*			Milhaud	*Quatrième Symphonie*	81	1b [30]
	Petit Orchestre	34	7	Schönberg	*A Survivor from Warsaw*	11	51
				Siegmeister	*Ozark Set*	63	3

Tuba

COMPOSER	WORK	PAGE	MEASURE	COMPOSER	WORK	PAGE	MEASURE
Honegger	*Le Roi David*	7	1	Milhaud	*La Mort d'un Tyran*	40	2

Horn and Trumpet

COMPOSER	WORK	PAGE	MEASURE	COMPOSER	WORK	PAGE	MEASURE
Bax	*Fourth Symphony*	147	2	Mihalovici	*Toccata pour Piano et*		
Cesana	*Second American*				*Orchestre*	136	4b [530]
	Symphony	137	1b [26]	Poulenc	*Aubade*	17	[10] 1f
Copland	*Third Symphony*	135	[117]	Rosenthal	*Les Petits Métiers*	2	3
Ferroud	*Au Parc Monceau*	10	3	Siegmeister	*From my Window*	52	4
Gershwin	*Rhapsody in Blue*	40	2b [37]	Siegmeister	*Sunday in Brooklyn*	65	[30] 1f
Honegger	*Pacific 231*	2	8	Stravinsky	*Ebony Concerto*	39	[33]
Maganini	*An Ornithological Suite*	13	[E]	White	*Five Miniatures*	9	1

Horn and Trombone

COMPOSER	WORK	PAGE	MEASURE
Moross	*Paeans*	16	2

131

BRASSES

Trumpet and Cornet

COMPOSER	WORK	PAGE	MEASURE
Stravinsky	*Petrouchka Suite*	114	4

Trumpet and Trombone

COMPOSER	WORK	PAGE	MEASURE	COMPOSER	WORK	PAGE	MEASURE
Britten	*Sinfonia da Requiem*	44	[30]	**Mihalovici**	*Divertissement pour Petit Orchestre*	42	11
Fitelberg	*Nocturne for Orchestra*	42	2b [239]				
Golestan	*Concerto Roumain pour Violon et Orchestre*	35	3b [200]	**Milhaud**	*Concerto pour Piano et Orchestre*	46	[65] 3f
McKay	*Sinfonietta No. 4*	32	2	**Milhaud**	*Ière Symphonie*	59	1b [180]
				Varèse	*Intégrales*	18	2

Trumpet and Tuba

COMPOSER	WORK	PAGE	MEASURE
Honegger	*Symphonie pour Orchestre*	106	2b [20]

Trombone and Tuba

COMPOSER	WORK	PAGE	MEASURE	COMPOSER	WORK	PAGE	MEASURE
Knipper	*Symphony No. 4*	52	[2] 1f	**Schönberg**	*Fünf Orchesterstücke*	5	1b [4]
Milhaud	*Ière Symphonie*	39	[60] 2f			11	5
						17	[16] 2f

Horn, Trumpet, and Trombone

COMPOSER	WORK	PAGE	MEASURE	COMPOSER	WORK	PAGE	MEASURE
Britten	*Sinfonia da Requiem*	36	[25]	**Moross**	*Paeans*	5	7b [E]
Casella	*Paganiniana*	176	1	**Poot**	*Symphonie*	99	3b [43]
Copland	*Concerto for Piano and Orchestra*	67	[50] 2f	**Rosenthal**	*Les Petits Métiers*	4	2
Golestan	*Concerto Roumain pour Violon et Orchestre*	43	2	**Siegmeister**	*From my Window*	57	3
				Strauss, R.	*Don Quixote*	52	3
Grofé	*Grand Canyon Suite*	33	4	**Strauss, R.**	*Suite from "Le Bourgeois Gentil-*	123	1
		137	3		*homme"*	127	2
		152	[15]	**Thomson**	*Orchestra Suite from "The Plow that*		
Honegger	*Suite d'Orchestre, "L'Impératrice aux Rochers"*	43	1		*Broke the Plains"*	35	[32]
Ibert	*Divertissement*	43	12	**Varèse**	*Intégrales*	18	3

Horn, Trombone, and Tuba

COMPOSER	WORK	PAGE	MEASURE	COMPOSER	WORK	PAGE	MEASURE
Siegmeister	*Sunday in Brooklyn*	94	[120] 1f	**Siegmeister**	*Western Suite*	39	2

Trumpet, Trombone, and Tuba

COMPOSER	WORK	PAGE	MEASURE
Honegger	*Rugby*	20	2

Horn, Trumpet, Trombone, and Tuba

COMPOSER	WORK	PAGE	MEASURE	COMPOSER	WORK	PAGE	MEASURE
Britten	*Sinfonia da Requiem*	51	[34]	**Milhaud**	*Concerto pour Violon- celle et Orchestre*	42	[105] 1f
Honegger	*Suite d'Orchestre, "L'Impératrice aux Rochers"*	46	[10]	**Shostakovich**	*Symphony No. 1*	08	[14]

Chapter 25

TRILLS AND TREMOLI

English	Italian	French	German
Tremolo	Tremolo	Trémolo	Tremolo
trem.	*trem.*	*trém.*	*trem.*
Trill	Trillo	Trille	Triller
tr.	*tr.*	*tr.*	*Tr.*
Trill with note below	Trillare al nota di sotto	Trillez avec la note en bas	Mit der unteren Note trillern
Major trill	Trillo maggiore	Trille majeur	Ganzton Triller
maj. tr.	*tr. mag.*	*tr. maj.*	
Minor trill	Trillo minore	Trille mineur	Halbton Triller
min. tr.	*tr. min.*	*tr. min.*	

Horn

COMPOSER	WORK	PAGE	MEASURE	COMPOSER	WORK	PAGE	MEASURE
Bach–	*Fugue in G minor—*			**Fitelberg**	*Nocturne for Orchestra*	**42**	2b [239]
Stokowski	*The Shorter*	**11**	2	**Gershwin**	*An American in Paris*	**68**	2
Balakirev–				**Handel**	*Water Music in F*	**14**	2
Casella	*Islamey*	**15**	[11]			**33**	19
Barber	*Overture to "The*			**Hindemith**	*Konzertmusik für*		
	School for Scandal"	**36**	1		*Streichorchester und*		
Bloch	*America*	**116**	[66]		*Blechbläser*	**75**	2
Bloch	*Schelomo*	**73**	3	**Hindemith**	*Mathis der Maler*	**40**	3
Bloch	*Trois Poèmes Juifs*	**64**	[3]	**Hindemith**	*Symphonic Metamor-*		
		78	1b [13]		*phosis of Themes*		
Britten	*Sinfonia da Requiem*	**25**	6b [18]		*by Weber*	**21**	7
Casella	*La Donna Serpente,*	**18**	[26] 2f	**Honegger**	*Le Chant de Nigamon*	**55**	3
	II. Serie	**49**	1	**Ibert**	*La Ballade de la Geôle*		
		67	[76]		*de Reading*	**57**	[40]
Chabrier	*Joyeuse Marche*	**6**	[B]	**d'Indy**	*Deuxième Symphonie*	**23**	[11] 4f
		24	[I]		*en Si♭*	**69**	2
Debussy	*Iberia*	**12**	3			**124**	6
Debussy	*La Mer*	**137**	4			**179**	1
Debussy	*Rondes de Printemps*	**21**	[12]			**187**	2
Dukas	*La Péri*	**46**	[7]	**d'Indy**	*Istar, Variations*		
Dvořák	*Symphony No. 4*	**58**	3		*Symphoniques*	**3**	[A]
		133	[C] 5f	**d'Indy**	*Jour d'été à la Montagne*	**39**	3
		171	[R] 5f	**d'Indy**	*Symphony on a French*	**13**	[E] 1f
Enesco	*Ière Rhapsodie Roumaine*	**24**	3		*Mountain Air*	**84**	2b [M]
Ferroud	*Au Parc Monceau*	**5**	[2]			**101**	4

BRASSES

Horn (contd.)

COMPOSER	WORK	PAGE	MEASURE	COMPOSER	WORK	PAGE	MEASURE
Inghelbrecht	*Pour le jour de la première neige au vieux Japon*	16	[8]	Respighi	*Feste Romane*	132	[41] 1f
		38	[2b]23]			151	[47] 2f
Inghelbrecht	*Rapsodie de Printemps*	21	[9]	Respighi	*The Pines of Rome*	18	4b [5]
		44	2	Respighi	*Vetrate di Chiesa*	59	4
Mahler	*Das Lied von der Erde*	9	[7] 4f	Riegger	*Symphony No. 3*	34	[175] 1f
		29	[35] 2f	Roussel	*Évocations, I*	43	2b [12]
		64	[6] 5f	Roussel	*Suite en Fa*	77	4
		95	[14]	Roussel	*Symphonie en Sol mineur*	133	3b [78]
Mahler	*Symphony No. 3*	39	4	Schelling	*A Victory Ball*	65	2b [18]
Mahler	*Symphony No. 6*	120	[81]	Schmitt	*Étude pour le "Palais Hanté" d'Edgar Poe*	49	3
Mahler	*Symphony No. 7*	184	4	Schmitt	*Rapsodie Viennoise*	26	2b [13]
Mahler	*Symphony No. 8*	108	[60] 4f	Schmitt	*Ronde burlesque*	18	[9] 2f
		127	[85] 1f	Schönberg	*A Survivor from Warsaw*	9	41
		178	5b [162]			14	66
Mahler	*Symphony No. 9*	17	4	Shepherd	*Horizons*	89	5b [I]
		27	I	Shostakovich	*Symphony No. 5*	13	[17] 3f
		61	13			146	[121] 4f
		99	I	Sibelius	*Symphony No. 3*	67	[19] 2f
Miaskovsky	*Symphony No. 22*	85	4	Siegmeister	*From my Window*	57	4
Milhaud	*Iᵉʳᵉ Symphonie*	84	[60] 1f	Strauss, R.	*Also Sprach Zarathustra*	84	I
Mussorgsky-Ravel	*Pictures at an Exhibition*	19	[17]	Strauss, R.	*Eine Alpensinfonie*	87	[86]
Parodi	*Preludio ad una Commedia*	59	5b [AF]	Strauss, R.	*Ein Heldenleben*	121	I
				Strauss, R.	*Symphonia Domestica*	53	4b [70]
Pizzetti	*Concerto dell'Estate*	25	I	Strauss, R.	*Till Eulenspiegel's Merry Pranks*	60	I
Ravel	*La Valse*	70	2b [51]	Stravinsky	*Le Sacre du Printemps*	55	I
Ravel	*Rapsodie Espagnole*	19	2b [9]	Tippett	*Symphony No. I*	130	I
		72	[21] 3f	Villa-Lobos	*Chôros No. 8*	36	3
Read	*Symphony No. I*	60	I	Walton	*Symphony*	54	[34] 7f
Respighi	*Ballata delle Gnomidi*	53	[16]			105	[78] 2f
		80	3			171	7
Respighi	*Belfagor, Ouverture per Orchestra*	43	7	Weingartner	*Lustige Ouvertüre*	58	4
				Zimbalist	*American Rhapsody*	45	[33] 1f
						59	[38] 2f

Trumpet

COMPOSER	WORK	PAGE	MEASURE	COMPOSER	WORK	PAGE	MEASURE
Antheil	*Over the Plains*	63	[38]	Creston	*Two Choric Dances*	73	[275] 3f
Antheil	*Symphony No. 5*	73	[2] 4f	Debussy	*Iberia*	88	[56] 2f
		113	2b [29]	Ferguson	*Partita for Orchestra*	101	4
Bartók	*Concerto for Orchestra*	72	[84]	Fernandez	*Batuque*	18	[15]
		75	[112]	Gershwin	*An American in Paris*	77	I
Bartók	*Vier Orchesterstücke*	53	[20] 3f	Handel	*Music for the Royal Fireworks*	2	2
Bartók	*Violin Concerto*	18	[111]	Hindemith	*Kammermusik No. 1*	32	[70] 3f
Britten	*Four Sea Interludes from "Peter Grimes"*	28	1b [4]			107	4
Casella	*Elegia Eroica*	26	[34]	Ibert	*Escales*	87	2b [77]
Casella	*La Donna Serpente, II. Serie*	23	[30]	Ibert	*Féerique*	33	[22]
Caturla	*Trois Danses Cubaines*	51	2b [6]	d'Indy	*Deuxième Symphonie en Sib*	71	I

134

TRILLS AND TREMOLI

Trumpet (contd.)

COMPOSER	WORK	PAGE	MEASURE	COMPOSER	WORK	PAGE	MEASURE
d'Indy	Jour d'été à la Montagne	27	[12]	Strauss, R.	Also Sprach Zarathustra	86	1
Khachaturian	Masquerade Suite	62	1			124	1
Mahler	Symphony No. 1	77	8	Strauss, R.	Symphonia Domestica	33	[41] 6f
Mahler	Symphony No. 3	180	8			69	9
Mahler	Symphony No. 6	30	[18]	Stravinsky	Scherzo Fantastique	61	2b [86]
Mahler	Symphony No. 9	155	[43]	Taylor	Through the Looking		
Mihalovici	Divertissement pour				Glass	100	5
	Petit Orchestre	39	4	Tippett	Symphony No. 1	131	3
Poot	Symphonie	27	4	Toch	Pinocchio	27	[50]
Ravel	La Valse	96	[73]	Turner	Fanfare, Chorale and		
		131	[101]		Finale	30	3b [240]
Respighi	The Fountains of Rome	12	[4]	Villa-Lobos	Amazonas	74	[31]
Roussel	Le Festin de l'Araignée	33	7	Walton	Concerto for Violin and		
Roussel	Suite en Fa	33	4b [16]		Orchestra	143	[70]
Sessions	Suite from "The Black			Weingartner	Lustige Ouvertüre	58	5
	Maskers"	14	[12]	Zimbalist	American Rhapsody	44	3

Cornet

COMPOSER	WORK	PAGE	MEASURE	COMPOSER	WORK	PAGE	MEASURE
Berlioz	The Roman Carnival			Villa-Lobos	Danses Africaines	10	[5] 2f
	Overture	59	438				

Trombone

COMPOSER	WORK	PAGE	MEASURE	COMPOSER	WORK	PAGE	MEASURE
Ravel	Rapsodie Espagnole	77	1	Sibelius	Tapiola	45	2
Schönberg	A Survivor from Warsaw	2	7	Stravinsky	Fire-Bird Suite (1919)	75	[18] 1f

Tuba

COMPOSER	WORK	PAGE	MEASURE
Wagner, R.	Prelude to "Die Meistersinger"	44	1

Horn and Trumpet

COMPOSER	WORK	PAGE	MEASURE	COMPOSER	WORK	PAGE	MEASURE
Antheil	McKonkey's Ferry	1	1	Mahler	Symphony No. 5	10	2
Bloch	Schelomo	31	3b [15]	Mahler	Symphony No. 6	86	[53]
Bloch	Trois Poèmes Juifs	39	4	Poot	Jazz-Music	39	6
Diamond	Fourth Symphony	101	2	Ravel	Daphnis et Chloé,		
Gershwin	Concerto in F for Piano				Suite No. 2	125	2
	and Orchestra	116	3	Respighi	Ballata delle Gnomidi	5	3
Handel	Music for the Royal			Shostakovich	Symphony No. 1	82	[33] 2f
	Fireworks	42	1	Siegmeister	Ozark Set	86	1
Harsanyi	Suite pour Orchestre	1	3	Stravinsky	Petrouchka Suite	96	[83]
Hindemith	Symphonic Meta-			Verdi	Messa da Requiem	22	2
	morphosis of Themes	23	[M]			228	49
	by Weber	27	[P] 3f	Walton	Concerto for Violin and		
Honegger	Prélude pour "La				Orchestra	82	[42] 1f
	Tempête"	34	[12] 2f	Walton	Symphony	111	14
Mahler	Symphony No. 2	46	2	Zimbalist	American Rhapsody	49	2

BRASSES

Horn and Cornet

COMPOSER	WORK	PAGE	MEASURE
Villa-Lobos	*Chôros No. 10*	5	[C]

Horn and Trombone

COMPOSER	WORK	PAGE	MEASURE	COMPOSER	WORK	PAGE	MEASURE
Stravinsky	*Fire-Bird Suite* (1919)	65	1b [39]	**Villa-Lobos**	*Chôros No. 8*	125	2

Trumpet and Cornet

COMPOSER	WORK	PAGE	MEASURE
Mohaupt	*Town Piper Music*	17	2b [11]

Trumpet and Trombone

COMPOSER	WORK	PAGE	MEASURE
Kodály	*Háry János Suite*	53	[4]

Horn, Trumpet, and Cornet

COMPOSER	WORK	PAGE	MEASURE
Stravinsky	*Petrouchka Suite*	116	[101]

Horn, Trumpet, and Trombone

COMPOSER	WORK	PAGE	MEASURE	COMPOSER	WORK	PAGE	MEASURE
Bach– Stokowski	*Fugue in G minor—The Shorter*	21	[14]	**Stravinsky** **Wellesz**	*Le Sacre du Printemps* *Symphony in C*	56 87	1b [64] 3b [360a]

Chapter 26

GLISSANDI

(for terminology and notation see Chapter 8, page 68)

Horn

COMPOSER	WORK	PAGE	MEASURE	COMPOSER	WORK	PAGE	MEASURE
Alfvén	A Legend of the Skerries	34	4	**Mohaupt**	Town Piper Music	7	5
Barber	First Symphony	36	[15]	**Parodi**	Preludio ad una		
Barber	Medea	59	[45]		Commedia	36	1b [R]
Britten	Serenade for Tenor,			**Piston**	Suite for Orchestra	21	4
	Horn and Strings	22	[17] 2f	**Poot**	Symphonie	91	1b [40]
Britten	Sinfonia da Requiem	35	4	**Prokofieff**	March and Scherzo from		
		52	4b [35]		"The Love of the	20	[5] 4f
Casella	La Donna Serpente,	1	2		Three Oranges"	28	[12]
	II. Serie	39	1b [50]	**Prokofieff**	Piano Concerto No. 3	28	1b [22]
		56	[69]	**Rosenthal**	Les Petits Métiers	65	3
Casella	Paganiniana	64	[33] 1f	**Roussel**	Symphonie en Sol		
Diamond	Timon of Athens	18	119		mineure	86	2b [54]
Gershwin	An American in Paris	21	4	**Sessions**	Suite from "The Black		
Gould	Latin-American				Maskers"	85	1b [84]
	Symphonette	22	5b [Q]	**Sessions**	Symphony for		
Gould	Philharmonic Waltzes	43	[500]		Orchestra (No. 1)	66	[104] 2f
Honegger	Le Roi David	6	4	**Sessions**	Symphony No. II	101	1b [A]
Honegger	Symphonie Liturgique	107	2			136	2
Ibert	Divertissement	16	[8]	**Stravinsky**	Feuerwerk	19	[19] 1f
		19	[9] 7f	**Stravinsky**	Fire-Bird Suite (1919)	74	[17]
Ibert	Féerique	29	[19] 2f	**Stravinsky**	Le Sacre du Printemps	27	[36]
Janssen	New Year's Eve in					47	[58] 4f
	New York	81	4			62	[72] 1f
Kodály	Háry János Suite	1	2			85	[103]
Knipper	Symphony No. 4	18	1b [15]	**Stravinsky**	Symphony in Three	91	[157]
Mahler	Symphony No. 4	158	42		Movements	97	[163]
Mahler	Symphony No. 6	153	[105] 3f	**Villa-Lobos**	Amazonas	11	2
Mahler	Symphony No. 7	129	[130] 1f			31	1b [12]
Mihalovici	Toccata pour Piano et					41	5
	Orchestre	6	2	**Villa-Lobos**	Chôros No. 8	49	1
Milhaud	Le Bal Martiniquais	9	4b [40]			72	2
Milhaud	Ière Symphonie	44	3b [90]	**Villa-Lobos**	Chôros No. 10	83	2
Milhaud	IIe Symphonie	30	2b [75]	**Varèse**	Hyperprism	13	3
Milhaud	Saudades do Brazil	56	2	**Varèse**	Intégrales	45	2

Trumpet

COMPOSER	WORK	PAGE	MEASURE	COMPOSER	WORK	PAGE	MEASURE
Dukelsky	Symphony No. 3	144	2	**Mahler**	Symphony No. 6	154	3
Gould	Philharmonic Waltzes	38	[463]	**Riisager**	Torgot Dance	31	[135] 1f

137

BRASSES

Trombone

COMPOSER	WORK	PAGE	MEASURE	COMPOSER	WORK	PAGE	MEASURE
Bartók	Concerto for Orchestra	73	[90]	Milhaud	Suite Provençale	17	[30] 3f
Bartók	Concerto for Piano and					45	[10]
	Orchestra	35	1b [38]	Milhaud	Two Marches	6	1b [20]
Bartók	Dance Suite	17	7	Moeran	Symphony in G minor	28	[14]
		24	56	Moore	In Memoriam	38	[X]
Bartók	Violin Concerto	43	[294]	Moross	Biguine	22	5
Berg	Violin Concerto	72	[110] 1f			31	2
		93	[200]	Moross	Paeans	7	1b [G]
Bloch	America	144	3	Pierné	Divertissements sur un		
Britten	Sinfonia da Requiem	26	2b [19]		Thème Pastorale	18	1b [13]
Britten	The Young Person's			Pierné	Viennoise	45	1b [Ff]
	Guide to the			Poot	Jazz-Music	11	4
	Orchestra	60	[L]	Poot	Symphonie	42	[23] 2f
Chávez	Sinfonia India	70	4b [97]			61	[29]
Copland	Dance Symphony	74	1b [45]	Poulenc	Concert Champêtre		
Copland	First Symphony	18	[8]		pour Clavecin et		
Coppola	Suite Intima	57	1		Orchestre	38	4
Debussy	Iberia	110	5	Prokofieff	Cinderella Suite No. 1	156	[131]
Diamond	Timon of Athens	6	34	Prokofieff	Symphony No. 5	200	[111] 2f
Dunn	Overture on Negro			Ravel	Alborada del Gracioso	42	3
	Themes	12	[E]	Ravel	Boléro	28	2
Elgar	Concerto for Violon-					50	[15] 3f
	cello and Orchestra	85	[60]			65	3
Gershwin	An American in Paris	14	[12] 4f	Ravel	Concerto pour la main	73	3
		45	[41]		gauche	97	[53] 4f
Gould	Latin-American			Ravel	Concerto pour Piano et	19	7
	Symphonette	69	3b [K]		Orchestre	62	5
Harsanyi	Suite pour Orchestre	62	[70] 2f			70	[8]
Honegger	Mouvement			Ravel	La Valse	126	[98] 1f
	Symphonique No. 3	49	1	Ravel	Rapsodie Espagnole	65	[16]
Honegger	Suite d'Orchestre,					89	1
	"L'Impératrice aux	40	[7] 2f	Read	First Overture	57	[20]
	Rochers"	44	[9]	Respighi	Feste Romane	15	1
Honegger	Symphonie pour					123	5
	Orchestre	106	2b [20]	Revueltas	Sensemayá	25	[27]
Ibert	Escales	54	6	Riisager	Torgot Dance	3	1
Inghelbrecht	La Métamorphose d'Ève	35	3			20	[95]
Inghelbrecht	Sinfonia Breve No. 1	43	[25] 1f	Rivier	Ouverture pour un don		
Khachaturian	Masquerade Suite	65	5		Quichotte	17	[8] 2f
		71	3	Rosenthal	Les Petits Métiers	1	1
Lambert	The Rio Grande	6	1b [3]			28	1
		13	[7] 3f			94	[F]
		22	1b [11]	Schönberg	Fünf Orchesterstücke	37	2
Loeffler	Evocation	12	[V]	Shostakovich	The Golden Age, Ballet	21	[21] 4f
Milhaud	La Création du Monde	3	[3] 6f		Suite	44	[52] 6f
		16	1	Siegmeister	Western Suite	32	1
Milhaud	Opus Americanum			Slonimsky	My Toy Balloon	28	2
	No. 2	79	[570] 1f	Stravinsky	Chant du Rossignol	24	[25] 2f
Milhaud	Ière Symphonie	7	1b [25]			79	[92] 2f
		23	2	Stravinsky	Ebony Concerto	25	[10]
Milhaud	Saudades do Brazil	13	6	Stravinsky	Fire-Bird Suite (1919)	37	[12] 5f
Milhaud	Suite Française	27	[35] 5f			65	[39]

GLISSANDI

Trombone (contd.)

COMPOSER	WORK	PAGE	MEASURE	COMPOSER	WORK	PAGE	MEASURE
Stravinsky	*Histoire du Soldat*	26	[14] 2f	Varèse	*Hyperprism*	3	4
Stravinsky	*Le Sacre du Printemps*	42	3	Varèse	*Intégrales*	32	[15]
		125	[173] 3f			41	1
		132	2b [184]	Villa-Lobos	*Amazonas*	75	2
Stravinsky	*Pulcinella Suite*	52	[85] 1f	Villa-Lobos	*Chôros No.* 10	9	[D]
		55	[93] 3f	Villa-Lobos	*Uirapurú*	3	1
Taylor	*Through the Looking*	108	4	Wagenaar	*Sinfonietta for Small*		
	Glass	120	2b [9]		*Orchestra*	5	[3] 1f
Turner	*Fanfare, Chorale and*	4	5	Weiss	*American Life*	3	1
	Finale	30	[240]	White	*Five Miniatures*	8	1

Tuba

COMPOSER	WORK	PAGE	MEASURE	COMPOSER	WORK	PAGE	MEASURE
Mahler	*Symphony No.* 7	138	[147] 5f	Strauss, R.	*Don Quixote*	99	6
Schmitt	*Ronde burlesque*	57	[30] 1f			154	2

Horn and Trumpet

COMPOSER	WORK	PAGE	MEASURE	COMPOSER	WORK	PAGE	MEASURE
Gillis	*Symphony No.* 5½	72	1	Shostakovich	*Symphony No.* 1	84	7
Grofé	*Grand Canyon Suite*	61	[C] 2f	Siegmeister	*From my Window*	58	2
Mohaupt	*Town Piper Music*	15	[9]	Siegmeister	*Sunday in Brooklyn*	94	[120] 1f
Read	*Sketches of the City*	39	4				

Horn and Trombone

COMPOSER	WORK	PAGE	MEASURE	COMPOSER	WORK	PAGE	MEASURE
Bartók	*Concerto for Orchestra*	147	[624]	Revueltas	*Sensemayá*	27	[28]
Inghelbrecht	*La Valse Retrouvée*	48	[65] 6f	Stravinsky	*Chant du Rossignol*	3	1
Knipper	*Symphony No.* 4	91	[9]	Stravinsky	*Le Sacre du Printemps*	91	[111]
		104	[19] 4f			128	[177]
Mahler	*Symphony No.* 3	92	[69] 3f	Villa-Lobos	*Amazonas*	15	3
Poot	*Symphonie*	48	3	Walton	*Façade, Suite No.* 1	2	5
Respighi	*Feste Romane*	17	[5]	Walton	*Symphony*	112	[82] 9f

Horn and Tuba

COMPOSER	WORK	PAGE	MEASURE
Inghelbrecht	*El Greco*	1	5

Trumpet and Trombone

COMPOSER	WORK	PAGE	MEASURE	COMPOSER	WORK	PAGE	MEASURE
Casella	*Paganiniana*	64	[33]	Khachaturian	*Gayne Ballet Suite*	6	2
Cesana	*Second American*				*No.* 1	17	4
	Symphony	155	[38] 1f	Kodály	*Háry János Suite*	49	[1]
Chávez	*Sinfonia India*	76	4b [103]			53	[4]
Gould	*Spirituals*	14	[C] 1f	McKay	*Sinfonietta No.* 4	4	1b [A]
		39	1b [K]			29	4
Guarnieri	*Brazilian Dance*	21	1	Riisager	*Torgot Dance*	25	3b [115]
Inghelbrecht	*La Métamorphose d'Ève*	18	[16] 2f	Rosenthal	*Les Petits Métiers*	8	1

BRASSES

Trombone and Tuba

COMPOSER	WORK	PAGE	MEASURE	COMPOSER	WORK	PAGE	MEASURE
Bloch	*America*	116	[66] 1f	**Kodály**	*Háry János Suite*	55	1
Delius	*Eventyr, Once Upon a*					60	3
	Time	24	4	**Mahler**	*Symphony No. 3*	11	[7]
Janssen	*New Year's Eve in*						
	New York	31	[12]				

Horn, Trumpet, and Trombone

COMPOSER	WORK	PAGE	MEASURE	COMPOSER	WORK	PAGE	MEASURE
Bartók	*Violin Concerto*	133	1b [594]	**Ibert**	*La Ballade de la Geôle*		
Dukelsky	*Symphony No. 3*	114	2b [48]		*de Reading*	58	7
Ferroud	*Au Parc Monceau*	5	[2] 2f	**Siegmeister**	*Western Suite*	64	1b [30]
Grofé	*Grand Canyon Suite*	53	1	**Varèse**	*Intégrales*	47	[22] 2f
				Villa-Lobos	*Amazonas*	63	1

Horn, Cornet, and Trombone

COMPOSER	WORK	PAGE	MEASURE
Villa-Lobos	*Chóros No. 10*	51	1

Horn, Trombone, and Tuba

COMPOSER	WORK	PAGE	MEASURE
Inghelbrecht	*El Greco*	7	3b [5]

Horn, Trumpet, Trombone, and Tuba

COMPOSER	WORK	PAGE	MEASURE	COMPOSER	WORK	PAGE	MEASURE
Gould	*Latin-American*			**Parodi**	*Preludio ad una*		
	Symphonette	123	1		*Commedia*	60	5

Chapter 27

BELLS UP

(for terminology see Chapter 9, page 72)

Horn

COMPOSER	WORK	PAGE	MEASURE	COMPOSER	WORK	PAGE	MEASURE
Albéniz	*Catalonia, Suite No.* I	**12**	[16]	**Mahler**	*Das Lied von der Erde*	**126**	[47]
Albéniz–				**Mahler**	*Symphony No.* I	**51**	[5] 6f
Arbós	*El Albaicín*	**27**	[Q]			**156**	3
Albéniz–	*Fête-Dieu à Séville*	**11**	3	**Mahler**	*Symphony No.* 2	**40**	5
Arbós		**27**	1	**Mahler**	*Symphony No.* 3	**4**	5b [1]
Albéniz–						**100**	74
Arbós	*Triana*	**29**	4	**Mahler**	*Symphony No.* 5	**64**	5
Antheil	*Over the Plains*	**28**	3			**90**	[22]
Bernstein	*"Jeremiah" Symphony*	**11**	[11] 2f			**134**	[10] 1f
		26	1			**165**	4
Bloch	*Hiver – Printemps*	**35**	[8] 1f	**Mahler**	*Symphony No.* 6	**105**	[70]
Bruckner	*Symphony No.* 6	**168**	411			**181**	[120]
Casella	*La Donna Serpente,*			**Mahler**	*Symphony No.* 7	**221**	6b [260]
	I. Serie	**39**	[36] 2f			**253**	[293]
Cesana	*Second American*	**26**	[20]	**Mahler**	*Symphony No.* 8	**20**	2
	Symphony	**64**	[6]			**65**	[80]
Chávez	*Sinfonia de Antigona*	**7**	[5]			**84**	3b [21]
Copland	*Third Symphony*	**153**	[130]	**Mahler**	*Symphony No.* 9	**48**	[15] 4f
Coppola	*Interlude Dramatique*	**51**	[26]			**149**	2
Diamond	*Music for Shakespeare's*			**Miaskovsky**	*Symphony No.* 6	**74**	[48] 1f
	"Romeo and Juliet"	**3**	1			**141**	[11]
Diamond	*Timon of Athens*	**28**	192			**176**	[34]
Dunn	*Overture on Negro*	**24**	[K]			**236**	5
	Themes	**31**	[N]	**Milhaud**	*Quatrième Symphonie*	**85**	1b [50]
de Falla	*El Retablo de Maese*			**Milhaud**	*Saudades do Brazil*	**44**	8
	Pedro	**108**	[97]	**Pick-**	*Notturno e Rondo*	**10**	[3] 1f
de Falla	*Three Dances from "The*			Mangiagalli	*Fantastico*	**40**	1
	Three-Cornered Hat"	**87**	1b [32]	**Poulenc**	*Concert Champêtre pour*	**17**	[12]
Hanson	*"Merry Mount" Suite*	**29**	3		*Clavecin et Orchestre*	**42**	[29]
Hanson	*Symphony No.* 2,			**Rachmaninoff**	*The Bells*	**88**	7b [91]
	"Romantic"	**41**	3b [P]	**Read**	*Sketches of the City*	**28**	3
Harsanyi	*Suite pour Orchestre*	**73**	3b [155]			**39**	2
Janssen	*New Year's Eve in*			**Read**	*Symphony No.* I	**7**	4
	New York	**82**	[34]			**32**	4
Khachaturian	*Concerto for Piano and*					**72**	1
	Orchestra	**130**	[348]			**119**	[43] 1f
Khachaturian	*Gayne Ballet Suite*	**84**	[14] 1f	**Rieti**	*L'Arca di Noè*	**12**	1b [11]
	No. 2	**96**	1			**34**	[32]
Knipper	*Symphony No.* 4	**12**	[8] 1f	**Riisager**	*Torgot Dance*	**27**	3

141

BRASSES

Horn (contd.)

COMPOSER	WORK	PAGE	MEASURE	COMPOSER	WORK	PAGE	MEASURE
Roussel	*Évocations, II*	23	7	Siegmeister	*Western Suite*	16	1
Roussel	*Pour une Fête de*					33	[35]
	Printemps	47	2	Stravinsky	*Feuerwerk*	29	4
Schönberg	*Fünf Orchesterstücke*	58	3b [12]	Stravinsky	*Le Sacre du Printemps*	35	2b [46]
Schuman, W.	*Symphony No. IV*	57	271			85	[103]
Scriabin	*Piano Concerto in F♯*	62	3			95	[116] 2f
	minor	66	[18]			106	[134]
Sessions	*Suite from "The Black*					127	[176]
	Maskers"	72	[69]	Stravinsky	*Petrouchka Suite*	93	[80] 1f
Sessions	*Symphony for Orchestra*	30	[48]	Tchaikovsky	*Manfred-Symphonie*	14	2
	(No. 1)	71	[111] 3f			57	1
Shepherd	*Horizons*	65	2	Varèse	*Intégrales*	12	1
Shostakovich	*Symphony No. 3*	59	[73]	Walton	*Symphony*	191	[142] 1f
Siegmeister	*Sunday in Brooklyn*	37	[70]				
		86	[95]				

Trumpet

COMPOSER	WORK	PAGE	MEASURE	COMPOSER	WORK	PAGE	MEASURE
Casella	*La Donna Serpente,*			Mahler	*Symphony No. 4*	47	[17]
	I. Serie	39	[36]	Mahler	*Symphony No. 5*	10	6
Casella	*La Donna Serpente,*	39	[50]			155	[22]
	II. Serie	82	[87]			217	[22]
Charpentier	*Impressions d'Italie*	154	[52] 1f	Mahler	*Symphony No. 7*	56	2
Diamond	*Fourth Symphony*	23	[125] 1f	Mahler	*Symphony No. 8*	216	[217]
Janssen	*New Year's Eve in*			Mahler	*Symphony No. 9*	53	5
	New York	86	[35]	Milhaud	*2me Suite Symphonique*	147	1
Mahler	*Symphony No. 2*	7	2b [2]	Milhaud	*Saudades do Brazil*	3	1
		36	[18]			35	1
		99	[40]	Schönberg	*Fünf Orchesterstücke*	14	2b [12]
		161	7			42	[5] 2f
		204	[48]	Schuman, W.	*Symphony No. IV*	60	286
Mahler	*Symphony No. 3*	12	[8]	Varèse	*Intégrales*	23	[10] 4f
		43	1				
		222	7				

Trombone

COMPOSER	WORK	PAGE	MEASURE	COMPOSER	WORK	PAGE	MEASURE
Mahler	*Symphony No. 9*	47	3	Strauss, R.	*Death and Transfigura-*		
Moross	*Biguine*	22	5		*tion*	51	2

Horn and Trumpet

COMPOSER	WORK	PAGE	MEASURE	COMPOSER	WORK	PAGE	MEASURE
Gould	*Latin-American*			Mahler	*Symphony No. 6*	243	[156]
	Symphonette	115	[26]	Mahler	*Symphony No. 9*	176	2
Janssen	*New Year's Eve in*	17	[7]	Milhaud	*Quatrième Symphonie*	34	2
	New York	90	[36]	Stravinsky	*Feuerwerk*	18	3b [18]
Mahler	*Symphony No. 2*	134	3	Varèse	*Hyperprism*	17	7
		181	[26] 7f	Varèse	*Intégrales*	27	[12]
Mahler	*Symphony No. 4*	121	[89]				
		144	[12]				

BELLS UP

Trumpet and Trombone

COMPOSER	WORK	PAGE	MEASURE	COMPOSER	WORK	PAGE	MEASURE
Bartók	*Dance Suite*	86	94	**Cesana**	*Second American*	118	[14]
					Symphony	152	[36]

Horn, Trumpet, and Trombone

COMPOSER	WORK	PAGE	MEASURE	COMPOSER	WORK	PAGE	MEASURE
Mahler	*Symphony No. 5*	43	[18]	**Weinberger**	*Polka and Fugue from*		
Schuman, W.	*Symphony No. III*	43	354		*"Schwanda, the Bag-*		
Schuman, W.	*Symphony No. IV*	30	247		*piper"*	64	1b [215]

Horn, Trombone, and Tuba

COMPOSER	WORK	PAGE	MEASURE
Siegmeister	*From my Window*	56	2b [40]

Horn, Trumpet, Trombone, and Tuba

Tansman	*Deux Moments*		
	Symphoniques	42	2

Chapter 28

OFF-STAGE

(for terminology see Chapter 11, page 75)

1 Horn

COMPOSER	WORK	PAGE	MEASURE
MacDowell	*2nd Suite (Indian)*	**74**	[A]
		78	[E] 6f

1 Trumpet

COMPOSER	WORK	PAGE	MEASURE	COMPOSER	WORK	PAGE	MEASURE
Beethoven	*Leonore Overture No. 2*	**50**	392	**Respighi**	*The Pines of Rome*	**36**	4
Beethoven	*Leonore Overture No. 3*	**30**	272	**Respighi**	*Vetrate di Chiesa*	**50**	[14]
Mahler	*Symphony No. 1*	**5**	1	**Schelling**	*A Victory Ball*	**122**	18
Prokofieff	*Alexander Nevsky*	**107**	4b [61]				

2 Trumpets

COMPOSER	WORK	PAGE	MEASURE	COMPOSER	WORK	PAGE	MEASURE
Dvořák	*Die Waldtaube*	**15**	[5] 2f	**Mahler**	*Symphony No. 2*	**175**	[22]

3 Trumpets

COMPOSER	WORK	PAGE	MEASURE	COMPOSER	WORK	PAGE	MEASURE
Loeffler	*A Pagan Poem*	**37**	[N] 2f	**Strauss, R.**	*Ein Heldenleben*	**81**	[42]
		66	[I] 1f				
		95	[20]				

4 Trumpets

COMPOSER	WORK	PAGE	MEASURE	COMPOSER	WORK	PAGE	MEASURE
Verdi	*Messa da Requiem*	**43**	93	**Weinberger**	*Polka and Fugue from "Schwanda, the Bagpiper"*	**57**	[185]

1 Cornet

COMPOSER	WORK	PAGE	MEASURE
Prokofieff	*Lieutenant Kijé*	**13**	[14]
		86	[53]
		100	[73]

1 Trombone

COMPOSER	WORK	PAGE	MEASURE
Prokofieff	*Alexander Nevsky*	**53**	4b [34]

OFF-STAGE

2 Trombones

COMPOSER	WORK	PAGE	MEASURE
Rosenthal	*Les Petits Métiers*	**1**	1

1 Posthorn

Mahler	*Symphony No. 3*	**172**	17

2 Roman Horns (Flicorni)

Respighi	*The Pines of Rome*	**72**	[20] 4f

3 Roman Trumpets (Buccine)

Respighi	*Feste Romane*	**1**	4

1 Horn and 1 Trumpet

COMPOSER	WORK	PAGE	MEASURE	COMPOSER	WORK	PAGE	MEASURE
Mahler	*Symphony No. 2*	**144**	1	**Ravel**	*Daphnis et Chloé, Suite No. 1*	**14**	[88]

1 Horn and 4 Trumpets

Mahler	*Symphony No. 2*	**185**	[29]

2 Trumpets and 2 Trombones

Pizzetti	*Introduzione all' "Agamennone" di Eschilo*	**50**	1

4 Trumpets and 3 Trombones

Mahler	*Symphony No. 8*	**73**	[91]
		216	[218]

12 Horns, 2 Trumpets, and 2 Trombones

Strauss, R.	*Eine Alpensinfonie*	**24**	5b [19]

Chapter 29

JAZZ EFFECTS

English	Italian	French	German
"Flare"	—	—	—

Trumpet

COMPOSER	WORK	PAGE	MEASURE
Janssen	*New Year's Eve in New York*	40	1b [16]

English	Italian	French	German
"Growl"	—	—	—

Trumpet

Gould	*Latin-American Symphonette*	84	10

Trombone

Gould	*Latin-American Symphonette*	96	3b [12]

English	Italian	French	German
"Lip slur"	—	—	—

Trumpet

Stravinsky	*Ebony Concerto*	25	1b [10]
		28	1b [16]

Trombone

Gould	*Latin-American Symphonette*	22	5b [Q]
		68	5

JAZZ EFFECTS

English	Italian	French	German
"Rip"	—	—	—

rip   rip

Trumpet

COMPOSER	WORK	PAGE	MEASURE
Gould	*Spirituals*	**3**	[A]

Trumpet and Trombone

COMPOSER	WORK	PAGE	MEASURE	COMPOSER	WORK	PAGE	MEASURE
Gould	*Philharmonic Waltzes*	**1**	6	**Gould**	*Spirituals*	**5**	[C] 5f

Horn, Trumpet, and Trombone

COMPOSER	WORK	PAGE	MEASURE
Gould	*Latin-American Symphonette*	**124**	4

English	Italian	French	German
"Smear"	—	—	—

smear

Trombone

COMPOSER	WORK	PAGE	MEASURE
Gillis	*The Alamo*	**31**	5

Horn, Trumpet, and Trombone

COMPOSER	WORK	PAGE	MEASURE
Gould	*Philharmonic Waltzes*	**27**	4

English	Italian	French	German
Vibrato	Vibrato	Faire vibrer le son	Vibrierend

(for further terminology see Chapter 13, page 77)

Horn

COMPOSER	WORK	PAGE	MEASURE	COMPOSER	WORK	PAGE	MEASURE
Albéniz–Arbós	*Évocation*	**13**	2	**Mohaupt**	*Town Piper Music*	**45**	[46]

Trumpet

COMPOSER	WORK	PAGE	MEASURE	COMPOSER	WORK	PAGE	MEASURE
Enesco	*2ᵉ Rhapsodie Roumaine*	**14**	[9]	**Inghelbrecht**	*La Métamorphose d'Ève*	**20**	1b [17]

BRASSES

Trombone

COMPOSER	WORK	PAGE	MEASURE	COMPOSER	WORK	PAGE	MEASURE
Delannoy	*Figures Sonores*	25	7	**Milhaud**	*Cinq Études pour Piano*		
Ibert	*Divertissement*	20	[1ɔ]		*et Orchestre*	18	[A]
Inghelbrecht	*La Valse Retrouvée*	6	[38] 1f	**Siegmeister**	*Sunday in Brooklyn*	10	[35]
Martinet	*Orphée*	7	[3] 2f				

English	Italian	French	German
"Laughing"	"Ridente"	"Riant"	"Wie Gelächter"
"Wah-wah"	—	"Woo-woo"	—

Trumpet

COMPOSER	WORK	PAGE	MEASURE
Siegmeister	*Sunday in Brooklyn*	40	3b [85]

Trombone

Varèse	*Hyperprism*	14	[8] 4f

English	Italian	French	German
"Wow"	—	"Oua-oua"	—
		"Wau-wau"	—

Trumpet

COMPOSER	WORK	PAGE	MEASURE	COMPOSER	WORK	PAGE	MEASURE
Gilli	*Symphony No. 5½*	4	[A] 1f	**Ibert**	*Divertissement*	60	8b [7]
		12	5				

Trombone

Gillis	*Symphony No. 5½*	17	5

Trumpet and Trombone

Gillis	*Symphony No. 5½*	30	[N] 6f

Chapter 30

MISCELLANEOUS EFFECTS

Horn

English	Italian	French	German
Coarsely blown	Suonare ruvido	Sonorité grossière	Grob geblasen

COMPOSER	WORK	PAGE	MEASURE
Bax	*Second Symphony*	**116**	1

English	Italian	French	German
Full-throated	Risonante di piena gola	De pleine gorge	Aus vollen Hals

COMPOSER	WORK	PAGE	MEASURE
Varèse	*Intégrales*	**40**	3

English	Italian	French	German
Like a bell	Come campana	Comme une cloche	Wie eine Glocke

COMPOSER	WORK	PAGE	MEASURE
de Falla	*El Retablo de Maese Pedro*	**71**	[72] 1f

English	Italian	French	German
Like screaming	Alla maniera stridente	Comme des cris perçants	Wie schreiend

COMPOSER	WORK	PAGE	MEASURE
Schuman, W.	*Undertow*	**39**	[480] 4f

English	Italian	French	German
Natural notes	Note aperte	Notes naturelles	Natur Noten (ohne Ventil)
To be played on natural harmonics	Note naturale		Naturtöne
			Wie ein Naturlaut

COMPOSER	WORK	PAGE	MEASURE	COMPOSER	WORK	PAGE	MEASURE
Britten	*Serenade for Tenor, Horn and Strings*	**1** **38**	1 6	**Vaughan Williams**	*Pastoral Symphony*	**48**	[L] 1f
Respighi	*Metamorphoseon, XII Modi*	**43**	[22]				

BRASSES

Trumpet

English	Italian	French	German
English	*Italian*	*French*	*German*
Coarsely	In modo grossolano	Grossier	Grob

COMPOSER	WORK	PAGE	MEASURE
Holst	*Beni Mora, Oriental Suite*	**37**	4

English	Italian	French	German
English	*Italian*	*French*	*German*
Dark tone	Suono tenebroso	Timbre sombre	Dunkler Ton

COMPOSER	WORK	PAGE	MEASURE
Persichetti	*The Hollow Men*	**7**	5

English	Italian	French	German
English	*Italian*	*French*	*German*
Muted, in imitation of an antique cornet	Con sordino, imitando il cornetto antico	Avec sourdine, imitant le cornet antique	Gedämpft, ein antikes Cornett nachahmend

COMPOSER	WORK	PAGE	MEASURE
Respighi	*Antiche Danze ed Arie, 2ª Suite*	**15**	1

English	Italian	French	German
English	*Italian*	*French*	*German*
No vibrato / Without vibrato	Non-vibrato / Senza vibrato	Non-vibrant / Sans vibrer	Nicht vibrierend

COMPOSER	WORK	PAGE	MEASURE
Siegmeister	*Wilderness Road*	**4**	1

Trombone

English	Italian	French	German
English	*Italian*	*French*	*German*
Biting	Mordace	Mordant	Scharf / Spitzig

COMPOSER	WORK	PAGE	MEASURE
Stravinsky	*Ebony Concerto*	**25**	1b [10]

English	Italian	French	German
English	*Italian*	*French*	*German*
In the jazz style	In stilo jazz	Dans le style jazz	Im Jazzstil

COMPOSER	WORK	PAGE	MEASURE
Poot	*Jazz-Music*	**10**	[5]

English	Italian	French	German
English	*Italian*	*French*	*German*
Nearly sliding between the notes	Quasi glissando	Presque glissant entre les notes	Fast gleitend zwischen den Noten

COMPOSER	WORK	PAGE	MEASURE
Rudhyar	*Sinfonietta*	**32**	1

MISCELLANEOUS EFFECTS

Trombone (contd.)

English	Italian	French	German
No glissando	Non-glissando	Non-glissant	Nicht glissando

COMPOSER	WORK	PAGE	MEASURE
Schuman, W.	*American Festival Overture*	20	[225] 1f
		31	1b [325]

English	Italian	French	German
Push the sound	Avanzare il suono	Poussez le son	Den Ton forcieren

Inghelbrecht	*Rapsodie de Printemps*	45	[23] 4f

English	Italian	French	German
Quarter-tones	Quarto di toni	Quart de tons	Vierteltöne

$$(\flat \tfrac{1}{2} \natural)$$

Varèse	*Hyperprism*	15	[9]

English	Italian	French	German
Like staccato—panting	Quasi staccato—palpitando	Comme staccato—haletant	Wie staccato—keuchend

Rudhyar	*Sinfonietta*	18	2

Tuba

English	Italian	French	German
Like pizzicato	Quasi pizzicato	Comme pizzicato	Wie pizzicato

COMPOSER	WORK	PAGE	MEASURE	COMPOSER	WORK	PAGE	MEASURE
Bax	*Second Symphony*	92	3	**Bax**	*Sixth Symphony*	12	2
Bax	*Fourth Symphony*	5	[3]				

Chapter 31

BRASS TERMINOLOGY

English	*Italian*	*French*	*German*
Change to E	Muta in E	Change en Mi	Wechseln in E
Change to F	Mutano in F	Changez en Fa	In F ändern
1st Horn take mute	Corno I mette il sordino	La Ière Cor met la sourdine	Horn 1 nimmt Dämpfer
1st and 2nd Horns muted	Corni I e II colle sordine	Sourdines aux Ière et 2e Cors	Hörner 1, 2 mit Dämpfer
4 Horns muted	Corni I–IV con sordini	Les 4 Cors avec sourdines	Hörner 1–4 gedämpft
Horns [Trpts.; Trbns.] muted	Corni [Tbe.; Trbni.] con sord.	Sourds. aux 4 Cors [Tpttes.; Tbnes.]	Hörner [Tromp.; Pos.] m.D.

152

PART IV

Percussion

Pics.

Fl. 1

Cl. I
in A

Harp

S. Vln.

Vlns. I

Vlns. II

Vls.

Vcs.

Comodo, ♩ = 120

105

S. Vln.

Vlns. I

Vlns. II

Vcs.

*col legno

Timp.

S. Dr.

S. Vln.

Vlns. I

Vlns. II

Vcs.

* with wooden sticks, to be played at the edge of the head
* baguettes en bois, à être éxécuté sur le bord de la membrane

** at the edge of the head
** au bord de la membrane

BARTÓK. VIOLIN CONCERTO

MILHAUD. LES CHOEPHORES (IV. Présages)

Reproduced by permission of Heugel & Cie., Paris, France, owners of the copyright of "L'Orestie d'Eschyle,"
translated by Paul Claudel, of which "Les Choéphores" is Part II

INTRODUCTION

I F THE BRASS INSTRUMENTS have seemingly assumed the dominant role in twentieth-century orchestration the percussion instruments are assuredly not far behind in importance, as any hearing of a contemporary score will unmistakably prove. But it must be stated at once that the use of the former is generally accomplished with more skill and intelligence than the latter, for the merely "good" instrumentator inevitably tends to over-orchestrate as far as the percussion section is concerned. The more restrained and sensitive employment of the countless percussion instruments now at the composer's disposal, however, can quite immeasurably enhance the coloration and over-all effectiveness of a score. It is the intention of the present section to show instances of the diverse and fascinating effects possible—and by now even common—in modern scoring.

As the timpani are without question the most important of all the percussion, the beginning of the section in Chapter 32 is devoted to illustrations of extended range (above F♯ and below E); chords—or more properly, intervals—produced by one player as well as by two or more; dampening the tone quickly; methods of striking—such as playing on or very near to the rim, which gives a sound of little or no resonance; muffled or muted drums; pedal *glissandi* effects; the various kinds of sticks called for; rolls (*tremoli*) on two drums; striking the drum-head with two sticks; and finally, various miscellaneous indications to the player and special effects.

Chapter 33 is given over to the pitched percussion instruments—bells, glockenspiel, marimba, vibraphone and xylophone—with examples catalogued of *glissandi* and *tremolandi* effects; muffled or muted sounds; off-stage passages; stick types; and, lastly, miscellaneous effects, such as a *glissando* across the resonators of the xylophone. The cymbals (pair and suspended), and the drums (bass, snare, and tenor) are grouped together in Chapters 34 and 35, with sections given on dampening the tone quickly, as in the timpani; methods of striking or clashing; muffling or muting; off-stage; and miscellaneous, special effects called for in study scores. It is a rather curious fact that composers have been far more explicit in designating specific stick types for striking the suspended cymbal than for any other percussion instrument, even including the timpani.

The same general procedure is followed in Chapter 36, devoted to gong, tambourine, and triangle, and Chapter 37 lists effects—including methods of playing and stick types—used for the less frequently called-for percussion instruments, such as wood blocks, maracas, and tom-tom. The remainder of the chapter merely lists places in contemporary scores where the more unusual percussion instruments have been used—guitar, antique cymbals, wind-machine, and so forth. The final chapter, as in the preceding sections, lists terminology of a miscellaneous nature.

Chapter 32

TIMPANI

(1) EXTENDED RANGE

COMPOSER	WORK	PAGE	MEASURE
Milhaud	La Création du Monde	11	[13]
		32	[33]

COMPOSER	WORK	PAGE	MEASURE
Milhaud	La Création du Monde	11	[13]
		32	[33]
		56	1b [54]

COMPOSER	WORK	PAGE	MEASURE
Martinet	Orphée	54	[19] 1f
Stravinsky	Le Sacre du Printemps	29	2b [39]
		46	[57]
		106	[134]

COMPOSER	WORK	PAGE	MEASURE
Janáček	Sinfonietta	4	[1] 7f
		103	[10] 2f
Schelling	A Victory Ball	30	2
Stravinsky	Le Sacre du Printemps	126	2b [175]

COMPOSER	WORK	PAGE	MEASURE
Chávez	Sinfonia de Antigona	8	6
		13	2b [15]
		19	4
Copland	Third Symphony	153	3b [130]
Engel	The Creation	40	3
Kabalevsky	Suite from "Colas Breugnon"	114	1b [38]
Kodály	Galanta Dances	64	607

COMPOSER	WORK	PAGE	MEASURE
Revueltas	Cuauhnahuac	2	[3] 1f
		10	3
Villa-Lobos	Amazonas	4	3

COMPOSER	WORK	PAGE	MEASURE
Debussy	La Mer	136	[63]
Janáček	Sinfonietta	5	[2] 5f
		104	6
Mahler	Symphony No. 9	24	5
Milhaud	2me Suite Symphonique	80	1
Moross	Paeans	2	[A] 1f
Revueltas	Sensemayá	7	[11]
		38	[36]
Rudhyar	Sinfonietta	11	1

COMPOSER	WORK	PAGE	MEASURE
Berg	Violin Concerto	48	[240] 3f
Bliss	Concerto for Piano and Orchestra	174	[112]
Casella	La Donna Serpente, II. Serie	49	1
		71	[80]
Copland	First Symphony	46	[33] 3f
Coppola	Scherzo Fantasque	56	5
Debussy	Rondes de Printemps	18	11
Dello Joio	Variations, Chaconne, and Finale	48	1
Engel	The Creation	7	2
		27	1
		74	[48]
Gould	Spirituals	9	1
Harsanyi	Suite pour Orchestre	66	[105] 2f
Inghelbrecht	El Greco	56	[47]
Ives	"The Fourth of July" from Symphony, "Holidays"	15	[L]
Janáček	Sinfonietta	4	[1] 7f
		103	[10] 2f

159

PERCUSSION

(1) EXTENDED RANGE (contd.)

COMPOSER	WORK	PAGE	MEASURE
Lambert	*The Rio Grande*	12	[6] 7f
Luening	*Two Symphonic Interludes*	9	[35] 2f
Mahler	*Symphony No. 2*	41	4
Milhaud	*Concerto pour Piano et Orchestre*	41	[35]
Milhaud	*2ᵐᵉ Suite Symphonique*	63	1
		96	2
Milhaud	*La Mort d'un Tyran*	1	1
Milhaud	*Opus Americanum No. 2*	90	3b [640]
Milhaud	*Quatrième Symphonie*	82	1b [35]
Milhaud	*Saudades do Brazil*	59	1
Milhaud	*Sérénade pour Orchestre*	33	1
		71	[15]
Prokofieff	*Ala et Lolly (Scythian Suite)*	5	2
		87	[56] 2f
Prokofieff	*March and Scherzo from "The Love of the Three Oranges"*	5	[3] 3f
Schelling	*A Victory Ball*	109	[34] 1f
Schuman, W.	*Symphony No. IV*	18	179
		60	286
Shostakovich	*Symphony No. 3*	68	[80]
Siegmeister	*Sunday in Brooklyn*	62	2
Strauss, R.	*Symphonia Domestica*	19	[24]
Stravinsky	*Le Sacre du Printemps*	139	[201] 3f
Stravinsky	*Les Noces*	87	[95] 5f
Taylor	*Through the Looking Glass*	108	5
Walton	*Façade, Suite No. 1*	46	[D]

COMPOSER	WORK	PAGE	MEASURE
Bloch	*Schelomo*	6	4
Britten	*Sinfonia da Requiem*	46	[31] 2f
Diamond	*Music for Shakespeare's "Romeo and Juliet"*	57	[40] 2f
Fernandez	*Batuque*	2	[1]
		11	[9]
Harsanyi	*Suite pour Orchestre*	76	3b [185]
Hindemith	*Symphony in E-Flat*	35	[18] 3f
Mahler	*Songs of a Wayfarer*	54	78
Mahler	*Symphony No. 2*	31	[15]
		141	2b [4]
Mahler	*Symphony No. 3*	83	[61]
		176	[31]
Mahler	*Symphony No. 7*	90	[81] 6f
		112	4b [103]

COMPOSER	WORK	PAGE	MEASURE
Mahler	*Symphony No. 8*	3	3b [1]
		72	[89]
		122	[81]
		218	7
Prokofieff	*Peter and the Wolf*	60	[44] 4f
Respighi	*Metamorphoseon, XII Modi*	7	[3]
		74	3
Respighi	*Vetrate di Chiesa*	93	4
Schreker	*The Birthday of the Infanta, Suite*	19	3b [75]
Schuman, W.	*Undertow*	46	1b [570]
Shostakovich–Stokowski	*Prelude in E-Flat minor*	2	1
		8	[7]
Strauss, R.	*Eine Alpensinfonie*	117	[112]
Ward	*Jubilation—An Overture*	2	1
		14	1

COMPOSER	WORK	PAGE	MEASURE
Bach–Stokowski	*Fugue in G minor—The Shorter*	20	[13]
Bernstein	*"Jeremiah" Symphony*	16	4b [4]
Bloch	*Schelomo*	3	3
Bloch	*Trois Poèmes Juifs*	79	3
Britten	*Four Sea Interludes from "Peter Grimes"*	33	[6]
Britten	*Sinfonia da Requiem*	22	7
		52	2b [35]
Carpenter	*Sea Drift*	1	1
Copland	*Third Symphony*	152	[129] 3f
Harsanyi	*Suite pour Orchestre*	51	[30]
Mahler	*Symphony No. 3*	5	[2]
		14	[10]
		22	[17]
		42	3
		223	[23]
Mahler	*Symphony No. 4*	176	113
Mahler	*Symphony No. 5*	67	6
Mahler	*Symphony No. 7*	64	[55] 1f
Mahler	*Symphony No. 9*	26	[10]
		55	4
		75	4
		122	[33]
Sowerby	*Prairie*	48	2

COMPOSER	WORK	PAGE	MEASURE
Mahler	*Symphony No. 2*	144	10
Mahler	*Symphony No. 5*	19	5

TIMPANI

(1) EXTENDED RANGE (contd.)

COMPOSER	WORK	PAGE	MEASURE
Mahler	*Symphony No. 7*	246	[286] 2f
Sowerby	*Prairie*	62	10

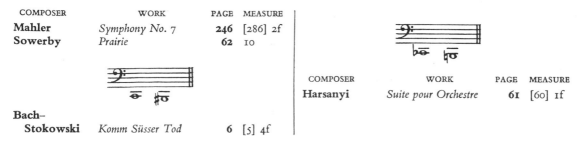

COMPOSER	WORK	PAGE	MEASURE
Harsanyi	*Suite pour Orchestre*	61	[60] 1f

COMPOSER	WORK	PAGE	MEASURE
Bach–
Stokowski	*Komm Süsser Tod*	6	[5] 4f

(2) CHORDS (INTERVALS)

1 Player

COMPOSER	WORK	PAGE	MEASURE		COMPOSER	WORK	PAGE	MEASURE
Antheil	*Over the Plains*	51	[30]		**Delius**	*Appalachia*	24	1
		59	[36]				108	464
Barber	*Second Symphony*	34	6b [24]		**Diamond**	*Fourth Symphony*	31	[170]
Bartók	*Concerto for Orchestra*	53	[34]		**Diamond**	*Music for Shakespeare's*		
Bartók	*Second Suite*	91	1			*"Romeo and Juliet"*	19	1b [115]
		114	3		**Diamond**	*Timon of Athens*	18	118
Bax	*First Symphony*	57	1		**Elgar**	*Sea Pictures*	5	[B]
		65	[C]		**Enesco**	*2ᵉ Rhapsodie Roumaine*	5	[3] 1f
		80	[K] 1f		**de Falla**	*Three Dances from "The*		
Bax	*Fifth Symphony*	48	[52]			*Three-Cornered Hat"*	30	[6]
Bax	*Tintagel*	3	1		**Fitelberg**	*Nocturne for Orchestra*	29	3
Beethoven	*Symphony No. 9*	157	153		**Fitelberg**	*Symphony No. 1*	14	[58] 1f
Benjamin	*Overture to an Italian*	4	[B]				44	[287] 6f
	Comedy	21	[J]		**Griffes**	*The Pleasure Dome of*		
Berlioz	*Symphonie Fantastique*	126	3			*Kubla Khan*	53	[V]
Bernstein	*"Jeremiah" Symphony*	10	[10]		**Grofé**	*Grand Canyon Suite*	170	2
		16	4b [4]		**Guarnieri**	*Negro Dance*	3	[20] 1f
Bizet	*L'Arlésienne Suite*	27	45		**Harsanyi**	*Suite pour Orchestre*	63	2b [80]
	No. 1	30	76		**Hindemith**	*Konzert für Orchester*	53	5
Bloch	*Hiver–Printemps*	40	[12]		**Holst**	*Beni Mora, Oriental*	16	[7] 1f
Bloch	*Schelomo*	1	3			*Suite*	21	1
Brahms	*Ein deutsches Requiem*	30	17				33	[4]
		51	161		**Honegger**	*Le Dit des Jeux du*		
		78	299			*Monde*	45	[1] 8f
Britten	*Sinfonia da Requiem*	46	[31] 2f		**Inghelbrecht**	*La Valse Retrouvée*	25	5
Casella	*Elegia Eroica*	16	1b [11]		**Inghelbrecht**	*Pour le jour de la*		
Copland	*El Salón México*	14	[15] 2f			*première neige au*		
		38	[36] 2f			*vieux Japon*	34	6b [20]
Copland	*Four Dance Episodes*				**Inghelbrecht**	*Rapsodie de Printemps*	23	[10]
	from "Rodeo"	46	4b [42]		**Ives**	*A Set of Pieces*	7	[D]
Copland	*Third Symphony*	26	1		**Khachaturian**	*Gayne Ballet Suite*		
		95	[86] 8f			*No. 2*	104	3
		154	1		**Knipper**	*Symphony No. 4*	79	1
Debussy	*Le Martyre de Saint*						100	[17]
	Sébastien	54	[23]		**Mahler**	*Symphony No. 1*	14	3

PERCUSSION

1 Player (contd.)

COMPOSER	WORK	PAGE	MEASURE	COMPOSER	WORK	PAGE	MEASURE
Mahler	Symphony No. 6	54	[33]	Sibelius	Symphony No. 3	41	7
Mahler	Symphony No. 7	228	3b [266]	Sibelius	Symphony No. 5	65	[S]
Mahler	Symphony No. 9	68	[19] 6f	Sibelius	Tapiola	35	[L] 3f
Martinet	Orphée	77	[12]			55	569
Milhaud	La Mort d'un Tyran	18	76	Sibelius	The Swan of Tuonela	12	[G]
		26	111	Skilton	Suite Primeval, Part 1	24	1
Milhaud	Sérénade pour Orchestre	14	3b [9]	Slonimsky	My Toy Balloon	23	4
Moross	Paeans	4	[C] 2f			30	6
		6	[F]	Stillman-	Gulliver—His Journey	11	[B]
Parodi	Preludio ad una			Kelley	to Lil'iput	121	6
	Commedia	59	5b [AF]	Strauss, R.	Don Juan	44	[L]
Poot	Symphonie	14	3	Strauss, R.	Till Eulenspiegel's		
Prokofieff	Ala et Lolly (Scythian				Merry Pranks	32	[24]
	Suite)	12	[4]	Stravinsky	Chant du Rossignol	20	[21]
Rachmaninoff	Die Toteninsel	30	7	Stravinsky	Les Noces	46	[55]
Read	Symphony No. I	78	1			129	3
Respighi	Belfagor, Ouverture per			Stravinsky	Oedipus Rex	85	1b [117]
	Orchestra	27	1			96	[129]
Respighi	Feste Romane	55	1	Stravinsky	Symphonie de Psaumes	1	1
Respighi	Metamorphoseon, XII			Vaughan	Symphony in E minor		
	Modi	23	4	Williams	(No. 6)	80	[14] 4f
Rudhyar	Sinfonietta	19	5	Verdi	Messa da Requiem	141	699
Schelling	A Victory Ball	22	4	Villa-Lobos	Amazonas	4	3
Schuman, W.	Undertow	43	[530] 1f			46	[19] 1f
Sessions	Symphony for Orchestra			Villa-Lobos	Chôros No. 8	67	[27] 1f
	(No. 1)	10	3b [14]	Villa-Lobos	Chôros No. 10	40	2
Shostakovich–						92	4
Stokowski	Prelude in E-Flat minor	2	1	Villa-Lobos	Danses Africaines	5	1
Sibelius	Pelleas and Melisande	25	3	Wagner, R.	Good Friday Spell		
Sibelius	Symphony No. 1	7	1		from "Parsifal"	15	122
		35	1				

2 Players

COMPOSER	WORK	PAGE	MEASURE	COMPOSER	WORK	PAGE	MEASURE
Bartók	Violin Concerto	101	[293]	Mahler	Symphony No. 3	5	[2]
Berg	Violin Concerto	51	2			79	[57]
Berlioz	Roméo et Juliette	53	5	Mahler	Symphony No. 6	238	[153] 1f
		91	4	Parodi	Preludio ad una		
		251	2		Commedia	30	[P]
Berlioz	Symphonie Fantastique	129	7	Schuman, W.	Symphony No. IV	60	286
Holst	The Planets	89	[VII] 8f	Stravinsky	Le Sacre du Printemps	99	[121] 1f
		143	1	Wagner, R.	Funeral Music from		
		161	[IX]		"Götterdämmerung"	17	59
Mahler	Symphony No. 2	114	[49]	Walton	Symphony	183	[137]
		141	2b [4]			190	3

3 Players

COMPOSER	WORK	PAGE	MEASURE	COMPOSER	WORK	PAGE	MEASURE
Berlioz	Benvenuto Cellini	2	1	Davidson	Auto Accident	9	4
	Overture	6	9	Stravinsky	Le Sacre du Printemps	109	[138]
		24	5				
		47	1				
		54	4				

TIMPANI

4 Players

COMPOSER	WORK	PAGE	MEASURE
Stravinsky	*Le Sacre du Printemps*	85	[103] 1f

(3) DAMPENED

English	Italian	French	German
Choke(d)	Secco	Étouffé(s)	Dämpfen
Damp(en)	Smorzate	Étouffez (le son)	Gleich abdämpfen
Dampened	Soffocato (subito)	Sec	Kurz
Damp [muffle] instantly		Très sec	Schnell abdämpfen
Dry			
Off			
Short			
Stop (quickly)			

COMPOSER	WORK	PAGE	MEASURE	COMPOSER	WORK	PAGE	MEASURE
Albéniz-Arbós	*El Albaicín*	8	[C]	Liszt	*Eine Faust-Symphonie*	12	1
						184	3
Casella	*La Donna Serpente, II. Serie*	5	[5]	Mahler	*Symphony No. 1*	77	10
				Mahler	*Symphony No. 5*	246	5
Copland	*El Salón México*	44	[41] 6f	Mahler	*Symphony No. 7*	119	1
Copland	*Four Dance Episodes from "Rodeo"*	46	4b [42]	McDonald	*Rhumba from 2nd Symphony*	30	6
Copland	*Statements*	14	[2]	Moore	*Symphony in A major*	125	5
Diamond	*Fourth Symphony*	20	1b [115]	Rivier	*Ouverture pour un don Quichotte*	76	7
Dunn	*Overture on Negro Themes*	44	[T] 8f	Sessions	*Suite from "The Black Maskers"*	47	6b [47]
Franck	*Le Chasseur Maudit*	97	426			64	[63]
Gruenberg	*The Enchanted Isle*	57	2b [235]	Stillman-Kelley	*New England Symphony*	98	2
Ibert	*Ouverture de Fête*	5	[1]	Stravinsky	*Le Sacre du Printemps*	26	1b [35]
		27	2	Stravinsky	*Les Noces*	25	2b [30]
Kay	*Suite for Orchestra*	11	[7]			70	2b [79]
Lalo	*Symphonie Espagnole*	41	4			91	[98]
		62	2	Stravinsky	*Renard*	69	[46] 2f
		87	[D]				

(4) METHODS OF STRIKING

English	Italian	French	German
At (the) rim of head	All'estremita della membrana	Au bord de la membrane [peau]	Am Rand des Felles
At (the) edge of (the) head	Sul bordo della membrana	Blousée	
Close to (the) rim		Blouser	
Near (the) rim		Blousez	
On the edge of the skin		Sur le bord de la membrane [peau]	
Struck near rim			

ORDINARY METHOD OF STRIKING

English	Italian	French	German
Strike in usual manner	Colpete al ordinario	Frappées, comme à l'ordinaire	Gewöhnlicher schlagen
		Frappez à la manière ordinaire	

COMPOSER	WORK	PAGE	MEASURE	COMPOSER	WORK	PAGE	MEASURE
Bartók	*Violin Concerto*	66	[105] 1f	Milhaud	*Concerto pour Violoncelle et Orchestre*	32	[60] 4f
		89	[182] 3f				
Kodály	*Galanta Dances*	12	1b [120]	Milhaud	*IIe Symphonie*	47	1
Milhaud	*Concerto pour Piano et Orchestre*	37	2	Milhaud	*Introduction et Marche Funèbre*	22	[105] 3f

PERCUSSION

(4) METHODS OF STRIKING (contd.)

COMPOSER	WORK	PAGE	MEASURE	COMPOSER	WORK	PAGE	MEASURE
Milhaud	*Quatrième Symphonie*	82	1b [35]	**Russell**	*Fugue for Eight*		
		96	[95]		*Percussion Instruments*	6	8
Milhaud	*Saudades do Brazil*	10	9	**Villa-Lobos**	*Danses Africaines*	62	[9]
Milhaud	*Suite Provençale*	37	[5]				

English	*Italian*	*French*	*German*
(Hit) in center (of head) Hit in middle Roll at center (of head) Roll in middle (of head)	Nel mezzo della membrana	Au centre Au milieu de la membrane [peau]	In der Mitte des Felles

(for further terminology see Chapter 35, page 198)

Gershwin	*An American in Paris*	79	[65]	**Russell**	*Fugue for Eight Per-*	4	[D] 8f
					cussion Instruments	6	8

English	*Italian*	*French*	*German*
Rubbed in a circle with wire-brush	Fregato in circola con scovolo di fil di ferro	Frôlez dans un arc avec balai métallique	Mit einer Drahtbürste im Kreis leicht gerieben

COMPOSER	WORK	PAGE	MEASURE
Inghelbrecht	*La Métamorphose d'Ève*	17	6

English	*Italian*	*French*	*German*
Strike on copper kettle (of timpani)	Colpete sul timballo di rame	Frappez sur la timbale de cuivre	An der Seite des Kessels schlagen

Russell	*Fugue for Eight* *Percussion Instruments*	3	[C]

English	*Italian*	*French*	*German*
Strike on metal rim around head	Colpete sul orlo di metallo della membrana	Frappez sur le cercle métallique de la peau	Am Metallrand um Fell schlagen

Russell	*Fugue for Eight* *Percussion Instruments*	2	[B] 8f

English	*Italian*	*French*	*German*
Sweep wire-brush across head near rim	Passate uno scovolo di fil di ferro sulla membrana presso del orlo	Balayez un balai métallique à travers de la peau	Mit Drahtbürste nah dem Rand übers Fell streichen

Russell	*Fugue for Eight* *Percussion Instruments*	2	[B]

English	*Italian*	*French*	*German*
Trill with pennies [coins]	Trillo colle monete	Trillez avec des pièces de monnaie	Mit Münzen trillern

Bax	*Second Symphony*	82	2b [4]	**Bax**	*In the Faery Hills*	36	18
Bax	*Fourth Symphony*	84	3b [7]				

English	*Italian*	*French*	*German*
With (the) fingernails	Colle unghie	Avec les ongles	Mit dem Nagel

Bax	*November Woods*	52	1	**Bax**	*Tintagel*	16	[G]
Bax	*Second Symphony*	45	5	**Lambert**	*The Rio Grande*	50	[26] 8f
Bax	*The Garden of Fand*	10	[C]				
		77	2				

TIMPANI

(5) MUFFLED

English	Italian	French	German
Muffled	Con sordino	Sons voilés	Abdämpfen
Muffle on	*con sord.*	Sourdine	Bedeckt
	Coperto(i)	*sourd.*	Dumpf
	Velato	Un voile sur la peau de la	Gedämpft
		timbale	*ged.*
		Voilée	

Muffle Off

English	Italian	French	German
Muffle off	Modo ordinario	Naturel	Gewöhnlich
Natural	*modo ord.*	*nat.*	*gew.*
nat.	Senza sordino	Sans sourdine	Dämpfung ab
Remove muffle	*senza sord.*	*sans sourd.*	

COMPOSER	WORK	PAGE	MEASURE	COMPOSER	WORK	PAGE	MEASURE
Barber	*Medea*	39	1	**Milhaud**	*Two Marches*	1	1
Berg	*Three Excerpts from*	42	[315] 1f			9	2b [30]
	"Wozzeck"	56	1b [380]	**Read**	*Sketches of the City*	3	1
Borodin	*Polovetzian Dances from*	49	[M]	**Rogers**	*Elegy*	8	[6] 12f
	"Prince Igor"	78	[T]	**Schreker**	*The Birthday of the*		
Charpentier	*Impressions d'Italie*	20	[20] 3f		*Infanta, Suite*	5	[15] 3f
Dvořák	*Die Waldtaube*	5	2	**Shostakovich**	*Symphony No. 1*	85	[36] 1f
Knipper	*Symphony No. 4*	51	[1]	**Shostakovich**	*Symphony No. 6*	82	[81]
Mahler	*Symphony No. 1*	78	[1]	**Thomson**	*Orchestra Suite from*		
		88	4b [13]		*"The Plow that*		
Mahler	*Symphony No. 2*	54	[26] 3f		*Broke the Plains"*	34	[30]
Mahler	*Symphony No. 3*	5	[2]	**Walton**	*Concerto for Violin and*	20	2
		51	8b [35]		*Orchestra*	47	2b [25]
						135	[66] 1f

(6) PEDAL GLISSANDI

English	Italian	French	German
Pedal glissando	Glissando colla pedale	Glissando avec le levier	Glissando mit Pedal
Pedal Timpani—glissando		Glissando pour la Timbale à	
		levier	

COMPOSER	WORK	PAGE	MEASURE	COMPOSER	WORK	PAGE	MEASURE
Bartók	*Concerto for Orchestra*	109	[255]	**Gould**	*Latin-American*		
Bartók	*Music for Strings, Per-*	27	[185]		*Symphonette*	47	1b [8]
	cussion and Celesta	41	[338]	**Gould**	*Spirituals*	14	[C] 1f
		66	4	**Moross**	*Paeans*	4	[C]
		71	[31]			12	2
Bartók	*Violin Concerto*	12	[72]	**Read**	*Symphony No. I*	97	1b [37]
		43	[293]			103	1b [39]
		91	[202]	**Russell**	*Fugue for Eight*		
Casella	*Elegia Eroica*	13	2		*Percussion Instruments*	7	[F] 11f
		15	[10]	**Siegmeister**	*Sunday in Brooklyn*	41	[90]
Davidson	*Auto Accident*	6	2	**Stravinsky**	*Renard*	30	124
		9	2			146	[90]

PERCUSSION

(7) STICK TYPES

English	Italian	French	German
Bass drum stick(s)	Bacchetta(e) di Gran cassa [Mazza della Gran cassa]	Mailloche de Grosse Caisse [Tampon de la Grosse Caisse]	Grosse Trommel Stock [Grosse Trommelschlägel]
Cane stick(s)	Bacchetta(e) di canna	Baguette(s) en canne	Rohrschlägel
Cane stick with fibre head	Bacchetta di giunco con la testa di capoc	Baguette en jonc à tête de [en] capoc	Rohrstäbchen mit Kopf aus Kapok
Cotton stick(s)	Bacchetta(e) di cotone	Baguette(s) de coton	Baumwollschlägel
Cymbal stick	Bacchetta di Piatto	Baguette de Cymbale	Beckenschlägel
Drumstick(s)	Mazza(e)	Mailloche(s) [Tampon(s)]	Klöpper [Schlägel; Trommelstock]
Felt stick(s)	Bacchetta(e) di feltro	Baguette(s) en feutre	Filzschlägel
Felt timpani stick(s)	Bacchetta(e) di Timpani a feltro	Baguette(s) de Timbale en feutre	Filz Paukenschlägel
Half-hard rubber stick(s)	Bacchetta(e) di gommaelastica mezza-dura	Baguette(s) de caoutchouc semi-dur	Halbharte Gummischlägel
Hard stick(s)	Bacchetta(e) dure	Baguette(s) dur(es)	Schwerer Schlägel
Hard felt stick(s)	Bacchetta(e) di feltro duro	Baguette(s) en feutre dur	Schlägel mit hartem Filz
Hard leather stick(s)	Bacchetta(e) di pelle dure	Baguette(s) de cuir dur	Hartlederschlägel
Hard rubber stick(s)	Bacchetta(e) di gommaelastica dura	Baguette(s) de caoutchouc dur	Hartgummischlägel [Hartkautschukschlägel]
Heavy mallet [Wooden hammer]	Maglio [Mazzetta]	Marteau	Holzhammer
Iron stick(s)	Bacchetta(e) di ferro	Baguette(s) en fer [Morceau de fil de fer]	Eisenschlägel
Knife-blade	Lama di coltello	Lame d'un canif	Messerklinge
Leather stick(s)	Bacchetta(e) di pelle	Baguette(s) en cuir	Lederschlägel
Light stick(s)	Bacchetta(e) leggiere	Baguette(s) légère(s)	Leichter Schlägel
Medium hard stick(s)	Bacchetta(e) media-dura	Baguette(s) assez dur(es)	Ziemlichschwerer Schlägel
Medium hard felt stick(s)	Bacchetta(e) di feltro medio-duro	Baguette(s) en feutre assez dur(es)	Schlägel mit ziemlich hartem Filz
Medium hard leather stick(s)	Bacchetta(e) di pelle medio-dure	Baguette(s) en cuir assez dur(es)	Schlägel mit ziemlich hartem Leder
Medium soft felt stick(s)	Bacchetta(e) di feltro medio-molle	Baguette(s) en feutre assez molle(s)	Schlägel mit ziemlich weichen Filz
Metal stick(s)	Bacchetta(e) di metallo [Battuta(e) metale]	Baguette(s) en [de] métal	Metallschlägel
Ordinary [Regular, Usual] beater(s) [hammer(s); mallet(s); stick(s); striker(s)]	Bacchetta(e) ordinaria	Baguette(s) normale(s) [Baguette(s) ordinaire(s)]	Gewöhnlicher Klöpper [Schlägel]
Padded stick(s)	Bacchetta(e) a bambagia	Baguette(s) ouateuse(s)	Wattierterschlägel
Plush stick(s)	Bacchetta(e) felpate	Baguette(s) de peluche	Plüschschlägel
Quarter-hard rubber stick(s)	Bacchetta(e) di gommaelastica quarta-dura	Baguette(s) en caoutchouc quart-dur	Schlägel mit viertelhartem Gummi
Rattan stick(s)	Bacchetta(e) di canna	Baguette(s) en rotin	Rohrschlägel
Rawhide stick(s)	Bacchetta(e) di pelle cruda	Baguette(s) en peau [cuir brut]	Naturleder Schlägel
Rawhide timpani stick(s)	Bacchetta(e) di Timpani a pelle cruda	Baguette(s) de Timbale en peau	Naturleder Paukenschlägel
Rubber (covered) stick(s)	Bacchetta(e) di gommaelastica	Baguette(s) en caoutchouc	Gummischlägel
Short [small] stick	Piccola bacchetta [Mazzette]	Petite baguette [mailloche]	Kleiner Schlägel
Small wood stick	Piccola bacchetta di legno	Petite baguette en bois	Kleiner Holzschlägel
Snare [side] drum stick(s)	Bacchetta(e) di Tamburo militare	Baguette(s) de Caisse claire	Kleine Trommel Stock
Soft stick(s)	Bacchetta(e) molle	Baguette(s) douce(s)	Weicher Schlägel
Soft felt stick(s)	Bacchetta(e) di feltro molle	Baguette(s) en feutre douce(s)	Weichenfilzschlägel
Soft felt timpani stick(s)	Bacchetta(e) di Timpani molle a feltro	Baguette(s) de Timbale en feutre douce(s)	Weichenfilz Paukenschlägel
Soft timpani stick(s)	Bacchetta(e) di Timpani molle	Baguette(s) de Timbale douce(s)	Weicher Paukenschlägel

TIMPANI

(7) STICK TYPES (contd.)

English	Italian	French	German
Sponge stick(s)	Bacchetta(e) di spugna	Baguette(s) d'éponge [Baguette(s) en éponge]	Schwammschlägel
Sponge timpani stick(s)	Bacchetta(e) di Timpani a spugna	Baguette(s) de Timbale en éponge	Schwamm-Paukenschlägel
Steel stick(s)	Bacchetta(e) d'acciaio	Baguette(s) d'acier	Stahlschlägel
Stick(s) with fibre head [knob]	Bacchetta(e) di capoc	Baguette(s) en capoc	Schlägel mit Kopf aus Kapok
Switch [Rod]	Verghe(i)	Verges	Rute [Ruthe]
Thick stick(s)	Bacchetta(e) grosse	Baguette(s) épaisse(s)	Dicker Schlägel
Thick timpani stick(s)	Bacchetta(e) di Timpani grosse	Baguette(s) de Timbales épaisse(s)	Dicker Paukenschlägel
Thin stick(s)	Bacchetta(e) sottile	Baguette(s) mince(s)	Dünne Ruten
Thin metal stick	Piccola bacchetta di metallo	Bâton mince d'acier	Dünner Metallschlägel
Thin stick with sponge head	Piccola bacchetta con la testa di spugna	Baguette mince à petite tête en éponge	Kleines Stäbchen mit kleinem Schwammkopf
Thin wood stick	Piccola bacchetta di legno	Baguette mince en bois	Kleiner Holzschlägel
Timpani stick(s)	Bacchetta(e) di Timpano(i) [Battuta di Timpano]	Baguette(s) de Timbale(s)	Paukenschlägel
Triangle stick	Bacchetta di Triangolo [Ferro del Triangolo]	Baguette de Triangle [Tringle du Triangle]	Triangelschlägel [Metallstäbchen]
Two-headed stick [Double stick]	Bacchetta a due capi	Double mailloche	Zweiköpfige Schlägel
Very hard stick(s)	Bacchetta(e) molto dure	Baguette(s) très dure(s)	Sehr schwerer Schlägel
Very hard timpani stick(s)	Bacchetta(e) di Timpani molto dure	Baguette(s) de Timbale(s) très dure(s)	Sehr schwerer Paukenschlägel
Very soft stick(s)	Bacchetta(e) molto molle	Baguette(s) très douce(s)	Sehr weicher Schlägel
Very soft timpani stick(s)	Bacchetta(e) di Timpani molto molle	Baguette(s) de Timbale(s) très douce(s)	Sehr weicher Paukenschlägel
Wire-brush [Brush(es)]	Scovolo di fil di ferro	Balai métallique [Brosse en fil de métal]	Drahtbürste
Wood(en) stick(s)	Bacchetta(e) di legno	Baguette(s) de [en] bois	Holzschlägel
Wood(en) timpani stick(s)	Bacchetta(e) di Timpani a legno	Baguette(s) de Timbale(s) en bois	Holz-Paukenschläge
Wool stick(s)	Bacchetta(e) di lana	Baguette(s) en laine	Wollschlägel
Xylophone stick(s)	Bacchetta(e) di Zilafono	Baguette(s) de Xylophone	Xylophonschlägel

FELT STICKS

COMPOSER	WORK	PAGE	MEASURE	COMPOSER	WORK	PAGE	MEASURE
Britten	The Young Person's Guide to the Orchestra	44	2	Holst	The Ballet from "The Perfect Fool"	25	[22] 1f
Holst	Beni Mora, Oriental Suite	19	2	Holst	The Planets	7	2b [II]
						179	1

HARD STICKS

COMPOSER	WORK	PAGE	MEASURE	COMPOSER	WORK	PAGE	MEASURE
Albéniz–Arbós	El Albaicín	8	[C]	Copland	Lincoln Portrait	4	4b [30]
Barber	Second Symphony	34	6b [24]	Copland	Statements	12	3
Britten	The Young Person's Guide to the Orchestra	68	4	Copland	Third Symphony	107	4
Copland	El Salón México	9	5b [11]	Harris	Third Symphony	80	5
		44	[41] 6f	Harris	When Johnny Comes Marching Home	53	1
				Loeffler	Evocation	27	[23]

PERCUSSION

HARD STICKS (contd.)

COMPOSER	WORK	PAGE	MEASURE	COMPOSER	WORK	PAGE	MEASURE
Piston	*Concerto for Orchestra*	23	2	Revueltas	*Sensemayá*	7	[11]
		29	[3]	Schuman, W.	*Symphony No. IV*	60	286
		48	2	Siegmeister	*Sunday in Brooklyn*	23	1
Read	*Sketches of the City*	21	1				

HARD FELT STICKS

COMPOSER	WORK	PAGE	MEASURE
Russell	*Fugue for Eight Percussion Instruments*	4	[D] 8f

HARD LEATHER STICKS

Harris	*When Johnny Comes Marching Home*	33	[180] 2f

MEDIUM HARD STICKS

Loeffler	*Evocation*	1	1

MEDIUM SOFT FELT STICKS

Russell	*Fugue for Eight Percussion Instruments*	1	8b [A]

ORDINARY STICKS

COMPOSER	WORK	PAGE	MEASURE	COMPOSER	WORK	PAGE	MEASURE
Casella	*Italia*	21	[18]	Mahler	*Symphony No. 7*	33	27]
Dunn	*Overture on Negro Themes*	20	4b [1]	Schreker	*The Birthday of the Infanta, Suite*	50	[305] 3f

PADDED STICKS

Johnson	*Imagery*	1	1

SMALL WOOD(EN) STICKS

Schreker	*The Birthday of the Infanta, Suite*	5	[15] 3f

SNARE DRUM STICKS

COMPOSER	WORK	PAGE	MEASURE	COMPOSER	WORK	PAGE	MEASURE
Bartók	*Violin Concerto*	89	[185]	Fitelberg	*Symphony No. 1*	14	[58] 1f
Britten	*Four Sea Interludes from "Peter Grimes"*	74	[9] 3f			44	[287] 6f
				Loeffler	*Evocation*	47	[52] 3f
Britten	*Sinfonia da Requiem*	59	[41]	Milhaud	*Saudades do Brazil*	10	9
Britten	*The Young Person's Guide to the Orchestra*	36	1	Moeran	*Symphony in G minor*	176	2
				Moore	*Symphony in A major*	72	4
				Stravinsky	*Le Sacre du Printemps*	85	[103] 1f
Diamond	*Timon of Athens*	22	140			92	1b [113]
Elgar	*Variations, "Enigma"*	88	[56] 1f	Stravinsky	*Petrouchka Suite*	39	[28] 2f
Fitelberg	*Nocturne for Orchestra*	9	[53]			145	[121]
		51	[309]	Vaughan Williams	*Pastoral Symphony*	51	[A]

TIMPANI

SOFT STICKS

COMPOSER	WORK	PAGE	MEASURE	COMPOSER	WORK	PAGE	MEASURE
Bernstein	"Jeremiah" Symphony	24	[14]	**Piston**	Concerto for Orchestra	23	2
Harris	When Johnny Comes			**Piston**	Symphony No. 2	50	6
	Marching Home	1	3	**Still**	Bells	17	1

SPONGE STICKS

COMPOSER	WORK	PAGE	MEASURE	COMPOSER	WORK	PAGE	MEASURE
Albéniz–Arbós	El Albaicín	39	[AA] 1f	**Ibert**	Escales	2	[1] 1f
Berlioz	Benvenuto Cellini	6	9			46	[41] 1f
	Overture	44	3	**Ibert**	Féerique	16	2
Berlioz	Harold en Italie	4	4	**Ibert**	La Ballade de la Geôle		
		60	5		de Reading	97	5
Berlioz	Roméo et Juliette	24	7	**Liszt**	Eine Faust-Symphonie	35	[K] 1f
		112	5			90	1
		212	8	**Mahler**	Symphony No. 2	50	3b [25]
Berlioz	Symphonie Fantastique	37	6	**Mahler**	Symphony No. 7	142	[154] 2f
		46	7	**Parodi**	Preludio ad una		
		129	7		Commedia	17	3b [I]
		160	1	**Rabaud**	La Procession Nocturne	9	5b [6]
Berlioz	The Roman Carnival			**Ravel**	Shéhérazade	38	[19]
	Overture	12	75	**Roussel**	Évocations, I	16	4
Berlioz	Three Pieces from "The	36	12	**Roussel**	Évocations, II	53	7
	Damnation of Faust"	40	3	**Roussel**	Évocations, III	95	[49] 4f
		47	2	**Roussel**	Pour une Fête de		
Bloch	America	116	[66]		Printemps	39	3
Casella	Italia	18	[10] 2f	**Roussel**	Symphonie en Sol		
Chabrier	España, Rhapsodie	20	[D]		mineur	67	[39] 5f
Charpentier	Impressions d'Italie	77	[3]	**Schreker**	The Birthday of the		
de Falla	El Retablo de Maese				Infanta, Suite	29	[125] 1f
	Pedro	44	[50]	**Strauss, R.**	Macbeth	17	8
Holst	Beni Mora, Oriental			**Strauss, R.**	Symphonia Domestica	118	[155]
	Suite	48	[12] 3f	**Strauss, R.**	Till Eulenspiegel's		
					Merry Pranks	55	[38] 4f

TIMPANI STICKS

COMPOSER	WORK	PAGE	MEASURE
Stravinsky	Le Sacre du Printemps	86	[104]

TRIANGLE STICK

Russell	Fugue for Eight		
	Percussion Instruments	2	[B] 8f

VERY HARD STICKS

Bernstein	"Jeremiah" Symphony	21	[10] 7f
		42	[35]

WIRE-BRUSH

Russell	Fugue for Eight		
	Percussion Instruments	2	[B]

PERCUSSION

WOOD(EN) STICKS

COMPOSER	WORK	PAGE	MEASURE	COMPOSER	WORK	PAGE	MEASURE
Atterberg	Ballade und Passacaglia	15	1	Mahler	Das Lied von der Erde	67	[8]
Balakirev–				Mahler	Symphony No. 2	36	[18]
Casella	Islamey	45	[43] 3f			114	[49]
Bartók	Violin Concerto	66	[106]			134	3
Bax	First Symphony	23	[F]	Mahler	Symphony No. 3	177	[32]
Bax	Second Symphony	53	3b [31]	Mahler	Symphony No. 5	108	3
Bax	Fifth Symphony	17	[11] 4f			170	4
		98	2b [1]	Mahler	Symphony No. 6	17	1b [10]
Berlioz	Benvenuto Cellini	17	1			67	[40] 3f
	Overture	47	1			202	4
Berlioz	Harold en Italie	31	1	Mahler	Symphony No. 7	32	[26] 1f
		126	1			139	[148]
		164	5			208	[247] 4f
Berlioz	Symphonie Fantastique	115	6	Piston	Symphony No. 2	12	[55]
		150	2			42	1
Bloch	America	114	1	Ravel	Shéhérazade	32	1
Britten	The Young Person's			Read	Symphony No. 1	89	7
	Guide to the			Rogers	Characters from Hans		
	Orchestra	61	[M]		Christian Andersen	27	5
Chabrier	España, Rhapsodie	3	7	Rogers	Once Upon a Time,		
Charpentier	Impressions d'Italie	71	1		Five Fairy Tales	41	1
Copland	Third Symphony	132	[115]	Schreker	The Birthday of the	22	[90]
Diamond	Fourth Symphony	70	[95] 3f		Infanta, Suite	40	[215]
		88	1	Sessions	Suite from "The Black		
Diamond	Timon of Athens	6	33		Maskers"	48	[48]
		12	77	Strauss, R.	Death and Transfigura-		
		33	233		tion	51	2
Dunn	Overture on Negro			Strauss, R.	Don Juan	4	2
	Themes	15	3	Strauss, R.	Macbeth	13	[C]
Elgar	Falstaff	75	3b [75]	Strauss, R.	Salomé's Dance	1	1
		101	2b [100]	Strauss, R.	Symphonia Domestica	69	11
de Falla	El Retablo de Maese					81	[105]
	Pedro	54	57			116	[152]
de Falla	Three Dances from			Strauss, R.	Till Eulenspiegel's	28	7
	"The Three-				Merry Pranks	53	[37] 2f
	Cornered Hat"	26	[3]	Stravinsky	Fire-Bird Suite (1919)	24	1
Gold	Allegorical Overture	1	2			36	[11] 1f
		30	1			64	[38]
Holst	Beni Mora, Oriental	5	4b [2]	Tansman	Sonatine Trans-		
	Suite	33	[4]		atlantique, III	3	[16]
Holst	The Ballet from "The			Vaughan	A London Symphony	31	[T]
	Perfect Fool"	25	[22] 1f	Williams		179	[Q]
Holst	The Planets	1	1	Vaughan	Job, A Masque for	21	2b [O]
		166	2	Williams	Dancing	50	[Cc]
		184	[VII]			60	[Gg]
Knipper	Symphony No. 4	51	1	Vaughan	Overture to "The		
Liszt	Eine Faust-Symphonie	8	4	Williams	Wasps"	42	307
		38	5	Walton	Façade, Suite No. 1	49	[F] 3f
		98	10			69	1b [J]
Luening	Two Symphonic Inter-						
	ludes	12	[45] 1f				

TIMPANI

WOOD TIMPANI STICKS

COMPOSER	WORK	PAGE	MEASURE
Hindemith	*Konzert für Orchester*	51	1

(8) 2-TIMPANI ROLL

* Correct notation

1 Player

COMPOSER	WORK	PAGE	MEASURE	COMPOSER	WORK	PAGE	MEASURE
Antheil	*Over the Plains*	17	2	**Loeffler**	*A Pagan Poem*	107	4
		30	[18]	**Moross**	*Paeans*	16	2
		62	3	**Read**	*Sketches of the City*	7	1b [4]
Antheil	*Symphony No. 5*	57	3	**Respighi**	*Ballata delle Gnomidi*	66	3
Barber	*Medea*	10	4	**Respighi**	*Vetrate di Chiesa*	90	3
Bartók	*Concerto for Orchestra*	53	[34]	**Russell**	*Fugue for Eight*	4	[D] 8f
Britten	*Sinfonia da Requiem*	59	[41]		*Percussion Instruments*	8	[G] 15f
Debussy	*Iberia*	88	1b [56]	**Schelling**	*A Victory Ball*	64	3
Debussy	*Jeux*	117	[81]			114	2b [36]
Debussy	*La Mer*	4	[2]			119	[38]
		82	[43]	**Schmitt**	*Mirages pour Orchestre,*	28	5
		85	[44] 4f		*No. 1*	36	2
		104	[51]	**Scriabin**	*Le Poème de l'Extase*	140	[29]
Debussy	*Nuages*	17	[10] 2f	**Scriabin**	*Prométhée, Le Poème*		
Debussy–	*Six Épigraphes*				*du Feu*	47	[31]
Ansermet	*Antiques*	16	[C]	**Sessions**	*Suite from "The Black*		
Delius	*Eventyr, Once Upon a*				*Maskers"*	71	[68]
	Time	21	4	**Shostakovich**	*Symphony No. 6*	22	1b [27]
Grofé	*Grand Canyon Suite*	135	1	**Sibelius**	*Symphony No. 5*	65	[S] 2f
		144	[13]			81	2b [E]
		152	[15]	**Sibelius**	*Symphony No. 7*	74	3
Harris	*When Johnny Comes*			**Sibelius**	*Tapiola*	39	[M] 2f
	Marching Home	60	2b [330]	**Sibelius**	*The Tempest, First Suite*	27	7
Honegger	*Le Dit des Jeux du*	8	[3] 3f			55	[A] 1f
	Monde	46	[2] 8f	**Stravinsky**	*Scènes de Ballet*	79	[127]
Honegger	*Le Roi David*	7	1	**Vaughan**	*Symphony in F minor*		
		16	1	**Williams**	*(No. 4)*	3	2b [2]
Ives	*"The Fourth of July"*			**Vaughan**	*Symphony in E minor*		
	from Symphony,			**Williams**	*(No. 6)*	95	[10]
	"Holidays"	17	[M] 1f	**Verdi**	*Messa da Requiem*	206	15
Khachaturian	*Gayne Ballet Suite*			**Walton**	*Symphony*	121	[90]
	No. 2	101	[26]			185	5

2 Players

COMPOSER	WORK	PAGE	MEASURE	COMPOSER	WORK	PAGE	MEASURE
Berg	*Violin Concerto*	51	2	**Mahler**	*Symphony No. 6*	237	[152] 4f
Davidson	*Auto Accident*	6	1	**Schönberg**	*Fünf Orchesterstücke*	11	1
Delius	*The Song of the High*	5	[2]	**Sibelius**	*Die Okeaniden*	2	1
	Hills	12	4b [8]	**Stravinsky**	*Le Sacre du Printemps*	73	[80]
Mahler	*Symphony No. 2*	31	[15]	**Walton**	*Symphony*	190	3

PERCUSSION

3 Players

COMPOSER	WORK	PAGE	MEASURE
Delius	*The Song of the High Hills*	33	[27] 3f

(9) WITH TWO STICKS

English	Italian	French	German
Double stick With two [2] sticks	Con due [2] bacchette	Avec deux [2] baguettes	Mit zwei [2] Schlägel

COMPOSER	WORK	PAGE	MEASURE	COMPOSER	WORK	PAGE	MEASURE
Berg	*Three Excerpts from "Wozzeck"*	52	1b [365]	**Diamond**	*Timon of Athens*	12	77
Bloch	*Trois Poèmes Juifs*	39	[3]			16	106
Britten	*Sinfonia da Requiem*	1	1			20	126
		20	3b [15]	**Ibert**	*Féerique*	15	5b [11]
Charpentier	*Impressions d'Italie*	71	1	**Mahler**	*Symphony No. 4*	146	318
Diamond	*Elegy in Memory of Maurice Ravel*	5	[30] 2f	**Mahler**	*Symphony No. 6*	238	[153] 1f
				Schelling	*A Victory Ball*	81	[25]
Diamond	*Music for Shakespeare's "Romeo and Juliet"*	3 13	1 [85] 1f	**Schreker**	*The Birthday of the Infanta, Suite*	34	[175]

(10) OTHER EFFECTS

English	Italian	French	German
Beat with maracas	Colpete colle marache	Frappez avec les maracas	Mit Maracas schlagen

Bernstein	*"Jeremiah" Symphony*	44	[37]

English	Italian	French	German
Two players (on same part)	Due esecutori [suonatori]	Deux exécutants	Zwei Spieler

Mahler	*Symphony No. 8*	70 217	3b [87] [219] 1f

Chapter 33

BELLS, GLOCKENSPIEL, MARIMBA, VIBRAPHONE, AND XYLOPHONE

(1) GLISSANDI

(for terminology see Chapter 8, page 68)

Glockenspiel

COMPOSER	WORK	PAGE	MEASURE	COMPOSER	WORK	PAGE	MEASURE
Read	*Sketches of the City*	23	2	**Siegmeister**	*Sunday in Brooklyn*	94	[120]

Xylophone

COMPOSER	WORK	PAGE	MEASURE	COMPOSER	WORK	PAGE	MEASURE
Bax	*Fourth Symphony*	115	[4] 5f	**Prokofieff**	*Ala et Lolly (Scythian Suite)*	47	2
Benjamin	*From San Domingo*	16	4			83	[54]
Benjamin	*Jamaican Rhumba*	17	5	**Prokofieff**	*Alexander Nevsky*	36	[24] 2f
Britten	*Sinfonia da Requiem*	52	3b [35]	**Ravel**	*Rapsodie Espagnole*	50	4
Britten	*The Young Person's Guide to the Orchestra*	46 / 61	11 / [M]	**Revueltas**	*Sensemayá*	31	[31]
				Riisager	*Torgot Dance*	3	1
						32	[140]
Cadman	*American Suite*	6	4b [5]	**Russell**	*Fugue for Eight Percussion Instruments*	3	[C]
Casella	*Paganiniana*	128	1				
Cesana	*Second American Symphony*	29	[22] 1f	**Sessions**	*Symphony for Orchestra (No. 1)*	48 / 66	[74] / [104]
Copland	*Dance Symphony*	46	[26] 11f	**Siegmeister**	*Western Suite*	37	2
Gould	*Latin-American Symphonette*	123	1	**Skilton**	*Suite Primeval, Part 1*	15 / 28	1b [B] / 7
Hanson	*"Merry Mount" Suite*	21	5	**Slonimsky**	*My Toy Balloon*	29	3
Holst	*The Ballet from "The Perfect Fool"*	37	2	**Stravinsky**	*Fire-Bird Suite (1919)*	38	[13]
				Stravinsky	*Les Noces*	47 / 81	3b [56] / 3
Kabalevsky	*Suite from "Colas Breugnon"*	109 / 112	[34] 3f / 3	**Stravinsky**	*Petrouchka Suite*	45 / 49	1b [34] / 1b [37]
Lambert	*The Rio Grande*	5 / 22	1 / 1b [11]	**Stravinsky**	*Scherzo à la Russe*	6 / 27	2b [6] / [22] 1f
Martinet	*Orphée*	1	1	**Taylor**	*Through the Looking Glass*	60	2
Mihalovici	*Divertissement pour Petit Orchestre*	41	2b [P]	**Walton**	*Façade, Suite No. 1*	60	1b [E]

173

PERCUSSION

Bells and Xylophone

COMPOSER	WORK	PAGE	MEASURE
Russell	*Fugue for Eight Percussion Instruments*	4	[D] 9f

Glockenspiel and Xylophone

COMPOSER	WORK	PAGE	MEASURE	COMPOSER	WORK	PAGE	MEASURE
Kodály	*Háry János Suite*	94	4	**Villa-Lobos**	*Uirapurú*	3	1
Rogers	*Once Upon a Time, Five Fairy Tales*	64	4				

(2) MUFFLED

English	Italian	French	German
Cover the metal with a silk cloth	Coprire le lamine con un pannello di seta	Couvrez les plaques avec une voile de soie	Mit einem Seidentuch die Platten überdeckt
Dampened with one hand; struck with the other			
Muffled with a piece of cloth	Coperto con un pezzo di tela	Voilée avec une pièce de toile	Gedämpft mit einem Seidentuch überdeckt
Muted: one player grasps tubes while another player strikes them			

Bells (Chimes)

Cowell	*Short Symphony (No. 4)*	5 13	1b [B] 4b [E]	**Moore**	*In Memoriam*	4	[C]

Glockenspiel

Schreker	*The Birthday of the Infanta, Suite*	18	[70]	**Stillman-Kelley**	*Gulliver—His Voyage to Lilliput*	88	1

Xylophone

Schreker	*The Birthday of the Infanta, Suite*	27	2b [110]	**Stillman-Kelley**	*Gulliver—His Voyage to Lilliput*	87	2

(3) OFF-STAGE

(for terminology see Chapter 11, page 75)

Bells

Mahler	*Symphony No. 3*	192	1	**Tchaikovsky**	*Manfred-Symphonie*	179	163
Mahler	*Symphony No. 6*	152 225	3 9				

BELLS, GLOCKENSPIEL, MARIMBA, VIBRAPHONE, AND XYLOPHONE

(4) STICK TYPES

(for terminology see Chapter 32, pages 166–7)

DRUM STICK

Bells

COMPOSER	WORK	PAGE	MEASURE
Balakirev–Casella	*Islamey*	64	[66]

HALF-HARD RUBBER STICKS

Bells

Russell	*Fugue for Eight Percussion Instruments*	3	[C] 7f

Xylophone

Russell	*Fugue for Eight Percussion Instruments*	I	9

HARD STICKS

Bells

Still	*Bells*	6	2

Vibraphone

Copland	*Music for Radio*	I	I

Xylophone

COMPOSER	WORK	PAGE	MEASURE	COMPOSER	WORK	PAGE	MEASURE
Cowell	*Short Symphony (No. 4)*	33	1	Rogers	*Once Upon a Time, Five Fairy Tales*	15	5b [12]

HARD RUBBER STICKS

Bells and Xylophone

Russell	*Fugue for Eight Percussion Instruments*	8	[G] 2f

175

PERCUSSION

LIGHT STICKS

Xylophone

COMPOSER	WORK	PAGE	MEASURE
Diamond	*Timon of Athens*	**17**	107

METAL STICKS

Bells

COMPOSER	WORK	PAGE	MEASURE	COMPOSER	WORK	PAGE	MEASURE
Copland	*Third Symphony*	**152**	[129] 1f	**Russell**	*Fugue for Eight*		
Holst	*The Planets*	**119**	[III] 7f		*Percussion Instruments*	**4**	[D] 9f

Glockenspiel

Maganini	*South Wind*	**2**	2

QUARTER-HARD RUBBER STICKS

Xylophone

Russell	*Fugue for Eight*		
	Percussion Instruments	**5**	[E] 1f

RATTAN STICKS

Xylophone

Rogers	*Once Upon a Time,*	**14**	3b [11]
	Five Fairy Tales	**30**	[19] 4f

RUBBER STICKS

Glockenspiel

Diamond	*Music for Shakespeare's*			**Diamond**	*Timon of Athens*	**23**	14f
	"Romeo and Juliet"	**28**	[55] 4f				

Xylophone

Chávez	*Sinfonia India*	**37**	[52]
		64	[90] 2f

SOFT STICKS

Bells

Siegmeister	*Sunday in Brooklyn*	**19**	[65] 2f	**Still**	*Bells*	**1**	4
						19	1b [21]

176

BELLS, GLOCKENSPIEL, MARIMBA, VIBRAPHONE, AND XYLOPHONE

Marimba

COMPOSER	WORK	PAGE	MEASURE	COMPOSER	WORK	PAGE	MEASURE
Gould	*Latin-American Symphonette*	**101**	[15] 1f	**Still**	*Bells*	**13** **20**	[13] [22]

Vibraphone

COMPOSER	WORK	PAGE	MEASURE
Still	*Bells*	**1** **4**	1 [5]

Xylophone

COMPOSER	WORK	PAGE	MEASURE	COMPOSER	WORK	PAGE	MEASURE
Hanson	*"Merry Mount" Suite*	**35**	[1]	**Siegmeister**	*Western Suite*	**71**	[50] 1f

SOFT FELT STICKS

Bells

Holst	*The Planets*	**125**	[VI]

STEEL STICKS

Bells

Cesana	*Second American Symphony*	**104**	[5]

TRIANGLE STICK

Bells

Rogers	*Characters from Hans Christian Andersen*	**16**	1b [9]

Glockenspiel

Rogers	*Characters from Hans Christian Andersen*	**6**	1

WOOD(EN) STICKS

Bells

Daniels	*Deep Forest*	**1**	5

Glockenspiel

Debussy–Ansermet	*Six Épigraphes Antiques*	**34**	2

177

PERCUSSION

(5) TREMOLANDI

Bells

COMPOSER	WORK	PAGE	MEASURE	COMPOSER	WORK	PAGE	MEASURE
Albéniz–Arbós	Fête-Dieu à Séville	11	5	**Siegmeister**	Sunday in Brooklyn	75	[60] 1f
		27	3				

Glockenspiel

COMPOSER	WORK	PAGE	MEASURE	COMPOSER	WORK	PAGE	MEASURE
Busoni	Rondo Arlecchinesco	11	3b [10]	**Read**	First Overture	57	[20] 2f
Converse	American Sketches	121	2	**Read**	Sketches of the City	21	3
Gould	Spirituals	41	2			26	[4] 2f
Grofé	Grand Canyon Suite	95	3	**Respighi**	The Fountains of Rome	11	2
		100	[4]	**Rogers**	Once Upon a Time,		
Ibert	Féerique	33	[22]		Five Fairy Tales	64	4
Inghelbrecht	El Greco	58	3	**Schreker**	The Birthday of the		
Janssen	New Year's Eve in				Infanta, Suite	54	[335]
	New York	51	[20] 1f	**Strauss, R.**	Also Sprach Zarathustra	107	2
Mahler	Symphony No. 6	119	7	**Strauss, R.**	Don Juan	14	4b [D]
Mahler	Symphony No. 7	27	2	**Weinberger**	Polka and Fugue from		
		229	[267]		"Schwanda, the		
Pizzetti	Concerto dell'Estate	45	[17]		Bagpiper"	2	[5] 1f
Ravel	Daphnis et Chloé,						
	Suite No. 2	125	1				

Marimba

COMPOSER	WORK	PAGE	MEASURE
Gould	Latin-American Symphonette	101	[15] 1f

Xylophone

COMPOSER	WORK	PAGE	MEASURE	COMPOSER	WORK	PAGE	MEASURE
Barber	Medea	19	[17] 5f	**Lambert**	The Rio Grande	18	[9]
Britten	Sinfonia da Requiem	48	[32]	**Liadov**	Baba-Yaga	14	4
Cadman	American Suite	5	[4]	**Liadov**	Kikimora	43	[44]
		18	5	**Mihalovici**	Divertissement pour		
Casella	La Donna Serpente,				Petit Orchestre	41	3b [P]
	II. Serie	49	1	**Pescara**	Tibet	24	3
Converse	American Sketches	13	[8] 2f	**Read**	First Overture	5	3
Copland	Dance Symphony	46	[26] 11f	**Revueltas**	Sensemayá	29	[30]
Diamond	Music for Shakespeare's					40	[37]
	"Romeo and Juliet"	16	[100] 1f	**Rogers**	Once Upon a Time,	14	3b [11]
Dukas	La Péri	64	[9]		Five Fairy Tales	30	[19] 4f
		119	[18] 2f			64	3
Dukelsky	Symphony No. 3	59	[24]	**Saint-Saëns**	Le Carnaval des		
Gillis	Symphony No. 5½	37	2b [R]		Animaux	50	5
Hanson	"Merry Mount" Suite	87	7	**Schmitt**	Mirages pour	9	[4]
Kabalevsky	Suite from "Colas				Orchestre, No. 2	41	[23]
	Breugnon"	152	[20]	**Schönberg**	A Survivor from Warsaw	2	9

178

Xylophone (contd.)

COMPOSER	WORK	PAGE	MEASURE	COMPOSER	WORK	PAGE	MEASURE
Sessions	Suite from "The Black Maskers"	33	3	**Wagenaar**	Sinfonietta for Small Orchestra	36	[9]
Sessions	Symphony No. II	37	2	**Wagner, J.**	Symphony Number One	40	4
Siegmeister	Sunday in Brooklyn	84	[90] 1f	**Walton**	Façade, Suite No. 1	51	4
Skilton	Suite Primeval, Part I	15	[B]			62	6
Stravinsky	Les Noces	44	[53]	**White**	Five Miniatures	6	4
Toch	The Chinese Flute	31	3				

Bells and Xylophone

COMPOSER	WORK	PAGE	MEASURE
Russell	Fugue for Eight Percussion Instruments	8	[G] 14f

(6) OTHER EFFECTS

Glockenspiel

English	Italian	French	German
Two, if necessary (ad lib.)	Due, anche se necessario (ad lib.)	Deux, si nécessaire (ad lib.)	Zwei, wenn nötig (ad lib.)

Riegger	Symphony No. 3	155	4b [185]

Vibraphone

English	Italian	French	German
Low (slow vibrato)	Vibrato lento	Vibrez lentement	Langsam vibrierend

Gould	Latin-American Symphonette	101	[15] 1 f

English	Italian	French	German
Pedal off; no resonance	Senza pedale; non risonanza	Sans pédale; non résonnant	Ohne Pedal; keine Resonanz

Gould	Spirituals	18	[G] 6f

Xylophone

English	Italian	French	German
Draw a bow across sharp edge at end of bar	Suonare col arco sul taglio del legno	Exécuté avec une archet sur la pointe du bois	Mit dem Bogen auf der scharfen Kaute des Holzes spielen

Russell	Fugue for Eight Percussion Instruments	4	[D]

English	Italian	French	German
Glissando across the resonators	Glissando sui risonatori	Glissez sur les résonateurs	Glissando über die Resonatoren

Russell	Fugue for Eight Percussion Instruments	4	[D] 9f

Chapter 34

CYMBALS

(1) DAMPENED

(for terminology and notation see Chapter 32, page 163)

COMPOSER	WORK	PAGE	MEASURE
Albéniz	Catalonia, Suite No. 1	39	[48]
Berlioz	Three Pieces from "The Damnation of Faust"	61	1
Bloch	America	118	[67] 1f
Casella	La Donna Serpente, I. Serie	33	1b [32]
Casella	La Donna Serpente, II. Serie	4 49	[4] [64]
Dunn	Overture on Negro Themes	44	[T] 8f
Dvořák	Carnival Overture	79	6
Enesco	Ière Rhapsodie Roumaine	65	1
Franck	Le Chasseur Maudit	50	1
Gershwin	An American in Paris	4	[3]
Gillis	Symphony No. 5½	14 64	6 2
Gould	Philharmonic Waltzes	1	6
Hanson	"Merry Mount" Suite	42	[5]
Ibert	Ouverture de Fête	43	[15]
Janssen	New Year's Eve in New York	31	[12]
Lambert	The Rio Grande	20	[10]
Lekeu	Fantaisie sur Deux Airs Populaires Angevins	11 14	6 [E]
Loeffler	Evocation	28	[24] 2f
Mahler	Symphony No. 1	77	10

COMPOSER	WORK	PAGE	MEASURE
Mahler	Symphony No. 5	246	5
Mahler	Symphony No. 7	80	[68] 2f
Malipiero	Impressioni dal Vero, 3^a Parte	31	9
Malipiero	Pause del Silenzio	29	177
Piston	Concerto for Orchestra	27 40	2 4
Piston	Suite from the Ballet, "The Incredible Flutist"	23	3
Respighi	Feste Romane	153	5
Rivier	Ouverture pour un don Quichotte	76	7
Schelling	A Victory Ball	35 100	3 [31]
Sessions	Suite from "The Black Maskers"	45	1b [45]
Siegmeister	Sunday in Brooklyn	39 59 86	4b [80] [10] 3f [95] 1f
Siegmeister	Western Suite	69	[45] 1f
Stravinsky	Les Noces	25 90	1b [30] 2
Stravinsky	Ragtime	15	[38] 7f
Stravinsky	Renard	76	1b [50]
Varèse	Hyperprism	6	1

(2) METHODS OF STRIKING

English	Italian	French	German
At (the) edge	All'estremità	Au bord	Am Rand
At (the) rim	In margine	Blousée	Auf dem Rand
On (the) edge	Sul bordo	Blouser	
(R)	Sull'orlo	Blousez	
		Blousez avec baguette(s)	
		Cymbale blousée	
		Sur le bord [rebord]	

CYMBALS

(2) METHODS OF STRIKING (contd.)

COMPOSER	WORK	PAGE	MEASURE	COMPOSER	WORK	PAGE	MEASURE
Bartók	*Concerto for Orchestra*	147	[625]	**Rivier**	*Ouverture pour un don*	4	[1] 2f
Bartók	*Concerto for Piano and*	19	1b [21]		*Quichotte*	46	[21] 1f
	Orchestra	52	2	**Rogers**	*Characters from Hans*		
		54	3b [5]		*Christian Andersen*	6	1
Bartók	*Violin Concerto*	85	[126]	**Varèse**	*Intégrales*	2	1
Rivier	*Chant Funèbre*	5	2b [3]			32	[15] 2f
Rivier	*Danse*	6	7b [6]	**Weiss**	*American Life*	14	2
		22	[19] 2f				

English	Italian	French	German
Barely touched	Appena toccata	A peine frôlé	Leicht berühren
Lightly rubbed		Frôlé	

COMPOSER	WORK	PAGE	MEASURE
Gershwin	*Concerto in F for Piano and Orchestra*	15	2b [11]

English	Italian	French	German
Brushed with a silver coin	Toccata colla moneta d'argenta	Broussez avec une pièce d'argent	Mit einer Silbermünze leicht berühren

White	*Five Miniatures*	3	3

English	Italian	French	German
Brushed with stick	Toccata colla bacchetta	Broussez avec la baguette	Mit einem Stock leicht berühren

McDonald	*Rhumba from 2nd Symphony*	6	3

English	Italian	French	German
Clash(ed)	A 2	A l'ordinaire	Becken gewöhnlich
Crash(ed)	Due [2] Piatti	Avec plateaux	Beide Schalen
Cymbal-pair	Due [2] piatti al [nel] modo	Cymbales à main	Gewöhnlich
Struck together	ordinario	Cymbale contre Cymbale	Mit den Tellern
Together	Modo ordinario	Cymbales plateaux	Mit Teller(n)
Two [2] cymbals (free)	Ordinario	Frappée à l'ordinaire	Normal
Two [2] cymbals clashed	Piatti a due [a 2]	Jeu ordinaire	Piatti ausklingen
Two [2] plate clash [crash]	Piatto con [contro] piatto	Les deux [2] cymbales	Zwei [2] Becken mit Teller(n)
Without stick		[plateaux]	
With plates		Sans baguette(s)	
		Une paire	

Albéniz–Arbós	*El Albaicín*	27	4b [Q]
Bartók	*Concerto for Piano and*		
	Orchestra	47	[49]
Bax	*The Garden of Fand*	71	2
Berg	*Violin Concerto*	50	1b [255]
Bloch	*America*	55	1
		118	[67] 1f

Britten	*Sinfonia da Requiem*	17	[13]
		61	[42]
Casella	*Italia*	30	[29]
Casella	*La Donna Serpente,*	9	[14]
	I. Serie	28	[29]
Casella	*La Donna Serpente,*	4	[4]
	II. Serie	49	[64]

PERCUSSION

(2) METHODS OF STRIKING (contd.)

COMPOSER	WORK	PAGE	MEASURE
Casella	*Paganiniana*	61	2
Chabrier	*España, Rhapsodie*	25	6
Copland	*Four Dance Episodes from "Rodeo"*	38	1b [36]
Cowell	*Short Symphony (No. 4)*	73	[P]
Delannoy	*Figures Sonores*	49	4
de Falla	*Three Dances from "The Three-Cornered Hat"*	61	[11]
Gershwin	*Rhapsody in Blue*	5	[3]
		41	1
Goossens	*Sinfonietta*	59	[30]
Grofé	*Grand Canyon Suite*	161	[18]
Hanson	*"Merry Mount" Suite*	7	[4]
Harsanyi	*Ouverture Symphonique*	3	[10]
Hindemith	*Symphony in E-Flat*	24	2
Holst	*A Somerset Rhapsody*	19	[11]
Ibert	*Escales*	26	[21] 4f
		82	[71]
Ibert	*Féerique*	31	[21]
Ibert	*La Ballade de la Geôle de Reading*	22	[14]
		35	[23]
		64	[46] 1f
Ireland	*A London Overture*	53	[35]
Johnson	*Imagery*	48	2
Liadov	*Baba-Yaga*	37	5
Lopatnikoff	*Sinfonietta*	56	1
		90	3
Mahler	*Symphony No. 1*	124	1b [24]
		157	[52]
Mahler	*Symphony No. 2*	7	2b [2]
Mahler	*Symphony No. 3*	4	5b [1]
		36	4
		88	[66] 3f
Mahler	*Symphony No. 7*	43	2b [37]
Mahler	*Symphony No. 8*	55	[64]

COMPOSER	WORK	PAGE	MEASURE
Martinet	*Orphée*	83	2
Milhaud	*Deuxième Concerto pour Violoncelle et Orchestre*	115	[120] 2f
Milhaud	*Les Choéphores*	127	3
Milhaud	*2me Suite Symphonique*	85	5b [44]
Moeran	*Symphony in G minor*	64	4b [34]
Moore	*Village Music*	20	3
Mussorgsky	*Night on the Bald Mountain*	46	[M]
Pierné	*Divertissements sur un Thème Pastoral*	62	[40]
Poot	*Symphonie*	84	2
Respighi	*Feste Romane*	106	4
Roussel	*Suite en Fa*	14	[7]
		51	[22]
Saint-Saëns	*La Jeunesse d'Hercule*	73	7
Schelling	*A Victory Ball*	20	3
		100	[31]
Schlein	*Dance Overture*	12	2b [170]
Shostakovich	*The Golden Age, Ballet Suite*	59	3
Sibelius	*The Tempest, Prelude*	14	1
Siegmeister	*Western Suite*	26	2b [10]
		46	2
		61	1b [20]
Strauss, R.	*Don Juan*	7	5
Stravinsky	*Ragtime*	15	[38] 7f
Tchaikovsky	*Hamlet*	29	4
Tchaikovsky	*Manfred-Symphonie*	206	41
Thomson	*Louisiana Story Suite*	74	65
Thomson	*Orchestra Suite from "The Plow that Broke the Plains"*	13	[8] 1f
Toch	*The Chinese Flute*	41	1
Vaughan Williams	*Pastoral Symphony*	79	4b [V]

English	Italian	French	German
Attach the cymb. to the foot-beater	I Piatto uniti alla (gran) cassa	Accrochez la Cymb. au pied	Becken an der grosse Trommel befestigt (aber ohne Trommel geschlagen)
Cymbal (struck) attached to bass drum	Piatto fissato alla (gran) cassa	Cymbale fixée à la Grosse caisse	Becken angebunden—von Einem geschlagen
Cymbal, fixed		Grosse caisse à pied avec cymbale	Die Becken an der grossen Trommel anzuhängen
Cymbal alone	Piatto solo	Cymbale seule	Becken allein

Berg	*Violin Concerto*	42	2b [205]	Ives	*Three Places in New England*	
Harsanyi	*Ouverture Symphonique*	33	1b [135]			21	1

182

CYMBALS

(2) METHODS OF STRIKING (contd.)

COMPOSER	WORK	PAGE	MEASURE	COMPOSER	WORK	PAGE	MEASURE
Mahler	*Symphony No. 1*	81	[6]	**Mahler**	*Symphony No. 7*	231	[269]
Mahler	*Symphony No. 3*	17	6b [13]	**Rogers**	*Once Upon a Time,*		
		68	1b [49]		*Five Fairy Tales*	3	[2]
		93	[70]	**Stravinsky**	*Histoire du Soldat*	39	1
Mahler	*Symphony No. 5*	15	3				

English	*Italian*	*French*	*German*
Hit with triangle	Colpo con triangolo	Frappée avec la triangle	Mit dem Triangel geschlagen

COMPOSER	WORK	PAGE	MEASURE
Walton	*Façade, Suite No. 1*	34	4

English	*Italian*	*French*	*German*
In the air	In aria	En l'air	In der Luft

COMPOSER	WORK	PAGE	MEASURE	COMPOSER	WORK	PAGE	MEASURE
Albéniz–Arbós	*El Albaicín*	8	[C]	**Dukelsky**	*Symphony No. 3*	73	1b [30]
		28	1b [R]			149	3
Albéniz–Arbós	*Fête-Dieu à Séville*	11	5	**Slonimsky**	*My Toy Balloon*	23	1

English	*Italian*	*French*	*German*
On (the) center	Sul mezzo	Au milieu	In der Mitte
On (the) dome	Sulla cupola	Sur la protubérance	Auf die Kuppel

COMPOSER	WORK	PAGE	MEASURE	COMPOSER	WORK	PAGE	MEASURE
Bartók	*Concerto for Piano and*			**Bartók**	*Violin Concerto*	109	[386]
	Orchestra	53	[4] 3f	**Varèse**	*Intégrales*	2	1

English	*Italian*	*French*	*German*
Rubbed together	Trillo (a 2)	Agitées l'une contre l'autre	Triller (zu 2)
Trill(ed)	tr.	Frôlée(s) [Frôlez]	Tr.
tr.		Frôlées l'une contre l'autre	
Trill a 2		Frottée(s) [Frottez]	
Two [2] plates together		Frottées l'une contre l'autre	

COMPOSER	WORK	PAGE	MEASURE	COMPOSER	WORK	PAGE	MEASURE
Bartók	*Second Rhapsody for*			**Rosenthal**	*Les Petits Métiers*	64	1
	Violin and Orchestra	37	[25] 2f	**Varèse**	*Hyperprism*	3	6
Bartók	*Violin Concerto*	53	[385]	**Varèse**	*Intégrales*	10	2
Mahler	*Symphony No. 6*	257	5b [163]			17	[7] 3f
Mussorgsky–	*Pictures at an*			**Varèse**	*Ionisation*	14	[9] 1f
Ravel	*Exhibition*	83	2	**Vaughan**			
Respighi	*Feste Romane*	91	5	**Williams**	*A London Symphony*	96	1
Rogers	*Once Upon a Time,*						
	Five Fairy Tales	57	1b [33]				

PERCUSSION

(2) METHODS OF STRIKING (contd.)

English	Italian	French	German
Struck with the wood	Colpete con legno	Frappée avec le bois	Mit Holz geschlagen
With (the) handle of (the) stick	Col mancio della mazza	Avec le manche de la mailloche	Mit dem Stiel des Klöppels
With wooden end of (the) stick	Coll'estremità di legno della bacchetta	Coup avec le bois d'une baguette	Ein Becken mit dem Holzschaft des Schlägels berühren

COMPOSER	WORK	PAGE	MEASURE	COMPOSER	WORK	PAGE	MEASURE
Bartók	Concerto for Piano and Orchestra	53	[4] 3f	d'Indy	Jour d'été à la Montagne	102	[49]
Bartók	Deux Images	41	[15] 7f	Inghelbrecht	Pour le jour de la première neige au vieux Japon	21	[11] 1f
Bartók	Deux Portraits	29	[8]				
		35	[12] 1f				
Bartók	Vier Orchesterstücke	48	[16] 5f	Inghelbrecht	Rapsodie de Printemps	2	2
Debussy–Ansermet	Six Épigraphes Antiques	11	3	Milhaud	Les Choéphores	120	3
				Schmitt	Rapsodie Viennoise	23	6

English	Italian	French	German
With (the) hand	Colla mano	Avec la main	Mit der Hand

COMPOSER	WORK	PAGE	MEASURE
Bartók	Dance Suite	43	[31]

English	Italian	French	German
With thick end of (the) stick	Coll'estremità grossa della bacchetta	Avec l'extrémité grosse de la baguette	Mit dem dicken Ende des Stockes

COMPOSER	WORK	PAGE	MEASURE	COMPOSER	WORK	PAGE	MEASURE
Barber	Medea	46	36	Bartók	Concerto for Orchestra	20	3
		60	3			75	[112]
						147	[625]

English	Italian	French	German
With thin end of (the) stick	Coll'estremità sottile della bacchettta	Avec l'extrémité mince de la baguette	Mit dem dünnen Ende des Stockes

COMPOSER	WORK	PAGE	MEASURE
Bartók	Violin Concerto	109	[386]

(3) STICK TYPES

(for terminology see Chapter 32, pages 166–7)

BASS DRUM STICKS

COMPOSER	WORK	PAGE	MEASURE	COMPOSER	WORK	PAGE	MEASURE
Barber	Second Essay for Orchestra	38	1	Ravel	Daphnis et Chloé, Suite No. 2	65	[192]
Debussy	Jeux	64	[43]	Saint-Saëns	La Jeunesse d'Hercule	67	2
Debussy	La Mer	132	[61]	Walton	Portsmouth Point Overture	2	1
Debussy	Rondes de Printemps	18	1b [11]				
MacDowell	2nd Suite (Indian)	83	[C] 2f				

CYMBALS

DRUMSTICKS

COMPOSER	WORK	PAGE	MEASURE	COMPOSER	WORK	PAGE	MEASURE
Albéniz–Arbós	*El Albaicín*	27	[Q] 2f	**d'Indy**	*Symphony on a French*		
Albéniz–Arbós	*Fête-Dieu à Séville*	35	9		*Mountain Air*	71	3
		41	2	**Inghelbrecht**	*El Greco*	6	[3]
Albéniz–Arbós	*Navarre*	3	4	**Ireland**	*Symphonic Rhapsody,*	5	4
Bax	*First Symphony*	11	[C]		*"Mai-Dun"*	48	4
Bax	*Third Symphony*	12	[11] 1f	**Janssen**	*New Year's Eve in*		
		110	[28] 7f		*New York*	44	1
Bax	*Fourth Symphony*	54	5	**Lekeu**	*Fantaisie sur Deux Airs*		
Bax	*In the Faery Hills*	57	3		*Populaires Angevins*	9	[C]
Bax	*The Garden of Fand*	17	2	**Malipiero**	*Impressioni dal Vero,*		
Casella	*La Donna Serpente,*				*3ª Parte*	1	2
	II. Serie	49	1	**Malipiero**	*Pause del Silenzio*	28	167
Casella	*Paganiniana*	87	[14]	**Malipiero**	*Seconda Sinfonia*		
		154	[29]		*(Elegiaca)*	40	[560] 2f
Cesana	*Second American*			**Martinet**	*Orphée*	77	[12] 3f
	Symphony	136	[25]	**Moeran**	*Symphony in G minor*	45	6
Chabrier	*España, Rhapsodie*	12	7			100	1
Daniels	*Deep Forest*	12	[K]	**Parodi**	*Preludio ad una*		
Delius	*Eventyr, Once Upon a*	12	4		*Commedia*	22	1
	Time	31	1b [11]	**Ravel**	*Ma Mère l'Oye*	32	5
Gershwin	*An American in Paris*	30	[28]	**Respighi**	*Belfagor, Ouverture per*		
Hindemith	*Neues vom Tage*	5	[A]		*Orchestra*	11	[4]
		23	[E]	**Schönberg**	*A Survivor from Warsaw*	11	50
Honegger	*Le Dit des Jeux du*			**Varèse**	*Intégrales*	5	2
	Monde	45	4	**Walton**	*Façade, Suite No. 1*	51	4
Honegger	*Le Roi David*	67	[6]				

FELT STICKS

COMPOSER	WORK	PAGE	MEASURE	COMPOSER	WORK	PAGE	MEASURE
Cesana	*Second American*	16	[14]	**Holst**	*The Ballet from "The*		
	Symphony	133	3		*Perfect Fool"*	26	5
Holst	*Beni Mora, Oriental*			**Holst**	*The Planets*	167	[II]
	Suite	29	11				

HARD STICKS

COMPOSER	WORK	PAGE	MEASURE	COMPOSER	WORK	PAGE	MEASURE
Converse	*American Sketches*	17	4	**Copland**	*Lincoln Portrait*	33	[190] 1f
		63	[9] 1f	**Copland**	*Statements*	4	[3]
Copland	*An Outdoor Overture*	44	[260] 1f	**Copland**	*Third Symphony*	26	3
Copland	*Appalachian Spring*	40	5			64	2b [49]
Copland	*Billy the Kid Ballet*			**Dukelsky**	*Symphony No. 3*	58	4
	Suite	20	[14]	**Gershwin**	*An American in Paris*	10	3
Copland	*El Salón México*	1	1	**Grofé**	*Grand Canyon Suite*	142	[12]
		16	[16]	**Morris**	*Prospice Symphony*	40	3
		39	[37]	**Piket**	*Curtain Raiser to an*	4	3
Copland	*First Symphony*	46	[33] 2f		*American Play*	13	2
Copland	*Four Dance Episodes*	1	1			41	[270]
	from "Rodeo"	50	5	**Siegmeister**	*From my Window*	47	4
		69	1	**Siegmeister**	*Ozark Set*	82	[85]

185

PERCUSSION

HARD STICKS (contd.)

COMPOSER	WORK	PAGE	MEASURE	COMPOSER	WORK	PAGE	MEASURE
Siegmeister	Sunday in Brooklyn	23	2	Taylor	Ballet Music from		
		59	[10] 3		"Casanova"	21	3
		86	[95] 1f	Thomson	Louisiana Story Suite	18	103
Siegmeister	Western Suite	11	1	Thomson	Orchestra Suite from		
		39	1		"The Plow that Broke		
		69	[45] 1f		the Plains"	31	[26]
Still	Poem for Orchestra	5	4	Vaughan			
Stravinsky	Chant du Rossignol	20	[21] 3f	Williams	A London Symphony	164	3

HARD RUBBER XYLOPHONE MALLETS

COMPOSER	WORK	PAGE	MEASURE
Sowerby	Prairie	30	[176]

HEAVY MALLET [WOODEN HAMMER]

COMPOSER	WORK	PAGE	MEASURE	COMPOSER	WORK	PAGE	MEASURE
Lambert	The Rio Grande	37	[5]	Pick-Mangiagalli	Notturno e Rondo Fantastico	19	2

IRON STICKS

COMPOSER	WORK	PAGE	MEASURE	COMPOSER	WORK	PAGE	MEASURE
Respighi	Ballata delle Gnomidi	11	3	Respighi	Feste Romane	114	[34] 2f
		62	[18] 1f				

LEATHER STICKS

COMPOSER	WORK	PAGE	MEASURE	COMPOSER	WORK	PAGE	MEASURE
Piston	Suite for Orchestra	7	[B]	Poulenc	Concerto pour deux		
		26	5		Pianos et Orchestre	106	[68]

METAL STICKS

COMPOSER	WORK	PAGE	MEASURE	COMPOSER	WORK	PAGE	MEASURE
Copland	Third Symphony	111	[100] 2f	Strang	Percussion Music	21	1
Kay	Suite for Orchestra	27	2b [26]	Stravinsky	Les Noces	88	[96] 4f
Starokadomsky	Concerto for Orchestra	88	1b [62]				

ORDINARY [REGULAR, USUAL] STICKS

COMPOSER	WORK	PAGE	MEASURE	COMPOSER	WORK	PAGE	MEASURE
Albéniz	Catalonia, Suite No. 1	51	[63] 1f	Casella	La Donna Serpente,		
Bax	In the Faery Hills	23	2		I. Serie	17	[19]
Bax	Second Symphony	113	2	Cowell	Short Symphony (No. 4)	1	2
Bax	Sixth Symphony	8	4	Chabrier	España, Rhapsodie	24	5
		25	2b [21]	Chabrier	Joyeuse Marche	12	6
Bloch	America	33	5			24	1b [I]
		114	1	Chabrier	Suite Pastorale	65	4
Bloch	Evocations	22	[17] 5f	de Falla	Three Dances from "The		
Borodin	Polovetzian Dances				Three-Cornered		
	from "Prince Igor"	26	[E]		Hat"	42	[3]

CYMBALS

ORDINARY [REGULAR, USUAL] STICKS (contd.)

COMPOSER	WORK	PAGE	MEASURE	COMPOSER	WORK	PAGE	MEASURE
Gershwin	An American in Paris	3	[2]	Ravel	Concerto pour Piano et	3	[1]
		50	[45] 4f		Orchestre	76	7
Gershwin	Concerto in F for Piano	15	2b [11]	Ravel	Ma Mère l'Oye	51	7
	and Orchestra	67	4	Respighi	Ballata delle Gnomidi	1	1
		90	[9] 4f	Respighi	Feste Romane	94	4
Harris	Third Symphony	42	1			139	[43]
Ibert	Escales	25	[20]	Respighi	The Fountains of Rome	32	[11] 2f
		81	[70]	Respighi	The Pines of Rome	35	[10] 3f
Ireland	A London Overture	5	[2]	Rieti	L'Arca di Noè	13	3
		44	[28]	Rieti	Sinfonia No. 5	13	[14] 4f
Kabalevsky	Symphony No. 2	5	3			39	[46]
		40	[36]	Rimsky-Korsakoff	Dance of the Buffoons	10	12
Khachaturian	Gayne Ballet Suite No. 1-A	27	[13]	Rimsky-Korsakoff	Le Coq d'Or Suite	6	[1] 2f
Kodály	Háry János Suite	32	2			102	[60]
Kodály	Psalmus Hungaricus	31	2	Rimsky-Korsakoff	Scheherazade	182	230
		52	[31] 1f	Rimsky-Korsakoff	Symphony No. 2, "Antar"	11	4b [G]
Liadov	Baba-Yaga	36	4	Saint-Saëns	Danse Macabre	5	[A] 4f
Mussorgsky	Night on the Bald Mountain	35	[H]	Saint-Saëns	3e Symphonie en Ut mineur	86	2b [E]
		53	269	Schönberg	Theme and Variations	57	271
Pierné	Divertissements sur un Thème Pastorale	54	2b [35]	Shepherd	Horizons	12	4
Prokofieff	Alexander Nevsky	137	[81] 1f			64	3
		145	[85]			95	3
Prokofieff	Cinderella Suite No. 1	68	[52]			150	[P] 2f
		97	[78] 5f	Sibelius	Lemminkainen Journeys Homeward	25	[F]
Prokofieff	Peter and the Wolf	50	[39]				
		68	[48] 1f	Sibelius	The Tempest, First Suite	49	2
Prokofieff	Romeo and Juliet, Suite No. 1	64	[42]	Smetana	The Moldau	85	321
Prokofieff	Summer Day Suite	58	2	Stravinsky	Feuerwerk	18	3b [18]
Prokofieff	Symphony No. 5	74	[42]	Tchaikovsky	Hamlet	28	2
		206	[113]				

PADDED STICKS

COMPOSER	WORK	PAGE	MEASURE
Johnson	Imagery	45	3

PLUSH STICKS

COMPOSER	WORK	PAGE	MEASURE
Casella	Paganiniana	139	[19] 2f

RAWHIDE STICKS

COMPOSER	WORK	PAGE	MEASURE
Milhaud	Les Choéphores	131	1

RAWHIDE TIMPANI STICKS

COMPOSER	WORK	PAGE	MEASURE
Milhaud	Les Choéphores	101	1

PERCUSSION

SHORT STICKS

COMPOSER	WORK	PAGE	MEASURE
Gershwin	Concerto in F for Piano and Orchestra	11	[8]

SNARE DRUM STICKS

COMPOSER	WORK	PAGE	MEASURE	COMPOSER	WORK	PAGE	MEASURE
Barber	Medea	46	[36]	Milhaud	Cinq Études pour Piano et Orchestre	5	1
		60	3	Piston	Concerto for Orchestra	34	8
Bartók	Concerto for Orchestra	20	3	Poot	Symphonie	41	4
		75	[112]			83	5
		147	[625]	Poulenc	Concerto pour deux		
Bartók	Violin Concerto	109	[386]		Pianos et Orchestre	75	[48]
Casella	La Donna Serpente, I. Serie	26	3b [27]	Prokofieff	Ala et Lolly (Scythian Suite)	3	1
Copland	Concerto for Piano and Orchestra	35	[24]			107	[72]
		61	[47]	Prokofieff	Romeo and Juliet, Suite No. 1	118	4
Copland	Dance Symphony	82	2	Russell	Fugue for Eight Percussion Instruments	2	[B]
Copland	Music for the Theatre	9	3			7	[F] 9f
		38	5	Schmitt	Mirages pour Orchestre, No. 2	22	3b [12]
		47	3	Sessions	Suite from "The Black Maskers"	33	3
		74	6			106	1
Delannoy	Figures Sonores			Skilton	Suite Primeval, Part I	28	7
de Falla	Three Dances from "The Three-Cornered Hat"	92	3	Sowerby	Prairie	34	3
Fernandez	Batuque	11	[9]	Stravinsky	Petrouchka Suite	14	[5]
Gershwin	An American in Paris	94	6	Thomson	Louisiana Story Suite	82	90
Grofé	Grand Canyon Suite	21	[8]	Varèse	Hyperprism	17	7
Hindemith	Symphony in E-Flat	1	4	Varèse	Intégrales	3	1b [1]
Johnson	Imagery	46	5			26	1
Kabalevsky	The Comedians	94	[83]			32	[15] 2f
Loeffler	Evocation	9	[Q] 1f	Vaughan Williams	A London Symphony	9	1b [D]
Lopatnikoff	Sinfonietta	7	4			70	2b [TT]
		28	1b [120]	Walton	Façade, Suite No. 2	1	1
		80	2				

SOFT STICKS

COMPOSER	WORK	PAGE	MEASURE	COMPOSER	WORK	PAGE	MEASURE
Antheil	Symphony No. 5	38	[22] 4f	Copland	Dance Symphony	29	[15]
Barber	First Symphony	83	4	Copland	Statements	13	3
Barber	Music for a Scene from Shelley	1	1			27	[3] 5f
		13	76	Copland	Third Symphony	35	1b [27]
Barber	Overture to "The School for Scandal"	1	4	Debussy-Ansermet	Six Épigraphes Antiques	11	3
Barber	Second Essay for Orchestra	33	[20]			27	2
Britten	Four Sea Interludes from "Peter Grimes"	2	1	Dello Joio	Variations, Chaconne, and Finale	59	[80] 1f
Britten	Sinfonia da Requiem	12	3b [9]	Dukelsky	Symphony No. 3	25	1b [11]
		35	3			94	[39] 4f
Carter	Holiday Overture	20	2			134	5
Copland	Concerto for Piano and Orchestra	53	2	Engel	The Creation	13	3
						25	1
						45	[26]
				Ferguson	Partita for Orchestra	36	1

CYMBALS

SOFT STICKS (contd.)

COMPOSER	WORK	PAGE	MEASURE	COMPOSER	WORK	PAGE	MEASURE
Gillis	Symphony No. 5½	72	1	Stravinsky	Les Noces	18	[21]
Ibert	Divertissement	9	10	Thomson	Louisiana Story Suite	7	33
Ireland	A London Overture	2	1			59	142
		23	4	Thomson	Orchestra Suite from		
Jacobi	Music Hall Overture	36	3		"The Plow that		
Janssen	New Year's Eve in				Broke the Plains"	27	2b [21]
	New York	64	[25] 2f	Thomson	The Seine at Night	26	[13] 1f
Moore	In Memoriam	18	[L]	Vaughan	A London Symphony	14	3b [G]
Moore	Village Music	28	[30]	Williams		50	[FF] 5f
Moross	Biguine	12	3			191	[W]
Morris	Prospice Symphony	55	1b [265]	Vaughan	Overture to "The		
Piston	Concerto for Orchestra	26	3b [2]	Williams	Wasps"	4	[B]
Ruggles	Sun-Treader	5	[15]	Vaughan	Symphony in E minor		
Shepherd	Horizons	89	3b [I]	Williams	(No. 6)	111	[22]
Siegmeister	From my Window	10	2b [50]	Walton	Façade, Suite No. 1	18	3
		39	1b [20]			50	[G] 1f
Siegmeister	Sunday in Brooklyn	38	2b [75]	Walton	Façade, Suite No. 2	26	4
Siegmeister	Western Suite	49	1	Walton	Portsmouth Point		
		77	2b [70]		Overture	10	[8]
Strang	Percussion Music	24	11	Weiss	American Life	5	2
Stravinsky	Fire-Bird Suite (1919)	60	[33] 1f				

SOFT FELT TIMPANI STICK

COMPOSER	WORK	PAGE	MEASURE
Russell	Fugue for Eight Percussion Instruments	5	[E] 1f

SOFT TIMPANI STICKS

COMPOSER	WORK	PAGE	MEASURE	COMPOSER	WORK	PAGE	MEASURE
Dohnányi	Variations on a Nursery Song	23	6	Hindemith	Ballet Overture, Cupid and Psyche	11	[I]
Enesco	Ière Rhapsodie Roumaine	19	[10] 2f				
		59	4				

SPONGE STICKS

COMPOSER	WORK	PAGE	MEASURE	COMPOSER	WORK	PAGE	MEASURE
Albéniz-Arbós	El Albaicín	7	[B]	Golestan	Concerto Roumain pour Violon et Orchestre	35	1b [200]
Berlioz	Roméo et Juliette	217	1	Goossens	Sinfonietta	81	2
Berlioz	Symphonie Fantastique	231	7	Hindemith	Mathis der Maler	11	[6] 1f
Berlioz	Three Pieces from "The			Hindemith	Symphony in E-Flat	16	8
	Damnation of Faust"	52	1	Honegger	Musique pour le		
Chabrier	Bourrée Fantastique	34	5		"Phaedre" de G.		
Chabrier	España, Rhapsodie	26	2		D'Annunzio	15	1
Chávez	Sinfonia India	34	[47]	Inghelbrecht	Sinfonia Breve No. 1	6	[4] 2f
Debussy	Jeux	67	6	Khachaturian	Gayne Ballet Suite	16	2
Diamond	Timon of Athens	33	233		No. 1	47	3b [5]
Dohnányi	Variations on a Nursery	86	[54] 6f	Khachaturian	Gayne Ballet Suite	18	[8]
	Song	125	6b [79]		No. 1-A	43	[4]
						82	[11]

PERCUSSION

SPONGE STICKS (contd.)

COMPOSER	WORK	PAGE	MEASURE	COMPOSER	WORK	PAGE	MEASURE
Khachaturian	*Gayne Ballet Suite*			**Milhaud**	*IIe Symphonie*	46	[190] 6f
	No. 2	38	I	**Moross**	*Paeans*	4	[C]
Lambert	*The Rio Grande*	5	I			10	I
Mahler	*Symphony No. I*	83	8b [9]	**Mussorgsky–**			
		91	[16]	**Ravel**	*Pictures at an Exhibition*	87	[71]
Mahler	*Symphony No. 2*	7	[2]	**Poulenc**	*Concerto pour deux*		
Mahler	*Symphony No. 3*	17	7b [13]		*Pianos et Orchestre*	36	I
		34	4	**Ravel**	*Daphnis et Chloé,*	32	[103]
		111	[5]		*Suite No. I*	61	[127]
Mahler	*Symphony No. 4*	27	149	**Ravel**	*Daphnis et Chloé,*	51	[180]
		73	8		*Suite No. 2*	78	[201]
		157	36	**Ravel**	*La Valse*	96	[73]
Mahler	*Symphony No. 5*	18	8	**Ravel**	*Shéhérazade*	32	I
		68	2b [11]			38	[19]
		112	I	**Ravel**	*Tzigane*	3	[4]
Mahler	*Symphony No. 6*	86	[53] 4f	**Ravel**	*Valses Nobles et*	9	[7] 3f
		149	I		*Sentimentales*	56	[55] 2f
Mahler	*Symphony No. 7*	42	[36] 3f	**Read**	*Symphony No. I*	I	I
		118	[111] 4f	**Rimsky–**			
Mahler	*Symphony No. 8*	52	[59]	**Korsakoff**	*Capriccio Espagnol*	42	I
		217	[219] 2f	**Roussel**	*Le Festin de l'Araignée*	44	3
Milhaud	*2me Suite Symphonique*	84	3b [43]	**Schreker**	*The Birthday of the*	18	[70]
Milhaud	*Les Choéphores*	162	I		*Infanta, Suite*	29	[125] 1f
Milhaud	*Opus Americanum*					61	[370] 1f
	No. 2	36	3b [225]	**Strauss, R.**	*Don Quixote*	74	3
Milhaud	*Ière Symphonie*	22	[85] 1f				
		70	[120] 4f				

STICK WITH FIBRE HEAD

COMPOSER	WORK	PAGE	MEASURE
Stravinsky	*Ragtime*	4	[2] 2f

TIMPANI STICKS

COMPOSER	WORK	PAGE	MEASURE	COMPOSER	WORK	PAGE	MEASURE
Aubert	*Saisons*	4	1b [4]	**Debussy**	*Fêtes*	57	5
Barber	*Second Symphony*	36	[26] 4f	**Debussy**	*Gigues*	2	4b [1]
		89	3b [29]	**Debussy**	*Jeux*	2	[1]
Bartók	*Concerto for Piano and*	19	1b [21]	**Debussy**	*La Mer*	121	1b [58]
	Orchestra	52	2	**Debussy**	*Le Martyre de Saint*		
Bloch	*Schelomo*	32	2		*Sébastien*	44	[20] 1f
Casella	*La Donna Serpente,*			**Debussy**	*Rapsodie pour Orchestre*		
	II. Serie	53	[67]		*et Saxophone*	20	2b [6]
Chávez	*Sinfonia de Antigona*	5	[2]	**Debussy**	*Rondes de Printemps*	4	[1] 1f
		13	[15] 1f	**Debussy–**	*Petite Suite*	6	2b [3]
Copland	*Dance Symphony*	77	I	**Busser**		49	I
Coppola	*Interlude Dramatique*	44	I	**Delannoy**	*Figures Sonores*	10	2
Coppola	*Suite Intima*	13	2	**Dukas**	*La Péri*	14	I
		36	2			72	[11]
Coppola	*Symphonie en La*					126	I
	mineur	9	5b [6]	**Dvořák**	*Die Waldtaube*	15	1b [5]

CYMBALS

TIMPANI STICKS (contd.)

COMPOSER	WORK	PAGE	MEASURE	COMPOSER	WORK	PAGE	MEASURE
Dvořák	*Der Wassermann*	7	[1]	**Riisager**	*Torgot Dance*	19	2b [90]
de Falla	*Nuits dans les Jardins d'Espagne*	20	[14]	**Rimsky-Korsakoff**	*Russian Easter Overture*	9	1
Fitelberg	*Symphony No. 1*	54	[31]			35	[K] 9f
Gretchaninoff	*Troisième Symphonie*	220	[28] 2f			74	3
Griffes	*The Pleasure Dome of Kubla Khan*	13	[F]	**Rivier**	*Chant Funèbre*	5	2b [3]
		39	2	**Rivier**	*Ouverture pour un don Quichotte*	49	[23]
Griffes	*The White Peacock*	13	1	**Rosenthal**	*Les Petits Métiers*	74	4
Grofé	*Grand Canyon Suite*	119	1	**Roussel**	*Évocations, III*	34	2
Harsanyi	*Suite pour Orchestre*	69	[125]	**Roussel**	*Le Festin de l'Araignée*	21	1b [26]
Hindemith	*Symphony in E-Flat*	36	3b [19]	**Roussel**	*4me Symphonie*	65	3
		118	3b [61]	**Roussel**	*Rapsodie Flamande*	26	5
Honegger	*Chant du Joie*	19	[9]	**Roussel**	*Suite en Fa*	2	[1]
Honegger	*Mouvement Symphonique No. 3*	1	1			83	[43]
Honegger	*Pacific 231*	1	1	**Roussel**	*Symphonie en Sol mineur*	11	[7] 5f
Honegger	*Suite d'Orchestre, "L'Impératrice aux Rochers"*	27	[2]			64	4
						87	4
						99	2
Ibert	*Escales*	4	[2] 1f	**Rudhyar**	*Sinfonietta*	30	7
		32	1b [27]	**Satie–Debussy**	*Gymnopédies*	4	2
Ibert	*Féerique*	3	[2] 1f	**Schelling**	*A Victory Ball*	9	2
d'Indy	*Symphony on a French Mountain Air*	75	[H]			36	7
		110	[Z] 10f	**Schlein**	*Dance Overture*	7	[60]
Knipper	*Symphony No. 4*	18	1b [15]	**Schmitt**	*Mirages pour Orchestre, No. 2*	77	[42] 1f
Lekeu	*Fantaisie sur Deux Airs Populaires Angevins*	40	5	**Sessions**	*Suite from "The Black Maskers"*	16	[14]
Luening	*Two Symphonic Interludes*	3	[5] 3f	**Sessions**	*Symphony for Orchestra (No. 1)*	48	[74] 2f
MacDowell	*2nd Suite (Indian)*	100	3b [K]	**Shostakovich**	*Symphony No. 5*	134	3
Maganini	*An Ornithological Suite*	31	3	**Shostakovich**	*Symphony No. 7*	59	3
Mahler	*Symphony No. 2*	171	3			152	[173] 7f
Mahler	*Symphony No. 6*	166	4	**Shostakovich**	*Symphony No. 9*	88	[67] 6f
Mahler	*Symphony No. 7*	80	[68] 1f	**Shostakovich**	*The Golden Age, Ballet Suite*	36	3
Miaskovsky	*Symphony No. 6*	125	10			53	[62]
Milhaud	*La Mort d'un Tyran*	12	49			62	[71]
Milhaud	*Sérénade pour Orchestre*	28	[5] 6f	**Sibelius**	*En Saga*	5	1
		44	[4]			83	[U]
Moore	*In Memoriam*	7	2b [E]	**Stravinsky**	*Chant du Rossignol*	35	[35]
Nystedt	*The Land of Suspense*	30	3b [12]	**Stravinsky**	*Petrouchka Suite*	101	[88]
Piston	*Concerto for Orchestra*	37	1			153	3b [129]
Poot	*Jazz-Music*	31	[12]	**Stravinsky**	*Scherzo Fantastique*	9	[9]
Poot	*Symphonie*	21	[10] 4f			55	[78]
		68	2b [31]	**Szymanowski**	*Symphonie Concertante pour Piano et Orchestre*	9	2b [5]
Poulenc	*Concert Champêtre pour Clavecin et Orchestre*	82	2b [9]			25	1
Poulenc	*Concerto pour deux Pianos et Orchestre*	24	[18]	**Tansman**	*Deux Moments Symphoniques*	11	2b [4]
Rabaud	*Divertissement sur des Chansons Russes*	17	[10] 2f	**Tchaikovsky**	*Francesca da Rimini*	19	8
		26	1			111	4
Respighi	*The Fountains of Rome*	10	[3]				

PERCUSSION

TIMPANI STICKS (contd.)

COMPOSER	WORK	PAGE	MEASURE	COMPOSER	WORK	PAGE	MEASURE
Tchaikovsky	*Manfred-Symphonie*	14	1	Wagenaar	*Sinfonietta for Small*	13	4
		204	3		*Orchestra*	36	[9]
		256	240	Walton	*Portsmouth Point*		
Tchaikovsky	*Mozartiana*	25	3		*Overture*	4	[3] 2f
Tchaikovsky	*Nutcracker Suite*	27	4	White	*Five Miniatures*	9	1

TRIANGLE STICK

COMPOSER	WORK	PAGE	MEASURE	COMPOSER	WORK	PAGE	MEASURE
Berg	*Violin Concerto*	10	1b [55]	Russell	*Three Dance Move-*		
Dukelsky	*Symphony No. 3*	121	2		*ments*	16	4
Harsanyi	*Suite pour Orchestre*	55	1	Schmitt	*Étude pour le "Palais*		
		82	2b [240]		*Hanté" d'Edgar Poe*	66	1
Inghelbrecht	*Pour le jour de la*			Schmitt	*Rapsodie Viennoise*	10	1
	première neige au			Stravinsky	*Fire-Bird Suite* (1919)	52	[26] 1f
	vieux Japon	28	[16]	Stravinsky	*Les Noces*	42	[51]
Khachaturian	*Gayne Ballet Suite*			Szymanowski	*Symphonie Concertante*	5	[2] 1f
	No. 1-A	36	3		*pour Piano et*	30	[17]
Lambert	*The Rio Grande*	11	3		*Orchestre*	67	[5]
Mahler	*Symphony No. 3*	144	2b [7]	Thomson	*Orchestra Suite from*		
Piston	*Concerto for Orchestra*	44	[9] 2f		*"The Plow that*		
Rogers	*Characters from Hans*	6	1		*Broke the Plains"*	29	[23] 2f
	Christian Andersen	11	2	Wagenaar	*Sinfonietta for Small*		
Rogers	*Once Upon a Time,*				*Orchestra*	17	[16]
	Five Fairy Tales	57	1b [33]				

TWO-HEADED STICK

COMPOSER	WORK	PAGE	MEASURE
Lambert	*The Rio Grande*	26	5b [E]

VERY SOFT TIMPANI STICKS

COMPOSER	WORK	PAGE	MEASURE
Hindemith	*Symphonic Meta-*		
	morphosis of Themes		
	by Weber	45	2

WIRE-BRUSH

COMPOSER	WORK	PAGE	MEASURE	COMPOSER	WORK	PAGE	MEASURE
Copland	*El Salón México*	3	[2]	Rogers	*Once Upon a Time,*		
Copland	*Four Dance Episodes*				*Five Fairy Tales*	30	[19] 2f
	from "Rodeo"	11	1	Siegmeister	*Western Suite*	12	[40] 1f
Engel	*The Creation*	67	1			57	3
Gershwin	*Rhapsody in Blue*	11	[9]	Stravinsky	*Ebony Concerto*	11	[14]
Inghelbrecht	*Sinfonia Breve No. 1*	53	[31]			26	11
		75	[42] 3f			39	[33]
				Walton	*Façade, Suite No. 2*	5	[C]

CYMBALS

WOOD(EN) STICKS

COMPOSER	WORK	PAGE	MEASURE	COMPOSER	WORK	PAGE	MEASURE
Bartók	*Dance Suite*	49	120	**Saint-Saëns**	*La Jeunesse d'Hercule*	19	1
		80	54	**Schelling**	*A Victory Ball*	5	1
		92	149			30	2
Bartók	*Second Rhapsody for Violin and Orchestra*	37	[25]	**Schuman, W.**	*Undertow*	43	6b [530]
Bartók	*Violin Concerto*	18	[111]	**Sessions**	*Suite from "The Black Maskers"*	64	[63]
		92	[208]	**Sessions**	*Symphony No. II*	102	2
Benjamin	*From San Domingo*	5	[A]	**Skilton**	*Suite Primeval, Part II*	81	3
Britten	*Sinfonia da Requiem*	53	5b [36]	**Strauss, R.**	*Also Sprach Zarathustra*	114	3
Casella	*Italia*	5	3	**Strauss, R.**	*Don Juan*	3	5
		28	[27] 2f			14	5b [D]
Chabrier	*España, Rhapsodie*	35	[H]			66	1
Ferguson	*Partita for Orchestra*	45	1			92	[Cc]
Harsanyi	*Suite pour Orchestre*	1	3	**Strauss, R.**	*Eine Alpensinfonie*	44	2
Honegger	*Horace Victorieux*	40	[16] 4f			118	[I]
Inghelbrecht	*El Greco*	17	2b [13]			139	[123]
Inghelbrecht	*Pour le jour de la première neige au vieux Japon*	24	4	**Strauss, R.**	*Ein Heldenleben*	107	4
		42	1b [26]			205	1
Inghelbrecht	*Rapsodie de Printemps*	25	1	**Strauss, R.**	*Macbeth*	32	[K]
Ireland	*A London Overture*	13	2b [7]			54	2
Knipper	*Symphony No. 4*	102	[18] 2f	**Strauss, R.**	*Salomé's Dance*	6	[H]
Lambert	*The Rio Grande*	16	1			34	1b [g]
MacDowell	*2nd Suite (Indian)*	94	3	**Stravinsky**	*Histoire du Soldat*	19	1
Mahler	*Symphony No. 1*	92	4b [17]			24	[10]
Mahler	*Symphony No. 2*	34	[17]	**Stravinsky**	*Les Noces*	1	1
Mahler	*Symphony No. 5*	108	3			24	[29]
Martinet	*Orphée*	63	4b [3]			57	6b [63]
		90	[19]	**Toch**	*Fünf Stücke für Kammerorchester*	54	[18] 2f
Milhaud	*2ᵐᵉ Suite Symphonique*	144	[68]				
Milhaud	*La Création du Monde*	4	3b [5]	**Walton**	*Façade, Suite No. 2*	25	11
Milhaud	*Les Choéphores*	107	[IV]			32	2
Milhaud	*Saudades do Brazil*	15	2	**Walton**	*Portsmouth Point Overture*	38	2b [27]
Rachmaninoff	*The Bells*	9	[8]	**Whithorne**	*Fata Morgana*	29	3b [24]
Russell	*Three Dance Movements*	19	[F] 1f	**Whithorne**	*The Dream Pedlar*	32	[17]

WOOD STICK WITH RUBBER BANDS AROUND ONE END

COMPOSER	WORK	PAGE	MEASURE
Russell	*Three Dance Movements*	15	3

WOOD(EN) TIMPANI STICKS

COMPOSER	WORK	PAGE	MEASURE	COMPOSER	WORK	PAGE	MEASURE
Mahler	*Symphony No. 1*	95	1	**Schelling**	*A Victory Ball*	78	3

XYLOPHONE MALLETS

COMPOSER	WORK	PAGE	MEASURE
Thomson	*Louisiana Story Suite*	23	137

PERCUSSION

(4) OTHER EFFECTS

English	Italian	French	German
Dampened by holding with fingers	Assordate col il dita	Étouffez avec les doigts	Mit den Fingern gedämpft

	COMPOSER	WORK	PAGE	MEASURE
	McDonald	*Three Poems for Orchestra*	**20**	[6]

English	Italian	French	German
Hissing	Cigolio	Sifflement	Zischend

COMPOSER	WORK	PAGE	MEASURE
Strauss, R.	*Ein Heldenleben*	**29**	4

English	Italian	French	German
Hold a wire-brush against vibrating cymbal	Tenete uno scovolo di fil di ferro contro il piatto vibrando	Tenez un balai métallique contre la cymbale vibrante	Eine Drahtbürste gegen das vibrierende Becken halten

COMPOSER	WORK	PAGE	MEASURE
Russell	*Fugue for Eight Percussion Instruments*	**6**	3

English	Italian	French	German
Hold cymbals together after striking	Tenete i piatti insieme dopo avendo colputo	Après avoir frappé les cymbales tenez-les ensembles	Becken nach Anschlag zusammen halten

COMPOSER	WORK	PAGE	MEASURE
Russell	*Fugue for Eight Percussion Instruments*	**4**	[D]

English	Italian	French	German
Muffled [Muted]	Con sordino	Sourdine	Gedämpft

(for further terminology see Chapter 32, page 165)

COMPOSER	WORK	PAGE	MEASURE	COMPOSER	WORK	PAGE	MEASURE
Bartók	*Deux Portraits*	**20**	[2]	**Cowell**	*Short Symphony (No. 4)*	**5**	1b [B]
		35	[12] 1f	**Varèse**	*Intégrales*	**2**	1

English	Italian	French	German
Retain hold of edge—after stopping tone shake cymbal violently	Tenete l'orlo dopo avendo assordato il suono e scuotete il piatto	Retenez au bord—après avoir étouffé le son secouez violemment	Becken am Rand halten (nach dem Ton abgedämpft ist) und lebhaft schütteln

COMPOSER	WORK	PAGE	MEASURE
Green	*Three Inventories of Casey Jones*	**12**	17

English	Italian	French	German
"Stomp the beat"	—	—	—

COMPOSER	WORK	PAGE	MEASURE
Siegmeister	*Sunday in Brooklyn*	**66**	1

194

CYMBALS

English	Italian	French	German
English	*Italian*	*French*	*German*
Stop [dampen] half-way, and full	Assordate a mezza, e tutta	Étouffez à demi, et tout à fait	Halb und ganz dämpfen

COMPOSER	WORK	PAGE	MEASURE
Green	*Three Inventories of Casey Jones*	11	1

English	*Italian*	*French*	*German*
Strike with back of a saw-blade on cymbal; draw saw across cymbal	Colpete col rovescio d'una lama di sega; tirate la sega sopra il piatto	Frappez avec l'envers d'une lame de scie; traînez la scie à travers une cymbale	Mit dem Rücken einer Säge auf das Becken schlagen; Säge über das Becken ziehen

COMPOSER	WORK	PAGE	MEASURE
Russell	*Three Dance Movements*	18	5b [E]

English	*Italian*	*French*	*German*
Swishing	Strosciando	Cinglant	Peitschend

COMPOSER	WORK	PAGE	MEASURE
Stravinsky	*Ebony Concerto*	39	[33]

English	*Italian*	*French*	*German*
Tremolo on cymbal with a 'cello bow	Tremolo sulla piatto coll'arco di violoncello	Trémolo sur une cymbale avec l'archet d'un violoncelle	Tremolo auf einem Becken-teller mit einem Violoncellbogen

COMPOSER	WORK	PAGE	MEASURE
Schönberg	*Fünf Orchesterstücke*	45	1

Chapter 35

BASS, SNARE, AND TENOR DRUMS

(1) DAMPENED

(for terminology and notation see Chapter 32, page 163)

Bass Drum

COMPOSER	WORK	PAGE	MEASURE	COMPOSER	WORK	PAGE	MEASURE
Copland	Four Dance Episodes from "Rodeo"	46	4b [42]	Roger-Ducasse	Poème Symphonique sur le nom de Gabriel Fauré	28	4
Franck	Le Chasseur Maudit	50	1				
Mahler	Symphony No. 5	246	7	Stravinsky	Le Sacre du Printemps	57	3b [65]
Poulenc	Concerto pour deux	2	[1]			125	[174]
	Pianos et Orchestre	55	2	Stravinsky	Les Noces	82	[91]
Respighi	Feste Romane	153	5	Stravinsky	Scherzo à la Russe	3	1
Rivier	Ouverture pour un don Quichotte	76	7			35	[30] 3f

Snare Drum

COMPOSER	WORK	PAGE	MEASURE	COMPOSER	WORK	PAGE	MEASURE
Bernstein	"Jeremiah" Symphony	23	[13]	Lalo	Symphonie Espagnole	152	[M]

Bass and Snare Drums

COMPOSER	WORK	PAGE	MEASURE	COMPOSER	WORK	PAGE	MEASURE
Copland	Dance Symphony	56	[33]	Copland	El Salón México	44	[41] 6f

(2) METHODS OF STRIKING

English	Italian	French	German
At the edge (of the head)	Sul bordo (della membrana)	Au bord (de la membrane)	Am Rand (des Felles)

(for further terminology see Chapter 32, page 163)

Bass Drum

COMPOSER	WORK	PAGE	MEASURE
Stravinsky	Le Sacre du Printemps	93	[114]

Snare Drum

COMPOSER	WORK	PAGE	MEASURE	COMPOSER	WORK	PAGE	MEASURE
Bartók	Music for Strings, Percussion and Celesta	28	199	Ravel	Concerto pour Piano et Orchestre	70	[9] 2f
Bartók	Second Rhapsody for Violin and Orchestra	43	[32]	Rogers	Once Upon a Time, Five Fairy Tales	14	1
Bartók	Violin Concerto	51	[374]			17	[13]
		66	[106]			20	[14] 1f
Parodi	Preludio ad una Commedia	38	1	Russell	Fugue for Eight Percussion Instruments	2	[B]

BASS, SNARE, AND TENOR DRUMS

English	Italian	French	German
At (the) rim	All'estremità	A la jante	Am Rand
On (the) rim (of the drum)	In margine	Sur le bois (du Tambour)	Rand mit Holz
On (the) wood	Sul bordo	Sur le bord	geschlagen
Rim [R]		Sur le cercle	
Strike (the) rim			

Bass Drum

COMPOSER	WORK	PAGE	MEASURE	COMPOSER	WORK	PAGE	MEASURE
Janssen	New Year's Eve in New York	8	1	Russell	Three Dance Movements	15	[A]
						20	4
Russell	Fugue for Eight Percussion Instruments	7	[F]	Stravinsky	Histoire du Soldat	19	[1] 1f
						24	2b [11]

Snare Drum

COMPOSER	WORK	PAGE	MEASURE	COMPOSER	WORK	PAGE	MEASURE
Bartók	Concerto for Piano and Orchestra	7	[7] 1f	Piston	Concerto for Orchestra	22	2
		30	[33]	Poot	Jazz-Music	10	3b [5]
		52	2	Poot	Symphonie	40	5
Bernstein	"Jeremiah" Symphony	25	[16]			86	[39]
Britten	Four Sea Interludes from "Peter Grimes"	66	[7] 3f	Rosenthal	Les Petits Métiers	34	3
				Russell	Fugue for Eight Percussion Instruments	1	8b [A]
Cesana	Second American Symphony	155	[38] 2f			4	[D] 9f
Copland	Appalachian Spring	29	1	Russell	Three Dance Movements	20	4
		32	[29]	Schmitt	La Tragédie de Salomé	58	6
Copland	Concerto for Piano and Orchestra	31	[21]	Schmitt	Mirages pour Orchestre, No. 2	18	2
		63	[48]			60	2b [33]
Copland	Four Dance Episodes from "Rodeo"	84	4b [13]	Schmitt	Rapsodie Viennoise	47	1
Copland	Music for the Theatre	32	[23] 2f	Schmitt	Ronde burlesque	15	3
		38	1			39	2
Copland	Statements	31	[6] 4f	Siegmeister	From my Window	47	[40]
Cowell	Short Symphony (No. 4)					56	1b [40]
		46	[I]	Siegmeister	Ozark Set	23	2b [15]
Davidson	Auto Accident	6	7			65	2
Diamond	Timon of Athens	7	39	Siegmeister	Sunday in Brooklyn	25	[25] 1f
		10	61			57	[5]
Gould	Latin-American Symphonette	2	4			83	3
		55	1b [A]	Siegmeister	Western Suite	8	3b [30]
		124	4			12	[40] 1f
Gould	Spirituals	26	12	Taylor	Through the Looking Glass	100	3
Moore	In Memoriam	4	[C]	Varèse	Hyperprism	3	6
Nystedt	The Land of Suspense	7	3			13	3
Parodi	Preludio ad una Commedia	27	[O]	Varèse	Ionisation	7	3b [5]
						16	[11]
				Villa-Lobos	Chôros No. 8	50	[21]

English	Italian	French	German
Barely touched	Appena toccata	A peine frôlé	Leicht berühren
Lightly rubbed		Frôlé	

Bass Drum

COMPOSER	WORK	PAGE	MEASURE	COMPOSER	WORK	PAGE	MEASURE
Milhaud	Concerto pour Piano et Orchestre	47	[70]	Milhaud	Les Choéphores	101	1
						117	1
Milhaud	Deuxième Concerto pour Violoncelle et Orchestre	55	[60]	Milhaud	Saudades do Brazil	41	1
				Milhaud	Sérénade pour Orchestre	25	2b [3]

197

PERCUSSION

English	Italian	French	German
Center of (the) head	Nel mezzo della membrana	Au milieu de la membrane	In der Mitte des Felles
In the center [middle]		[peau]	
Near (the) center			

(for further terminology see Chapter 32, page 164)

Bass Drum

COMPOSER	WORK	PAGE	MEASURE	COMPOSER	WORK	PAGE	MEASURE
Russell	*Fugue for Eight*	4	[D] 8f	**Stravinsky**	*Histoire du Soldat*	19	[1] 1f
	Percussion Instruments	7	[F]			24	2b [11]
		8	[G] 1f				

Snare Drum

Bartók	*Concerto for Piano and*	7	1b [7]	**Bartók**	*Second Rhapsody for*		
	Orchestra	52	2		*Violin and Orchestra*	44	2

English	Italian	French	German
"Flam" stroke	—	—	—

Snare Drum

COMPOSER	WORK	PAGE	MEASURE
Schuman, W.	*Prayer in Time of War*	26	347

English	Italian	French	German
Laid on side	Sul lato	Placé à plat	Auf die Seite gedreht

Bass Drum

COMPOSER	WORK	PAGE	MEASURE
Inghelbrecht	*El Greco*	1	1

English	Italian	French	German
Lay 1 stick on head of drum—strike with the other (stick)	Mettete una bacchetta sulla membrana—colpetela col altro	Appuyer une baguette sur la peau—frappez-la avec l'autre	Ein Schlägel um Fell—mit dem andern geschlagen

Snare Drum

COMPOSER	WORK	PAGE	MEASURE
Milhaud	*La Création du Monde*	25	[27] 6f

English	Italian	French	German
On both sides [skins]	Dalle due parti	Sur tous les deux côtés	Auf beiden Fellen

Bass Drum

COMPOSER	WORK	PAGE	MEASURE
Schönberg	*Fünf Orchesterstücke*	12	[10]

BASS, SNARE, AND TENOR DRUMS

English	Italian	French	German
On the bell [body]	Sulla cassa	Contre le pupitre	Auf dem Holzrand der
On the frame [hoop]		Sur la caisse	Trommel
On the shell [wood]		Sur le cadre	Auf dem Holzstäbchen
On (the) side			Auf den hölzernen Rahmen
			Auf Holz geschlägen

Bass Drum

COMPOSER	WORK	PAGE	MEASURE	COMPOSER	WORK	PAGE	MEASURE
Mahler	*Symphony No. 2*	80	[28] 11f	**Varèse**	*Intégrales*	17	[7] 1f
Mahler	*Symphony No. 6*	116	[79]				

Snare Drum

COMPOSER	WORK	PAGE	MEASURE	COMPOSER	WORK	PAGE	MEASURE
Albéniz	*Catalonia, Suite No. 1*	38	[47]	**Poulenc**	*Concerto pour deux*		
Debussy	*Gigues*	5	7		*Pianos et Orchestre*	76	2
Gershwin	*Rhapsody in Blue*	18	[14]	**Ravel**	*Alborada del Gracioso*	39	[32]
Janssen	*New Year's Eve in*			**Rosenthal**	*Les Petits Métiers*	137	1
	New York	40	4	**Walton**	*Façade, Suite No. 2*	3	2
Moross	*Paeans*	6	[F]			26	10
Mussorgsky–							
Ravel	*Pictures at an Exhibition*	57	[53]				

Tenor Drum

COMPOSER	WORK	PAGE	MEASURE	COMPOSER	WORK	PAGE	MEASURE
Rogers	*Once Upon a Time,*			**Varèse**	*Intégrales*	19	[8] 2f
	Five Fairy Tales	57	1b [33]			37	1

English	Italian	French	German
On (the) head	Sulla membrana	Position ordinaire	Auf das Fell
On (the) skin	Modo ordinario	Sur la peau	Gewöhnlich
		Sur membrane	

Snare Drum

COMPOSER	WORK	PAGE	MEASURE	COMPOSER	WORK	PAGE	MEASURE
Copland	*Third Symphony*	104	[94] 1f	**Siegmeister**	*From my Window*	48	[5]
Cowell	*Short Symphony*					56	1b [40]
	(No. 4)	46	[I]	**Siegmeister**	*Ozark Set*	25	[20]
Janssen	*New Year's Eve in*	28	[11]	**Siegmeister**	*Sunday in Brooklyn*	26	2b [30]
	New York	59	[23]			57	[5]
Moross	*Paeans*	6	[F]	**Siegmeister**	*Western Suite*	9	3
Piston	*Symphony No. 2*	80	3			25	5
Poot	*Jazz-Music*	10	5	**Varèse**	*Hyperprism*	3	6
Russell	*Three Dance Move-*					13	3
	ments	20	4				

Tenor Drum

COMPOSER	WORK	PAGE	MEASURE	COMPOSER	WORK	PAGE	MEASURE
Rogers	*Once Upon a Time,*			**Varèse**	*Intégrales*	19	[8] 2f
	Five Fairy Tales	57	1b [33]			37	1

PERCUSSION

English	Italian	French	German
Rim shot	—	—	—
Shot			

Snare Drum

COMPOSER	WORK	PAGE	MEASURE	COMPOSER	WORK	PAGE	MEASURE
Carter	*Holiday Overture*	37	3	**Gould**	*Latin-American*	28	3b [V]
		69	3		*Symphonette*	58	1b [C]
Copland	*Four Dance Episodes*	13	1b [13]			114	[25]
	from "Rodeo"	43	[39]	**Gould**	*Philharmonic Waltzes*	13	[129] 5f
		83	[12]	**Gould**	*Spirituals*	3	[A]
Copland	*Third Symphony*	34	[26]			13	[A] 8f
		43	[32]			35	3
		61	[47]	**Piston**	*Symphony No. 2*	78	1
		105	[95]			109	4
Dello Joio	*Variations, Chaconne,*	11	[90] 2f	**Schuman, W.**	*Symphony No. III*	72	373
	and Finale	62	[110] 1f	**Schuman, W.**	*Symphony No. IV*	8	49
Gershwin	*An American in Paris*	46	4	**Schuman, W.**	*Undertow*	41	2b [500]
Gillis	*Symphony No. 5½*	14	6	**Siegmeister**	*From my Window*	48	[5] 3f
Gould	*American Salute*	19	[I] 2f	**Siegmeister**	*Sunday in Brooklyn*	24	[20] 1f
						39	4b [80]
						77	3

Snare and Tenor Drums

COMPOSER	WORK	PAGE	MEASURE
Copland	*Third Symphony*	70	5

English	Italian	French	German
Roll(ed) with the fingers	Rullo col il dita	Roulé avec les doigts	Wirbel mit den Fingern
With the fingertips	Sulle punte delle dita	Avec les pointes des doigts	Mit Fingerspitzen

Snare Drum

Russell	*Fugue for Eight*	2	[B]
	Percussion Instruments	6	8

English	Italian	French	German
Drag with wire-brush	Strisciate con scovolo di fil di	Effleurez [glissez] avec un	Mit einem Drahtbürste gleiten
Slide [swish] with brush	ferro	balai métallique	

Snare Drum

Russell	*Three Dance Movements*	15	I	**Siegmeister**	*Sunday in Brooklyn*	20	I
Siegmeister	*Ozark Set*	69	[35]			29	[40]

English	Italian	French	German
Struck with the wood	Col mancio della mazza	Frappée avec le bois	Mit dem Stiel des Klöppels

(for further terminology see Chapter 34, page 184)

Bass Drum

Hindemith	*Konzert für Orchester*	31	1b [100]

BASS, SNARE, AND TENOR DRUMS

English	*Italian*	*French*	*German*
Bass drum alone (with Cymb. detached)	A piede	A pied	Mit dem Fuss
With foot-beater [foot-pedal]		Gr. C. seule (avec Cymb. décrochée)	

Bass Drum

COMPOSER	WORK	PAGE	MEASURE	COMPOSER	WORK	PAGE	MEASURE
Delannoy	*Figures Sonores*	59	[28]	Thomson	*Orchestra Suite from "The Plow that		
Russell	*Three Dance Move-*				*Broke the Plains"*	28	[22]
	ments	15	1				

(3) MUFFLED

(for terminology see Chapter 32, page 165)

Bass Drum

| Barber | *Medea* | 39 | 1 | Thomson | *Orchestra Suite from "The Plow that* | | |
| Bartók | *Deux Portraits* | 39 | 6 | | *Broke the Plains"* | 28 | [22] |

Snare Drum

Bartók	*Deux Portraits*	20	[2] 7f	Moore	*In Memoriam*	27	2b [R]
		25	[6]	Pizzetti	*Introduzione all' "Agamennone" di*		
Berg	*Three Excerpts from "Wozzeck"*	57	2		*Eschilo*	44	[18]
Bloch	*Schelomo*	66	[41]	Poulenc	*Concerto pour deux*		
Bloch	*Trois Poèmes Juifs*	62	[1]		*Pianos et Orchestre*	51	[37]
Cesana	*Second American*	98	4	Respighi	*Ballata delle Gnomidi*	42	[13]
	Symphony	139	[27]	Rogers	*Once Upon a Time, Five Fairy Tales*	35	1b [22]
Cowell	*Short Symphony (No. 4)*	13	4b [E]	Strauss, R.	*Till Eulenspiegel's Merry Pranks*	54	8
Debussy	*Iberia*	35	[22]	Thomson	*Louisiana Story Suite*	26	152
Delius	*Eventyr, Once Upon a Time*	43	1b [16]	Thomson	*Orchestra Suite from "The Plow that*		
Elgar	*Falstaff*	147	1		*Broke the Plains"*	56	[52] 2f
de Falla	*El Retablo de Maese Pedro*	1 / 18	1 / [17]	Varèse	*Hyperprism*	3	4
Gould	*Latin-American Symphonette*	37	1	Varèse	*Ionisation*	21	[13] 3f
				Vaughan Williams	*Symphony in E minor (No. 6)*	57 / 71	3 / [11] 3f
Gould	*Spirituals*	20	[A]	Walton	*Concerto for Violin and Orchestra*	20 / 135	2 / [66] 1f
Mahler	*Symphony No. 5*	14	4				
		33	[12]				
		43	[18]				

Tenor Drum

| Milhaud | *Quatrième Symphonie* | 85 | [50] 1f | Milhaud | *Two Marches* | 1 | 1 |
| Milhaud | *Suite Provençale* | 45 | [10] | | | 9 | 2b [30] |

PERCUSSION

(4) OFF-STAGE

(for terminology see Chapter 11, page 75)

Snare Drum

COMPOSER	WORK	PAGE	MEASURE	COMPOSER	WORK	PAGE	MEASURE
Balakirev–				**Strauss, R.**	*Macbeth*	80	[Ee]
Casella	*Islamey*	38	[37]	**Stravinsky**	*Petrouchka Suite*	39	[28] 2f
Mahler	*Symphony No. 3*	77	[54] 2f				

Snare and Tenor Drums

COMPOSER	WORK	PAGE	MEASURE
Knipper	*Symphony No. 4*	51	[1]

(5) STICK TYPES

(for terminology see Chapter 32, pages 166–7)

CANE STICK WITH FIBRE HEAD

Snare Drum

Stravinsky	*Histoire du Soldat*	1	1b [1]
		14	1b [1]

Tenor Drum

Stravinsky	*Histoire du Soldat*	4	[8]
		20	[2]

Bass and Tenor Drums

Stravinsky	*Histoire du Soldat*	53	[4]

DRUM STICKS

Bass Drum

COMPOSER	WORK	PAGE	MEASURE	COMPOSER	WORK	PAGE	MEASURE
Pierné	*Viennoise*	22	1	**Rivier**	*Danse*	50	[38]
Piston	*Concerto for Orchestra*	50	10	**Roussel**	*Rapsodie Flamande*	52	1b [27]
Poulenc	*Concerto pour deux*			**Roussel**	*Suite en Fa*	14	[7]
	Pianos et Orchestre	66	2b [43]	**Stravinsky**	*Ragtime*	4	[2] 3f

FELT STICKS

Bass Drum

Holst	*The Ballet from "The*	25	[22] 1f
	Perfect Fool"	38	2b [29]

BASS, SNARE, AND TENOR DRUMS

Snare Drum

COMPOSER	WORK	PAGE	MEASURE
Stravinsky	*Chant du Rossignol*	60	1b [62]

Snare and Tenor Drums

Varèse	*Ionisation*	6	1b [4]

FELT TIMPANI STICKS

Snare Drum

Russell	*Fugue for Eight Percussion Instruments*	1	[A] 8f

HARD STICKS

Bass Drum

COMPOSER	WORK	PAGE	MEASURE	COMPOSER	WORK	PAGE	MEASURE
Copland	*Third Symphony*	107	2	**Rogers**	*Once Upon a Time, Five Fairy Tales*	50	[29]

HARD FELT STICKS

Bass Drum

Russell	*Fugue for Eight Percussion Instruments*	8	[G] 1f

Snare Drum

Stravinsky	*Histoire du Soldat*	51	2

Bass, Snare, and Tenor Drums

Stravinsky	*Histoire du Soldat*	62	[2]

MEDIUM HARD FELT STICKS

Bass Drum

Russell	*Fugue for Eight Percussion Instruments*	4	[D]

PERCUSSION

ORDINARY [REGULAR, USUAL] STICKS

Bass Drum

COMPOSER	WORK	PAGE	MEASURE
Weingartner	*Lustige Ouvertüre*	**22**	1

Snare Drum

Milhaud	*Ière Symphonie*	**58**	[170] 1f

Tenor Drum

Milhaud	*Ière Symphonie*	**25**	3

RAWHIDE TIMPANI STICKS

Bass Drum

Milhaud	*Les Choéphores*	**101**	1

SHORT [SMALL] STICKS

Bass Drum

Pierné	*Viennoise*	**44**	1

SNARE DRUM STICKS

Bass Drum

COMPOSER	WORK	PAGE	MEASURE	COMPOSER	WORK	PAGE	MEASURE
Britten	*Four Sea Interludes from "Peter Grimes"*	**80**	[12]	**Russell**	*Fugue for Eight Percussion Instruments*	**7**	[F] 11f
Britten	*Sinfonia da Requiem*	**26**	1b [19]	**Stravinsky**	*Le Sacre du Printemps*	**85**	[103] 1f
Rosenthal	*Les Petits Métiers*	**137**	1				

Tenor Drum

Diamond	*Elegy in Memory of Maurice Ravel*	**8**	[55]	**Rogers**	*Once Upon a Time, Five Fairy Tales*	**46**	[27]

SNARE DRUM STICKS, WRAPPED WITH FELT

Bass Drum

McDonald	*Rhumba from 2nd Symphony*	**3**	[10] 2f

BASS, SNARE, AND TENOR DRUMS

SOFT STICKS

Bass Drum

COMPOSER	WORK	PAGE	MEASURE	COMPOSER	WORK	PAGE	MEASURE
Converse	*American Sketches*	97	[2] 2f	Janssen	*New Year's Eve in New York*	65	[26]
Debussy– Ansermet	*Six Épigraphes Antiques*	11	1				

Snare Drum

Moross	*Biguine*	13	[C]	Rogers	*Once Upon a Time, Five Fairy Tales*	40	3

Tenor Drum

COMPOSER	WORK	PAGE	MEASURE
Diamond	*Elegy in Memory of Maurice Ravel*	6	[40]

SOFT FELT TIMPANI STICKS

Bass Drum

Russell	*Fugue for Eight Percussion Instruments*	6	1

SOFT TIMPANI STICKS

Bass Drum

Piston	*Concerto for Orchestra*	24	3b [1]

SPONGE STICKS

Bass Drum

COMPOSER	WORK	PAGE	MEASURE	COMPOSER	WORK	PAGE	MEASURE
Dohnányi	*Variations on a Nursery Song*	112	2	Mahler	*Symphony No. 7*	202	[242] 4f
				Read	*Symphony No. I*	1	1
Mahler	*Symphony No. 3*	4	[1]	Roussel	*Évocations, III*	13	[6]

Snare Drum

Lambert	*The Rio Grande*	23	[A]

SPONGE TIMPANI STICKS

Bass Drum

Berlioz	*Symphonie Fantastique*	163	3
		187	5
		208	5

PERCUSSION

Tenor Drum

COMPOSER	WORK	PAGE	MEASURE
Milhaud	*Les Choéphores*	106	4

STICK WITH FIBRE HEAD

Bass Drum

COMPOSER	WORK	PAGE	MEASURE	COMPOSER	WORK	PAGE	MEASURE
Stravinsky	*Histoire du Soldat*	14	1b [1]	Stravinsky	*Ragtime*	3	[1]
		19	[1] 1f			11	[27]
		24	2b [11]				

Tenor Drum

Stravinsky	*Histoire du Soldat*	49	[33]

SWITCH [ROD]

Bass Drum

COMPOSER	WORK	PAGE	MEASURE	COMPOSER	WORK	PAGE	MEASURE
Mahler	*Symphony No. 2*	80	[28] 11f	Varèse	*Intégrales*	17	[7] 1f
Mahler	*Symphony No. 7*	202	[242] 4f				

THICK TIMPANI STICKS

Bass Drum

Inghelbrecht	*El Greco*	1	1

THIN STICK WITH SPONGE HEAD

Tenor Drum

Stravinsky	*Histoire du Soldat*	49	[34]

TIMPANI STICKS

Bass Drum

COMPOSER	WORK	PAGE	MEASURE	COMPOSER	WORK	PAGE	MEASURE
Bax	*Third Symphony*	44	7b [45]	Bloch	*America*	9	[5] 1f
Bax	*Fourth Symphony*	145	3b [30]			63	2b [33]
Bax	*Fifth Symphony*	1	1			144	2
		68	[44] 2f	Bloch	*Evocations*	18	1
Bax	*Sixth Symphony*	28	5b [24]	Bloch	*Schelomo*	45	[27]
		105	4	Dukas	*La Péri*	40	1
Bax	*The Garden of Fand*	41	[K]			98	[14 bis]
Bax	*Tintagel*	37	1b [Q]			127	3

BASS, SNARE, AND TENOR DRUMS

Bass Drum (contd.)

COMPOSER	WORK	PAGE	MEASURE	COMPOSER	WORK	PAGE	MEASURE
de Falla	Three Dances from			Roussel	Rapsodie Flamande	50	1b [26]
	"The Three-	46	[5] 3f	Roussel	Suite en Fa	12	1
	Cornered Hat"	68	[15] 2f			66	[31]
Fitelberg	Nocturne for Orchestra	21	[114]	Roussel	Symphonie en Sol	32	[19] 2f
Halffter	Deux Esquisses	4	5		mineur	137	5
	Symphoniques	23	4	Rudhyar	Sinfonietta	10	3
Hill	Lilacs	37	2	Schelling	A Victory Ball	68	[20]
Honegger	Le Chant de Nigamon	36	[125]	Schreker	The Birthday of the	49	2b [285]
Honegger	Le Dit des Jeux du	40	4		Infanta, Suite	90	[465]
	Monde	75	1	Shepherd	Horizons	115	[B] 2f
Ibert	La Ballade de la Geôle	1	1	Sibelius	En Saga	17	2
	de Reading	85	[62]	Sibelius	Finlandia	19	[L]
Janssen	New Year's Eve in			Sibelius	Lemminkainen		
	New York	24	[10]		Journeys Homeward	26	1
Knipper	Symphony No. 4	27	[21]	Sibelius	Pelleas and Melisande	9	3
MacDowell	2nd Suite (Indian)	10	[C]	Sibelius	Symphony No. 1	24	1
		73	4			95	12b [K]
		113	5	Sibelius	The Swan of Tuonela	3	1b [A]
Martinet	Orphée	60	[1]	Sibelius	The Tempest,		
		87	[18] 1f		First Suite	60	1
Milhaud	Les Choéphores	162	1	Sibelius	The Tempest, Prelude	3	1
Milhaud	Opus Americanum			Smetana	The Moldau	70	271
	No. 2	97	[675]	Strauss, R.	Also Sprach Zarathustra	202	10
Milhaud	Ière Symphonie	28	1b [105]	Strauss, R.	Don Quixote	150	2
Milhaud	Saudades do Brazil	33	4	Strauss, R.	Eine Alpensinfonie	107	[103] 4f
Parodi	Preludio ad una	6	[C]	Stravinsky	Le Sacre du Printemps	92	1b [113]
	Commedia	39	[S] 4f	Szymanowski	Symphonie Concertante		
Rabaud	La Procession Nocturne	1	1		pour Piano et	21	2
Ravel	Rapsodie Espagnole	4	[3] 1f		Orchestre	58	[7] 1f
		27	3	Tchaikovsky	Manfred-Symphonie	3	3
		81	[27]			67	331
Rivier	Danse	23	[20]			248	186
Rivier	Ouverture pour un don			Thomson	Louisiana Story Suite	42	90
	Quichotte	17	[8] 2f			82	89
Roger-				Villa-Lobos	Danses Africaines	33	[15]
Ducasse	Sarabande	2	[1]	Weingartner	Lustige Ouvertüre	7	1
Roussel	4me Symphonie	15	3			50	[22]

Snare Drum

COMPOSER	WORK	PAGE	MEASURE	COMPOSER	WORK	PAGE	MEASURE
Bartók	Concerto for Piano and			Walton	Façade, Suite No. 1	42	1
	Orchestra	52	2			50	[G] 8f
Milhaud	Quatrième Symphonie	84	[45] 1f				

Tenor Drum

COMPOSER	WORK	PAGE	MEASURE	COMPOSER	WORK	PAGE	MEASURE
Milhaud	Concerto pour Violon-			Milhaud	IIe Symphonie	69	[C]
	celle et Orchestre	12	1	Milhaud	Suite Provençale	18	1
Milhaud	Ière Symphonie	20	[80] 1f				

207

PERCUSSION

Snare and Tenor Drums

COMPOSER	WORK	PAGE	MEASURE
Milhaud	*IIe Symphonie*	**5**	[45] 1f

TRIANGLE STICK

Bass Drum

Stravinsky	*Histoire du Soldat*	**46**	[25]

Tenor Drum

Stravinsky	*Histoire du Soldat*	**46**	[24]

Bass and Snare Drums

Walton	*Portsmouth Point Overture*	**34**	3b [24]

TWO-HEADED STICK

Bass Drum

COMPOSER	WORK	PAGE	MEASURE	COMPOSER	WORK	PAGE	MEASURE
Dukas	*L'Apprenti Sorcier*	**38**	[36]	**Stravinsky**	*Fire-Bird Suite (1919)*	**24**	1

WIRE-BRUSH

Bass Drum

Russell	*Three Dance Movements*	**15**	[A]

Snare Drum

COMPOSER	WORK	PAGE	MEASURE	COMPOSER	WORK	PAGE	MEASURE
Copland	*Appalachian Spring*	**28**	[26]	**Piston**	*Suite for Orchestra*	**16**	[F]
Copland	*Four Dance Episodes from "Rodeo"*	**23**	[23]	**Read**	*First Overture*	**22**	2
Copland	*Statements*	**27**	[3] 5f	**Rogers**	*Once Upon a Time, Five Fairy Tales*	**14**	1
Creston	*Two Choric Dances*	**43**	[95] 4f	**Rosenthal**	*Les Petits Métiers*	**78**	[A] 2f
Dukelsky	*Symphony No. 3*	**48**	1			**117**	1
Gershwin	*An American in Paris*	**32**	[30]	**Russell**	*Fugue for Eight Percussion Instruments*	**2**	[B] 8f
		50	[45] 5f				
		72	[61]	**Russell**	*Three Dance Movements*	**15**	1
Gershwin	*Concerto in F for Piano and Orchestra*	**62**	[6]	**Siegmeister**	*Ozark Set*	**69**	[35]
Gillis	*Symphony No. 5½*	**4**	2b [A]	**Siegmeister**	*Sunday in Brooklyn*	**20**	1
		56	1			**29**	[40]
		73	4			**90**	3
Gould	*Latin-American Symphonette*	**61**	[F]	**Siegmeister**	*Western Suite*	**25**	[5]
Gould	*Spirituals*	**17**	[E]	**Thomson**	*Orchestra Suite from "The Plow that Broke the Plains"*	**21**	1
Janssen	*New Year's Eve in New York*	**28**	[11]			**32**	[28]
		59	[23]	**Walton**	*Façade, Suite No. 1*	**43**	[A]
Lambert	*The Rio Grande*	**13**	[7] 4f	**Walton**	*Façade, Suite No. 2*	**3**	[A]
		40	[20]	**Weiss**	*American Life*	**9**	[D]

208

BASS, SNARE, AND TENOR DRUMS

WOOD(EN) STICKS

Bass Drum

COMPOSER	WORK	PAGE	MEASURE	COMPOSER	WORK	PAGE	MEASURE
Holst	Beni Mora, Oriental Suite	29	11	Rogers	Once Upon a Time, Five Fairy Tales	23	2
Holst	The Ballet from "The Perfect Fool"	4 38	3b [4] 2b [29]	Stravinsky Varèse	Le Sacre du Printemps Ionisation	110 6	[139] [4]
Lambert	The Rio Grande	24	[B] 5f	Walton	Portsmouth Point Overture	4	[3] 2f
Mahler	Symphony No. 6	116	[79]				
Milhaud	La Création du Monde	22	[24] 1f				

Snare Drum

COMPOSER	WORK	PAGE	MEASURE	COMPOSER	WORK	PAGE	MEASURE
Moross	Biguine	29	5	Stravinsky	Ragtime	3	2b [1]
Stravinsky	Histoire du Soldat	57	4			5	[5]
						14	[36] 3f

Tenor Drum

COMPOSER	WORK	PAGE	MEASURE
Stravinsky	Histoire du Soldat	58	14

Bass and Snare Drums

	WORK	PAGE	MEASURE
Walton	Portsmouth Point Overture	34	3b [24]

Snare and Tenor Drums

	WORK	PAGE	MEASURE
Stravinsky	Les Noces	24	[29]

WOOD(EN) TIMPANI STICKS

Snare Drum

	WORK	PAGE	MEASURE
Riisager	Torgot Dance	6	[20] 1f

Bass and Snare Drums

	WORK	PAGE	MEASURE
Hindemith	Konzert für Orchester	51	2

(6) WITHOUT SNARES

English	Italian	French	German
Loosen snares	Corde del Tamburo lasciare	Avec les cordes lâches [relâchées]	Ohne Schnarrseite
Slacken(ed) snares	Senza corda(e)	Détimbrée(s)	
Snares muffled	Senza timbro	Sans corde(s)	
Snares loose(ned)		Sans timbre(s)	
Snares off			
Snares slack(ened)			
No snares			
Without snares			
With snares loose(ned)			
With snares slack(ened)			

PERCUSSION

Snares On

English	Italian	French	German
Snares on	Con corda(e)	Avec corde(s)	Mit Schnarrseite
Tight(en) snares	Con timbro	Avec timbre(s)	
With snares		Très timbrée	

Snare Drum

COMPOSER	WORK	PAGE	MEASURE	COMPOSER	WORK	PAGE	MEASURE
Barber	*Medea*	47	[37]	Chávez	*Sinfonia India*	26	[33]
Barber	*Second Essay for*					33	[45]
	Orchestra	39	[22]	Creston	*Two Choric Dances*	43	[95] 4f
Bartók	*Concerto for Orchestra*	29	1	Gillis	*Symphony No. 5½*	43	3
		36	[120]	Holst	*A Somerset Rhapsody*	25	[14] 3f
Bartók	*Concerto for Piano and*	7	1b [7]	Ives	*Three Places in New*		
	Orchestra	52	2		*England*	21	1
Bartók	*Concerto No. 3 for*			Khachaturian	*Gayne Ballet Suite*		
	Piano and Orchestra	10	[54]		*No. 1-A*	36	3
Bartók	*Second Rhapsody for*			Knipper	*Symphony No. 4*	51	3b [1]
	Violin and Orchestra	43	[32]	Moore	*In Memoriam*	2	1b [B]
Bartók	*Violin Concerto*	34	[226]	Piket	*Curtain Raiser to an*		
		63	[84]		*American Play*	16	[80] 6f
		74	[37]	Piston	*Concerto for Orchestra*	38	4b [7]
Bax	*First Symphony*	57	1	Piston	*Suite for Orchestra*	36	3
Bax	*Second Symphony*	5	1b [2]	Russell	*Fugue for Eight*		
Bax	*Third Symphony*	39	[40] 3f		*Percussion Instruments*	1	[A]
		110	[28] 7f	Schuman, W.	*Prayer in Time of War*	25	341
Bax	*Fourth Symphony*	40	3	Shepherd	*Horizons*	112	1
Bax	*Fifth Symphony*	106	[7] 3f	Siegmeister	*From my Window*	46	[50] 1f
Bax	*Sixth Symphony*	30	[27]	Stravinsky	*Histoire du Soldat*	1	1b [1]
Britten	*Four Sea Interludes*					14	1b [1]
	from "Peter Grimes"	74	[9] 3f			51	2
Britten	*Passacaglia from "Peter*			Stravinsky	*Ragtime*	3	[1]
	Grimes"	16	1b [6]	Stravinsky	*Scherzo à la Russe*	27	[22]
Britten	*Sinfonia da Requiem*	36	[25]	Thomson	*Louisiana Story Suite*	64	15
						79	79

Tenor Drum

COMPOSER	WORK	PAGE	MEASURE	COMPOSER	WORK	PAGE	MEASURE
Chávez	*Sinfonia India*	24	[27]	Stravinsky	*Histoire du Soldat*	3	7
						4	8
						46	24

Snare and Tenor Drums

COMPOSER	WORK	PAGE	MEASURE	COMPOSER	WORK	PAGE	MEASURE
Chávez	*Sinfonia de Antigona*	8	[6]	Stravinsky	*Les Noces*	2	[2]

Snare Drum and Tarolle (Small Side Drum)

COMPOSER	WORK	PAGE	MEASURE	COMPOSER	WORK	PAGE	MEASURE
Poulenc	*Concert Champêtre pour*	16	[11] 5f	Poulenc	*Concerto pour deux*	1	1
	Clavecin et Orchestre	37	[26]		*Pianos et Orchestre*	84	1
		92	1b [16]			105	2b [67]

(7) OTHER EFFECTS

Bass Drum

English	Italian	French	German
Cannon shot(s)	Colpo(i) di cannone	Comme un canon	Wie eine Kanone
Like a cannon	Quasi cannone		

	COMPOSER	WORK	PAGE	MEASURE
	Prokofieff	*Lieutenant Kijé*	4	[6]

English	Italian	French	German
Out of tune (without pitch or resonance)	Scordata	Mal accordé	Verstimmt

Verdi	*Messa da Requiem*	208 43

English	Italian	French	German
Played delicately with the fingers, like a five-finger exercise	Teneramente, coi quintupolo dita, come un esercizio	Joué délicatement avec les doigts, comme une étude pour les cinq doigts	Zart mit den Fingern gespielt, wie eine 5-Fingerübung

	WORK		
Stillman-Kelley	*Gulliver—His Voyage to Lilliput*	80 [C] 6f	106 [Y] 4f

English	Italian	French	German
Rub a rosined glove or cloth over a snare drum stick with tip of stick pressed against center of drum head	Fregate con uno guanto resinato sopra una bacchetta di tamburo spingendo la punta della bacchetta nel medio della membrana	Frottez avec un gant résineux sur une baguette de tambour en pressant le bout de la baguette contre le milieu de la peau	Mit einem harzigen Handschuh über einem Trommelschlägel reiben mit dem Punkt des Schlägels am Mitte des Fells drückend

Russell	*Fugue for Eight Percussion Instruments*	7 [F] 11f	

English	Italian	French	German
Two [2] players	Due [2] esecutori [suonatori]	Deux [2] exécutants	Zwei [2] Schläger

Berlioz	*Symphonie Fantastique*	208 5

Snare Drum

English	Italian	French	German
Place a handkerchief over drum head	Coprire la membrana col fazzoletto	Mettez un mouchoir sur la peau	Mit einem Taschentuch an der Felle bedeckt

Russell	*Fugue for Eight Percussion Instruments*	1 1	

PERCUSSION

Snare Drum (contd.)

English	Italian	French	German
Place a piece of paper on the drum head	Coprire la membrana colla carta	Mettez un papier sur la peau	Mit einem Papier an der Felle bedeckt

COMPOSER	WORK	PAGE	MEASURE
Russell	*Fugue for Eight Percussion Instruments*	**3**	[C]

English	Italian	French	German
"Ride" solo	—	—	—

COMPOSER	WORK	PAGE	MEASURE
Gould	*Spirituals*	**26**	9

English	Italian	French	German
Roll—beginning at center—gradually going to the rim	Rullo—dal medio all'orlo poco a poco	Roulez—commençant au milieu de la peau en allant peu à peu vers le bord	Wirbel—von der Mitte allmählich bis zum Rand

COMPOSER	WORK	PAGE	MEASURE
Bartók	*Concerto for Piano and Orchestra*	**59**	5b [13]

English	Italian	French	German
Roll—beginning at the rim—gradually going to center	Rullo—dall'orlo al medio poco a poco	Roulez—commençant au bord en allant peu à peu vers le milieu	Wirbel—vom Rand allmählich bis zur Mitte

COMPOSER	WORK	PAGE	MEASURE
Bartók	*Concerto for Piano and Orchestra*	**53**	[2] 3f

English	Italian	French	German
3 Drums	3 Casse	3 Caisses	3 Trommeln
	I: f; II: mf; III: p.		

COMPOSER	WORK	PAGE	MEASURE
Schelling	*A Victory Ball*	**75**	1

English	Italian	French	German
Tuned high	Accordato in alto	Accordé en haut	Hoch gestimmt

COMPOSER	WORK	PAGE	MEASURE
Vaughan Williams	*Symphony in E minor (No. 6)*	**83**	3

English	Italian	French	German
With a thin piece of felt on middle of drum head	Con una minuto frammento di feltro nel medio della membrana	Avec un morceau mince de feutre au milieu de la peau	Mit dünnem Filzstück auf der Mitte des Fells

COMPOSER	WORK	PAGE	MEASURE
Russell	*Fugue for Eight Percussion Instruments*	1	[A] 8f

Chapter 36

GONG, TAMBOURINE, AND TRIANGLE

(1) DAMPENED

(for terminology and notation see Chapter 32, page 163)

Tambourine

COMPOSER	WORK	PAGE	MEASURE	COMPOSER	WORK	PAGE	MEASURE
Albéniz–Arbós	Fête-Dieu à Séville	6	1b [B]	**Dvořák**	Carnival Overture	79	6
		30	[J]	**Milhaud**	Opus Americanum No. 2	33	[205] 3f

Triangle

COMPOSER	WORK	PAGE	MEASURE	COMPOSER	WORK	PAGE	MEASURE
Ireland	Symphonic Rhapsody, "Mai-Dun"	41	2	**Lalo**	Symphonie Espagnole	49	4
						62	2
Kay	Suite for Orchestra	71	[79]	**Mahler**	Symphony No. 5	246	5

Gong and Tambourine

COMPOSER	WORK	PAGE	MEASURE
Respighi	Feste Romane	153	5

(2) METHODS OF STRIKING

English	Italian	French	German
Brush the head [skin] with the thumb	Col pollice (sulla membrana)	Avec le pouce	Das Fell mit dem Daumen streifen
Rub head [skin] with thumb		Frôlez la membrane avec le pouce	Mit dem Daumen (über das Fell)
Stroke(d)		Le trille (tr.) indique le pouce	
Thumb (trill)			
With (the) thumb			

Tambourine

COMPOSER	WORK	PAGE	MEASURE	COMPOSER	WORK	PAGE	MEASURE
Dukas	La Péri	46	[7]	**Siegmeister**	Sunday in Brooklyn	61	3
		64	[9]	**Siegmeister**	Western Suite	44	3
Griffes	The Pleasure Dome of Kubla Khan	27	1			99	1
				Siegmeister	Wilderness Road	9	[40]
McDonald	Rhumba from 2nd Symphony	8	[40]	**Stravinsky**	Fire-Bird Suite (1919)	55	[28]
Milhaud	La Création du Monde	12	1	**Stravinsky**	Les Noces	8	1b [10]
Milhaud	La Mort d'un Tyran	1	1			24	[29]
Milhaud	Saudades do Brazil	20	11	**Stravinsky**	Renard	2	[III]
Poulenc	Concert Champêtre pour Clavecin et Orchestre	107	[28]			44	[26]
						114	1b [73]
Schreker	The Birthday of the Infanta, Suite	5	[15] 1f	**Stravinsky**	Scherzo à la Russe	27	[22]
		56	2b [355]	**Tchaikovsky**	Nutcracker Suite	75	2b [A]
				Varèse	Ionisation	3	6

213

PERCUSSION

Tambourine (contd.)

English	Italian	French	German
Brush [flick] the jingles	*Sulle tintinnie*	*Effleurez [tintez] les cliquetis*	*Auf den Schellen*
On the jingles		*Sur les tintements*	

COMPOSER	WORK	PAGE	MEASURE	COMPOSER	WORK	PAGE	MEASURE
Lambert	*The Rio Grande*	**26**	[E] 6f	**Walton**	*Façade, Suite No. 1*	**55**	1

English	Italian	French	German
Fist	*Col pugno*	*L'accent (>) indique le coup*	*Mit der Faust*
With (the) fist		*frappé avec le poing*	

Gould	*Philharmonic Waltzes*	**8**	[74] 3f	**Prokofieff**	*Cinderella Suite No. 1*	**119**	[95]
		36	7	**Prokofieff**	*Lieutenant Kijé*	**48**	[41]
Milhaud	*La Création du Monde*	**12**	1				

English	Italian	French	German
On (the) knee	*Col ginocchio*	*Avec le genou*	*Auf dem Knie gestreichen*
Strike on knee	*Colpo sul ginocchio*	*Frappez sur le genou*	*Mit dem Knie*
With (the) knee		*Le coup frappé avec le genou*	

Ibert	*Escales*	**19**	4	**Stravinsky**	*Chant du Rossignol*	**61**	[63] 1f
		91	[80] 2f	**Stravinsky**	*Les Noces*	**126**	[130]
Sessions	*Suite from "The Black*			**Stravinsky**	*Renard*	**2**	[III]
	Maskers"	**10**	1b [7]			**69**	[46] 2f
Sessions	*Symphony for*	**23**	[35] 2f				
	Orchestra (No. 1)	**66**	[104] 1f				

English	Italian	French	German
On the rim	*Sull'orlo*	*Sur bord*	*Am Rand*

(for further terminology see Chapter 32, page 163, and Chapter 35, page 197)

Gong

Rogers	*Once Upon a Time,*			**Strang**	*Percussion Music*	**23**	18
	Five Fairy Tales	**61**	[36]				

Tambourine

Khachaturian	*Gayne Ballet Suite*			**Lambert**	*The Rio Grande*	**8**	6
	No. 1-A	**22**	[10] 2f			**51**	[27] 7f

Tambourine (contd.)

English	Italian	French	German
On the skin	Sulla membrana	Sur la peau	Auf das Fell

COMPOSER	WORK	PAGE	MEASURE	COMPOSER	WORK	PAGE	MEASURE
Khachaturian	Gayne Ballet Suite No. 1-A	22	[10] 2f	Schreker	The Birthday of the Infanta, Suite	5 56 71	[15] 1f 2b [355] 1

English	Italian	French	German
Shake (hoop)	Agitare Trillo	Agité Agitez Secoué(er) Secouez	Schütteln

COMPOSER	WORK	PAGE	MEASURE	COMPOSER	WORK	PAGE	MEASURE
Bax	First Symphony	32 101	[JJ] 4	Ireland	A London Overture	71	[49]
				Milhaud	La Mort d'un Tyran	27	113
Bax	Third Symphony	43	1b [44]	Milhaud	Le Bal Martiniquais	9	4b [40]
Bax	Sixth Symphony	114	[33]	Mussorgsky–	Pictures at an		
Bax	The Garden of Fand	32	[H]	Ravel	Exhibition	57	[53]
Ibert	Escales	14 55	[9] [48]	Siegmeister	Western Suite	98	1b [90]
				Stravinsky	Chant du Rossignol	34	[34] 1f
Ibert	Féerique	29	[19]	Stravinsky	Petrouchka Suite	75	[60]

English	Italian	French	German
Strike Struck	Colpo Colpete	Frappée(s) Frapper Frappez	Schlagen

COMPOSER	WORK	PAGE	MEASURE	COMPOSER	WORK	PAGE	MEASURE
Ibert	Escales	26	[21]	Milhaud	Quatrième Symphonie	88	2b [65]
Ibert	Féerique	38	2	Milhaud	La Mort d'un Tyran	27 40	113 8
Malipiero	Impressioni dal Vero, 3ª Parte	17	[8]	Milhaud	Le Bal Martiniquais	9	4b [40]
Milhaud	Deuxième Concerto pour Violoncelle et Orchestre	15	1	Milhaud Mussorgsky– Ravel	Opus Americanum No. 2 Pictures at an Exhibition	33 57	[205] 3f [53]
Milhaud	IIe Symphonie	35 77	[110] 2f [G] 1f				

English	Italian	French	German
With (the) fingers [fingertips]	Col il dita	Avec les doigts	Mit den Fingern

COMPOSER	WORK	PAGE	MEASURE	COMPOSER	WORK	PAGE	MEASURE
McDonald	Rhumba from 2nd Symphony	7	[33]	Rogers	Once Upon a Time, Five Fairy Tales	35	[22]
McDonald	Three Poems for Orchestra	30	2b [77]				

English	Italian	French	German
With (the) hand	Colla mano	Avec la main	Mit der Hand

COMPOSER	WORK	PAGE	MEASURE	COMPOSER	WORK	PAGE	MEASURE
Elgar	Cockaigne, Concert Overture	37	[21]	Riisager	Torgot Dance	25	[115]

PERCUSSION

Tambourine (contd.)

English	Italian	French	German
English	*Italian*	*French*	*German*
With (the) knuckles	Colla nocce	Avec les jointures	Mit den Knöcheln

COMPOSER	WORK	PAGE	MEASURE
Siegmeister	*Ozark Set*	**10**	2

(3) MUFFLED [MUTED]

(for terminology see Chapter 32, page 165)

Gong

Bartók	*Deux Portraits*	**36**	1

Tambourine

Mahler	*Symphony No. 3*	**17**	8b [13]

Triangle

COMPOSER	WORK	PAGE	MEASURE	COMPOSER	WORK	PAGE	MEASURE
Bartók	*Deux Portraits*	**20**	[2] 7f	**Russell**	*Fugue for Eight*		
		34	[11] 1f		*Percussion Instruments*	**4**	[D]

(4) OFF-STAGE

(for terminology see Chapter 11, page 75)

Tambourine

Stravinsky	*Petrouchka Suite*	**39**	[28]

Triangle

Inghelbrecht	*Rapsodie de Printemps*	**1**	1	**Mahler**	*Symphony No. 2*	**175**	[22]

(5) STICK TYPES

(for terminology see Chapter 32, pages 166–7)

BASS DRUM STICK

Gong

Milhaud	*Ière Symphonie*	**64**	[60] 1f	**Strauss, R.**	*Macbeth*	**71**	4
Strang	*Percussion Music*	**23**	24				

GONG, TAMBOURINE, AND TRIANGLE

CANE STICK WITH FIBRE HEAD [KNOB]

Tambourine

COMPOSER	WORK	PAGE	MEASURE
Stravinsky	Histoire du Soldat	4	[8]
		14	[2] 1f

CYMBAL STICK

Tambourine

Creston	Two Choric Dances	64	[240] 2f

HAMMER

Triangle

Russell	Three Dance Movements	19	[F] 4f

HARD STICK

Gong

Rogers	Characters from Hans Christian Andersen	10	1b [6]

Tambourine

Siegmeister	Western Suite	94	2b [75]

IRON STICK

Triangle

Stravinsky	Chant du Rossignol	42	[43]

PADDED STICK

Tambourine

Johnson	Imagery	4	4
		41	4

RUBBER STICK [STRIP]

Gong

Moross	Paeans	14	[M]

PERCUSSION

SNARE DRUM STICK

Gong

COMPOSER	WORK	PAGE	MEASURE
Stravinsky	*Petrouchka Suite*	**14**	[5]

Tambourine

Respighi	*The Pines of Rome*	**24**	[7]

SOFT STICK

Gong

COMPOSER	WORK	PAGE	MEASURE	COMPOSER	WORK	PAGE	MEASURE
Grofé	*Grand Canyon Suite*	**115**	3	**Strang**	*Percussion Music*	**23**	18

Tambourine

Siegmeister	*Ozark Set*	**80**	[80]

SPONGE STICK

Gong

Elgar	*Sea Pictures*	**5**	[B]	**Mahler**	*Symphony No. 3*	**72**	[51]
Mahler	*Symphony No. 1*	**78**	[3] 4f	**Mahler**	*Symphony No. 6*	**259**	[164]
Mahler	*Symphony No. 2*	**31**	[15]				

THIN STICK

Tambourine

Schreker	*The Birthday of the Infanta, Suite*	**71**	1

THIN METAL STICK

Triangle

Bartók	*Violin Concerto*	**87**	[145]

THIN WOOD STICK

Triangle

Bartók	*Violin Concerto*	**86**	[135]

218

GONG, TAMBOURINE, AND TRIANGLE

TIMPANI STICK

Gong

COMPOSER	WORK	PAGE	MEASURE	COMPOSER	WORK	PAGE	MEASURE
Bloch	*Schelomo*	33	2	**Ibert**	*Féerique*	15	[11]
Grofé	*Grand Canyon Suite*	165	[19]	**Milhaud**	*Ière Symphonie*	29	3b [110]
Honegger	*Le Roi David*	46	1	**Strauss, R.**	*Macbeth*	57	[V]

TRIANGLE STICK

Gong

Rogers	*Characters from Hans*			**Strauss, R.**	*Salomé's Dance*	2	[B]
	Christian Andersen	17	1	**Stravinsky**	*Le Sacre du Printemps*	85	[103]
Strauss, R.	*Macbeth*	59	[W]				

Tambourine

COMPOSER	WORK	PAGE	MEASURE
Stravinsky	*Histoire du Soldat*	46	[24]

WOOD(EN) STICK

Gong

de Falla	*El Retablo de Maese Pedro*	15	[10] 8f

Triangle

COMPOSER	WORK	PAGE	MEASURE	COMPOSER	WORK	PAGE	MEASURE
Bartók	*Second Rhapsody for*	9	[5]	**Stravinsky**	*Les Noces*	57	6b [63]
	Violin and Orchestra	42	[31] 1f	**Stravinsky**	*Renard*	76	[50]
Stravinsky	*Le Sacre du Printemps*	20	[29]	**Walton**	*Façade, Suite No. 1*	23	7

(6) OTHER EFFECTS

Gong

English	*Italian*	*French*	*German*
Kept in vibration by friction on the edge	Mantenuto in vibrazione per fregamento sull'orlo	Faites vibrer en frottant au bord	Durch Reibung an der Kante in Schwingung gehalten

Griffes	*The Pleasure Dome of Kubla Khan*	1	1

English	*Italian*	*French*	*German*
Laid horizontal—without resonance	Orizzontalmente—senza risonanza	Placé à plat—sans résonance	Ohne Resonanz—horizontal gelegt

de Falla	*El Retablo de Maese Pedro*	15	[10] 8f

PERCUSSION

English	*Italian*	*French*	*German*
Rapid glissando with triangle stick, describing an arc on the surface of the instrument	Glissando rapido circolando sulla superficie del'instrumento colla bacchetta di triangolo	Glissez rapidement avec la baguette du triangle, décrivant un arc sur la surface de l'instrument	Schnelles Glissando mit Triangelschlägel im Bogen an der Oberfläche des Instrumentes ausgeführt

COMPOSER	WORK	PAGE	MEASURE
Stravinsky	*Le Sacre du Printemps*	85	[103]
		87	[106]

Tambourine

English	*Italian*	*French*	*German*
Let drop on the floor	Lasciate cadere sul palco	Tenir (le Tamb. de B.) tout bas au sol et le faire tomber	Auf den Boden werfen

Stravinsky	*Petrouchka Suite*	153	2b [129]

English	*Italian*	*French*	*German*
Placed on snare drum	Mettere sulla tamburo militare	Mettez sur la caisse claire	Auf der kleinen Trommel

Siegmeister	*Western Suite*	94	2b [75]

English	*Italian*	*French*	*German*
Without jingles	Senza tintinnie	Sans tintements	Ohne Schellen

de Falla	*El Retablo de Maese Pedro*	36	[41]

Triangle

English	*Italian*	*French*	*German*
Muffle notes by holding l.h. against triangle	Assordate i toni mettendo la m.s. contra il triangolo	Étouffez les tons en mettant la m.g. contre la triangle	Töne durch linke Hand am Triangel gedämpft

Russell	*Fugue for Eight Percussion Instruments*	6	4

English	*Italian*	*French*	*German*
Wrapped tightly in a cloth—hold tightly in the hand	Involguto strettamente in tela—tenare strettamente nella mano	Bien enveloppé de toile—tenez fermement à la main	Fest in Stoff gewickelt—fest in der Hand gehalten

Stillman-Kelley	*Gulliver—His Voyage to Lilliput*	85	6b [H]

Chapter 37

OTHER PERCUSSION INSTRUMENTS

(for terminology see Nomenclature of Instruments, pages 7–10)

(1) METHODS OF PLAYING OR STRIKING

English	*Italian*	*French*	*German*
Near the center	Nell mezzo della membrana	Au milieu de la peau	In der Mitte des Fells

(for further terminology see Chapter 32, page 164)

Hand Drum

COMPOSER	WORK	PAGE	MEASURE
Antheil	*Over the Plains*	**51**	[30]

English	*Italian*	*French*	*German*
On the frame	Sulla cassa	Sur la caisse	Auf dem Holzrand

(for further terminology see Chapter 35, page 199)

Tom-Tom

Revueltas	*Sensemayá*	**1**	1

English	*Italian*	*French*	*German*
Played behind the bridge	Sonato dietro il ponticello	Jouez en arrière du chevalet	Hinter dem Steg spielen

Cimbalom

Stravinsky	*Renard*	**4**	1

English	*Italian*	*French*	*German*
Plucked with the fingertips	Pizzicato con il dita	Pizzicato avec les doigts	Mit den Fingern Pizzicato

Cimbalom

Bartók	*First Rhapsody for Violin and Orchestra*	**4**	[1]

English	*Italian*	*French*	*German*
Rasped and beaten	Raspato e battuto	Râpé et frappé	Gekratzt und geschlagen

Reco-Reco [Rasper]

Villa-Lobos	*Uirapurú*	**44**	1

PERCUSSION

English	*Italian*	*French*	*German*
Roll with the fingers	Rullo col il dita	Roulé avec les doigts	Wirbel mit den Fingern

Small Drums

COMPOSER	WORK	PAGE	MEASURE
Berlioz	*Harold en Italie*	**147**	5

English	*Italian*	*French*	*German*
With (the) handle of the stick	Col mancio della mazza	Avec la manche de la mailloche	Mit dem Stiel des Klöppels

(for further terminology see Chapter 34, page 184)

Cimbalom

Bartók	*First Rhapsody for Violin and Orchestra*	**6**	[2] 1f

(2) MUFFLED [MUTED]

(for terminology see Chapter 32, page 165)

Wood Blocks

Stillman-Kelley	*Gulliver—His Voyage to Lilliput*	**85**	[H]

(3) OFF-STAGE

(for terminology see Chapter 11, page 75)

Cowbells

COMPOSER	WORK	PAGE	MEASURE	COMPOSER	WORK	PAGE	MEASURE
Mahler	*Symphony No. 6*	**35**	[21] 2f	**Mahler**	*Symphony No. 7*	**92**	[84]
		182	[121]				

Harmonium

Inghelbrecht	*Rapsodie de Printemps*	**1**	1

(4) STICK TYPES

(for terminology see Chapter 32, pages 166–7)

FELT STICKS

Bongos [Cuban Drums]

Varèse	*Ionisation*	**4**	[1]

222

OTHER PERCUSSION INSTRUMENTS

Tom-Tom

COMPOSER	WORK	PAGE	MEASURE
Stravinsky	*Ebony Concerto*	**4**	[4]
		22	[3]

HARD STICKS

Tom-Tom

Revueltas	*Sensemayá*	**38**	[36]

HEAVY HAMMER

Anvil [or Steel Pipe]

Russell	*Three Dance Movements*	**18**	[E] 4f

Steel Plate

Bloch	*America*	**141**	[80] 2f

LEATHER STICKS

Cimbalom

Stravinsky	*Renard*	**5**	[1]

ORDINARY [REGULAR, USUAL] STICKS

Castanets

Siegmeister	*Ozark Set*	**78**	1

RUBBER (-COVERED) STICKS

Pop Bottles

Green	*Three Inventories of Casey Jones*	**12**	1

Tom-Tom

Russell	*Three Dance Movements*	**16**	4b [4]

SMALL HAMMER

Anvil

Bloch	*America*	**128**	[73]

223

PERCUSSION

SNARE DRUM STICKS

Tom-Tom

COMPOSER	WORK	PAGE	MEASURE	COMPOSER	WORK	PAGE	MEASURE
Russell	*Three Dance Movements*	17	2	Stravinsky	*Ebony Concerto*	34	[28]

Wood Blocks

COMPOSER	WORK	PAGE	MEASURE
Russell	*Three Dance Movements*	17	2

SOFT WOOD HAMMER

Steel Plate

Bloch	*America*	155	[89]	1f

SPONGE STICKS

Bongos

Varèse	*Ionisation*	21	[13]	4f

TIMPANI STICKS

Tabor

Milhaud	*Ière Symphonie*	55	1b	[155]

TRIANGLE STICK

Ginger-ale Bottle

Russell	*Three Dance Movements*	17	[C]

VERY HARD LEATHER STICKS

Tarolle [Small Side Drum]

Poulenc	*Concert Champêtre pour Clavecin et Orchestre*	16	[11]	5f

WOOD(EN) STICKS

Bongos

Varèse	*Ionisation*	12	[8]

OTHER PERCUSSION INSTRUMENTS

Cimbalom

COMPOSER	WORK	PAGE	MEASURE
Stravinsky	*Renard*	**5**	[1]

Tom-Tom

Russell	*Three Dance Movements*	**18**	1

(5) OTHER EFFECTS

English	*Italian*	*French*	*German*
Break bottle!	Fracassate la bottiglia!	Brisez la bouteille!	Flasche zerbrechen!

Bottle

Russell	*Three Dance Movements*	**19**	2b [G]

English	*Italian*	*French*	*German*
4 Hands	A 4 mani	A 4 mains	4-Händig Zu 4 Händen

Clavicembalo

Respighi	*Antiche Danze ed Arie,* *2ª Suite*	**1**	1

English	*Italian*	*French*	*German*
Glissando across (wood) blocks	Glissando sui legni	Glissez sur les blocs	Gleitend über die Holzkasten

Wood Blocks

Riisager	*Torgot Dance*	**21**	3

English	*Italian*	*French*	*German*
Glissando on string with nail of l.h. thumb	Glissando sulla corda colla unghie delle pollice sinistra	Glissez sur la corde avec l'ongle de la pouce gauche	Glissando auf der Saite mit dem Nagel des linken Hand

Cimbalom

Bartók	*First Rhapsody for* *Violin and Orchestra*	**28**	[13] 3f

English	*Italian*	*French*	*German*
Harmonics	Armonici	Sons harmoniques	Flageolett

Guitar

Schreker	*The Birthday of the* *Infanta, Suite*	**31**	2b [140]

225

PERCUSSION

English	Italian	French	German
Pricked with a pin	Punturato con uno spillo	Piquez avec une épingle	Mit einer Nadel stecken

Toy Balloons

COMPOSER	WORK	PAGE	MEASURE
Slonimsky	*My Toy Balloon*	**23**	4

English	Italian	French	German
(Glass) smashed with a mallet; emptied on a hard surface	Fracassate con uno maglio; vuotate il verraio spezzato sopra una superficie	Écrasez avec un maillet; videz le verre brisé sur une surface dure	Mit Hammer zerschlagen; Glas auf hartem Boden ausgeleert

Glass Plates

Davidson	*Auto Accident*	**9**	4

(6) OTHER KEYED PERCUSSION INSTRUMENTS

Color Organ

Scriabin	*Prométhée, Le Poème du Feu*	**3**	1

Harmonium

COMPOSER	WORK	PAGE	MEASURE	COMPOSER	WORK	PAGE	MEASURE
Hindemith	*Kammermusik No. 1*	**1**	2	**Shostakovich**	*The Golden Age, Ballet Suite*	**47**	[57]
Mahler	*Symphony No. 8*	**139**	[106]	**Tchaikovsky**	*Manfred-Symphonie*	**300**	448

(7) OTHER PITCHED PERCUSSION INSTRUMENTS

Antique Cymbals

Berlioz	*Roméo et Juliette*	**218**	8	**Ravel**	*Alborada del Gracioso*	**14**	[9] 5f
Debussy	*Prélude à l'après-midi d'un Faune*	**27**	[10]	**Ravel**	*Daphnis et Chloé, Suite No. 1*	**62**	[128] 2f
Debussy-Ansermet	*Six Épigraphes Antiques*	**51**	2	**Stravinsky**	*Le Sacre du Printemps*	**20**	[29]
				Stravinsky	*Les Noces*	**127**	3

Cimbalom [Clavicembalo]

Bartók	*First Rhapsody for Violin and Orchestra*	**3**	1	**Rogers**	*Once Upon a Time, Five Fairy Tales*	**1**	4
de Falla	*El Retablo de Maese Pedro*	**3**	1	**Strauss, R.**	*Dance Suite after François Couperin*	**1**	1
				Stravinsky	*Ragtime*	**3**	1

226

OTHER PERCUSSION INSTRUMENTS

Cowbells

COMPOSER	WORK	PAGE	MEASURE	COMPOSER	WORK	PAGE	MEASURE
Gould	*Latin-American Symphonette*	78	1	Mahler	*Symphony No. 7*	253	[293] 1f
Lambert	*The Rio Grande*	24	2b [B]	Siegmeister	*From my Window*	56	1b [40]
Mahler	*Symphony No. 6*	134	[94] 2f	Strauss, R.	*Eine Alpensinfonie*	58	3b [51]

Cytharra [Zither]

COMPOSER	WORK	PAGE	MEASURE
Villa-Lobos	*Amazonas*	20	[7] 3f

Flexatone

Khachaturian	*Concerto for Piano and Orchestra*	65	[49]

Gramophone Record (Nightingale's song)

Respighi	*The Pines of Rome*	67	3

Guitar

COMPOSER	WORK	PAGE	MEASURE	COMPOSER	WORK	PAGE	MEASURE
Gould	*Latin-American Symphonette*	36	1	Thomson	*Orchestra Suite from "The Plow that Broke the Plains"*	15	1
Mahler	*Symphony No. 7*	155	4b [175]				

Harmonica

Saint-Saëns	*Le Carnaval des Animaux*	17	1

Jew's Harp

Ives	*"Washington's Birthday" from Symphony, "Holidays"*	10	[P]

Mandoline

Mahler	*Symphony No. 7*	158	[180]	Respighi	*Feste Romane*	79	[24] 2f

Musical Tumblers (water-tuned)

Davidson	*Auto Accident*	9	6

Sleighbells

COMPOSER	WORK	PAGE	MEASURE	COMPOSER	WORK	PAGE	MEASURE
Cadman	*American Suite*	41	4	Mahler	*Symphony No. 4*	1	1
Copland	*Billy the Kid Ballet Suite*	28	7	Respighi	*Feste Romane*	60	[17]
				Skilton	*Suite Primeval, Part II*	81	3
Elgar	*Cockaigne, Concert Overture*	27	[17]	Varèse	*Hyperprism*	3	1
				Varèse	*Intégrales*	1	1

PERCUSSION

Temple Bells

COMPOSER	WORK	PAGE	MEASURE
Davidson	*Auto Accident*	6	7

Violinophone

Villa-Lobos	*Uirapurú*	87	[23]

(8) OTHER UNPITCHED PERCUSSION INSTRUMENTS

Anvil [Steel Bar, Plate]

COMPOSER	WORK	PAGE	MEASURE	COMPOSER	WORK	PAGE	MEASURE
Gould	*Spirituals*	20	I	**Strang**	*Percussion Music*	21	4
Russell	*Three Dance Movements*	15	5	**Varèse**	*Hyperprism*	3	I

Auto [Taxi] Horn [Claxon]

COMPOSER	WORK	PAGE	MEASURE	COMPOSER	WORK	PAGE	MEASURE
Bloch	*America*	126	2	**Inghelbrecht**	*La Métamorphose d'Ève*	25	2
Gershwin	*An American in Paris*	4	[3] 6f				
		17	4b [15]				
		88	[72]				

Bouteillophone

Honegger	*Le Dit des Jeux du Monde*	27	I

Box filled with sand

Hindemith	*Kammermusik No. 1*	67	3

Chains

Varèse	*Intégrales*	I	I

Chinese Blocks [Drums]

COMPOSER	WORK	PAGE	MEASURE	COMPOSER	WORK	PAGE	MEASURE
Davidson	*Auto Accident*	6	9	**Varèse**	*Hyperprism*	3	I
Strang	*Percussion Music*	21	I	**Varèse**	*Intégrales*	I	I

Chocalho, Xocalho [Large Gourds]

COMPOSER	WORK	PAGE	MEASURE	COMPOSER	WORK	PAGE	MEASURE
Guarnieri	*Brazilian Dance*	5	[20] 4f	**Milhaud**	*Saudades do Brazil*	32	I

Claves [Cuban Sticks]

Gould	*Latin–American Symphonette*	I	3

228

OTHER PERCUSSION INSTRUMENTS

Coconut Shells (muffled on leather)

COMPOSER	WORK	PAGE	MEASURE
Grofé	*Grand Canyon Suite*	57	[A]

Cuckoo

Rosenthal	*Les Petits Métiers*	87	2

Drumsticks

Rogers	*Once Upon a Time, Five Fairy Tales*	1	1

Gourds, Maracas, Shakers

COMPOSER	WORK	PAGE	MEASURE	COMPOSER	WORK	PAGE	MEASURE
Engel	*The Creation*	46	3	**Prokofieff**	*Romeo and Juliet, Suite No. 2*	85	[52] 3f
Gould	*Latin-American Symphonette*	19	[N]	**Rosenthal**	*Les Petits Métiers*	113	2
McDonald	*Rhumba from 2nd Symphony*	9	1b [50]	**Strang**	*Percussion Music*	22	16

Guáchara, Güiro, Reco-Reco [Raspers]

COMPOSER	WORK	PAGE	MEASURE	COMPOSER	WORK	PAGE	MEASURE
Milhaud	*Saudades do Brazil*	4	2	**Villa-Lobos**	*Uirapurú*	44	1
Stravinsky	*Le Sacre du Printemps*	60	[70]				

Horse-hooves

Thomson	*Orchestra Suite from "The Plow that Broke the Plains"*	22	5b [17]

Jingles

COMPOSER	WORK	PAGE	MEASURE	COMPOSER	WORK	PAGE	MEASURE
Holst	*The Ballet from "The Perfect Fool"*	9	[7] 4f	**Ireland**	*A London Overture*	10	3b [5]

Large Bottle filled with Marbles

Green	*Three Inventories of Casey Jones*	12	20

Pop Bottles

Green	*Three Inventories of Casey Jones*	11	1

PERCUSSION

Rattle [Ratchet]

COMPOSER	WORK	PAGE	MEASURE	COMPOSER	WORK	PAGE	MEASURE
Davidson	*Auto Accident*	5	1	Rosenthal	*Les Petits Métiers*	28	1
de Falla	*El Retablo de Maese*			Schuman, W.	*Undertow*	31	3
	Pedro	36	41	Siegmeister	*Sunday in Brooklyn*	81	[80] 1f
Gould	*Philharmonic Waltzes*	18	[185]	Skilton	*Suite Primeval, Part I*	21	3
Jacobi	*Music Hall Overture*	7	[2]	Skilton	*Suite Primeval, Part II*	14	2
Milhaud	*La Mort d'un Tyran*	35	150	Strauss, R.	*Till Eulenspiegel's*		
Pizzetti	*Introduzione all'*				*Merry Pranks*	14	[9] 8f
	"Agamennone" di			Varèse	*Hyperprism*	3	1
	Eschilo	69	3	Walton	*Façade, Suite No. 1*	72	4
Rogers	*Characters from Hans*						
	Christian Andersen	27	5				

Sandpaper (blocks)

COMPOSER	WORK	PAGE	MEASURE	COMPOSER	WORK	PAGE	MEASURE
Gould	*Spirituals*	13	[A] 6f	Stillman-	*Gulliver—His Voyage*		
		18	1b [G]	Kelley	*to Lilliput*	119	3
				White	*Five Miniatures*	9	2

Siren

COMPOSER	WORK	PAGE	MEASURE	COMPOSER	WORK	PAGE	MEASURE
Davidson	*Auto Accident*	9	8	Varèse	*Ionisation*	3	1
Hindemith	*Kammermusik No. 1*	111	4				

Slapstick [Whip]

COMPOSER	WORK	PAGE	MEASURE	COMPOSER	WORK	PAGE	MEASURE
Britten	*Sinfonia da Requiem*	52	3b [35]	Milhaud	*La Mort d'un Tyran*	1	1
Britten	*The Young Person's*			Milhaud	*Le Bal Martiniquais*	21	[15] 3f
	Guide to the			Milhaud	*Sérénade pour*		
	Orchestra	47	10		*Orchestre*	71	[15] 4f
Copland	*Four Dance Episodes*			Russell	*Three Dance Move-*		
	from "Rodeo"	14	4b [14]		*ments*	17	1
Copland	*Statements*	15	4b [3]	Varèse	*Hyperprism*	3	1
Gershwin	*Concerto in F for*			Varèse	*Intégrales*	1	1
	Piano and Orchestra	31	[22] 2f				

Small Dinner Bell

COMPOSER	WORK	PAGE	MEASURE
Russell	*Three Dance Move-*		
	ments	15	5

String Drum, Cuica [Lion roar]

COMPOSER	WORK	PAGE	MEASURE	COMPOSER	WORK	PAGE	MEASURE
Guarnieri	*Savage Dance*	1	4	Varèse	*Hyperprism*	3	1

Switches

COMPOSER	WORK	PAGE	MEASURE	COMPOSER	WORK	PAGE	MEASURE
Mahler	*Symphony No. 7*	202	[242] 4f	Varèse	*Intégrales*	1	1

OTHER PERCUSSION INSTRUMENTS

Temple Blocks

COMPOSER	WORK	PAGE	MEASURE	COMPOSER	WORK	PAGE	MEASURE
Gould	*Latin-American Symphonette*	98	[13] 1f	Hanson	*"Merry Mount" Suite*	12	2b [78]
						41	4b [4]
Gould	*Philharmonic Waltzes*	16	[160]	Strang	*Percussion Music*	21	5

Tom-Tom [Indian Drum]

COMPOSER	WORK	PAGE	MEASURE	COMPOSER	WORK	PAGE	MEASURE
Hindemith	*Neues vom Tage*	15	2	Skilton	*Suite Primeval, Part I*	11	1
Inghelbrecht	*La Métamorphose d'Ève*	29	[21]	Skilton	*Suite Primeval, Part II*	7	1

Thunder-machine

COMPOSER	WORK	PAGE	MEASURE
Strauss, R.	*Eine Alpensinfonie*	141	[124]

Wind-machine

COMPOSER	WORK	PAGE	MEASURE	COMPOSER	WORK	PAGE	MEASURE
Grofé	*Grand Canyon Suite*	128	9	Strauss, R.	*Don Quixote*	111	1
Milhaud	*Les Choéphores*	125	3b [D]	Strauss, R.	*Eine Alpensinfonie*	110	2b [108]

Wood Blocks

COMPOSER	WORK	PAGE	MEASURE	COMPOSER	WORK	PAGE	MEASURE
Barber	*Second Symphony*	34	[24] 3f	Ravel	*Concerto pour la main gauche*	61	[33]
Copland	*Billy the Kid Ballet Suite*	32	2	Rogers	*Once Upon a Time, Five Fairy Tales*	14	1
Copland	*Four Dance Episodes from "Rodeo"*	12	[12] 6f	Russell	*Three Dance Movements*	15	[A]
		72	3				
Hanson	*"Merry Mount" Suite*	41	4b [4]	Strang	*Percussion Music*	22	9

Wooden Hammer on a Plank

COMPOSER	WORK	PAGE	MEASURE	COMPOSER	WORK	PAGE	MEASURE
Milhaud	*Les Choéphores*	163	3	Respighi	*Feste Romane*	114	[34]

Chapter 38

PERCUSSION TERMINOLOGY

Cymbals

English	Italian	French	German
Cymbal hung by its strap	Piatto sospeso dalla sua lascia	Une cymbale suspendue par sa courroie	Becken am Riemen hängend
Cymbal struck with drum-stick	Piatto colpo colla mazza	1 Cymbale frappée avec la mailloche	Teller mit Schlägel
Hung cymbal rolled with timpani sticks	I Piatto rullo con bacchette di Timpani	1 Cymbale roulée avec baguettes de Timbales	Ein Beckenteller mit Pauken-schlägel
Let vibrate gently by barely touching	Lasciate vibrare leggieramente —appena toccate	Laissez vibrer doucement en effleurant à peine les deux plateaux	Leicht vibrieren lassen—leicht berühren
Roll on suspended cymbal with sticks	Piatto sospeso rullo con bacchette	Roulement sur une cymbale avec des baguettes	Wirbel auf den Beckenteller mit Schlägel
Stick on cymbal	Piatto colla mazza	Baguette [mailloche] sur Cymbale	Schlägel auf den Becken
Suspended cymbal with stick	Piatto sospeso con bacchetta	Cymbale libre avec baguette	Becken frei mit Schlägel
Take the other cymbal	Prendete l'altro piatto	Prenez l'autre cymbale	Anderes Becken nehmen
With two [2] sticks on cymbal	Con due [2] bacchette a piatto	Avec deux [2] baguettes sur une cymbale	Mit zwei [2] Schlägel auf Becken

Drums

English	Italian	French	German
On the skin with thin sticks	Sulla membrana con bacchette sottile	Sur la peau avec des baguettes minces	Auf das Fell mit dünnen Ruten
On the snares	Sulle corde	Sur le(s) timbre(s)	Auf den Saiten
Played on the shell (of the drum) with handle of stick	Esecutato sulla cassa del tam-buro col mancio della mazza	Joué sur le cadre du tambour avec le manche de la mail-loche	Mit einem Holzstäbchen auf dem Holzrand der Trommel geschlagen
Roll on one side with soft sticks	Rullo sopra uno lato colle bacchette molle	Roulée sur un seul côté avec des baguettes molles	Mit weichen Schlägel auf einer Seite rollen
Well-tuned	Ben accordato	Bien accordé	Gut stimmen

Cymbals or Drums

English	Italian	French	German
Put stick aside	Lasciare la bacchetta	Laissez la baguette	Den Schlägel beiseite legen
Roll with sponge sticks	Rullo colle bacchette di spugna	Roulée avec des baguettes éponges	Wirbel mit den Schwamm-schlägel
Roll(ed) with two [2] sticks	Rullo con due [2] bacchette	Roulée avec deux [2] bag-uettes	Wirbel mit zwei [2] Schlägel
Take drumstick	Colla mazza	Prenez la mailloche	Mit der Schlägel
With stick(s)	Con bacchetta(e)	Avec baguette(s)	Mit Schlägel
With switches	Colli verghi	Avec verges	Mit Ruten

232

PERCUSSION TERMINOLOGY

Timpani

English	*Italian*	*French*	*German*
A to low E	Cambia A in E bassa	La au Mi bas [grave]	A nach E tief
C♯ to high F♯	C♯ in F♯ alta	Changez l'Ut♯ au Fa♯ haut	Cis in Fis hoch
Change C♯ to C♮	Muta C♯ in C♮	Changez Ut♯ en Ut♮	Cis nach C (züruckstimmen)
		Ut♯ change en Ut♮	
		La♯ Ut au Ut♮	
		Préparez Ut♮	
Lower C♯ to C♮	Cambia C♯ in C♮	Baissez Ut♯ à Ut♮	Cis nach C umstimmen
		Descendre le Ut♯ au Ut♮	Nach C umstimmen
		Ut♮ de Ut♯	
Raise C to C♯	Mutano C in C♯	L'Ut monte au Ut♯	C nach Cis umstimmen
		Monter(ez) l'Ut au Ut♯	
Tune G♯ to B	Muta G♯ in B	Changez Sol♯ en Si	Gis nach H stimmen
Tune high E to C	Muta E alta in C	Changez le Mi aigu en Do	Hoch E nach C umstimmen

General

Allow to vibrate	Lasciare vibrare	Frappez en laissant vibrer	Ausklingen lassen
Don't damp(en)	*l.v.*	Laissez vibrer	Klingen lassen
Let vibrate [ring; sound]	Si lasci vibrare	*l.v.*	Nicht abdämpfen
l.v.			
Let sound [tone] die away	Lascia svanire	Laisser mourir le son	Verklingen lassen
	Lasciar estinguere		
	Lasci spegnere		
Touched with stick	Toccato con una bacchetta	Touchée avec une baguette	Mit einem Stock berühren
With sticks only	Bacchette soli	Baguettes solos	Nur mit Schlägel

PART V

Keyboard Instruments

INTRODUCTION

I T IS AN INTERESTING and rather significant phenomenon that the piano, more than any other keyboard instrument, has become such an integral part of the orchestral fabric in the past half-century. Its frequent use in contemporary orchestration has given the new music an individual color and sonority unique in instrumental composition. And it is perhaps equally significant that it is the percussive character of the instrument that is most fully exploited. Whether or not, of course, this particular tonal emphasis will be overdone by composers and arrangers, and will finally become a commonplace mannerism remains to be seen. There is always the ever-present danger—against which every sensitive orchestrator must be on guard— that any purely technical device or color effect may become important for its own sake and not for its aptness or inevitability in the music being written or scored.

Although the keyboard instruments—celesta, organ, and piano—are normally grouped with the percussion section, at least so far as the arrangement on the score page is concerned, it was thought best to consider these instruments separately, as their "percussive" quality—even that of the piano—is secondary to their harmonic and melodic capacities. It should be evident, also, that these instruments are considered in the *Thesaurus* only in their role as orchestral members, not as solo or concerted instruments.

In addition to the more conventional devices, such as *glissandi* and *tremolandi*, some of the newer effects possible are catalogued in Chapter 39. These include tone-clusters, playing on the piano strings with the fingertips, the use of full organ for massive sonority, and the employing of the overtones (harmonics) in the piano. As the terminology applicable to the keyboard instruments can be found listed under each appropriate section of Part V, no final chapter of miscellaneous terms is necessary here, as is the case in the other divisions of the book.

Chapter 39

CELESTA, ORGAN, AND PIANO

(1) GLISSANDI

English	Italian	French	German
Glissando on (the) black keys	Glissando sulle taste nere	Glissez des touches noires	Glissando auf den schwarzen Tastatur
Glissando on (the) white keys	Glissando sulle taste bianche	Glissez des touches blanches	Glissando auf den weissen Tastatur
Glissando over the entire keyboard	Glissando sopra tutte i taste	Glissez sur toutes les touches	Glissando über die ganze Klaviatur

Celesta

COMPOSER	WORK	PAGE	MEASURE	COMPOSER	WORK	PAGE	MEASURE
Bartók	*Dance Suite*	89	2b [58]	**Ravel**	*Ma Mère l'Oye*	52	[5]
Ferroud	*Au Parc Monceau*	8	1b [3]	**Ravel**	*Rapsodie Espagnole*	51	[7] 1f
Morris	*Prospice Symphony*	64	3			76	1

Organ

COMPOSER	WORK	PAGE	MEASURE
Holst	*The Planets*	159	7

Piano

COMPOSER	WORK	PAGE	MEASURE	COMPOSER	WORK	PAGE	MEASURE
Bartók	*Vier Orchesterstücke*	59	2b [26]	**Dukelsky**	*Symphony No. 3*	55	[22]
Benjamin	*From San Domingo*	13	1b [E]			106	1b [44]
Britten	*Sinfonia da Requiem*	51	[34] 6f	**de Falla**	*El Amor Brujo*	20	[5]
Casella	*Pupazzetti*	51	[8] 9f	**de Falla**	*Nuits dans les Jardins*	31	[24]
Copland	*Dance Symphony*	67	[40] 7f		*d'Espagne*	64	2b [31]
Creston	*Two Choric Dances*	74	[280] 3f	**Gould**	*Philharmonic Waltzes*	1	5
Delannoy	*Figures Sonores*	1	3			47	5

CELESTA, ORGAN, AND PIANO

Piano (contd.)

COMPOSER	WORK	PAGE	MEASURE	COMPOSER	WORK	PAGE	MEASURE
Hindemith	Kammermusik No. 1	17	1	Siegmeister	Sunday in Brooklyn	27	2
Honegger	Symphonie Liturgique	86	1			94	[120] 1f
Kodály	Háry János Suite	4	1	Stravinsky	Chant du Rossignol	3	1
Lambert	The Rio Grande	5	1	Stravinsky	Fire-Bird Suite (1919)	8	[11]
		44	3			12	1b [14]
Moross	Paeans	4	[C]			45	[19]
Prokofieff	Ala et Lolly (Scythian Suite)	6	[2]			60	[33]
Prokofieff	Suite from the Ballet "Chout"	156	[204] 2f	Stravinsky	Les Noces	12	6
						68	[77]
Respighi	Feste Romane	106	4	Stravinsky	Scherzo à la Russe	6	2b [6]
Riegger	Dichotomy	27	[11] 4f	Stravinsky	Symphonie de Psaumes	52	2
Russell	Fugue for Eight Percussion Instruments	4	[D] 9f	Stravinsky	Symphony in Three Movements	3	1
Sessions	Symphony for Orchestra (No. 1)	48	[74]			59	[105]
		66	[104]			97	[163]
Siegmeister	From my Window	56	2b [40]	Taylor	Through the Looking Glass	101	4

Celesta and Piano

COMPOSER	WORK	PAGE	MEASURE	COMPOSER	WORK	PAGE	MEASURE
Villa-Lobos	Amazonas	39	[16] 3f	Villa-Lobos	Uirapurú	3	1
Villa-Lobos	Chôros No. 8	17	2			15	[5]
Villa-Lobos	Danses Africaines	85	[18]				

(2) TONE-CLUSTERS

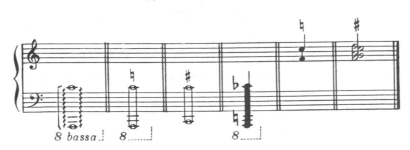

Organ

COMPOSER	WORK	PAGE	MEASURE
Schelling	A Victory Ball	81	[25]

Piano

COMPOSER	WORK	PAGE	MEASURE	COMPOSER	WORK	PAGE	MEASURE
Gould	Philharmonic Waltzes	1	6	Russell	Three Dance Movements	15	1
Ives	Three Places in New England	87	[J]			17	1
Moross	Paeans	2	[A]	Schuman, W.	Undertow	40	4b [490]
Russell	Fugue for Eight Percussion Instruments	8	[G]	Varèse	Ionisation	21	[13]

239

KEYBOARD INSTRUMENTS

(3) TREMOLANDI

Celesta

COMPOSER	WORK	PAGE	MEASURE	COMPOSER	WORK	PAGE	MEASURE
Albéniz–				**Loeffler**	Evocation	38	[39] 2f
Arbós	Triana	32	2	**Mahler**	Symphony No. 6	69	[41]
Bartók	Deux Images	16	[9] 5f			181	[120] 1f
Bartók	Music for Strings, Percussion and Celesta	130	[F] 1f	**Mahler**	Symphony No. 8	183	[171]
				Milhaud	Les Choéphores	38	1
Bartók	Vier Orchesterstücke	27	2	**Pescara**	Tibet	34	1b [12]
Bloch	Schelomo	63	2	**Read**	Sketches of the City	4	[1] 3f
		70	[44] 2f	**Respighi**	The Birds	45	2
Converse	American Sketches	120	3	**Respighi**	The Pines of Rome	12	3
Dukas	La Péri	119	[18]			66	1
Grofé	Grand Canyon Suite	95	3	**Respighi**	Vetrate di Chiesa	11	1
		100	[4]	**Schmitt**	Mirages pour Orchestre, No. 2	9	[4]
Halffter	Deux Esquisses Symphoniques	29	[C] 1f			41	[23]
Hill	Lilacs	3	1b [1]	**Schreker**	The Birthday of the Infanta, Suite	61	[370] 2f
Honegger	Le Roi David	150	[26]	**Shostakovich**	Symphony No. 6	23	3b [28]
Ibert	Escales	87	2b [77]	**Strauss, R.**	Salomé's Dance	38	[K] 3f
Ibert	La Ballade de la Geôle de Reading	77	1b [57]	**Vaughan Williams**	Pastoral Symphony	79	5b [V]

Piano

COMPOSER	WORK	PAGE	MEASURE	COMPOSER	WORK	PAGE	MEASURE
Barber	Medea	19	[17]	**Respighi**	Trittico Botticelliano	3	[1]
Bartók	Vier Orchesterstücke	83	[47]	**Respighi**	Vetrate di Chiesa	97	[29]
Bernstein	"Jeremiah" Symphony	36	[27]	**Saint-Saëns**	Le Carnaval des Animaux	1	1
Britten	Sinfonia da Requiem	51	[34]			50	1
		61	[42]	**Schönberg**	Pierrot Lunaire	8	[35]
Carter	Holiday Overture	61	[29] 3f			30	[10] 1f
Copland	Four Dance Episodes from "Rodeo"	42	1			47	3b [20]
				Sessions	Suite from "The Black Maskers"	33	3
Dukelsky	Symphony No. 3	121	5			42	[43]
Gould	Philharmonic Waltzes	18	[185] 3f	**Sessions**	Symphony No. II	36	[W]
Gould	Spirituals	41	6			146	2
Hindemith	Kammermusik No. 1	60	3	**Siegmeister**	Sunday in Brooklyn	66	1
Kay	Suite for Orchestra	11	2b [7]	**Stravinsky**	Chant du Rossignol	3	1
		91	[98]			9	[6]
Prokofieff	Ala et Lolly (Scythian Suite)	100	[69]			47	[48]
Prokofieff	Symphony No. 5	49	[24]	**Stravinsky**	Les Noces	18	[21]
Read	First Overture	1	2			44	[53]
		13	[4]	**Villa-Lobos**	Chôros No. 8	51	2
Respighi	Feste Romane	132	[41] 1f	**Wagenaar**	Sinfonietta for Small Orchestra	6	[4]

CELESTA, ORGAN, AND PIANO

Celesta and Piano

COMPOSER	WORK	PAGE	MEASURE	COMPOSER	WORK	PAGE	MEASURE
Mahler	*Symphony No. 8*	**144**	[112]	**Villa-Lobos**	*Amazonas*	**74**	[31]
		155	[127]				

(4) OTHER EFFECTS

Celesta

English	Italian	French	German
4 hands	A 4 mani	A 4 mains	4-Händig
			Zu 4 Händen

COMPOSER	WORK	PAGE	MEASURE
Stravinsky	*Petrouchka Suite*	**23**	[15]

English	Italian	French	German
Not arpeggiated	Non-arpeggio	Non arpégé	Nicht brechen

(for further terminology see Chapter 43, page 264)

Toch	*The Chinese Flute*	**32**	I

Organ

English	Italian	French	German
Full organ	Gran ripieno	Pleine orgue	Volles Werk

Mahler	*Symphony No. 2*	**209**	[51]	**Strauss, R.**	*Also Sprach*	**8**	I
Mahler	*Symphony No. 8*	**3**	I		*Zarathustra*		
		217	[220]	**Weinberger**	*Polka and Fugue from*		
Respighi	*Feste Romane*	**44**	I		*"Schwanda, the*		
					Bagpiper"	**57**	[185]

Piano

English	Italian	French	German
4 hands	A 4 mani	A 4 mains	4-Händig
			Zu 4 Händen

Bach–	*Prelude and Fugue in*			**Debussy**	*Printemps*	**I**	I
Respighi	*D major*	**I**	I	**Saint-Saëns**	*3e Symphonie en Ut*		
Bartók	*Dance Suite*	**43**	[31]		*mineur*	**126**	[S]
Bartók	*Music for Strings, Per-*						
	cussion and Celesta	**108**	[B]				

English	Italian	French	German
Glissando on the strings	Glissando sulle corde	Glissez sur les cordes	Glissando auf den Saiten

Gould	*Latin–American*		
	Symphonette	**53**	4

241

KEYBOARD INSTRUMENTS

Piano (contd.)

English	Italian	French	German
Harmonics (keys pressed down without sounding)	Armonici	Harmoniques	Flageolett
Hold [press] down keys silently	Sostenete le taste tacitamente	Baissez les touches sans sonner	Tasten stumm niederdrücken

COMPOSER	WORK	PAGE	MEASURE	COMPOSER	WORK	PAGE	MEASURE
Gould	Latin-American Symphonette	53	3	**Schönberg**	Pierrot Lunaire	15 / 45 / 52	[25] 3f / [10] / [25]

English	Italian	French	German
Like a harp	Quasi arpa	Comme une harpe	Wie eine Harfe

COMPOSER	WORK	PAGE	MEASURE
de Falla	El Amor Brujo	84	[45]

English	Italian	French	German
Muffle the strings with the l.h. palm—play with the r.h. Place fingers or palm of l.h. on strings	Assordate le corde colla palma della mano sinistra—suonate colla mano destra	Étouffez les cordes avec la paume de la main gauche—jouez avec la main droite	Saiten mit der linken Handfläche dämpfen—mit der rechten Hand spielen

Moross	Biguine	2	4	**Russell**	Fugue for Eight Percussion Instruments	6	7

English	Italian	French	German
Pizzicato on the strings with a fork—glissando	Pizzicato sulle corde colla forchetta—glissando	Pizzicato sur les cordes avec une fourchette—glissando	Pizzicato auf den Saiten mit einer Gabel—Glissando

Russell	Three Dance Movements	16	6b [B]

English	Italian	French	German
Pizzicato on the strings with the fingertips	Pizzicato sulle corde e sulle punte delle dita	Pizzicato sur les cordes avec les pointes des doigts	Pizzicato auf den Saiten mit Fingerspitzen

Russell	Fugue for Eight Percussion Instruments	3	[C]

English	Italian	French	German
Pizzicato with back of fingernail	Pizzicato colla unghia	Pizzicato avec l'ongle	Mit dem Nagel Pizzicato

Russell	Fugue for Eight Percussion Instruments	3	[C] 7f

CELESTA, ORGAN, AND PIANO

Piano (contd.)

English	Italian	French	German
English R. and L. pedals	*Italian* Due pedali	*French* Deux pédales	*German* Zwei Pedale

COMPOSER	WORK	PAGE	MEASURE
Stravinsky	*Scènes de Ballet*	**23**	[42]

English	*Italian*	*French*	*German*
Scratch strings lengthwise with a coin, like a banjo pick	Grattate le corde in lunghezza con una moneta, come media-tore	Grattez les cordes avec une pièce de monnaie, comme un plectrum [médiateur]	Saiten mit einer Münze (wie einem Plektrum) kratzen

Russell	*Fugue for Eight Percussion Instruments*	**2**	[B] 8f

English	*Italian*	*French*	*German*
Strike the strings with hard rubber mallets	Colpete le corde con magli di gomma elastica dura	Frappez les cordes avec des baguettes de caoutchouc dur	Die Saiten mit Hammern aus hartem Kautschuk schlagen

Russell	*Fugue for Eight Percussion Instruments*	**4**	[D]

English	*Italian*	*French*	*German*
Tinkling "Pianola" style	In stilo "Pianola"	Dans le style "Pianola"	Im Pianolastil

Gould	*Philharmonic Waltzes*	**15**	[146]

English	*Italian*	*French*	*German*
Tremolo by rocking a board from black to white keys	Tremolo dendolando un'asse dalle taste nere alle taste bianche	Roulez en balançant une planche des touches noires aux touches blanches	Tremolo durch Holzbrett von schwarzen auf weissen Tasten geschaukelt

Russell	*Fugue for Eight Percussion Instruments*	**18**	[E] 6f

English	*Italian*	*French*	*German*
Use a 4 ft. board to play all the keys	Suonate tutte le taste con un' asse lunga	Employez une planche longue pour jouer toutes les touches	Tastaturlanges Brett (um alle Tasten niederdrücken zu können)

Russell	*Fugue for Eight Percussion Instruments*	**18**	[E]

PART VI

Harp

Permission for reprint granted by Durand & Cie, Paris, France; U.S. copyright owners, Elkan-Vogel Co., Inc., Philadelphia, Pa.

RAVEL. RAPSODIE ESPAGNOLE

Permission for reprint granted by Durand & Cie., Paris, France; U.S. copyright owners, Elkan-Vogel Co., Inc., Philadelphia, Pa.

249

INTRODUCTION

I F THE CONTEMPORARY ORCHESTRATOR does not always employ the percussion instruments in his scores with rare imagination and skill, his use of the harp is even less adept and individual. It is safe to say that no other orchestral instrument is so generally misunderstood by orchestrators and composers and so ill-used in the overwhelming majority of modern works. Just why this should be is difficult to fathom, for the harp is certainly no less available than any other instrument in the orchestra, and harpists are only too glad to explain the technique of the instrument to any genuinely curious student of scoring.

To the average orchestrator the harp unfortunately means but one thing—*glissando*, and more *glissando*! Yet even this most overworked of all harp effects can—in the hands of a sensitive colorist—create unforgettable moments of sheer orchestral sound. Overdone and badly used as they generally are, harp *glissandi* yet remain the most characteristic device of the instrument. The present section, then, begins in Chapter 40 with examples of *glissando* in one and two hands, chord *glissandi* in either or both hands, and combinations. Chapter 41 is devoted to harmonics, subdivided into illustrations of single, double, triple, and quadruple harmonics (the latter three only possible in the left hand), and combinations, such as a single harmonic in the right hand and a double in the left.

Because of the physical nature of the harp, enharmonic doublings (homonyms) are possible on two adjacent strings; i.e.—F♯ and G♭. Listings of this characteristic and common harp device for one and two hands are given in Chapter 42. The percussive nature of the instrument is best shown in the use of *non-arpeggiato* chords (played without the customary rolling of the chord), illustrated in Chapter 43, while two methods of playing on the string: "près de la table" (near the sounding-board, low on the string), which gives a guitar-like tone; and "sons étouffés" (muffled or dampened sounds, achieved by stopping the string's vibration quickly with the palm), are catalogued in Chapters 44 and 45. Chapter 46 is taken up with examples of *tremolandi* and trills, and Chapter 47 with instances of sundry effects, such as playing with the fingernail or a plectrum, or sweeping across the strings with a stick. Again, as in the previous sections, the final chapter lists terminology not found under the other chapter headings.

For a detailed, highly fascinating discourse on some of the new and exotic effects now possible on the harp, the composer is advised to read Carlos Salzedo's *Modern Study of the Harp*. One can only wonder why orchestrators and arrangers have not as yet made some of these colorful devices (the "flux," "eolian tremolo," "timpanic sounds," for instance) a permanent and effective part of their orchestral technique.

Chapter 40

GLISSANDI

English	Italian	French	German
Glissando	Glissando	En glissant	Glissando
gliss.	*gliss., gl.*	Glissé	*Gliss., Gl.*
Slide	Strisciando	Glissez	
	Striscia(ta)		

(1) IN ONE HAND

COMPOSER	WORK	PAGE	MEASURE	COMPOSER	WORK	PAGE	MEASURE
Albéniz–				**Delius**	*Appalachia*	**62**	[P]
Arbós	*Triana*	**27**	I			**68**	[Q]
Antheil	*McKonkey's Ferry*	**22**	5	**Dukas**	*La Péri*	**22**	I
Barber	*Overture to "The*			**Dukas**	*L'Apprenti Sorcier*	**2**	1b [2]
	School for Scandal"	**20**	I			**64**	[52]
Bartók	*Concerto for Orchestra*	**9**	[171]	**Enesco**	*Ière Rhapsodie Roumaine*	**24**	4
		43	[228]	**de Falla**	*Nuits dans les Jardins*		
		47	[10]		*d'Espagne*	**21**	[15] 2f
Bartók	*Dance Suite*	**14**	123	**de Falla**	*Three Dances from "The*	**11**	4
		39	57		*Three-Cornered Hat"*	**42**	[3]
Bartók	*Deux Images*	**20**	I	**Glazounov**	*Violin Concerto in A*		
Bartók	*Deux Portraits*	**34**	[11]		*minor*	**24**	[14]
Bartók	*Hungarian Peasant Songs*	**7**	I	**Goossens**	*Sinfonietta*	**74**	5
Bartók	*Second Suite*	**86**	I	**Griffes**	*The Pleasure Dome of*		
Bax	*First Symphony*	**11**	2b [C]		*Kubla Khan*	**46**	[R]
Bax	*Third Symphony*	**38**	3b [39]	**Hanson**	*"Merry Mount" Suite*	**4**	2
Bax	*Sixth Symphony*	**81**	1b [8]			**21**	5
Bloch	*Evocations*	**59**	[42]			**82**	5
Bloch	*Schelomo*	**70**	[44] 2f	**Hanson**	*Symphony No. 1,*		
Bloch	*Trois Poèmes Juifs*	**67**	I		*"Nordic"*	**7**	[B] 5f
Britten	*The Young Person's*			**Hanson**	*Symphony No. 2,*		
	Guide to the Orchestra	**57**	[J]		*"Romantic"*	**77**	[G]
Casella	*Elegia Eroica*	**13**	2	**Holst**	*The Planets*	**179**	I
Casella	*Italia*	**58**	[53]	**Honegger**	*Horace Victorieux*	**53**	4
Debussy	*La Damoiselle Élue*	**67**	[30] 6f	**Ibert**	*Escales*	**2**	[I] 1f
Debussy	*Prélude à l'après-*	**I**	4			**30**	[25]
	midi d'un Faune	**26**	I			**79**	[68]

(1) IN ONE HAND (contd.)

COMPOSER	WORK	PAGE	MEASURE
d'Indy	*Deuxième Symphonie en Si♭*	14	[6]
d'Indy	*Istar, Variations Symphoniques*	39	1
Inghelbrecht	*Pour le jour de la première neige au vieux Japon*	4	[2]
Janssen	*New Year's Eve in New York*	41	[16]
Kabalevsky	*Suite from "Colas Breugnon"*	65	[57]
Khachaturian	*Gayne Ballet Suite No. 1-A*	22 55	[10] 4f 5
Khachaturian	*Gayne Ballet Suite No. 2*	84	[14]
Loeffler	*Evocation*	12 27	[V] 1f [23]
Loeffler	*Poem, La Bonne Chanson*	54	[25]
Mahler	*Das Lied von der Erde*	65 92 104	[7] 2f [11] 2f 2
Mahler	*Symphony No. 2*	79 122 139 195	[15] 10f 2b [53] 3 1b [42]
Mahler	*Symphony No. 3*	42 100	3 [74]
Mahler	*Symphony No. 5*	99	[27] 1f
Mahler	*Symphony No. 9*	14	1
Martinet	*Orphée*	44	[14]
Moeran	*Symphony in G minor*	55	[28]
Parodi	*Preludio ad una Commedia*	3	[A]
Prokofieff	*Ala et Lolly (Scythian Suite)*	6	[2] 1f
Prokofieff	*Alexander Nevsky*	117 154	[66] [91] 1f
Prokofieff	*Cinderella Suite No. 1*	148	4
Prokofieff	*Suite from the Ballet "Chout"*	155	[202]
Rachmaninoff	*The Bells*	22	2
Ravel	*Alborada del Gracioso*	30	[24] 1f
Ravel	*Concerto pour Piano et Orchestre*	11 29	6 22
Ravel	*Daphnis et Chloé, Suite No. 2*	1	[155]
Ravel	*La Valse*	77	1b [57]
Ravel	*Le Tombeau de Couperin*	17	[12] 2f
Ravel	*Ma Mère l'Oye*	25	[5]
Ravel	*Rapsodie Espagnole*	5 10 17 23 40 58	[4] [8] 3b [7] [12] 1f 2 [11]
Ravel	*Shéhérazade*	32	1
Ravel	*Tzigane*	18	[16]
Respighi	*The Fountains of Rome*	56	[19]
Respighi	*The Pines of Rome*	1	1
Rimsky-Korsakoff	*Capriccio Espagnol*	43	1
Rimsky-Korsakoff	*Le Coq d'Or Suite*	19	[12]
Rimsky-Korsakoff	*Scheherazade*	139 236	1 588
Rimsky-Korsakoff	*Symphony No. 2, "Antar"*	39 132 159	7 2 5
Roussel	*Évocations, III*	54	1
Roussel	*Le Festin de l'Araignée*	21	[26] 2f
Roussel	*Pour une Fête de Printemps*	36	1
Roussel	*4me Symphonie*	108	2b [62]
Roussel	*Suite en Fa*	102	[57]
Roussel	*Symphonie en Sol mineur*	28	[16]
Schelling	*A Victory Ball*	8	[1]
Schmitt	*Mirages pour Orchestre, No. 2*	9	[4] 1f
Schreker	*The Birthday of the Infanta, Suite*	63	[375]
Shepherd	*Horizons*	138	1
Shostakovich	*Symphony No. 6*	40	5
Sibelius	*Symphony No. 1*	97 129	[M] 4f 2
Sibelius	*The Tempest, First Suite*	9 57	1 3
Siegmeister	*From my Window*	27	[40] 1f
Strauss, R.	*Also Sprach Zarathustra*	33 198	2 9
Strauss, R.	*Don Quixote*	32 111	3 1
Strauss, R.	*Ein Heldenleben*	60	[32]
Stravinsky	*Fire-Bird Suite (1919)*	45 65	[19] [39]
Stravinsky	*Petrouchka Suite*	10	[3]
Szymanowski	*Symphonie Concertante pour Piano et Orchestre*	11	[6] 2f
Tchaikovsky	*Manfred-Symphonie*	271	310
Thomson	*The Seine at Night*	7	1b [4]

(1) IN ONE HAND (contd.)

COMPOSER	WORK	PAGE	MEASURE	COMPOSER	WORK	PAGE	MEASURE
Vaughan Williams	*A London Symphony*	30	[S]	**Vaughan Williams**	*Symphony in E minor (No. 6)*	52	[17] 3f
Vaughan Williams	*Job, A Masque for Dancing*	44 88	4 [Ww]	**Villa-Lobos**	*Danses Africaines*	85	[18]
Vaughan Williams	*Overture to "The Wasps"*	43	2	**Villa-Lobos**	*Uirapurú*	77	4
				Zimbalist	*American Rhapsody*	2	[1] 2f

(2) IN TWO HANDS

COMPOSER	WORK	PAGE	MEASURE	COMPOSER	WORK	PAGE	MEASURE
Albéniz-Arbós	*El Puerto*	6	1	**Dunn**	*Overture on Negro Themes*	3 30	4 1
Albéniz-Arbós	*Triana*	12	[D] 3f	**Elgar**	*Falstaff*	14	1b [13]
Antheil	*McKonkey's Ferry*	47	[28]	**Elgar**	*In the South, Concert Overture*	3 70	[2] 1f 3b [43]
Antheil	*Over the Plains*	7 25	1b [4] [14]	**Elgar**	*Symphony No. 1*	161	5
Aubert	*Saisons*	31	[18]	**Elgar**	*Symphony No. 2*	59 133	2 5
Barber	*First Symphony*	36 65	[15] 1	**de Falla**	*Nuits dans les Jardins d'Espagne*	39	4
Barber	*Medea*	20 73	1b [18] 5	**de Falla**	*Three Dances from "The Three-Cornered Hat"*	73	[20]
Barber	*Music for a Scene from Shelley*	13	75	**Ferguson**	*Partita for Orchestra*	7	[3]
Bartók	*Music for Strings, Percussion and Celesta*	59 72 125	471 [35] [170] 4f	**Grofé**	*Grand Canyon Suite*	30 33 128	2 5 [9]
Bartók	*Second Rhapsody for Violin and Orchestra*	30	[14]	**Guarnieri**	*Savage Dance*	16	1
Bartók	*Vier Orchesterstücke*	59	2b [26]	**Hanson**	*Symphony No. 1, "Nordic"*	53 66	[C] 1f 3
Bax	*First Symphony*	12 85	4 1b [A]	**Hanson**	*Symphony No. 2, "Romantic"*	132	3
Bax	*November Woods*	35 54	1 3	**Honegger**	*Horace Victorieux*	68	2
Bax	*The Garden of Fand*	19 66	1 3b [R]	**Honegger**	*Prélude, Fugue, Postlude*	37	[16]
Berg	*Violin Concerto*	69	2	**Ibert**	*Escales*	91	[80] 1f
Britten	*Four Sea Interludes from "Peter Grimes"*	24	1b [3]	**Ibert**	*Féerique*	20	[14]
Casella	*La Donna Serpente, I. Serie*	32	3	**Inghelbrecht**	*El Greco*	2 15 36 56	1b [1] 2 3 1b [47]
Caturla	*Trois Danses Cubaines*	42	[18] 5f	**Inghelbrecht**	*La Valse Retrouvée*	24 39	2 [59] 6f
Debussy	*Fêtes*	23	1b [2]	**Kabalevsky**	*Suite from "Colas Breugnon"*	118 128	1 [10]
Debussy	*Iberia*	102	1b [64]				
Debussy	*Jeux*	115	[80] 5f	**Maganini**	*An Ornithological Suite*	13	[E]
Debussy	*La Mer*	30	1b [15]				

HARP

(2) IN TWO HANDS (contd.)

COMPOSER	WORK	PAGE	MEASURE	COMPOSER	WORK	PAGE	MEASURE
Mahler	Symphony No. 7	70	3	**Schelling**	A Victory Ball	9	2
Miaskovsky	Symphony No. 8	113	[15]			40	1b [9]
Parodi	Preludio ad una	12	2b [F]			81	[25]
	Commedia	36	1b [R]	**Schmitt**	Mirages pour Orchestre,		
		55	4		No. 2	79	[4]
Pierné	Viennoise	15	3	**Scriabin**	Prométhée, Le Poème		
Pizzetti	Concerto dell'Estate	10	2b [4]		du Feu	56	6b [38]
		35	5	**Sibelius**	Die Okeaniden	11	[E]
Pizzetti	Introduzione all'			**Sibelius**	Pohjola's Daughter	13	5
	"Agamennone" di					25	1b [H]
	Eschilo	34	7b [15]	**Sibelius**	Symphony No. 6	19	2
Prokofieff	Ala et Lolly (Scythian					59	7
	Suite)	107	[72]	**Sibelius**	The Tempest,		
Ravel	Alborada del Gracioso	5	[3]		Second Suite	12	8
		31	2	**Siegmeister**	From my Window	56	2b [40]
Ravel	Daphnis et Chloé,			**Sowerby**	Concert Overture for	5	1b [A]
	Suite No. 1	19	4		Orchestra	57	1b [Y]
Ravel	La Valse	19	[13]	**Strauss, R.**	Also Sprach Zarathustra	26	3
		22	[15] 1f	**Strauss, R.**	Don Juan	64	[S]
		70	3b [51]			79	[X]
		91	[68]			94	6
Ravel	Ma Mère l'Oye	52	5	**Strauss, R.**	Don Quixote	101	1
Ravel	Rapsodie Espagnole	49	1b [6]	**Strauss, R.**	Symphonia Domestica	122	2b [160]
		72	[21] 2f	**Stravinsky**	Chant du Rossignol	13	1
Ravel	Shéhérazade	13	2	**Stravinsky**	Feuerwerk	7	[7]
Ravel	Valses Nobles et	52	[51]	**Stravinsky**	Fire-Bird Suite (1919)	65	[39] 2f
	Sentimentales	63	[63]	**Stravinsky**	Petrouchka Suite	28	[19]
Read	Sketches of the City	21	2	**Stravinsky**	Symphonie de Psaumes	33	2
		29	1b [5]	**Szymanowski**	Symphonie Concertante		
Respighi	Belfagor, Ouverture per				pour Piano et		
	Orchestra	54	[19] 2f		Orchestre	78	[14] 2f
Respighi	The Fountains of Rome	24	1	**Turina**	La Procesión del Rocío	17	1
		32	[11]	**Vaughan**	Overture to "The		
Respighi	The Pines of Rome	10	[3] 2f	**Williams**	Wasps"	6	1b [C]
Rimsky-				**Villa-Lobos**	Uirapurú	15	[5]
Korsakoff	Russian Easter Overture	12	5	**Walton**	Concerto for Violin		
Roussel	Suite en Fa	74	5		and Orchestra	34	1b [18]
				White	Idyl for Orchestra	12	2

(3) CHORD—ONE HAND

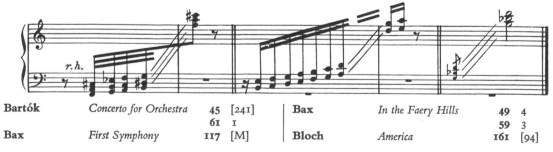

Composer	Work	Page	Measure	Composer	Work	Page	Measure
Bartók	Concerto for Orchestra	45	[241]	**Bax**	In the Faery Hills	49	4
		61	1			59	3
Bax	First Symphony	117	[M]	**Bloch**	America	161	[94]

GLISSANDI

(3) CHORD—ONE HAND (contd.)

COMPOSER	WORK	PAGE	MEASURE	COMPOSER	WORK	PAGE	MEASURE
Cesana	Second American	29	[22] 1f	Ravel	Daphnis et Chloé,		
	Symphony	155	2b [38]		Suite No. 2	62	[189] 3f
Debussy	Iberia	67	2b [45]	Ravel	Rapsodie Espagnole	24	[13]
Debussy	La Mer	39	[20]			63	1b [14]
		76	[39]	Respighi	Trittico Botticelliano	22	4
Enesco	Ière Rhapsodie			Rimsky-			
	Roumaine	15	1b [8]	Korsakoff	Capriccio Espagnol	55	3
Guarnieri	Savage Dance	6	3b [30]	Rimsky-			
Harsanyi	Suite pour Orchestre	12	2b [45]	Korsakoff	Le Coq d'Or Suite	8	[3]
Ibert	La Ballade de la Geôle	9	1b [7]	Rimsky-			
	de Reading	58	7	Korsakoff	Scheherazade	100	3b [Q]
		64	[46]	Schelling	A Victory Ball	20	1b [3]
Ibert	Ouverture de Fête	3	1			58	[15]
		47	3			65	2b [18]
Inghelbrecht	Pour le jour de la			Scriabin	Prométhée, Le Poème du		
	première neige au				Feu	37	1b [25]
	vieux Japon	46	[28] 3f	Stravinsky	Chant du Rossignol	10	[7] 2f
Milhaud	Four Sketches	8	[45]			48	2b [50]
Milhaud	Le Bal Martiniquais	6	1b [25]	Stravinsky	Fire-Bird Suite (1919)	60	[33] 1f
		9	4b [40]			73	[15]
Milhaud	Ière Symphonie	41	[70] 2f	Thomson	The Seine at Night	20	3
				Wagner, J.	Symphony Number One	21	2

(4) CHORD—TWO HANDS

COMPOSER	WORK	PAGE	MEASURE	COMPOSER	WORK	PAGE	MEASURE
Bartók	Music for Strings,			Pizzetti	Introduzione all'		
	Percussion and Celesta	144	284		"Agamennone" di		
Bartók	Violin Concerto	72	1b [29]		Eschilo	18	[8] 2f
Casella	La Donna Serpente,			Poot	Symphonie	11	6
	II. Serie	39	1b [50]			30	2
Cesana	Second American			Ravel	Ma Mère l'Oye	32	5
	Symphony	56	[40]	Read	Sketches of the City	38	1b [10]
Debussy	La Mer	72	5	Schelling	A Victory Ball	23	1b [4]
Inghelbrecht	Rapsodie de Printemps	32	[15]	Stravinsky	Scherzo Fantastique	11	[13]
						55	[78]

HARP

(5) COMBINATIONS

COMPOSER	WORK	PAGE	MEASURE
Bartók	*Music for Strings,*		
	Percussion and Celesta	77	[40]
Bartók	*Violin Concerto*	40	[280]
		95	[222]
Casella	*La Donna Serpente,*	5	1b [5]
	II. Serie	26	1b [33]
		74	1b [82]

COMPOSER	WORK	PAGE	MEASURE
Ferroud	*Au Parc Monceau*	11	[4] 1f
Honegger	*Chant de Joie*	25	1b [12]
Ibert	*La Ballade de la Geôle*	12	3
	de Reading	82	2
Villa-Lobos	*Amazonas*	75	2
Villa-Lobos	*Danses Africaines*	22	4

Chapter 41

HARMONICS

English	Italian	French	German
Harmonic(s)	Armonico(i)	En harmoniques	Flageolett
harms.	*arm.*	Harmonique(s)	*Flag.*
In harmonics	Suono(i) flautato(i)	*harm.*	Mit Flageolett
		Sons harmoniques	

NATURAL SOUNDS

Natural (sounds)	Non-armonici	Son(s) naturel(s)	Gewöhnlich

(for further terminology see Chapter 9, page 72, and Chapter 20, page 112)

(1) SINGLE—IN EITHER HAND

COMPOSER	WORK	PAGE	MEASURE	COMPOSER	WORK	PAGE	MEASURE
Albéniz–				**Bloch**	*Trois Poèmes Juifs*	53	[8] 2f
Arbós	*El Albaicín*	19	2b [J]			60	[10]
Albéniz–				**Britten**	*Four Sea Interludes*		
Arbós	*El Puerto*	33	4		*from "Peter Grimes"*	40	[1]
Albéniz–				**Casella**	*Elegia Eroica*	32	[47]
Arbós	*Évocation*	17	2	**Chabrier**	*España, Rhapsodie*	2	4
Albéniz–				**Chausson**	*Symphonie en Si bémol*		
Arbós	*Triana*	10	3		*majeur*	18	[E] 4f
Barber	*First Symphony*	46	[21]	**Copland**	*Appalachian Spring*	19	[15]
Barber	*Medea*	2	[1] 2f			67	[55]
Barber	*Overture to "The*					82	[73] 7f
	School for Scandal"	17	[E]	**Copland**	*Billy the Kid Ballet*		
Bax	*In the Faery Hills*	59	4		*Suite*	51	[30]
Bax	*Third Symphony*	78	6b [14]	**Copland**	*First Symphony*	28	[16]
Bax	*Sixth Symphony*	21	[17]	**Copland**	*Third Symphony*	90	[83]
		89	1			137	[120]
Berlioz	*Harold en Italie*	121	2	**Debussy**	*Jeux*	7	[5]
Berlioz	*Roméo et Juliette*	201	3	**Debussy**	*Nuages*	14	8
Berlioz	*Three Pieces from "The*			**Debussy**	*Prélude à l'après–midi*	14	1b [6]
	Damnation of Faust"	29	1		*d'un Faune*	31	[12] 2f
Bizet	*Roma*	5	1	**Debussy**	*Première Rhapsodie*	9	3
Bloch	*America*	70	5			15	[5]
Bloch	*Evocations*	75	3	**Debussy**	*Rondes de Printemps*	1	1
Bloch	*Schelomo*	60	2b [36]	**Debussy**	*Sirènes*	111	2
		62	3b [38]				

257

HARP

(1) SINGLE—IN EITHER HAND (contd.)

COMPOSER	WORK	PAGE	MEASURE	COMPOSER	WORK	PAGE	MEASURE
Diamond	Fourth Symphony	9	3b [50]	Ravel	Ma Mère l'Oye	15	[5]
		15	1b [85]			24	[14]
		45	[80]			35	19
Diamond	Music for Shakespeare's			Ravel	Rapsodie Espagnole	2	[1]
	"Romeo and Juliet"	66	[115] 2f			11	[9]
Dukas	L'Apprenti Sorcier	1	3			31	[3]
Ferguson	Partita for Orchestra	63	[6] 5f			81	[27]
Ferroud	Au Parc Monceau	16	[3]	Ravel	Valses Nobles et Senti-		
Franck	Les Éolides	67	6		mentales	38	[35]
Grofé	Grand Canyon Suite	91	[1] 2f	Reger	Variations on a Theme	33	5
		107	3		of Mozart	50	1
Holst	The Planets	43	[VII]	Respighi	Concerto Gregoriano per		
		122	[V]		Violino e Orchestra	29	[17]
Honegger	Horace Victorieux	2	3	Respighi	The Fountains of Rome	10	[3] 3f
Ibert	Escales	36	[31] 1f			64	[23] 6f
Ibert	La Ballade de la Geôle			Respighi	The Pines of Rome	37	6
	de Reading	86	2			67	9
d'Indy	Deuxième Symphonie			Respighi	Vetrate di Chiesa	11	2
	en Si♭	112	[54] 4f			71	[19] 1f
d'Indy	Symphony on a French			Rimsky-			
	Mountain Air	25	[K]	Korsakoff	Russian Easter Overture	4	3b [B]
Inghelbrecht	Rapsodie de Printemps	1	1	Rimsky-	Symphony No. 2,		
Khachaturian	Gayne Ballet Suite			Korsakoff	"Antar"	160	[P] 2f
	No. 2	57	[14]	Rivier	3 Pastorales	23	[9]
Liszt	Eine Faust-Symphonie	147	[S] 1f	Roger-			
		158	3	Ducasse	Le Joli Jeu de Furet	42	[11]
Liszt	Les Préludes	23	91	Rosenthal	Les Petits Métiers	58	2
Loeffler	Evocation	19	[10]	Roussel	Évocations, I	1	1
		42	[44]	Roussel	Évocations, II	69	[31]
Mahler	Das Lied von der Erde	107	[18] 3f	Roussel	Suite en Fa	83	[43]
Mahler	Symphony No. 3	125	7	Schreker	The Birthday of the	31	[135] 1f
Mahler	Symphony No. 4	143	308		Infanta, Suite	55	[345] 2f
Milhaud	IIᵉ Symphonie	76	[125] 2f			88	[455] 2f
Mussorgsky-				Shostakovich	Symphony No. 5	108	[96]
Ravel	Pictures at an Exhibition	58	[54]	Sibelius	Die Okeaniden	3	3
Pizzetti	Concerto dell'Estate	83	[32] 6f			26	1
		103	2	Sibelius	Symphony No. 1	58	3
		117	[49]	Sibelius	Symphony No. 6	38	[I] 1f
Prokofieff	Romeo and Juliet,	63	1			46	1
	Suite No. 2	81	[49]	Strauss, R.	Don Juan	10	2b [C]
Ravel	Concerto pour Piano et					14	4b [D]
	Orchestre	29	[22]			42	8
Ravel	Daphnis et Chloé,	4	[74]	Stravinsky	Chant du Rossignol	8	[5]
	Suite No. 1	44	[113]			14	[11]
Ravel	Daphnis et Chloé,					41	[42] 3f
	Suite No. 2	41	[172] 1f	Stravinsky	Fire-Bird Suite (1919)	4	[5] 2f
Ravel	La Valse	44	[31]			69	[5] 2f
Ravel	Le Tombeau de	11	2	Stravinsky	Petrouchka Suite	74	1b [60]
	Couperin	24	[7] 1f	Szymanowski	Symphonie Concertante		
		38	[5]		pour Piano et		
					Orchestre	7	[4] 1f

HARMONICS

(1) SINGLE—IN EITHER HAND (contd.)

COMPOSER	WORK	PAGE	MEASURE	COMPOSER	WORK	PAGE	MEASURE
Thomson	*The Seine at Night*	13	2b [8]	Villa-Lobos	*Uirapurú*	43	[9]
Vaughan Williams	*A London Symphony*	6	[C] 1f			81	1
		181	3	Walton	*Concerto for Violin and Orchestra*	75	4
Vaughan Williams	*Symphony in E minor (No. 6)*	155	1b [9]			105	4
				White	*Idyl for Orchestra*	12	5
				Zimbalist	*American Rhapsody*	1	4

(2) DOUBLE

COMPOSER	WORK	PAGE	MEASURE	COMPOSER	WORK	PAGE	MEASURE
Alfvén	*A Legend of the Skerries*	29	1	Ravel	*La Valse*	37	[25] 3f
Bartók	*Dance Suite*	16	143	Ravel	*Le Tombeau de Couperin*	19	[1] 1f
Bloch	*Evocations*	52	[38] 2f			26	[9] 1f
Debussy	*Jeux*	117	[81]	Ravel	*Ma Mère l'Oye*	10	3
Debussy	*Rondes de Printemps*	12	2			45	9
Debussy-Ansermet	*Six Épigraphes Antiques*	4	3	Ravel	*Rapsodie Espagnole*	9	[7]
				Ravel	*Shéhérazade*	26	1b [13]
Debussy-Busser	*Petite Suite*	9	8			38	[19] 3f
Holst	*The Planets*	113	1	Ravel	*Valses Nobles et Senti- mentales*	7	[5]
		182	[VI]			18	[16]
Mahler	*Symphony No. 3*	182	2	Rogers	*Characters from Hans Christian Andersen*	15	2
		188	4	Rosenthal	*Les Petits Métiers*	29	3
Miaskovsky	*Symphony No. 8*	96	2	Sibelius	*The Bard*	18	[L] 1f
Moore	*In Memoriam*	23	[O]	Sibelius	*The Tempest, Second Suite*	3	3
Parodi	*Preludio ad una Commedia*	40	4			50	7
Pizzetti	*Concerto dell'Estate*	14	[6]	Strauss, R.	*Eine Alpensinfonie*	55	[47] 2f
Prokofieff	*Symphony No. 6*	86	1b [54]	Strauss, R.	*Rosenkavalier Waltzes —First Sequence*	20	[21]
Ravel	*Alborada del Gracioso*	14	[9] 4f				
		22	[17] 2f	Stravinsky	*Scherzo Fantastique*	46	[67]
Ravel	*Boléro*	4	[2]	Tchaikovsky	*Manfred-Symphonie*	91	153
Ravel	*Daphnis et Chloé, Suite No. 2*	45	[176]	Vaughan Williams	*A London Symphony*	142	[V] 8f
		87	[204] 3f				

(3) TRIPLE

COMPOSER	WORK	PAGE	MEASURE	COMPOSER	WORK	PAGE	MEASURE
Ibert	*Escales*	46	[41]	Strauss, R.	*Salomé's Dance*	9	3b [L]
Mahler	*Das Lied von der Erde*	80	[22] 7f	Walton	*Concerto for Violin and Orchestra*	130	[65]
Ravel	*Rapsodie Espagnole*	73	[22]				

HARP

(4) QUADRUPLE

COMPOSER	WORK	PAGE	MEASURE	COMPOSER	WORK	PAGE	MEASURE
Mahler	Symphony No. 2	**139**	3	**Ravel**	Rapsodie Espagnole	**74**	1
Ravel	Daphnis et Chloé, Suite No. 1	**8**	[78]				

(5) COMBINATIONS—TWO HANDS

COMPOSER	WORK	PAGE	MEASURE	COMPOSER	WORK	PAGE	MEASURE
Bax	Fourth Symphony	**41**	[28] 2f	**Ravel**	Daphnis et Chloé	**5**	[75]
		47	[37] 2f		Suite No. 1	**34**	5
		63	[50] 4f			**47**	[116]
Bax	Fifth Symphony	**25**	2	**Ravel**	Daphnis et Chloé,	**43**	[174]
		73	5		Suite No. 2	**57**	[184]
Bloch	Evocations	**53**	1	**Ravel**	La Valse	**66**	[48]
Casella	La Donna Serpente, I. Serie	**1**	1	**Ravel**	Rapsodie Espagnole	**15**	[5]
						61	1b [13]
Copland	Third Symphony	**25**	9			**73**	[22]
Debussy	Gigues	**34**	1b [20]			**74**	1
Debussy–				**Ravel**	Shéhérazade	**36**	[18] 1f
Busser	Petite Suite	**14**	5	**Ravel**	Valses Nobles et Senti-	**18**	[16] 4f
Dukas	La Péri	**41**	2		mentales	**42**	1b [39]
Glazounov	Violin Concerto in A minor	**53**	3			**67**	[67]
Holst	The Planets	**131**	2	**Respighi**	Metamorphoseon, XII Modi	**55**	[29] 11f
Mahler	Das Lied von der Erde	**140**	[64]	**Rimsky-**			
Mahler	Symphony No. 2	**139**	3	**Korsakoff**	Scheherazade	**253**	627
		184	[28] 1f	**Rosenthal**	Les Petits Métiers	**27**	2
Mahler	Symphony No. 3	**58**	[42] 3f			**61**	2
Mahler	Symphony No. 4	**36**	182			**136**	1
		117	56	**Schönberg**	Fünf Orchesterstücke	**28**	3b [11]
Martinet	Orphée	**1**	5	**Schmitt**	Mirages pour Orchestre,		
		90	[19]		No. 2	**78**	2b [43]
Moore	Symphony in A major	**64**	[47]	**Scriabin**	Prométhée, Le Poème	**45**	3b [30]
Mussorgsky-	Pictures at an Exhibition	**10**	[9]		du Feu	**50**	5
Ravel		**17**	4b [16]	**Sibelius**	The Tempest,		
		96	[78] 5f		First Suite	**39**	3
Rachmaninoff	The Bells	**2**	1	**Stillman-**	New England		
		30	[29] 1f	**Kelley**	Symphony	**79**	[U] 4f
Ravel	Concerto pour Piano et			**Stravinsky**	Ebony Concerto	**19**	1b [4]f
	Orchestre	**58**	[9]	**Stravinsky**	Feuerwerk	**11**	[10] 1

HARMONICS

(5) COMBINATIONS—TWO HANDS (contd.)

COMPOSER	WORK	PAGE	MEASURE	COMPOSER	WORK	PAGE	MEASURE
Stravinsky	*Firebird Ballet Suite*	18	[20]	Vaughan	*Job, A Masque for*		
	(1945)	33	3b [42]	Williams	*Dancing*	2	5
Tchaikovsky	*Mozartiana*	11	7	Vaughan	*Pastoral Symphony*	14	4
Tchaikovsky	*Suite from the Ballet,*			Williams		83	2
	"The Sleeping			Walton	*Concerto for Violin and*		
	Beauty"*	26	5		*Orchestra*	95	[48]

Chapter 42

HOMONYMS (ENHARMONICS)

(1) IN ONE HAND

COMPOSER	WORK	PAGE	MEASURE	COMPOSER	WORK	PAGE	MEASURE
Bartók	*Music for Strings, Percussion and Celesta*	**93**	[75]	**Ravel**	*Concerto pour la main gauche*	**2**	[1]
Bax	*Second Symphony*	**106**	[19] 3f	**Ravel**	*Daphnis et Chloé, Suite No. 2*	**43**	[174]
Bloch	*America*	**24**	3			**45**	[176]
Britten	*Sinfonia da Requiem*	**36**	[25] 1f	**Ravel**	*Le Tombeau de Couperin*	**17**	[12]
		55	[37]			**19**	[1] 1f
Casella	*La Donna Serpente, I. Serie*	**1**	1			**22**	[4]
						26	[9] 1f
Copland	*Third Symphony*	**93**	2			**28**	[12] 1f
Debussy	*Rapsodie pour Orchestre et Saxophone*	**44**	[10] 1f	**Ravel**	*Ma Mère l'Oye*	**10**	3
						21	[10]
Dukas	*La Péri*	**94**	2	**Ravel**	*Rapsodie Espagnole*	**7**	[5] 2f
de Falla	*Nuits dans les Jardins d'Espagne*	**77**	[43]			**41**	2
						43	[3] 3f
Honegger	*Le Roi David*	**126**	[19]	**Ravel**	*Valses Nobles et Sentimentales*	**67**	[67]
d'Indy	*Deuxième Symphonie en Si♭*	**114**	[56]	**Read**	*Symphony No. I*	**135**	[47] 2f
				Respighi	*Trittico Botticelliano*	**3**	[1]
Mussorgsky– Ravel	*Pictures at an Exhibition*	**96**	[78] 4f	**Rogers**	*Once Upon a Time, Five Fairy Tales*	**14**	2
						19	5
Ravel	*Alborada del Gracioso*	**22**	[17] 2f	**Ropartz**	*Soir sur les Chaumes*	**33**	3

(2) IN TWO HANDS

COMPOSER	WORK	PAGE	MEASURE	COMPOSER	WORK	PAGE	MEASURE
Bartók	*Music for Strings, Percussion and Celesta*	**85**	[65]	**Bloch**	*Trois Poèmes Juifs*	**48**	3
Bloch	*Schelomo*	**38**	[22] 3f	**Casella**	*Italia*	**49**	[45]
				Copland	*Third Symphony*	**18**	[13]

HOMONYMS (ENHARMONICS)

(2) IN TWO HANDS (contd.)

COMPOSER	WORK	PAGE	MEASURE	COMPOSER	WORK	PAGE	MEASURE
Debussy	Iberia	35	[22]	Prokofieff	March and Scherzo		
Debussy	Le Martyre de Saint	13	6		from "The Love of	13	1
	Sébastien	25	[10]		the Three Oranges"	24	3b [9]
Dukas	La Péri	25	1	Ravel	Alborada del Gracioso	10	[6]
de Falla	Nuits dans les Jardins	25	[18]			33	[27]
	d'Espagne	40	[5]	Ravel	Daphnis et Chloé,	1	5
Ferguson	Partita for Orchestra	2	2		Suite No. 1	8	[78]
Ferroud	Au Parc Monceau	12	7			38	[108]
Halffter	Deux Esquisses			Ravel	Daphnis et Chloé,		
	Symphoniques	8	2		Suite No. 2	44	[175] 1f
Hill	Lilacs	19	[8]	Ravel	La Valse	2	3
Holst	The Planets	44	5			75	[54]
		162	4			80	[59]
Honegger	Horace Victorieux	35	3	Read	Symphony No. I	83	4
Ibert	La Ballade de la Geôle			Ruggles	Sun-Treader	49	[231]
	de Reading	86	2	Schmitt	Étude pour le "Palais		
d'Indy	Istar, Variations				Hanté" d' Edgar Poe	66	6
	Symphoniques	15	[G] 2f	Stravinsky	Chant du Rossignol	27	[28]
Mahler	Symphony No. 2	208	[50]			43	[44]
Mussorgsky–						54	[58]
Ravel	Pictures at an Exhibition	12	[11]			67	[74]
Parodi	Preludio ad una			Stravinsky	Scherzo Fantastique	63	[88]
	Commedia	7	3	Szymanowski	Symphonie Concertante		
					pour Piano et Orchestre	82	[17]

Chapter 43

NON-ARPEGGIATO

English	Italian	French	German
Do not roll	Non-arpeggiando	N'arpéger pas	Immer ungebrochen
Dry	*non-arpegg.*	Ne jamais arpéger les accords	Nicht arpeggieren
Not arpeggiated	Non-arpeggiato	Non arpégé	Nicht brechen [gebrochen]
Unbroken	Secco	Sans arpéger	Nicht harpeggi(e)rt
	Senza arpeggiare	Sec	Ohne Brechung

COMPOSER	WORK	PAGE	MEASURE	COMPOSER	WORK	PAGE	MEASURE
Albéniz– Arbós	*Navarra*	1	1	**de Falla**	*Nuits dans les Jardins d'Espagne*	43	[8]
Alfvén	*Midsommarvaka*	7	[2]	**de Falla**	*Three Dances from*	28	2b [4]
Atterberg	*Ballade und Passacaglia*	16	71		*"The Three-Cornered*	40	[2]
Balakirev– Casella	*Islamey*	15	[11]		*Hat"*	78	2
Barber	*Medea*	39	1	**Ferguson**	*Partita for Orchestra*	23	3
		83	3	**Hanson**	*"Merry Mount" Suite*	10	[76]
Barraine	*Deuxième Symphonie*	48	[1]	**Ibert**	*La Ballade de la Geôle de Reading*	75	[55]
Bax	*Third Symphony*	106	[22] 3f	**Inghelbrecht**	*Pour le jour de la première neige au*		
		113	[32] 7f		*vieux Japon*	21	[11] 1f
Bax	*Fourth Symphony*	115	[4] 6f	**Janssen**	*New Year's Eve in*	9	[4]
Bax	*Sixth Symphony*	20	4b [16]		*New York*	21	1
Berg	*Violin Concerto*	6	1b [30]	**Khachaturian**	*Gayne Ballet Suite*		
		16	1b [85]		*No. 1*	47	[5]
		72	[110] 1f	**Khachaturian**	*Gayne Ballet Suite*		
		93	[205]		*No. 1-A*	5	2
Bloch	*Hiver–Printemps*	23	3	**Khachaturian**	*Gayne Ballet Suite*		
Bloch	*Schelomo*	77	[48] 4f		*No. 2*	8	[6]
Bloch	*Trois Poèmes Juifs*	9	[3]	**Mahler**	*Das Lied von der Erde*	6	1
Casella	*Elegia Eroica*	16	2b [11]			26	[30] 8f
Casella	*Italia*	20	3b [16]			67	[8] 1f
Casella	*La Donna Serpente, II. Serie*	47	[60] 2f			74	[13] 2f
Charpentier	*Impressions d'Italie*	27	3b [4]			89	[8]
		32	[8] 3f	**Mahler**	*Songs of a Wayfarer*	50	64
		122	4	**Mahler**	*Symphony No. 1*	13	[9]
Debussy– Ansermet	*Six Épigraphes Antiques*	37	[A]	**Mahler**	*Symphony No. 2*	53	4
						74	[13] 4f

NON-ARPEGGIATO

COMPOSER	WORK	PAGE	MEASURE	COMPOSER	WORK	PAGE	MEASURE
Mahler	Symphony No. 3	52	[36] 3f	**Rachmaninoff**	The Bells	1	4
		108	1b [3]			14	[13]
		118	[10]	**Ravel**	Shéhérazade	43	1
		208	[10] 3f	**Read**	Symphony No. I	32	4
Mahler	Symphony No. 4	36	182			94	[36] 7f
		166	72	**Rimsky-**	Russian Easter Overture	73	[U]
		172	95	**Korsakoff**		79	[V]
Mahler	Symphony No. 5	113	[33] 1f	**Roger-**		5	4
		227	[27]	**Ducasse**	Sarabande	31	[17]
Mahler	Symphony No. 6	116	[79]	**Rogers**	Once Upon a Time,		
		182	2b [121]		Five Fairy Tales	3	[2]
Mahler	Symphony No. 7	109	7	**Schelling**	A Victory Ball	92	[28a] 1f
		181	2b [217]	**Schlein**	Dance Overture	14	1b [205]
Mahler	Symphony No. 8	177	[161]	**Schmitt**	Mirages pour Orchestre,		
Mahler	Symphony No. 9	36	[13] 3f		No. 1	4	1
Martinet	Orphée	1	5	**Schmitt**	Mirages pour Orchestre,		
		7	[3]		No. 2	2	3
		90	[19]	**Schönberg**	A Survivor from		
Milhaud	Cinq Symphonies pour				Warsaw	12	54
	Petit Orchestre	11	[15] 2f	**Shostakovich**	Symphony No. 5	8	1b [9]
Milhaud	Concerto pour Piano et			**Shostakovich**	Symphony No. 6	10	[9]
	Orchestre	36	1b [15]	**Siegmeister**	Sunday in Brooklyn	13	[45]
Milhaud	Deuxième Concerto					42	1
	pour Violoncelle et			**Strauss, R.**	Symphonia Domestica	39	[54]
	Orchestre	6	[10]			59	[76] 1f
Milhaud	Ière Symphonie	1	1	**Stravinsky**	Chant du Rossignol	75	[83]
Moore	Symphony in A major	60	3	**Stravinsky**	Ebony Concerto	39	[33]
		63	4	**Stravinsky**	Fire-Bird Suite (1919)	66	3
Pierné	Divertissements sur un			**Stravinsky**	Firebird Ballet Suite		
	Thème Pastorale	60	[39] 2f		(1945)	20	[22]
Poot	Symphonie	10	7	**Stravinsky**	Orpheus	13	[29]
Prokofieff	Cinderella Suite No. 1	15	[5]			15	[34]
		20	[8]	**Stravinsky**	Petrouchka Suite	15	[6]
		96	[77]			31	[21]
Prokofieff	Lieutenant Kijé	25	[15]	**Stravinsky**	Symphonie de Psaumes	1	1
Prokofieff	Romeo and Juliet,					32	2b [5]
	Suite No. 1	79	[51]			49	2b [17]
Prokofieff	Romeo and Juliet,	36	[21]	**Stravinsky**	Symphony in Three		
	Suite No. 2	39	[24]		Movements	70	[123]
		66	[44]	**Thomson**	The Seine at Night	16	[9]
		100	2	**Vaughan**	Job, A Masque for		
Prokofieff	Suite from the Ballet			**Williams**	Dancing	54	[Ee]
	"Chout"	25	[30]	**Whithorne**	The Dream Pedlar	65	9

Chapter 44

"PRÈS DE LA TABLE"

English	Italian	French	German
Like a guitar	Alla chitarra [clavecin]	A la guitarra	Resonanz(tisch)
Low on strings	Come guitarra	Près de la table	
Near soundingboard	Presso la tavola	Table	
Near the sound-board	Quasi guitaro		
	Sulla tavola		

NATURAL SOUNDS

Natural (sounds)	Modo ordinario	Son(s) naturel(s)	Gewöhnlich

(for further terminology see Chapter 9, page 72, and Chapter 20, page 112)

COMPOSER	WORK	PAGE	MEASURE	COMPOSER	WORK	PAGE	MEASURE
Albéniz– Arbós	El Albaicín	5	[A] 1f	**de Falla**	Three Dances from "The Three-Cornered Hat"	2	[1]
		14	2b [F]			15	[11] 4f
Albéniz– Arbós	Navarra	1	5			25	[2]
		33	4	**Ferroud**	Au Parc Monceau	4	4
Albéniz– Arbós	Triana	8	2			12	1
Bartók	Concerto for Orchestra	22	[438]	**Ibert**	Escales	15	[10]
Bartók	Music for Strings, Percussion and Celesta	93	[75]			20	[14]
						40	[35]
Bartók	Violin Concerto	12	[74]	**Ibert**	Féerique	8	[5]
		45	[302]			16	2
		123	[555]	**Ibert**	La Ballade de la Geôle de Reading	49	[34]
Britten	Four Sea Interludes from "Peter Grimes"	74	[9] 3f	**Inghelbrecht**	La Métamorphose d'Ève	10	[8]
Britten	Sinfonia da Requiem	25	[18] 2f			29	[21]
Britten	The Young Person's Guide to the Orchestra	17	2	**Inghelbrecht**	Pour le jour de la première neige au vieux Japon	14	2b [7]
Chabrier	España, Rhapsodie	6	2	**Loeffler**	A Pagan Poem	10	8b [D]
Copland	Appalachian Spring	56	[46]	**Loeffler**	Evocation	4	[F]
Copland	Third Symphony	75	[61]			17	[6] 2f
Debussy	Gigues	12	[7] 2f			46	[50] 2f
Debussy	Jeux	38	[27] 2f	**Mahler**	Das Lied von der Erde	117	2
Debussy	Rondes de Printemps	49	[25]	**Mahler**	Symphony No. 1	22	3
		52	[27] 2f			27	[20] 2f
Diamond	Music for Shakespeare's "Romeo and Juliet"	39	1b [20]	**Mahler**	Symphony No. 7	133	7b [137]
Dukas	La Péri	69	2			162	[186]
de Falla	Nuits dans les Jardins d'Espagne	3	1	**Parodi**	Preludio ad una Commedia	5	[B] 1f
				Pizzetti	Concerto dell'Estate	99	[41]
				Ravel	Alborada del Gracioso	1	1
						12	[8]
						25	[20]

266

"PRÈS DE LA TABLE"

COMPOSER	WORK	PAGE	MEASURE	COMPOSER	WORK	PAGE	MEASURE
Rogers	*Characters from Hans*	7	1	**Stravinsky**	*Scherzo à la Russe*	10	[9] 2f
	Christian Andersen	15	3	**Stravinsky**	*Symphonie de Psaumes*	30	3b [4]
Rogers	*Once Upon a Time,*					45	1b [14]
	Five Fairy Tales	18	1	**Stravinsky**	*Symphony in Three*		
Schreker	*The Birthday of the*				*Movements*	72	[129]
	Infanta, Suite	42	1b [230]	**Szymanowski**	*Symphonie Concertante*	5	[2] 4f
Stravinsky	*Chant du Rossignol*	15	[15]		*pour Piano et*	29	[16] 4f
		67	[74]		*Orchestre*	64	1
		75	[83]			109	[39] 1f
Stravinsky	*Firebird Ballet Suite*			**Thomson**	*The Seine at Night*	16	[9]
	(1945)	30	[36] 1f	**Wagenaar**	*Sinfonietta for Small*		
Stravinsky	*Orpheus*	1	1		*Orchestra*	31	1b [1]
		5	[7] 3f	**Walton**	*Concerto for Violin*	47	2b [25]
		31	[80]		*and Orchestra*	56	[29]
		57	[143]				

Chapter 45

"SONS ÉTOUFFÉS"

English	Italian	French	German
Damp(en)	Con sordino	Étouffé(s)	Abdämpfen
Muffled	c.s.	Étouffez	Gedämpft
Plucked and stopped	Secco	Sec	ged.
Stop(ped)	Staccato	Sons étouffés	Scharf abreissen
		Très sec	Schnell abdämpfen

COMPOSER	WORK	PAGE	MEASURE	COMPOSER	WORK	PAGE	MEASURE
Barber	Medea	4	[3]	**Ravel**	Daphnis et Chloé,	50	[179] 1f
		8	[6]		Suite No. 2	53	[181]
		43	[35]			62	[189] 4f
Bax	First Symphony	89	3	**Schelling**	A Victory Ball	47	4
Bax	Sixth Symphony	69	[13]	**Schreker**	The Birthday of the		
		77	[4] 6f		Infanta, Suite	96	[490]
Britten	Four Sea Interludes			**Siegmeister**	Sunday in Brooklyn	16	2b [55]
	from "Peter Grimes"	85	3			42	1
Britten	The Young Person's			**Stravinsky**	Chant du Rossignol	11	[9]
	Guide to the					18	[18]
	Orchestra	13	4			70	2b [78]
Chabrier	Joyeuse Marche	21	[H]	**Stravinsky**	Ebony Concerto	17	1b [2]
Charpentier	Impressions d'Italie	70	[19] 8f			22	[3]
		95	[16] 6f	**Stravinsky**	Fire-Bird Suite (1919)	10	1
Debussy	Jeux	87	4b [59]			21	[10]
de Falla	Three Dances from					31	4b [4]
	"The Three-Cornered					33	[6]
	Hat"	89	[33] 4f	**Stravinsky**	Firebird Ballet Suite	23	[26]
Inghelbrecht	La Métamorphose d'Ève	25	2		(1945)	30	[36] 1f
Lalo	Symphonie Espagnole	41	4	**Stravinsky**	Orpheus	6	[12]
		62	2	**Stravinsky**	Petrouchka Suite	84	[72]
Loeffler	Evocation	13	[X]	**Stravinsky**	Scherzo à la Russe	13	[16] 1f
		20	[12]	**Stravinsky**	Symphony in Three	109	[181] 1f
		28	[24] 1f		Movements	87	[152]
Mahler	Das Lied von der Erde	127	3b [48]	**Szymanowski**	Symphonie Concertante		
Mahler	Symphony No. 2	74	[13] 1f		pour Piano et	10	1
Milhaud	Concerto pour Piano				Orchestre	64	[1]
	et Orchestre	36	1b [15]	**Thomson**	The Seine at Night	17	4
Milhaud	Iᵉʳᵉ Symphonie	19	3b [75]	**Villa-Lobos**	Amazonas	62	[26]
Parodi	Preludio ad una			**Walton**	Concerto for Violin	20	2
	Commedia	5	[B] 1f		and Orchestra	47	2b [25]
Ravel	Concerto pour Piano					56	[29]
	et Orchestre	77	[14] 8f			135	[66] 1f
				Weingartner	Lustige Ouvertüre	19	6

Chapter 46

TREMOLANDI AND TRILLS

English	Italian	French	German
Tremolo	Bisb[p]igliando	Trémolo	Tremolo
trem.	Tremolo	*trem.*	*Trem.*
Trill	*trem.*	Trille	Triller
tr.	Trillo	*tr.*	*Tr.*
	tr.		

COMPOSER	WORK	PAGE	MEASURE	COMPOSER	WORK	PAGE	MEASURE
Albéniz–Arbós	*Triana*	32	3	**Honegger**	*Horace Victorieux*	8	[3]
Bartók	*Concerto for Orchestra*	60	[66]			35	3
Bartók	*Deux Images*	5	1	**Honegger**	*Le Roi David*	7	1
Bartók	*Music for Strings,*			**Howe**	*Stars*	6	1
	Percussion and Celesta	85	[65]	**Ibert**	*Escales*	15	[10]
Bax	*First Symphony*	110	[K]	**Ibert**	*La Ballade de la Geôle*		
Bax	*Second Symphony*	100	6b [16]		*de Reading*	30	1b [19]
Bax	*Fifth Symphony*	28	[18] 1f	**d'Indy**	*Jour d'été à la Montagne*	75	[37]
Bax	*In the Faery Hills*	54	4	**Inghelbrecht**	*La Métamorphose d'Ève*	17	6
Bloch	*America*	24	3			41	[27]
Bloch	*Schelomo*	38	[22] 3f	**Loeffler**	*Evocation*	18	1b [8]
		64	[39] 1f			43	2b [45]
Converse	*American Sketches*	13	[8]	**Mahler**	*Das Lied von der Erde*	16	1b [17]
Cras	*Journal de Bord*	52	2			19	[20] 4f
Debussy	*Le Martyre de Saint*			**Mahler**	*Symphony No. 2*	189	[34] 3f
	Sébastien	65	4			208	[50]
Delius	*Appalachia*	16	76	**Mahler**	*Symphony No. 3*	169	5
		29	140	**Mahler**	*Symphony No. 4*	44	[16]
Delius	*Paris*	6	2	**Mahler**	*Symphony No. 5*	102	2
Dukas	*La Péri*	72	[11]	**Mahler**	*Symphony No. 8*	195	[186] 2f
Dvořák	*Die Waldtaube*	46	[17] 1f			205	2
Enesco	*Ière Rhapsodie Roumaine*	2	[1] 4f	**Mahler**	*Symphony No. 9*	27	2
Gould	*Latin-American*			**Rachmaninoff**	*The Bells*	46	1
	Symphonette	102	[16] 2f	**Respighi**	*The Pines of Rome*	12	3
Gould	*Spirituals*	41	6			66	1
Harsanyi	*Suite pour Orchestre*	59	[45] 1f	**Respighi**	*Trittico Botticelliano*	3	[1]
Holst	*The Planets*	162	4	**Ropartz**	*Soir sur les Chaumes*	33	3
		167	[11]	**Schönberg**	*A Survivor from Warsaw*	9	43

HARP

COMPOSER	WORK	PAGE	MEASURE	COMPOSER	WORK	PAGE	MEASURE
Strauss, R.	*Also Sprach Zarathustra*	**74**	6	**Stravinsky**	*Scherzo Fantastique*	**63**	[88]
Strauss, R.	*Don Juan*	**73**	[V]	**Vaughan**	*Overture to "The*		
Strauss, R.	*Symphonia Domestica*	**67**	[84] 1f	**Williams**	*Wasps"*	**66**	447

Chapter 47

MISCELLANEOUS EFFECTS

English
Glissando with an appropriately shaped wooden (if possible metal) stick

Italian
Glissando con una bacchetta di legno (di metallo se si' a possibile) convenevolmente formata

French
Glissez avec une baguette de bois (de métal si c'est possible) de forme convenable

German
Glissando mit einem zweckmässig geformten Holzschlägel (Metallschlägel wenn möglich)

COMPOSER	WORK	PAGE	MEASURE
Bartók	*Concerto for Orchestra*	**22**	[438]

English
L.h. near soundingboard; r.h. normal

Italian
M.s. sulla tavola; m.d. ordinario

French
M.g. près de la table; m.d. au naturel

German
L.H. Resonanztisch; R.H. gewöhnlich

Stravinsky	*Scherzo à la Russe*	**10**	[10]

English
Pedal glissando

Italian
Glissando colla pedale

French
Glissando avec le levier

German
Glissando mit Pedal

Rogers	*Once Upon a Time, Five Fairy Tales*	**45**	3

English
Pinch the string

Italian
Pizzicato la corda

French
Pincer la corde

German
Die Saite kneipen

Stravinsky	*Symphonie de Psaumes*	**45**	1b [14]

English
Place a piece of paper between the strings

Italian
Mettete un frammento di carta fra le corde

French
Mettez un papier entre les cordes

German
Ein Stück Papier zwischen den Saiten stecken

Albéniz–Arbós	*El Albaicín*	**3**	1

English
Tune lowest string to B♭

Italian
Accordate la corda la più bassa in Si♭

French
Accordez la corde la plus basse en Si♭

German
Stimmt die tiefste Saite nach B

Berg	*Three Excerpts from "Wozzeck"*	**42**	[315] 4f

271

HARP

English	Italian	French	German
With plectrum	Con mediatore	Avec médiateur	Mit Mediator

COMPOSER	WORK	PAGE	MEASURE	COMPOSER	WORK	PAGE	MEASURE
Mahler	*Das Lied von der Erde*	102	[7]	**Mahler**	*Symphony No. 6*	151	[104] 1f
Mahler	*Symphony No. 3*	51	2b [35]			224	[144] 1f
				Mahler	*Symphony No. 7*	162	[187]

English	Italian	French	German
With the fingernail	Colla unghia	Sons d'ongles	Mit dem Nagel

COMPOSER	WORK	PAGE	MEASURE
Copland	*Appalachian Spring*	20	[16]
Rogers	*Characters from Hans Christian Andersen*	17	1

Bartók *Violin Concerto* 55 [10]

Stravinsky *Petrouchka Suite* 134 [114]

Chapter 48

HARP TERMINOLOGY

English	Italian	French	German
Gently vibrate (the string)	Vibrato dolce	Faites doucement vibrer (la corde)	Weich vibrierend
Glissando—scale of C major	Glissando—in Do maggiore	Glissando—gamme de Do majeur Glissez en Ut maj.	Glissando—C dur
Glissando—scale of A minor	Glissando—in La minore	Glissando—gamme de La mineur Glissez en La min.	Glissando—A moll
Harmonics: Actual pitch [sound]; At [real] pitch; Sound; Sounding where written; Written sounds	Armonici: Come è scritto; Non un'ottava più alta; Suono	Harmoniques: A l'octave [hauteur] réelle; Effet; Sons écrits [réels]	Flageolett: Klang; Klingt wie notieren [angegeben]; Nicht eine Oktave höher
In D major	Muta in Re maggiore	En Ré majeur	Wechseln in D dur
Put in F♯ minor	Muta in F♯ minore	Accordez en Fa♯ mineur	Im Fis moll vorbereiten

PART VII

Strings

277

INTRODUCTION

IN SPITE OF the dominant role assumed by the winds and brasses in twentieth-century instrumentation, and notwithstanding the ever-growing importance of the percussion, the harp, and the keyed instruments to the contemporary orchestrator, for the composer at least, the strings still remain the solid nucleus of the modern symphony orchestra. Judging from the symphonic literature of the past the reason is not difficult to discover, for it may be stated in two words—tonal tolerance. By this is meant that the ear does not tire of the tone color and sonority of the string instruments, either singly or as an ensemble, as rapidly and as thoroughly as of brass and woodwind, to say nothing of the percussion. It is not surprising, therefore, that the string section of the symphonic organization today is almost the same—at least in make-up if not in size—as it was in the earliest days of orchestral development. A glance at the charts on pages 29-34 showing the evolution of modern orchestral balance will bear this statement out.

To the "good," or even to the merely "average" orchestrator, the understanding and generally comprehensive mastery of string technique from the standpoint of the various devices at the player's command, and effects possible, is an absolute necessity. It is doubtful, indeed, if any one single instrument in the rest of the orchestra can produce such a diversity of effect and amazing range of tone color as does any one of the four different string instruments. And it is a certainty that no other choir or section as a whole can duplicate the extraordinary range and homogeneity of sound which the strings alone are capable of producing. Proof is to be found in the large number of chapters devoted to string devices and technique—almost a third of the total number in the *Thesaurus*. For that very reason a thorough knowledge of the various effects possible and devices commonly employed by the strings should be the first goal and achievement of any student of the craft of instrumentation.

Inasmuch as extreme ranges in the strings, individually and collectively, are common, characteristic, and fairly easy of execution, no attempt has been made to parallel those in the wind and brass sections of the book. Therefore Chapter 49, the first of the section on the strings, is concerned with examples of the various bowing techniques. For the sake of both simplicity and practicality the numerous (and to the non-string player, confusing) variations of bowing have been reduced to four basic types: *détaché*—literally, detached or separate bows; *legato*—smoothly connected single bows, or groups of notes slurred together; *marcato* and *martelé*—accented bowing, with varying degrees of pressure on the string; and *spiccato* and *staccato*—not identical, of course, but closely allied in the separation of each note. The string player will no doubt find grounds for violent objection to such seeming over-simplification, but for the orchestrator the more subtle refinements and ramifications of these four basic types are largely unnecessary to his scoring technique. It must likewise be added that orchestral string players seldom conscientiously observe the composer's markings anyway, no matter how painstakingly and meticulously indicated in their parts! Nor do conductors and concertmasters always see eye to eye, even in routine bowing matters. Perhaps, then, it is not to be wondered at that so few orchestrators go to the trouble of carefully marking all bowing in their scorcs, for the fruits of such devoted labor all too often are futility and frustration!

Concluding the chapter on bowing technique are such devices as *saltando*—short note groups taken with a "bouncing" bow; directions to play at the heel of the bow (*au talon*), for sharp accent and "bite," and with the tip of the bow (*punta d'arco*), to produce lightness and delicacy; striking the strings sharply with the bow; playing with the full bow—from tip to nut, and also using only the middle part of the bow; the employment of what might be termed "reverse" bowing—that is, the accented beat or beats of the bar, normally taken with the down-bow (⊓) are instead played with the up-bow (∨), followed on the weaker beats by the naturally heavier down-bow; and finally the consecutive use of both down-bows and groups of up-bows —used respectively for maximum, strong accent, and for the direct opposite.

In this, as in all other string chapters to come, the examples are catalogued according to section—Violin I, II, Violin I and II, Viola, Violoncello, Bass, and all combinations of the five component parts of the string group. *Solo* and *Soli* strings refer, of course, to players within the group, *not* to soloists in concerto works. In fact, no devices as used anywhere in concerto solo parts have been included in the *Thesaurus*, as it was not the purpose of the volume to show examples of virtuoso, soloistic writing.

Two common and contrasting methods of playing on the string occupy Chapters 50 and 51. In addition to the more conventional uses of *pizzicato*—arpeggiated, or deliberately rolled; in rapid chords; taken with the left hand (usually on open strings, played while the right hand is occupied with bowing); on harmonics; and with exaggerated *vibrato*—some of the newer plucked effects have been listed. These include the "nail" *pizzicato* (the string actually plucked by the fingernail); the "snap" *pizzicato*—achieved by plucking the string with such force that it rebounds against the fingerboard, and like the "nail" *pizzicato* invented by, or at least first extensively used by Bartók; the jazz "slap" *pizzicato*, done with the palm; the "thumb" *pizzicato*, produced by softly stroking the string with the fleshy part of the thumb—the most delicate sound imaginable!; *pizzicato* with two fingers, which nearly approximates to the "snap" *pizzicato*; and finally, *pizzicato glissando*, where the finger slides up (or down) on the string immediately after plucking the note or chord. The chapter is concluded with examples of *pizzicato* and *non-pizzicato* combined; that is, cellos *arco* and basses *pizzicato* on the same part—a most frequent and effective string device.

The chapter on *tremoli* includes the familiar bow and finger *tremoli*; the simultaneous bow-finger *tremolo* (actually, a kind of detached trill); *tremoli* played *glissandi* and on harmonics, and the employment of bow and finger *tremoli* combined—that is, Violin I playing bow *tremolo* and Violin II playing the same notes finger *tremolo*. Examples of measured *tremoli* (properly speaking, not a true *tremolo* as the note values for the repetitions are indicated) are quite common in classical and romantic orchestral literature, and illustrations of the use of *tremoli* combined with *non-tremoli* are plentiful in the scores of all periods.

Three rather closely allied tonal effects are next catalogued in Chapters 52, 53, and 54: *col legno* (playing with the back or wooden part of the bow); *sul ponticello* (playing on or very near to the bridge); and *sul tasto* (played on the fingerboard). All three methods are used in *tremoli, non-tremoli, glissandi,* for harmonics, and the latter two in *pizzicati.* Examples are also cited of the combination of one effect with the other, such as the cellos playing *sul ponticello, arco,* and the basses duplicating the same notes *col legno.* Although not catalogued, mention might be made of the author's use in his Symphony No. III of the string struck with the ivory tip of the bow, which produces a kind of super-refined *col legno* effect.

Muting in the string orchestra, either as a whole section or by groups, is so common as to preclude any listing in this *Thesaurus* of instances of such a familiar device. Chapter 55, however, gives a few illustrations of the use of *con sordini* and *senza sordini* combined—i.e., Violin I muted, and Violin II unmuted—and two correlated muting devices: the players are directed to put on their mutes stand by stand (or player by player) in succession, so that there is no cessation of sound but only a gradual softening of the string timbre. The reverse procedure, quite naturally, is both feasible and effective.

No facet of string technique is more mysterious and baffling to the uninitiated than that of harmonics—both natural and artificial. There seem to be almost as many ways used to notate harmonics as there are available notes to be so played. Some of the best composers and orchestrators, even including that master craftsman, Ravel, have at times taken the easy way out of the dilemma by writing the note desired at actual pitch, and merely indicating by means of a "o," or the word, "harmonic," the effect wished. But this method is not only slipshod and careless—it is also actually inaccurate. A single note, for example, may be sounded as a harmonic in three or four different ways, each by means of a separate string, finger, and place on the string to be considered, and each method produces a subtly different tone color. This D:

for instance, may be produced as a *natural* harmonic on both the G and D strings of the violin (see page 409), and as an *artificial* harmonic on the G string—in two different ways (see page 444), and on the D string (see page 449). Thus this one note alone can be taken as a harmonic sound in five different ways. The student should ask any competent string player to demonstrate this for him. He should then be able to perceive the slight but nonetheless important variation in timbre of each—as well as the relative degree of difficulty in so playing—and resolve hereafter to notate all harmonics both specifically and accurately. Chapters 56 and 57, then, are grouped according to the exact and individual notation as found in the various scores, and each group is prefaced with an example of the notation in question and the resulting sound.

Chapter 58 is concerned with illustrations of multiple *divisi,* which is the subdivision of any one of the five component parts of the string section into three or more voices. The standard division into two parts is so common, of course, that there is no point in attempting to list the places where they occur. These multiple *divisi* examples, from 3 up to and including 12 separate voices, are grouped according to the specific combinations called for.

With a smaller number of individual wind and brass instruments in the orchestra's make-up, all are frequently called upon to perform solo roles. But this is equally true of the strings, for notwithstanding the numerical superiority of these instruments their employment as *solo* and *soli* voices is an important part of the orchestrator's tonal palette. Chapter 59 is given over to listing the uses of *solo* parts (one instrument only from any one of the five string divisions, individually or in combination), and Chapter 60 to those of *soli* parts (two or more like string instruments designated on a particular passage).

Because chord notation in the strings is sometimes confusing to the student orchestrator who is not thoroughly conversant with string technique, Chapter 61 gives some examples of such stopping notation. Novices in the craft of instrumentation tend to write quadruple stops as though all four notes could be prolonged at will. The two most common, standardized forms of chord notation are, therefore, illustrated chiefly for their benefit.

Like the harp, but generally limited to three notes for each instrument, the strings are also able to produce enharmonics, or double-stopped unisons. These are accomplished by playing on each of the three upper open strings, and by fingering the same note on the adjacent lower string—that is,

Examples of this device are listed in Chapter 62.

Glissandi and *portamenti* effects are catalogued in Chapter 63 according to the most common orchestral uses: normal *glissando*; slow or measured *glissando*; in harmonics, and sliding to a harmonic. Examples of *glissandi* combined with *tremolo, sul tasto, col legno, sul ponticello,* and *pizzicato* will be found, of course, under these individual chapters.

Chapter 64 gives the few instances where solo strings have been directed to play off-stage, and Chapter 67 deals with reverse arpeggio, or attacking the notes of a chord from the highest to the lowest notes instead of the usual opposite.

Although string performers as a rule avoid the use of the open strings (excepting, quite naturally, the lowest one), composers sometimes indicate their specific use because of certain technical problems or because they want the open string's distinctive tone quality. The customary sign for the open string is the small "o," placed over, under, or at the side of the note—as illustrated throughout Chapter 65. Ordinarily there should be no confusing these notes with the same sign which is used to designate harmonics, as with but one exception on each of the four instruments the open-string notes could not possibly be taken as harmonics. Usually the context of the passage is enough to explain whether this one exception is meant as open string or as a harmonic. The specific indication to play on any particular string—i.e., *sul G'*, or *sul IV corda*—is also done, of course, with the distinctive tone color of the indicated string in mind, and such instances are catalogued in Chapter 66.

A relatively modern device of string technique is *scordatura*, or the re-tuning of one or more of the instrument's four strings. Examples of the violins, violas, and violoncellos employing this unusual device are listed in Chapter 68, as well as the classical and early romantic scores that call for notes in the basses lower than the conventional bottom E. These extra notes—Eb down to C, and in the modern orchestra, B—are possible either on a five-stringed bass, by means of a mechanical extension attached to the neck of the instrument, or by tuning down the lowest string. But even though composers from Haydn to Stravinsky have consistently written bass notes lower than E, bass players have been notoriously indifferent to the adjusting of their instruments accordingly. It is strange, indeed, that the development of bass technique has not kept pace with that of the other string instruments. For all its size and bulk the bass does not contribute proportionately in sheer weight and mass of sound to the body of string tone, owing not a little to the players' reluctance to develop the lowest range of their instrument.

Chapter 69 deals with *senza vibrato*, which is playing with a dead, expressionless tone, and Chapter 70 lists various miscellaneous effects for the strings, such as tapping on the back of the instrument with the fingertips, or the employment of quarter tones. The final chapter again lists miscellaneous terminology for the section not included in the previous chapters.

Chapter 49

BOWING

(1) DÉTACHÉ

English	Italian	French	German
Bow on string	Alla corda	Détaché (à la corde)	Gestrichen
Detached (on the string)	Arco per arco		Strich für Strich
Separate bows	Non-legato		
	Non-spiccato		
	Non-staccato		

Violin I

COMPOSER	WORK	PAGE	MEASURE	COMPOSER	WORK	PAGE	MEASURE
Arnell	*Sinfonia*	14	[4] 2f	**Mason**	*Chanticleer – Festival Overture*	9	[5]
Beethoven	*Symphony No. 3, "Eroica"*	139	183	**Ravel**	*Le Tombeau de Couperin*	46	3
Beethoven	*Symphony No. 6, "Pastoral"*	16	247	**Rimsky-Korsakoff**	*Le Coq d'Or Suite*	21	9
Bizet	*Symphony No. 1*	63	5	**Rimsky-Korsakoff**	*Scheherazade*	50	112
Cherubini	*Anakreon Overture*	47	2			216	[V]
Cimarosa	*Overture to "The Secret Marriage"*	1	4	**Rossini**	*La Scala di Seta, Overture*	16	217
Dukas	*L'Apprenti Sorcier*	41	[38]	**Schumann, R.**	*Symphony No. 2*	62	1
Dvořák	*Carnival Overture*	42	[M]	**Shostakovich**	*The Golden Age, Ballet Suite*	21	[21] 6f
Haydn	*Symphony No. 2 in D major, "London"*	8	86	**Stravinsky**	*Petrouchka Suite*	8	[2]
Mahler	*Symphony No. 2*	20	4	**Thomas**	*Mignon Overture*	11	4

Solo Violin

COMPOSER	WORK	PAGE	MEASURE
Stravinsky	*Histoire du Soldat*	23	3b [9]

Violin II

COMPOSER	WORK	PAGE	MEASURE	COMPOSER	WORK	PAGE	MEASURE
Bartók	*Concerto for Orchestra*	79	[8]	**Haydn**	*Symphony No. 2 in D major, "London"*	12	145
Beethoven	*Symphony No. 3, "Eroica"*	109	143	**Mozart**	*Symphony No. 28 in C major*	18	1
Berlioz	*The Roman Carnival Overture*	41	300	**Smetana**	*Overture to "The Bartered Bride"*	41	398
Dvořák	*Carnival Overture*	4	5				

STRINGS

Violin I and II

COMPOSER	WORK	PAGE	MEASURE	COMPOSER	WORK	PAGE	MEASURE
Antheil	*McKonkey's Ferry*	40	2b [24]	Liszt	*Eine Faust-Symphonie*	3	[A]
Bach, J. C.	*Sinfonia in B♭ major*	8	50			18	1
		23	21	Mozart	*Clarinet Concerto in A major*	3	21
Barber	*First Symphony*	52	[24]				
Barber	*Overture to "The School for Scandal*	25	4	Mozart	*Symphony No. 40 in G minor*		
		31	[J]			47	36
Bartók	*Concerto for Orchestra*	85	[59]	Piston	*First Symphony*	74	41
Beethoven	*Egmont Overture*	29	248	Rachmaninoff	*Rapsodie pour Piano et Orchestre*		
Beethoven	*Piano Concerto No. 3*	97	242			77	5b [55]
Beethoven	*Symphony No. 4*	9	85	Rieti	*Sinfonia No. 5*	5	3b [4]
Beethoven	*Symphony No. 9*	210	435	Rimsky-Korsakoff	*Capriccio Espagnol*	75	2b [U]
Brahms	*Academic Festival Overture*	48	3	Rimsky-Korsakoff	*Le Coq d'Or Suite*	76	5
Bruckner	*Symphony No. 7*	83	172			96	57
Diamond	*Timon of Athens*	27	176	Rimsky-Korsakoff	*Russian Easter Overture*	40	[L]
Dvořák	*Symphony No. 4*	68	[C]				
Elgar	*Variations, "Enigma"*	38	[25]	Rimsky-Korsakoff	*Scheherazade*	160	[B]
Franck	*Symphony in D minor*	141	300	Saint-Saëns	*Danse Macabre*	39	4
Gluck	*Overture to "Iphigénie en Aulide"*	4	34	Schlein	*Dance Overture*	6	1
Gould	*Philharmonic Waltzes*	43	[500] 1f	Schubert	*Symphony No. 6*	67	53
Grofé	*Grand Canyon Suite*	131	[10]			86	322
Haydn	*Symphony No. 6 in G major, "Surprise"*	41	[L]	Shostakovich	*Symphony No. 9*	118	1b [90]
				Stravinsky	*Petrouchka Suite*	18	4b [9]
Haydn	*Symphony No. 13 in G major*	41	66			33	[23] 4f
				Stravinsky	*Scherzo Fantastique*	54	[76]
Khachaturian	*Gayne Ballet Suite No. 2*	93	[22]	Weber	*Der Freischütz Overture*	8	[B]

Viola

COMPOSER	WORK	PAGE	MEASURE	COMPOSER	WORK	PAGE	MEASURE
Bach–Respighi	*Prelude and Fugue in D major*	20	7	Mozart	*Symphony No. 40 in G minor*	1	1
Beethoven	*Overture to Prometheus*	16	181	Rimsky-Korsakoff	*Dance of the Buffoons*	4	[A]
Beethoven	*Symphony No. 8*	68	19	Rimsky-Korsakoff	*Scheherazade*	204	[R]
Copland	*Third Symphony*	13	4				

Violoncello

COMPOSER	WORK	PAGE	MEASURE	COMPOSER	WORK	PAGE	MEASURE
Debussy	*Iberia*	81	1	Dvořák	*Concerto for Violin in A minor*	86	285

Bass

COMPOSER	WORK	PAGE	MEASURE
Beethoven	*Symphony No. 6, "Pastoral"*	90	64

Violin I and Viola

COMPOSER	WORK	PAGE	MEASURE	COMPOSER	WORK	PAGE	MEASURE
Copland	*Appalachian Spring*	75	[62] 8f	Rachmaninoff	*Symphony No. 2*	36	7
Gould	*Philharmonic Waltzes*	1	1	Rossini	*La Scala di Seta, Overture*	1	2
Martinet	*Orphée*	71	[9]				

BOWING

Violin II and Viola

COMPOSER	WORK	PAGE	MEASURE	COMPOSER	WORK	PAGE	MEASURE
Becker	Soundpiece No. 2	3	1	Chávez	Sinfonia India	9	[9]
Beethoven	Piano Concerto No. 2	2	16	Dvořák	Symphony No. 4	147	7
Beethoven	Piano Concerto No. 4	20	134	Franck	Le Chasseur Maudit	48	2
Beethoven	Piano Concerto No. 5	126	106	Miaskovsky	Symphony No. 6	237	[1]
Beethoven	Symphony No. 1	48	8	Poulenc	Concert Champêtre pour		
Beethoven	Symphony No. 5	95	[D]		Clavecin et Orchestre	12	[9]
Beethoven	Symphony No. 9	170	187				

Violin I, II, and Viola

COMPOSER	WORK	PAGE	MEASURE	COMPOSER	WORK	PAGE	MEASURE
Barber	Second Symphony	64	1	Hindemith	Nobilissima Visione	66	[42]
Bax	Fifth Symphony	113	[13] 1f	Kalinnikov	Symphony No. 1	28	2
Beethoven	Symphony No. 9	18	[D]			174	[P]
Bizet	Symphony No. 1	75	12	Piston	First Symphony	90	172
Brahms	Symphony No. 2	99	32	Poot	Jazz-Music	34	[13]
Brahms	Violin Concerto in			Rachmaninoff	Symphony No. 2	191	[74] 4f
	D major	5	[B]	Read	First Overture	1	3
Bruckner	Symphony No. 3	143	[U]	Sibelius	Lemminkainen Journeys	36	[I]
Copland	First Symphony	51	[37] 2f		Homeward	55	[P]
Copland	Four Dance Episodes			Sibelius	Symphony No. 6	35	[G]
	from "Rodeo"	37	[35] 7f	Strauss, R.	Ein Heldenleben	119	[63]
Dvořák	Carnival Overture	59	3			189	1
Franck	Symphony in D minor	30	239	Tchaikovsky	Symphony No. 6,		
Glière	Russian Sailors' Dance	16	[110]		"Pathétique"	11	70
Grétry–Mottl	Ballet Suite, "Céphale			Thomas	Mignon Overture	27	3
	et Procris"	49	[Y] 3f	Weber	Euryanthe Overture	1	1
Hindemith	Mathis der Maler	35	[3]				

Violin I and Violoncello

COMPOSER	WORK	PAGE	MEASURE
Elgar	Variations, "Enigma"	111	[73]

Viola and Violoncello

COMPOSER	WORK	PAGE	MEASURE	COMPOSER	WORK	PAGE	MEASURE
Beethoven	Coriolanus Overture	13	118	Elgar	Introduction and Allegro		
Debussy	Iberia	100	[62]		for Strings	31	[18] 2f
Dvořák	Carnival Overture	16	[E]	Gershwin	An American in Paris	72	4b [61]
Dvořák	Symphony No. 5,			Riegger	Symphony No. 3	73	2b [20]
	"From the New			Stravinsky	Le Sacre du Printemps	66	[75]
	World"	93	4				

Violoncello and Bass

COMPOSER	WORK	PAGE	MEASURE	COMPOSER	WORK	PAGE	MEASURE
Beethoven	Piano Concerto No. 4	130	568	Mendelssohn	Fingal's Cave Overture	43	[H]
Beethoven	Symphony No. 5	60	141	Shostakovich	Symphony No. 3	22	[26]
Mahler	Symphony No. 5	190	10b [7]	Sibelius	Symphony No. 1	126	[K]

Violin I, Viola, and Violoncello

COMPOSER	WORK	PAGE	MEASURE	COMPOSER	WORK	PAGE	MEASURE
Ibert	Divertissement	42	[9]	Stravinsky	Petrouchka Suite	81	[67] 7f
d'Indy	Deuxième Symphonie						
	en Sib	150	[71]				

STRINGS

Violin II, Viola, and Violoncello

COMPOSER	WORK	PAGE	MEASURE
Schubert	Symphony No. 8, "Unfinished"	57	244

Violin I, II, Viola, and Violoncello

COMPOSER	WORK	PAGE	MEASURE	COMPOSER	WORK	PAGE	MEASURE
Bartók	Concerto for Orchestra	94	[126]	Piston	Concertino for Pianoforte and Chamber Orchestra	4	2
Becker	Soundpiece No. 2	13	[14]	Piston	Concerto for Orchestra	37	2
Borodin	Symphony No. 2	122	1	Piston	First Symphony	116	322
Brahms	Symphony No. 1	38	327	Prokofieff	Ala et Lolly (Scythian Suite)	4	1
Britten	Passacaglia from "Peter Grimes"	25	2	Rabaud	Divertissement sur des Chansons Russes	82	3
Copland	Third Symphony	109	[99]	Schuman, W.	American Festival Overture	31	[325] 1f
Dvořák	Symphony No. 5, "From the New World"	150	2	Schuman, W.	Prayer in Time of War	9	167
Elgar	Concerto for Violin and Orchestra	84	1b [97]	Shostakovich	Symphony No. 7	63	1
Elgar	Symphony No. 1	74	[64]	Sibelius	Karelia-Suite	26	[B]
Hindemith	Kammermusik No. 1	92	[200] 3f	Sibelius	Symphony No. 1	75	1
Hindemith	Nobilissima Visione	40	10	Sibelius	Symphony No. 3	8	[4]
Hindemith	Symphony in E-Flat	11	8	Sibelius	Tapiola	4	12
		45	[25] 4f	Smetana	Blanik	47	2
Inghelbrecht	El Greco	21	2b [17]	Stravinsky	Scènes de Ballet	50	1
Kabalevsky	Suite from "Colas Breugnon"	62	[53] 3f	Tchaikovsky	Capriccio Italien	98	2
Levant	Nocturne	16	57	Tchaikovsky	Francesca da Rimini	28	1
Mahler	Symphony No. 5	221	[24]	Tchaikovsky	Manfred-Symphonie	62	319
Mendelssohn	Fingal's Cave Overture	16	76	Tchaikovsky	Piano Concerto No. 1, in Bb minor	36	341
Milhaud	Cinq Symphonies pour Petit Orchestre	45	1	Tchaikovsky	Symphony No. 4	171	187

Violin II, Violoncello, and Bass

COMPOSER	WORK	PAGE	MEASURE
Mahler	Symphony No. 3	167	[23]

Viola, Violoncello, and Bass

COMPOSER	WORK	PAGE	MEASURE	COMPOSER	WORK	PAGE	MEASURE
Bartók	Concerto for Orchestra	31	[57]	Mohaupt	Town Piper Music	40	8b [36]
Beethoven	Piano Concerto No. 3	75	33	Rimsky-Korsakoff	Capriccio Espagnol	78	4
Haydn	Symphony No. 17 in C major, "L'Ours"	28	101	Schumann, R.	Symphony No. 2	136	93
Hindemith	Mathis der Maler	20	[16]				

Violin II, Viola, Violoncello, and Bass

COMPOSER	WORK	PAGE	MEASURE	COMPOSER	WORK	PAGE	MEASURE
Beethoven	Piano Concerto No. 4	79	49	Tchaikovsky	Symphony No. 6, "Pathétique"	31	175

Violin I, II, Viola, Violoncello, and Bass

COMPOSER	WORK	PAGE	MEASURE	COMPOSER	WORK	PAGE	MEASURE
Aubert	Saisons	49	[27]	Beethoven	Leonore Overture No. 3	30	268
Beethoven	Leonore Overture No. 2	48	382			50	530

BOWING

Violin I, II, Viola, Violoncello, and Bass (contd.)

COMPOSER	WORK	PAGE	MEASURE	COMPOSER	WORK	PAGE	MEASURE
Beethoven	Overture to Prometheus	24	249	Haydn	Symphony No. 6 in	9	100
Beethoven	Piano Concerto No. 1	71	37		G major, "Surprise"	31	[K]
Beethoven	Piano Concerto No. 3	57	37	Ibert	Ouverture de Fête	41	1
Beethoven	Piano Concerto No. 5	152	302	Inghelbrecht	Sinfonia Breve No. 1	14	2
		171	439	Lopatnikoff	Sinfonietta	53	1
Beethoven	Symphony No. 3,			Mahler	Symphony No. 5	236	[32]
	"Eroica"	127	1	Mendelssohn	Ruy Blas Overture	11	1
Beethoven	Symphony No. 4	91	1	Miaskovsky	Sinfonietta for String		
		123	335		Orchestra	25	[19]
Beethoven	Symphony No. 5	15	273	Moeran	Sinfonietta	40	[56]
		23	408	Moeran	Symphony in G minor	60	3b [32]
Beethoven	Symphony No. 7	31	195			135	[92]
		133	[B]	Mozart	Bassoon Concerto in		
Beethoven	Symphony No. 9	260	763		Bb major	4	32
		293	920	Mozart	Symphony No. 28 in		
Beethoven	Violin Concerto in	2	34		C major	28	[J]
	D major	22	315	Mozart	Symphony No. 35 in		
Berlioz	Benvenuto Cellini				D major, "Haffner"	34	20
	Overture	50	3	Mozart	Symphony No. 40 in	8	88
Brahms	Symphony No. 3	95	81		G minor	40	1
Brahms	Variations on a Theme			Mozart	Symphony No. 41 in		
	by Haydn	65	457		C major, "Jupiter"	53	19
Bruckner	Symphony No. 1	85	[B]	Mussorgsky	Night on the Bald		
		114	2b [330]		Mountain	72	351
Bruckner	Symphony No. 2	75		Piston	Concerto for Orchestra	3	1
		110	1	Piston	Prelude and Fugue	32	1
Bruckner	Symphony No. 3	89	[A]	Poot	Symphonie	1	1
Bruckner	Symphony No. 6	112	[B]	Rossini	Semiramide, Overture	75	3
Bruckner	Symphony No. 8	127	[Q]	Schubert	Symphony No. 4	36	269
		158	[I]	Schubert	Symphony No. 7	6	78
Bruckner	Symphony No. 9	174	145			83	121
Cowell	Short Symphony (No. 4)	60	[A] 5f	Schumann, R.	Symphony No. 1	162	301
Delius	Eventyr, Once Upon a			Schumann, R.	Symphony No. 4	120	211
	Time	32	4	Smetana	From Bohemia's Woods		
Dello Joio	Variations, Chaconne,				and Fields	60	5
	and Finale	21	[170] 1f	Smetana	Overture to "The		
Diamond	Fourth Symphony	24	[130]		Bartered Bride"	1	5
Dvořák	Carnival Overture	12	1	Smetana	Tabor	48	332
de Falla	Three Dances from			Stillman-	New England		
	"The Three-Cornered			Kelley	Symphony	11	[C]
	Hat"	37	1	Strauss, R.	Ein Heldenleben	94	[49]
Franck	Symphony in D minor	4	29	Tchaikovsky	March Slav	77	1
Glinka	Russlan and Ludmilla			Tchaikovsky	Mozartiana	55	250
	Overture	35	229	Tchaikovsky	Romeo and Juliet	18	1
Grétry–Mottl	Ballet Suite, "Céphale			Tchaikovsky	Symphony No. 3	96	1
	et Procris"	14	1b [E]			118	[P]
Haydn	Symphony No. 2 in			Tchaikovsky	Symphony No. 4	130	2
	D major, "London"	35	138	Wagner, R.	Entrance of the Guests		
Haydn	Symphony No. 4 in				from "Tannhäuser"	23	2b [D]
	D major, "Clock"	3	45	Weber	Euryanthe Overture	25	175
		49	34	Weber	Oberon Overture	8	41
		67	261				

287

STRINGS

(2) LEGATO

English	Italian	French	German
Legato (bowing)	Legato [ligato]	A la corde	Gezogen
Smooth (bows)	Non-marcato	L'archet bien à la corde	Lang gestrichen
	Non-spiccato	Legato	Legato
	Non-staccato	Très à la corde	Mit liegendem Bogen

Violin I

COMPOSER	WORK	PAGE	MEASURE	COMPOSER	WORK	PAGE	MEASURE
Beethoven	Egmont Overture	3	15	Mendelssohn	Symphony No. 4, "Italian"	50	5
Beethoven	Symphony No. 9	237	655				
Liszt	Les Préludes	13	47	Ravel	Daphnis et Chloé, Suite No. 2	8	[157]
Mahler	Das Lied von der Erde	39	1				
Mahler	Symphony No. 5	139	[13]				

Violin II

COMPOSER	WORK	PAGE	MEASURE	COMPOSER	WORK	PAGE	MEASURE
Mendelssohn	Overture to "A Midsummer Night's Dream"	54	[H]	Respighi	The Fountains of Rome	1	1

Violin I and II

COMPOSER	WORK	PAGE	MEASURE	COMPOSER	WORK	PAGE	MEASURE
Beethoven	Piano Concerto No. 5	11	49	Mozart	Clarinet Concerto in A major	35	1
Beethoven	Symphony No. 1	45	85	Mozart	Symphony No. 28 in C major	24	102
Beethoven	Symphony No. 2	14	81	Mozart	Symphony No. 35 in D major, "Haffner"	3	19
Beethoven	Symphony No. 7	96	155	Mozart	Symphony No. 39 in Eb major	8	[B] 1f
Beethoven	Violin Concerto in D major	21	301			51	54
Dvořák	Symphony No. 5, "From the New World"	88	17	Mozart	Symphony No. 41 in C major, "Jupiter"	40	1
Franck	Le Chasseur Maudit	22	1			52	1
d'Indy	Deuxième Symphonie en Sib	59	[28] 4f	Weber	Der Freischütz Overture	2	9
Kabalevsky	Suite from "Colas Breugnon"	92	[19]				

Viola

COMPOSER	WORK	PAGE	MEASURE	COMPOSER	WORK	PAGE	MEASURE
Beethoven	Symphony No. 6, "Pastoral"	118	80	Rachmaninoff	Symphony No. 2	124	1

Violoncello

COMPOSER	WORK	PAGE	MEASURE	COMPOSER	WORK	PAGE	MEASURE
Franck	Le Chasseur Maudit	60	275	Schuman, W.	Symphony No. III	10	89
Mahler	Das Lied von der Erde	41	3				

BOWING

Violin I and Viola

COMPOSER	WORK	PAGE	MEASURE	COMPOSER	WORK	PAGE	MEASURE
Beethoven	Leonore Overture No. 2	40	306	Ravel	Rapsodie Espagnole	1	1

Violin II and Viola

COMPOSER	WORK	PAGE	MEASURE	COMPOSER	WORK	PAGE	MEASURE
Flotow	Alessandro Stradella Overture	3	24	Saint-Saëns	3ᵉ Symphonie en Ut mineur	137	[V]
Haydn	Symphony No. 2 in D major, "London"	40	72				

Violin I, II, and Viola

COMPOSER	WORK	PAGE	MEASURE	COMPOSER	WORK	PAGE	MEASURE
Beethoven	Piano Concerto No. 3	100	265	Cowell	Short Symphony (No. 4)	61	4b [B]
Beethoven	Symphony No. 3, "Eroica"	145	270	Engel	The Creation	20	3b [9]
Beethoven	Symphony No. 5	4	63	Hill	Sinfonietta for String Orchestra	6	[100]
Beethoven	Symphony No. 6, "Pastoral"	5 138	67 196	Mendelssohn	Fingal's Cave Overture	35	194
Berlioz	Symphonie Fantastique	215	4	Mussorgsky	Polonaise from "Boris Godunov"	10	1
Brahms	Variations on a Theme by Haydn	56	406	Ravel	Rapsodie Espagnole	15	[5]
				Riegger	Dichotomy	46	1
Bruckner	Symphony No. 6	20	[H]	Schumann, R.	Symphony No. 4	70	65

Violin I and Violoncello

COMPOSER	WORK	PAGE	MEASURE	COMPOSER	WORK	PAGE	MEASURE
Beethoven	Coriolanus Overture	4	52	Hindemith	Mathis der Maler	50	[6]
Beethoven	Symphony No. 6, "Pastoral"	96	97				

Violin I, II, and Violoncello

COMPOSER	WORK	PAGE	MEASURE
Wagner, R.	Overture to "Tannhäuser"	22	[B]

Viola and Violoncello

COMPOSER	WORK	PAGE	MEASURE	COMPOSER	WORK	PAGE	MEASURE
Beethoven	Egmont Overture	22	[C]	Respighi	The Birds	37	2
Beethoven	Symphony No. 5	34	50	White	Idyl for Orchestra	1	1
Bizet	Roma	57	1				

Violoncello and Bass

COMPOSER	WORK	PAGE	MEASURE
Beethoven	Symphony No. 9	165	92

Violin I, Viola, and Violoncello

COMPOSER	WORK	PAGE	MEASURE	COMPOSER	WORK	PAGE	MEASURE
Brahms	Symphony No. 2	3	[A]	Hindemith	Mathis der Maler	1	[1]
Elgar	Variations, "Enigma"	85	[54]				

Violin II, Viola, and Violoncello

COMPOSER	WORK	PAGE	MEASURE
Haydn	Symphony No. 2 in D major, "London"	52	[S]

STRINGS

Violin I, II, Viola, and Violoncello

COMPOSER	WORK	PAGE	MEASURE	COMPOSER	WORK	PAGE	MEASURE
Beethoven	Piano Concerto No. 4	46	260	Diamond	Fourth Symphony	1	1
Beethoven	Symphony No. 3 "Eroica"	2	9	Dvořák	Symphony No. 5, "From the New World"	58	1
Beethoven	Symphony No. 4	47	[B]	Franck	Symphony in D minor	26	213
		57	72	Grieg	Peer Gynt Suite No. 1	4	[A]
Beethoven	Symphony No. 8	57	1	Harris	Third Symphony	23	1
Beethoven	Symphony No. 9	15	114	Haydn	Symphony No. 2 in D major, "London"	46	73
		54	382	Hindemith	Kammermusik No. 1	23	2
Berlioz	The Roman Carnival Overture	40	279	Honegger	Le Dit des Jeux du Monde	78	1
Bizet	L'Arlésienne Suite No. 2	1	3	Kalinnikov	Symphony No. 1	57	[W]
Brahms	Concerto for Violin and Violoncello	11	1	Liszt	Eine Faust-Symphonie	127	[E] 1f
Brahms	Ein deutsches Requiem	245	48	Mozart	Symphony No. 41 in C major, "Jupiter"	80	360
Brahms	Symphony No. 3	55	[E] 1f	Rachmaninoff	Piano Concerto No. 3	134	[75]
Brahms	Symphony No. 4	16	3b [E]	Rieti	Sinfonia Tripartita	32	[24]
		129	[B]	Smetana	The Moldau	11	56
Brahms	Violin Concerto in D major	1	9	Stillman-Kelley	New England Symphony	66	[O]
Chausson	Symphonie en Si bèmol majeur	85	[D]	Wagner, R.	Eine Faust-Overture	9	39
Debussy	Prélude à l'après-midi d'un Faune	17	1	Wagner, R.	The Flying Dutchman Overture	34	219

Violin I, II, Violoncello, and Bass

COMPOSER	WORK	PAGE	MEASURE
Schumann, R.	Symphony No. 2	1	1

Viola, Violoncello, and Bass

COMPOSER	WORK	PAGE	MEASURE	COMPOSER	WORK	PAGE	MEASURE
Bartók	Concerto for Orchestra	2	[35]	Brahms	Ein deutsches Requiem	5	1
Bartók	Violin Concerto	115	[450]	Haydn	Symphony No. 6 in G major, "Surprise"	1	10
Beethoven	Overture to Prometheus	20	217				

Violin I, II, Viola, Violoncello, and Bass

COMPOSER	WORK	PAGE	MEASURE	COMPOSER	WORK	PAGE	MEASURE
Bartók	Music for Strings, Percussion and Celesta	1	1	Beethoven	Symphony No. 5	52	1
Becker	Soundpiece No. 2	4	[2]	Beethoven	Symphony No. 7	52	340
Beethoven	Piano Concerto No. 1	6	63			167	350
		52	15	Beethoven	Symphony No. 9	117	422
Beethoven	Piano Concerto No. 3	5	58	Bizet	Roma	98	1
Beethoven	Piano Concerto No. 4	18	119	Brahms	Ein deutsches Requiem	101	129
Beethoven	Piano Concerto No. 5	98	540			178	40
Beethoven	Symphony No. 2	86	157	Brahms	Symphony No. 1	95	1
Beethoven	Symphony No. 3, "Eroica"	114	216	Brahms	Symphony No. 2	113	135
				Britten	Four Sea Interludes from "Peter Grimes"	83	[13] 1f
Beethoven	Symphony No. 4	68	58	Bruckner	Symphony No. 2	141	[W]

BOWING

Violin I, II, Viola, Violoncello, and Bass (contd.)

COMPOSER	WORK	PAGE	MEASURE	COMPOSER	WORK	PAGE	MEASURE
Cimarosa	Overture to "The Secret Marriage"	25	9	Mozart	Symphony No. 41 in C major, "Jupiter"	39	65
Copland	Music for the Theatre	5	[2]	Mozart	Titus Overture	10	4
Dvořák	Concerto for Violin in A minor	47	69	Schumann, R.	Symphony No. 1	58	438
Haydn	Symphony No. 4 in D major, "Clock"	13	[E]	Schumann, R.	Symphony No. 2	110	1
				Shostakovich	Piano Concerto	12	[11]
Mozart	Overture to "The Marriage of Figaro"	1	1	Sibelius	Symphony No. 7	29	1
				Smetana	Vysehrad	7	35
Mozart	Symphony No. 35 in D major, "Haffner"	43	134	Stillman-Kelley	Gulliver—His Voyage to Lilliput	6	1
				Vaughan Williams	Symphony in D major (No. 5)	11	5

(3) MARCATO—MARTELÉ

English	Italian	French	German
Accented (bows)	Marcato	Martelé	Markiert (gestrichen)
Marked	Martellato	Marteler	
	Martello		

Violin I

COMPOSER	WORK	PAGE	MEASURE
Chávez	Sinfonia India	9	[9]

Violin I and II

COMPOSER	WORK	PAGE	MEASURE	COMPOSER	WORK	PAGE	MEASURE
Debussy	Fêtes	18	1	Mozart	Symphony No. 41 in C major, "Jupiter"	70	[E]
d'Indy	Deuxième Symphonie en Sib	91	5	Rachmaninoff	Symphony No. 2	88	1
Maganini	Symphony for Chamber Orchestra	11	[E] 1f	Strauss, R.	Death and Transfiguration	47	2
Mahler	Symphony No. 5	202	2				

Viola

COMPOSER	WORK	PAGE	MEASURE
Charpentier	Impressions d'Italie	34	9

Violoncello

COMPOSER	WORK	PAGE	MEASURE
Trapp	Symphonie No. 4	33	1

Violin II and Viola

COMPOSER	WORK	PAGE	MEASURE	COMPOSER	WORK	PAGE	MEASURE
de Falla	Three Dances from "The Three-Cornered Hat"	27	2	Schreker	The Birthday of the Infanta, Suite	23	[95] 1f

291

STRINGS

Soli Violin II and Viola

COMPOSER	WORK	PAGE	MEASURE
Stravinsky	*Pulcinella Suite*	**25**	1b [32]

Violin I, II, and Viola

COMPOSER	WORK	PAGE	MEASURE	COMPOSER	WORK	PAGE	MEASURE
Bruckner	*Symphony No. 9*	**61**	400	**Franck**	*Symphony in D minor*	**127**	187
		130	556	**Smetana**	*Blanik*	**59**	2
Copland	*First Symphony*	**49**	10b [36]	**Schumann, R.**	*Symphony No. 1*	**167**	331
Cowell	*Short Symphony*	**1**	1	**Strauss, R.**	*Till Eulenspiegel's*		
	(No. 4)	**77**	1b [S]		*Merry Pranks*	**26**	1
Elgar	*Falstaff*	**108**	[109]	**Walton**	*Symphony*	**84**	[60] 3f
Enesco	*Ière Rhapsodie*						
	Roumaine	**20**	[11]				

Violin I, II, and Violoncello

Rimsky-Korsakoff	*Le Coq d'Or Suite*	**48**	2

Viola and Violoncello

COMPOSER	WORK	PAGE	MEASURE	COMPOSER	WORK	PAGE	MEASURE
Schönberg	*Theme and Variations*	**42**	205	**Wellesz**	*Symphony in C*	**27**	2b [200]
Wagner, R.	*Tannhäuser Overture*	**41**	257				

Violoncello and Bass

COMPOSER	WORK	PAGE	MEASURE	COMPOSER	WORK	PAGE	MEASURE
Elgar	*Symphony No. 2*	**117**	[121]	**Ibert**	*Escales*	**29**	[24]
Grieg	*Piano Concerto in*			**Thomson**	*Louisiana Story Suite*	**61**	5
	A minor	**14**	[D] 2f	**Wagner, R.**	*Eine Faust-Overture*	**5**	21

Violin I, Viola, and Violoncello

Wagner, R.	*Eine Faust-Overture*	**37**	303

Violin II, Viola, and Violoncello

COMPOSER	WORK	PAGE	MEASURE	COMPOSER	WORK	PAGE	MEASURE
Dukas	*L'Apprenti Sorcier*	**55**	[47]	**James**	*Suite for String*		
					Orchestra	**6**	[D] 5f

Violin I, II, Viola, and Violoncello

COMPOSER	WORK	PAGE	MEASURE	COMPOSER	WORK	PAGE	MEASURE
Bizet	*Intermezzi from*			**Chasins**	*Rush Hour in Hong*		
	"Carmen"	**21**	6		*Kong*	**6**	[A] 4f
Brahms	*Symphony No. 3*	**38**	[L]	**Chávez**	*Sinfonia India*	**42**	[58]
Brahms	*Violin Concerto in*			**Copland**	*Music for Radio*	**1**	1
	D major	**4**	78	**Copland**	*Statements*	**32**	[7] 4f
Britten	*Four Sea Interludes*			**Elgar**	*Introduction and Allegro*		
	from "Peter Grimes"	**24**	[3]		*for Strings*	**18**	11

BOWING

Violin I, II, Viola, and Violoncello (contd.)

COMPOSER	WORK	PAGE	MEASURE	COMPOSER	WORK	PAGE	MEASURE
Ferguson	*Partita for Orchestra*	70	1	Schumann, R.	*Symphony No. 2*	143	140
Herrmann	*Sinfonietta for String Orchestra*	12	2	Stravinsky	*Fire-Bird Suite (1919)*	56	[30]
Honegger	*Prélude, Fugue, Postlude*	9	[4]	Tchaikovsky	*Symphony No. 6, "Pathétique"*	192	72
Prokofieff	*Ala et Lolly (Scythian Suite)*	41	[22]	Vaughan Williams	*Symphony in E minor (No. 6)*	101	[16]
Roussel	*4me Symphonie*	31	5	Wagner, R.	*Eine Faust-Overture*	28	229
Schuman, W.	*Symphony No. IV*	22	198				

Viola, Violoncello, and Bass

COMPOSER	WORK	PAGE	MEASURE	COMPOSER	WORK	PAGE	MEASURE
Bruckner	*Symphony No. 7*	70	[K]	Rimsky-Korsakoff	*Le Coq d'Or Suite*	88	[54] 1f
Prokofieff	*Symphony No. 5*	54	[28]				

Violin I, Viola, Violoncello, and Bass

COMPOSER	WORK	PAGE	MEASURE
Beethoven	*Symphony No. 9*	9	[B] 1f

Violin II, Viola, Violoncello, and Bass

Beethoven	*Piano Concerto No. 2*	54	69

Violin I, II, Viola, Violoncello, and Bass

COMPOSER	WORK	PAGE	MEASURE	COMPOSER	WORK	PAGE	MEASURE
Beethoven	*Egmont Overture*	1	2	Britten	*Four Sea Interludes from "Peter Grimes"*	74	[9] 3f
Beethoven	*Piano Concerto No. 1*	77	133	Britten	*Passacaglia from "Peter Grimes"*	27	[11]
Beethoven	*Symphony No. 3, "Eroica"*	26	[I]	Bruckner	*Symphony No. 1*	93	[E]
Beethoven	*Symphony No. 8*	105	[G]	Bruckner	*Symphony No. 3*	53	[W]
Beethoven	*Symphony No. 9*	41	297			127	3b [200]
		197	321	Bruckner	*Symphony No. 5*	125	[F] 2f
Berlioz	*Harold en Italie*	200	1	Bruckner	*Symphony No. 6*	134	235
Berlioz	*Three Pieces from "The Damnation of Faust"*	9	4	Bruckner	*Symphony No. 7*	60	27
Bizet	*L'Arlésienne Suite No. 2*	21	1	Copland	*Appalachian Spring*	49	[41]
Brahms	*Academic Festival Overture*	5	6	Dvořák	*Violin Concerto in A minor*	52	107
Brahms	*Concerto for Violin and Violoncello*	1	1	Elgar	*In the South, Concert Overture*	92	4
Brahms	*Symphony No. 1*	45	370	Elgar	*Introduction and Allegro for Strings*	45	1b [26]
		53	459	Elgar	*Variations, "Enigma"*	20	[11]
		158	391	de Falla	*Nuits dans les Jardins d'Espagne*	58	[23]
Brahms	*Symphony No. 2*	10	[E]	Gershwin	*An American in Paris*	77	4
Brahms	*Symphony No. 3*	97	[F]	Grieg	*Norwegian Dances*	39	1
Brahms	*Symphony No. 4*	70	37	Harris	*Third Symphony*	50	6
Brahms	*Tragic Overture*	20	1	Harsanyi	*Suite pour Orchestre*	66	[100] 1f
		39	5				

STRINGS

Violin I, II, Viola, Violoncello, and Bass (contd.)

COMPOSER	WORK	PAGE	MEASURE	COMPOSER	WORK	PAGE	MEASURE
Kabalevsky	*Symphony No. 2*	162	[61]	Roussel	*4me Symphonie*	118	1
Mahler	*Symphony No. 2*	31	[15]	Schubert	*Symphony No. 8,*		
		158	4		*"Unfinished"*	42	[A]
Moore	*Symphony in A major*	120	[79] 1f	Shostakovich	*Piano Concerto*	7	[5] 1f
Prokofieff	*Romeo and Juliet, Suite*			Sibelius	*Symphony No. 2*	1	1
	No. 1	114	[70]	Smetana	*Overture to "The*	18	180
Prokofieff	*Symphony No. 5*	62	3		*Bartered Bride"*	36	343
Rameau–				Smetana	*Sárka*	42	2
Mottl	*Ballet Suite*	32	[Y]	Strauss, R.	*Till Eulenspiegel's*		
Rimsky–					*Merry Pranks*	53	[37]
Korsakoff	*Capriccio Espagnol*	88	1	Stravinsky	*Petrouchka Suite*	150	6b [125]
Rivier	*Ouverture pour un don*			Wagner, R.	*Entrance of the Guests*		
	Quichotte	2	1		*from "Tannhäuser"*	8	5

(4) SPICCATO AND STACCATO

English	Italian	French	German
Short (bows)	Spiccato	Staccato	Abgestossen
Staccato	Staccato		Kurz (gestrichen)
			Scharf gestossen

Violin I

COMPOSER	WORK	PAGE	MEASURE	COMPOSER	WORK	PAGE	MEASURE
Bartók	*Concerto for Orchestra*	32	[63]	Rachmaninoff	*2d Concerto pour Piano*		
Beethoven	*Leonore Overture No. 2*	3	24		*et Orchestre*	88	[34]
Beethoven	*Overture to Prometheus*	3	17	Reger	*Variations on a Theme*		
Beethoven	*Symphony No. 1*	3	15		*of Mozart*	108	1
Beethoven	*Symphony No. 5*	72	6	Rieti	*Sinfonia No. 5*	53	[60] 1f
Beethoven	*Symphony No. 9*	117	[L]	Rimsky–			
Bruckner	*Symphony No. 4*	81	[D]	Korsakoff	*Capriccio Espagnol*	74	6
Bruckner	*Symphony No. 9*	118	345	Rimsky–			
Glinka	*Kamarinskaïa*	12	3b [5]	Korsakoff	*Scheherazade*	175	[H]
Haydn	*Symphony No. 1 in*			Rossini	*Semiramide, Overture*	19	112
	Eb major, "Drumroll"	31	16	Rossini	*The Barber of Seville,*		
Haydn	*Symphony No. 2 in*				*Overture*	16	82
	D major, "London"	29	70	Schubert	*Symphony No. 5*	10	120
Herrmann	*Sinfonietta for String*			Shostakovich	*Symphony No. 1*	4	[6] 1f
	Orchestra	3	8	Sibelius	*Symphony No. 3*	17	5
Liadov	*Eight Russian Popular*			Stillman–	*Gulliver—His Voyage*		
	Songs	22	5	Kelley	*to Lilliput*	94	[Q]
Mahler	*Symphony No. 3*	129	4b [17]	Verdi	*Messa da Requiem*	179	42
Mozart	*Symphony No. 35 in*						
	D major, "Haffner"	3	[A]				

Solo Violin

COMPOSER	WORK	PAGE	MEASURE
Stravinsky	*Histoire du Soldat*	7	2

BOWING

Violin II

COMPOSER	WORK	PAGE	MEASURE	COMPOSER	WORK	PAGE	MEASURE
Beethoven	Symphony No. 6, "Pastoral"	78	3	Mason	Chanticleer—Festival Overture	5	[3] 1f
Haydn	Symphony No. 7 in C major, "Le Midi"	1	1	Mozart	Symphony No. 35 in D major, "Haffner"	22	1
Haydn	Symphony No. 15 in B♭ major, "La Reine"	21	5	Parodi	Preludio ad una Commedia	51	[AB]
Hindemith	Mathis der Maler	83	1	Schumann, R.	Symphony No. 2	116	[Q]
				Shostakovich	Piano Concerto	4	[2]
				Stravinsky	Petrouchka Suite	105	[92]

Violin I and II

COMPOSER	WORK	PAGE	MEASURE	COMPOSER	WORK	PAGE	MEASURE
Barber	First Symphony	37	2	Mozart	Symphony No. 41 in C major, "Jupiter"	74	284
Bartók	Concerto for Orchestra	10	[192]	Mozart	Violin Concerto in B♭ major	19	17
		73	[95]	Piston	Symphony No. 2	106	1
Beethoven	Piano Concerto No. 2	60	41	Rachmaninoff	The Bells	29	4b [27]
Beethoven	Symphony No. 6, "Pastoral"	121	99	Reger	Variations on a Theme of Mozart	33	1
Bizet	Prelude to "Carmen"	1	1			67	3
Bizet	Symphony No. 1	20	[15] 4f	Rimsky-Korsakoff	Capriccio Espagnol	61	1
Bruckner	Symphony No. 4	60	[F]	Rimsky-Korsakoff	Scheherazade	214	[U]
Chausson	Symphonie en Si bémol majeur	40	15	Rossini	L'Italiani in Algeri, Overture	3	9
Copland	Appalachian Spring	45	[37]	Rossini	The Thieving Magpie, Overture	12	3
Copland	Third Symphony	30	[24]	Schubert	Symphony No. 6	61	205
Debussy	Fêtes	66	[20]			71	107
Debussy	La Mer	53	[27]	Schubert	Symphony No. 7	4	61
Elgar	Variations, "Enigma"	8	[5]	Sibelius	Symphony No. 1	69	[M] 1f
Franck	Le Chasseur Maudit	23	1	Sibelius	Symphony No. 3	28	[15] 2f
Gershwin	An American in Paris	17	4b [15]	Stravinsky	Jeu de Cartes	36	[71]
Haydn	Symphony No. 2 in D major, "London"	5	46			55	2b [102]
Haydn	Symphony No. 6 in G major, "Surprise"	23	1	Stravinsky	Scherzo à la Russe	24	[20]
Haydn	Symphony No. 16 in G major, "Oxford"	7	61	Tchaikovsky	Manfred-Symphonie	114	3
Haydn	Symphony No. 17 in C major, "L'Ours"	58	231	Vaughan Williams	Symphony in F minor (No. 4)	41	8
Khachaturian	Masquerade Suite	66	[3]	Verdi	Overture to "La Forza del Destino"	32	[N]
Liszt	Eine Faust-Symphonie	270	3	Wagner, R.	Prelude to "Die Meistersinger von Nürnberg"	8	39
Mahler	Symphony No. 4	139	278				
Mendelssohn	Midsummer Night's Dream Overture	1	8				
Mozart	Clarinet Concerto in A major	22	229				

Viola

COMPOSER	WORK	PAGE	MEASURE	COMPOSER	WORK	PAGE	MEASURE
Barber	Second Symphony	67	[4] 4f	Brahms	Symphony No. 1	121	[G]
Borodin	Symphony No. 1	130	3	Britten	Sinfonietta	28	[1] 2f

STRINGS

Viola (contd.)

COMPOSER	WORK	PAGE	MEASURE	COMPOSER	WORK	PAGE	MEASURE
Dvořák	Symphony No. 5, "From the New World"	131	4	Rossini	Tancredi, Overture	19	96
				Schubert	Symphony No. 8, "Unfinished"	6	[A] 4f
Glière	Russian Sailors' Dance	8	[62]	Sibelius	Symphony No. 3	14	[7] 7f
Haydn	Symphony No. 3 in Eb major	21	157	Stravinsky	"Dumbarton Oaks" Concerto	3	[4]
Milhaud	Saudades do Brazil	35	9	Tchaikovsky	Nutcracker Suite	2	8b [A]
Piston	Prelude and Allegro for Organ and Strings	16	[140] 1f	Tchaikovsky	Symphony No. 5	107	[E]
Rachmaninoff	Symphony No. 2	92	4b [35]	Vaughan Williams	Symphony in E minor (No. 6)	100	[14]
Rimsky-Korsakoff	Scheherazade	157	30				

Violoncello

COMPOSER	WORK	PAGE	MEASURE	COMPOSER	WORK	PAGE	MEASURE
Beethoven	Symphony No. 8	63	45	Sibelius	Symphony No. 2	48	3
Ibert	Escales	5	[3]	Wagner, R.	Prelude to "Die Meistersinger von Nürnberg"	32	138
Mahler	Symphony No. 5	208	3				
Rimsky-Korsakoff	Dance of the Buffoons	14	[E]				

Soli Violoncello

COMPOSER	WORK	PAGE	MEASURE
Schönberg	A Survivor from Warsaw	5	23

Violin I and Viola

COMPOSER	WORK	PAGE	MEASURE	COMPOSER	WORK	PAGE	MEASURE
Barber	Second Symphony	100	[37]	Stravinsky	Chant du Rossignol	44	2b [45]
Beethoven	Symphony No. 2	50	105	Stravinsky	Concerto en Ré pour Orchestre à Cordes	2	[3] 2f
Beethoven	Symphony No. 7	78	[B] 1f				
Schönberg	Kammersymphonie, Op. 9	78	[71]	Stravinsky	Petrouchka Suite	92	1

Violin II and Viola

COMPOSER	WORK	PAGE	MEASURE	COMPOSER	WORK	PAGE	MEASURE
Beethoven	Piano Concerto No. 3	107	339	Schubert	Symphony No. 4	74	85
Beethoven	Symphony No. 2	43	[A]			106	373
Beethoven	Symphony No. 4	42	6	Stravinsky	Fire-Bird Suite (1919)	9	1b [12]
Bizet	Symphony No. 1	5	[2]	Stravinsky	Ode	7	[12]
Ibert	Escales	20	[14]	Verdi	I Vespri Siciliani, Overture	43	185
Liszt	Piano Concerto No. 1	5	[A] 3f				
Rossini	La Scala di Seta, Overture	7	82				

Violin I, II, and Viola

COMPOSER	WORK	PAGE	MEASURE	COMPOSER	WORK	PAGE	MEASURE
Barber	Essay for Orchestra	8	3	Beethoven	Symphony No. 1	10	78
Beethoven	Piano Concerto No. 2	45	18			22	[E]
Beethoven	Piano Concerto No. 3	66	69	Beethoven	Symphony No. 5	33	32

BOWING

Violin I, II, and Viola (contd.)

COMPOSER	WORK	PAGE	MEASURE	COMPOSER	WORK	PAGE	MEASURE
Beethoven	Symphony No. 7	2	10	Nystedt	The Land of Suspense	17	2
Berlioz	Symphonie Fantastique	161	2	Rachmaninoff	Piano Concerto No. 3	119	6
Borodin	Symphony No. 2	57	7	Rachmaninoff	Symphony No. 2	159	6
		82	5	Riisager	Torgot Dance	22	[100] 3f
Brahms	Concerto for Violin and Violoncello	15	2	Roussel	Symphonie en Sol mineur	85	[53] 3f
Brahms	Tragic Overture	31	4	Saint-Saëns	3e Symphonie en Ut mineur	2	4
Copland	El Salón México	32	[31]				
Debussy	Fêtes	24	2	Schelling	A Victory Ball	107	[33]
de Falla	El Retablo de Maese Pedro	89	[83] 4f	Shostakovich	Symphony No. 5	51	[46]
				Sibelius	Symphony No. 6	9	[D]
de Falla	Nuits dans les Jardins d'Espagne	41	2b [6]	Smetana	Šárka	59	1
Harris	Third Symphony	33	[27] 3f	Stravinsky	Petrouchka Suite	155	5b [131]
Haydn	Symphony No. 6 in G major, "Surprise"	28	75	Stravinsky	Scènes de Ballet	34	[58]
				Tchaikovsky	Nutcracker Suite	35	[E] 2f
Hindemith	Konzert für Orchester	14	4			98	1
Hindemith	Mathis der Maler	14	[10]	Tchaikovsky	Overture Solennelle— 1812	66	4
d'Indy	Deuxième Symphonie en Sib	55	2				
Liszt	Les Préludes	8	35	Tchaikovsky	Symphony No. 6, "Pathétique"	101	1
Mendelssohn	Symphony No. 3, "Scotch"	57	523	Vaughan Williams	Symphony in E minor (No. 6)	117	[25]
Mendelssohn	Symphony No. 4, "Italian"	130	3	Verdi	Messa da Requiem	10	1
				Walton	Concerto for Viola and Orchestra	58	[51]

Violin I and Violoncello

COMPOSER	WORK	PAGE	MEASURE
Dvořák	Symphony No. 5, "From the New World"	124	4

Solo Violin and Violoncello

Schönberg	Pierrot Lunaire	73	[15] 1f

Violin I, II, and Violoncello

COMPOSER	WORK	PAGE	MEASURE	COMPOSER	WORK	PAGE	MEASURE
Mahler	Songs of a Wayfarer	40	22	Tchaikovsky	Symphony No. 6, "Pathétique"	108	41
Sibelius	Symphony No. 1	91	13	Walton	Symphony	92	9

Viola and Violoncello

COMPOSER	WORK	PAGE	MEASURE	COMPOSER	WORK	PAGE	MEASURE
Brahms	Symphony No. 4	151	177	Rossini	The Barber of Seville, Overture	18	15
Brahms	Variations on a Theme by Haydn	24	206	Saint-Saëns	Danse Macabre	13	[C]
Rimsky-Korsakoff	Scheherazade	178	[K]				

STRINGS

Violoncello and Bass

COMPOSER	WORK	PAGE	MEASURE	COMPOSER	WORK	PAGE	MEASURE
Beethoven	*Piano Concerto No. 5*	132	144	Mahler	*Symphony No. 8*	38	[42]
Egge	*Symphony No. 1*	27	2b [31]	Mendelssohn	*Symphony No. 4,*		
Elgar	*Variations, "Enigma"*	35	[23]		*"Italian"*	75	2
Fitelberg	*Nocturne for Orchestra*	11	[61]	Rachmaninoff	*2d Concerto pour Piano*		
Grétry–Mottl	*Ballet Suite, "Céphale*				*et Orchestre*	94	2
	et Procris"	32	1	Schmitt	*Étude pour le "Palais*		
Haydn	*Symphony No. 4 in*				*Hanté" d'Edgar Poe*	42	4
	D major, "Clock"	28	[L]	Vaughan	*Symphony in D major*		
Haydn	*Symphony No. 16 in*			Williams	*(No. 5)*	56	[14] 10f
	G major, "Oxford"	42	1	Walton	*Symphony*	14	[8] 8f
Mahler	*Symphony No. 4*	13	80				

Violin I, Viola, and Violoncello

COMPOSER	WORK	PAGE	MEASURE
Brahms	*Symphony No. 3*	72	[D]

Violin II, Viola, and Violoncello

COMPOSER	WORK	PAGE	MEASURE	COMPOSER	WORK	PAGE	MEASURE
Barber	*Second Symphony*	15	[9]	Schuman, W.	*American Festival*		
Mahler	*Symphony No. 2*	105	[43] 3f		*Overture*	15	[150]
				Toch	*Pinocchio*	13	[21]

Violin I, II, Viola, and Violoncello

COMPOSER	WORK	PAGE	MEASURE	COMPOSER	WORK	PAGE	MEASURE
Barber	*Overture to "The*			Liszt	*Eine Faust-Symphonie*	172	3
	School for Scandal"	30	[I]	Mendelssohn	*Symphony No. 4,*		
Beethoven	*Piano Concerto No. 4*	18	123		*"Italian"*	5	3
Beethoven	*Symphony No. 2*	6	25	Nicolai	*Overture to "The*		
Beethoven	*Symphony No. 3,*				*Merry Wives of*		
	"Eroica"	101	1		*Windsor"*	7	32
Beethoven	*Symphony No. 9*	291	917	Prokofieff	*Ala et Lolly (Scythian*		
Beethoven	*Violin Concerto in*				*Suite)*	68	[45]
	D major	11	166	Prokofieff	*Romeo and Juliet, Suite*		
Benjamin	*Jamaican Rhumba*	2	1		*No. 1*	75	[49] 5f
Berlioz	*Symphonie Fantastique*	23	12	Rameau–			
Brahms	*Symphony No. 2*	82	33	Mottl	*Ballet Suite*	16	1b [L]
Britten	*Les Illuminations*	6	1	Rimsky-			
Bruckner	*Symphony No. 9*	114	251	Korsakoff	*Scheherazade*	95	392
Chávez	*Sinfonia India*	63	[88]	Schumann, R.	*Piano Concerto in*		
Debussy	*Prélude à l'après-midi*				*A minor*	43	2
	d'un Faune	23	2	Siegmeister	*Western Suite*	40	[50]
Haydn	*Symphony No. 1 in*			Smetana	*Blanik*	43	1
	Eb major, "Drum-			Stravinsky	*Feuerwerk*	28	4b [28]
	roll"	36	9	Stravinsky	*Petrouchka Suite*	57	[43] 10f
Haydn	*Symphony No. 3 in*			Tchaikovsky	*Symphony No. 5*	71	24
	Eb major	2	11	Wagner, R.	*Bacchanale from*		
Holst	*The Planets*	30	[XI]		*"Tannhäuser"*	12	3
		63	[VII]	Wagner, R.	*Eine Faust-Overture*	52	379
Honegger	*Pacific 231*	16	109	Walton	*Façade, Suite No. 1*	45	[B]
Ibert	*La Ballade de la Geôle*			Walton	*Symphony*	100	[74]
	de Reading	80	[59]	Warlock	*Capriol Suite*	10	1

BOWING

Solo Quartet

COMPOSER	WORK	PAGE	MEASURE
Elgar	*Introduction and Allegro for Strings*	16	[10]

Violin I, II, Violoncello, and Bass

COMPOSER	WORK	PAGE	MEASURE	COMPOSER	WORK	PAGE	MEASURE
Beethoven	*Piano Concerto No. 5*	57	313	Haydn	*Symphony No. 4 in D major, "Clock"*	25	11

Viola, Violoncello, and Bass

COMPOSER	WORK	PAGE	MEASURE	COMPOSER	WORK	PAGE	MEASURE
Beethoven	*Piano Concerto No. 4*	7	56	Mozart	*Symphony No. 35 in D major, "Haffner"*	10	80
Borodin	*Symphony No. 2*	21	1	Saint-Saëns	*Danse Macabre*	27	1
Mozart	*Overture to "The Magic Flute"*	6	47	Walton	*Concerto for Viola and Orchestra*	20	1

Violin II, Viola, Violoncello, and Bass

COMPOSER	WORK	PAGE	MEASURE	COMPOSER	WORK	PAGE	MEASURE
Bartók	*Divertimento for String Orchestra*	1	1	Liszt	*Eine Faust-Symphonie*	103	[Kk]
Bruckner	*Symphony No. 6*	89	2	Stravinsky	*Scènes de Ballet*	12	[15]

Violin I, II, Viola, Violoncello, and Bass

COMPOSER	WORK	PAGE	MEASURE	COMPOSER	WORK	PAGE	MEASURE
Beethoven	*Consecration of the House Overture*	15	61	Brahms	*Symphony No. 3*	101	120
Beethoven	*Fidelio Overture*	33	250	Britten	*Four Sea Interludes from "Peter Grimes"*	80	[12]
Beethoven	*Leonore Overture No. 3*	3	24	Britten	*The Young Person's Guide to the Orchestra*	61	[M]
		5	33				
Beethoven	*Overture to Prometheus*	6	58	Bruckner	*Symphony No. 1*	91	[120]
Beethoven	*Piano Concerto No. 3*	1	2	Bruckner	*Symphony No. 5*	80	1
Beethoven	*Piano Concerto No. 4*	69	1	Copland	*An Outdoor Overture*	33	1b [205]
Beethoven	*Symphony No. 1*	17	161	Debussy	*La Mer*	129	4
		62	251	Dvořák	*Symphony No. 5, "From the New World"*	75	7
Beethoven	*Symphony No. 3, "Eroica"*	5	63				
		44	502				
		81	135	Franck	*Variations Symphoniques*	79	2
Beethoven	*Symphony No. 4*	11	121				
		63	100	Glinka	*March and Oriental Dances from "Russlan und Lud- mila"*	500	7
Beethoven	*Symphony No. 6, "Pastoral"*	65	1				
Beethoven	*Symphony No. 9*	83	10	Gluck	*Overture to "Iphigénie en Aulide"*	2	22
		219	[M]				
Beethoven	*Violin Concerto in D major*	40	68	Grétry–Mottl	*Ballet Suite, "Céphale et Procris"*	47	[X]
Bizet	*Symphony No. 1*	52	[3]	Grieg	*Norwegian Dances*	2	3
Bliss	*Concerto for Piano and Orchestra*	130	4b [72]	Grieg	*Piano Concerto in A minor*	4	7
Brahms	*Academic Festival Overture*	1	1				

STRINGS

Violin I, II, Viola, Violoncello, and Bass (contd.)

COMPOSER	WORK	PAGE	MEASURE	COMPOSER	WORK	PAGE	MEASURE
Haydn	Symphony No. 4 in D major, "Clock"	33	107	Piston	First Symphony	106	264
Haydn	Symphony No. 5 in D major	7	95	Piston	Prelude and Fugue	26	[N]
		18	237	Rachmaninoff	2d Concerto pour Piano et Orchestre	73	2b [29]
		26	56	Rachmaninoff	Symphony No. 2	60	5
Haydn	Symphony No. 6 in G major, "Surprise"	19	208	Saint-Saëns	Danse Macabre	36	6
Haydn	Symphony No. 11 in G major, "Military"	6	58	Schubert	Rosamunde Overture	18	[D]
		22	[H]	Schumann, R.	Piano Concerto in A minor	88	[M] 8f
Liszt	Eine Faust-Symphonie	279	[A]				
Lopatnikoff	Sinfonietta	14	[50]	Shostakovich	Symphony No. 3	40	[52]
		49	1b [210]	Siegmeister	Ozark Set	42	[75] 1f
Mahler	Symphony No. 2	59	1	Smetana	Blanik	3	2
Mahler	Symphony No. 5	169	[30] 12f	Stravinsky	Feuerwerk	5	[6] 1f
Mendelssohn	Fingal's Cave Overture	27	149	Stravinsky	Four Norwegian Moods	23	[31]
Mozart	Symphony No. 41 in C major, "Jupiter"	59	100	Stravinsky	Oedipus Rex	134	[192]
Pierné	Divertissements sur un Thème Pastorale	7	2	Walton	Façade, Suite No. 1	1	3
				Weber	Der Freischütz Overture	9	89
				Weber	Oberon Overture	11	[C] 1f

(5) SALTANDO

English	Italian	French	German
Bounce the bow	Balzato	En jetant l'archet	Mit (aufgeworfenem) spring-
Bouncing bow	Coll'arco slanciato e saltante	Jeté	endem Bogen
Rebounding (bow)	Gettando l'arco	Ricochet	Springbogen
	Gettato	Sautillé	Springender Bogen
	Saltando		spring. Bog.
	Saltante		
	Saltarello		
	Saltato		
	Saltellato		

Violin I

COMPOSER	WORK	PAGE	MEASURE	COMPOSER	WORK	PAGE	MEASURE
Gould	Philharmonic Waltzes	2	[16]	Rimsky-Korsakoff	Symphony No. 2, "Antar"	6	7
Ibert	Féerique	3	[2] 1f	Stravinsky	Fire-Bird Suite (1919)	8	[11]
		14	[10]			14	[17] 1f
Prokofieff	Cinderella Suite No. 1	17	[7]	Stravinsky	Le Sacre du Printemps	17	[24] 4f
Rimsky-Korsakoff	Scheherazade	122	91				
		131	119				

Solo Violin

COMPOSER	WORK	PAGE	MEASURE
Stravinsky	Histoire du Soldat	2	[5]
		22	[8]
		40	[4] 2f

BOWING

Violin II

COMPOSER	WORK	PAGE	MEASURE	COMPOSER	WORK	PAGE	MEASURE
Bloch	Trois Poèmes Juifs	8	2	Mussorgsky	Polonaise from "Boris Godunov"	18	1
Ibert	Escales	59	[54]	Ravel	Boléro	32	[11]

Violin I and II

COMPOSER	WORK	PAGE	MEASURE	COMPOSER	WORK	PAGE	MEASURE
Borodin	Polovetzian Dances from "Prince Igor"	38 / 63	1 / 51	Rimsky-Korsakoff	Capriccio Espagnol	40	[L] 2f
Gould	Latin-American Symphonette	56 / 72	[B] 1f / [L] 1f	Rosenthal	Les Petits Métiers	69 / 110	1 / 1
Ibert	La Ballade de la Geôle de Reading	28	[18]	Schönberg	A Survivor from Warsaw	18	85
Mahler	Das Lied von der Erde	74	[13] 1f	Schreker	The Birthday of the Infanta, Suite	71	1
Mahler	Symphony No. 7	226	[264]	Shepherd	Horizons	92	1b [K]
Mussorgsky	Polonaise from "Boris Godunov"	22	1	Strauss, R.	Eine Alpensinfonie	45	[41]
Poulenc	Concert Champêtre pour Clavecin et Orchestre	25	[21]	Strauss, R.	Ein Heldenleben	126	[66]
Ravel	Daphnis et Chloé, Suite No. 1	38	[108]	Stravinsky	Feuerwerk	23	[23]
Riisager	Torgot Dance	23	[105] 2f	Stravinsky	Scherzo Fantastique	14 / 57	2b [18] / [81]

Viola

COMPOSER	WORK	PAGE	MEASURE	COMPOSER	WORK	PAGE	MEASURE
Britten	Sinfonietta	27	[12]	Rimsky-Korsakoff	Scheherazade	144	178
Ibert	Divertissement	9	6	Rogers	Once Upon a Time, Five Fairy Tales	64	1
Mahler	Das Lied von der Erde	3	3	Stravinsky	Petrouchka Suite	58	[44]
Mahler	Symphony No. 3	111	[5] 1f				
Ravel	Boléro	27	[10]				
Rimsky-Korsakoff	Le Coq d'Or Suite	47	[32]				

Solo Viola

COMPOSER	WORK	PAGE	MEASURE
Schönberg	Pierrot Lunaire	57	2

Violoncello

COMPOSER	WORK	PAGE	MEASURE	COMPOSER	WORK	PAGE	MEASURE
Borodin	Polovetzian Dances from "Prince Igor"	50 / 58	[N] / [P]	Halffter	Deux Esquisses Symphoniques	23	4
				Stravinsky	Renard	24	[14] 1f

Bass

COMPOSER	WORK	PAGE	MEASURE	COMPOSER	WORK	PAGE	MEASURE
Sibelius	Symphony No. 5	109	6	Strauss, R.	Don Quixote	7	1

STRINGS

Violin I and Viola

COMPOSER	WORK	PAGE	MEASURE	COMPOSER	WORK	PAGE	MEASURE
Bloch	*America*	89	[52]	Chausson	*Symphonie en Si bémol*		
Borodin	*Symphony No. 2*	132	I		*majeur*	87	[E]
		161	[K]	Stravinsky	*Fire-Bird Suite* (1919)	16	I

Solo Violin I and Soli Viola

COMPOSER	WORK	PAGE	MEASURE
Schönberg	*A Survivor from Warsaw*	4	18

Violin II and Viola

COMPOSER	WORK	PAGE	MEASURE	COMPOSER	WORK	PAGE	MEASURE
Bartók	*Concerto for Orchestra*	30	[45]	Prokofieff	*Romeo and Juliet, Suite No. 2*	48	[30]
Bliss	*Concerto for Piano and Orchestra*	146	[86]	Rachmaninoff	*The Bells*	6	[5] 4f
Chasins	*Rush Hour in Hong Kong*	3	I	Ravel	*Rapsodie Espagnole*	70	[20] 1f
Gould	*Latin-American Symphonette*	87	[6]	Respighi	*Trittico Botticelliano*	12	[4]
Ippolitov-Ivanov	*Caucasian Sketches*	42	I	Rimsky-Korsakoff	*Le Coq d'Or Suite*	49	[33]
		57	[D]	Scriabin	*Le Poème de l'Extase*	18	3
Prokofieff	*Romeo and Juliet, Suite No. 1*	96	[60]	Sibelius	*The Tempest, First Suite*	32	5
				Stravinsky	*Petrouchka Suite*	141	[118]

Violin I, II, and Viola

COMPOSER	WORK	PAGE	MEASURE	COMPOSER	WORK	PAGE	MEASURE
Barber	*First Symphony*	34	[14]	Ravel	*Rapsodie Espagnole*	13	[2] 3f
Barber	*Overture to "The School for Scandal"*	14 / 29	[D] 9f / 7	Rachmaninoff	*Piano Concerto No. 3*	78	11
Britten	*The Young Person's Guide to the Orchestra*	44	I	Respighi	*The Birds*	3	[1]
				Riisager	*Torgot Dance*	12	2b [60]
Glazounov	*Violin Concerto in A minor*	39	[24]	Roger-Ducasse	*Le Joli Jeu de Furet*	32	2
Jacobi	*Music Hall Overture*	16	[8] 2f	Roussel	*Suite en Fa*	80	[41]
Kabalevsky	*The Comedians*	18	[9]	Shostakovich	*Symphony No. 7*	80	[76] 1f
Mahler	*Das Lied von der Erde*	51	[2]	Shostakovich	*The Golden Age, Ballet Suite*	7	[5]
Parodi	*Preludio ad una Commedia*	30	1b [P]	Sibelius	*En Saga*	5	I
						16	[C]
Prokofieff	*Romeo and Juliet, Suite No. 1*	75	[49] 1f	Sibelius	*Symphony No. 5*	124	[L]
				Sibelius	*Tapiola*	19	[G]
Ravel	*Alborada del Gracioso*	2	[1]	Stravinsky	*Fire-Bird Suite* (1919)	10	I
Ravel	*Daphnis et Chloé, Suite No. 2*	88	3	Taylor	*Through the Looking Glass*	116	[7]
Ravel	*Le Tombeau de Couperin*	21	[3]	Tchaikovsky	*Symphony No. 6, "Pathétique"*	17	101
				Thomson	*Louisiana Story Suite*	48	35

Violin I and Violoncello

COMPOSER	WORK	PAGE	MEASURE	COMPOSER	WORK	PAGE	MEASURE
Sibelius	*Symphony No. 5*	114	[G]	Stravinsky	*Chant du Rossignol*	8	[5] 5f
						46	[47]

BOWING

Violin II and Violoncello

COMPOSER	WORK	PAGE	MEASURE	COMPOSER	WORK	PAGE	MEASURE
Ibert	*Féerique*	24	[16]	Tchaikovsky	*Nutcracker Suite*	78	[C]
Piston	*First Symphony*	17	102				

Violin I, II, and Violoncello

COMPOSER	WORK	PAGE	MEASURE
Sibelius	*Tapiola*	25	[I]

Viola and Violoncello

COMPOSER	WORK	PAGE	MEASURE	COMPOSER	WORK	PAGE	MEASURE
MacDowell	*2nd Suite (Indian)*	61	[M]	Stravinsky	*Fire-Bird Suite* (1919)	52	[26]
Mahler	*Das Lied von der Erde*	71	3	Stravinsky	*Le Sacre du Printemps*	76	[86] 3f
Sibelius	*Symphony No. 1*	93	[G] 5f				

Viola and Bass

COMPOSER	WORK	PAGE	MEASURE
Sibelius	*Symphony No. 4*	26	5

Violoncello and Bass

COMPOSER	WORK	PAGE	MEASURE	COMPOSER	WORK	PAGE	MEASURE
Mahler	*Symphony No. 3*	79	[57]	Sibelius	*Lemminkainen Journeys Homeward*	59	4b [Q]
Prokofieff	*Cinderella Suite No. 1*	85	[65]				
		99	[80]	Stravinsky	*Firebird Ballet Suite* (1945)	23	[26]
Ravel	*Alborada del Gracioso*	39	[32]				

Violin I, Viola, and Violoncello

COMPOSER	WORK	PAGE	MEASURE
Britten	*Sinfonia da Requiem*	24	5

Violin II, Viola, and Violoncello

COMPOSER	WORK	PAGE	MEASURE	COMPOSER	WORK	PAGE	MEASURE
Berlioz	*Roméo et Juliette*	177	7	Prokofieff	*Lieutenant Kijé*	54	[46]
Mahler	*Symphony No. 2*	69	[9]				

Violin I, II, Viola, and Violoncello

COMPOSER	WORK	PAGE	MEASURE	COMPOSER	WORK	PAGE	MEASURE
Gould	*American Salute*	8	1	Rimsky-Korsakoff	*Capriccio Espagnol*	73	[T]
Janssen	*New Year's Eve in New York*	24	[10]	Roussel	*Évocations, II*	54	[23]
Mahler	*Symphony No. 3*	141	[5]	Sibelius	*En Saga*	1	1
Miaskovsky	*Symphony No. 6*	132	[5]	Stravinsky	*Fire-Bird Suite* (1919)	33	[6]
		147	[14]	Tchaikovsky	*Symphony No. 6, "Pathétique"*	5	42
		182	[37]				

Solo Violin I, II, Viola, and Violoncello

COMPOSER	WORK	PAGE	MEASURE
Britten	*Les Illuminations*	12	[6] 1f

STRINGS

Viola, Violoncello, and Bass

COMPOSER	WORK	PAGE	MEASURE	COMPOSER	WORK	PAGE	MEASURE
Gould	*Philharmonic Waltzes*	22	[246]	Rimsky-			
Mahler	*Symphony No. 7*	122	[118] 2f	Korsakoff	*Scheherazade*	227	[W]

Violin II, Viola, Violoncello, and Bass

COMPOSER	WORK	PAGE	MEASURE	COMPOSER	WORK	PAGE	MEASURE
Mahler	*Symphony No. 6*	31	5	Tchaikovsky	*Capriccio Italien*	33	3
Stravinsky	*Le Sacre du Printemps*	115	[149]				
		120	[162]				

Violin I, II, Viola, Violoncello, and Bass

COMPOSER	WORK	PAGE	MEASURE	COMPOSER	WORK	PAGE	MEASURE
Gould	*Latin-American Symphonette*	43	[5]	Martinet	*Orphée*	66	[5]
Ippolitov-				Moeran	*Sinfonietta*	50	1b [65]
Ivanov	*Caucasian Sketches*	72	[I]	Rachmaninoff	*2d Concerto pour Piano et Orchestre*	44	[16]
Mahler	*Symphony No. 2*	59	1	Shostakovich	*Piano Concerto*	8	[6] 1f
		89	9	Shostakovich	*Symphony No. 7*	113	[126]

(6) STRIKE WITH BOW

English	Italian	French	German
Hit [strike] with (the) bow	Battuto coll'arco	Frappé avec l'archet	Mit dem Bogen geschlagen
Struck with bow			

Violin I

COMPOSER	WORK	PAGE	MEASURE
Mahler	*Symphony No. 3*	108	3

Violoncello

Mahler	*Symphony No. 4*	159	45
		163	55

Violin II and Viola

Mahler	*Symphony No. 4*	158	42

Violin II, Viola, and Violoncello

Mahler	*Symphony No. 4*	174	101
		177	116

Viola, Violoncello, and Bass

Mahler	*Symphony No. 1*	58	2

Violin I, II, Viola, Violoncello, and Bass

Mahler	*Symphony No. 2*	38	[19] 4f	Mahler	*Symphony No. 5*	5	1b [1]

304

BOWING

(7) AU TALON

English	Italian	French	German
At heel (of bow)	Al tallone	A [au] talon	Am Frosch
At (the) frog	Col tallone	Avec le talon	
Frog (of bow)	Sul talone	Du talon	
Heel of bow	Talone	Talon (de l'archet)	
Near (the) frog			
On [at] the nut			

Violin I

COMPOSER	WORK	PAGE	MEASURE	COMPOSER	WORK	PAGE	MEASURE
Albéniz–Arbós	Fête-Dieu à Séville	7	5	Strauss, R.	Don Quixote	8	10
Bloch	America	91	[53]	Stravinsky	Fire-Bird Suite (1919)	34	2b [8]
Chabrier	Suite Pastorale	57	[I]	Stravinsky	Renard	62	[39]
Mahler	Das Lied von der Erde	121	[42]	Szymanowski	Symphonie Concertante pour Piano et Orchestre	76	[13]
Rivier	Rapsodie pour Violon-celle et Orchestre	2	2	Villa-Lobos	Amazonas	41	4
Rogers	Once Upon a Time, Five Fairy Tales	22	[15] 1f				

Solo Violin

COMPOSER	WORK	PAGE	MEASURE
Stravinsky	Histoire du Soldat	34	[17]
		43	[13]
		51	[1] 3f
		61	[1]

Violin I and II

COMPOSER	WORK	PAGE	MEASURE	COMPOSER	WORK	PAGE	MEASURE
Albéniz–Arbós	Fête-Dieu à Séville	24	[F]	Poulenc	Concert Champêtre pour Clavecin et Orchestre	11	4
		36	[N]				
Bloch	Evocations	22	[17]				
Chabrier	España, Rhapsodie	16	7	Prokofieff	Romeo and Juliet, Suite No. 1	113	3
Chausson	Symphonie en Si bémol majeur	29	2	Schlein	Dance Overture	4	1
Chávez	Sinfonia India	17	[16]	Skilton	Suite Primeval, Part I	28	2
Copland	Appalachian Spring	51	42	Strauss, R.	Don Quixote	56	1
Dohnányi	Ruralia Hungarica	27	[1]	Strauss, R.	Symphonia Domestica	7	[5] 3f
Enesco	Ière Rhapsodie Roumaine	41	[22]			69	16
				Stravinsky	Fire-Bird Suite (1919)	11	[13] 2f
Grieg	Norwegian Dances	5	[A] 2f	Stravinsky	Quatre Études pour Orchestre	2	4b [1]
		20	[F] 2f	Stravinsky	Ragtime	5	3b [5]

Viola

COMPOSER	WORK	PAGE	MEASURE	COMPOSER	WORK	PAGE	MEASURE
Bernstein	"Jeremiah" Symphony	44	[37]	Respighi	Feste Romane	124	[37]
Inghelbrecht	La Métamorphose d'Ève	17	2	Stravinsky	Apollon Musagète	36	[89]
Poulenc	Aubade	45	[37]				

Violoncello

COMPOSER	WORK	PAGE	MEASURE	COMPOSER	WORK	PAGE	MEASURE
Bartók	Concerto for Orchestra	43	[228]	Stravinsky	Oedipus Rex	107	[154]

STRINGS

Violin I and Viola

COMPOSER	WORK	PAGE	MEASURE	COMPOSER	WORK	PAGE	MEASURE
Albéniz–Arbós	El Albaicín	16	[G]	Honegger	Pacific 231	24	138
Delannoy	Figures Sonores	56	[26]				

Violin II and Viola

COMPOSER	WORK	PAGE	MEASURE
de Falla	El Retablo de Maese Pedro	5	2

Violin I, II, and Viola

COMPOSER	WORK	PAGE	MEASURE	COMPOSER	WORK	PAGE	MEASURE
Copland	Appalachian Spring	43	35	Prokofieff	Symphony No. 6	31	22
Copland	First Symphony	22	[10] 3f	Read	Symphony No. I	110	1
Copland	Four Dance Episodes from "Rodeo"	22	[21]	Rieti	Sinfonia Tripartita	68	2b [71]
Dukas	L'Apprenti Sorcier	41	[38] 2f	Schelling	A Victory Ball	66	8
Gershwin	An American in Paris	5	4	Schlein	Dance Overture	24	[375] 1f
Honegger	Horace Victorieux	46	[19] 2f	Schuman, W.	Symphony No. IV	21	195
Moeran	Sinfonietta	62	5b [81]	Stravinsky	"Dumbarton Oaks" Concerto	8	1b [12]
Poot	Symphonie	91	[40]	Walton	Symphony	75	[51]
Poulenc	Concert Champêtre pour Clavecin et Orchestre	33	[25] 4f				

Viola and Violoncello

COMPOSER	WORK	PAGE	MEASURE	COMPOSER	WORK	PAGE	MEASURE
Copland	Third Symphony	57	[43] 2f	Read	Symphony No. I	107	1
Elgar	Falstaff	117	2b [117]	Siegmeister	From my Window	22	3b [20]
Poot	Symphonie	51	4				

Violoncello and Bass

COMPOSER	WORK	PAGE	MEASURE	COMPOSER	WORK	PAGE	MEASURE
Debussy	La Mer	102	[50]	Stravinsky	Oedipus Rex	9	[9] 3f
		134	[62]	Stravinsky	Orpheus	51	[134] 1f
Diamond	Timon of Athens	14	88	Stravinsky	Pulcinella Suite	52	2b [87]
Poulenc	Concert Champêtre pour Clavecin et Orchestre	77	[4]				

Violin II, Viola, and Violoncello

COMPOSER	WORK	PAGE	MEASURE
Rachmaninoff	Rapsodie pour Piano et Orchestre	48	6b [36]

Violin I, II, Viola, and Violoncello

COMPOSER	WORK	PAGE	MEASURE	COMPOSER	WORK	PAGE	MEASURE
Berg	Three Excerpts from "Wozzeck"	55	[375]	Chabrier	Joyeuse Marche	22	2
Britten	Sinfonia da Requiem	30	[21]	Chausson	Symphonie en Si bémol majeur	72	1
		44	[30] 1f	Copland	Statements	32	[7] 4f
Cesana	Second American Symphony	39	4b [30]	Elgar	Falstaff	63	[65]
				Honegger	Pacific 231	15	[8]

BOWING

Violin I, II, Viola, and Violoncello (contd.)

COMPOSER	WORK	PAGE	MEASURE	COMPOSER	WORK	PAGE	MEASURE
Moeran	Sinfonietta	17	[32] 3f	Piston	First Symphony	7	1
Piston	Concertino for Piano			Prokofieff	Peter and the Wolf	15	13
	and Chamber			Stravinsky	Oedipus Rex	113	[163]
	Orchestra	12	1b [70]	Stravinsky	Symphony in C	55	2b [104]
Piston	Concerto for Orchestra	29	[3]	Walton	Portsmouth Point		
					Overture	22	[16]

Viola, Violoncello, and Bass

COMPOSER	WORK	PAGE	MEASURE	COMPOSER	WORK	PAGE	MEASURE
Poulenc	Aubade	20	2	Siegmeister	Sunday in Brooklyn	24	[20]
Rogers	Characters from Hans						
	Christian Andersen	27	5				

Violin I, II, Viola, Violoncello, and Bass

COMPOSER	WORK	PAGE	MEASURE	COMPOSER	WORK	PAGE	MEASURE
Albéniz–				Prokofieff	Symphony No. 6	158	[120]
Arbós	Navarra	1	1	Siegmeister	Sunday in Brooklyn	61	2
Cesana	Second American	98	4			82	2b [85]
	Symphony	152	[36]	Stravinsky	Pulcinella Suite	63	[103] 3f
Inghelbrecht	La Métamorphose d'Ève	40	2			71	[113] 6f
Mahler	Symphony No. 8	39	[43]	Szymanowski	Symphonie Concertante		
Poulenc	Concert Champêtre				pour Piano et		
	pour Clavecin et				Orchestre	111	4
	Orchestre	87	1b [12]				

(8) PUNTA D'ARCO

English	Italian	French	German
At the end of the bow	Al punto	A la pointe	An der Spitze des Bogens
At the point (of the bow)	A punta d'arco	Avec la pointe (de l'archet)	An der Spitze gestrichen
At the tip (of the bow)	Colla punta	De la pointe (de l'archet)	Spitze (des Bogens)
End of (the) bow	Colle punte dell'arco	Du bout de l'archet	
Point (of the bow)	Coll'punto	Pointe (de l'archet)	
Tip of (the) bow	Col punto del arco	Vers la pointe	
	Punta (d'arco)		
	Punta dell'arco		
	Sul punta [punto del arco]		

Violin I

COMPOSER	WORK	PAGE	MEASURE	COMPOSER	WORK	PAGE	MEASURE
Barber	Overture to "The			Dukas	Symphonie en Ut majeur	42	[15] 5f
	School for Scandal"	2	4	Gould	Philharmonic Waltzes	2	[16]
Bartók	Concerto No. 3 for			d'Indy	Istar, Variations		
	Piano and Orchestra	36	[72]		Symphoniques	38	[P]
Berlioz	Symphonie Fantastique	2	13	Kabalevsky	Symphony No. 2	109	[16]
Bruckner	Symphony No. 7	123	1	Prokofieff	Classical Symphony	8	[6]
Busoni	Rondo Arlecchinesco	31	1b [28]			29	[24]
Chabrier	Suite Pastorale	27	4	Riegger	Symphony No. 3	2	[10] 1f
Chasins	Rush Hour in Hong			Scriabin	Prométhée, Le Poème		
	Kong	3	1		du Feu	48	[32] 2f
Chausson	Symphonie en Si bémol			Stravinsky	Jeu de Cartes	53	[97] 2f
	majeur	8	4	Stravinsky	Le Sacre du Printemps	76	1b [87]
Copland	El Salón México	23	5	Stravinsky	Ode	5	[7]
Copland	Music for Radio	50	2	Stravinsky	Petrouchka Suite	41	[30] 4f
Debussy	Rondes de Printemps	8	[4]	Stravinsky	Renard	105	[66]
Delius	North Country Sketches	5	5b [4]	Walton	Façade, Suite No. 1	11	[A]

307

STRINGS

Soli Violin I

COMPOSER	WORK	PAGE	MEASURE	COMPOSER	WORK	PAGE	MEASURE
Diamond	*Timon of Athens*	**34**	250	Rogers	*Once Upon a Time, Five Fairy Tales*	**1**	[1]

Violin II

COMPOSER	WORK	PAGE	MEASURE	COMPOSER	WORK	PAGE	MEASURE
Balakirev– Casella	*Islamey*	**15**	[11]	Mussorgsky	*Polonaise from "Boris Godunov"*	**18**	1
Bartók	*Concerto for Orchestra*	**79**	[8]	Rogers	*Characters from Hans Christian Andersen*	**6**	3
Copland	*Third Symphony*	**115**	[103] 2f				
Dukas	*Symphonie en Ut majeur*	**94**	[E]	Sibelius	*Tapiola*	**42**	427

Violin I and II

COMPOSER	WORK	PAGE	MEASURE	COMPOSER	WORK	PAGE	MEASURE
Bartók	*Concerto for Orchestra*	**10**	[192]	Miaskovsky	*Sinfonietta for String Orchestra*	**39**	[17] 4f
		90	[96]	Moross	*Paeans*	**9**	[J]
Bruckner	*Symphony No. 4*	**137**	2b [360]				
Bruckner	*Symphony No. 7*	**138**	[N]	Rogers	*Characters from Hans Christian Andersen*	**26**	1b [13]
Chávez	*Sinfonia India*	**1**	1	Roussel	*Évocations, II*	**1**	1
		58	[82]			**65**	[29]
Copland	*Third Symphony*	**39**	[30]	Roussel	*Le Festin de l'Araignée*	**8**	[7] 4f
		88	[78]	Shepherd	*Horizons*	**92**	1b [K]
Debussy	*Rondes de Printemps*	**11**	[6]	Sibelius	*Rakastava*	**6**	1
Debussy– Ansermet	*Six Épigraphes Antiques*	**31**	[C] 1f	Sibelius	*Symphony No. 1*	**55**	13
Dunn	*Overture on Negro Themes*	**27**	9	Sibelius	*Symphony No. 4*	**45**	5b [E]
				Stravinsky	*Chant du Rossignol*	**27**	[28]
Gould	*Latin–American Symphonette*	**56**	[B] 1f	Stravinsky	*Symphony in C*	**80**	[171]
				Walton	*Concerto for Viola and Orchestra*	**5**	[5] 2f
Gould	*Spirituals*	**15**	5			**45**	[39]
Ibert	*Féerique*	**11**	[7]				

Viola

COMPOSER	WORK	PAGE	MEASURE	COMPOSER	WORK	PAGE	MEASURE
Bartók	*Concerto for Orchestra*	**43**	[231]	Charpentier	*Impressions d'Italie*	**140**	[43] 2f
Bartók	*Violin Concerto*	**28**	[194]	Inghelbrecht	*Rapsodie de Printemps*	**6**	[2]
Bruckner	*Symphony No. 3*	**102**	7b [10]				

Violoncello

COMPOSER	WORK	PAGE	MEASURE	COMPOSER	WORK	PAGE	MEASURE
Ibert	*Escales*	**5**	[3]	Stravinsky	*Pulcinella Suite*	**10**	[8]
Sibelius	*Symphony No. 4*	**5**	[D] 5f				
		13	3				

Violin I and Viola

COMPOSER	WORK	PAGE	MEASURE	COMPOSER	WORK	PAGE	MEASURE
Bruckner	*Symphony No. 7*	**156**	[W]	Stravinsky	*Danses Concertantes*	**51**	[83] 1f

BOWING

Violin II and Viola

COMPOSER	WORK	PAGE	MEASURE	COMPOSER	WORK	PAGE	MEASURE
Bartók	*Concerto for Orchestra*	30	[28]	**Roussel**	*Le Festin de l'Araignée*	18	[23]
Dvořák	*Die Waldtaube*	15	[5] 2f	**Stravinsky**	*Apollon Musagète*	22	[55]

Violin I, II, and Viola

COMPOSER	WORK	PAGE	MEASURE	COMPOSER	WORK	PAGE	MEASURE
Charpentier	*Impressions d'Italie*	88	[11]	**Ravel**	*Shéhérazade*	27	2
Debussy	*Jeux*	21	4	**Sibelius**	*Tapiola*	19	[G]
Dunn	*Overture on Negro*			**Sibelius**	*The Bard*	11	[G]
	Themes	5	[A]	**Sibelius**	*The Tempest,*		
Golestan	*Concerto Roumain pour*				*Second Suite*	30	[A] 2f
	Violon et Orchestre	11	5	**Stravinsky**	*Orpheus*	40	[109]
Martinet	*Orphée*	88	1	**Walton**	*Concerto for Viola and*		
Prokofieff	*Classical Symphony*	74	[58] 2f		*Orchestra*	58	[51]

Violin I, II, and Violoncello

COMPOSER	WORK	PAGE	MEASURE
Walton	*Symphony*	92	9

Viola and Violoncello

COMPOSER	WORK	PAGE	MEASURE	COMPOSER	WORK	PAGE	MEASURE
Albéniz–				**Debussy**	*Le Martyre de Saint*		
Arbós	*Fête-Dieu à Séville*	3	2		*Sébastien*	62	1
Debussy	*La Mer*	37	[19] 2f	**Whithorne**	*Fata Morgana*	61	[61] 1f

Violoncello and Bass

COMPOSER	WORK	PAGE	MEASURE	COMPOSER	WORK	PAGE	MEASURE
Debussy	*Fêtes*	69	4	**Egge**	*Symphony No. 1*	27	2b [31]
Diamond	*Fourth Symphony*	96	2	**Sibelius**	*Violin Concerto*	39	4b [10]

Violin I, Viola, and Violoncello

COMPOSER	WORK	PAGE	MEASURE	COMPOSER	WORK	PAGE	MEASURE
Stravinsky	*Danses Concertantes*	86	[135]	**Stravinsky**	*Feuerwerk*	11	1b [10]

Violin II, Viola, and Violoncello

COMPOSER	WORK	PAGE	MEASURE
Poulenc	*Concert Champêtre pour Clavecin et Orchestre*	10	[8]

Violin I, II, Viola, and Violoncello

COMPOSER	WORK	PAGE	MEASURE	COMPOSER	WORK	PAGE	MEASURE
Bartók	*Violin Concerto*	86	[135]	**Tchaikovsky**	*Nutcracker Suite*	56	[B]
Sibelius	*Pelleas and Melisande*	27	[B] 8f	**Walton**	*Symphony*	100	[74]
Sibelius	*Symphony No. 7*	10	[D]				

Violin I, Violoncello, and Bass

COMPOSER	WORK	PAGE	MEASURE
Walton	*Concerto for Viola and Orchestra*	27	1

STRINGS

Soli Viola, Violoncello, and Bass

COMPOSER	WORK	PAGE	MEASURE
Sibelius	*Violin Concerto*	**86**	[3]

Violin I, II, Viola, Violoncello, and Bass

COMPOSER	WORK	PAGE	MEASURE	COMPOSER	WORK	PAGE	MEASURE
Debussy	*Sirènes*	**84**	[4] 2f	**Schuman, W.**	*Undertow*	**34**	[440] 5f
Piston	*Concerto for Orchestra*	**48**	2				

Soli Violin I, II, Viola, Violoncello, and Bass

Whithorne	*Fata Morgana*	**47**	[50]

(9) FULL BOW

English	Italian	French	German
Full bow(s)	Con l'arco in tutta la sua lunghezza	Avec toute la longueur de l'archet	Breit gezogen [ausstreichen]
Full bow on each note	Con larga arcata	Glisser tout le long de l'archet	Ganze Bogen(länge)
Full length of bow	Con molto arco	L'archet de [en] toute sa longueur	Grosse Strich
Glide (the) full bow	Con tutta la lunghezza dell'arco	Tout l'archet sur chaque note	Lange Bogen
Long bow(s)	Gran arco		Lang gezogen
Whole bow(s)	Grande arcata		Mit breitem Strich
With full bow	Tutto l'arco		Mit der ganzen Länge des Bogens
			Viel Bogen (wechseln)
			Viel Bogenwechsel

Violin I

Stravinsky	*Ragtime*	**5**	[5]

Violoncello

Stravinsky	*Orpheus*	**2**	[2] 2f

Violin I, II, and Viola

Respighi	*Metamorphoseon, XII Modi*	**73**	3

Violin I, II, Viola, and Violoncello

Vaughan Williams	*Pastoral Symphony*	**99**	1b [L]

Violin II, Viola, Violoncello, and Bass

Bartók	*Concerto for Piano and Orchestra*	**87**	[28]

BOWING

(10) MIDDLE OF THE BOW

English	*Italian*	*French*	*German*
Center of bow	A metà arco	Au [du] milieu de l'archet	Auf der mitte des Bogens
Middle of (the) bow			Bogenmitte

Solo Violin I

COMPOSER	WORK	PAGE	MEASURE
Stravinsky	*Orpheus*	4	[5]

Violin I, II, and Viola

Stravinsky	*Ode*	5	[8]

(11) REVERSE BOWING

Violin I

COMPOSER	WORK	PAGE	MEASURE	COMPOSER	WORK	PAGE	MEASURE
Bax	*Sixth Symphony*	57	1b [6]	Rachmaninoff	*Piano Concerto No. 3*	71	[40] 6f
Elgar	*Variations, "Enigma"*	48	[31] 1f	Shostakovich	*Symphony No. 6*	84	[82]
Grieg	*Norwegian Dances*	28	7			92	2
Prokofieff	*March and Scherzo from "The Love of the Three Oranges"*	3	[1] 1f	Tchaikovsky	*Manfred-Symphonie*	152	9

Solo Violin

Stravinsky	*Histoire du Soldat*	34	[16]
		43	[13]

Soli Violin I

Casella	*Paganiniana*	91	1b [1]

Violin II

Bartók	*Second Rhapsody for Violin and Orchestra*	29	[11]	Stravinsky	*Apollon Musagète*	13	[34]

Violin I and II

COMPOSER	WORK	PAGE	MEASURE	COMPOSER	WORK	PAGE	MEASURE
Barber	*First Symphony*	21	1b [9]	Mahler	*Symphony No. 2*	50	[25]
Carter	*Holiday Overture*	21	1b [9]	Milhaud	*Saudades do Brazil*	35	9
Copland	*Music for Radio*	51	[34]			41	6
Elgar	*Cockaigne, Concert Overture*	24	3	Mussorgsky	*Polonaise from "Boris Godunov"*	1	5
de Falla	*Three Dances from "The Three-Cornered Hat"*	1	1	Prokofieff	*Classical Symphony*	13	2
		49	2	Rimsky-Korsakoff	*Scheherazade*	158	[A]
						227	[W]
Kabalevsky	*Symphony No. 2*	4	[2]	Sibelius	*Symphony No. 6*	53	3
		50	[44]				

311

STRINGS

Viola

COMPOSER	WORK	PAGE	MEASURE	COMPOSER	WORK	PAGE	MEASURE
Bartók	*First Rhapsody for Violin and Orchestra*	3	1	Rogers	*Once Upon a Time, Five Fairy Tales*	64	1
Persichetti	*The Hollow Men*	7	6	Roussel	*Symphonie en Sol mineur*	36	6

Violoncello

COMPOSER	WORK	PAGE	MEASURE
Copland	*Quiet City*	13	[14] 1f

Violin I and Viola

Miaskovsky	*Sinfonietta for String Orchestra*	13	[38]	Rogers	*Once Upon a Time, Five Fairy Tales*	32	[20]
Mussorgsky	*Polonaise from "Boris Godunov"*	17	1	Taylor	*Through the Looking Glass*	21	2
Ravel	*La Valse*	29	[20]	Turner	*Gregorian Overture for String Orchestra*	3	37

Violin II and Viola

Bartók	*First Rhapsody for Violin and Orchestra*	39	[31]	de Falla	*El Amor Brujo*	90	[52]
Copland	*Third Symphony*	80	[71]	Stravinsky	*Fire-Bird Suite* (1919)	9	1b [12]

Violin I, II, and Viola

Bartók	*Dance Suite*	51	37	Hindemith	*Mathis der Maler*	44	[3]
Chávez	*Sinfonia de Antigona*	17	4b [25]	Khachaturian	*Masquerade Suite*	47	5 2f
Copland	*Concerto for Piano and Orchestra*	27	2	Mahler	*Symphony No. 7*	107	5b [99]
Gould	*Spirituals*	5	[C]	Rachmaninoff	*Symphony No. 2*	132	3
Hanson	*Symphony No. 1, "Nordic"*	4	[A] 1f	Rogers	*Elegy*	4	7
				Ruggles	*Sun-Treader*	2	[6]
				Sibelius	*Symphony No. 4*	16	[B] 1f

Violin I, II, and Violoncello

Sibelius	*Symphony No. 6*	40	1

Viola and Violoncello

Barber	*Medea*	75	[54]	Knipper	*Symphony No. 4*	99	2
Bartók	*Dance Suite*	33	[23]	Tchaikovsky	*Manfred-Symphonie*	178	156
Bartók	*Second Rhapsody for Violin and Orchestra*	21	1				

Violin I, II, Viola, and Violoncello

Becker	*Concerto Arabesque for Piano and Orchestra*	14	1	Britten	*Serenade for Tenor, Horn and Strings*	1 / 5	15 / 12
Bliss	*Concerto for Piano and Orchestra*	78	2	Copland	*Four Dance Episodes from "Rodeo"*	7	2b [6]

BOWING

Violin I, II, Viola, and Violoncello (contd.)

COMPOSER	WORK	PAGE	MEASURE	COMPOSER	WORK	PAGE	MEASURE
Debussy	*Jeux*	85	4b [57]	Schelling	*A Victory Ball*	117	2b [37]
Grieg	*Norwegian Dances*	53	6	Toch	*The Chinese Flute*	46	2
		71	11	Vaughan	*Job, A Masque for*		
Martinet	*Orphée*	25	[4] 1f	Williams	*Dancing*	53	4
Prokofieff	*Symphony No. 5*	116	3				

Soli Violin I, II, Viola, and Violoncello

COMPOSER	WORK	PAGE	MEASURE
Britten	*Les Illuminations*	12	[6] 1f

Viola, Violoncello, and Bass

Sibelius	*Violin Concerto*	75	1

Violin II, Viola, Violoncello, and Bass

Britten	*The Young Person's Guide to the Orchestra*	24	1

Violin I, II, Viola, Violoncello, and Bass

Bax	*First Symphony*	79	8	**Prokofieff**	*Piano Concerto No. 3*	98	[76] 2f
Khachaturian	*Concerto for Piano and Orchestra*	59	[496]				

(12) SUCCESSIVE DOWN-BOWS

Violin I

COMPOSER	WORK	PAGE	MEASURE	COMPOSER	WORK	PAGE	MEASURE
Borodin	*Polovetzian Dances from "Prince Igor"*	98	51	Sessions	*Symphony No. II*	34	[U]
				Stravinsky	*Concerto en Ré pour Violon et Orchestre*	61	[124]
Elgar	*Variations, "Enigma"*	98	[63]				
Gershwin	*An American in Paris*	32	4b [30]	Stravinsky	*"Dumbarton Oaks" Concerto*	3	[4]
Mahler	*Das Lied von der Erde*	74	[13] 1f				
Prokofieff	*Symphony No. 5*	64	[34] 1f	Stravinsky	*Fire-Bird Suite (1919)*	14	3
Ravel	*Menuet Antique*	1	1	Tchaikovsky	*Symphony No. 6, "Pathétique"*	30	171
Revueltas	*Sensemayá*	26	1				

Solo Violin I

Shostakovich	*Symphony No. 9*	30	[22] 2f	**Stravinsky**	*Histoire du Soldat*	4	[8]
						19	1
						36	[25]

313

STRINGS

Violin II

COMPOSER	WORK	PAGE	MEASURE
Roussel	*Symphonie en Sol*	**1**	1
	mineur	**13**	3

Violin I and II

COMPOSER	WORK	PAGE	MEASURE	COMPOSER	WORK	PAGE	MEASURE
Albéniz–Arbós	*El Puerto*	**13**	4b [E]	**Rimsky-Korsakoff**	*Capriccio Espagnol*	**16**	5
Bach, J. C.	*Sinfonia in Bb major*	**14**	122	**Rimsky-Korsakoff**	*Scheherazade*	**193**	306
Britten	*The Young Person's Guide to the Orchestra*	**26**	4	**Rozsa**	*Concerto for String Orchestra*	**6**	[57]
Gershwin	*An American in Paris*	**4**	[3] 6f	**Sessions**	*Symphony for Orchestra (No. 1)*	**58**	[91]
Gershwin	*Concerto in F for Piano and Orchestra*	**12**	3	**Stravinsky**	*Fire-Bird Suite (1919)*	**35**	[10]
Ibert	*Escales*	**40**	[35]	**Stravinsky**	*Orpheus*	**37**	[97]
Riegger	*Dichotomy*	**23**	2b [9]	**Stravinsky**	*Quatre Études pour Orchestre*	**2**	[1]

Viola

COMPOSER	WORK	PAGE	MEASURE	COMPOSER	WORK	PAGE	MEASURE
Borodin	*Polovetzian Dances from "Prince Igor"*	**49**	91	**Chabrier**	*España, Rhapsodie*	**4**	[A] 3f

Violoncello

COMPOSER	WORK	PAGE	MEASURE	COMPOSER	WORK	PAGE	MEASURE
Bartók	*Concerto for Orchestra*	**43**	[228]	**Gershwin**	*An American in Paris*	**20**	[17] 1f
Chávez	*Sinfonia India*	**16**	[15]	**Siegmeister**	*Sunday in Brooklyn*	**23**	1
Copland	*Third Symphony*	**111**	[100] 2f				

Bass

COMPOSER	WORK	PAGE	MEASURE	COMPOSER	WORK	PAGE	MEASURE
Bartók	*Second Rhapsody for Violin and Orchestra*	**21**	1	**Ravel**	*Rapsodie Espagnole*	**88**	[31]

Violin I and Viola

COMPOSER	WORK	PAGE	MEASURE	COMPOSER	WORK	PAGE	MEASURE
Honegger	*Pacific 231*	**24**	138	**Roussel**	*Symphonie en Sol mineur*	**39**	[25] 3f

Violin I, II, and Viola

COMPOSER	WORK	PAGE	MEASURE	COMPOSER	WORK	PAGE	MEASURE
Antheil	*Symphony No. 5*	**22**	2	**Enesco**	*Ière Rhapsodie Roumaine*	**67**	[33] 6f
Bax	*First Symphony*	**103**	[G]	**de Falla**	*Three Dances from "The Three-Cornered Hat"*	**34**	[9]
Borodin	*Polovetzian Dances from "Prince Igor"*	**91**	[X]	**Glière**	*Russian Sailors' Dance*	**1**	1
Copland	*Billy the Kid Ballet Suite*	**56**	2	**Hindemith**	*Kammermusik No. 1*	**20**	[10] 1f

BOWING

Violin I, II, and Viola (contd.)

COMPOSER	WORK	PAGE	MEASURE	COMPOSER	WORK	PAGE	MEASURE
Honegger	*Horace Victorieux*	29	3	Roussel	*Le Festin de l'Araignée*	11	[10] 4f
d'Indy	*Symphony on a French Mountain Air*	94	[S]	Shostakovich	*Symphony No. 6*	101	4
Janssen	*New Year's Eve in New York*	23	3	Stillman-Kelley	*New England Symphony*	123	3
Lopatnikoff	*Sinfonietta*	13	1	Stravinsky	*Fire-Bird Suite (1919)*	75	[18] 6f
Mahler	*Das Lied von der Erde*	4	1	Stravinsky	*Le Sacre du Printemps*	41	[53]
Prokofieff	*Symphony No. 5*	75	[43]	Stravinsky	*Orpheus*	50	[133]
Prokofieff	*Symphony No. 6*	125	[91]	Stravinsky	*Symphony in Three Movements*	21	[29] 2f
Ravel	*La Valse*	112	2	Tansman	*Short Suite*	13	7
Revueltas	*Sensemayá*	9	[13]	Tchaikovsky	*Symphony No. 2*	115	[C]
Riisager	*Torgot Dance*	4	4b [10]	Walton	*Façade, Suite No. 1*	46	[D]

Violin I and Violoncello

Strauss, R.	*Also Sprach Zarathustra*	70	1	Stravinsky	*Symphony in C*	3	[4]

Violin I, II, and Violoncello

COMPOSER	WORK	PAGE	MEASURE
Roussel	*Symphonie en Sol mineur*	32	[19] 2f

Violin I, II, and Bass

Prokofieff	*Symphony No. 6*	148	[109]

Viola and Violoncello

Honegger	*Pacific 231*	5	[3]	Siegmeister	*From my Window*	22	3b [20]
Mahler	*Das Lied von der Erde*	71	3	Tchaikovsky	*Hamlet*	1	6
Sessions	*Symphony No. II*	43	3				

Violoncello and Bass

Bartók	*Concerto for Orchestra*	113	[317]	Ibert	*Escales*	26	[21]
Cesana	*Second American Symphony*	98	4			53	[47]
Copland	*Dance Symphony*	28	3	Rivier	*Ouverture pour un don Quichotte*	2	1

Violin I, Viola, and Violoncello

Ravel	*Rapsodie Espagnole*	5	[4]

Violin II, Viola, and Violoncello

Bartók	*Dance Suite*	2	9	Stravinsky	*Le Sacre du Printemps*	38	[49]
Sessions	*Suite from "The Black Maskers"*	70	1	Whithorne	*Fata Morgana*	15	[14]

315

STRINGS

Violin I, II, Viola, and Violoncello

COMPOSER	WORK	PAGE	MEASURE	COMPOSER	WORK	PAGE	MEASURE
Arnell	*Sinfonia*	85	1b [26]	Prokofieff	*Suite from the Ballet "Chout"*	142	[184] 3f
Britten	*Sinfonia da Requiem*	39	[27]	Prokofieff	*Violin Concerto No. 2*	64	[55]
Chabrier	*Joyeuse Marche*	22	2	Schuman, W.	*American Festival Overture*	1	1
Copland	*Concerto for Piano and Orchestra*	43	3	Sessions	*Symphony No. II*	59	1b [Mm]
Debussy	*Iberia*	45	3b [30]	Shostakovich	*Symphony No. 6*	42	2b [49]
de Falla	*Three Dances from "The Three-Cornered Hat"*	25	[2]	Sibelius	*Symphony No. 1*	52 67	[D] 1f [K]
Hanson	*Symphony No. 1, "Nordic"*	77	[J]	Stravinsky	*Le Sacre du Printemps*	112 122	1b [143] [167]
Harris	*When Johnny Comes Marching Home*	40	[220]	Stravinsky	*Symphony in C*	24	1b [41]
Honegger	*Pacific 231*	15	[8]	Tchaikovsky	*Capriccio Italien*	5	6
Knipper	*Symphony No. 4*	111	[28] 5f	Tchaikovsky	*Manfred-Symphonie*	200	11
Piston	*Symphony No. 2*	115	2	Tchaikovsky	*Symphony No. 5*	135	58
Prokofieff	*Peter and the Wolf*	45	3	Tchaikovsky	*Symphony No. 6, "Pathétique"*	62	297

Solo Quartet

COMPOSER	WORK	PAGE	MEASURE
Elgar	*Introduction and Allegro for Strings*	31	[18]

Violin I, II, Violoncello, and Bass

COMPOSER	WORK	PAGE	MEASURE	COMPOSER	WORK	PAGE	MEASURE
Britten	*Serenade for Tenor, Horn and Strings*	22	[17] 2f	Walton	*Portsmouth Point Overture*	11	[9]

Viola, Violoncello, and Bass

COMPOSER	WORK	PAGE	MEASURE	COMPOSER	WORK	PAGE	MEASURE
Bartók	*Concerto for Orchestra*	64	[93]	Honegger	*Mouvement Symphonique, No. 3*	17	[6]
Bartók	*Dance Suite*	3	25	Mussorgsky	*Night on the Bald Mountain*	60	300
Britten	*Sinfonia da Requiem*	31	[22]	Riegger	*Dichotomy*	25	[10]
Casella	*La Donna Serpente, I. Serie*	19	[20]	Stravinsky	*Petrouchka Suite*	115	[100]
Honegger	*Concertino pour Piano et Orchestre*	11	[6]	Walton	*Portsmouth Point Overture*	18	2b [14]

Violin I, Viola, Violoncello, and Bass

COMPOSER	WORK	PAGE	MEASURE
Stravinsky	*"Dumbarton Oaks" Concerto*	27	[53] 2f

Violin II, Viola, Violoncello, and Bass

COMPOSER	WORK	PAGE	MEASURE
Hindemith	*Symphonische Tänze*	1	3

BOWING

Violin I, II, Viola, Violoncello, and Bass

COMPOSER	WORK	PAGE	MEASURE	COMPOSER	WORK	PAGE	MEASURE
Antheil	Symphony No. 5	43	4b [26]	Moeran	Sinfonietta	39	1
Bartók	Concerto for Orchestra	94	[123]	Mohaupt	Town Piper Music	42	2b [42]
Bartók	Concerto for Piano and					50	7b [54]
	Orchestra	17	5	Mussorgsky–	Pictures at an		
Benjamin	Overture to an Italian			Ravel	Exhibition	98	[80]
	Comedy	26	[M]	Poot	Symphonie	23	8b [11]
Bliss	Concerto for Piano and			Prokofieff	Romeo and Juliet,		
	Orchestra	12	4		Suite No. 1	131	2
Borodin	Symphony No. 1	11	[D]	Prokofieff	Symphony No. 5	172	[99]
		37	[N]	Prokofieff	Violin Concerto No. 2	21	[20] 5f
		113	4	Read	Sketches of the City	24	[2]
Borodin	Symphony No. 2	3	4	Revueltas	Cuauhnahuac	7	[10] 2f
		34	[K]	Respighi	The Birds	58	1
		145	[G]	Rivier	Ouverture pour un don		
Britten	Sinfonietta	34	[11] 2f		Quichotte	31	[13]
Bruckner	Symphony No. 3	35	[O]	Rosenthal	Les Petits Métiers	13	2b [C]
Bruckner	Symphony No. 4	138	[P] 3f	Roussel	Suite en Fa	35	2
Bruckner	Symphony No. 5	150	4b [390]	Roussel	Symphonie en Sol		
Carter	Holiday Overture	54	[26]		mineur	71	4
Copland	Music for the Theatre	39	2	Schuman, W.	American Festival		
de Falla	El Amor Brujo	100	3		Overture	15	[165] 2f
de Falla	El Retablo de Maese			Shepherd	Horizons	127	1
	Pedro	9	3	Shostakovich	Piano Concerto	44	[56] 2f
Gould	American Salute	21	[K]	Shostakovich	Symphony No. 7	28	1
Gould	Latin-American			Siegmeister	Ozark Set	58	1
	Symphonette	112	[24]	Siegmeister	Sunday in Brooklyn	27	1
Gretchaninoff	Troisième Symphonie	64	[29]			75	[60] 2f
Hindemith	Mathis der Maler	57	3	Siegmeister	Western Suite	57	1
Honegger	Horace Victorieux	67	1			87	[50]
Honegger	Symphonie pour Cordes	36	4b [10]	Sowerby	Concert Overture for		
Honegger	Symphonie pour	27	4		Orchestra	60	1
	Orchestre	42	4	Starokadom-			
Kabalevsky	Symphony No. 2	171	[66]	sky	Concerto for Orchestra	14	4b [13]
Kalinnikov	Symphony No. 1	9	2	Stravinsky	Apollon Musagète	24	[58]
		193	[Z]	Stravinsky	Four Norwegian Moods	32	1b [42]
Knipper	Symphony No. 4	56	[8]	Stravinsky	Le Sacre du Printemps	85	[103] 1f
Kodály	Háry János Suite	67	3	Stravinsky	Orpheus	48	[128] 2f
		71	[I]	Stravinsky	Petrouchka Suite	14	[5]
		86	89			126	[108] 3f
Liadov	Eight Russian Popular			Tansman	Short Suite	3	8
	Songs	32	2	Tchaikovsky	Symphony No. 6,		
Mahler	Symphony No. 5	110	[32]		"Pathétique"	125	109
		234	4	Turner	Gregorian Overture for		
Mahler	Symphony No. 7	186	2b [225]		String Orchestra	22	263
Mahler	Symphony No. 8	37	[41]	Vaughan	Job, A Masque for		
Mason	Chanticleer—Festival			Williams	Dancing	16	6
	Overture	1	1	Villa-Lobos	Uirapurú	7	[3] 1f
Miaskovsky	Symphony No. 22	83	[117]	Wellesz	Symphony in C	2	4

317

STRINGS

(13) SUCCESSIVE UP-BOWS

Violin I

COMPOSER	WORK	PAGE	MEASURE	COMPOSER	WORK	PAGE	MEASURE
Bach, C. P. E.	Concerto for Orchestra	17	[9] 3f	Miaskovsky	Sinfonietta for String		
Bach, J. C.	Sinfonia in B♭ major	14	120		Orchestra	8	3b [22]
Barber	Overture to "The	2	7	Prokofieff	Classical Symphony	8	[6]
	School for Scandal"	17	[E]			29	[24]
Chabrier	Suite Pastorale	27	4	Prokofieff	Peter and the Wolf	3	[1]
Chávez	Sinfonia de Antigona	15	[18] 2f	Ravel	La Valse	48	[35]
Copland	Third Symphony	71	7b [55]	Roussel	Symphonie en Sol		
Fitelberg	Nocturne for Orchestra	14	1		mineur	8	3
Ibert	Escales	22	2	Scriabin	Le Poème de l'Extase	28	1
d'Indy	Istar, Variations Sym-			Shostakovich	Symphony No. 6	84	[82] 2f
	phoniques	26	[L] 2f			90	[89]

Solo Violin

COMPOSER	WORK	PAGE	MEASURE
Stravinsky	Histoire du Soldat	5	[10]
		17	[5]
		25	[12]

Violin II

COMPOSER	WORK	PAGE	MEASURE	COMPOSER	WORK	PAGE	MEASURE
Copland	Third Symphony	128	[112]	Stravinsky	Symphony in C	41	2

Solo Violin II

COMPOSER	WORK	PAGE	MEASURE
Ibert	Escales	51	[45] 1f

Violin I and II

COMPOSER	WORK	PAGE	MEASURE	COMPOSER	WORK	PAGE	MEASURE
Diamond	Rounds for String	2	[15] 3f	Schelling	A Victory Ball	92	[28a] 10f
	Orchestra	12	[170] 2f	Schuman, W.	Undertow	18	1b [210]
Gershwin	An American in Paris	73	6	Sibelius	Symphony No. 6	24	[M]
Kabalevsky	The Comedians	42	[28]	Sibelius	Symphony No. 7	74	8
Kabalevsky	Symphony No. 2	145	4	Starokadom-			
Mahler	Symphony No. 4	124	[5]	sky	Concerto for Orchestra	59	1b [18]
Prokofieff	Peter and the Wolf	13	[10] 4f	Stravinsky	Concerto en Ré pour		
		76	[52] 2f		Violon et Orchestre	8	[16] 1f
Prokofieff	Suite from the Ballet			Stravinsky	Quatre Études pour		
	"Chout"	19	4		Orchestre	2	4b [1]
Ravel	Daphnis et Chloé,			Walton	Façade, Suite No. 1	23	7
	Suite No. 2	57	[184]				

318

BOWING

Viola

COMPOSER	WORK	PAGE	MEASURE	COMPOSER	WORK	PAGE	MEASURE
Albéniz–Arbós	*El Puerto*	13	[E]	Jacobi	*Music Hall Overture*	13	3
Cadman	*American Suite*	27	4	Rachmaninoff	*Symphony No. 2*	189	[73]
						200	[78] 2f

Violoncello

COMPOSER	WORK	PAGE	MEASURE	COMPOSER	WORK	PAGE	MEASURE
Britten	*Les Illuminations*	48	[4]	Schuman, W.	*Undertow*	39	[480] 4f
Prokofieff	*Cinderella Suite No. 1*	123	8b [101]				

Solo Violoncello

COMPOSER	WORK	PAGE	MEASURE
Mahler	*Das Lied von der Erde*	43	[9] 2f

Bass

COMPOSER	WORK	PAGE	MEASURE	COMPOSER	WORK	PAGE	MEASURE
Britten	*Four Sea Interludes from "Peter Grimes"*	76	[10]	Mahler	*Symphony No. 4*	167	78
				Stravinsky	*Le Sacre du Printemps*	24	[33]

Violin I and Viola

COMPOSER	WORK	PAGE	MEASURE	COMPOSER	WORK	PAGE	MEASURE
Borodin	*Symphony No. 3*	30	2	Stravinsky	*Danses Concertantes*	58	[92]
Delannoy	*Figures Sonores*	18	[7]	Walton	*Concerto for Viola and Orchestra*	41	2
Ibert	*Escales*	54	5				

Solo Violin I and Viola

COMPOSER	WORK	PAGE	MEASURE
Copland	*El Salón México*	23	2

Violin II and Viola

COMPOSER	WORK	PAGE	MEASURE	COMPOSER	WORK	PAGE	MEASURE
Copland	*Billy the Kid Ballet Suite*	51	[30] 7f	Prokofieff	*Symphony No. 5*	68	[39]
Gershwin	*Concerto in F for Piano and Orchestra*	63	[7] 7f	Prokofieff	*Symphony No. 6*	105	[69]
Prokofieff	*Classical Symphony*	59	3	Rogers	*Once Upon a Time, Five Fairy Tales*	22	[15] 2f
		82	[64]	Stravinsky	*Apollon Musagète*	22	[52] 1f

Violin I, II, and Viola

COMPOSER	WORK	PAGE	MEASURE	COMPOSER	WORK	PAGE	MEASURE
Antheil	*McKonkey's Ferry*	6	5	Mahler	*Symphony No. 7*	106	[98] 1f
Copland	*Appalachian Spring*	32	[29]	Prokofieff	*Cinderella Suite No. 1*	42	[29]
Copland	*El Salón México*	6	[7] 1f	Rachmaninoff	*Rapsodie pour Piano et Orchestre*	33	[29]
Copland	*Four Dance Episodes from "Rodeo"*	22	[21]	Rachmaninoff	*Symphony No. 2*	190	1
Elgar	*Introduction and Allegro for Strings*	1	3	Ravel	*La Valse*	23	[16]
Honegger	*Pacific 231*	13	[7]	Sibelius	*Symphony No. 3*	37	2b [6]
Jacobi	*Music Hall Overture*	36	3			45	[15]
Khachaturian	*Concerto for Piano and Orchestra*	51	[379]	Stravinsky	*Oedipus Rex*	35	[45]

319

STRINGS

Violin I and Violoncello

COMPOSER	WORK	PAGE	MEASURE	COMPOSER	WORK	PAGE	MEASURE
Mahler	Das Lied von der Erde	134	[57] 9f	Scriabin	Le Poème de l'Extase	34	[5] 1f

Violin II and Violoncello

COMPOSER	WORK	PAGE	MEASURE	COMPOSER	WORK	PAGE	MEASURE
Diamond	Rounds for String Orchestra	19	3b [270]	Prokofieff	Lieutenant Kijé	95	[63]

Violin I, II, and Violoncello

COMPOSER	WORK	PAGE	MEASURE	COMPOSER	WORK	PAGE	MEASURE
Sibelius	Pelleas and Melisande	31	[B] 9f	Walton	Portsmouth Point Overture	23	[17] 1f

Viola and Violoncello

COMPOSER	WORK	PAGE	MEASURE	COMPOSER	WORK	PAGE	MEASURE
Prokofieff	Cinderella Suite No. 1	59	[45] 4f	Walton	Portsmouth Point Overture	35	5b [25]
Rogers	Characters from Hans Christian Andersen	14	[8]				

Soli Viola and Violoncello

COMPOSER	WORK	PAGE	MEASURE
Ravel	La Valse	63	[46] 3f

Violoncello and Bass

COMPOSER	WORK	PAGE	MEASURE	COMPOSER	WORK	PAGE	MEASURE
Britten	Serenade for Tenor, Horn and Strings	18	[14] 3f	Prokofieff	Classical Symphony	42	[34] 2f
Ireland	A London Overture	10	4b [5]	Shostakovich	Symphony No. 6	53	[58] 2f
Miaskovsky	Symphony No. 8	76	[10]	Tchaikovsky	Symphony No. 6, "Pathétique"	50	247
Moeran	Sinfonietta	1	[1]				

Violin II, Viola, and Violoncello

COMPOSER	WORK	PAGE	MEASURE	COMPOSER	WORK	PAGE	MEASURE
Prokofieff	Piano Concerto No. 3	65	[48] 1f	Walton	Portsmouth Point Overture	4	[3] 1f
		74	[57]				
Stravinsky	Petrouchka Suite	131	[112]				

Violin I, II, Viola, and Violoncello

COMPOSER	WORK	PAGE	MEASURE	COMPOSER	WORK	PAGE	MEASURE
Copland	Concerto for Piano and Orchestra	43	4	Shostakovich	Symphony No. 7	89	[88] 2f
Copland	Third Symphony	78	4	Stillman-Kelley	New England Symphony	95	1
Diamond	Rounds for String Orchestra	5	3b [70]	Stravinsky	Quatres Études pour Orchestre	23	[3]
Ireland	Symphonic Rhapsody, "Mai-Dun"	22	3	Stravinsky	Suite No. 1 for Small Orchestra	13	1
Mahler	Symphony No. 5	210	7	Taylor	Through the Looking Glass	47	[4]
Prokofieff	Piano Concerto No. 3	13	[9]				
Prokofieff	Symphony No. 6	82	4				

BOWING

Violin I, Violoncello, and Bass

COMPOSER	WORK	PAGE	MEASURE
Walton	*Concerto for Viola and*	22	[20] 3f
	Orchestra	27	1

Violin II, Violoncello, and Bass

COMPOSER	WORK	PAGE	MEASURE
Stravinsky	*Apollon Musagète*	10	[25]

Violin I, II, Violoncello, and Bass

COMPOSER	WORK	PAGE	MEASURE
Prokofieff	*Symphony No. 6*	150	[111] 3f

Violin II, Viola, Violoncello, and Bass

COMPOSER	WORK	PAGE	MEASURE
Prokofieff	*Symphony No. 6*	127	8

Violin I, II, Viola, Violoncello, and Bass

COMPOSER	WORK	PAGE	MEASURE	COMPOSER	WORK	PAGE	MEASURE
Britten	*Les Illuminations*	24	[1] 2f	Miaskovsky	*Symphony No. 6*	243	[7]
Britten	*The Young Person's Guide to the Orchestra*	61	[M] 2f	Prokofieff	*Piano Concerto No. 3*	130	[99]
				Prokofieff	*Symphony No. 6*	158	2
Elgar	*Concerto for Violin and Orchestra*	19	[22]	Sibelius	*Pohjola's Daughter*	39	5

Chapter 50

PIZZICATI

English	Italian	French	German
Pizzicato	Pizzicato	Pizzicato	Pizzicato
pizz.	*pizz.*	*pizz.*	*Pizz.*

ARCO

Bow	Arco	Archet	Bogen
With (the) bow	Con l'arco	Avec l'archet	Mit Bogen
	Riprendere l'arco	Reprendre l'archet	

(1) ARPEGGIATO

Arpeggiate	Arpeggiato	Arpégé	Harpeggiert
Roll	Ben arpeggiando gli accordi	Arpégez le pizzicato	
	Quasi arpa		

Violin I

COMPOSER	WORK	PAGE	MEASURE	COMPOSER	WORK	PAGE	MEASURE
Chabrier	*Suite Pastorale*	26	5	**Poulenc**	*Deux Marches et un*		
Debussy	*La Damoiselle Élue*	50	2		*Intermède*	**6**	[10]
Elgar	*Variations, "Enigma"*	37	1	**Ravel**	*Le Tombeau de Couperin*	**41**	2b [10]
de Falla	*El Amor Brujo*	40	1	**Ravel**	*Rapsodie Espagnole*	**37**	[10] 1f
Maganini	*An Ornithological Suite*	44	3			**70**	[20] 1f
Poot	*Symphonie*	**12**	[6] 2f	**Stravinsky**	*Le Sacre du Printemps*	**76**	1b [87]

Violin II

COMPOSER	WORK	PAGE	MEASURE	COMPOSER	WORK	PAGE	MEASURE
Alfvén	*Midsommarvaka*	60	[24] 2f	**Rimsky-**			
Ibert	*La Ballade de la Geôle*			**Korsakoff**	*Scheherazade*	236	588
	de Reading	44	[30]	**Villa-Lobos**	*Chôros No. 8*	**24**	[10] 1f
Rimsky-	*Russian Easter Overture*	36	1				
Korsakoff		74	8				

Violin I and II

COMPOSER	WORK	PAGE	MEASURE	COMPOSER	WORK	PAGE	MEASURE
Rimsky-				**Rimsky-**			
Korsakoff	*Le Coq d'Or Suite*	47	[32]	**Korsakoff**	*Scheherazade*	**6**	24
				Stravinsky	*Petrouchka Suite*	**81**	[67] 6f

322

PIZZICATI

Viola

COMPOSER	WORK	PAGE	MEASURE	COMPOSER	WORK	PAGE	MEASURE
Dvořák	Symphony No. 4	70	[D]	Ravel	La Valse	94	1
Parodi	Preludio ad una	3	[A]	Rimsky-			
	Commedia	43	[U]	Korsakoff	Capriccio Espagnol	49	[N]

Violoncello

COMPOSER	WORK	PAGE	MEASURE	COMPOSER	WORK	PAGE	MEASURE
Barber	First Symphony	40	[18]	Poulenc	Aubade	27	5
Berg	Violin Concerto	20	[110] 1f	Poulenc	Concerto pour deux		
Chávez	Sinfonia India	48	[64]		Pianos et Orchestre	33	[26]
Debussy	Jeux	41	2	Ravel	Daphnis et Chloé,	43	[112]
Debussy	La Damoiselle Élue	18	1		Suite No. 1	60	[126]
Debussy	La Mer	34	[16]	Ravel	Daphnis et Chloé,		
Diamond	Music for Shakespeare's	4	[10] 4f		Suite No. 2	39	[170] 2f
	"Romeo and Juliet"	26	[40]	Ravel	La Valse	6	[5]
Dohnányi	Variations on a					44	[31]
	Nursery Song	109	1b [69]			77	[57]
Dvořák	Concerto for Violoncello			Ravel	Le Tombeau de Couperin	21	[3]
	and Orchestra	46	15	Ravel	Rapsodie Espagnole	12	1
Elgar	Symphony No. 2	138	[137]	Read	Prelude and Toccata	25	3b [9]
Grétry–Mottl	Ballet Suite, "Céphale			Respighi	Feste Romane	80	7
	et Procris"	33	[O]	Respighi	The Birds	29	[12] 7f
Maganini	An Ancient Greek			Respighi	Trittico Botticelliano	17	1
	Melody	2	2	Stravinsky	Le Sacre du Printemps	108	[135]
Mahler	Symphony No. 9	23	3	Walton	Façade, Suite No. 2	13	[A]
McDonald	Bataan	10	2b [25]				

Soli Violoncello

COMPOSER	WORK	PAGE	MEASURE
Casella	Paganiniana	109	[12]

Bass

COMPOSER	WORK	PAGE	MEASURE	COMPOSER	WORK	PAGE	MEASURE
Britten	Serenade for Tenor, Horn and Strings	12	1b [9]	Szymanowski	Symphonie Concertante pour Piano et Orchestre	33	[18]

Violin I and Viola

COMPOSER	WORK	PAGE	MEASURE	COMPOSER	WORK	PAGE	MEASURE
Ravel	Daphnis et Chloé, Suite No. 2	45	[176]	Ravel	Introduction et Allegro	35	[27] 4f

Violin II and Viola

COMPOSER	WORK	PAGE	MEASURE	COMPOSER	WORK	PAGE	MEASURE
Elgar	Concerto for Violin and Orchestra	6	[5] 1f	Ravel	La Valse	63	[46]
Maganini	Tuolumne	18	1	Ravel	Rapsodie Espagnole	13	[2] 3f
Ravel	Boléro	23	[9]	Schönberg	Theme and Variations	13	51

STRINGS

Violin I, II, and Viola

COMPOSER	WORK	PAGE	MEASURE	COMPOSER	WORK	PAGE	MEASURE
Brahms	*Symphony No. 2*	53	509	Rimsky-Korsakoff	*Capriccio Espagnol*	4	7
Ibert	*Escales*	83	[72]	Schmitt	*Mirages pour Orchestre, No. 1*	32	3b [15]
Poulenc	*Concerto pour deux Pianos et Orchestre*	59	4b [40]	Toch	*Fünf Stücke für Kammerorchester*	20	[5]
Ravel	*La Valse*	89	[66]				
Ravel	*Valses Nobles et Sentimentales*	22	[19]				

Violin I and Violoncello

Ravel	*Daphnis et Chloé, Suite No. 2*	40	1	Rivier	*3 Pastorales*	17	[4]

Violin II and Violoncello

COMPOSER	WORK	PAGE	MEASURE
Read	*First Overture*	23	[8] 1f

Violin I, II, and Violoncello

La Violette	*Largo Lyrico*	2	1

Viola and Violoncello

Elgar	*Concerto for Violin and Orchestra*	58	[64] 3f	Stravinsky	*Pulcinella Suite*	26	[33]
Moeran	*Symphony in G minor*	156	[105]	Walton	*Concerto for Viola and Orchestra*	2	[2] 1f
Stravinsky	*Le Sacre du Printemps*	82	[97]				

Violin II, Viola, and Violoncello

Elgar	*Concerto for Violoncello and Orchestra*	13	[11]	Ravel	*Rapsodie Espagnole*	54	[9]
Moross	*Paeans*	2	[A]	Rimsky-Korsakoff	*Capriccio Espagnol*	68	8

Soli Violin II, Viola, and Violoncello

Stravinsky	*Pulcinella Suite*	29	[39]

Violin I, II, Viola, and Violoncello

Britten	*Les Illuminations*	5	8	Ravel	*Rapsodie Espagnole*	27	3
Debussy	*La Mer*	51	[26]			74	3
Dohnányi	*Ruralia Hungarica*	41	[10]	Rimsky-Korsakoff	*Scheherazade*	132	124
Elgar	*Concerto for Violin and Orchestra*	91	2b [104]			151	209
Ibert	*Escales*	79	[68]	Respighi	*Metamorphoseon, XII Modi*	39	[19] 7f
Milhaud	*Deuxième Concerto pour Violon et Orchestre*	98	[65]	Rosenthal	*Les Petits Métiers*	114	1
Ravel	*Alborada del Gracioso*	29	1	Walton	*Concerto for Violin and Orchestra*	51	5
Ravel	*Daphnis et Chloé, Suite No. 2*	52	2				

324

PIZZICATI

Violin I, II, Violoncello, and Bass

COMPOSER	WORK	PAGE	MEASURE
Poulenc	*Concert Champêtre pour Clavecin et Orchestre*	**26**	I

Viola, Violoncello, and Bass

COMPOSER	WORK	PAGE	MEASURE
Britten	*Sinfonietta*	**15**	3

Violin I, II, Viola, Violoncello, and Bass

COMPOSER	WORK	PAGE	MEASURE	COMPOSER	WORK	PAGE	MEASURE
Britten	*Serenade for Tenor, Horn and Strings*	**22**	[17]	**Poulenc**	*Concert Champêtre pour Clavecin et Orchestre*	**5** **46**	[3] [32]

(2) CHORDS

English	*Italian*	*French*	*German*
Held like a guitar	Al banjo Quasi chitarra	A la guitarra Le Violon [l'Alto] sous le bras —quasi guitarra L'instrument en guitare	Wie eine Gitarre

Violin I

COMPOSER	WORK	PAGE	MEASURE	COMPOSER	WORK	PAGE	MEASURE
Inghelbrecht	*La Métamorphose d'Ève*	18	[16] 4f	**Villa-Lobos**	*Chôros No. 10*	61 76	1 2

Violin II

COMPOSER	WORK	PAGE	MEASURE
Inghelbrecht	*La Valse Retrouvée*	4	[37]

Violin I and II

COMPOSER	WORK	PAGE	MEASURE
Inghelbrecht	*La Métamorphose d'Ève*	35	I

Viola

COMPOSER	WORK	PAGE	MEASURE
Szymanowski	*Symphonie Concertante pour Piano et Orchestre*	32	3

Violoncello

COMPOSER	WORK	PAGE	MEASURE	COMPOSER	WORK	PAGE	MEASURE
Bartók	*Dance Suite*	7	[5]	**Diamond**	*Rounds for String Orchestra*	42	2b [175]
Bartók	*Violin Concerto*	127	[583]				

STRINGS

Violin I and Viola

COMPOSER	WORK	PAGE	MEASURE
Maganini	*At the Setting of the Sun*	**16**	[I]

Violin II and Viola

COMPOSER	WORK	PAGE	MEASURE	COMPOSER	WORK	PAGE	MEASURE
Stravinsky	*Le Sacre du Printemps*	**22**	[31]	**Stravinsky**	*Petrouchka Suite*	**45**	[34]

Violin I, II, and Viola

COMPOSER	WORK	PAGE	MEASURE	COMPOSER	WORK	PAGE	MEASURE
Bax	*Fourth Symphony*	**108**	3	**Maganini**	*At the Setting of the Sun*	**12**	2b [G]
Hanson	*"Merry Mount" Suite*	**11**	[77]	**McKay**	*Sinfonietta No. 4*	**81**	[N] 2f
Honegger	*Le Roi David*	**126**	[19]	**Prokofieff**	*Lieutenant Kijé*	**48**	[41]

Violin I, II, and Violoncello

COMPOSER	WORK	PAGE	MEASURE	COMPOSER	WORK	PAGE	MEASURE
Rimsky-Korsakoff	*Capriccio Espagnol*	**53**	1b [O]	**Stillman-Kelley**	*Gulliver—His Voyage to Lilliput*	**119** **132**	3 [H]

Viola and Violoncello

COMPOSER	WORK	PAGE	MEASURE	COMPOSER	WORK	PAGE	MEASURE
Bartók	*Concerto for Orchestra*	**79**	5	**Sibelius**	*Symphony No. 1*	**81**	1
Britten	*Les Illuminations*	**18**	1			**99**	1

Violoncello and Bass

COMPOSER	WORK	PAGE	MEASURE
Křenek	*Symphonic Elegy*	**11**	245

Violin II, Viola, and Violoncello

COMPOSER	WORK	PAGE	MEASURE	COMPOSER	WORK	PAGE	MEASURE
Ravel	*Boléro*	**54**	[16]	**Szymanowski**	*Symphonie Concertante pour Piano et Orchestre*	**69**	4
Rimsky-Korsakoff	*Capriccio Espagnol*	**68**	8				

Violin I, II, Viola, and Violoncello

COMPOSER	WORK	PAGE	MEASURE	COMPOSER	WORK	PAGE	MEASURE
Balakirev-Casella	*Islamey*	**60**	[61]	**Gershwin**	*Concerto in F for Piano and Orchestra*	**55**	[3]
Bartók	*Music for Strings, Percussion and Celesta*	**95**	1	**Sibelius**	*En Saga*	**75**	1
Debussy	*Iberia*	**88**	[56]	**Sibelius**	*Symphony No. 1*	**107**	3
		102	[64]	**Sibelius**	*The Tempest, First Suite*	**34**	2
				Tchaikovsky	*Symphony No. 4*	**126**	383

Violin II, Viola, Violoncello, and Bass

COMPOSER	WORK	PAGE	MEASURE
Schelling	*A Victory Ball*	**34**	3

PIZZICATI

(3) GLISSANDO

English	Italian	French	German
Pizz. on one string	Pizz. sul una corda	Pizz. sur une corde	Pizz. auf einer Saite
Slide the finger	Pizz. strisciando	Pizz. en glissant	Pizz. u. mit dem
	il dita	le doigt	Finger gleiten

Violin I

COMPOSER	WORK	PAGE	MEASURE
Stravinsky	*Renard*	48	187

Viola

COMPOSER	WORK	PAGE	MEASURE	COMPOSER	WORK	PAGE	MEASURE
Casella	*Pupazzetti*	8	[3]	**Stravinsky**	*Renard*	64	2b [41]
Milhaud	*Saudades do Brazil*	60	1				

Violoncello

COMPOSER	WORK	PAGE	MEASURE	COMPOSER	WORK	PAGE	MEASURE
Cowell	*Symphonic Set*	32	[50]	**Stravinsky**	*Chant du Rossignol*	24	[25] 2f
Gould	*Latin-American*					38	1b [38]
	Symphonette	52	[12] 2f			67	[74]
Poot	*Symphonie*	12	[6] 2f	**Stravinsky**	*Quatre Études pour*		
		48	3		*Orchestre*	15	2b [5]
				Stravinsky	*Renard*	73	[48] 2f

Solo Violoncello

COMPOSER	WORK	PAGE	MEASURE
Schönberg	*Pierrot Lunaire*	24	2b [20]
		66	[10] 1f

Soli Violoncello

COMPOSER	WORK	PAGE	MEASURE
Bartók	*Concerto for Orchestra*	58	3b [57]

Bass

COMPOSER	WORK	PAGE	MEASURE	COMPOSER	WORK	PAGE	MEASURE
Halffter	*Deux Esquisses Symphoniques*	10	2b [C]	**Read**	*Symphony No. I*	103	1b [39]

Violin I, II, and Viola

COMPOSER	WORK	PAGE	MEASURE
Tansman	*Sonatine Trans-atlantique, II*	9	5

Violin II and Violoncello

COMPOSER	WORK	PAGE	MEASURE
Bartók	*Dance Suite*	3	23

327

STRINGS

Viola and Violoncello

COMPOSER	WORK	PAGE	MEASURE
Stravinsky	*Renard*	**24**	[14]

Violoncello and Bass

COMPOSER	WORK	PAGE	MEASURE	COMPOSER	WORK	PAGE	MEASURE
Barber	*Second Symphony*	**45**	[31] 1f	**Read**	*First Overture*	**57**	[20]
Poot	*Symphonie*	**55**	5				

Violin I, II, Viola, and Violoncello

Stravinsky	*Renard*	**29**	[18]

Violin I, II, Viola, Violoncello, and Bass

Bartók	*Music for Strings,*	**11**	1
	Percussion and Celesta	**25**	169

(4) LEFT-HAND

English	Italian	French	German
Left hand	Mano sinistra	Main gauche	Linke Hand
l.h.	m.s.	m.g.	L.H.
By means of the l.h.			Mit Zuhilfenahme der linken Hand
The sign + indicates pizz. with left hand	+ = segno per il pizz. colla mano sinistra	Le signe + indique le pizz. exécuté par la main gauche Le signe + veut dire pizz. avec la main gauche Les notes marquées + pizz. avec la m.g. Les notes marquées + seront jouées pizz. de la m.g.	+ = Zeichen für ein pizz. mit der linken Hand

Violin I

Alfvén	*Midsommarvaka*	**60**	[24] 2f	**Gould**	*Latin-American*		
Bloch	*Trois Poèmes Juifs*	**9**	[3] 3f		*Symphonette*	**53**	4
Borodin	*Symphony No. 3*	**56**	[10] 4f	**Rosenthal**	*Les Petits Métiers*	**138**	3
		70	[18] 4f	**Villa-Lobos**	*Amazonas*	**34**	4
Casella	*Paganiniana*	**54**	[29] 1f	**Villa-Lobos**	*Chôros No. 8*	**24**	[10] 2f
Ferroud	*Au Parc Monceau*	**43**	3	**Villa-Lobos**	*Uirapurú*	**45**	2

Solo Violin

Schönberg	*Pierrot Lunaire*	**50**	[15]	**Stravinsky**	*Histoire du Soldat*	**10**	[17] 8f
						33	1b [14]
						44	[17] 3f
						50	[37] 8f

PIZZICATI

Violin II

COMPOSER	WORK	PAGE	MEASURE	COMPOSER	WORK	PAGE	MEASURE
Balakirev–				**Rimsky-**			
Casella	*Islamey*	**27**	[25] 2f	**Korsakoff**	*Capriccio Espagnol*	**56**	[P]
Casella	*Paganiniana*	**160**	[32]	**Stravinsky**	*Apollon Musagète*	**27**	66
Honegger	*Le Roi David*	**201**	7	**Stravinsky**	*Jeu de Cartes*	**56**	[105] 2f
Ravel	*Rapsodie Espagnole*	**36**	[9] 1f				

Violin I and II

COMPOSER	WORK	PAGE	MEASURE	COMPOSER	WORK	PAGE	MEASURE
Shostakovich	*Symphony No. 9*	**117**	[89] 1f	**Stravinsky**	*Symphony in C*	**21**	[34] 2f

Viola

COMPOSER	WORK	PAGE	MEASURE	COMPOSER	WORK	PAGE	MEASURE
Berg	*Violin Concerto*	**66**	[65] 2f	**Skilton**	*Suite Primeval, Part I*	**15**	1b [B]

Violoncello

COMPOSER	WORK	PAGE	MEASURE	COMPOSER	WORK	PAGE	MEASURE
Bartók	*Violin Concerto*	**50**	[369]	**Stravinsky**	*Renard*	**18**	1b [10]
Fitelberg	*Symphony No. 1*	**69**	[136] 2f			**65**	1b [42]
d'Indy	*Tableaux de Voyage*	**35**	1				

Violin I and Viola

COMPOSER	WORK	PAGE	MEASURE
Stravinsky	*Danses Concertantes*	**78**	[125]

Violin II and Viola

COMPOSER	WORK	PAGE	MEASURE
Albéniz–			
Arbós	*El Albaicín*	**6**	2

Violin I, II, and Viola

COMPOSER	WORK	PAGE	MEASURE	COMPOSER	WORK	PAGE	MEASURE
Albéniz–	*Triana*	**5**	1b [A]	**Rimsky-**			
Arbós		**37**	1	**Korsakoff**	*Scheherazade*	**98**	411

Viola and Violoncello

COMPOSER	WORK	PAGE	MEASURE
Ravel	*Rapsodie Espagnole*	**72**	[21] 2f

Solo Viola and Violoncello

COMPOSER	WORK	PAGE	MEASURE
Schönberg	*Pierrot Lunaire*	**41**	[15]

Violoncello and Bass

COMPOSER	WORK	PAGE	MEASURE
Parodi	*Preludio ad una Commedia*	**33**	[Q]

STRINGS

(5) NAIL

English	Italian	French	German
With (the) nail	Colla unghia	Avec l'ongle	Mit dem Nagel
☉ = pizz. with the finger-nail at the extreme upper end of the string drawn below the finger which touches it	☉ = pizz. coll'unghia al capo della corda tirata sotto il dita toccando	☉ = pizz. avec l'ongle au bout extrême supérieur de la corde tiré au-dessous du doigt touchant	☉ = Pizz. mit dem Nagel am aufstersten Ende der Saite knapp unterhalb des Griff-fingers gerissen

Violin I, II, Viola, and Violoncello

COMPOSER	WORK	PAGE	MEASURE
Bartók	*Music for Strings, Percussion and Celesta*	24	157

(6) ON HARMONICS

English	Italian	French	German
Pizz. on harmonics	Pizz. sull'armonici	Pizz. sur les sons harmoniques	Pizz. auf Flageolett

Violin II

COMPOSER	WORK	PAGE	MEASURE
Rimsky-Korsakoff	*Scheherazade*	64	194

Viola

COMPOSER	WORK	PAGE	MEASURE
Rimsky-Korsakoff	*Scheherazade*	67	221

Violoncello

COMPOSER	WORK	PAGE	MEASURE	COMPOSER	WORK	PAGE	MEASURE
Glazounov	*Violin Concerto in A minor*	67	[44] 1f	**Poulenc**	*Concerto pour deux Pianos et Orchestre*	34	[27]
Ibert	*Escales*	40	[35]	**Stravinsky**	*Chant du Rossignol*	38	[38] 1f
Mussorgsky	*Night on the Bald Mountain*	79 86	[W] 440	**Stravinsky**	*Quatre Études pour Orchestre*	13	3b [3]

Bass

COMPOSER	WORK	PAGE	MEASURE	COMPOSER	WORK	PAGE	MEASURE
Britten	*Sinfonia da Requiem*	3	[2] 13f	**Rogers**	*Once Upon a Time, Five Fairy Tales*	37	3
Britten	*Sinfonietta*	42	[16] 5f	**Stravinsky**	*Renard*	18	1b [10]
Debussy	*Jeux*	77	[51]			65	1b [42]
Debussy-Ansermet	*Six Épigraphes Antiques*	37	[A] 1f				

PIZZICATI

Solo Bass

COMPOSER	WORK	PAGE	MEASURE		COMPOSER	WORK	PAGE	MEASURE
Rogers	*Once Upon a Time, Five Fairy Tales*	20	[14] 2f		**Stravinsky**	*Histoire du Soldat*	2	[3] 2f
		29	3				7	I
							13	I
							33	[15] 4f
							47	[29]
							53	[4]

Violin II and Viola

COMPOSER	WORK	PAGE	MEASURE
Rogers	*Once Upon a Time, Five Fairy Tales*	36	5b [23]

Violin I, II, and Viola

Mahler	*Symphony No. 9*	60	20

Viola and Violoncello

COMPOSER	WORK	PAGE	MEASURE		COMPOSER	WORK	PAGE	MEASURE
Inghelbrecht	*Sinfonia Breve No. 1*	36	2		**Stravinsky**	*Pulcinella Suite*	11	[10]
Janssen	*New Year's Eve in New York*	60	I					

Solo Violoncello and Bass

Stravinsky	*Chant du Rossignol*	15	[13]		**Stravinsky**	*Pulcinella Suite*	12	[13] 2f

Violin II, Viola, and Violoncello

Inghelbrecht	*Sinfonia Breve No. 1*	58	[34]

(7) "SLAP"

English	Italian	French	German
Slap (a la jazz)	Colpo col mano (alla jazz)	En frappant la table de la paume—à la jazz	Mit dem Hand schlagen—im
Strike with the hand			Jazzstil

Bass

Balogh	*Portrait of a City*	17	[M] 3f		**Inghelbrecht**	*Sinfonia Breve No. 1*	45	4
							69	I

Violoncello and Bass

Cesana	*Second American Symphony*	151	[35] 4f		**Riisager**	*Torgot Dance*	16	[75] 1f

STRINGS

(8) "SNAP"

English	Italian	French	German
Let string snap	Fate scappiero la corda	Faites claquer la corde	Die Saite schnappen lassen
Let string strike fingerboard	⊕ indica uno pizz. forte dimodo	⊕ indique un ferme et vig-	⊕ bezeichnet ein Pizz. bei
⊕ indicates a strong pizz. so	che la corda ribalza dalla	oureux pizz. faisant rebon-	welchem die Saite auf das
that the string rebounds off	tastiera	dir la corde sur la touche	Griffbrett anschlägt
the fingerboard		⊕ indique un pizz. auquel la	⊕ = ein starkes Pizz.
Pizz. allowing the string to		corde frappe la touche	
slap the fingerboard		⊕ = pizz. fort jusqu'à ce que	
		la corde frappe la touche	

Bass

COMPOSER	WORK	PAGE	MEASURE	COMPOSER	WORK	PAGE	MEASURE
Bartók	Divertimento for String	26	[103] 6f	Diamond	Rounds for String	24	2
	Orchestra	35	[403]		Orchestra	34	[100] 1f
Bartók	Music for Strings,	125	175			42	2b [175]
	Percussion and Celesta	138	[H]	Diamond	Timon of Athens	22	140

Solo Bass

COMPOSER	WORK	PAGE	MEASURE
Bartók	Music for Strings, Percussion and Celesta	20	116

Violin I, II, and Viola

Diamond	Timon of Athens	12	77

Violin I, II, and Violoncello

Bartók	Violin Concerto	66	[105]

Violoncello and Bass

COMPOSER	WORK	PAGE	MEASURE	COMPOSER	WORK	PAGE	MEASURE
Bartók	Divertimento for String Orchestra	42	[583]	Diamond	Rounds for String Orchestra	26	[25] 1f
Diamond	Fourth Symphony	50	2b [15]	Gershwin	Rhapsody in Blue	11	[9]

Violin I, II, Viola, and Violoncello

COMPOSER	WORK	PAGE	MEASURE	COMPOSER	WORK	PAGE	MEASURE
Bartók	Music for Strings, Percussion and Celesta	28	199	Diamond	Fourth Symphony	47	1

Viola, Violoncello, and Bass

Bartók	Music for Strings, Percussion and Celesta	81	49

PIZZICATI

Violin I, Viola, Violoncello, and Bass

COMPOSER	WORK	PAGE	MEASURE
Bartók	*Music for Strings, Percussion and Celesta*	93	75

Violin I, II, Viola, Violoncello, and Bass

Bartók	*Violin Concerto*	51	[373]
		137	[613]

(9) THUMB

English	Italian	French	German
With the thumb	Col pollice	Avec le pouce	Mit dem Daumen

Viola

Sibelius	*Pelleas and Melisande*	15	1

(10) TREMOLANDO

English	Italian	French	German
Strum(ming)	Pizzicando	Tapotant	Klimpernd

Violin I

Bax	*Mediterranean*	3	5

Violin I and II

Grofé	*Grand Canyon Suite*	122	[6]

Violin I, II, and Viola

COMPOSER	WORK	PAGE	MEASURE	COMPOSER	WORK	PAGE	MEASURE
Bax	*Third Symphony*	27	[25] 3f	**Sowerby**	*From the Northland*	23	2b [F]

Viola and Violoncello

Bax	*Tintagel*	28	[M] 2f

Violin I, II, Viola, and Violoncello

Elgar	*Concerto for Violin and Orchestra*	88	[102]

Violin I, II, Viola, Violoncello, and Bass

Rimsky-Korsakoff	*Scheherazade*	60	[F]
		82	[L]

STRINGS

(11) VIBRATO

English	Italian	French	German
Let vibrate	Fa risaltare il suono	Faire vibrer le son	Vibrieren lassen
l.v.	Tenuto	Laissez vibrer	
Vibrate	Vibrando	l.v.	
vib.	Vibrato	Vibrer	
	vib.	vib.	

Violin I

COMPOSER	WORK	PAGE	MEASURE
Inghelbrecht	Sinfonia Breve No. 1	63	6

Solo Violin

COMPOSER	WORK	PAGE	MEASURE
Stravinsky	Histoire du Soldat	21	[5]

Violin I and II

COMPOSER	WORK	PAGE	MEASURE
Britten	The Young Person's Guide to the Orchestra	45	3

Viola

COMPOSER	WORK	PAGE	MEASURE	COMPOSER	WORK	PAGE	MEASURE
Chávez	Sinfonia India	25	[29]	**Mihalovici**	Divertissement pour Petite Orchestre	35	4b [N]
Inghelbrecht	La Métamorphose d'Ève	27	[20] 5f				

Violoncello

COMPOSER	WORK	PAGE	MEASURE	COMPOSER	WORK	PAGE	MEASURE
Albéniz– Arbós	El Puerto	32	[M]	**Harris**	Third Symphony	1	2b [3]
Britten	Serenade for Tenor, Horn and Strings	25	[20]	**Parodi**	Preludio ad una Commedia	3	[A]
Copland	Dance Symphony	13	5	**Rogers**	Elegy	8	[6] 9f
Debussy	La Mer	99	1	**Schuman, W.**	Symphony No. IV	57	271
Dello Joio	Variations, Chaconne, and Finale	43	[105] 1f	**Sessions**	Symphony No. II	81	[M] 5f
				Stravinsky	Chant du Rossignol	7	[4]
Diamond	Music for Shakespeare's "Romeo and Juliet"	21	[10] 2f	**Stravinsky**	Oedipus Rex	79	2b [107]
Gould	Philharmonic Waltzes	29	[339] 14f	**Stravinsky**	Suite No. 1 for Small Orchestra	12	[12] 4f

Bass

COMPOSER	WORK	PAGE	MEASURE	COMPOSER	WORK	PAGE	MEASURE
Copland	Four Dance Episodes from "Rodeo"	69	1	**Gould**	Spirituals	13	[A]
						21	[C]
Debussy	Iberia	77	[50] 2f	**Harris**	Third Symphony	3	[6]
Diamond	Fourth Symphony	15	[85]			94	2
		88	1	**Maganini**	An Ornithological Suite	42	13b [E]
Diamond	Music for Shakespeare's "Romeo and Juliet"	5	4b [20]	**Parodi**	Preludio ad una Commedia	45	[V]

334

PIZZICATI

Bass (contd.)

COMPOSER	WORK	PAGE	MEASURE	COMPOSER	WORK	PAGE	MEASURE
Piston	*Symphony No. 1*	54	44	Schuman, W.	*Symphony No. III*	66	330
		65	143	Sibelius	*Pelleas and Melisande*	15	1
Poulenc	*Concert Champêtre pour*	101	1	Stravinsky	*Chant du Rossignol*	66	[73]
	Clavecin et Orchestre	114	[33]	Stravinsky	*Orpheus*	7	[13]

Solo Bass

COMPOSER	WORK	PAGE	MEASURE
Stravinsky	*Histoire du Soldat*	48	[32]

Violin II and Viola

Copland	*Billy the Kid Ballet Suite*	41	[25] 4f

Violin I, II, and Viola

Rosenthal	*Les Petits Métiers*	133	[E]

Violin II and Violoncello

Stravinsky	*Fire-Bird Suite* (1919)	8	[11] 1f

Violin I, II, and Violoncello

Inghelbrecht	*La Métamorphose d'Ève*	19	4

Violin I and Bass

Jolivet	*Andante pour Orchestre à Cordes*	6	[25] 1f

Violoncello and Bass

COMPOSER	WORK	PAGE	MEASURE	COMPOSER	WORK	PAGE	MEASURE
Debussy	*La Mer*	100	3	Stravinsky	*Chant du Rossignol*	18	[18] 1f
Parodi	*Preludio ad una Commedia*	24	[N]	Stravinsky	*Fire-Bird Suite* (1919)	20	[7]
Piston	*Symphony No. 2*	56	1	Szymanowski	*Symphonie Concertante pour Piano et Orchestre*	25	1
Shostakovich	*Symphony No. 9*	39	[28] 1f				
Sibelius	*The Tempest, First Suite*	37	[C]				

Viola, Violoncello, and Bass

COMPOSER	WORK	PAGE	MEASURE	COMPOSER	WORK	PAGE	MEASURE
Bernstein	*"Jeremiah" Symphony*	61	[20]	Harris	*When Johnny Comes Marching Home*	29	[160] 3f

STRINGS

Soli Viola, Violoncello, and Bass

COMPOSER	WORK	PAGE	MEASURE
Chávez	*Sinfonia India*	27	[35]

Violin II, Viola, and Violoncello

COMPOSER	WORK	PAGE	MEASURE
Walton	*Façade, Suite No. 1*	35	[B]

Violin I, II, Viola, and Violoncello

COMPOSER	WORK	PAGE	MEASURE	COMPOSER	WORK	PAGE	MEASURE
Britten	*Serenade for Tenor, Horn and Strings*	3	2b [2]	Sibelius	*The Tempest, Second Suite*	50	7
Diamond	*Fourth Symphony*	65	1	Stravinsky	*Fire-Bird Suite (1919)*	11	[13] 1f
Harris	*When Johnny Comes Marching Home*	51	5	Stravinsky	*Oedipus Rex*	112	[162]

Violin II, Viola, and Bass

COMPOSER	WORK	PAGE	MEASURE
Harris	*When Johnny Comes Marching Home*	26	3

Violin II, Viola, Violoncello, and Bass

COMPOSER	WORK	PAGE	MEASURE	COMPOSER	WORK	PAGE	MEASURE
Kay	*Suite for Orchestra*	67	[74]	Schuman, W.	*Symphony for Strings*	15	95

Violin I, II, Viola, Violoncello, and Bass

COMPOSER	WORK	PAGE	MEASURE	COMPOSER	WORK	PAGE	MEASURE
Diamond	*Fourth Symphony*	32	1	Schuman, W.	*Symphony No. III*	64	311
Guarnieri	*Negro Dance*	21	[120] 3f	Shostakovich	*Symphony No. 9*	50	[40] 5f
Harris	*Third Symphony*	15	2b [16]				

(12) WITH TWO FINGERS

English	Italian	French	German
Pizz. with two [2] fingers	Pizz. col due [2] dita	Pizz. avec deux [2] doigts	Pizz. mit zwei [2] Fingern

Violin I

COMPOSER	WORK	PAGE	MEASURE
Schönberg	*Kammersymphonie, Op. 9*	41	[38]

Violin II

COMPOSER	WORK	PAGE	MEASURE
Stravinsky	*Ragtime*	9	2b [20]

PIZZICATI

Violin I and II

COMPOSER	WORK	PAGE	MEASURE	COMPOSER	WORK	PAGE	MEASURE
Stravinsky	*Quatre Études pour Orchestre*	51	4	Stravinsky	*Ragtime*	4	[3] 3f

Viola

COMPOSER	WORK	PAGE	MEASURE
Stravinsky	*Ragtime*	15	[38] 3f

Violoncello

COMPOSER	WORK	PAGE	MEASURE	COMPOSER	WORK	PAGE	MEASURE
Bartók	*First Rhapsody for Violin and Orchestra*	33	[20] 2f	Stravinsky	*Pulcinella Suite*	69	[111] 3f

Solo Violoncello

COMPOSER	WORK	PAGE	MEASURE
Stravinsky	*Pulcinella Suite*	22	[27]
		30	[41] 1f

(13) PIZZICATO AND NON-PIZZICATO COMBINED

English	*Italian*	*French*	*German*
Div.—½ arco	Div.—1° arco	Div.—1ères archet	Div.—I mit Bog.
—½ pizz.	—2° pizz.	—2mes pizz.	—II Pizz.

Violin I divisi (pizz. and non-pizz.)

COMPOSER	WORK	PAGE	MEASURE	COMPOSER	WORK	PAGE	MEASURE
Albéniz-Arbós	*Triana*	19	2	Mahler	*Symphony No. 4*	172	95
Charpentier	*Impressions d'Italie*	114	[27]	Sessions	*Symphony No. II*	121	2

Violin I pizz.—Violin II non-pizz.

COMPOSER	WORK	PAGE	MEASURE	COMPOSER	WORK	PAGE	MEASURE
Antheil	*Symphony No. 5*	94	1b [15]	Schelling	*A Victory Ball*	87	[27]
Bartók	*Second Rhapsody for Violin and Orchestra*	29	[11]	Sibelius	*The Swan of Tuonela*	9	7
Egge	*Piano Concerto No. 2*	25	2b [18]	Stravinsky	*Quatre Études pour Orchestre*	17	[6]
Ferroud	*Au Parc Monceau*	15	[2]				

Violin I pizz.—Violin II and Viola non-pizz.

COMPOSER	WORK	PAGE	MEASURE	COMPOSER	WORK	PAGE	MEASURE
Martinet	*Orphée*	1	5	Stravinsky	*Renard*	146	1b [90]
Prokofieff	*Symphony No. 5*	20	3b [11]				

337

STRINGS

Soli Violin I divisi (pizz. and non-pizz.)

COMPOSER	WORK	PAGE	MEASURE
Szymanowski	*Symphonie Concertante pour Piano et Orchestre*	**13**	[7] 2f

Violin II pizz.—Violin I non-pizz.

COMPOSER	WORK	PAGE	MEASURE	COMPOSER	WORK	PAGE	MEASURE
Britten	*Four Sea Interludes from "Peter Grimes"*	**15**	[1]	**Mahler**	*Symphony No. 5*	**122**	2
Copland	*Appalachian Spring*	**47**	1b [39]	**Mahler**	*Symphony No. 6*	**37**	1
Debussy	*Jeux*	**25**	1b [18]	**Mahler**	*Symphony No. 7*	**11**	[6]
de Falla	*Nuits dans les Jardins d'Espagne*	**67**	[34]	**Miaskovsky**	*Symphony No. 6*	**130**	[3]
Fitelberg	*Nocturne for Orchestra*	**14**	1	**Respighi**	*Belfagor, Ouverture per Orchestra*	**27**	1
Honegger	*Pacific 231*	**17**	113	**Stravinsky**	*Chant du Rossignol*	**8**	[5] 5f
		33	165	**Stravinsky**	*Feuerwerk*	**7**	[7]
				Stravinsky	*Scènes de Ballet*	**16**	[27]
Mahler	*Symphony No. 3*	**108**	[3]	**Wellesz**	*Symphony in C*	**44**	[320] 4f

Violin II divisi (pizz. and non-pizz.)

Křenek	*Symphonic Elegy*	**5**	124	**Rieti**	*Sinfonia No. 5*	**46**	[53]

Violin II pizz.—Solo Violin I and II non-pizz.

Stravinsky	*Pulcinella Suite*	**36**	[56]

Violin II pizz.—Viola non-pizz.

COMPOSER	WORK	PAGE	MEASURE	COMPOSER	WORK	PAGE	MEASURE
Bizet	*L'Arlésienne Suite No. 1*	**39**	1	**Ravel**	*Daphnis et Chloé, Suite No. 2*	**59**	[186]
Debussy	*Rondes de Printemps*	**54**	[28] 2f				

Violin II pizz.—Violin I and Viola non-pizz.

d'Indy	*Deuxième Symphonie en Sib*	**15**	4

Violin II pizz.—Viola and Violoncello non-pizz.

Martinet	*Orphée*	**7**	[3]

Violin I and II divisi (pizz. and non-pizz.)

Albéniz-Arbós	*El Albaicín*	**7**	[B]	**Strauss, R.**	*Till Eulenspiegel's Merry Pranks*	**47**	[33]
				Walton	*Façade, Suite No. 1*	**43**	[A]

338

PIZZICATI

Violin I and II pizz.—Viola non-pizz.

COMPOSER	WORK	PAGE	MEASURE
de Falla	Nuits dans les Jardins d'Espagne	15	2

Violin I and II pizz.—Viola and Violoncello non-pizz.

Chabrier	Bourrée Fantastique	1	1

Viola pizz.—Violin II non-pizz.

COMPOSER	WORK	PAGE	MEASURE	COMPOSER	WORK	PAGE	MEASURE
Mahler	Symphony No. 4	164	63	Rosenthal	Les Petits Métiers	75	1
Prokofieff	Piano Concerto No. 3	19	[13] 1f	Sibelius	Rakastava	6	1
Riisager	Torgot Dance	5	3b [15]				

Viola pizz.—Violin I and II non-pizz.

Stravinsky	Chant du Rossignol	27	[28]

Viola divisi (pizz. and non-pizz.)

Barber	Music for a Scene from Shelley	10	60	Debussy	Rondes de Printemps	31	[17]
Bloch	Evocations	66	[46]	Ives	Three Places in New England	4	2
Copland	Dance Symphony	6	[4]	Respighi	Feste Romane	65	5
Debussy	Gigues	14	[8]	Respighi	The Pines of Rome	73	2

Soli Viola divisi (pizz. and non-pizz.)

Casella	Paganiniana	100	[7] 1f	Chávez	Sinfonia India	25	[29]

Viola pizz.—Violoncello non-pizz.

Bizet	L'Arlésienne Suite No. 1	42 53	29 122	Szymanowski	Symphonie Concertante pour Piano et Orchestre	45	[24] 1f
Kodály	Psalmus Hungaricus	50	[30]				
Ravel	Tzigane	18	[16]				

Violoncello pizz.—Violin II non-pizz.

Rosenthal	Les Petits Métiers	78	[A]

Violoncello pizz.—Viola non-pizz.

Chabrier	Bourrée Fantastique	5	[2]	Hill	Sinfonietta for String Orchestra	10	1b [15]
de Falla	El Amor Brujo	41	1	Kodály	Marosszék Dances	39	3b [180]
de Falla	Nuits dans les Jardins d'Espagne	41	2b [6]	Prokofieff	Ala et Lolly (Scythian Suite)	17	[8]

STRINGS

Violoncello divisi (pizz. and non-pizz.)

COMPOSER	WORK	PAGE	MEASURE	COMPOSER	WORK	PAGE	MEASURE
Albéniz-Arbós	Fête-Dieu à Séville	16	1	Kabalevsky	Symphony No. 2	100	7
Barber	First Symphony	6	4	Kalinnikov	Symphony No. 1	115	1
Bax	Sixth Symphony	21	[17]	Liadov	Baba-Yaga	22	1
Bloch	Trois Poèmes Juifs	26	[15]	Mahler	Symphony No. 5	105	8
Borodin	Symphony No. 2	165	[M]	Revueltas	Cuauhnahuac	1	[2] 3f
Charpentier	Impressions d'Italie	37	2b [3]	Schönberg	Fünf Orchesterstücke	5	[4]
Copland	El Salón México	21	[22]	Schuman, W.	Symphony No. IV	57	271
Debussy	Iberia	20	1	Scriabin	Piano Concerto in F♯ minor	10	[6]
Dvořák	Der Wassermann	7	[1]	Sessions	Suite from "The Black Maskers"	36	1
Hanson	"Merry Mount" Suite	48	[8]	Stravinsky	Le Sacre du Printemps	24	[33]
Harris	Third Symphony	1	2b [3]	Walton	Concerto for Viola and Orchestra	69	[61]
Harris	When Johnny Comes Marching Home	1	3				
Ibert	Escales	73	[64]				

Violoncello pizz.—Bass non-pizz.

COMPOSER	WORK	PAGE	MEASURE	COMPOSER	WORK	PAGE	MEASURE
Bloch	Trois Poèmes Juifs	40	1	Rogers	Once Upon a Time, Five Fairy Tales	55	[32]
de Falla	Nuits dans les Jardins d'Espagne	63	[30]	Schuman, W.	Symphony No. IV	24	216
Loeffler	Evocation	10	2b [R]	Sessions	Symphony for Orchestra (No. 1)	9	[12]
Milhaud	Introduction et Marche Funèbre	22	[105] 3f	Stravinsky	Symphony in C	42	[78] 1f
Prokofieff	Summer Day Suite	70	[35]	Stravinsky	Symphony in Three Movements	61	[109]
Rachmaninoff	Piano Concerto No. 3	32	[16] 5f				

Violoncello pizz.—Violin II and Viola non-pizz.

COMPOSER	WORK	PAGE	MEASURE
Elgar	Concerto for Violoncello and Orchestra	100	[70] 4f

Violoncello pizz.—Violoncello and Bass non-pizz.

Britten	Les Illuminations	48	[5]

Violoncello pizz.—Solo Violoncello and Bass non-pizz.

Stravinsky	Concerto en Ré pour Orchestre à Cordes	26	[81]

Solo Violoncello pizz.—Violoncello non-pizz.

James	Suite for String Orchestra	1	1

340

PIZZICATI

Solo Violoncello pizz.—Solo Bass non-pizz.

COMPOSER	WORK	PAGE	MEASURE
Rogers	*Once Upon a Time, Five Fairy Tales*	11	[8]

Bass pizz.—Violoncello non-pizz.

COMPOSER	WORK	PAGE	MEASURE	COMPOSER	WORK	PAGE	MEASURE
Alfvén	*Midsommarvaka*	31	[13] 6f	**Honegger**	*Pacific 231*	10	73
Barber	*Second Symphony*	7	3	**Honegger**	*Symphonie pour Cordes*	36	[10] 5f
Barraine	*Deuxième Symphonie*	8	3	**Ibert**	*Divertissement*	13	[3] 8f
Bartók	*First Rhapsody for*					46	[2]
	Violin and Orchestra	9	[7]	**Khachaturian**	*Concerto for Piano and*		
Beethoven	*Piano Concerto No. 4*	103	299		*Orchestra*	30	[240]
Beethoven	*Piano Concerto No. 5*	39	210	**Khachaturian**	*Masquerade Suite*	31	[1]
		83	463	**Kodály**	*Háry János Suite*	40	1
Bizet	*L'Arlésienne Suite*					102	1
	No. 1	26	29	**Lalo**	*Symphonie Espagnole*	39	6
Borodin	*Symphony No. 2*	166	3			109	4
Brahms	*Ein deutsches Requiem*	224	294	**Liszt**	*Eine Faust-Symphonie*	93	[Ee] 3f
Britten	*Sinfonia da Requiem*	39	[27]	**Mahler**	*Symphony No. 5*	175	3
Copland	*Appalachian Spring*	64	[51]	**Milhaud**	*Concertino de Printemps*	14	[85] 1f
Copland	*El Salón México*	6	[7]	**Milhaud**	*Deuxième Concerto*		
Copland	*Music for the Theatre*	40	2b [30]		*pour Violoncelle et*		
		47	4		*Orchestre*	53	[50]
Copland	*Third Symphony*	131	[114] 10f	**Milhaud**	*Introduction et Marche*		
Debussy	*Danses Sacrée et Profane*	15	5		*Funèbre*	6	[25] 2f
		25	2	**Milhaud**	*Ière Symphonie*	6	2
Debussy	*La Mer*	11	[5]	**Milhaud**	*Saudades do Brazil*	57	4
Dvořák	*Symphony No. 4*	169	1	**Milhaud**	*Two Marches*	23	4
Egge	*Symphony No. 1*	13	1b [15]	**Poulenc**	*Concert Champêtre pour*		
de Falla	*El Amor Brujo*	90	[52] 4f		*Clavecin et Orchestre*	40	[28]
de Falla	*Nuits dans les Jardins*			**Prokofieff**	*Cinderella Suite No. 1*	123	8b [101]
	d'Espagne	7	[4] 2f	**Prokofieff**	*Piano Concerto No. 3*	3	[2]
de Falla	*Three Dances from*			**Prokofieff**	*Suite from the Ballet*	8	[7]
	"The Three-				*"Chout"*	29	[35]
	Cornered Hat"	7	[5]	**Prokofieff**	*Summer Day Suite*	81	[43]
Gershwin	*An American in Paris*	3	[2]	**Rachmaninoff**	*Piano Concerto No. 3*	82	2
		67	[57]	**Rimsky-**	*Capriccio Espagnol*	70	5
Harris	*When Johnny Comes*	13	3	**Korsakoff**		73	[T]
	Marching Home	26	3	**Rosenthal**	*Les Petits Métiers*	137	1
		36	3	**Roussel**	*Le Festin de l'Araignée*	40	4b [58]
Harrison	*Alleluia for Orchestra*	2	3			54	[69]
Herrmann	*Sinfonietta for String*			**Satie–Debussy**	*Gymnopédies*	2	5
	Orchestra	12	2	**Schreker**	*The Birthday of the*		
Hill	*Sinfonietta for String*				*Infanta, Suite*	28	[120] 1f
	Orchestra	12	[50] 1f	**Schuman, W.**	*Symphony No. IV*	5	35
Hindemith	*Theme and Four Varia-*	12	[9] 5f	**Sibelius**	*En Saga*	22	2
	tions, "The Four	33	[25] 1f	**Sibelius**	*Symphony No. 6*	61	5
	Temperaments"	54	1	**Siegmeister**	*Ozark Set*	51	4b [25]
Honegger	*Concertino pour Piano*			**Stravinsky**	*Oedipus Rex*	95	[128]
	et Orchestre	31	[20]	**Stravinsky**	*Scènes de Ballet*	35	[60]
Honegger	*Le Dit des Jeux du*			**Tansman**	*Deux Moments*		
	Monde	65	[8] 2f		*Symphoniques*	11	[4]

STRINGS

Bass pizz.—Violoncello non-pizz. (contd.)

COMPOSER	WORK	PAGE	MEASURE	COMPOSER	WORK	PAGE	MEASURE
Taylor	Ballet Music from "Casanova"	22	[J]	Vaughan Williams	Symphony in D major (No. 5)	93	4
Vaughan Williams	A London Symphony	81	3b [E]	Walton	Concerto for Viola and Orchestra	1	1
		108	2				
Vaughan Williams	Job, A Masque for Dancing	6	[B]	Walton	Symphony	12	[7]
				Wolf	Der Feuerreiter	20	48
Vaughan Williams	Symphony in F minor (No. 4)	17	3				

Bass divisi (pizz. and non-pizz.)

COMPOSER	WORK	PAGE	MEASURE	COMPOSER	WORK	PAGE	MEASURE
Albéniz–Arbós	Triana	7	[B]	Prokofieff	Romeo and Juliet, Suite No. 1	75	[49] 1f
		25	2				
Bloch	Trois Poèmes Juifs	18	[10]	Prokofieff	Romeo and Juliet, Suite No. 2	66	3
Bloch	Voice in the Wilderness	22	1b [18]			110	3
Borodin	On the Steppes of Central Asia	13	4b [E]	Prokofieff	Suite from the Ballet "Chout"	4	2b [1]
Debussy	Gigues	22	[13]	Prokofieff	Summer Day Suite	66	[32]
		28	2b [16]	Prokofieff	Violin Concerto No. 2	33	[32]
Debussy	Iberia	9	[5]	Rachmaninoff	Piano Concerto No. 1	72	[49]
		26	[17] 4f	Rachmaninoff	Symphony No. 2	141	3
Debussy	Rondes de Printemps	7	1	Rachmaninoff	The Bells	96	6b [100]
Dukas	La Péri	60	1	Ravel	Concerto pour Piano et Orchestre	44	[35]
Dukas	Symphonie en Ut majeur	160	[H] 2f	Ravel	La Valse	1	5
Dukelsky	Symphony No. 3	122	[52]	Rimsky-Korsakoff	Le Coq d'Or Suite	16	[9]
de Falla	Nuits dans les Jardins d'Espagne	19	4b [13]	Rivier	Chant Funèbre	5	[3]
de Falla	Three Dances from "The Three-Cornered Hat"	1	3	Schuman, W.	Symphony No. IV	2	19
				Scriabin	Le Divin Poème	275	1
				Sessions	Symphony No. II	61	[Nn]
Glazounov	Violin Concerto in A minor	18	4	Sibelius	En Saga	27	[G]
Harris	Third Symphony	4	1	Sibelius	Violin Concerto	82	4
		15	1	Sowerby	Concert Overture for Orchestra	28	[K]
		22	1				
Honegger	Chant de Joie	1	1	Strauss, R.	Suite from "Le Bourgeois Gentil-homme"	81	1
Honegger	Horace Victorieux	27	10				
Ives	A Set of Pieces	20	1				
Ives	Three Places in New England	2	2	Stravinsky	Concerto en Ré pour Orchestre à Cordes	25	[80]
Kodály	Marosszék Dances	56	4b [270]	Stravinsky	Concerto en Ré pour Violon et Orchestre	61	[123]
Kodály	Te Deum	38	2b [225]	Stravinsky	"Dumbarton Oaks" Concerto	20	[39]
Milhaud	Introduction et Marche Funèbre	4	[15] 4f	Stravinsky	Fire-Bird Suite (1919)	1	1
Milhaud	Ière Symphonie	28	1b [105]			67	2b [2]
		111	1b [165]	Stravinsky	Le Sacre du Printemps	7	[10]
Milhaud	IIe Symphonie	88	1b [70]			80	[90]
Pierné	Viennoise	3	[A]	Stravinsky	Symphony in C	70	[145]
		15	3	Walton	Concerto for Viola and Orchestra	8	4
Pizzetti	Concerto dell'Estate	19	4				
Prokofieff	Classical Symphony	36	1	Zimbalist	American Rhapsody	22	[16] 2f
		49	[41]				

342

PIZZICATI

Soli Bass divisi (pizz. and non-pizz.)

COMPOSER	WORK	PAGE	MEASURE
Diamond	*Timon of Athens*	**23**	147

Violin I and Viola pizz.—**Violin II and Viola** non-pizz.

Antheil	*Symphony No. 5*	**102**	[21]

Violin II and Viola pizz.—**Violin I** non-pizz.

COMPOSER	WORK	PAGE	MEASURE	COMPOSER	WORK	PAGE	MEASURE
Prokofieff	*Romeo and Juliet, Suite No. 2*	**62**	[50]	**Stravinsky**	*Fire-Bird Suite (1919)*	**6** **12**	[9] [14]

Violin II and Viola divisi (pizz. and non-pizz.)

Barraine	*Deuxième Symphonie*	**55**	5	**Copland**	*Appalachian Spring*	**6**	[7] 7f
Blancafort	*Mati de Festa a Puig-Gracios*	**I**	I	**Debussy**	*Jeux*	**13**	4b [10]

Violin II and Viola pizz.—**Violin I and Violoncello** non-pizz.

Copland	*Third Symphony*	**77**	1b [67]	**Kodály**	*Galanta Dances*	**21**	[181]

Violin I, II, and Viola pizz.—**Violin II and Viola** non-pizz.

Debussy	*Première Rhapsodie*	**18**	3

Violin I, II, and Viola divisi (pizz, and non-pizz.)

Bloch	*Trois Poèmes Juifs*	**37**	2	**Schönberg**	*Fünf Orchesterstücke*	**53**	[6]
Bruckner	*Symphony No. 4*	**87**	[140] 3f	**Schuman, W.**	*Symphony No. IV*	**8**	47
de Falla	*El Amor Brujo*	**9** **19**	[3] 3f 4	**Scriabin**	*Prométhée, Le Poème du Feu*	**74**	4b [56]
Liadov	*The Enchanted Lake*	**I**	I	**Tansman**	*Sonatine Trans-atlantique, III*	**5**	6
Rogers	*Once Upon a Time, Five Fairy Tales*	**20**	[14] 1f				

Violin I and Violoncello divisi (pizz. and non-pizz.)

Mahler	*Symphony No. 8*	**155**	[127]

Violin II and Violoncello pizz.—**Violin I and Viola** non-pizz.

Stravinsky	*Concerto in Ré pour Orchestre à Cordes*	**I**	I

Violin II and Violoncello pizz.—**Violin II and Viola** non-pizz.

Barber	*Medea*	**43**	1b [35]

STRINGS

Violin II and Violoncello pizz.—Viola and Violoncello non-pizz.

COMPOSER	WORK	PAGE	MEASURE
Bloch	*Trois Poèmes Juifs*	13	4b [6]

Violin II and Violoncello pizz.—Viola and Bass non-pizz.

Stravinsky	*Oedipus Rex*	101	[139]

Violin I, II, and Violoncello pizz.—Violin I, II, and Viola non-pizz.

Siegmeister	*Western Suite*	104	1

Violin I, II, and Violoncello pizz.—Violin II, Viola, and Violoncello non-pizz.

COMPOSER	WORK	PAGE	MEASURE	COMPOSER	WORK	PAGE	MEASURE
Copland	*Third Symphony*	98	[90]	Debussy	*La Damoiselle Élue*	11	[4] 2f

Violin I and Bass pizz.—Violin II and Violoncello non-pizz.

Debussy-Ansermet	*Six Épigraphes Antiques*	8	1	de Falla	*Nuits dans les Jardins d'Espagne*	3	1

Viola and Violoncello pizz.—Violin I and II non-pizz.

Gould	*Philharmonic Waltzes*	17	[172]

Viola and Violoncello divisi (pizz. and non-pizz.)

Fitelberg	*Nocturne for Orchestra*	21	[114] 1f	Prokofieff	*Piano Concerto No. 3*	128	[98]
Honegger	*Le Dit des Jeux du Monde*	34	4	Rogers	*Once Upon a Time, Five Fairy Tales*	5	[3]
Ives	*"Washington's Birthday" from Symphony, "Holidays"*	6	[H]	Schelling	*A Victory Ball*	5	1
				Schuman, W.	*Prayer in Time of War*	2	38
				Siegmeister	*Ozark Set*	58	1

Viola and Violoncello pizz.—Soli Viola and Violoncello non-pizz.

Milhaud	*Saudades do Brazil*	68	1

Viola and Bass pizz.—Violin I, II, and Violoncello non-pizz.

Bloch	*America*	139	[79]

Violoncello and Bass divisi (pizz. and non-pizz.)

Debussy	*Jeux*	103	[71]	Dukas	*La Péri*	5	[1]
Debussy	*Rondes de Printemps*	34	2	Fitelberg	*Symphony No. 1*	103	[218]
Diamond	*Fourth Symphony*	6	[30] 1f	Harris	*Third Symphony*	9	4

PIZZICATI

Violoncello and Bass divisi (pizz. and non-pizz.) (contd.)

COMPOSER	WORK	PAGE	MEASURE	COMPOSER	WORK	PAGE	MEASURE
Harris	When Johnny Comes			Rachmaninoff	Die Toteninsel	3	1
	Marching Home	29	[160] 3f	Rogers	Characters from Hans		
Ives	Three Places in New	7	[C]		Christian Andersen	25	2
	England	32	4	Rogers	Once Upon a Time,		
Kabalevsky	Suite from "Colas	7	1		Five Fairy Tales	48	[28]
	Breugnon"	31	4	Schuman, W.	Symphony for Strings	14	58
Kabalevsky	Symphony No. 2	14	2	Scriabin	Le Poème de l'Extase	32	[4]
		59	[50]	Strauss, R.	Till Eulenspiegel's		
		93	[20]		Merry Pranks	40	2b [29]
Khachaturian	Masquerade Suite	34	[7]	Stravinsky	Concerto en Ré pour		
Maganini	Tuolumne	2	2b [A]		Orchestre à Cordes	17	[58]
Mahler	Das Lied von der Erde	107	[18]	Stravinsky	Concerto en Ré pour		
Mahler	Symphony No. 5	5	[1] 2f		Violon et Orchestre	58	[119]
		30	[11]	Stravinsky	"Dumbarton Oaks"		
Mahler	Symphony No. 7	42	[35]		Concerto	22	2b [44]
Martinet	Orphée	87	[18]	Stravinsky	Scènes de Ballet	51	[82]
Miaskovsky	Sinfonietta for Strings	29	[26] 4f	Szymanowski	Symphonie Concertante		
Moeran	Sinfonietta	56	4b [74]		pour Piano et		
Prokofieff	Cinderella Suite No. 1	68	[52]		Orchestre	97	2b [30]
Prokofieff	Symphony No. 5	107	[61]	Walton	Concerto for Viola and		
		112	1		Orchestra	10	[9]
		130	[73]	Walton	Symphony	177	[132] 1f

Violin I, Viola, and Violoncello pizz.—Violin II, Viola, and Violoncello non-pizz.

COMPOSER	WORK	PAGE	MEASURE
Debussy	Jeux	11	[8]

Violin II, Viola, and Violoncello pizz.—Violin I non-pizz.

Gillis	Symphony No. 5½	52	[A]

Violin II, Viola, and Violoncello pizz.—Violin I, Viola, and Violoncello non-pizz.

Franck	Le Chasseur Maudit	91	408

Violin II, Viola, and Violoncello divisi (pizz. and non-pizz.)

Bruckner	Symphony No. 4	98	10b [A]	Franck	Le Chasseur Maudit	77	348

Violin I, II, Viola, and Violoncello divisi (pizz. and non-pizz.)

Chávez	Sinfonia India	34	[47]	Schuman, W.	Symphony for Strings	15	91
d'Indy	Deuxième Symphonie			Schuman, W.	Symphony No. III	38	330
	en Sib	12	6	Siegmeister	Sunday in Brooklyn	61	2
Saint-Saëns	Suite Algérienne	56	3	Stravinsky	Petrouchka Suite	58	1b [44]

Violin I, Violoncello, and Bass divisi (pizz. and non-pizz.)

Miaskovsky	Sinfonietta for Strings	2	4b [8]

345

STRINGS

Violin II, Violoncello, and Bass pizz.—**Violin I, Violoncello, and Bass** non-pizz.

COMPOSER	WORK	PAGE	MEASURE
Prokofieff	*Classical Symphony*	**40**	24

Violin I, II, Violoncello, and Bass pizz.—**Violin I, II, Viola, and Violoncello** non-pizz.

| **Delius** | *Three Orchestral Pieces* | **24** | 1b [2] |

Viola, Violoncello, and Bass divisi (pizz. and non-pizz.)

COMPOSER	WORK	PAGE	MEASURE	COMPOSER	WORK	PAGE	MEASURE
Siegmeister	*Sunday in Brooklyn*	**41**	1b [90]	**Tansman**	*Sonatine Trans-atlantique, I*	**13**	2
Stravinsky	*Concerto en Ré pour Violon et Orchestre*	**13**	[27]	**Tansman**	*Sonatine Trans-atlantique, II*	**1**	[9] 7f

Violin I, II, Viola, Violoncello, and Bass pizz.—**Solo Violin I, II, Viola, and Violoncello** non-pizz.

| **Britten** | *Sinfonia da Requiem* | **62** | [43] |

Violin I, II, Viola, Violoncello, and Bass divisi (pizz. and non-pizz.)

| **Schuman, W.** | *Symphony No. III* | **79** | 408 |

Tutti pizz.—**Solo Quintet** non-pizz.

| **Stravinsky** | *Orpheus* | **30** | [77] |

346

Chapter 51

TREMOLI

English	*Italian*	*French*	*German*
Tremolo	Tremolo	Trémolo	Tremolo
trem.	*trem.*	*trém.*	*Trem.*
Fast trem.	Trem. rapido	Trém. serré	Schnelles Trem.

(I) BOW

Violin I and II

COMPOSER	WORK	PAGE	MEASURE	COMPOSER	WORK	PAGE	MEASURE
Beethoven	*Piano Concerto No. 3*	89	168	**Mussorgsky**	*Night on the Bald*		
Bruckner	*Symphony No. 2*	89	9b [10]		*Mountain*	23	120
Dvořák	*Symphony No. 5,*			**Rimsky-**			
	"From the New			**Korsakoff**	*Le Coq d'Or Suite*	72	I
	World"	5	5	**Rimsky-**			
				Korsakoff	*Scheherazade*	99	416

Viola

COMPOSER	WORK	PAGE	MEASURE	COMPOSER	WORK	PAGE	MEASURE
Berlioz	*Symphonie Fantastique*	57	I	**Delius**	*Sea Drift*	30	9

Bass

COMPOSER	WORK	PAGE	MEASURE
Strauss, R.	*Death and Transfigura-*		
	tion	14	2b [D]

Violin I and Viola

COMPOSER	WORK	PAGE	MEASURE	COMPOSER	WORK	PAGE	MEASURE
Britten	*Passacaglia from "Peter*			**Hindemith**	*Mathis der Maler*	66	[17]
	Grimes"	21	9				

Violin II and Viola

COMPOSER	WORK	PAGE	MEASURE	COMPOSER	WORK	PAGE	MEASURE
Beethoven	*Egmont Overture*	32	287	**Dvořák**	*Symphony No. 5,*		
Beethoven	*Piano Concerto No. 3*	3	26		*"From the New*		
Beethoven	*Symphony No. 1*	26	277		*World"*	59	[2]
Borodin	*Symphony No. 2*	98	[C]	**Liszt**	*Piano Concerto No. 2*	41	3
Bruckner	*Symphony No. 4*	77	I	**Rimsky-**			
				Korsakoff	*Scheherazade*	245	607

STRINGS

Violin I, II, and Viola

COMPOSER	WORK	PAGE	MEASURE	COMPOSER	WORK	PAGE	MEASURE
Bartók	Concerto for Orchestra	1	6	Liadov	Eight Russian Popular	18	1
Beethoven	Symphony No. 3,				Songs	50	[9] 6f
	"Eroica"	168	431	Liadov	The Enchanted Lake	11	[6] 1f
Beethoven	Symphony No. 6,	11	175	Liszt	Piano Concerto No. 1	31	37
	"Pastoral"	98	107	Mussorgsky	Introduction to		
Berlioz	Symphonie Fantastique	113	1		"Khovantchina"	14	1
Bruckner	Symphony No. 5	110	[E]	Piston	First Symphony	59	95
Bizet	Prelude to "Carmen"	14	6	Ravel	Rapsodie Espagnole	3	[2] 5f
Debussy	La Damoiselle Élue	28	2	Shostakovich	Symphony No. 1	61	1
Debussy	Rondes de Printemps	1	1	Sibelius	Symphony No. 4	7	2
Dvořák	Symphony No. 5,			Sibelius	Symphony No. 5	6	1
	"From the New			Sibelius	The Swan of Tuonela	6	[D]
	World"	116	[3]	Wagner, R.	Rienzi Overture	43	262
Franck	Symphony in D minor	43	1	Weber	Der Freischütz Overture	3	30
Grieg	Piano Concerto in			Weber	Konzertstücke für		
	A minor	79	[K]		Klavier und		
Ibert	Escales	19	3		Orchester	7	7

Viola and Violoncello

Franck	Symphony in D minor	2	13	Wagner, R.	Prelude and Love Death		
					from "Tristan und		
					Isolde"	21	112

Violoncello and Bass

COMPOSER	WORK	PAGE	MEASURE
Beethoven	Symphony No. 6,		
	"Pastoral"	78	1

Violin I, Viola, and Violoncello

d'Indy	Istar, Variations		
	Symphoniques	3	[A]

Violin I, II, Viola, and Violoncello

COMPOSER	WORK	PAGE	MEASURE	COMPOSER	WORK	PAGE	MEASURE
Bartók	Concerto No. 3 for			Liszt	Eine Faust-Symphonie	6	2
	Piano and Orchestra	72	[500] 16f	Prokofieff	Suite from the Ballet		
Bartók	Music for Strings,				"Chout"	123	[157]
	Percussion and Celesta	8	78	Ravel	Rapsodie Espagnole	19	[9]
Bax	Fifth Symphony	141	[37]	Rimsky-			
Bax	The Garden of Fand	47	1	Korsakoff	Scheherazade	86	328
Brahms	Violin Concerto in			Rimsky-	Symphony No. 2,		
	D major	22	361	Korsakoff	"Antar"	10	4b [F]
Debussy	La Mer	2	1	Roussel	Évocations, III	93	[47]
		11	3	Schumann, R.	Symphony No. 1	135	117
		49	[25] 3f	Tchaikovsky	Francesca da Rimini	37	1
Debussy	Sirènes	74	[1]	Tchaikovsky	Symphony No. 6,		
		87	[5]		"Pathétique"	199	115
Grieg	Piano Concerto in			Wagner, R.	Eine Faust-Overture	39	311
	A minor	37	6b [A]				

348

TREMOLI

Violin II, Viola, and Bass

COMPOSER	WORK	PAGE	MEASURE
Franck	*Symphony in D minor*	**29**	229

Violin I, II, Viola, and Bass

Strauss, R.	*Ein Heldenleben*	**205**	1

Viola, Violoncello, and Bass

Stravinsky	*Scènes de Ballet*	**44**	[77]

Violin II, Viola, Violoncello, and Bass

de Falla	*El Amor Brujo*	**8**	2b [2]

Violin I, II, Viola, Violoncello, and Bass

COMPOSER	WORK	PAGE	MEASURE	COMPOSER	WORK	PAGE	MEASURE
Bartók	*Dance Suite*	**86**	94	d'Indy	*Istar, Variations Symphoniques*	**39**	2
Beethoven	*Symphony No. 3, "Eroica"*	**7**	75	Kabalevsky	*Suite from "Colas Breugnon"*	**123**	[4]
Beethoven	*Symphony No. 7*	**138**	[D]	Lalo	*Le Roi d'Ys Ouverture*	**9**	[C]
Beethoven	*Symphony No. 9*	**235**	650	Mahler	*Symphony No. 8*	**74**	[92]
Bizet	*L'Arlésienne Suite No. 1*	**21**	138	Mendelssohn	*Fingal's Cave Overture*	**46**	[I] 1f
Bloch	*America*	**103**	[60]	Mendelssohn	*Symphony No. 3, "Scotch"*	**17**	153
Bruckner	*Symphony No. 4*	**3**	1	Prokofieff	*Ala et Lolly (Scythian Suite)*	**12**	[4]
		147	[V]				
Bruckner	*Symphony No. 5*	**20**	5b [210]	Rachmaninoff	*2d Concerto pour Piano et Orchestre*	**40**	[13]
		47	5b [470]				
Bruckner	*Symphony No. 6*	**158**	367	Rimsky-Korsakoff	*Russian Easter Overture*	**12**	5
Bruckner	*Symphony No. 7*	**51**	[X]	Rimsky-Korsakoff	*Symphony No. 2, "Antar"*	**60**	[D]
Bruckner	*Symphony No. 8*	**46**	[360] 1f	Schumann, R.	*Symphony No. 1*	**127**	70
		219	[Ww]			**138**	149
Bruckner	*Symphony No. 9*	**155**	[A]	Scriabin	*Le Poème de l'Extase*	**51**	1
Debussy	*La Mer*	**18**	1	Shepherd	*Horizons*	**64**	3
Debussy	*Sirènes*	**104**	2	Sibelius	*The Bard*	**18**	4b [L]
Dvořák	*Concerto for Violoncello and Orchestra*	**103**	501	Sibelius	*The Tempest, Prelude*	**24**	[H]
				Sibelius	*Violin Concerto*	**37**	4
Dvořák	*Symphony No. 4*	**42**	[L]			**66**	1
Dvořák	*Symphony No. 5, "From the New World"*	**48**	[13]	Smetana	*Šárka*	**62**	5
		97	7	Strauss, R.	*Death and Transfiguration*	**85**	2
		138	3	Stravinsky	*Scènes de Ballet*	**79**	[127]
Dohnányi	*Variations on a Nursery Song*	**120**	6b [75]	Tchaikovsky	*Suite from the Ballet, "The Sleeping Beauty"*	**15**	1
Flotow	*Alessandro Stradella Overture*	**5**	36				
Franck	*Symphony in D minor*	**160**	5	Wagner, R.	*Prelude to Act III, "Lohengrin"*	**35**	112
Grofé	*Grand Canyon Suite*	**31**	[10]				
Haydn	*Symhony No. 1 in E♭ major, "Drumroll"*	**16**	10	Wagner, R.	*Rienzi Overture*	**14**	70
		31	11	Wagner, R.	*The Flying Dutchman Overture*	**17**	121
Haydn	*Symphony No. 11 in G major, "Military"*	**41**	161				
Haydn	*Symphony No. 13 in G major*	**24**	41	Weber	*Der Freischütz Overture*	**9**	91

STRINGS

(2) FINGER

Violin I

COMPOSER	WORK	PAGE	MEASURE	COMPOSER	WORK	PAGE	MEASURE
Debussy	La Mer	8	1	Loeffler	Evocation	29	2b [26]
Dvořák	Carnival Overture	30	13	Rimsky-			
d'Indy	Istar, Variations			Korsakoff	Le Coq d' Or Suite	6	[1] 2f
	Symphoniques	3	[A]	Wagner, R.	Bacchanale from	19	2
					"Tannhäuser"	51	3

Soli Violin I

COMPOSER	WORK	PAGE	MEASURE
Roussel	Évocations, III	55	[25]

Violin II

COMPOSER	WORK	PAGE	MEASURE	COMPOSER	WORK	PAGE	MEASURE
Beethoven	Piano Concerto No. 1	5	47	Liszt	Eine Faust-Symphonie	198	10
Dvořák	Slavonic Dances,			Mahler	Symphony No. 2	131	[4] 6f
	No. 1–4	19	117	Mozart	Piano Concerto in		
Dvořák	Symphony No. 4	70	[D]		D major, "Corona-		
Elgar	Symphony No. 1	98	[85]		tion"	24	216
Haydn	Violoncello Concerto	3	10	Prokofieff	Summer Day Suite	6	[1]
Honegger	Concertino pour Piano			Ravel	Rapsodie Espagnole	69	[19] 3f
	et Orchestre	17	[10]	Sibelius	Tapiola	42	427
Ibert	Escales	1	1	Wagner, R.	Bacchanale from		
d'Indy	Deuxième Symphonie				"Tannhäuser"	55	1
	en Sib	173	[82]	Walton	Concerto for Viola and	1	4
d'Indy	Symphony on a French				Orchestra	69	[61]
	Mountain Air	47	4				

Violin I and II

COMPOSER	WORK	PAGE	MEASURE	COMPOSER	WORK	PAGE	MEASURE
Bartók	Concerto for Orchestra	34	[87]	Dvořák	Violin Concerto in		
		43	[228]		A minor	15	106
		60	[63]	Gruenberg	The Enchanted Isle	72	[345] 1f
Bartók	Concerto No. 3 for			Mendelssohn	Fingal's Cave Overture	9	37
	Piano and Orchestra	34	[58]			22	96
Bartók	Music for Strings,			Mozart	Symphony No. 35 in		
	Percussion and Celesta	143	276		D major, "Haffner"	8	[C] 2f
Bartók	Second Rhapsody for			Mussorgsky	Night on the Bald		
	Violin and Orchestra	30	[14]		Mountain	2	5
Berlioz	Symphonie Fantastique	57	1	Ravel	Ma Mère l'Oye	24	[14]
Brahms	Tragic Overture	14	[E]	Sibelius	Violin Concerto	1	1
		51	3	Strauss, R.	Don Juan	95	2
Casella	Paganiniana	38	[20]	Stravinsky	"Dumbarton Oaks"		
Debussy	Sirènes	72	2		Concerto	20	[39]
Dvořák	Carnival Overture	25	1	Tchaikovsky	Manfred-Symphonie	14	1
Dvořák	Symphony No. 4	29	3	Vaughan	Symphony in D major		
Dvořák	Symphony No. 5,			Williams	(No. 5)	103	[9]
	"From the New			Wagner, R.	Tannhäuser Overture	15	84
	World"	146	6			33	196

350

TREMOLI

Viola

COMPOSER	WORK	PAGE	MEASURE	COMPOSER	WORK	PAGE	MEASURE
Bartók	Music for Strings, Percussion and Celesta	122	148	Ravel	Rapsodie Espagnole	47	[5]
Beethoven	Piano Concerto No. 5	5	17	Roussel	Le Festin de l'Araignée	60	[72]
Berlioz	Three Pieces from "The Damnation of Faust"	59	1	Roussel	Symphonie en Sol mineur	30	5
Dvořák	Symphony No. 2	36	[C]	Saint-Saëns	Omphale's Spinning Wheel	5	[B]
Dvořák	Symphony No. 4	7	3	Sibelius	Lemminkainen Journeys Homeward	4	1
Dvořák	Symphony No. 5, "From the New World"	5	4	Sibelius	Pelleas and Melisande	19	1
		14	2	Sibelius	Symphony No. 1	56	[F] 8f
de Falla	Nuits dans les Jardins d'Espagne	17	[10]	Sibelius	Symphony No. 4	14	1
Janáček	Sinfonietta	101	[9]	Sibelius	Symphony No. 7	45	6
Liadov	The Enchanted Lake	17	[9]	Strauss, R.	Don Quixote	78	1

Violoncello

COMPOSER	WORK	PAGE	MEASURE	COMPOSER	WORK	PAGE	MEASURE
Bloch	Schelomo	60	4b [35]	Scriabin	Le Poème de l'Extase	21	1
Debussy	La Mer	108	1	Strauss, R.	Also Sprach Zarathustra	165	1
Dvořák	Symphony No. 2	112	8				
Mussorgsky	Night on the Bald Mountain	6	26				

Bass

COMPOSER	WORK	PAGE	MEASURE	COMPOSER	WORK	PAGE	MEASURE
Bartók	Music for Strings, Percussion and Celesta	45	370	Flotow	Alessandro Stradella Overture	3	25
Debussy	Le Martyre de Saint Sébastien	62	1	Ravel	La Valse	1	1
				Sibelius	Karelia-Suite	24	[A]

Violin I and Viola

COMPOSER	WORK	PAGE	MEASURE	COMPOSER	WORK	PAGE	MEASURE
Bartók	Violin Concerto	104	[333]	Kodály	Psalmus Hungaricus	51	1
Bruckner	Symphony No. 2	116	[280]				

Violin II and Viola

COMPOSER	WORK	PAGE	MEASURE	COMPOSER	WORK	PAGE	MEASURE
Beethoven	Piano Concerto No. 4	2	20	Hill	Lilacs	31	[12]
Beethoven	Symphony No. 4	104	122	Mendelssohn	Fingal's Cave Overture	3	15
Bloch	America	2	1	Mendelssohn	Symphony No. 3, "Scotch"	38	355
Bruckner	Symphony No. 1	53	7b [110]				
Bruckner	Symphony No. 7	21	150	Mussorgsky-Ravel	Pictures at an Exhibition	112	[93]
Chausson	Symphonie en Si bémol majeur	7	1	Stravinsky	Feuerwerk	29	[30]
Dvořák	Concerto for Violoncello and Orchestra	5	45	Stravinsky	Fire-Bird Suite (1919)	71	[11]
				Stravinsky	Scènes de Ballet	72	[122]
Dvořák	Symphony No. 4	96	[A]	Stravinsky	Symphony in Three Movements	97	[163]
Dvořák	Symphony No. 5, "From the New World"	15	9				
		117	11	Wagner, R.	The Flying Dutchman Overture	32	211
de Falla	Three Dances from "The Three-Cornered Hat"	17	2				

STRINGS

Violin I, II, and Viola

COMPOSER	WORK	PAGE	MEASURE	COMPOSER	WORK	PAGE	MEASURE
Bax	In the Faery Hills	4	5	Liadov	Eight Russian Popular Songs	28	[5]
Bax	Third Symphony	42	[43] 1f	Liadov	The Enchanted Lake	26	[12]
Berlioz	Symphonie Fantastique	205	4	Loeffler	A Pagan Poem	19	2
Brahms	Symphony No. 1	102	[B] 1f	MacDowell	2nd Suite (Indian)	17	[H]
Brahms	Symphony No. 2	124	234	Moeran	Symphony in G minor	76	3
Chabrier	España, Rhapsodie	53	[M]	Ravel	Concerto pour la main gauche	95	2
Debussy	Prélude à l'après-midi d'un Faune	27	[10]	Ravel	Ma Mère l'Oye	52	[5]
Debussy	Rapsodie pour Orchestre et Saxophone	52	2	Respighi	The Pines of Rome	2	1
Dukas	L'Apprenti Sorcier	58	[49]	Schmitt	Mirages pour Orchestre, No. 1	33	3
de Falla	Nuits dans les Jardins d'Espagne	21	[15] 2f	Sibelius	En Saga	3	3
Franck	Les Éolides	40	1	Sibelius	Karelia-Suite	7	[F]
Fuleihan	Mediterranean	4	1	Sibelius	Symphony No. 6	17	[I]
Goossens	Sinfonietta	36	1	Sibelius	Violin Concerto	27	1
Kodály	Háry János Suite	42	[3]	Stravinsky	Scherzo Fantastique	11	[13]
				Tchaikovsky	Manfred-Symphonie	57	1

Violin II and Soli Viola

COMPOSER	WORK	PAGE	MEASURE
Read	Sketches of the City	17	[5] 2f

Violin II and Violoncello

COMPOSER	WORK	PAGE	MEASURE	COMPOSER	WORK	PAGE	MEASURE
Bartók	Concerto No. 3 for Piano and Orchestra	68	[452]	Ravel	Tzigane	18	[16]

Violin I, II, and Violoncello

COMPOSER	WORK	PAGE	MEASURE	COMPOSER	WORK	PAGE	MEASURE
Bartók	Concerto for Orchestra	8	[135]	Liszt	Piano Concerto No. 1	100	[O] 2f

Viola and Violoncello

COMPOSER	WORK	PAGE	MEASURE	COMPOSER	WORK	PAGE	MEASURE
Bartók	Violin Concerto	111	[408]	Dvořák	Symphony No.5, "From the New World"	100	1
Bax	Second Symphony	4	3	Elgar	Variations, "Enigma"	39	4b [26]
Beethoven	Symphony No. 6, "Pastoral"	3 / 20	37 / [G]	Fitelberg	Symphony No. 1	123	[371]
Bliss	Concerto for Piano and Orchestra	170	5	Hindemith	Kammermusik No. 4	40	[G] 2f
Bloch	Trois Poèmes Juifs	64	[3]	Respighi	The Birds	41	2
Dvořák	Carnival Overture	13	1	Stillman-Kelley	Gulliver—His Journey to Lilliput	7	[A]
Dvořák	Concerto for Violoncello and Orchestra	74	111	Tchaikovsky	Francesca da Rimini	18	1
				Wagner, R.	Magic Fire Music from "Die Walküre"	40	6

Violoncello and Bass

COMPOSER	WORK	PAGE	MEASURE	COMPOSER	WORK	PAGE	MEASURE
Hadyn	Symphony No. 1 in E♭ major, "Drumroll"	30	4	Sibelius	Lemminkainen Journeys Homeward	36	[I]
Ravel	Ma Mère l'Oye	36	[2] 4f	Vaughan Williams	Job, A Masque for Dancing	20	1
Sibelius	Finlandia	7	[D]				

TREMOLI

Violin I, Viola, and Violoncello

COMPOSER	WORK	PAGE	MEASURE
Mendelssohn	*Calm Sea and Prosperous Voyage, Overture*	22	169

Violin II, Viola, and Violoncello

COMPOSER	WORK	PAGE	MEASURE	COMPOSER	WORK	PAGE	MEASURE
Bartók	*Deux Images*	20	1	Rossini	*William Tell Overture*	25	149
Debussy	*La Mer*	33	3	Wagner, R.	*Forest Murmurs from "Siegfried"*	4	36
Hindemith	*Mathis der Maler*	65	3b [16]				
Inghelbrecht	*Rapsodie de Printemps*	18	1	Wagner, R.	*The Flying Dutchman Overture*	36	225
Mahler	*Symphony No. 6*	149	2				
Ravel	*Daphnis et Chloé, Suite No. 1*	11	[81]				

Violin I, II, Viola, and Violoncello

COMPOSER	WORK	PAGE	MEASURE	COMPOSER	WORK	PAGE	MEASURE
Beethoven	*Fidelio Overture*	3	23	Ravel	*Ma Mère l'Oye*	10	1
Britten	*Les Illuminations*	53	[10] 1f	Respighi	*Feste Romane*	96	[29] 3f
Britten	*The Young Person's Guide to the Orchestra*	34	9	Rimsky-Korsakoff	*Russian Easter Overture*	11	[D]
Debussy	*La Mer*	15	2	Sibelius	*Symphony No. 2*	26	[N] 6f
		97	1	Sibelius	*Symphony No. 4*	63	[O]
Debussy	*Sirènes*	96	1	Sibelius	*Violin Concerto*	52	[12] 4f
Dvořák	*Symphony No. 5, "From the New World"*	126	2			91	[5]
				Stravinsky	*Le Sacre du Printemps*	37	6
Ravel	*Daphnis et Chloé, Suite No. 1*	1	1	Thomson	*Louisiana Story Suite*	1	1
				Vaughan Williams	*The Lark Ascending*	15	8b [O]
Ravel	*Daphnis et Chloé, Suite No. 2*	65	[192]	Wagner, R.	*Forest Murmurs from "Siegfried"*	8	82
				Verdi	*Messa da Requiem*	208	43

Violin II, Viola, Violoncello, and Bass

COMPOSER	WORK	PAGE	MEASURE
Loeffler	*A Pagan Poem*	62	[Y] 2f

Violin I, II, Viola, Violoncello, and Bass

COMPOSER	WORK	PAGE	MEASURE	COMPOSER	WORK	PAGE	MEASURE
Bartók	*Music for Strings, Percussion and Celesta*	20	115	Vaughan Williams	*A London Symphony*	9	[D] 3f
Hanson	*"Merry Mount" Suite*	32	3	Verdi	*Messa da Requiem*	22	2

STRINGS

(3) BOW-FINGER (DÉTACHÉ TRILL OR INTERVAL)

English	Italian	French	German
Detached	Non-legato	Détaché	Gestossen

Violin I

COMPOSER	WORK	PAGE	MEASURE	COMPOSER	WORK	PAGE	MEASURE
Bartók	Concerto No. 3 for Piano and Orchestra	36	[72]	**Stravinsky**	Symphony in Three Movements	97	[163]
Fitelberg	Symphony No. 1	54	[31]	**Verdi**	Messa da Requiem	210	54

Violin II

COMPOSER	WORK	PAGE	MEASURE	COMPOSER	WORK	PAGE	MEASURE
Coppola	Suite Intima	48	3	**Mihalovici**	Divertissement pour Petit Orchestre	35	[N]
Dvořák	Serenade for Strings	23	6				
Haydn	Concerto in D major for Piano and Orchestra	1	7	**Mozart**	Clarinet Concerto in A major	2	16
		9	113			33	343
Haydn	Symphony No. 14 in D major	11	104	**Schreker**	The Birthday of the Infanta, Suite	61	[370] 2f
Kodály	Háry János Suite	10	[2]	**Schubert**	Symphony No. 2	10	80
Kodály	Psalmus Hungaricus	18	[11]	**Stravinsky**	Petrouchka Suite	8	[2]
		51	1			28	[19]
Mahler	Symphony No. 2	131	[4] 6f	**Wellesz**	Symphony in C	17	[115]

Violin I and II

COMPOSER	WORK	PAGE	MEASURE	COMPOSER	WORK	PAGE	MEASURE
Brahms	Symphony No. 2	143	397	**Schubert**	Symphony No. 2	41	441
Saint-Saëns	Suite Algérienne	9	2	**Whithorne**	Fata Morgana	29	1b [24]

Viola

COMPOSER	WORK	PAGE	MEASURE	COMPOSER	WORK	PAGE	MEASURE
Delannoy	Figures Sonores	68	[33]	**Holst**	Beni Mora, Oriental Suite	9	[4]
Dvořák	Symphony No. 5, "From the New World"	17	5	**Poulenc**	Concerto pour deux Pianos et Orchestre	39	[30]
Griffes	The Pleasure Dome of Kubla Khan	38	[N]			96	[60]

Violoncello

COMPOSER	WORK	PAGE	MEASURE	COMPOSER	WORK	PAGE	MEASURE
Dvořák	Serenade for Strings	24	8	**Stravinsky**	Petrouchka Suite	90	5

Solo Bass

COMPOSER	WORK	PAGE	MEASURE
Herrmann	Sinfonietta for String Orchestra	5	[H] 3f

TREMOLI

Violin I and Viola

COMPOSER	WORK	PAGE	MEASURE	COMPOSER	WORK	PAGE	MEASURE
Liszt	*Eine Faust-Symphonie*	54	[R]	Skilton	*Suite Primeval, Part II*	80	2
Sibelius	*Finlandia*	23	[N] 4f				

Violin II and Viola

COMPOSER	WORK	PAGE	MEASURE	COMPOSER	WORK	PAGE	MEASURE
Haydn	*Symphony No. 14 in D major*	8	71	Schumann, R.	*Concerto for Violoncello and Orchestra*	43	331
Mendelssohn	*Calm Sea and Prosperous Voyage, Overture*	32	275	Sibelius	*Symphony No. 7*	37	[N]
				Stravinsky	*Petrouchka Suite*	89	[76]

Violin I, II, and Viola

COMPOSER	WORK	PAGE	MEASURE	COMPOSER	WORK	PAGE	MEASURE
Bloch	*America*	149	4	Stravinsky	*Scènes de Ballet*	76	[124]
Fuleihan	*Mediterranean*	4	9	Verdi	*Messa da Requiem*	81	322
Liszt	*Tasso, Lamento e Trionfo*	46	340	Wagner, R.	*Entrance of the Gods into Valhalla from "Das Rheingold"*	31	[E]
Nystedt	*The Land of Suspense*	46	4				
Schubert	*Symphony No. 8, "Unfinished"*	19	[D] 2f	Wagner, R.	*Forest Murmurs from "Siegfried"*	16	120
Shostakovich	*Symphony No. 3*	14	[16]	Wagner, R.	*Ride of the Valkyries from "Die Walküre"*	22	47
Stravinsky	*Petrouchka Suite*	75	[60]			36	84

Viola and Violoncello

COMPOSER	WORK	PAGE	MEASURE
Fitelberg	*Symphony No. 1*	57	[40]

Violoncello and Bass

COMPOSER	WORK	PAGE	MEASURE
Gould	*Spirituals*	40	[L]

Violin I, Viola, and Violoncello

COMPOSER	WORK	PAGE	MEASURE
Strauss, R.	*Dance Suite after François Couperin*	86	4

Violin I, II, Viola, and Violoncello

COMPOSER	WORK	PAGE	MEASURE	COMPOSER	WORK	PAGE	MEASURE
Britten	*Sinfonia da Requiem*	30	[21]	Sibelius	*Symphony No. 5*	14	[G]
		49	[33]			17	1
Griffes	*The Pleasure Dome of Kubla Khan*	48	[S]	Stravinsky	*Concerto en Ré pour Orchestre à Cordes*	32	[98] 2f
Lopatnikoff	*Sinfonietta*	43	[180] 1f	Stravinsky	*Petrouchka Suite*	64	[51]
Respighi	*The Fountains of Rome*	12	4	Tchaikovsky	*Symphony No. 3*	123	[R] 4f
Respighi	*Vetrate di Chiesa*	58	2	Vaughan Williams	*Overture to "The Wasps"*	43	2
Shostakovich	*Symphony No. 7*	54	[49]				
Sibelius	*Karelia–Suite*	1	1	Verdi	*Messa da Requiem*	249	175
		10	4				

355

STRINGS

Viola, Violoncello, and Bass

COMPOSER	WORK	PAGE	MEASURE
Holst	The Ballet from "The Perfect Fool"	25	[22] 1f

Violin II, Viola, Violoncello, and Bass

COMPOSER	WORK	PAGE	MEASURE
Milhaud	Concerto pour Piano et Orchestre	46	[65] 3f

(4) GLISSANDO

Violin I

COMPOSER	WORK	PAGE	MEASURE	COMPOSER	WORK	PAGE	MEASURE
Debussy	Jeux	78	2b [52]	Mahler	Das Lied von der Erde	95	1b [14]
Debussy	Rondes de Printemps	6	[3]	Rogers	Characters from Hans Christian Andersen	15	4
Jolivet	Andante pour Orchestre à Cordes	9	[40]				

Solo Violin

COMPOSER	WORK	PAGE	MEASURE
Stravinsky	Histoire du Soldat	55	10

Violin I and II

COMPOSER	WORK	PAGE	MEASURE	COMPOSER	WORK	PAGE	MEASURE
Britten	The Young Person's Guide to the Orchestra	19	8	Cras	Journal de Bord	56	4
				Debussy	Jeux	115	[80]

Violin II and Viola

COMPOSER	WORK	PAGE	MEASURE	COMPOSER	WORK	PAGE	MEASURE
Debussy	Gigues	31	[18] 1f	Inghelbrecht	Sinfonia Breve No. 1	6	[4] 2f

Violin I, II, and Viola

COMPOSER	WORK	PAGE	MEASURE	COMPOSER	WORK	PAGE	MEASURE
Inghelbrecht	Sinfonia Breve No. 1	12	5	Read	Sketches of the City	35	5

Violoncello

COMPOSER	WORK	PAGE	MEASURE	COMPOSER	WORK	PAGE	MEASURE
Debussy	Première Rhapsodie	39	3	Debussy	Rondes de Printemps	31	[17] 3f

Bass

COMPOSER	WORK	PAGE	MEASURE	COMPOSER	WORK	PAGE	MEASURE
Janssen	New Year's Eve in New York	31	[12]	Moross	Paeans	5	4b [E]

TREMOLI

Violoncello and Bass

COMPOSER	WORK	PAGE	MEASURE
Debussy	*Le Martyre de Saint Sébastien*	**29**	[12]

Violin II, Viola, and Violoncello

Bartók	*Violin Concerto*	**5**	[36]

Violin I, II, Viola, and Violoncello

COMPOSER	WORK	PAGE	MEASURE	COMPOSER	WORK	PAGE	MEASURE
Debussy–Ansermet	*Six Épigraphes Antiques*	**65**	3	**Read**	*Sketches of the City*	**21**	2
Harris	*When Johnny Comes Marching Home*	**26**	1			**26**	1b [4]

(5) MEASURED

English	Italian	French	German
Non tremolo	Non-tremolo	Non-trémolo	Nicht tremolierend
non trem.	non-trem.	non-trém.	nicht trem.
	Tremolo misurato	Trémolo très régulier	

Violin I

Mussorgsky	*Night on the Bald Mountain*	6	26	**Prokofieff**	*Lieutenant Kijé*	**15**	[17]

Violin II

Honegger	*Le Chant de Nigamon*	8	4	**Strauss, R.**	*Don Quixote*	**21**	1
Shostakovich	*Symphony No. 1*	34	[6]				

Violin I and II

Antheil	*Over the Plains*	25	[14]	**Haydn**	*Symphony No. 7 in C major, "Le Midi"*	47	76
Beethoven	*Egmont Overture*	42	331	**Mahler**	*Symphony No. 8*	105	[56]
Beethoven	*Symphony No. 2*	9	34	**Mendelssohn**	*A Midsummer Night's Dream Overture*	32	334
Beethoven	*Symphony No. 4*	64	101				
Beethoven	*Symphony No. 6, "Pastoral"*	108	26	**Ravel**	*Concerto pour la main gauche*	62	[34] 1f
		127	133				
Bizet	*Symphony No. 1*	50	[1]	**Schubert**	*Symphony No. 8, "Unfinished"*	1	9
Cimarosa	*Overture to "The Secret Marriage"*	29	1	**Sibelius**	*Rakastava*	6	1
Cras	*Âmes d'Enfants*	8	1b [4]	**Turner**	*Gregorian Overture for String Orchestra*	14	173
Franck	*Symphony in D minor*	19	145				
Grieg	*Piano Concerto in A minor*	16	89				

STRINGS

Viola

COMPOSER	WORK	PAGE	MEASURE	COMPOSER	WORK	PAGE	MEASURE
Beethoven	*Leonore Overture No. 3*	6	37	d'Indy	*Istar, Variations Symphoniques*	46	[V]
Beethoven	*Symphony No. 9*	17	125	d'Indy	*Symphony on a French*		
Berlioz	*The Roman Carnival*				*Mountain Air*	55	[I] 3f
	Overture	3	28	Sibelius	*Violin Concerto*	7	[2]
Bloch	*Schelomo*	32	1	Stravinsky	*Concerto en Ré pour*		
Bruckner	*Symphony No. 3*	5	1		*Orchestre à Cordes*	22	[70]
		58	[X]				

Violin I and Viola

COMPOSER	WORK	PAGE	MEASURE	COMPOSER	WORK	PAGE	MEASURE
Albéniz– Arbós	*Triana*	19	2	Milhaud	*Sérénade pour Orchestre*	10	1
Elgar	*Concerto for Violoncello*			Prokofieff	*Romeo and Juliet, Suite No. 2*	71	[46]
	and Orchestra	40	2	Scriabin	*Le Poème de l'Extase*	5	4

Violin II and Viola

COMPOSER	WORK	PAGE	MEASURE	COMPOSER	WORK	PAGE	MEASURE
Beethoven	*Egmont Overture*	3	15	Haydn	*Symphony No. 2 in*		
Beethoven	*Symphony No. 3, "Eroica"*	1	3		*D major, "London"*	4	6
Beethoven	*Symphony No. 5*	130	390	d'Indy	*Deuxième Symphonie en Si♭*	4	1
Beethoven	*Symphony No. 7*	146	[G] 1f	Lekeu	*Fantaisie sur Deux Airs*		
Beethoven	*Symphony No. 8*	3	13		*Populaires Angevins*	21	[H]
Beethoven	*Symphony No. 9*	156	[C]	Mozart	*Symphony No. 41 in*		
Beethoven	*Violin Concerto in*				*C major, "Jupiter"*	33	23
	D major	17	248	Mozart	*Titus Overture*	24	2
Bruch	*Violin Concerto in*			Mozart	*Violin Concerto No. V*		
	G minor	68	1		*in A major*	1	1
Cadman	*Dark Dancers of the*			Mussorgsky–			
	Mardi Gras	40	3	Ravel	*Pictures at an Exhibition*	75	2
Dvořák	*Concerto for Violoncello*			Prokofieff	*Romeo and Juliet, Suite*		
	and Orchestra	92	333		*No. 2*	60	[39]
Dvořák	*Symphony No. 2*	19	[F] 2f	Rimsky–			
Dvořák	*Symphony No. 4*	81	[H]	Korsakoff	*Russian Easter Overture*	14	2
Dvořák	*Violin Concerto in*			Schubert	*Symphony No. 5*	2	5
	A minor	43	41	Shostakovich	*Piano Concerto*	35	[45]
Franck	*Le Chasseur Maudit*	60	277	Sibelius	*Symphony No. 5*	99	6

Violin I, II, and Viola

COMPOSER	WORK	PAGE	MEASURE	COMPOSER	WORK	PAGE	MEASURE
Beethoven	*Leonore Overture No. 2*	44	348	Bizet	*Symphony No. 1*	8	[4]
Beethoven	*Leonore Overture No. 3*	59	594	Brahms	*Ein deutsches Requiem*	75	287
Beethoven	*Piano Concerto No. 3*	25	257	Brahms	*Symphony No. 1*	25	[F]
Beethoven	*Symphony No. 3, "Eroica"*	84	160	Brahms	*Symphony No. 2*	124	234
Beethoven	*Symphony No. 8*	100	260	Brahms	*Tragic Overture*	9	[C]
Berlioz	*Three Pieces from "The*					28	[K] 1f
	Damnation of Faust"	16	5	Bruch	*Violin Concerto in*		
					G minor	45	[H]

TREMOLI

Violin I, II, and Viola (contd.)

COMPOSER	WORK	PAGE	MEASURE	COMPOSER	WORK	PAGE	MEASURE
Bruckner	*Symphony No. 1*	3	1	Liszt	*Tasso, Lamento e*		
Bruckner	*Symphony No. 2*	152	2		*Trionfo*	70	487
Carse	*A Romantic Legend*	1	6	Rossini	*L'Italiani in Algeri,*		
Debussy	*Jeux*	21	4		*Overture*	41	2
Debussy	*Première Rhapsodie*	42	[11]	Rossini	*Semiramide, Overture*	26	147
Gold	*Allegorical Overture*	40	2	Shostakovich	*Symphony No. 1*	46	1
Grieg	*Peer Gynt Suite No. 1*	30	[B]	Tchaikovsky	*Symphony No. 2*	157	[Q]
Kabalevsky	*Suite from "Colas*			Verdi	*Messa da Requiem*	167	177
	Breugnon"	136	[7]	Wagner, R.	*Prelude to Act III,*		
					"Lohengrin"	18	16

Violin II and Violoncello

COMPOSER	WORK	PAGE	MEASURE
Beethoven	*Symphony No. 9*	1	1

Viola and Violoncello

COMPOSER	WORK	PAGE	MEASURE	COMPOSER	WORK	PAGE	MEASURE
Dvořák	*Symphony No. 5, "From the New World"*	91	[5] 8f	Honegger	*Symphonie pour Cordes*	24	[5]
				Ives	*Third Symphony*	28	1
				Milhaud	*Saudades do Brazil*	66	12

Viola and Bass

COMPOSER	WORK	PAGE	MEASURE
Gluck	*Overture to "Alceste"*	2	12

Violoncello and Bass

COMPOSER	WORK	PAGE	MEASURE	COMPOSER	WORK	PAGE	MEASURE
Beethoven	*Symphonie No. 1*	54	108	Borodin	*Symphony No. 2*	48	[O]
Berlioz	*Symphonie Fantastique*	15	1	Dvořák	*Symphony No. 2*	79	1
Bizet	*L'Arlésienne Suite No. 2*	56	174	Rimsky-Korsakoff	*Symphony No. 2, "Antar"*	78	[K]

Violin II, Viola, and Violoncello

COMPOSER	WORK	PAGE	MEASURE
d'Indy	*Deuxième Symphonie en Si♭*	106	1

Violin I, II, Viola, and Violoncello

COMPOSER	WORK	PAGE	MEASURE	COMPOSER	WORK	PAGE	MEASURE
Becker	*Concerto for Horn and Orchestra*	3	9	Kay	*Suite for Orchestra*	54	[57]
Beethoven	*Fidelio Overture*	3	23	Liszt	*Les Préludes*	26	119
Beethoven	*Leonore Overture No. 3*	34	330	Mussorgsky-Ravel	*Pictures at an Exhibition*	87	[71]
Berlioz	*Symphonie Fantastique*	21	2	Piston	*Concerto for Orchestra*	22	3
Brahms	*Symphony No. 4*	144	137	Riegger	*Symphony No. 3*	58	3
Flotow	*Alessandro Stradella Overture*	10	90	Schmitt	*Étude pour le "Palais Hanté" d'Edgar Poe*	11	[5]
Franck	*Symphony in D minor*	106	1	Tchaikovsky	*Symphony No. 2*	12	1

STRINGS

Viola, Violoncello, and Bass

COMPOSER	WORK	PAGE	MEASURE	COMPOSER	WORK	PAGE	MEASURE
Bartók	*Dance Suite*	70	3	Rossini	*L'Italiani in Algeri,*		
Beethoven	*Symphony No. 1*	12	98		*Overture*	10	2
Haydn	*Symphony No. 6 in*			Smetana	*Overture to "The*		
	G major, "Surprise"	55	[R]		*Bartered Bride"*	41	398
Haydn	*Symphony No. 15 in*	5	43	Stillman-	*New England*		
	B♭ major, "La Reine"	10	115	Kelley	*Symphony*	7	9
		17	231				

Violin II, Viola, Violoncello, and Bass

COMPOSER	WORK	PAGE	MEASURE	COMPOSER	WORK	PAGE	MEASURE
Beethoven	*Symphony No. 2*	2	12	Haydn	*Symphony No. 11 in*		
		82	119		*G major, "Military"*	70	280
Haydn	*Symphony No. 3 in*			Schubert	*Symphony No. 4*	66	5
	E♭ major	32	47	Schubert	*Symphony No. 6*	12	89
Haydn	*Symphony No. 4 in*			Sibelius	*En Saga*	18	5
	D major, "Clock"	12	[D]				

Violin I, II, Viola, Violoncello, and Bass

COMPOSER	WORK	PAGE	MEASURE	COMPOSER	WORK	PAGE	MEASURE
Bartók	*Concerto for Orchestra*	14	[258]	Moeran	*Symphony in G minor*	47	6b [24]
Bartók	*Music for Strings,*			Piston	*Concertino for Pianoforte*		
	Percussion and Celesta	56	449		*and Chamber Orchestra*	64	[442]
Beethoven	*Piano Concerto No. 3*	2	24	Rachmaninoff	*2d Concerto pour Piano*		
Beethoven	*Symphony No. 3,*				*et Orchestre*	108	1
	"Eroica"	7	75	Rimsky-			
Beethoven	*Symphony No. 4*	26	[G]	Korsakoff	*Russian Easter Overture*	38	1
Beethoven	*Violin Concerto in*			Rossini	*The Thieving Magpie,*		
	D major	8	[C]		*Overture*	62	1
Berlioz	*Benvenuto Cellini*			Schubert	*Symphony No. 4*	37	272
	Overture	19	4			90	223
Grieg	*Piano Concerto in*			Schubert	*Symphony No. 6*	32	357
	A minor	54	99			46	109
Haydn	*Symphony No. 1 in*	42	14	Sibelius	*Symphony No. 1*	12	3b [G]
	E♭ major, "Drumroll"	52	9	Stillman-	*New England*		
Hindemith	*Kammermusik No. 1*	69	1	Kelley	*Symphony*	148	3
Liszt	*Eine Faust-Symphonie*	287	1	Vaughan	*Symphony in D major*		
Mendelssohn	*A Midsummer Night's*			Williams	*(No. 5)*	18	1
	Dream Overture	34	358	Verdi	*Overture to "La Forza*		
Mendelssohn	*Ruy Blas Overture*	20	4b [D]		*del Destino"*	31	200
Mendelssohn	*Symphony No. 3,*						
	"Scotch"	115	[B]				

TREMOLI

(6) ON HARMONICS

English	Italian	French	German
Trem. on harmonics	Trem. sull'armonici	Trém. sur les sons harmoniques	Trem. auf Flageolett

Violin I

COMPOSER	WORK	PAGE	MEASURE	COMPOSER	WORK	PAGE	MEASURE
Bloch	Schelomo	32	2	Khachaturian	Gayne Ballet Suite		
Britten	The Young Person's				No. 2	42	[4]
	Guide to the Orchestra	49	5	Miaskovsky	Symphony No. 8	60	1b [60]
Debussy	Gigues	12	1b [7]	Roussel	Évocations, III	57	6b [27]
Debussy–	Six Épigraphes			Roussel	Pour une Fête de		
Ansermet	Antiques	22	1		Printemps	20	1
Dukas	La Péri	14	1	Saminsky	Litanies des Femmes	3	1
		90	1	Scarlatti–	Toccata, Bourrée et	23	[13]
Ibert	La Ballade de la Geôle			Casella	Gigue	29	[24]
	de Reading	62	[44] 5f	Stravinsky	Le Sacre du Printemps	24	[33]

Soli Violin I

COMPOSER	WORK	PAGE	MEASURE	COMPOSER	WORK	PAGE	MEASURE
Casella	Paganiniana	100	[7] 1f	de Falla	El Retablo de Maese		
Dukas	La Péri	39	[6]		Pedro	61	[66] 3f
		77	1	Rogers	Elegy	6	[5]

Violin II

COMPOSER	WORK	PAGE	MEASURE	COMPOSER	WORK	PAGE	MEASURE
Casella	Paganiniana	19	[10]	Roussel	Le Festin de l'Araignée	60	[72]
Rogers	Once Upon a Time,						
	Five Fairy Tales	61	[36]				

Violin I and II

COMPOSER	WORK	PAGE	MEASURE	COMPOSER	WORK	PAGE	MEASURE
Bloch	Hiver–Printemps	24	3b [2]	Siegmeister	From my Window	38	2b [15]
Mahler	Symphony No. 6	81	1b [49]	Siegmeister	Sunday in Brooklyn	70	1b [45]
Miaskovsky	Symphony No. 6	117	2b [74]	Villa-Lobos	Amazonas	2	3
Schreker	The Birthday of the						
	Infanta, Suite	40	[215]				

Viola

COMPOSER	WORK	PAGE	MEASURE	COMPOSER	WORK	PAGE	MEASURE
Bloch	America	2	1	Strauss, R.	Eine Alpensinfonie	80	5b [74]
		150	[84]	Stravinsky	Chant du Rossignol	43	1b [44]
Mahler	Symphony No. 9	50	6	Stravinsky	Orpheus	16	[39]
Parodi	Preludio ad una			Stravinsky	Petrouchka Suite	153	[129]
	Commedia	14	[G]	Walton	Concerto for Violin and		
Poulenc	Concert Champêtre				Orchestra	43	[22] 1f
	pour Clavecin et						
	Orchestre	121	[40] 1f				

STRINGS

Violoncello

COMPOSER	WORK	PAGE	MEASURE	COMPOSER	WORK	PAGE	MEASURE
Debussy	*Jeux*	**77**	[51] 2f	**Honegger**	*Pacific 231*	**1**	1
Debussy	*Le Martyre de Saint*			**Sibelius**	*Symphony No. 7*	**45**	4
	Sébastien	**12**	1	**Stravinsky**	*Fire-Bird Suite* (1919)	**70**	[9] 1f

Soli Violoncello

COMPOSER	WORK	PAGE	MEASURE
Rogers	*Characters from Hans Christian Andersen*	**9**	[5]

Bass

COMPOSER	WORK	PAGE	MEASURE	COMPOSER	WORK	PAGE	MEASURE
Bartók	*Deux Portraits*	**34**	[11] 1f	**Prokofieff**	*Lieutenant Kijé*	**13**	[14]
Debussy	*Le Martyre de Saint*					**100**	[73]
	Sébastien	**15**	[6]				

Violin I, II, and Viola

COMPOSER	WORK	PAGE	MEASURE	COMPOSER	WORK	PAGE	MEASURE
Goossens	*Sinfonietta*	**54**	2	**Siegmeister**	*Ozark Set*	**80**	[80]
Read	*Sketches of the City*	**4**	[1] 3f	**Stravinsky**	*Le Sacre du Printemps*	**84**	[101]

Violin I and Violoncello

COMPOSER	WORK	PAGE	MEASURE	COMPOSER	WORK	PAGE	MEASURE
Stravinsky	*Fire-Bird Suite* (1919)	**23**	[14] 7f	**Stravinsky**	*Le Sacre du Printemps*	**74**	[82] 1f
						83	[100]

Violin I and Bass

COMPOSER	WORK	PAGE	MEASURE
Bartók	*Deux Images*	**20**	1

Viola and Violoncello

COMPOSER	WORK	PAGE	MEASURE	COMPOSER	WORK	PAGE	MEASURE
Bax	*First Symphony*	**69**	1	**Ferroud**	*Au Parc Monceau*	**37**	2
Debussy	*Le Martyre de Saint*						
	Sébastien	**61**	[27]				

Soli Viola and Violoncello

COMPOSER	WORK	PAGE	MEASURE
Casella	*Paganiniana*	**110**	[13]

Violoncello and Bass

COMPOSER	WORK	PAGE	MEASURE	COMPOSER	WORK	PAGE	MEASURE
Miaskovsky	*Symphony No. 8*	**124**	[23]	**Parodi**	*Preludio ad una Commedia*	**36**	[R]
Mussorgsky–Ravel	*Pictures at an Exhibition*	**95**	[77] 1f	**Stravinsky**	*Chant du Rossignol*	**41**	[42] 3f
				Stravinsky	*Fire-Bird Suite* (1919)	**71**	[11]

TREMOLI

Violin II, Viola, and Solo Violoncello

COMPOSER	WORK	PAGE	MEASURE
Rogers	*Once Upon a Time,* *Five Fairy Tales*	21	5

Violin I, II, Viola, and Violoncello

COMPOSER	WORK	PAGE	MEASURE	COMPOSER	WORK	PAGE	MEASURE
Borodin	*Symphony No.* 1	18	[H]	Villa-Lobos	*Amazonas*	9	[3]
Honegger	*Pacific* 231	2	8			12	[4]
Parodi	*Preludio ad una* *Commedia*	60	2				

Violin I, II, Viola, Violoncello, and Bass

Sibelius	*Pelleas and Melisande*	9	[A]

(7) BOW AND FINGER COMBINED

Violin I Bow—Violin II Finger

COMPOSER	WORK	PAGE	MEASURE	COMPOSER	WORK	PAGE	MEASURE
Bloch	*America*	17	2b [9]	Kodály	*Háry János Suite*	10	[2]

Violin I Bow—Violin II and Viola Finger

Bloch	*America*	24	3

Violin II Bow—Violin I Finger

COMPOSER	WORK	PAGE	MEASURE	COMPOSER	WORK	PAGE	MEASURE
Barber	*Music for a Scene from* *Shelley*	10	59	Szymanowski	*Symphonie Concertante* *pour Piano et* *Orchestre*	48	1
Bloch	*America*	165	[96]				
Bloch	*Schelomo*	68	[43]				

Violin II divisi (Bow and Finger)

COMPOSER	WORK	PAGE	MEASURE	COMPOSER	WORK	PAGE	MEASURE
Delius	*Brigg Fair*	140	5	Rogers	*Characters from Hans* *Christian Andersen*	16	2b [9]

Violin II Bow—Viola Finger

COMPOSER	WORK	PAGE	MEASURE	COMPOSER	WORK	PAGE	MEASURE
Bloch	*Schelomo*	21	[9]	Kodály	*Psalmus Hungaricus*	7	[4]
Hanson	*Symphonie No.* 1, *"Nordic"*	38	4			35	[22]

STRINGS

Violin I and II divisi (Bow and Finger)

COMPOSER	WORK	PAGE	MEASURE
Ravel	*La Valse*	**3**	1

Viola Bow—Violin II Finger

COMPOSER	WORK	PAGE	MEASURE	COMPOSER	WORK	PAGE	MEASURE
Bloch	*Hiver–Printemps*	**9**	[3] 2f	**Mahler**	*Symphony No. 2*	**131**	[4] 6f
Debussy	*La Mer*	**16**	[8]	**Stravinsky**	*Fire-Bird Suite* (1919)	**3**	[3]
Dvořák	*Violin Concerto in A minor*	**15**	106	**Strauss, R.**	*Also Sprach Zarathustra*	**66**	3

Viola Bow—Violin I and II Finger

COMPOSER	WORK	PAGE	MEASURE
Delius	*Brigg Fair*	**32**	[28] 1f

Viola divisi (Bow and Finger)

COMPOSER	WORK	PAGE	MEASURE	COMPOSER	WORK	PAGE	MEASURE
Scriabin	*Prométhée, Le Poème du Feu*	**11**	[5]	**Stravinsky**	*Chant du Rossignol*	**14** **51**	[11] [53]

Violoncello Bow—Viola Finger

COMPOSER	WORK	PAGE	MEASURE
Debussy	*Rapsodie pour Orchestre et Saxophone*	**53**	1

Violin I and Viola divisi (Bow and Finger)

COMPOSER	WORK	PAGE	MEASURE
Strauss, R.	*Ein Heldenleben*	**60**	[32]

Violin II and Viola Bow—Violin I and Viola Finger

COMPOSER	WORK	PAGE	MEASURE
Honegger	*Le Roi David*	**87**	[3] 2f

Violin II and Viola divisi (Bow and Finger)

COMPOSER	WORK	PAGE	MEASURE
Strauss, R.	*Ein Heldenleben*	**70**	[35]

Violin I, Viola, and Violoncello divisi (Bow and Finger)

COMPOSER	WORK	PAGE	MEASURE
Stravinsky	*Fire-Bird Suite* (1919)	**5**	[6]

TREMOLI

(8) TREMOLO AND NON-TREMOLO COMBINED

Violin I divisi (trem. and non-trem.)

COMPOSER	WORK	PAGE	MEASURE	COMPOSER	WORK	PAGE	MEASURE
Bloch	*Trois Poèmes Juifs*	64	[3]	Stillman-	*Gulliver—His Voyage*		
Mahler	*Symphony No. 3*	226	4b [27]	Kelley	*to Lilliput*	86	1
Mahler	*Symphony No. 8*	161	[142]	Strauss, R.	*Eine Alpensinfonie*	12	7
Prokofieff	*Alexander Nevsky*	130	[73]	Thomson	*The Seine at Night*	13	2b [8]

Violin I trem.—Soli Violin I non-trem.

COMPOSER	WORK	PAGE	MEASURE
Bloch	*America*	17	2b [9]

Violin I trem.—Violin II non-trem.

COMPOSER	WORK	PAGE	MEASURE	COMPOSER	WORK	PAGE	MEASURE
Dvořák	*Symphony No. 2*	133	6	Stravinsky	*"Dumbarton Oaks"*		
Mahler	*Symphony No. 8*	28	[29]		*Concerto*	22	[43] 3f

Violin I trem.—Violoncello non-trem.

COMPOSER	WORK	PAGE	MEASURE
Bloch	*Concerto Grosso*	11	[14] 5f

Violin II trem.—Violin I non-trem.

COMPOSER	WORK	PAGE	MEASURE	COMPOSER	WORK	PAGE	MEASURE
Bartók	*Concerto for Orchestra*	99	[175]	Schönberg	*Kammersymphonie,*		
Bloch	*Schelomo*	34	[16]		*Op. 9*	119	2
Brahms	*Concerto for Violin and*			Sibelius	*The Swan of Tuonela*	6	5b [D]
	Violoncello	13	103	Strauss, R.	*Eine Alpensinfonie*	134	120
Debussy	*Le Martyre de Saint*			Szymanowski	*Symphonie Concertante*		
	Sébastien	29	[12]		*pour Piano et*		
Honegger	*Prélude pour "La*				*Orchestre*	25	1
	Tempête"	27	[9]	Wagner, R.	*Prelude and Love Death*		
Mahler	*Symphony No. 6*	45	3		*from "Tristan und*		
Read	*Symphony No. I*	11	1		*Isolde"*	38	44
		44	2	Wellesz	*Symphony in C*	69	2b [135]
Rogers	*Once Upon a Time,*						
	Five Fairy Tales	47	2				

Violin II trem.—Soli Violin I non-trem.

COMPOSER	WORK	PAGE	MEASURE
Szymanowski	*Symphonie Concertante pour Piano et Orchestre*	13	[7] 2f

365

STRINGS

Violin II divisi (trem. and non-trem.)

COMPOSER	WORK	PAGE	MEASURE	COMPOSER	WORK	PAGE	MEASURE
de Falla	*Three Dances from "The Three-Cornered Hat"*	64	3	Scriabin	*Prométhée, Le Poème du Feu*	11	[5]
				Thomson	*The Seine at Night*	19	2

Violin II trem.—Viola non-trem.

COMPOSER	WORK	PAGE	MEASURE	COMPOSER	WORK	PAGE	MEASURE
Debussy	*Jeux*	99	[68] 1f	Rachmaninoff	*Piano Concerto No. 3*	88	[49] 1f
Haydn	*Symphony No. 15 in Bb major, "La Reine"*	31	[B] 2f				

Violin II trem.—Violin I and Violoncello non-trem.

COMPOSER	WORK	PAGE	MEASURE
Balakirev–Casella	*Islamey*	15	[11]

Violin I and II divisi (trem. and non-trem.)

COMPOSER	WORK	PAGE	MEASURE	COMPOSER	WORK	PAGE	MEASURE
de Falla	*Nuits dans les Jardins d'Espagne*	32	2	Honegger	*Le Dit des Jeux du Monde*	83	[3]
Honegger	*Horace Victorieux*	12	[4] 4f	Ibert	*La Ballade de la Geôle de Reading*	2	2b [2]

Violin I and II trem.—Soli Violin I and II non-trem.

COMPOSER	WORK	PAGE	MEASURE
Dukas	*La Péri*	128	[19 bis]

Violin I and II trem.—Viola non-trem.

COMPOSER	WORK	PAGE	MEASURE	COMPOSER	WORK	PAGE	MEASURE
Bruckner	*Symphony No. 1*	9	2b [80]	Haydn	*Symphony No. 18 in F# minor, "Farewell"*	2	13
Bruckner	*Symphony No. 5*	128	2				
Debussy	*Le Martyre de Saint Sébastien*	64	[28]	Mendelssohn	*Symphony No. 3, "Scotch"*	50	463
Haydn	*Symphony No. 7 in C major, "Le Midi"*	2	11	Mozart	*Symphony No. 39 in Eb major*	16	170
		12	99			25	[L] 1f
		20	13				
Haydn	*Symphony No. 17 in C major, "L'Ours"*	47	73	Vaughan Williams	*Symphony in F minor (No. 4)*	16	[11] 4f
		56	210				

Violin I and II trem.—Viola and Violoncello non-trem.

COMPOSER	WORK	PAGE	MEASURE
Beethoven	*Symphony No. 2*	71	97

Violin I and II trem.—Violoncello and Bass non-trem.

COMPOSER	WORK	PAGE	MEASURE
Enesco	*Ière Rhapsodie Roumaine*	82	3b [39]

TREMOLI

Viola trem.—Violin II non-trem.

COMPOSER	WORK	PAGE	MEASURE	COMPOSER	WORK	PAGE	MEASURE
Bloch	*America*	2		de Falla	*Nuits dans les Jardins*		
Dvořák	*Violin Concerto in*				*d'Espagne*	46	[11] 4f
	A minor	21	151	Reger	*Variations on a Theme*		
Elgar	*Symphony No. 1*	168	[150]		*of Mozart*	61	3
				Strauss, R.	*Eine Alpensinofnie*	87	85

Viola divisi (trem. and non-trem.)

COMPOSER	WORK	PAGE	MEASURE	COMPOSER	WORK	PAGE	MEASURE
Bloch	*Evocations*	13	2	Stravinsky	*Le Sacre du Printemps*	81	[94] 2f
Shostakovich	*Symphony No. 1*	73	[20]				

Viola trem.—Violoncello non-trem.

COMPOSER	WORK	PAGE	MEASURE	COMPOSER	WORK	PAGE	MEASURE
Albéniz–	*El Puerto*	7	[B]	Liszt	*Eine Faust-Symphonie*	255	[Rr]
Arbós		26	[J] 2f	Liszt	*Les Préludes*	37	160
Bach–	*Passacaglia and Fugue*			Mahler	*Symphony No. 3*	79	[57] 3f
Respighi	*in C minor*	14	[10] 1f	Prokofieff	*Piano Concerto No. 3*	137	[108]
Brahms	*Symphony No. 1*	86	89	Rossini	*The Barber of Seville,*		
Cras	*Journal de Bord*	66	5		*Overture*	14	72
de Falla	*Three Dances from*			Schönberg	*Fünf Orchesterstücke*	26	[9]
	"The Three-			Schubert	*Symphony No. 4*	52	179
	Cornered Hat"	1	3	Schumann, R.	*Symphony No. 2*	188	520
Ives	*Three Places in New*			Schumann, R.	*Symphony No. 3*	22	4b [F]
	England	56	[Q]	Smetana	*The Moldau*	87	333
Jacobi	*Music Hall Overture*	13	5				

Viola trem.—Bass non-trem.

COMPOSER	WORK	PAGE	MEASURE
Ibert	*Divertissement*	5	[4]

Viola trem.—Violin I, II, and Violoncello non-trem.

COMPOSER	WORK	PAGE	MEASURE
d'Indy	*Istar, Variations*		
	Symphoniques	40	[R] 2f

Viola trem.—Violoncello and Bass non-trem.

COMPOSER	WORK	PAGE	MEASURE	COMPOSER	WORK	PAGE	MEASURE
Beethoven	*Consecration of the*			Liszt	*Eine Faust-Symphonie*	219	6
	House Overture	73	272	Mendelssohn	*Symphony No. 3,*		
Beethoven	*Coriolanus Overture*	11	[D]		*"Scotch"*	49	455
		15	140	Schumann, R.	*Symphony No. 4*	20	118
d'Indy	*Deuxième Symphonie*						
	en Si♭	179	1				

STRINGS

Violoncello divisi (trem. and non-trem.)

COMPOSER	WORK	PAGE	MEASURE	COMPOSER	WORK	PAGE	MEASURE
Antheil	*Serenade for String Orchestra*	10	[19]	Dukas	*Polyeucte, Ouverture*	41	2
Bloch	*Evocations*	29	[23] 3f	de Falla	*Nuits dans les Jardins d'Espagne*	54	[20] 2f
Chabrier	*Ouverture de "Gwendoline"*	52	[18]	Honegger	*Pacific 231*	1	1
Debussy	*Le Martyre de Saint Sébastien*	38	[17]	Pizzetti	*Concerto dell'Estate*	105	1
				Thomson	*The Seine at Night*	16	3b [9]

Violoncello trem.—Bass non-trem.

COMPOSER	WORK	PAGE	MEASURE	COMPOSER	WORK	PAGE	MEASURE
Barber	*First Symphony*	11	[4] 2f	Liszt	*Piano Concerto No. 1*	57	[I]
Bartók	*Concerto for Orchestra*	128	[468]	Mahler	*Das Lied von der Erde*	4	2
Bartók	*Divertimento for String Orchestra*	22	[70] 3f	Mahler	*Symphony No. 8*	39	[43]
Berlioz	*Harold en Italie*	35	4	Mendelssohn	*Symphony No. 3, "Scotch"*	158	420
Berlioz	*Symphonie Fantastique*	57	3	Miaskovsky	*Symphony No. 22*	59	[97] 1f
Bizet	*Roma*	180	1	Mozart	*Clarinet Concerto in A major*	52	129
Bloch	*Schelomo*	29	2b [14]	Nystedt	*The Land of Suspense*	24	[8]
		60	4b [35]	Poulenc	*Concert Champêtre pour Clavecin et Orchestre*	14	[10] 2f
Brahms	*Academic Festival Overture*	9	78	Read	*First Overture*	39	2
Brahms	*Concerto for Violin and Violoncello*	5	67	Rimsky-Korsakoff	*Russian Easter Overture*	101	2
Brahms	*Piano Concerto No. 1*	161	4	Roussel	*Évocations, I*	29	7
Brahms	*Song of the Fates*	13	55	Roussel	*Évocations, III*	93	[47]
Brahms	*Symphony No. 2*	130	301	Schumann, R.	*Symphony No. 1*	135	117
Bruch	*Violin Concerto in G minor*	24	[E]	Schumann, R.	*Symphony No. 2*	47	298
Bruckner	*Symphony No. 7*	12	[D]	Schumann, R.	*Symphony No. 3*	41	[L]
Bruckner	*Symphony No. 9*	47	333	Schumann, R.	*Symphony No. 4*	34	[G] 1f
Chabrier	*Ouverture de "Gwendoline"*	12	[4]			47	277
Chabrier	*Suite Pastorale*	10	7	Sibelius	*Symphony No. 5*	39	[D]
Cowell	*Symphonic Set*	11	2b [25]	Smetana	*From Bohemia's Woods and Fields*	85	2
Dvořák	*Violin Concerto in A minor*	102	484	Smetana	*Libuša Overture*	10	1
de Falla	*Three Dances from "The Three-Cornered Hat"*	67	3	Smetana	*Vyšehrad*	20	107
						37	184
Franck	*Le Chasseur Maudit*	114	6	Tchaikovsky	*Suite from the Ballet, "The Sleeping Beauty"*	45	1
Hill	*Sinfonietta for String Orchestra*	15	[110] 3f	Vaughan Williams	*A London Symphony*	177	1
Honegger	*Prélude pour "La Tempête"*	7	1	Wagner, R.	*Bacchanale from "Tannhäuser"*	51	3
d'Indy	*Deuxième Symphonie en Sib*	111	1	Wagner, R.	*Eine Faust-Overture*	15	78
		169	[80]	Wagner, R.	*Prelude and Love Death from "Tristan und Isolde"*	38	43
d'Indy	*Symphony on a French Mountain Air*	28	1				
		49	[F]	Wagner, R.	*Rienzi Overture*	22	120
Lekeu	*Fantaisie sur Deux Airs Populaires Angevins*	30	[L]	Wagner, R.	*The Flying Dutchman Overture*	50	277
Liszt	*Eine Faust-Symphonie*	115	[Pp]				
Liszt	*Hungarian Rhapsody No. 2*	50	1				

368

TREMOLI

Bass trem.—Violoncello non-trem.

COMPOSER	WORK	PAGE	MEASURE	COMPOSER	WORK	PAGE	MEASURE
Bartók	Second Suite	21	7b [19]	Schumann, R.	Symphony No. 3	72	41
Mahler	Symphony No. 5	44	3	Walton	Symphony	158	3

Bass divisi (trem. and non-trem.)

Bartók	Concerto for Orchestra	130	[498]	Prokofieff	Summer Day Suite	66	[32]
de Falla	Nuits dans les Jardins			Shepherd	Horizons	124	1
	d'Espagne	19	4b [13]	Thomson	Louisiana Story Suite	47	26
Prokofieff	Piano Concerto No. 3	2	[1]				

Violin I and Viola divisi (trem. and non-trem.)

Bax	The Garden of Fand	67	5	Prokofieff	Ala et Lolly (Scythian		
Halffter	Deux Esquisses				Suite)	65	[42] 2f
	Symphoniques	3	3b [A]				

Violin II and Viola trem.—Violin I non-trem.

COMPOSER	WORK	PAGE	MEASURE
Barber	Medea	64	[48] 3f

Violin II and Viola divisi (trem. and non-trem.)

Debussy	Jeux	64	[43] 2f	Reger	Variations on a Theme		
Elgar	Variations, "Enigma"	113	4b [74]		of Mozart	104	1

Violin II and Viola trem.—Violin I and Violoncello non-trem.

d'Indy	Istar, Variations			Wagner, R.	Rienzi Overture	4	34
	Symphoniques	42	[T]			6	46

Violin II and Viola trem.—Violin I, Violoncello, and Bass non-trem.

Bartók	Hungarian Peasant		
	Songs	6	[4] 2f

Violin I, II, and Viola divisi (trem. and non-trem.)

Copland	Lincoln Portrait	8	2	Scriabin	Le Divin Poème	202	1
		12	4				

Violin I, II, and Viola trem.—Violoncello and Bass non-trem.

Beethoven	Symphony No. 3,			Beethoven	Symphony No. 5	98	145
	"Eroica"	171	447	Cherubini	Anakreon Overture	16	8

Violin I and Violoncello divisi (trem. and non-trem.)

Revueltas	Sensemayá	40	[37]

369

STRINGS

Violin II and Violoncello trem.—**Violin I and Violoncello** non-trem.

COMPOSER	WORK	PAGE	MEASURE
Scriabin	*Deuxième Symphonie*	**112**	1b [66]

Violin II and Violoncello divisi (trem. and non-trem.)

Debussy–Ansermet	*Six Épigraphes Antiques*	**59**	3

Viola and Violoncello trem.—**Violin I** non-trem.

Bloch	*Schelomo*	**57**	4

Viola and Violoncello trem.—**Violin I and II** non-trem.

Bartók	*Concerto for Orchestra*	**141**	[573]

Viola and Violoncello divisi (trem. and non-trem.)

COMPOSER	WORK	PAGE	MEASURE	COMPOSER	WORK	PAGE	MEASURE
Debussy	*Jeux*	**112**	3	**Fitelberg**	*Nocturne for Orchestra*	**21**	[114] 1f
de Falla	*Nuits dans les Jardins d'Espagne*	**61**	[27] 1f				

Viola and Violoncello trem.—**Bass** non-trem.

Beethoven	*Symphony No. 9*	**75**	513	**Bizet**	*L'Arlésienne Suite No. 1*	**4**	1

Violoncello and Bass trem.—**Soli Violoncello** non-trem.

Moeran	*Symphony in G minor*	**30**	3b [15]

Violoncello and Bass divisi (trem. and non-trem.)

Antheil	*Symphony No. 5*	**74**	3b [3]	**Mahler**	*Symphony No. 5*	**30**	[11]

Violoncello and Bass trem.—**Soli Violoncello and Bass** non-trem.

Moeran	*Symphony in G minor*	**173**	[117] 1f	**Szymanowski**	*Symphonie Concertante pour Piano et Orchestre*	**65**	6b [3]

Violin I, Viola, and Violoncello divisi (trem. and non-trem.)

de Falla	*Nuits dans les Jardins d'Espagne*	**16**	[9]

TREMOLI

Violin I, Viola, and Violoncello trem.—Violin II, Viola, and Bass non-trem.

COMPOSER	WORK	PAGE	MEASURE
Pizzetti	*Concerto dell'Estate*	**64**	[23]

Violin II, Viola, and Violoncello divisi (trem. and non-trem.)

de Falla	*Nuits dans les Jardins d'Espagne*	**69**	[35]

Violin I, II, Viola, and Violoncello divisi (trem. and non-trem.)

COMPOSER	WORK	PAGE	MEASURE	COMPOSER	WORK	PAGE	MEASURE
Bartók	*Violin Concerto*	**86**	[135]	**Honegger**	*Musique pour la "Phaedre" de G. D'Annunzio*	**22**	[6]
de Falla	*Three Dances from "The Three-Cornered Hat"*	**71**	[18]	**Scriabin**	*Deuxième Symphonie*	**126**	[73]
				Thomson	*The Seine at Night*	**6**	4

Violin I, Viola, and Bass divisi (trem. and non-trem.)

Debussy	*Première Rhapsodie*	**43**	4

Violin II, Violoncello, and Bass divisi (trem. and non-trem.)

Halffter	*Deux Esquisses Symphoniques*	**13**	3

Violin I, Viola, Violoncello, and Bass divisi (trem. and non-trem.)

de Falla	*Nuits dans les Jardins d'Espagne*	**30**	[23]

371

Chapter 52

COL LEGNO

English	*Italian*	*French*	*German*
Drawn [tapped] with (the) bow stick	Col legno [ligno]	Avec le bois	Col legno gestrichen
With (the) back of (the) bow	Col legno battuto [tratto]	Avec le dos de l'archet	Mit dem Holz zu Streichen
With hair and stick at point with stick towards player	Con la bacchetta	Sur le bois	

NORMAL BOWING

Naturally	Al solito	A la corde	Gewöhnlich
Natural (position)	Il corde col arco naturale	A l'ordinaire	*gewöhn.*
nat. pos.	(In) modo ordinario	Au naturel	Natürlich
Normal bowing	*modo ord., ord.*	Jeu ordinaire	*nat.*
Ordinary position	Loco	*jeu ord.*	Normal
ord. pos.	Non col legno	Naturel	
	Posizione ordinaria	*nat.*	
	pos. ord.	Position naturelle [normale]	
		pos. nat., p.n.	
		Position ordinaire	
		Pos^{on} ordre, pos. ord.	
		Son normal	

(1) GLISSANDO

Violin II

COMPOSER	WORK	PAGE	MEASURE
Rogers	*Characters from Hans Christian Andersen*	**27**	3

Violin I and II

Harsanyi	*Suite pour Orchestre*	**69**	[125] 1f

(2) ON HARMONICS

Bass

Stravinsky	*Fire-Bird Suite* (1919)	**35**	[10]

COL LEGNO

(3) TREMOLO

Violin II

COMPOSER	WORK	PAGE	MEASURE	COMPOSER	WORK	PAGE	MEASURE
Schönberg	Kammersymphonie, Op. 9	**42**	[40]	**Strauss, R.**	Also Sprach Zarathustra	**75**	1

Violoncello

COMPOSER	WORK	PAGE	MEASURE
Schönberg	A Survivor from Warsaw	**1**	3

Violin II, Viola, and Violoncello

Schönberg	Kammersymphonie, Op. 9	**89**	1b [78]

Violin I, II, Violoncello, and Bass

Honegger	Concertino pour Piano et Orchestre	**23**	[14]

Violin I, II, Viola, Violoncello, and Bass

Sibelius	The Swan of Tuonela	**14**	[H]

(4) NON-TREMOLO

English	Italian	French	German
Non tremolo	Col legno battuto	Non-trémolo	Nicht tremolierend
non trem.	Col legno tratto	*non-trém.*	*nicht trem.*
	Non-tremolo		
	non-trem.		

Violin I

COMPOSER	WORK	PAGE	MEASURE	COMPOSER	WORK	PAGE	MEASURE
Copland	Four Dance Episodes from "Rodeo"	**12**	[12] 2f	**Mahler**	Symphony No. 1	**91**	3b [16]
		27	[27] 3f	**Schönberg**	Theme and Variations	**27**	108
Ibert	Escales	**39**	[34]				

Solo Violin I

COMPOSER	WORK	PAGE	MEASURE	COMPOSER	WORK	PAGE	MEASURE
Debussy	Iberia	**92**	[58]	**Schönberg**	Pierrot Lunaire	**17**	[10] 2f

Violin II

COMPOSER	WORK	PAGE	MEASURE	COMPOSER	WORK	PAGE	MEASURE
Balogh	Portrait of a City	**15**	5b [H]	**Ibert**	Escales	**21**	[16]
Copland	Dance Symphony	**11**	4b [6]			**55**	[48]
		17	6	**Ibert**	La Ballade de la Geôle		
Copland	First Symphony	**8**	1		de Reading	**43**	[29]
		63	6	**Milhaud**	2me Suite Symphonique	**88**	3

373

STRINGS

Violin II (contd.)

COMPOSER	WORK	PAGE	MEASURE	COMPOSER	WORK	PAGE	MEASURE
Prokofieff	Suite from the Ballet "Chout"	143	[185]	Schönberg	Theme and Variations	28	120
Schönberg	Kammersymphonie,	41	[39]	Skilton	Suite Primeval, Part I	15	[B]
	Op. 9	78	[71] 1f	Wagenaar	Sinfonietta for Small Orchestra	3	5

Violin I and II

COMPOSER	WORK	PAGE	MEASURE	COMPOSER	WORK	PAGE	MEASURE
Albéniz–Arbós	Triana	27	3	Mahler	Symphony No. 6	32	[19]
Atterberg	Ballade und Passacaglia	30	3	Milhaud	Concerto pour Piano et Orchestre	36	1b [15]
Bartók	Music for Strings, Percussion and Celesta	111	90	Schelling	A Victory Ball	46	[11]
				Schlein	Dance Overture	23	1b [360]
Berg	Three Excerpts from "Wozzeck"	50	2	Schreker	The Birthday of the Infanta, Suite	21	[85] 3f
Copland	Third Symphony	57	[43] 2f	Siegmeister	Sunday in Brooklyn	31	1b [50]
Inghelbrecht	La Métamorphose d'Ève	33	[23] 4f	Stillman-Kelley	Gulliver—His Voyage to Lilliput	90	[L]
Mahler	Symphony No. 4	37	185			101	3
		162	53				

Viola

COMPOSER	WORK	PAGE	MEASURE	COMPOSER	WORK	PAGE	MEASURE
Bloch	Schelomo	24	[11]	Rimsky-Korsakoff	Le Coq d'Or Suite	46	[31]
Copland	Two Pieces for String Orchestra	10	3b [75]				

Violoncello

COMPOSER	WORK	PAGE	MEASURE	COMPOSER	WORK	PAGE	MEASURE
Bartók	Music for Strings, Percussion and Celesta	109	83	Rachmaninoff	The Bells	107	[113] 5f
Bax	Fourth Symphony	146	2b [31]	Rimsky-Korsakoff	Le Coq d'Or Suite	49	4b [33]
Berg	Three Excerpts from "Wozzeck"	25	[20] 3f	Schmitt	Mirages pour Orchestre, No. 1	18	2
Berg	Violin Concerto	25	[135] 2f	Sessions	Symphony No. II	127	3
Copland	Third Symphony	105	[95] 2f	Strauss, R.	Don Quixote	46	3
Ibert	Féerique	16	2	Stravinsky	Fire-Bird Suite (1919)	34	[9]
Parodi	Preludio ad una Commedia	39	[S] 2f	Wagenaar	Sinfonietta for Small Orchestra	9	[6] 2f
Prokofieff	Romeo and Juliet, Suite No. 1	123	[78] 1f				

Soli Violoncello

COMPOSER	WORK	PAGE	MEASURE	COMPOSER	WORK	PAGE	MEASURE
Berg	Three Excerpts from "Wozzeck"	14	[365] 2f	Stillman-Kelley	Gulliver—His Voyage to Lilliput	77	[A]
Schönberg	A Survivor from Warsaw	8	35				

Bass

COMPOSER	WORK	PAGE	MEASURE	COMPOSER	WORK	PAGE	MEASURE
Antheil	Over the Plains	51	[30] 3f	Milhaud	Saudades do Brazil	70	2
Berlioz	Roméo et Juliette	183	20	Schönberg	A Survivor from Warsaw	4	16
Honegger	Quatrième Symphonie	5	5				

COL LEGNO

Violin I and Viola

COMPOSER	WORK	PAGE	MEASURE	COMPOSER	WORK	PAGE	MEASURE
Schönberg	A Survivor from Warsaw	7	32	Schmitt	Ronde burlesque	54	[29] 2f

Violin II and Viola

COMPOSER	WORK	PAGE	MEASURE	COMPOSER	WORK	PAGE	MEASURE
Albéniz–Arbós	Fête-Dieu à Séville	6	[B]	Prokofieff	Summer Day Suite	53	[25] 6f
Bax	Third Symphony	16	[15] 5f	Rachmaninoff	The Bells	5	[4] 2f
Copland	Two Pieces for String Orchestra	8	1b [50]	Ravel	Rapsodie Espagnole	70	3
				Respighi	Ballata delle Gnomidi	13	[3]
Maganini	An Ornithological Suite	44	3	Schmitt	Mirages pour Orchestre, No. 1	22	[10]
Mahler	Symphony No. 4	79	56				
Mahler	Symphony No. 7	94	[86]	Stravinsky	Petrouchka Suite	141	[118]
Mussorgsky	Night on the Bald Mountain	21	[E]	Szymanowski	Symphonie Concertante pour Piano et Orchestre	76	[13]
		35	[H]				

Violin I, II, and Viola

COMPOSER	WORK	PAGE	MEASURE	COMPOSER	WORK	PAGE	MEASURE
Bax	First Symphony	10	2	Mahler	Symphony No. 4	88	126
Bax	Second Symphony	51	[29] 1f			167	[7]
Bax	Fifth Symphony	40	1b [27]	Mahler	Symphony No. 6	62	[38]
Berg	Violin Concerto	56	[20]			96	[64]
Berlioz	Symphonie Fantastique	220	1	Malipiero	Impressioni dal Vero, 1ª Parte	18	44
Britten	Passacaglia from "Peter Grimes"	16	[6]	Prokofieff	Cinderella Suite No. 1	105	[83]
Chabrier	España, Rhapsodie	35	[H]	Prokofieff	Peter and the Wolf	68	[48] 5f
Dohnányi	Variations on a Nursery Song	80	[49]	Prokofieff	Piano Concerto No. 3	96	[75]
Holst	Beni Mora, Oriental Suite	4	3b [1]	Rachmaninoff	Rapsodie pour Piano et Orchestre	27	8b [24]
Holst	The Ballet from "The Perfect Fool"	7	[6]	Roger-Ducasse	Le Joli Jeu de Furet	30	1
				Schmitt	Ronde burlesque	15	2
Ibert	Escales	79	[68] 1f	Stravinsky	Petrouchka Suite	143	[119]
		83	[72] 1f	Vaughan Williams	Overture to "The Wasps"	34	246
Liszt	Todtentanz für Piano und Orchester	62	1				

Solo Violin and Violoncello

COMPOSER	WORK	PAGE	MEASURE
Schönberg	Pierrot Lunaire	31	1

Soli Violin I and Violoncello

COMPOSER	WORK	PAGE	MEASURE
Berg	Three Excerpts from "Wozzeck"	17	[385] 4f

Violin I, II, and Violoncello

COMPOSER	WORK	PAGE	MEASURE	COMPOSER	WORK	PAGE	MEASURE
Bax	First Symphony	93	[D] 1f	Mahler	Symphony No. 4	33	172

STRINGS

Violin I and Bass

COMPOSER	WORK	PAGE	MEASURE
Mahler	*Symphony No. 3*	**171**	[26]

Viola and Violoncello

COMPOSER	WORK	PAGE	MEASURE	COMPOSER	WORK	PAGE	MEASURE
Bax	*Fourth Symphony*	**28**	2b [18]	**Loeffler**	*Evocation*	**27**	[23]
Berg	*Violin Concerto*	**8**	[45]	**Mahler**	*Symphony No. 3*	**111**	[5] 3f
Gould	*Latin-American*					**179**	[33]
	Symphonette	**51**	[11]	**Respighi**	*Ballata delle Gnomidi*	**60**	2
Inghelbrecht	*Pour le jour de la*			**Stravinsky**	*Le Sacre du Printemps*	**17**	[24]
	première neige au			**Stringfield**	*A Negro Parade*	**1**	1
	vieux Japon	**12**	[6] 1f				

Solo Viola and Violoncello

COMPOSER	WORK	PAGE	MEASURE
Schönberg	*Pierrot Lunaire*	**35**	[5] 2f

Viola and Bass

COMPOSER	WORK	PAGE	MEASURE
Piston	*Suite for Orchestra*	**16**	[F]

Soli Viola and Violoncello

COMPOSER	WORK	PAGE	MEASURE
Schönberg	*Suite for String .Orchestra*	**22**	382

Violoncello and Bass

COMPOSER	WORK	PAGE	MEASURE	COMPOSER	WORK	PAGE	MEASURE
Bloch	*Schelomo*	**14**	[5] 1f	**Parodi**	*Preludio ad una*		
Delannoy	*Figures Sonores*	**36**	3		*Commedia*	**5**	[B] 1f
Gould	*Latin-American*			**Sessions**	*Suite from "The Black*		
	Symphonette	**45**	[6] 3f		*Maskers"*	**13**	[11]
Ibert	*Divertissement*	**44**	1	**Stringfield**	*A Negro Parade*	**25**	[11]

Violin I, Viola, and Violoncello

COMPOSER	WORK	PAGE	MEASURE	COMPOSER	WORK	PAGE	MEASURE
Bax	*Tintagel*	**22**	4	**Mahler**	*Symphony No. 3*	**159**	[18] 3f

Violin II, Viola, and Violoncello

COMPOSER	WORK	PAGE	MEASURE	COMPOSER	WORK	PAGE	MEASURE
Bax	*First Symphony*	**53**	4	**Ibert**	*Escales*	**37**	1
Gould	*Latin-American*			**Rachmaninoff**	*Symphony No. 2*	**80**	5
	Symphonette	**83**	[3]			**112**	5

COL LEGNO

Violin I, II, Viola, and Violoncello

COMPOSER	WORK	PAGE	MEASURE	COMPOSER	WORK	PAGE	MEASURE
Bartók	Dance Suite	6	52	Gould	Latin-American		
Bartók	Violin Concerto	85	[122]		Symphonette	103	[18] 3t
Bloch	Schelomo	66	[41]	Ibert	Escales	52	1
Caturla	Trois Danses Cubaines	19	5	Jacobi	Concertino for Piano and		
Cesana	Second American				String Orchestra	60	[35] 4f
	Symphony	80	[8]	Prokofieff	Peter and the Wolf	74	3
Copland	Billy the Kid Ballet Suite	32	5	Rosenthal	Les Petits Métiers	6	2
Debussy	Jeux	58	4b [40]	Still	Bells	12	[12]

Violin II, Violoncello, and Bass

COMPOSER	WORK	PAGE	MEASURE
Holst	Beni Mora, Oriental Suite	33	[4]

Violin I, II, Violoncello, and Bass

COMPOSER	WORK	PAGE	MEASURE	COMPOSER	WORK	PAGE	MEASURE
Prokofieff	Ala et Lolly (Scythian Suite)	42	[23]	Sessions	Suite from "The Black Maskers"	20	9b [18]
Prokofieff	Suite from the Ballet "Chout"	40	[55]				

Viola, Violoncello, and Bass

COMPOSER	WORK	PAGE	MEASURE	COMPOSER	WORK	PAGE	MEASURE
Albéniz–Arbós	Triana	11	1	Prokofieff	Piano Concerto No. 3	61	[45] 1f
				Schönberg	A Survivor from Warsaw	3	10
Bloch	Voice in the Wilderness	22	1b [18]	Sessions	Symphony No. II	134	1b [T]
Prokofieff	Cinderella Suite No. 1	49	5	Villa-Lobos	Danses Africaines	62	[9]

Violin I, Viola, Violoncello, and Bass

COMPOSER	WORK	PAGE	MEASURE	COMPOSER	WORK	PAGE	MEASURE
Berg	Three Excerpts from "Wozzeck"	38	1b [290]	Mahler	Symphony No. 2	85	[31] 8f

Violin II, Viola, Violoncello, and Bass

COMPOSER	WORK	PAGE	MEASURE	COMPOSER	WORK	PAGE	MEASURE
Bartók	Dance Suite	12	109	Prokofieff	Piano Concerto No. 3	133	[103]
Bloch	Schelomo	17	[6]	Schönberg	Kammersymphonie,		
Honegger	Concertino pour Piano				Op. 9	50	4
	et Orchestre	35	[23]	Shostakovich	Piano Concerto	50	[64] 2f

Violin I, II, Viola, Violoncello, and Bass

COMPOSER	WORK	PAGE	MEASURE	COMPOSER	WORK	PAGE	MEASURE
Bartók	Dance Suite	73	15	Holst	The Planets	1	1
Bartók	Second Rhapsody for			Ireland	A London Overture	34	[20]
	Violin and Orchestra	37	[25]	Ireland	Symphonic Rhapsody,		
Bartók	Vier Orchesterstücke	111	5		"Mai-Dun"	7	2
Britten	The Young Person's			Mahler	Symphony No. 2	83	3b [30]
	Guide to the			Mahler	Symphony No. 3	103	4
	Orchestra	47	3	Mahler	Symphony No. 5	46	1
Copland	Concerto for Piano and			Mahler	Symphony No. 6	116	[79]
	Orchestra	47	1	Martinet	Orphée	66	[5]

STRINGS

Violin I, II, Viola, Violoncello, and Bass (contd.)

COMPOSER	WORK	PAGE	MEASURE	COMPOSER	WORK	PAGE	MEASURE
Mihalovici	Divertissement pour	17	1	Prokofieff	Romeo and Juliet,	102	[63] 4f
	Petite Orchestre	29	3b [L]		Suite No. 1	108	[67]
		47	11	Saint-Saëns	Danse Macabre	12	7
Poulenc	Concert Champêtre pour			Siegmeister	Western Suite	89	[55] 1f
	Clavecin et Orchestre	19	[15]				

(5) COL LEGNO AND PIZZICATO COMBINED

Violin I col legno—Violin II pizz.

COMPOSER	WORK	PAGE	MEASURE
Mahler	Symphony No. 2	85	[31] 8f

Violin II col legno—Violin I pizz.

Mahler	Symphony No. 3	117	1b [9]

Violin II divisi (col legno and pizz.)

Schelling	A Victory Ball	54	[14]

Violin II col legno—Viola pizz.

Siegmeister	From my Window	40	[25] 1f

Violin I and II col legno—Viola pizz.

Honegger	Concertino pour Piano et		
	Orchestre	23	[14] 1f

Violoncello divisi (col legno and pizz.)

Honegger	Concertino pour Piano		
	et Orchestre	42	[27]

Violoncello col legno—Bass pizz.

Bartók	Dance Suite	6	[4]	Gould	Latin-American		
Bax	November Woods	51	4		Symphonette	83	[3]

COL LEGNO

Bass col legno—Violoncello pizz.

COMPOSER	WORK	PAGE	MEASURE	COMPOSER	WORK	PAGE	MEASURE
Delannoy	Figures Sonores	5	[2]	Mussorgsky	Night on the Bald Mountain	36	184

Bass divisi (col legno and pizz.)

COMPOSER	WORK	PAGE	MEASURE
Villa-Lobos	Amazonas	64	[27]

Violin I and Viola col legno—Violin II and Violoncello pizz.

Schönberg	A Survivor from Warsaw	7	32

Violin II and Viola col legno—Violin I and II pizz.

Bosmans	La Vie en Bleu	8	8

Violin I, II, and Viola divisi (col legno and pizz.)

COMPOSER	WORK	PAGE	MEASURE	COMPOSER	WORK	PAGE	MEASURE
Poot	Jazz-Music	10	[5]	Poot	Symphonie	47	[25]
		18	[8]				

Violin II and Violoncello col legno—Violin I and Violoncello pizz.

Mahler	Symphony No. 3	135	1

Violoncello and Bass divisi (col legno and pizz.)

Parodi	Preludio ad una Commedia	24	[N]

Violin I, II, Viola, and Violoncello divisi (col legno and pizz.)

COMPOSER	WORK	PAGE	MEASURE	COMPOSER	WORK	PAGE	MEASURE
Debussy	Jeux	58	4b [40]	Moross	Biguine	8	2

(6) COL LEGNO AND MODO ORDINARIO (ARCO) COMBINED

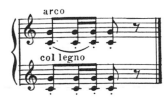

Violin II col legno—Violin I arco

Benjamin	From San Domingo	15	[F]

STRINGS

Violin I and II divisi (col legno and arco)

COMPOSER	WORK	PAGE	MEASURE
Sibelius	*The Swan of Tuonela*	**14**	[H]

Viola col legno—Violin II arco

Mahler	*Symphony No. 3*	**165**	[22] 4f

Bass col legno—Violoncello arco

Honegger	*Concertino pour Piano et Orchestre*	**24**	[15]

Violin II and Viola col legno—Violin I and II arco

Ibert	*La Ballade de la Geôle de Reading*	**59**	[41]

Violin II and Viola divisi (col legno and arco)

Parodi	*Preludio ad una Commedia*	**7**	3

Viola and Violoncello col legno—Soli Violin I arco

Stravinsky	*Le Sacre du Printemps*	**17**	[24]

Violin I, II, Viola, and Violoncello divisi (col legno and arco)

COMPOSER	WORK	PAGE	MEASURE	COMPOSER	WORK	PAGE	MEASURE
de Falla	*El Amor Brujo*	**14**	[B]	**Mihalovici**	*Toccata pour Piano et Orchestre*	**99**	[380]

Chapter 53

SUL PONTICELLO

English	Italian	French	German
Bridge	Al ponticello	Au chevalet	Am Steg
Close to (the) bridge	*al pontic.*	Chevalet	*a.s.*
On [near] the bridge	Sul ponticello	Près du chevalet	Auf dem Steg
	sul pont.	Sur [vers] le chevalet	Zum Steg

NATURAL POSITION

Natural (position)	Modo ordinario	Jeu ordinaire	Gewöhnlich
	Non sul pont.		

(for further terminology see Chapter 52, page 372)

(1) BACK OF THE BRIDGE

English	Italian	French	German
Back of (the) bridge	Dietro il ponticello	En arrière du chevalet	Hinter dem Steg
Below [behind] the bridge	Sub ponticello		
	sub. pont.		
On the four strings between the nut and bridge	Sulle quattro corde fra noce e ponticello	Dans les quatres cordes entre le tire-corde et la chevalet	Auf den Vier Saiten zwischen Frosch u. Steg

Solo Violin I

COMPOSER	WORK	PAGE	MEASURE
Grofé	*Grand Canyon Suite*	**53**	5

Viola and Violoncello

Slonimsky	*My Toy Balloon*	**24**	4

Violin II, Viola, Violoncello, and Bass

Villa-Lobos	*Amazonas*	**24**	[9] 2f

(2) GLISSANDO

English	Italian	French	German
Gliss.—gliding over the string near the bridge	Gliss.—passando leggeramente sopra la corda al ponticello	Glissez en effleurant la corde du côté du chevalet	Gliss. über die Saite nah am Steg gleitend

Violin I and II

Villa-Lobos	*Uirapurú*	**49**	2b [11]

381

STRINGS

Viola

COMPOSER	WORK	PAGE	MEASURE
Stravinsky	*Chant du Rossignol*	**24**	[25] 1f

Violoncello

Milhaud	*Ière Symphonie*	**6**	1
		22	[85] 1f

Violin II and Viola

Inghelbrecht	*Sinfonia Breve No. 1*	**6**	[4] 2f

Violin I, II, and Viola

COMPOSER	WORK	PAGE	MEASURE	COMPOSER	WORK	PAGE	MEASURE
Inghelbrecht	*Sinfonia Breve No. 1*	**12**	5	**Ives**	*"The Fourth of July" from Symphony, "Holidays"*	**33**	[X]

Violin I, II, and Violoncello

Stravinsky	*Petrouchka Suite*	**153**	4b [129]

Viola and Violoncello

Ravel	*Rapsodie Espagnole*	**40**	2

Viola, Violoncello, and Bass

Bartók	*Violin Concerto*	**123**	[557]

(3) ON HARMONICS

Violin I

Stravinsky	*Le Sacre du Printemps*	**74**	[82] 1f

Soli Violin I

de Falla	*El Retablo de Maese Pedro*	**31**	1
		61	[66] 3f

Violin I and II

Villa-Lobos	*Amazonas*	**2**	3

Viola

COMPOSER	WORK	PAGE	MEASURE	COMPOSER	WORK	PAGE	MEASURE
Parodi	*Preludio ad una Commedia*	**14**	[G]	**Halffter**	*Deux Esquisses Symphoniques*	**8**	2
				Read	*Symphony No. I*	**38**	2

382

SUL PONTICELLO

Soli Bass

COMPOSER	WORK	PAGE	MEASURE
Halffter	*Deux Esquisses Symphoniques*	19	1

Violin II and Viola

Milhaud	*Ière Symphonie*	7	1b [25]

Violin I, II, and Viola

Read	*Sketches of the City*	4	[1] 3f

Violoncello and Bass

Miaskovsky	*Symphony No. 8*	124	[23]

Violin I, Viola, and Violoncello

Berg	*Three Excerpts from "Wozzeck"*	56	1b [380]

Violin I, II, Viola, and Violoncello

Honegger	*Pacific 231*	1	1

(4) PIZZICATO

Violin I and II

Debussy	*Gigues*	24	4b [14]

Violoncello

Inghelbrecht	*La Métamorphose d'Ève*	17	2

Violin II and Violoncello

Antheil	*Serenade for String Orchestra*	2	[3] 4f

Viola and Violoncello

Inghelbrecht	*Sinfonia Breve No. 1*	36	2

Violin II, Viola, and Violoncello

Inghelbrecht	*Sinfonia Breve No. 1*	58	[34]

Violin I, II, Viola, and Violoncello

Berg	*Violin Concerto*	77	[125]

STRINGS

Violin I, II, Viola, Violoncello, and Bass

COMPOSER	WORK	PAGE	MEASURE	COMPOSER	WORK	PAGE	MEASURE
Antheil	*Serenade for String Orchestra*	23	[39]	**Siegmeister**	*Sunday in Brooklyn*	28	[35] 1f

(5) TREMOLO

Violin I

COMPOSER	WORK	PAGE	MEASURE	COMPOSER	WORK	PAGE	MEASURE
Bartók	*Divertimento for String Orchestra*	12	[141]	**Poulenc**	*Concert Champêtre pour Clavecin et Orchestre*	100	[23]
Bloch	*Concerto Grosso*	11	[14] 5f	**Respighi**	*The Fountains of Rome*	56	[19]
Casella	*La Donna Serpente, I. Serie*	5	[7] 5f	**Rogers**	*Characters from Hans Christian Andersen*	14	1b [8]
Debussy	*Gigues*	12	[7] 2f	**Rudhyar**	*Five Stanzas*	3	[A] 6f
Debussy	*Iberia*	39	2b [24]			20	[B']
		51	[34] 4f	**Schmitt**	*Mirages pour Orchestre, No. 2*	22	[12]
Dukas	*La Péri*	40	1	**Sessions**	*Symphony No. II*	63	[Pp]
de Falla	*Three Dances from "The Three-Cornered Hat"*	15	[11]	**Shostakovich**	*Symphony No. 7*	85	[85]
				Stravinsky	*Le Sacre du Printemps*	74	[82] 1f
Grofé	*Grand Canyon Suite*	35	1			109	1b [138]
		49	[8]			120	[164] 1f
Inghelbrecht	*Rapsodie de Printemps*	2	5	**Stravinsky**	*Scherzo Fantastique*	33	[49] 2f
		7	1b [3]	**Thomson**	*The Seine at Night*	13	2b [8]
Mahler	*Das Lied von der Erde*	108	1	**Walton**	*Symphony*	79	[54]
Mahler	*Symphony No. 3*	172	9				

Solo Violin

COMPOSER	WORK	PAGE	MEASURE
Schönberg	*Pierrot Lunaire*	7	2b [25]
		17	[10]

Violin II

COMPOSER	WORK	PAGE	MEASURE	COMPOSER	WORK	PAGE	MEASURE
Albéniz–Arbós	*El Puerto*	19	2	**Mahler**	*Symphony No. 1*	119	[21] 6f
Bartók	*Concerto for Orchestra*	23	[462]	**Rachmaninoff**	*Piano Concerto No. 3*	88	[49] 1f
Bloch	*Trois Poèmes Juifs*	75	[10] 2f	**Respighi**	*The Fountains of Rome*	58	[20]
Copland	*Dance Symphony*	46	[26] 11f	**Rogers**	*Characters from Hans Christian Andersen*	6	3
Copland	*First Symphony*	4	[5]				
Dukas	*La Péri*	77	1	**Rogers**	*Once Upon a Time, Five Fairy Tales*	47	2
de Falla	*El Amor Brujo*	92	[55]	**Rosenthal**	*Les Petits Métiers*	75	1
de Falla	*Three Dances from "The Three-Cornered Hat"*	85	[30]	**Rozsa**	*Concerto for String Orchestra*	6	[47]
Ferroud	*Au Parc Monceau*	24	1	**Schönberg**	*Kammersymphonie, Op. 9*	31	[29]
		36	[12]	**Sessions**	*Suite from "The Black Maskers"*	51	[50] 1f
Honegger	*Concertino pour Piano et Orchestre*	17	[10]			83	[82]
				Sessions	*Symphony No. II*	112	[H] 1f
Honegger	*Suite d'Orchestre, "L'Impératrice aux Rochers"*	50	1	**Sibelius**	*Tapiola*	42	427
				Strauss, R.	*Also Sprach Zarathustra*	58	1
Levant	*Nocturne*	35	153	**Stravinsky**	*Le Sacre du Printemps*	61	4b [71]

384

SUL PONTICELLO

Violin II (contd.)

COMPOSER	WORK	PAGE	MEASURE	COMPOSER	WORK	PAGE	MEASURE
Thomson	*The Seine at Night*	19	2	Walton	*Concerto for Viola and Orchestra*	2	[2]
Vaughan Williams	*A London Symphony*	14	3b [G]	Walton	*Symphony*	71	[46] 6f
						120	1b [90]

Violin I and II

COMPOSER	WORK	PAGE	MEASURE	COMPOSER	WORK	PAGE	MEASURE
Bartók	*Dance Suite*	42	73	Prokofieff	*Summer Day Suite*	52	2
Bax	*Tintagel*	15	3	Rachmaninoff	*The Bells*	46	1
Bloch	*Trois Poèmes Juifs*	65	2	Read	*Sketches of the City*	6	[3]
Debussy	*Iberia*	44	[29]	Read	*Symphony No. I*	49	1
Debussy	*Rondes de Printemps*	1	1	Revueltas	*Sensemayá*	35	[33]
Dukas	*La Péri*	14	1	Rossini	*Tancredi, Overture*	19	96
		133	[20]			27	142
de Falla	*Nuits dans les Jardins d'Espagne*	47	[12]	Schelling	*A Victory Ball*	89	2
Ferroud	*Au Parc Monceau*	9	3	Sessions	*Suite from "The Black Maskers"*	13	[10]
Honegger	*Le Chant de Nigamon*	52	[178] 1f			23	[23]
Ibert	*La Ballade de la Geôle de Reading*	44	[30] 4f	Sessions	*Symphony No. II*	69	2b [C]
Maganini	*South Wind*	12	[L]	Stillman-Kelley	*Gulliver—His Voyage to Lilliput*	71	[D]
Mahler	*Symphony No. 3*	51	[35]	Vaughan Williams	*A London Symphony*	9	1b [D]
Mahler	*Symphony No. 9*	141	[39]	Vaughan Williams	*Symphony in E minor (No. 6)*	140	[44] 5f
Parodi	*Preludio ad una Commedia*	10	2	Villa-Lobos	*Uirapurú*	49	2b [11]
Pescara	*Tibet*	23	[8]	Walton	*Symphony*	34	2b [21]
Pizzetti	*Concerto dell'Estate*	14	[6]				

Soli Violin I and II

COMPOSER	WORK	PAGE	MEASURE
Stillman-Kelley	*New England Symphony*	48	3

Viola

COMPOSER	WORK	PAGE	MEASURE	COMPOSER	WORK	PAGE	MEASURE
Albéniz-Arbós	*Triana*	24	[G]	de Falla	*Nuits dans les Jardins d'Espagne*	3	1
Antheil	*Symphony No. 5*	73	2b [2]			62	[28]
Balogh	*Portrait of a City*	3	5	Grofé	*Grand Canyon Suite*	40	[4]
Bartók	*Concerto for Orchestra*	1	8	Jacobi	*Music Hall Overture*	26	[15]
		51	[22]	Khachaturian	*Gayne Ballet Suite No. 2*	42	[4]
Bartók	*Second Rhapsody for Violin and Orchestra*	30	[14]	Prokofieff	*Summer Day Suite*	59	[28] 1f
Bax	*The Garden of Fand*	18	2b [E]	Rosenthal	*Les Petits Métiers*	111	2
Bloch	*Schelomo*	8	[3]	Roussel	*Le Festin de l'Araignée*	40	4b [58]
Debussy	*Gigues*	14	[8]	Roussel	*Symphonie en Sol mineur*	21	1
Debussy	*Iberia*	64	4			41	3
Dukas	*Symphonie en Ut majeur*	166	2			131	[77] 1f
				Saint-Saëns	*La Jeunesse d'Hercule*	13	8
Elgar	*Symphony No. 2*	29	[33]	Schönberg	*A Survivor from Warsaw*	9	42

385

STRINGS

Viola (contd.)

COMPOSER	WORK	PAGE	MEASURE	COMPOSER	WORK	PAGE	MEASURE
Schönberg	Fünf Orchesterstücke	27	1b [10]	Thomson	The Seine at Night	14	2
Skilton	Suite Primeval, Part II	7	1	Vaughan	Symphony in D major		
Strauss, R.	Symphonia Domestica	63	[81] 1f	Williams	(No. 5)	39	5
Szymanowski	Symphonie Concertante pour Piano et Orchestre	6	[3]				

Violoncello

COMPOSER	WORK	PAGE	MEASURE	COMPOSER	WORK	PAGE	MEASURE
Bax	Third Symphony	36	[36] 4f	Revueltas	Sensemayá	40	[37]
Bax	Sixth Symphony	74	[2]	Rimsky-Korsakoff	Scheherazade	193	310
Berg	Violin Concerto	16	1b [80]	Shepherd	Horizons	71	8
Britten	Les Illuminations	44	[1]	Still	Dismal Swamp	22	[15] 4f
Debussy-Ansermet	Six Épigraphes Antiques	61	[B] 2f	Stillman-Kelley	Gulliver—His Voyage to Lilliput	67	2
Elgar	Falstaff	74	[74]	Strauss, R.	Don Juan	10	6
Jolivet	Andante pour Orchestre à Cordes	9	[40]	Stravinsky	Firebird Ballet Suite (1945)	50	[62]
Prokofieff	Symphony No. 5	117	[66] 1f	Thomson	The Seine at Night	16	3b [9]
		128	2				

Solo Violoncello

COMPOSER	WORK	PAGE	MEASURE
Schönberg	Pierrot Lunaire	27	3b [15]

Bass

COMPOSER	WORK	PAGE	MEASURE	COMPOSER	WORK	PAGE	MEASURE
Debussy	Iberia	88	[56]	Schönberg	A Survivor from Warsaw	6	26
Debussy	La Mer	82	[43]	Sibelius	Pelleas and Melisande	9	3
Inghelbrecht	El Greco	1	1				

Violin I and Viola

COMPOSER	WORK	PAGE	MEASURE	COMPOSER	WORK	PAGE	MEASURE
Berg	Three Excerpts from "Wozzeck"	31	[45] 4f	Respighi	Ballata delle Gnomidi	6	[1]
Bloch	Evocations	50	3	Respighi	Feste Romane	60	[17]
de Falla	Nuits dans les Jardins d'Espagne	4	[2]	Roussel	Évocations, I	14	2
		67	[34]	Stravinsky	Petrouchka Suite	93	[80]

Violin II and Viola

COMPOSER	WORK	PAGE	MEASURE	COMPOSER	WORK	PAGE	MEASURE
Bax	First Symphony	50	8	Dukas	Symphonie en Ut majeur	91	6b [D]
Chabrier	Suite Pastorale	27	10				
Debussy	Gigues	33	[19] 3f	Elgar	Symphony No. 1	24	5
Delius	Appalachia	2	11	Honegger	Quatrième Symphonie	43	[2]
Delius	A Song Before Sunrise	9	6b [E]	d'Indy	Symphony on a French Mountain Air	4	[A]
Dukas	La Péri	127	3				

386

SUL PONTICELLO

Violin II and Viola (contd.)

COMPOSER	WORK	PAGE	MEASURE	COMPOSER	WORK	PAGE	MEASURE
Inghelbrecht	Sinfonia Breve No. 1	6	[4] 2f	Sessions	Symphony No. II	35	[V]
Malipiero	Impressioni dal Vero, 1ª Parte	8	[3]	Strauss, R.	Don Juan	73	[V]
Prokofieff	Symphony No. 6	153	[115]	Strauss, R.	Macbeth	11	I
Prokofieff	Violin Concerto No. 2	86	[82]	Tansman	Deux Moments Symphoniques	50	4
Read	Symphony No. I	31	[13]	Walton	Façade, Suite No. 2	24	I
Roussel	Suite en Fa	83	[43]	Walton	Symphony	73	[48]

Violin I, II, and Viola

COMPOSER	WORK	PAGE	MEASURE	COMPOSER	WORK	PAGE	MEASURE
Antheil	Serenade for String Orchestra	11	[21]	d'Indy	Deuxième Symphonie en Sib	37	6
Bartók	Concerto for Orchestra	58	[54]	Inghelbrecht	Sinfonia Breve No. 1	12	5
Bax	First Symphony	57	I			54	[32]
		80	[K]	Kabalevsky	Symphony No. 2	168	[65] 1f
Bax	Sixth Symphony	7	[5]	MacDowell	2nd Suite (Indian)	23	[K]
Bloch	Schelomo	49	3	Mahler	Symphony No. 3	15	[11]
Chabrier	Ouverture de "Gwendoline"	23	[7]			158	[17]
Charpentier	Impressions d'Italie	142	[44] 6f	Mahler	Symphony No. 7	83	I
Debussy	La Mer	56	2	Milhaud	2me Suite Symphonique	92	4
Debussy	Le Martyre de Saint Sébastien	17	4	Prokofieff	Summer Day Suite	66	[32]
Delius	A Song of Summer	19	[140] 3f	Ravel	Shéhérazade	27	2
Dukas	L'Apprenti Sorcier	30	[30] 3f	Read	Symphony No. I	11	3
de Falla	El Retablo de Maese Pedro	101	[92] 3f	Rosenthal	Les Petits Métiers	43	3
de Falla	Nuits dans les Jardins d'Espagne	12	[7]			54	2
		38	[4]	Sessions	Suite from "The Black Maskers"	96	[91]
Gershwin	Concerto in F for Piano and Orchestra	67	4	Shostakovich	Symphony No. 1	72	[19]
Golestan	Concerto Roumain pour Violon et Orchestre	55	[S]	Siegmeister	From my Window	23	3b [25]
Grieg	Piano Concerto in A minor	58	141	Siegmeister	Ozark Set	84	I
Gruenberg	The Enchanted Isle	I	I	Stringfield	A Negro Parade	30	[14] 1f
Holst	The Planets	170	3	Taylor	Through the Looking Glass	92	[12]
Honegger	Le Chant de Nigamon	36	[125]	Vaughan Williams	A London Symphony	34	[V] 1f
Howe	Stars	6	4	Vaughan Williams	Overture to "The Wasps"	13	123
				Walton	Concerto for Viola and Orchestra	13	2

Violin II and Violoncello

COMPOSER	WORK	PAGE	MEASURE	COMPOSER	WORK	PAGE	MEASURE
Elgar	Introduction and Allegro for Strings	25	[15] 3f	Kodály	Psalmus Hungaricus	18	[11]
				Miaskovsky	Sinfonietta for String Orchestra	22	[12]

Violin I, II, and Violoncello

COMPOSER	WORK	PAGE	MEASURE	COMPOSER	WORK	PAGE	MEASURE
Maganini	South Wind	5	10	Rimsky-Korsakoff	Le Coq d'Or Suite	20	[14]

STRINGS

Viola and Violoncello

COMPOSER	WORK	PAGE	MEASURE	COMPOSER	WORK	PAGE	MEASURE
Barber	*Music for a Scene from*			**Gould**	*Spirituals*	7	3b [E]
	Shelley	16	98	**Grofé**	*Grand Canyon Suite*	168	1
Bartók	*Violin Concerto*	11	[67]	**Kabalevsky**	*Suite from "Colas*		
		22	[156]		*Breugnon"*	37	[27]
Debussy	*Le Martyre de Saint*			**Respighi**	*The Pines of Rome*	65	[17]
	Sébastien	62	1	**Rosenthal**	*Les Petits Métiers*	95	2
Gould	*Latin-American*			**Taylor**	*Through the Looking*	81	[5]
	Symphonette	17	[L]		*Glass*	87	[9]

Solo Viola and Violoncello

COMPOSER	WORK	PAGE	MEASURE
Schönberg	*Pierrot Lunaire*	43	[30] 3f

Violoncello and Bass

COMPOSER	WORK	PAGE	MEASURE	COMPOSER	WORK	PAGE	MEASURE
Bartók	*Music for Strings,*			**Griffes**	*The Pleasure Dome of*		
	Percussion and Celesta	68	17		*Kubla Khan*	1	1
Debussy	*La Mer*	104	[51]	**Thomson**	*Louisiana Story Suite*	45	5

Soli Violoncello and Bass

COMPOSER	WORK	PAGE	MEASURE
Elgar	*Falstaff*	145	[145]

Violin II, Viola, and Violoncello

COMPOSER	WORK	PAGE	MEASURE	COMPOSER	WORK	PAGE	MEASURE
Atterberg	*The Wise and the*			**Prokofieff**	*Alexander Nevsky*	6	[1]
	Foolish Virgins	38	1	**Rimsky-**			
Bax	*Second Symphony*	5	1b [2]	**Korsakoff**	*Le Coq d'Or Suite*	105	[62]
Elgar	*Symphony No. 1*	59	[52] 4f	**Schreker**	*The Birthday of the*		
Gillis	*Symphony No. 5½*	44	2b [A]		*Infanta, Suite*	55	2b [340]

Violin I, II, Viola, and Violoncello

COMPOSER	WORK	PAGE	MEASURE	COMPOSER	WORK	PAGE	MEASURE
Antheil	*Over the Plains*	28	3	**Holst**	*The Planets*	178	[IV]
Bartók	*Concerto for Orchestra*	129	[482]	**Knipper**	*Symphony No. 4*	28	[22]
Bax	*Third Symphony*	52	[53] 1f	**Read**	*Symphony No. I*	95	1
		111	2b [29]	**Respighi**	*The Pines of Rome*	56	3
Bloch	*America*	108	[63]	**Saint-Saëns**	*Le Carnaval des*		
Britten	*Sinfonia da Requiem*	13	7b [10]		*Animaux*	32	2b [4]
Britten	*The Young Person's*			**Schönberg**	*Fünf Orchesterstücke*	53	[6]
	Guide to the			**Siegmeister**	*Sunday in Brooklyn*	75	[60]
	Orchestra	47	8	**Vaughan**	*A London Symphony*	50	[FF] 5f
Coppola	*Scherzo Fantasque*	10	[5] 1f	**Williams**		93	[K]
Debussy	*Jeux*	78	4b [52]	**Vaughan**	*Overture to "The*		
Enesco	*2ᵉ Rhapsodie Roumaine*	10	7b [7]	**Williams**	*Wasps"*	29	212

SUL PONTICELLO

Violin II, Viola, and Bass

COMPOSER	WORK	PAGE	MEASURE
Walton	*Symphony*	130	[99]

Violin I, Violoncello, and Bass

Holst	*The Planets*	184	[VII]

Violin I, II, Violoncello, and Bass

Casella	*Italia*	14	[5]

Viola, Violoncello, and Bass

COMPOSER	WORK	PAGE	MEASURE	COMPOSER	WORK	PAGE	MEASURE
Antheil	*Over the Plains*	17	2	**Schönberg**	*A Survivor from Warsaw*	14	67
Bax	*Second Symphony*	72	[41]	**Vaughan**			
Britten	*The Young Person's Guide to the Orchestra*	36	1	**Williams**	*Pastoral Symphony*	20	4

Violin I, Viola, Violoncello, and Bass

Bartók	*Concerto for Orchestra*	42	[219]

Violin II, Viola, Violoncello, and Bass

Debussy	*Iberia*	80	[52]	**Szymanowski**	*Symphonie Concertante pour Piano et Orchestre*	11	[6] 2f
Kabalevsky	*Suite from "Colas Breugnon"*	167	[29]	**Walton**	*Symphony*	101	1
Mahler	*Symphony No. 2*	31	[15] 5f				
Still	*Bells*	10	[8] 5f				

Violin I, II, Viola, Violoncello, and Bass

Bartók	*Music for Strings, Percussion and Celesta*	80	45	**Taylor**	*Through the Looking Glass*	45	[2]
Bax	*First Symphony*	12	2	**Turner**	*Gregorian Overture for String Orchestra*	12	145
Prokofieff	*Peter and the Wolf*	28	[23] 2f	**Vaughan**			
Rimsky-Korsakoff	*Symphony No. 2, "Antar"*	60	[D]	**Williams**	*A London Symphony*	179	[Q]

(6) NON-TREMOLO

Violin I

Debussy	*Iberia*	30	1	**Schönberg**	*Fünf Orchesterstücke*	27	1b [10]
de Falla	*Three Dances from "The Three-Cornered Hat"*	15	[11]	**Stillman-Kelley**	*New England Symphony*	63	[L] 5f
Prokofieff	*Suite from the Ballet "Chout"*	103	1	**Stravinsky**	*Le Sacre du Printemps*	60	[70]
		119	[151]			121	[165]

389

STRINGS

Soli Violin I

COMPOSER	WORK	PAGE	MEASURE
Copland	Concerto for Piano and Orchestra	40	[31]

Violin II

COMPOSER	WORK	PAGE	MEASURE	COMPOSER	WORK	PAGE	MEASURE
Parodi	Preludio ad una Commedia	51	[AB]	Roussel	Symphonie en Sol mineur	11 / 116	[7] 4f / [70] 3f
				Schönberg	Theme and Variations	28	122

Violin I and II

COMPOSER	WORK	PAGE	MEASURE	COMPOSER	WORK	PAGE	MEASURE
Fernandez	Batuque	4	[3] 3f	Rogers	Once Upon a Time, Five Fairy Tales	17	3b [13]
Ferroud	Au Parc Monceau	1	1				
Grieg	The Last Spring	2	[B]	Rudhyar	Sinfonietta	12	5
Loeffler	Evocation	40	[42]	Schreker	The Birthday of the Infanta, Suite	55	[345] 2f
Prokofieff	Alexander Nevsky	68	1				
Prokofieff	Cinderella Suite No. 1	38	1b [25]				

Viola

COMPOSER	WORK	PAGE	MEASURE	COMPOSER	WORK	PAGE	MEASURE
Bax	Second Symphony	10	2b [4]	Inghelbrecht	La Valse Retrouvée	4	[37]
Copland	Two Pieces for String Orchestra	13	[110] 3f	Mahler	Das Lied von der Erde	44	[11] 4f
				Prokofieff	Alexander Nevsky	50	[32] 2f
Debussy	Jeux	2	1	Walton	Façade, Suite No. 2	3	[A]
Halffter	Deux Esquisses Symphoniques	21	1b [A]	Walton	Symphony	92	8

Violoncello

COMPOSER	WORK	PAGE	MEASURE	COMPOSER	WORK	PAGE	MEASURE
Berg	Violin Concerto	66	[65] 6f	Mahler	Symphony No. 4	35	180
Berlioz	Roméo et Juliette	219	9	Rimsky-Korsakoff	Scheherazade	251	619
Debussy	Iberia	81	1				

Violin I and Viola

COMPOSER	WORK	PAGE	MEASURE	COMPOSER	WORK	PAGE	MEASURE
Delannoy	Figures Sonores	60	2	de Falla	Three Dances from "The Three-Cornered Hat"	85	[30]
Delius	Summer Night on the River	13	5				

Violin II and Viola

COMPOSER	WORK	PAGE	MEASURE	COMPOSER	WORK	PAGE	MEASURE
Bax	Second Symphony	124	2	Fitelberg	Symphony No. 1	119	[346]
Debussy	Iberia	77	[50]	Kabalevsky	Symphony No. 2	29	[24]
Debussy	La Mer	134	[62]	Prokofieff	Symphony No. 5	128	2
Debussy	Rondes de Printemps	49	[25]	Roussel	Suite en Fa	95	2b [52]
Egge	Piano Concerto No. 2	50	[42]				

SUL PONTICELLO

Violin I, II, and Viola

COMPOSER	WORK	PAGE	MEASURE	COMPOSER	WORK	PAGE	MEASURE
Berg	Three Excerpts from "Wozzeck"	14	2b [370]	Prokofieff	Cinderella Suite No. 1	52 79	1b [39] [60]
de Falla	Three Dances from "The Three-Cornered Hat"	42	[3]	Prokofieff	Romeo and Juliet, Suite No. 1	123	[78] 2f
Milhaud	Ière Symphonie	7	1b [25]	Prokofieff	Summer Day Suite	86	5
Parodi	Preludio ad una Commedia	30	1b [P]	Schelling	A Victory Ball	66	8
				Stravinsky	Le Sacre du Printemps	139	[201] 2f

Soli Violin I, II, and Viola

COMPOSER	WORK	PAGE	MEASURE
Stillman-Kelley	New England Symphony	125	14

Violin I and Violoncello

COMPOSER	WORK	PAGE	MEASURE
Blancafort	Mati de Festa a Puig-Gracios	7	[7]

Solo Violin and Violoncello

COMPOSER	WORK	PAGE	MEASURE
Schönberg	Pierrot Lunaire	32	1b [15]

Violin II and Violoncello

COMPOSER	WORK	PAGE	MEASURE
Stravinsky	Le Sacre du Printemps	108	[135] 2f

Violin I, II, and Violoncello

COMPOSER	WORK	PAGE	MEASURE
Stravinsky	Petrouchka Suite	153	4b [129]

Viola and Violoncello

COMPOSER	WORK	PAGE	MEASURE	COMPOSER	WORK	PAGE	MEASURE
Jolivet	Andante pour Orchestre à Cordes	9	[40]	Loeffler	Evocation	41	[43]
				Prokofieff	Summer Day Suite	54	[26]
Levant	Nocturne	35	154	Prokofieff	Symphony No. 5	165	4b [93]

Solo Viola and Violoncello

COMPOSER	WORK	PAGE	MEASURE
Schönberg	Pierrot Lunaire	35	[5]

Violoncello and Bass

COMPOSER	WORK	PAGE	MEASURE	COMPOSER	WORK	PAGE	MEASURE
Prokofieff	Romeo and Juliet, Suite No. 1	124	[79]	Schelling	A Victory Ball	69	[21]
				Stravinsky	Petrouchka Suite	80	[66]

STRINGS

Violin I, Viola, and Violoncello

COMPOSER	WORK	PAGE	MEASURE	COMPOSER	WORK	PAGE	MEASURE
Prokofieff	Suite from the Ballet "Chout"	III	[143]	Walton	Symphony	101	1

Soli Violin I, Viola, and Violoncello

COMPOSER	WORK	PAGE	MEASURE
Stravinsky	Orpheus	57	[143]

Violin II, Viola, and Violoncello

Bartók	Dance Suite	34	26	Prokofieff	Peter and the Wolf	22	[18] 1f

Violin I, II, Viola, and Violoncello

Bartók	Music for Strings, Percussion and Celesta	24	155	Jolivet	Andante pour Orchestre à Cordes	3	[10] 1f
Becker	Concerto for Horn and Orchestra	3	9	Mahler	Symphony No. 3	23	[18]
				Mahler	Symphony No. 4	106	274
Debussy–Busser	Petite Suite	53	3	Prokofieff	Peter and the Wolf	16	6
Dukas	L'Apprenti Sorcier	48	12			42	[35] 1f
de Falla	El Amor Brujo	63	4b [36]	Rudhyar	Sinfonietta	8	1
de Falla	Three Dances from					39	5
	"The Three-	25	[2]	Schönberg	A Survivor from Warsaw	14	70
	Cornered Hat"	56	[8]	Stravinsky	Petrouchka Suite	40	[29] 7f
Gould	Latin-American			Walton	Concerto for Viola and Orchestra	11	[10]
	Symphonette	22	[Q]	Walton	Symphony	157	[120]
Inghelbrecht	La Métamorphose d'Ève	18	[16] 1f				

Violin II, Violoncello, and Bass

MacDowell	2nd Suite (Indian)	46	[D]

Viola, Violoncello, and Bass

Prokofieff	Alexander Nevsky	53	[34]	Walton	Concerto for Viola and Orchestra	24	3

Violin I, II, Viola, Violoncello, and Bass

Berg	Three Excerpts from "Wozzeck"	37	1b [285]	Prokofieff	Romeo and Juliet, Suite No. 1	81	[53]
Prokofieff	Alexander Nevsky	56	[36]	Sibelius	En Saga	47	5
Prokofieff	Cinderella Suite No. 1	45	[32]	Siegmeister	Sunday in Brooklyn	27	1
		61	[47]			74	2

392

SUL PONTICELLO

(7) SUL PONTICELLO AND COL LEGNO COMBINED

Violoncello divisi (sul pont. and col legno)

COMPOSER	WORK	PAGE	MEASURE	COMPOSER	WORK	PAGE	MEASURE
Parodi	*Preludio ad una Commedia*	**17**	[I]	**Schönberg**	*A Survivor from Warsaw*	**1**	3

(8) SUL PONTICELLO AND MODO ORDINARIO COMBINED

Violin II divisi (sul pont. and modo ord.)

COMPOSER	WORK	PAGE	MEASURE
Mahler	*Symphony No. 8*	**171**	[154]

Violin I and II divisi (sul pont. and modo ord.)

Cadman	*American Suite*	**18**	5

Violoncello divisi (sul pont. and modo ord.)

Revueltas	*Sensemayá*	**40**	[37]

Violin II and Viola divisi (sul pont. and modo ord.)

Rogers	*Once Upon a Time, Five Fairy Tales*	**14** **19**	3b [11] 6

Violin I, Viola, Violoncello divisi (sul pont. and modo ord.)

Elgar	*Concerto for Violin and Orchestra*	**88**	[101]

393

Chapter 54

SUL TASTO

English	Italian	French	German
Fingerboard	Flautando	Sur la touche	Am Griffbrett
Flute-like	Flautato	Touche	*am Griff., Griffbr.*
On [over] the fingerboard	*flaut.*	Vers la touche	
	Sulla tastiera		
	Sul tasto		
	sul tast.		
	Suoni flautati		

NATURAL POSITION

Natural (position)	Modo ordinario	Jeu ordinaire	Gewöhnlich
	Non sul tasto		

(for further terminology see Chapter 52, page 372)

(1) GLISSANDO
Violin I and II

COMPOSER	WORK	PAGE	MEASURE
Parodi	*Preludio ad una Commedia*	**15**	[H]

Viola

COMPOSER	WORK	PAGE	MEASURE	COMPOSER	WORK	PAGE	MEASURE
Ravel	*Daphnis et Chloé, Suite No. 1*	**6**	[76]	**Ravel**	*Shéhérazade*	**27**	2

Violoncello

COMPOSER	WORK	PAGE	MEASURE	COMPOSER	WORK	PAGE	MEASURE
Halffter	*Deux Esquisses Symphoniques*	**9**	2	**Ravel**	*Daphnis et Chloé, Suite No. 1*	**7**	3b [77]

Soli Violoncello and Bass

COMPOSER	WORK	PAGE	MEASURE
Ravel	*Rapsodie Espagnole*	**59**	2b [12]

Violin I, Viola, and Violoncello

COMPOSER	WORK	PAGE	MEASURE
Ravel	*Rapsodie Espagnole*	**61**	[13] 1f

Violin II, Viola, and Violoncello

COMPOSER	WORK	PAGE	MEASURE
Mussorgsky–Ravel	*Pictures at an Exhibition*	**10**	[9]

394

SUL TASTO

Viola, Violoncello, and Bass

COMPOSER	WORK	PAGE	MEASURE	COMPOSER	WORK	PAGE	MEASURE
Ravel	Daphnis et Chloé, Suite No. 1	3	[73]	Ravel	Valses Nobles et Sentimentales	70	[71]

(2) ON HARMONICS
Violin I

COMPOSER	WORK	PAGE	MEASURE
Ravel	Shéhérazade	50	1b [3]

Violin I and II

COMPOSER	WORK	PAGE	MEASURE	COMPOSER	WORK	PAGE	MEASURE
Milhaud	Saudades do Brazil	77	5	Read	Symphony No. 1	104	1

Violoncello

Ravel	Shéhérazade	23	[12]

Violoncello and Bass

Casella	Elegia Eroica	29	6

Violin I, Viola, and Violoncello

Stravinsky	Le Sacre du Printemps	73	1b [81]

(3) PIZZICATO
Violin II

Debussy	Gigues	35	[21]

Violin II and Violoncello

Mahler	Symphony No. 6	226	[145]

Violoncello and Bass

Berg	Three Excerpts from "Wozzeck"	41	[305] 1f

Violin I, II, Viola, and Violoncello

Berg	Violin Concerto	77	[125]

(4) TREMOLO
Violin I

COMPOSER	WORK	PAGE	MEASURE	COMPOSER	WORK	PAGE	MEASURE
Debussy	Iberia	25	[16]	Debussy	Sirènes	96	1
		31	[20]	de Falla	Nuits dans les Jardins d'Espagne	26	[19] 10f
		37	[23] 2f	de Falla	Three Dances from		
		78	[51] 2f		"The Three-		
Debussy	Jeux	52	5		Cornered Hat"	3	[2]
Debussy	La Damoiselle Élue	45	[18]				

STRINGS

Violin I (contd.)

COMPOSER	WORK	PAGE	MEASURE	COMPOSER	WORK	PAGE	MEASURE
Ibert	Escales	22	5	Roussel	Évocations, III	68	[34]
Ibert	La Ba'lade de la Geôle			Stravinsky	Fire-Bird Suite (1919)	1	[1] 2f
	de Reading	7	[6]	Walton	Concerto for Violin and		
Mahler	Symphony No. 6	36	8		Orchestra	108	[54]

Soli Violin I

COMPOSER	WORK	PAGE	MEASURE
Rogers	Once Upon a Time, Five Fairy Tales	14	[11]

Violin II

COMPOSER	WORK	PAGE	MEASURE	COMPOSER	WORK	PAGE	MEASURE
Bloch	Trois Poèmes Juifs	5	[1]	Ravel	Daphnis et Chloé,		
Britten	Les Illuminations	2	3		Suite No. 1	4	[74]
Debussy	Iberia	64	1	Ravel	Ma Mère l'Oye	7	5
		69	3	Ravel	Rapsodie Espagnole	67	[18]
Debussy	Jeux	7	[5]	Stravinsky	Fire-Bird Suite (1919)	68	[4]
Ibert	Escales	14	[9]	Stravinsky	Le Sacre du Printemps	83	2b [100]
Mahler	Das Lied von der Erde	44	[11] 4f	Walton	Concerto for Viola and		
					Orchestra	17	[15]

Violin I and II

COMPOSER	WORK	PAGE	MEASURE	COMPOSER	WORK	PAGE	MEASURE
Chausson	Symphonie en Si bémol majeur	21	[F] 4f	Ravel	Shéhérazade	23	[12]
Debussy	Gigues	35	[21]	Ravel	Valses Nobles et Sentimentales	54	[53]
Debussy	La Mer	85	1b [44]	Read	Symphony No. 1	23	[11]
de Falla	Three Dances from "The Three-Cornered Hat"	5	[3]	Roussel	Évocations, I	48	[14] 3f
				Stravinsky	Chant du Rossignol	71	[79]
Poulenc	Concert Champêtre pour Clavecin et Orchestre	89	[13]	Szymanowski	Symphonie Concertante pour Piano et Orchestre	48	1
Ravel	Daphnis et Chloé, Suite No. 1	6	[76]	Vaughan Williams	Overture to "The Wasps"	32	229
Ravel	Introduction et Allegro	15	[9]	Walton	Concerto for Viola and Orchestra	2	4b [2]
Ravel	Ma Mère l'Oye	24	[14]				
Ravel	Rapsodie Espagnole	3	[2] 5f				

Viola

COMPOSER	WORK	PAGE	MEASURE	COMPOSER	WORK	PAGE	MEASURE
Bloch	Trois Poèmes Juifs	43	[2]	Halffter	Deux Esquisses Symphoniques	8	2
		85	[18] 1f	Jolivet	Andante pour Orchestre à Cordes	8	1b [35]
Britten	Sinfonietta	27	[12]				
Chabrier	España, Rhapsodie	26	[F]	Ravel	La Valse	2	1
Charpentier	Impressions d'Italie	61	[9]	Ravel	Ma Mère l'Oye	25	1
Dukas	La Péri	94	1	Ravel	Rapsodie Espagnole	47	[5]
de Falla	El Amor Brujo	20	[5]	Stravinsky	Fire-Bird Suite (1919)	5	[6]

SUL TASTO

Violoncello

COMPOSER	WORK	PAGE	MEASURE	COMPOSER	WORK	PAGE	MEASURE
Debussy	Iberia	80	[52] 2f	Ibert	Escales	18	[12]
Debussy	La Mer	11	[5]	Mahler	Symphony No. 6	151	[104] 1f
Dukas	La Péri	40	1	Ravel	Daphnis et Chloé, Suite No. 2	101	[210]
de Falla	Three Dances from "The Three-Cornered Hat"	13	[10]	Walton	Symphony	38	[23]

Bass

COMPOSER	WORK	PAGE	MEASURE	COMPOSER	WORK	PAGE	MEASURE
Debussy	Nuages	16	[9]	de Falla	Nuits dans les Jardins d'Espagne	19	4b [13]

Violin I and Viola

COMPOSER	WORK	PAGE	MEASURE	COMPOSER	WORK	PAGE	MEASURE
de Falla	Nuits dans les Jardins d'Espagne	17	[11]	Stravinsky	"Dumbarton Oaks" Concerto	20	[39]

Violin II and Viola

COMPOSER	WORK	PAGE	MEASURE	COMPOSER	WORK	PAGE	MEASURE
Bartók	Concerto for Orchestra	99	[175]	Malipiero	Impressioni dal Vero, 1ª Parte	39	[2]
Cras	Journal de Bord	2	4	Ravel	La Valse	79	[58]
Debussy	Gigues	22	2b [13]	Stravinsky	Le Sacre du Printemps	81	[94]
Debussy	Jeux	77	[51]	Walton	Concerto for Viola and Orchestra	19	[16]
Debussy	La Mer	33	4				
		108	3				
Debussy–Ansermet	Six Épigraphes Antiques	56	[A]	Walton	Concerto for Violin and Orchestra	43	[22] 1f

Violin I, II, and Viola

COMPOSER	WORK	PAGE	MEASURE	COMPOSER	WORK	PAGE	MEASURE
Aubert	Saisons	23	[14] 4f	Ravel	Daphnis et Chloé, Suite No. 1	8	[78]
		62	[33] 2f			10	[80]
Bloch	Schelomo	48	[29]	Ravel	Rapsodie Espagnole	9	[7]
Debussy	La Damoiselle Élue	28	2	Read	Sketches of the City	7	[4]
Debussy–Ansermet	Six Épigraphes Antiques	48	[E]	Sibelius	Symphony No. 4	7	2
Dukas	La Péri	126	1	Sibelius	Symphony No. 5	6	1
Dukas	Symphonie en Ut majeur	128	2b [R]	Sibelius	Symphony No. 6	23	[K] 7f
				Siegmeister	From my Window	6	4b [30]
Mahler	Songs of a Wayfarer	46	43	Vaughan Williams	Fantasia on a Theme by Thomas Tallis	18	[U] 1f

Viola and Violoncello

COMPOSER	WORK	PAGE	MEASURE	COMPOSER	WORK	PAGE	MEASURE
Debussy	Jeux	28	[20] 4f	Mahler	Symphony No. 2	23	5
Debussy	Nuages	15	4	Ravel	Menuet Antique	12	[9] 1f
Debussy	Première Rhapsodie	38	3	Sessions	Symphony No. II	27	[Q]

Violoncello and Bass

COMPOSER	WORK	PAGE	MEASURE	COMPOSER	WORK	PAGE	MEASURE
Britten	Sinfonia da Requiem	59	[40]	Ravel	Ma Mère l'Oye	36	[2] 4f
Debussy	La Mer	105	[52]	Ravel	Rapsodie Espagnole	41	1
Debussy	Sirènes	110	1			59	1

STRINGS

Violin II, Viola, and Violoncello

COMPOSER	WORK	PAGE	MEASURE	COMPOSER	WORK	PAGE	MEASURE
Bartók	*Violin Concerto*	111	[415]	Stravinsky	*Petrouchka Suite*	42	[32] 3f
Debussy	*Prélude à l'après-midi d'un Faune*	3	[1]				

Violin I, II, Viola, and Violoncello

COMPOSER	WORK	PAGE	MEASURE	COMPOSER	WORK	PAGE	MEASURE
Bartók	*Music for Strings, Percussion and Celesta*	73	36	Ravel	*Daphnis et Chloé, Suite No. 1*	1	1
Debussy	*Prélude à l'après-midi d'un Faune*	27	[10]	Ravel	*Ma Mère l'Oye*	10	1
Debussy	*Sirènes*	76	2	Read	*Symphony No. I*	73	[29]
Janssen	*New Year's Eve in New York*	51	[20] 1f	Sibelius	*Die Okeaniden*	13	3
				Sibelius	*Symphony No. 4*	68	[W]
				Sibelius	*Symphony No. 5*	95	3
				Stravinsky	*Fire-Bird Suite (1919)*	70	[9]

Violin I, II, Violoncello, and Bass

COMPOSER	WORK	PAGE	MEASURE
Whithorne	*The Dream Pedlar*	22	[11]

Viola, Violoncello, and Bass

COMPOSER	WORK	PAGE	MEASURE	COMPOSER	WORK	PAGE	MEASURE
de Falla	*El Amor Brujo*	7	[1]	Walton	*Concerto for Viola and Orchestra*	3	[3]
Siegmeister	*Western Suite*	21	[80] 1f	Whithorne	*The Dream Pedlar*	65	4

Violin II, Viola, Violoncello, and Bass

COMPOSER	WORK	PAGE	MEASURE	COMPOSER	WORK	PAGE	MEASURE
Debussy	*Première Rhapsodie*	12	2	Scriabin	*Prométhée, Le Poème du Feu*	3	1
de Falla	*Nuits dans les Jardins d'Espagne*	55	3b [22]				

Violin I, II, Viola, Violoncello, and Bass

COMPOSER	WORK	PAGE	MEASURE	COMPOSER	WORK	PAGE	MEASURE
Debussy	*Sirènes*	104	2	Halffter	*Deux Esquisses Symphoniques*	16	[F]

(5) NON-TREMOLO

Violin I

COMPOSER	WORK	PAGE	MEASURE	COMPOSER	WORK	PAGE	MEASURE
Chasins	*Rush Hour in Hong Kong*	3	1	Mahler	*Symphony No. 2*	69	[9]
Chausson	*Symphonie en Si bémol majeur*	57	2	Mahler	*Symphony No. 3*	226	3b [27]
				Mahler	*Symphony No. 4*	61	28
Debussy–Ansermet	*Six Épigraphes Antiques*	4	3	Mahler	*Symphony No. 5*	38	5
Delannoy	*Figures Sonores*	32	[14]	Mahler	*Symphony No. 7*	159	[181] 1f
Ibiamond	*Fourth Symphony*	29	[155]	Ravel	*Rapsodie Espagnole*	24	1b [13]
Dert	*La Ballade de la Geôle de Reading*	7	[6]			37	[10] 3f
		28	[18]	Rossini	*La Scala di Seta, Overture*	18	336
Janssen	*New Year's Eve in New York*	28	[11]	Schlein	*Dance Overture*	6	6b [35]
Mahler	*Das Lied von der Erde*	97	[1] 1f	Siegmeister	*Ozark Set*	15	[60] 1f
Mahler	*Songs of a Wayfarer*	67	[31]	Walton	*Façade, Suite No. 1*	18	1
				Walton	*Symphony*	77	11

SUL TASTO

Solo Violin

COMPOSER	WORK	PAGE	MEASURE	COMPOSER	WORK	PAGE	MEASURE
Schönberg	*Pierrot Lunaire*	31	1b [5]	Stravinsky	*Histoire du Soldat*	43	[12] 3f

Soli Violin I

Debussy	*Iberia*	94	2b [59]	Respighi	*Metamorphoseon, XII*		
Gould	*Philharmonic Waltzes*	29	[339] 14f		*Modi*	42	[21₁]

Violin II

Albéniz Arbós	*Triana*	24	[G]	Jolivet	*Andante pour Orchestre à Cordes*	3	[10] 2f
Berg	*Violin Concerto*	83	2b [160]	Mahler	*Das Lied von der Erde*	36	[46]
Copland	*Dance Symphony*	32	[16]	Mahler	*Symphony No. 5*	127	13
Debussy	*Iberia*	20	I	Rudhyar	*Sinfonietta*	6	6
Dukas	*Symphonie en Ut majeur*	94	[E]	Stravinsky	*Pulcinella Suite*	31	[42]

Violin I and II

Debussy	*Rapsodie pour Orchestre et Saxophone*	41	[G]	Mussorgsky-Ravel	*Pictures at an Exhibition*	41	[35]
Debussy-Ansermet	*Six Épigraphes Antiques*	31	[C] 1f	Piston	*Prelude and Allegro for Organ and Strings*	14	I
de Falla	*El Amor Brujo*	20	[5]	Ravel	*Daphnis et Chloé,*		
Mahler	*Das Lied von der Erde*	53	[6]		*Suite No. 2*	57	[184]
		129	[51]	Ravel	*Rapsodie Espagnole*	29	[1]
Mahler	*Symphony No. 1*	116	1b [15]	Read	*Symphony No. I*	40	3
Mahler	*Symphony No. 4*	82	78	Rogers	*Characters from Hans Christian Andersen*	4	I
Mahler	*Symphony No. 7*	64	[55] 2f				
Mahler	*Symphony No. 8*	59	4	Rogers	*Elegy*	I	12
		210	[205]	Siegmeister	*Western Suite*	19	[65] 2f
Mahler	*Symphony No. 9*	172	I	Stravinsky	*Pulcinella Suite*	10	[8] 3f
				Tippett	*Symphony No. I*	133	2

Soli Violin I and II

COMPOSER	WORK	PAGE	MEASURE
Szymanowski	*Symphonie Concertante pour Piano et Orchestre*	13	[7] 2f

Viola

Mahler	*Songs of a Wayfarer*	53	75	Walton	*Concerto for Viola and Orchestra*	7	[7]
Ravel	*Daphnis et Chloé, Suite No. 2*	58	[185]			17	[15]
Ravel	*Rapsodie Espagnole*	81	2b [27]	Walton	*Symphony*	71	[46] 3f

Soli Viola

Stravinsky	*Le Sacre du Printemps*	72	[79] 4f

STRINGS

Violoncello

COMPOSER	WORK	PAGE	MEASURE	COMPOSER	WORK	PAGE	MEASURE
Charpentier	*Impressions d'Italie*	18	[16]	Mahler	*Symphony No. 5*	70	3
Debussy	*Iberia*	68	[46]	Ravel	*La Valse*	66	[48]
		75	2	Rivier	*Rapsodie pour Violon-*		
Debussy	*Rondes de Printemps*	1	1		*celle et Orchestre*	3	[1]
Jolivet	*Andante pour Orchestre*						
	à Cordes	10	1				

Solo Violoncello

COMPOSER	WORK	PAGE	MEASURE
Schönberg	*Pierrot Lunaire*	27	[15] 2f

Bass

COMPOSER	WORK	PAGE	MEASURE	COMPOSER	WORK	PAGE	MEASURE
Debussy	*Gigues*	28	2b [16]	Ravel	*Daphnis et Chloé,*		
Debussy	*Iberia*	58	[39] 2f		*Suite No. 1*	1	1
		76	2	Ravel	*Rapsodie Espagnole*	45	[4]
		80	[52] 2f	Ravel	*Shéhérazade*	23	[12]

Violin I and Viola

COMPOSER	WORK	PAGE	MEASURE
Rudhyar	*Five Stanzas*	17	[W] 3f

Violin II and Viola

COMPOSER	WORK	PAGE	MEASURE	COMPOSER	WORK	PAGE	MEASURE
Debussy	*Première Rhapsodie*	16	3	Ravel	*Rapsodie Espagnole*	64	[15] 2f

Violin I, II, and Viola

COMPOSER	WORK	PAGE	MEASURE	COMPOSER	WORK	PAGE	MEASURE
Debussy-Ansermet	*Six Épigraphes Antiques*	49	1	Schreker	*The Birthday of the Infanta, Suite*	88	[455]
Ferroud	*Au Parc Monceau*	4	3	Shepherd	*Horizons*	82	[E]
Křenek	*Symphonic Elegy*	5	121	Shostakovich	*Symphony No. 6*	79	[78]
Mihalovici	*Toccata pour Piano et Orchestre*	112	1	Sibelius	*Symphony No. 6*	35	[G]
				Turina	*La Procesión del Rocío*	40	3
Ravel	*Shéhérazade*	44	[4]	Walton	*Concerto for Viola and Orchestra*	1	4
Rudhyar	*Sinfonietta*	21	1				
Schmitt	*Ronde burlesque*	48	[26]	Walton	*Façade, Suite No. 1*	48	1

Violin I and Violoncello

COMPOSER	WORK	PAGE	MEASURE	COMPOSER	WORK	PAGE	MEASURE
Debussy	*Rondes de Printemps*	15	[8]	Rogers	*Once Upon a Time, Five Fairy Tales*	23	2
		36	3				
Mahler	*Symphony No. 8*	23	[21]				

Violin I, II, and Violoncello

COMPOSER	WORK	PAGE	MEASURE	COMPOSER	WORK	PAGE	MEASURE
Ibert	*La Ballade de la Geôle de Reading*	62	[44] 2f	Mahler	*Symphony No. 2*	200	[46]
				Mahler	*Symphony No. 3*	173	[28]

Viola and Violoncello

COMPOSER	WORK	PAGE	MEASURE	COMPOSER	WORK	PAGE	MEASURE
Debussy	*Première Rhapsodie*	33	[9]	Stravinsky	*Fire-Bird Suite* (1919)	22	[12] 4f
Mahler	*Das Lied von der Erde*	75	[14]	Stravinsky	*Orpheus*	16	[35]
Rudhyar	*Sinfonietta*	29	4	Walton	*Façade, Suite No. 1*	42	3

SUL TASTO

Viola and Bass

COMPOSER	WORK	PAGE	MEASURE
Ravel	*Alborada del Gracioso*	**14**	[9] 4f

Violoncello and Bass

COMPOSER	WORK	PAGE	MEASURE	COMPOSER	WORK	PAGE	MEASURE
Debussy	*Jeux*	**64**	[43]	**Ravel**	*Daphnis et Chloé,*	**8**	[78]
		89	3		*Suite No. 1*	**10**	[80]
Dukas	*La Péri*	**126**	1				

Violin I, Viola, and Violoncello

COMPOSER	WORK	PAGE	MEASURE	COMPOSER	WORK	PAGE	MEASURE
Berg	*Three Excerpts from*			**Debussy**	*Jeux*	**7**	[5]
	"Wozzeck"	**40**	3b [300]	**Debussy**	*Rondes de Printemps*	**56**	1
Debussy	*Gigues*	**22**	2b [13]	**Stravinsky**	*Le Sacre du Printemps*	**73**	[80] 2f

Soli Violin I, Viola, and Violoncello

Ravel	*Rapsodie Espagnole*	**9**	[7]

Violin II, Viola, and Violoncello

COMPOSER	WORK	PAGE	MEASURE	COMPOSER	WORK	PAGE	MEASURE
Debussy	*Iberia*	**51**	[34]	**Ravel**	*Daphnis et Chloé,*		
Ravel	*Concerto pour Piano et*				*Suite No. 1*	**15**	[91]
	Orchestre	**70**	1b [9]				

Violin I, II, Viola, and Violoncello

COMPOSER	WORK	PAGE	MEASURE	COMPOSER	WORK	PAGE	MEASURE
Bach–	*Passacaglia and Fugue*			**Ravel**	*Valses Nobles et*	**38**	[35]
Respighi	*in C minor*	**21**	[14] 1f		*Sentimentales*	**70**	[71]
Debussy	*Prélude à l'après-midi*			**Rogers**	*Once Upon a Time,*		
	d'un Faune	**23**	2		*Five Fairy Tales*	**32**	[20]
Mahler	*Symphony No. 3*	**52**	[36]	**Tippett**	*Symphony No. 1*	**27**	[17] 2f
Ravel	*Rapsodie Espagnole*	**17**	[7]				

Violin I, II, Viola I, II, and Violoncello I, II

Schönberg	*Verklärte Nacht*	**30**	4

Violin I, II, Viola, and Bass

Debussy	*Première Rhapsodie*	**26**	3

Violin I, II, Viola, Violoncello, and Bass

COMPOSER	WORK	PAGE	MEASURE	COMPOSER	WORK	PAGE	MEASURE
Casella	*Elegia Eroica*	**33**	[50]	**Respighi**	*Vetrate di Chiesa*	**11**	1
Ravel	*Valses Nobles et*			**Shostakovich**	*Symphony No. 6*	**116**	[109]
	Sentimentales	**18**	[16]				

Soli Violin I, II, Viola, Violoncello, and Bass

Whithorne	*Fata Morgana*	**47**	[50]

STRINGS

(6) SUL TASTO AND SUL PONTICELLO COMBINED

Violin II sul tasto—**Viola** sul pont.

COMPOSER	WORK	PAGE	MEASURE	COMPOSER	WORK	PAGE	MEASURE
Albéniz– **Arbós**	*Triana*	24	[G]	Debussy– **Ansermet**	*Six Épigraphes* *Antiques*	8	1

Violin I and II sul tasto—**Viola and Violoncello** sul pont.

COMPOSER	WORK	PAGE	MEASURE
Vaughan **Williams**	*Pastoral Symphony*	90	5b [F]

Chapter 55

MUTES

(for terminology see Chapter 19, page 104)

(1) MUTED AND OPEN COMBINED

English	Italian	French	German
Half [½] muted—half open	La prima [1ᵃ] metà con sord.—la secunda [2ᵃ] metà senza sord.	La première [1ère] moitié avec sourd.—la deuxième [2me] moitié sans sourd.	Die erste [1] Hälfte mit Dämpfer—die zweite [2] Hälfte ohne Dämpfer

Violin I divisi (con and senza sord.)

COMPOSER	WORK	PAGE	MEASURE
Bliss	Concerto for Piano and Orchestra	115	[63] 5f

Violin I con sord.—Solo Violin I senza sord.

COMPOSER	WORK	PAGE	MEASURE	COMPOSER	WORK	PAGE	MEASURE
Debussy	Jeux	73	[49] 1f	Mahler	Symphony No. 7	133	[137]
Debussy-Ansermet	Six Épigraphes Antiques	31	[C] 1f				

Violin II con sord.—Violin I senza sord.

COMPOSER	WORK	PAGE	MEASURE
Mahler	Symphony No. 3	135	[2]
		172	1

Violin II con sord.—Solo Violin I senza sord.

COMPOSER	WORK	PAGE	MEASURE
Mahler	Symphony No. 3	23	[18] 4f

Violin II con sord.—Viola senza sord.

COMPOSER	WORK	PAGE	MEASURE
Mahler	Symphony No. 8	153	1b [124]

Violin I and II divisi (con and senza sord.)

COMPOSER	WORK	PAGE	MEASURE
Dukas	Polyeucte, Ouverture	36	[R]

Soli Violin I and II divisi (con and senza sord.)

COMPOSER	WORK	PAGE	MEASURE
Albéniz-Arbós	El Albaicín	34	6

STRINGS

Soli Viola con sord.—Viola senza sord.

COMPOSER	WORK	PAGE	MEASURE
Mahler	Symphony No. 8	164	2b [148]

Violoncello con sord.—Solo Violoncello senza sord.

James	Suite for String Orchestra	1	1

Violoncello con sord.—Soli Violoncello senza sord.

Debussy-Ansermet	Six Épigraphes Antiques	24	1

Soli Violoncello divisi (con and senza sord.)

Walton	Façade, Suite No. 1	40	4

Bass con sord.—Soli Bass senza sord.

Albéniz–Arbós	Fête-Dieu à Séville	41	2

Violin I and Violoncello divisi (con and senza sord.)

Albéniz–Arbós	Fête-Dieu à Séville	16	1

Soli Violin I, Viola, and Violoncello con sord.—Violin I, II, Viola, and Violoncello senza sord.

COMPOSER	WORK	PAGE	MEASURE	COMPOSER	WORK	PAGE	MEASURE
Berg	Three Excerpts from "Wozzeck"	22	2b [5]	Debussy	Jeux	38	[27] 2f

Violin I, II, Viola, and Violoncello divisi (con and senza sord.)

COMPOSER	WORK	PAGE	MEASURE	COMPOSER	WORK	PAGE	MEASURE
Albéniz–Arbós	Évocation	19	[H]	Mahler	Symphony No. 4	78	2
Bergsma	Music on a Quiet Theme	1	1	Reger	Variations on a Theme of Mozart	3	5
				Schönberg	Fünf Orchesterstücke	34	[4]

Soli Violin I, II, Viola, and Violoncello con sord.—Violin I, II, Viola, and Violoncello senza sord.

Dukas	La Péri	128	[19 bis]

Violin I, II, Viola, Violoncello, and Bass divisi (con and senza sord.)

Elgar	Concerto for Violin and Orchestra	88	[101]

404

MUTES

IInd Orchestra con sord.—**Ist Orchestra** senza sord.

COMPOSER	WORK	PAGE	MEASURE
Turner	*Gregorian Overture for String Orchestra*	**2**	28

(2) MUTES ON GRADUALLY

English	*Italian*	*French*	*German*
Mutes on gradually [one by one]	Con sordini poco a poco	Mettez les sourdines une à une	Allmählich die Dämpfer aufsetzen
Put on mutes gradually [one by one]	Con sord. leggio a leggio	Mettez progressivement les sourdines	Allmählich Sordinen an
	Mettete le sordine uno dopo l'atro		*allm. Sord. an*

Soli Violin II

Whithorne	*The Dream Pedlar*	**57**	3

Viola

COMPOSER	WORK	PAGE	MEASURE	COMPOSER	WORK	PAGE	MEASURE
Bax	*The Garden of Fand*	**42**	5	**Thomson**	*Tango Lullaby*	**2**	14

Violoncello

Stillman-Kelley	*Gulliver—His Voyage to Lilliput*	**133**	[I]

Viola and Violoncello

Hindemith	*Symphonische Tänze*	**79**	4b [9]

Violoncello and Bass

Mussorgsky-Ravel	*Pictures at an Exhibition*	**51**	[45]

Violin I, II, Viola, and Violoncello

White	*Idyl for Orchestra*	**7**	[F]

Violin I, II, Viola, Violoncello, and Bass

Delius	*Appalachia*	**45**	196

405

STRINGS

(3) MUTES OFF GRADUALLY

English	Italian	French	German
Gradually remove mutes	Levano successivamente i	Les Vons. [Altos, Velles,	Allmählich Sordinen ab
Mutes off gradually [one by one]	sordini	C.Bs.] enlèveront leurs	allm. Sord. ab
Remove [take off] mutes gradually [one by one]	Senza sordini poco a poco	sourds. l'un après l'autre	Dämpfer allmählich ab
Remove mutes imperceptibly	Senza sord. leggio a leggio	Ôtez les sourdines petit à petit [une à une]	Dämpfer nach und nach abnehmen
	Togliere successivamente le sordine	Ôtez progressivement les sourdines	Nehmen nach und nach die Dämpfer ab

Violin I

COMPOSER	WORK	PAGE	MEASURE
Copland	*Billy the Kid Ballet Suite*	**53**	3b [33]

Violin II

COMPOSER	WORK	PAGE	MEASURE
Mahler	*Symphony No. 2*	**48**	2b [23]
		178	5

Violin I and II

COMPOSER	WORK	PAGE	MEASURE
Sibelius	*Tapiola*	**51**	515

Viola

COMPOSER	WORK	PAGE	MEASURE	COMPOSER	WORK	PAGE	MEASURE
Schreker	*The Birthday of the Infanta, Suite*	**43**	1b [240]	**Siegmeister**	*Sunday in Brooklyn*	**44**	2b [15]

Violoncello

COMPOSER	WORK	PAGE	MEASURE	COMPOSER	WORK	PAGE	MEASURE
Bloch	*Evocations*	**5**	[5] 2f	**Debussy–**	*Six Épigraphes*		
Busoni	*Rondo Arlecchinesco*	**7**	[7] 5f	**Ansermet**	*Antiques*	**3**	[B]

Violoncello and Bass

COMPOSER	WORK	PAGE	MEASURE	COMPOSER	WORK	PAGE	MEASURE
Mussorgsky–Ravel	*Pictures at an Exhibition*	**46**	[38]	**Ravel**	*Daphnis et Chloé, Suite No. 2*	**1**	[155]

Violin II, Viola, and Violoncello

COMPOSER	WORK	PAGE	MEASURE
Copland	*Music for Radio*	**36**	2

Violin I, II, Viola, Violoncello

COMPOSER	WORK	PAGE	MEASURE	COMPOSER	WORK	PAGE	MEASURE
Stillman-Kelley	*Gulliver—His Voyage to L'lliput*	**141**	[N]	**Thomson**	*The Seine at Night*	**33**	[17] 3f

Viola, Violoncello, and Bass

COMPOSER	WORK	PAGE	MEASURE
Mahler	*Symphony No. 8*	**210**	[205] 1f

MUTES

Violin I, II, Viola, Violoncello, and Bass

COMPOSER	WORK	PAGE	MEASURE	COMPOSER	WORK	PAGE	MEASURE
Harris	*Third Symphony*	48	[36]	**Tansman**	*Deux Moments*	3	[1] 4f
Ravel	*La Valse*	19	[13] 1f		*Symphoniques*	10	1
Stillman-	*Gulliver—His Voyage*			**Wagner, R.**	*Forest Murmurs from*		
Kelley	*to Lilliput*	35	[K]		*"Siegfried"*	8	82

Chapter 56

NATURAL HARMONICS

(for terminology see Chapter 41, page 257)

(1) "HARMONICS"

English	Italian	French	German
Harmonic on G [C; D; A; E] string	Armonico sul G [C; D; A; E] corda	Harmonique à Sol [Ut; Ré; La; Mi]	Flageolett auf der G-[C; D A; E] Saite

Harm.   Arm.   Harm.   Flag.

Violin I

COMPOSER	WORK	PAGE	MEASURE
Bartók	*Second Suite*	**5**	[3] 9f

Soli Violin I

Bartók	*Vier Orchesterstücke*	**27**	1

Violin II

Stravinsky	*Le Sacre du Printemps*	**77**	[87]

Violin I and II

Bartók	*Second Suite*	**9**	2b [8]

Soli Violin I and II

Wagner, R.	*Prelude to Act I, "Lohengrin"*	**1** **14**	2 1

Violoncello

Respighi	*Antiche Danze ed Arie, 2ª Suite*	**41**	6b [10]

Solo Violoncello

Stravinsky	*Concerto en Ré pour Violon et Orchestre*	**62**	[125]

NATURAL HARMONICS

Soli Violoncello

COMPOSER	WORK	PAGE	MEASURE
Schreker	The Birthday of the Infanta, Suite	57	3

Bass

COMPOSER	WORK	PAGE	MEASURE	COMPOSER	WORK	PAGE	MEASURE
Bartók	Deux Portraits	34	[11] 1f	Poulenc	Deux Marches et un Intermède	6	[10]
Griffes	The Pleasure Dome of Kubla Khan	14	[1] 1f				

Solo Bass

Stravinsky	Histoire du Soldat	12	1b [3]
		59	3

Violin I, II, and Viola

Hill	Sinfonietta for String Orchestra	16	1b [135]

Solo Viola and Violoncello

Wagner, R.	Forest Murmurs from "Siegfried"	20	139

(2)

English	Italian	French	German
Actual pitch [sound]	Come è scritto	A l'octave réelle	Klang
At pitch	Suono	Effet	Klingt wie notiert
Real pitch [sound]		Hauteur réelle	Wirklicher Ton [Töne]
Sounding where written		Pour l'oreille	
		Son(s) écrits [réels]	

Violin I

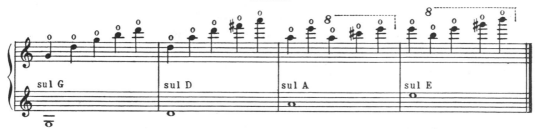

Bloch	Evocations	55	[40]	Copland	Billy the Kid Ballet	28	7	
Borodin	Polovetzian Dances from "Prince Igor"	4	23		Suite	55	[35]	2f
				Copland	Dance Symphony	7	3	
Britten	The Young Person's Guide to the			Copland	Statements	43	4	
				Copland	Two Pieces for String			
	Orchestra	45	7		Orchestra	7	[35]	
Casella	Paganiniana	163	[35]	Debussy	La Mer	80	[42]	7f

STRINGS

Violin I (contd.)

COMPOSER	WORK	PAGE	MEASURE	COMPOSER	WORK	PAGE	MEASURE
Debussy	*Nuages*	16	2b [9]	**Reger**	*Variations on a Theme*	2	3
Dukas	*La Péri*	14	1		*of Mozart*	9	[2]
Dukas	*L'Apprenti Sorcier*	42	9			15	1
Glinka	*March and Oriental*					82	1
	Dances from "Russlan			**Respighi**	*The Fountains of Rome*	1	1
	und Ludmila"	484	[19] 4f	**Respighi**	*Trittico Botticelliano*	7	[3]
Grieg	*Norwegian Dances*	13	8	**Respighi**	*Vetrate di Chiesa*	8	3
Holst	*The Planets*	50	6	**Rimsky-**	*Capriccio Espagnol*	56	[P]
		71	5	Korsakoff		80	2
Honegger	*Le Roi David*	67	[6]	**Rimsky-**			
Ibert	*Divertissement*	40	[7] 10f	Korsakoff	*Le Coq d'Or Suite*	30	8
Ibert	*Escales*	14	[9]	**Rimsky-**	*Scheherazade*	21	[E]
Inghelbrecht	*Pour le jour de la*			Korsakoff		64	181
	première neige au					98	410
	vieux Japon	13	3			131	120
Kodály	*Háry János Suite*	75	3			195	[O] 1f
Liadov	*Eight Russian Popular*					214	[U]
	Songs	19	10			247	611
Liadov	*Kikimora*	5	[8]			257	645
Loeffler	*Poem, La Bonne*			**Roussel**	*Le Festin de l'Araignée*	30	2
	Chanson	47	[19]	**Roussel**	*Symphonie en Sol*		
Mahler	*Songs of a Wayfarer*	12	[7] 3f		*mineur*	116	[70] 3f
Milhaud	*La Création du Monde*	56	[54] 5f	**Ruggles**	*Sun-Treader*	39	[185]
Milhaud	*Ière Symphonie*	4	[15] 2f	**Scarlatti-**			
Mussorgsky	*Night on the Bald*			Casella	*Toccata, Bourrée, et Gigue*	7	8b [9]
	Mountain	21	[E] 1f	**Scriabin**	*Le Poème de l'Extase*	29	1
Pierné	*Viennoise*	10	[F] 1f	**Scriabin**	*Prométhée, Le Poème du*		
Piston	*Suite from "The*				*Feu*	30	[21] 2f
	Incredible Flutist"	53	4	**Strauss, R.**	*Also Sprach*		
Prokofieff	*Classical Symphony*	8	[6] 1f		*Zarathustra*	146	4
		11	[9] 1f	**Stravinsky**	*Fire-Bird Suite (1919)*	23	[14] 7f
		59	1	**Stravinsky**	*Petrouchka Suite*	70	[56]
		86	161	**Stravinsky**	*Le Sacre du Printemps*	24	[33]
		90	[71]			83	[100] 2f
Ravel	*Rapsodie Espagnole*	83	1	**Stravinsky**	*Renard*	73	[48] 2f
Ravel	*Shéhérazade*	9	2	**Stravinsky**	*Scènes de Ballet*	7	1b [8]
Ravel	*Valses Nobles et*			**Tchaikovsky**	*Symphony No. 6,*		
	Sentimentales	55	3b [54]		*"Pathétique"*	74	22
Read	*Symphony No. I*	1	3				
		136	[48] 2f				

Solo Violin I

COMPOSER	WORK	PAGE	MEASURE	COMPOSER	WORK	PAGE	MEASURE
Strauss, R.	*Ein Heldenleben*	49	2	**Stravinsky**	*Chant du Rossignol*	21	[22]
						38	[38] 1f

Soli Violin I

COMPOSER	WORK	PAGE	MEASURE	COMPOSER	WORK	PAGE	MEASURE
Bartók	*Dance Suite*	43	[31]	**Stravinsky**	*Apollon Musagète*	24	[60]
Bartók	*Violin Concerto*	94	[219]				

410

NATURAL HARMONICS

Violin II

COMPOSER	WORK	PAGE	MEASURE	COMPOSER	WORK	PAGE	MEASURE
Bartók	Dance Suite	29	97	Rogers	Once Upon a Time,	1	[1]
Bloch	Trois Poèmes Juifs	12	4b [5]		Five Fairy Tales	11	[8]
		53	2b [8]	Roussel	Évocations, III	28	1
Britten	Les Illuminations	4	[4]	Roussel	Symphonie en Sol		
Dvořák	Carnival Overture	19	[F]		mineur	84	[52] 2f
Fauré	Pelléas et Mélisande	41	1	Strauss, R.	Also Sprach		
Inghelbrecht	Rapsodie de Printemps	40	6		Zarathustra	103	1
Loeffler	A Pagan Poem	25	1	Strauss, R.	Ein Heldenleben	159	3
Miaskovsky	Symphony No. 6	154	[19]	Stravinsky	Concerto en Ré pour		
Rachmaninoff	Rapsodie pour Piano				Orchestre à Cordes	32	2b [97]
	et Orchestre	21	[17]	Stravinsky	Petrouchka Suite	49	[37]
Read	Symphony No. I	104	1	Turner	Gregorian Overture for		
Respighi	The Birds	55	[25] 2f		String Orchestra	14	177

Soli Violin II

COMPOSER	WORK	PAGE	MEASURE
Roussel	Évocations, II	70	2b [32]

Violin I and II

COMPOSER	WORK	PAGE	MEASURE	COMPOSER	WORK	PAGE	MEASURE
Bartók	Music for Strings,			Prokofieff	Classical Symphony	35	204
	Percussion and Celesta	92	72	Reger	Variations on a Theme		
Bloch	Trois Poèmes Juifs	13	[6]		of Mozart	71	3
Britten	Four Sea Interludes from			Respighi	Concerto Gregoriano per	14	[6]
	"Peter Grimes"	32	2		Violino e Orchestra	32	6
Britten	The Young Person's			Respighi	The Birds	12	1b [5]
	Guide to the	19	8	Rimsky-			
	Orchestra	28	1	Korsakoff	Capriccio Espagnol	78	4
Copland	First Symphony	49	[36]	Roussel	Le Festin de l'Araignée	43	[60]
Enesco	Ière Rhapsodie Roumaine	38	5	Shostakovich	Symphony No. I	84	1b [35]
Inghelbrecht	Rapsodie de Printemps	6	[2]	Stravinsky	Firebird Ballet Suite		
Inghelbrecht	Sinfonia Breve No. I	21	7		(1945)	40	1b [52]
Milhaud	Ière Symphonie	105	2b [145]	Villa-Lobos	Chôros No. 8	99	[41]
Moore	Symphony in A major	69	[51]				

Viola

COMPOSER	WORK	PAGE	MEASURE	COMPOSER	WORK	PAGE	MEASURE
Bartók	First Rhapsody for			Britten	The Young Person's		
	Violin and Orchestra	8	[3]		Guide to the		
Bloch	Trois Poèmes Juifs	17	[9] 3f		Orchestra	67	2
Britten	Passacaglia from "Peter			Copland	Music for Radio	50	6
	Grimes"	3	1b [1]	Copland	Quiet City	15	[17] 4f

STRINGS

Viola (contd.)

COMPOSER	WORK	PAGE	MEASURE	COMPOSER	WORK	PAGE	MEASURE
Copland	*Third Symphony*	6	4	Ravel	*La Valse*	29	[20]
		141	1			59	[43]
Debussy–Ansermet	*Six Épigraphes Antiques*	53	3	Ravel	*Valses Nobles et Sentimentales*	42	[39]
Elgar	*Introduction and Allegro for Strings*	3	3	Roussel	*Évocations, I*	7	4
Honegger	*Horace Victorieux*	35	1	Scarlatti–Casella	*Toccata, Bourrée, et Gigue*	3	7b [3]
Honegger	*Musique pour le "Phaedre" de G. D'Annunzio*	27	2	Strauss, R.	*Also Sprach Zarathustra*	74	3
Inghelbrecht	*Rapsodie de Printemps*	2	3	Strauss, R.	*Don Quixote*	66	1
Khachaturian	*Gayne Ballet Suite No. 1-A*	4	1	Stravinsky	*Apollon Musagète*	28	[68]
Milhaud	*Le Bal Martiniquais*	1	1	Stravinsky	*Feuerwerk*	12	2b [11]
Milhaud	*Ière Symphonie*	12	[45] 2f	Stravinsky	*Le Sacre du Printemps*	9	[11]
Poulenc	*Concert Champêtre pour Clavecin et Orchestre*	121	[40] 1f	Stravinsky	*Petrouchka Suite*	153	[129]
				Stravinsky	*Pulcinella Suite*	31	[42]
Prokofieff	*Classical Symphony*	78	[61] 2f	Stravinsky	*Renard*	68	[45]
Ravel	*Alborada del Gracioso*	15	[10]	Stravinsky	*Symphony in Three Movements*	100	[166] 1f

Solo Viola

COMPOSER	WORK	PAGE	MEASURE
Schönberg	*Pierrot Lunaire*	57	2b [5]

Soli Viola

Ravel	*Rapsodie Espagnole*	60	6

Violoncello

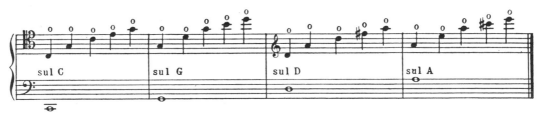

COMPOSER	WORK	PAGE	MEASURE	COMPOSER	WORK	PAGE	MEASURE
Bartók	*Concerto for Orchestra*	9	[149]	Britten	*Four Sea Interludes from "Peter Grimes"*	21	3
Bartók	*Concerto No. 3 for Piano and Orchestra*	34	[58]			28	[4] 1f
Bartók	*Second Rhapsody for Violin and Orchestra*	13	[7]	Britten	*Serenade for Tenor, Horn and Strings*	35	[29] 6f
				Caturla	*Trois Danses Cubaines*	43	[19]
Bartók	*Violin Concerto*	77	[59]	Copland	*Two Pieces for String Orchestra*	3	[55] 2f
Bloch	*America*	81	[47] 1f				
Bloch	*Voice in the Wilderness*	7	3	Debussy–Ansermet	*Six Épigraphes Antiques*	37	[A]
Borodin	*Polovetzian Dances from "Prince Igor"*	6	35	Elgar	*Variations, "Enigma"*	88	[56] 3f
		55	[O] 2f	Enesco	*2e Rhapsodie Roumaine*	2	[1] 1f
Borodin	*Symphony No. 2*	11	[C] 2f				

NATURAL HARMONICS

Violoncello (contd.)

COMPOSER	WORK	PAGE	MEASURE	COMPOSER	WORK	PAGE	MEASURE
Glazounov	Violin Concerto in A minor	75	[48]	Riegger	Symphony No. 3	3	1b [20]
Glinka	March and Oriental Dances from "Russlan und Ludmila"	497	10	Rimsky-Korsakoff	Russian Easter Overture	10	8
Ibert	Féerique	21	1	Rimsky-Korsakoff	Scheherazade	31	168
Inghelbrecht	La Métamorphose d'Ève	2	[1]	Rimsky-Korsakoff	Symphony No. 2, "Antar"	136	[C]
Khachaturian	Gayne Ballet Suite No. 1	28	[3] 5f	Roussel	Le Festin de l'Araignée	25	[28]
Loeffler	Evocation	19	[9] 1f	Roussel	Symphonie en Sol mineur	74	3
Mussorgsky	Night on the Bald Mountain	79	[W]	Scarlatti-Casella	Toccata, Bourrée, et Gigue	17	1
Mussorgsky-Ravel	Pictures at an Exhibition	53	5	Sessions	Symphony No. II	79	[K] 2f
Prokofieff	Peter and the Wolf	28	[23] 4f	Sibelius	Symphony No. 3	53	[6] 3f
Prokofieff	Summer Day Suite	52	6			57	[9]
Ravel	La Valse	53	1	Sibelius	Symphony No. 7	45	4
Ravel	Le Tombeau de Couperin	5	[4]	Stravinsky	Apollon Musagète	1	1b [2]
Ravel	Ma Mère l'Oye	6	1b [3]	Stravinsky	Chant du Rossignol	43	[44] 3f
		40	3	Stravinsky	Concerto en Ré pour Violon et Orchestre	39	[85] 2f
Reger	Variations on a Theme of Mozart	18	1	Stravinsky	Fire-Bird Suite (1919)	70	[9] 1f
Respighi	Vetrate di Chiesa	6	[2] 1f	Stravinsky	Quatre Études pour Orchestre	24	[4]
				Stravinsky	Renard	101	[64]

Solo Violoncello

COMPOSER	WORK	PAGE	MEASURE	COMPOSER	WORK	PAGE	MEASURE
Bloch	Concerto Grosso	15	1b [20]	Stravinsky	Orpheus	3	[4] 4f
Schönberg	Pierrot Lunaire	24	[15] 1f			10	[22] 1f
Strauss, R.	Don Quixote	38	1	Stravinsky	Quatre Études pour Orchestre	18	2b [8]
Stravinsky	Concerto en Ré pour Orchestre à Cordes	17	[60] 1f				

Soli Violoncello

COMPOSER	WORK	PAGE	MEASURE	COMPOSER	WORK	PAGE	MEASURE
Honegger	Concertino pour Piano et Orchestre	17	[10]	Ravel	Rapsodie Espagnole	59	3

Bass

Extension on E string, or 5 strings   sul E   sul A   sul D   sul G

* actual pitch

COMPOSER	WORK	PAGE	MEASURE	COMPOSER	WORK	PAGE	MEASURE
Bartók	Music for Strings, Percussion and Celesta	9	80	Bloch	Schelomo	62	1
						77	[48]

STRINGS

Bass (contd.)

COMPOSER	WORK	PAGE	MEASURE	COMPOSER	WORK	PAGE	MEASURE
Bloch	*Trois Poèmes Juifs*	60	10	Ravel	*Le Tombeau de*		
		74	1		*Couperin*	37	[3] 7f
Britten	*Passacaglia from "Peter*			Ravel	*Ma Mère l'Oye*	8	[7]
	Grimes"	29	[12] 4f	Ravel	*Rapsodie Espagnole*	11	[9] 7f
Debussy	*Jeux*	77	[51]			32	[4] 2f
Delannoy	*Figures Sonores*	50	2			38	[11] 3f
Diamond	*Fourth Symphony*	96	2	Riegger	*Dichotomy*	18	[6] 1f
Ferroud	*Au Parc Monceau*	40	[14] 3f	Rimsky-			
Honegger	*Chant de Joie*	12	3	Korsakoff	*Le Coq d'Or Suite*	41	[28]
Honegger	*Le Roi David*	8	1	Schönberg	*Kammersymphonie,*		
Honegger	*Suite d'Orchestre,*				*Op. 9*	88	[77]
	"L'Impératrice aux			Sibelius	*Symphony No. 6*	25	7
	Rochers"	16	1	Sibelius	*Tapiola*	33	333
Ibert	*Escales*	46	[41] 2f	Sibelius	*The Tempest,*		
Ibert	*Féerique*	10	[6]		*First Suite*	29	3
Ibert	*La Ballade de la Geôle*			Stravinsky	*Chant du Rossignol*	41	[42] 3f
	de Reading	84	1	Stravinsky	*Concerto en Ré pour*		
Inghelbrecht	*Sinfonia Breve No. 1*	11	6b [7]		*Orchestre à Cordes*	8	[27]
Knipper	*Symphony No. 4*	50	2	Stravinsky	*Firebird Ballet Suite*		
Kodály	*Háry János Suite*	5	25		*(1945)*	18	[20]
Kodály	*Marosszék Dances*	56	4b [270]	Stravinsky	*Le Sacre du Printemps*	7	[10]
Moore	*Symphony in A major*	58	[43]	Stravinsky	*Oedipus Rex*	71	[95] 7f
Mussorgsky-				Stravinsky	*Orpheus*	9	2b [21]
Ravel	*Pictures at an Exhibition*	110	[91]			34	[89] 3f
Prokofieff	*Romeo and Juliet,*			Stravinsky	*Scènes de Ballet*	68	[118] 1f
	Suite No. 2	71	[46]	Stravinsky	*Symphony in Three*		
Ravel	*Alborada del Gracioso*	36	[29] 5f		*Movements*	87	[152]
Ravel	*La Valse*	56	[40]				
		66	[48]				

Solo Bass

COMPOSER	WORK	PAGE	MEASURE	COMPOSER	WORK	PAGE	MEASURE
Britten	*Sinfonia da Requiem*	57	5	Stravinsky	*Histoire du Soldat*	7	1
						56	3
						59	3

Soli Bass

COMPOSER	WORK	PAGE	MEASURE	COMPOSER	WORK	PAGE	MEASURE
Ibert	*La Ballade de la Geôle*			Stillman-	*Gulliver—His Voyage*		
	de Reading	95	5b [71]	Kelley	*to Lilliput*	77	[A]

Violin I and Viola

COMPOSER	WORK	PAGE	MEASURE	COMPOSER	WORK	PAGE	MEASURE
Bloch	*Hiver—Printemps*	40	[12]	Stravinsky	*Danses Concertantes*	41	[65]
Borodin	*Symphony No. 2*	108	3	Tchaikovsky	*Variations on a Rokoko*		
Copland	*Lincoln Portrait*	2	2b [10]		*Theme*	21	171
Debussy-	*Six Épigraphes*						
Ansermet	*Antiques*	58	2				

414

NATURAL HARMONICS

Violin II and Viola

COMPOSER	WORK	PAGE	MEASURE	COMPOSER	WORK	PAGE	MEASURE
Barber	Medea	83	3	Ferroud	Au Parc Monceau	17	8
Bartók	Concerto for Piano and Orchestra	103	7	Kodály	Galanta Dances	44	[416]

Violin I, II, and Viola

Copland	Third Symphony	24	[18]	Rimsky-Korsakoff	Symphony No. 2, "Antar"	11	5b [G]
Mussorgsky	Night on the Bald Mountain	14 64	70 [S] 1f	Sibelius	Symphony No. 3	10	[5] 3f
Piston	Concerto for Orchestra	29	[3] 3f				

Violin I and Violoncello

Bartók	Concerto for Piano and Orchestra	102	[44]	Ravel	La Valse	64	2b [47]
Elgar	Variations, "Enigma"	49	4	Reger	Variations on a Theme of Mozart	34	4
Ravel	Daphnis et Chloé, Suite No. 2	103	1	Rogers	Elegy	7	4
				Sibelius	Symphony No. 6	7	[C] 4f

Solo Violin I and Violoncello

COMPOSER	WORK	PAGE	MEASURE
Strauss, R.	Don Quixote	61	3

Violin II and Violoncello

Bartók	Violin Concerto	58	[38]	Inghelbrecht	El Greco	50	1b [43]
Britten	Les Illuminations	17	1	Ravel	Daphnis et Chloé, Suite No. 1	8	[78]
de Falla	El Amor Brujo	37	[21]				
Glinka	Kamarinskaïa	13	[3]	Riegger	Symphony No. 3	38	[200]

Violin I, II, and Violoncello

Bloch	Trois Poèmes Juifs	84	[17]	Rimsky-Korsakoff	Scheherazade	148	194
Borodin	Symphony No. 3	35	[12] 10f				
Kodály	Háry János Suite	36	16	Stravinsky	Scènes de Ballet	15	[25] 1f

Soli Violin I, II, and Violoncello

Borodin	Polovetzian Dances from "Prince Igor"	2	14	Miaskovsky	Symphony No. 8	127	[27] 1f

Violin I and Bass

Copland	Lincoln Portrait	1	5

Violin II and Bass

Britten	Les Illuminations	51	2

Solo Violin and Bass

Stravinsky	Histoire du Soldat	34	[17] 1f

STRINGS

Viola and Violoncello

COMPOSER	WORK	PAGE	MEASURE	COMPOSER	WORK	PAGE	MEASURE
Britten	Passacaglia from "Peter Grimes"	28	1	Milhaud	Cinq Symphonies pour Petit Orchestre	9	1
Enesco	Ière Rhapsodie Roumaine	75	[36] 1f	Ravel	Daphnis et Chloé, Suite No. 2	1	2
Inghelbrecht	La Métamorphose d'Ève	8	[7]	Ravel	Rapsodie Espagnole	40	2
Inghelbrecht	Sinfonia Breve No. 1	58	[34]				

Viola and Bass

COMPOSER	WORK	PAGE	MEASURE	COMPOSER	WORK	PAGE	MEASURE
Bloch	Schelomo	8 / 59	[3] / 2	Stravinsky	Le Sacre du Printemps	77	[87]

Violoncello and Bass

COMPOSER	WORK	PAGE	MEASURE	COMPOSER	WORK	PAGE	MEASURE
Bartók	Concerto for Orchestra	90	[96]	Enesco	2e Rhapsodie Roumaine	23	2
Britten	Les Illuminations	44	1	Ravel	Ma Mère l'Oye	7	[5]
Britten	Serenade for Tenor, Horn and Strings	9 / 38	[6] / 3	Stravinsky	Danses Concertantes	45	[72]
				Stravinsky	Renard	18	1b [10]

Violin I, Viola, and Violoncello

COMPOSER	WORK	PAGE	MEASURE	COMPOSER	WORK	PAGE	MEASURE
Bartók	Concerto for Orchestra	31	[52]	Ravel	Rapsodie Espagnole	7	[5]
Bartók	Dance Suite	31 / 61	109 / 26	Shostakovich	Symphony No. 1	45	[24]
Berg	Three Excerpts from "Wozzeck"	56	1b [380]	Stravinsky	Le Sacre du Printemps	73	[80] 2f

Violin II, Viola, and Violoncello

COMPOSER	WORK	PAGE	MEASURE
Mussorgsky–Ravel	Pictures at an Exhibition	10	[9]

Violin I, II, Viola, and Violoncello

COMPOSER	WORK	PAGE	MEASURE	COMPOSER	WORK	PAGE	MEASURE
Bach–Respighi	Passacaglia and Fugue in C minor	4	[5]	Liadov	Baba-Yaga	1	1
Bartók	Vier Orchesterstücke	59	2b [26]	Piston	Suite for Orchestra	43	[D] 11f
Borodin	Symphony No. 1	18	[H]	Piston	Prelude and Allegro for Organ and Strings	15	[130] 3f
Borodin	Symphony No. 3	75	1	Stravinsky	Pulcinella Suite	12	[13] 2f
Janssen	New Year's Eve in New York	50	[19] 2f	Tchaikovsky	Serenade for Strings	40	16

Solo Quartet

COMPOSER	WORK	PAGE	MEASURE
Elgar	Introduction and Allegro for Strings	20	3

Violin I, Violoncello, and Bass

COMPOSER	WORK	PAGE	MEASURE	COMPOSER	WORK	PAGE	MEASURE
Copland	Third Symphony	90	2b [83]	Debussy–Ansermet	Six Épigraphes Antiques	21	2

NATURAL HARMONICS

Violin II, Violoncello, and Bass

COMPOSER	WORK	PAGE	MEASURE
Skilton	*Suite Primeval, Part II*	**6**	4

Violin I, II, Violoncello, and Bass

COMPOSER	WORK	PAGE	MEASURE
Stravinsky	*Le Sacre du Printemps*	**72**	[79] 11

Viola, Violoncello, and Bass

COMPOSER	WORK	PAGE	MEASURE	COMPOSER	WORK	PAGE	MEASURE
Britten	*Les Illuminations*	**16**	3	**Ravel**	*Concerto pour la main gauche*	**55**	1
Copland	*Third Symphony*	**56**	[42]	**Rosenthal**	*Les Petits Métiers*	**136**	4

Violin II, Viola, Violoncello, and Bass

COMPOSER	WORK	PAGE	MEASURE
Mahler	*Symphony No. 6*	**130**	2b [92]

Violin I, II, Viola, Violoncello, and Bass

COMPOSER	WORK	PAGE	MEASURE	COMPOSER	WORK	PAGE	MEASURE
Sibelius	*Pelleas and Melisande*	**9**	[A]	**Stravinsky**	*Fire-Bird Suite (1919)*	**3**	[3] 1f

(3)

Violin I

COMPOSER	WORK	PAGE	MEASURE
Villa-Lobos	*Amazonas*	**1**	4

Viola

COMPOSER	WORK	PAGE	MEASURE
Stravinsky	*Le Sacre du Printemps*	**16**	[23]

Bass

COMPOSER	WORK	PAGE	MEASURE
Casella	*Pupazzetti*	**14**	2b [1]

Soli Bass

COMPOSER	WORK	PAGE	MEASURE
Halffter	*Deux Esquisses Symphoniques*	**10**	[C]

STRINGS

Violoncello and Bass

COMPOSER	WORK	PAGE	MEASURE
Bartók	*Dance Suite*	**43**	[31]

(4) MINOR 3rd

Violin I

Parodi	*Preludio ad una Commedia*	**41**	[T]

Solo Viola

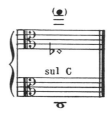

Milhaud	*Saudades do Brazil*	**57**	4

Bass

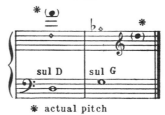

❋ actual pitch

COMPOSER	WORK	PAGE	MEASURE	COMPOSER	WORK	PAGE	MEASURE
Bloch	*Trois Poèmes Juifs*	49	[5]	**Ravel**	*La Valse*	55	[39] 2f
		74	1	**Ravel**	*Le Tombeau de*	25	1
Casella	*Elegia Eroica*	29	6		*Couperin*	27	[10] 1f
Halffter	*Deux Esquisses*					37	1b [3]
	Symphoniques	31	[D]	**Ravel**	*Ma Mère l'Oye*	1	5
Parodi	*Preludio ad una*			**Ravel**	*Rapsodie Espagnole*	7	[5] 5f
	Commedia	36	[R]	**Ravel**	*Tzigane*	5	[5] 4f
Ravel	*Concerto pour Piano et*					9	[8] 1f
	Orchestre	29	[23] 2f	**Roussel**	*Suite en Fa*	88	[47] 1f

418

NATURAL HARMONICS

(5) MAJOR 3rd
Violin I

COMPOSER	WORK	PAGE	MEASURE	COMPOSER	WORK	PAGE	MEASURE
Britten	*Les Illuminations*	16	1	**Ravel**	*Valses Nobles et*		
Ravel	*Shéhérazade*	50	1b [3]		*Sentimentales*	7	5

Solo Violin I

Ibert	*Divertissement*	9	3	**Ravel**	*Rapsodie Espagnole*	10	¡8j

Soli Violin I

Martinet	*Orphée*	41	[13]	**Ravel**	*Daphnis et Chloé,*		
					Suite No. 2	5	1

Viola

COMPOSER	WORK	PAGE	MEASURE
Inghelbrecht	*Sinfonia Breve No. 1*	21	7
Ravel	*Ma Mère l'Oye*	9	[9] 5f

Violoncello

COMPOSER	WORK	PAGE	MEASURE	COMPOSER	WORK	PAGE	MEASURE
Ravel	*Ma Mère l'Oye*	35	2b [2]	**Stravinsky**	*Le Sacre du Printemps*	62	1b [72]
Ravel	*Valses Nobles et*	6	[4]			83	[100]
	Sentimentales	20	[18] 7f				
		23	[22]				
		48	[47] 1f				
		61	[61] 5f				

419

STRINGS

Solo Violoncello

COMPOSER	WORK	PAGE	MEASURE	COMPOSER	WORK	PAGE	MEASURE
Casella	*Paganiniana*	**112**	[14] 3f	**Rogers**	*Characters from Hans Christian Andersen*	**16**	1b [9]

Bass

* actual pitch

Bartók	*Concerto for Orchestra*	**69**	[31]	**Ravel**	*Daphnis et Chloé, Suite No. 2*	**44**	[175]
Bartók	*Divertimento for String Orchestra*	**15**	[171] 1f	**Ravel**	*Le Tombeau de Couperin*	**27**	[10] 1f
Debussy–Ansermet	*Six Épigraphes Antiques*	**53** / **58**	3 / 2	**Ravel**	*Ma Mère l'Oye*	**10** / **15**	1 / 6
Ferroud	*Au Parc Monceau*	**23**	[5] 7f				
Halffter	*Deux Esquisses Symphoniques*	**14** / **23** / **31**	[E] / 4 / [D]	**Stravinsky**	*Concerto en Ré pour Orchestre à Cordes*	**8**	[27]
Mussorgsky–Ravel	*Pictures at an Exhibition*	**95**	[77] 1f	**Turner**	*Gregorian Overture for String Orchestra*	**19**	[233]

Solo Bass

COMPOSER	WORK	PAGE	MEASURE
Stravinsky	*Histoire du Soldat*	**11**	[2] 1f

Soli Bass

Stravinsky	*Le Sacre du Printemps*	**80**	[91]

Solo Violin I and Violoncello

Martinet	*Orphée*	**18**	2

Viola and Violoncello

Ravel	*Alborada del Gracioso*	**15**	[10]	**Ravel**	*Rapsodie Espagnole*	**73**	[22]
Ravel	*Daphnis et Chloé, Suite No. 2*	**40**	2	**Ravel**	*Shéhérazade*	**36**	[18] 1f

Violoncello and Bass

Ravel	*Rapsodie Espagnole*	**11**	[9] 7f

NATURAL HARMONICS

Violin II, Viola, and Violoncello

COMPOSER	WORK	PAGE	MEASURE
Stravinsky	*Le Sacre du Printemps*	**84**	[101]

Viola, Violoncello, and Bass

COMPOSER	WORK	PAGE	MEASURE	COMPOSER	WORK	PAGE	MEASURE
Britten	*Les Illuminations*	**17**	I	**Ravel**	*Valses Nobles et Sentimentales*	**24**	5b [23]

(6) PERFECT 4th

Violin I

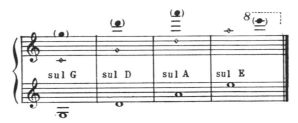

Bartók	Concerto for Piano and Orchestra	**103**	7	**Ravel**	Concerto pour Piano et Orchestre	**29**	[23] 2f
Bartók	Music for Strings, Percussion and Celesta	**130**	[F] 1f	**Ravel**	La Valse	**48**	[35]
						68	[50]
Bloch	Evocations	**55**	[40]	**Ravel**	Valses Nobles et	**7**	[5]
Bloch	Trois Poèmes Juifs	**12**	4b [5]		Sentimentales	**15**	[12] 4f
Casella	La Donna Serpente, II. Serie	**61**	[73]			**55**	3b [54]
						74	[75] 10f
Casella	Paganiniana	**167**	3b [38]	**Rosenthal**	Les Petits Métiers	**40**	3
Charpentier	Impressions d'Italie	**111**	[26]	**Roussel**	Évocations, III	**28**	3
Gould	Spirituals	**4**	[B] 2f	**Roussel**	4me Symphonie	**68**	I
Ibert	Divertissement	**45**	[I] 2f	**Saint-Saëns**	Omphale's Spinning Wheel	**44**	[Q] 14f
Inghelbrecht	El Greco	**50**	1b [43]				
Inghelbrecht	Pour le jour de la première neige au vieux Japon	**13**	3	**Scarlatti– Casella**	Toccata, Bourrée, et Gigue	**3**	7b [3]
Loeffler	Poem, La Bonne Chanson	**47**	[19]	**Schmitt**	Mirages pour Orchestre, No. 2	**76**	3
Milhaud	Ière Symphonie	**4**	[15] 2f	**Stravinsky**	Feuerwerk	**26**	[26]
Poot	Jazz-Music	**3**	1b [1]	**Stravinsky**	Petrouchka Suite	**45**	[34]
						128	[110]
Prokofieff	Ala et Lolly (Scythian Suite)	**76**	7	**Turner**	Gregorian Overture for String Orchestra	**14**	177
Ravel	Alborada del Gracioso	**17**	[12]				

Solo Violin I

COMPOSER	WORK	PAGE	MEASURE	COMPOSER	WORK	PAGE	MEASURE
Ibert	Divertissement	**8**	2	**Ravel**	Rapsodie Espagnole	**10**	[8]

STRINGS

Soli Violin I

COMPOSER	WORK	PAGE	MEASURE	COMPOSER	WORK	PAGE	MEASURE
Debussy	*Rondes de Printemps*	10	[5] 2f	**Roussel**	*Le Festin de l'Araignée*	25	[28] 7f
Ravel	*Daphnis et Chloé, Suite No. 2*	5	1				

Violin II

COMPOSER	WORK	PAGE	MEASURE	COMPOSER	WORK	PAGE	MEASURE
Bartók	*Dance Suite*	43	31	**Loeffler**	*Evocation*	47	[52] 3f
Britten	*Les Illuminations*	4	[4]	**Ravel**	*Shéhérazade*	7	[5]
		16	1	**Ravel**	*Tzigane*	12	[11]
Charpentier	*Impressions d'Italie*	81	7	**Roussel**	*Le Festin de l'Araignée*	60	[72]

Violin I and II

COMPOSER	WORK	PAGE	MEASURE	COMPOSER	WORK	PAGE	MEASURE
Glinka	*March and Oriental Dances from "Russlan und Ludmila"*	469	[14] 4f	**Halffter**	*Deux Esquisses Symphoniques*	14	[E]
				Milhaud	*Saudades do Brazil*	52	14
				Parodi	*Preludio ad una Commedia*	41	[T]

Viola

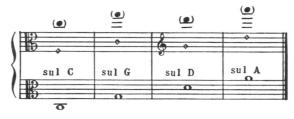

COMPOSER	WORK	PAGE	MEASURE	COMPOSER	WORK	PAGE	MEASURE
Bloch	*Trois Poèmes Juifs*	19	[11]	**Ravel**	*Le Tombeau de Couperin*	26	3b [9]
		17	[9] 3f				
Casella	*Pupazzetti*	28	[5]	**Rimsky-Korsakoff**	*Scheherazade*	253	627
Inghelbrecht	*Rapsodie de Printemps*	2	4	**Strauss, R.**	*Also Sprach Zarathustra*	74	3
Milhaud	*Le Bal Martiniquais*	1	1	**Stravinsky**	*Chant du Rossignol*	78	[90]
Ravel	*Daphnis et Chloé, Suite No. 2*	1	2	**Stravinsky**	*Feuerwerk*	11	[10] 1f

Violoncello

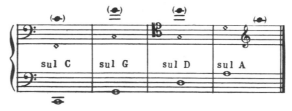

COMPOSER	WORK	PAGE	MEASURE	COMPOSER	WORK	PAGE	MEASURE
Ibert	*Escales*	14	[9]	**Ravel**	*Ma Mère l'Oye*	6	[3]
Parodi	*Preludio ad una Commedia*	36	[R]			9	[8] 5f
						35	2b [2]
Ravel	*Alborada del Gracioso*	15	[10]	**Ravel**	*Tzigane*	5	[5] 4f
Ravel	*Concerto pour Piano et Orchestre*	1	1	**Stravinsky**	*Chant du Rossignol*	41	[42] 3f
Ravel	*Le Tombeau de Couperin*	6	1	**Stravinsky**	*Le Sacre du Printemps*	83	[100]

NATURAL HARMONICS

Bass

* actual pitch

COMPOSER	WORK	PAGE	MEASURE	COMPOSER	WORK	PAGE	MEASURE
Bartók	Dance Suite	31	III	**Diamond**	Music for Shakespeare's "Romeo and Juliet"	66	[120] 3f
Bartók	Divertimento for String Orchestra	10	2b [120]	**de Falla**	El Amor Brujo	37	[21]
Bartók	Second Rhapsody for Violin and Orchestra	13	[7]	**Halffter**	Deux Esquisses Symphoniques	31	[D]
Bloch	Schelomo	8	[3]	**Ravel**	Le Tombeau de Couperin	11	2
		67	[42] 1f			37	[3] 7f
Bloch	Trois Poèmes Juifs	18	4b [10]	**Ravel**	Ma Mère l'Oye	1	5
		74	I			8	[7]
Britten	Serenade for Tenor, Horn and Strings	37	[31]			34	[1] 5f
Debussy–Ansermet	Six Épigraphes Antiques	53	3	**Ravel**	Rapsodie Espagnole	7	[5] 5f
		58	2			11	[9] 7f
				Stravinsky	Quatre Études pour Orchestre	1	4

Solo Bass

COMPOSER	WORK	PAGE	MEASURE
Stravinsky	Histoire du Soldat	11	[2]

Soli Bass

Casella	Elegia Eroica	34	[51]

Violin I and Viola

Ravel	Alborada del Gracioso	14	[9] 4f

Violin II and Viola

Bloch	Trois Poèmes Juifs	85	[18] 4f

Violin I and Violoncello

Milhaud	Saudades do Brazil	58	11	**Ravel**	Valses Nobles et Sentimentales	20	[18] 7f

Soli Violin I and Violoncello

Casella	Paganiniana	112	[14] 3f

Violin I, II, and Violoncello

Bloch	Trois Poèmes Juifs	32	I

Violin I and Bass

de Falla	El Amor Brujo	40	I	**Ravel**	Concerto pour la main gauche	59	I

STRINGS

Violin II and Bass

COMPOSER	WORK	PAGE	MEASURE
Ravel	Concerto pour la main gauche	55	1

Viola and Violoncello

COMPOSER	WORK	PAGE	MEASURE	COMPOSER	WORK	PAGE	MEASURE
Bloch	Trois Poèmes Juifs	69	[6] 1f	Stravinsky	Danses Concertantes	29	[45]
Debussy	Danses Sacrée et Profane	3	9	Stravinsky	Le Sacre du Printemps	62	1b [72]
Ravel	Daphnis et Chloé, Suite No. 2	49	[178] 1f				

Viola and Bass

COMPOSER	WORK	PAGE	MEASURE	COMPOSER	WORK	PAGE	MEASURE
Bloch	Trois Poèmes Juifs	49	[5]	Ravel	La Valse	55	[39] 2f

Violoncello and Bass

COMPOSER	WORK	PAGE	MEASURE
Bloch	Evocations	49	2

Violin I, Viola, and Violoncello

COMPOSER	WORK	PAGE	MEASURE	COMPOSER	WORK	PAGE	MEASURE
Bloch	Voice in the Wilderness	53	2	Ravel	Rapsodie Espagnole	73	[22]

Violin II, Viola, and Violoncello

COMPOSER	WORK	PAGE	MEASURE
Stravinsky	Le Sacre du Printemps	84	[101]

Violin I, II, Viola, and Violoncello

COMPOSER	WORK	PAGE	MEASURE	COMPOSER	WORK	PAGE	MEASURE
Britten	Les Illuminations	17	3	Parodi	Preludio ad una Commedia	60	3

Viola, Violoncello, and Bass

COMPOSER	WORK	PAGE	MEASURE	COMPOSER	WORK	PAGE	MEASURE
Ravel	Shéhérazade	9	1	Stravinsky	Petrouchka Suite	49	[37]

Violin I, II, Viola, Violoncello, and Bass

COMPOSER	WORK	PAGE	MEASURE
Roussel	Suite en Fa	88	[47]

(7) PERFECT 5th

Violin I

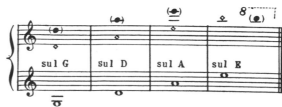

COMPOSER	WORK	PAGE	MEASURE	COMPOSER	WORK	PAGE	MEASURE
Bloch	Trois Poèmes Juifs	12	4b [5]	Ravel	Alborada del Gracioso	17	[12]
Britten	Les Illuminations	17	1	Ravel	La Valse	48	[35]
Ibert	Divertissement	45	[1]			68	[50]

NATURAL HARMONICS

Violin I (contd.)

COMPOSER	WORK	PAGE	MEASURE	COMPOSER	WORK	PAGE	MEASURE
Ravel	*Le Tombeau de Couperin*	45	[15] 1f	Roussel	*4ᵐᵉ Symphonie*	68	1
Ravel	*Valses Nobles et*	15	[12] 4f	Roussel	*Suite en Fa*	46	4
	Sentimentales	20	[18] 7f	Schmitt	*Mirages pour Orchestre,*		
		55	3b [54]		*No. 2*	76	3

Solo Violin I

COMPOSER	WORK	PAGE	MEASURE	COMPOSER	WORK	PAGE	MEASURE
Ibert	*Divertissement*	8	2	Ravel	*Rapsodie Espagnole*	10	[8]

Soli Violin I

COMPOSER	WORK	PAGE	MEASURE
Roussel	*Le Festin de l'Araignée*	25	[28] 9f

Violin II

COMPOSER	WORK	PAGE	MEASURE	COMPOSER	WORK	PAGE	MEASURE
Charpentier	*Impressions d'Italie*	III	[26]	Ravel	*Concerto pour la main*		
Ibert	*La Ballade de la Geôle*				*gauche*	55	1
	de Reading	97	[73]	Ravel	*Valses Nobles et*		
Parodi	*Preludio ad una*				*Sentimentales*	18	[16]
	Commedia	41	[T]	Rosenthal	*Les Petits Métiers*	40	3

Violin I and II

COMPOSER	WORK	PAGE	MEASURE	COMPOSER	WORK	PAGE	MEASURE
Halffter	*Deux Esquisses*			Ravel	*Valses Nobles et*		
	Symphoniques	14	[E]		*Sentimentales*	74	[75] 10f
Milhaud	*Saudades do Brazil*	52	14				

Viola

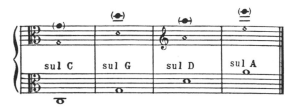

COMPOSER	WORK	PAGE	MEASURE	COMPOSER	WORK	PAGE	MEASURE
Bloch	*Trois Poèmes Juifs*	3	3	Ravel	*La Valse*	28	[19]
		17	[9] 8f			55	[39] 2f
Britten	*Les Illuminations*	29	1	Ravel	*Le Tombeau de*	21	[3] 2f
Casella	*La Donna Serpente,*				*Couperin*	25	2
	II. Serie	61	[73]			27	[10] 4f
Casella	*Paganiniana*	112	[14] 3f	Ravel	*Ma Mère l'Oye*	3	4
Charpentier	*Impressions d'Italie*	81	7	Ravel	*Rapsodie Espagnole*	73	[22]
Parodi	*Preludio ad una*			Scarlatti-	*Toccata, Bourrée, et*		
	Commedia	8	2b [D]	Casella	*Gigue*	21	[9]
Ravel	*Daphnis et Chloé,*						
	Suite No. 2	42	[173]				

425

STRINGS

Violoncello

COMPOSER	WORK	PAGE	MEASURE
Bloch	*Trois Poèmes Juifs*	13	[6]
Ibert	*Escales*	37	I
Poulenc	*Concerto pour deux*		
	Pianos et Orchestre	34	[27]
Ravel	*Alborada del Gracioso*	15	[10]
Ravel	*Le Tombeau de*	6	I
	Couperin	37	1b [3]
Ravel	*Shéhérazade*	23	[12]

COMPOSER	WORK	PAGE	MEASURE
Ravel	*Tzigane*	5	[5] 4f
Ravel	*Valses Nobles et*		
	Sentimentales	61	[61] 4f
Roussel	*Symphonie en Sol*	50	[31] 6f
	mineur	83	[51] 1f
Stravinsky	*Chant du Rossignol*	38	[38] 1f
		78	2b [90]

Bass

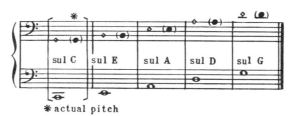

*actual pitch

COMPOSER	WORK	PAGE	MEASURE
Bartók	*Dance Suite*	27	75
		30	102
Britten	*Les Illuminations*	16	4
de Falla	*El Amor Brujo*	41	I
Ravel	*Le Tombeau de Couperin*	4	[3] 6f

COMPOSER	WORK	PAGE	MEASURE
Ravel	*Ma Mère l'Oye*	34	[1] 5f
Roussel	*Suite en Fa*	88	[47] 1f
Stravinsky	*Concerto en Ré pour*		
	Violon et Orchestre	39	[84]
Stravinsky	*Fire-Bird Suite (1919)*	27	[2]

Soli Bass

COMPOSER	WORK	PAGE	MEASURE
Stravinsky	*Le Sacre du Printemps*	62	1b [72]
		80	[91]

Violin I and Violoncello

COMPOSER	WORK	PAGE	MEASURE
Bartók	*Dance Suite*	43	[31]
Milhaud	*Saudades do Brazil*	58	11
Ravel	*Valses Nobles et*		
	Sentimentales	7	[5]

Violin II and Violoncello

COMPOSER	WORK	PAGE	MEASURE
Bartók	*Dance Suite*	31	III
Parodi	*Preludio ad una*		
	Commedia	9	I
Ravel	*Alborada del Gracioso*	14	[9] 4f
Ravel	*Concerto pour la main*		
	gauche	59	I

426

NATURAL HARMONICS

Violin I, II, and Violoncello

COMPOSER	WORK	PAGE	MEASURE
Mussorgsky–Ravel	Pictures at an Exhibition	110	[91]

Viola and Violoncello

COMPOSER	WORK	PAGE	MEASURE	COMPOSER	WORK	PAGE	MEASURE
Bloch	Trois Poèmes Juifs	19	[11]	Ravel	Tzigane	8	6
Ravel	Daphnis et Chloé, Suite No. 2	1	2				
		49	[178] 1f				

Violoncello and Bass

COMPOSER	WORK	PAGE	MEASURE	COMPOSER	WORK	PAGE	MEASURE
				Ravel	Valses Nobles et Sentimentales	22	[20]
Mussorgsky–Ravel	Pictures at an Exhibition	53	5				
Ravel	Rapsodie Espagnole	11	[9] 7f				

Violin I, Viola, and Violoncello

COMPOSER	WORK	PAGE	MEASURE
Ravel	Rapsodie Espagnole	74	1

Violin II, Viola, and Violoncello

COMPOSER	WORK	PAGE	MEASURE	COMPOSER	WORK	PAGE	MEASURE
Bloch	Trois Poèmes Juifs	32	1	Ravel	Tzigane	12	[11]

Solo Violin I, II, Viola, and Bass

COMPOSER	WORK	PAGE	MEASURE
Stravinsky	Pulcinella Suite	36	[56]

(8) MAJOR 6th

Violin I

* actual pitch is 8va

Ibert	Divertissement	45	[1] 2f	Ravel	Le Tombeau de Couperin	26	4b [9]
Milhaud	Saudades do Brazil	58	11				
Ravel	Concerto pour Piano et Orchestre	59	[10] 5f	Roussel	Suite en Fa	46	4

Solo Violin I

COMPOSER	WORK	PAGE	MEASURE
Ibert	Divertissement	8	2

Violin I and II

COMPOSER	WORK	PAGE	MEASURE
Milhaud	Saudades do Brazil	52	14

STRINGS

Viola

* actual pitch is 8va

COMPOSER	WORK	PAGE	MEASURE
Milhaud	*Le Bal Martiniquais*	**1**	1
Ravel	*Le Tombeau de*	**21**	[3] 2f
	Couperin	**26**	4b [9]
		27	[10] 2f
Ravel	*Tzigane*	**12**	[11]

Violoncello

* actual pitch is 8va

COMPOSER	WORK	PAGE	MEASURE
Mussorgsky–Ravel	*Pictures at an Exhibition*	**95**	[77] 1f
Ravel	*Tzigane*	**16**	1

Bass

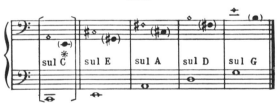

* actual pitch is 8va

COMPOSER	WORK	PAGE	MEASURE
Ravel	*Alborada del Gracioso*	**22**	[17] 2f
Ravel	*Le Tombeau de*	**36**	[2] 5f
	Couperin	**40**	[8]

Violin I and Violoncello

COMPOSER	WORK	PAGE	MEASURE	COMPOSER	WORK	PAGE	MEASURE
Ravel	*Alborada del Gracioso*	**14**	[9] 4f	**Ravel**	*Concerto pour la main gauche*	**59**	1

Viola and Violoncello

COMPOSER	WORK	PAGE	MEASURE	COMPOSER	WORK	PAGE	MEASURE
Mussorgsky–Ravel	*Pictures at an Exhibition*	**96**	[78] 5f	**Ravel**	*Alborada del Gracioso*	**17**	[12]

428

NATURAL HARMONICS

Viola and Bass

COMPOSER	WORK	PAGE	MEASURE
Ravel	*Le Tombeau de Couperin*	24	[7] 1f

Violin I, Viola, and Violoncello

Ravel	*Concerto pour Piano et Orchestre*	29	[23] 2f

(9) OCTAVE

Viola

Rimsky-Korsakoff	*Scheherazade*	253	627

Bass

* actual pitch

Roussel	*Suite en Fa*	88	[47]

Violoncello and Bass

Stravinsky	*Petrouchka Suite*	49	[37]

Soli Violoncello and Bass

Stravinsky	*Le Sacre du Printemps*	62	1b [72]

(10)

Violin I

COMPOSER	WORK	PAGE	MEASURE	COMPOSER	WORK	PAGE	MEASURE
Casella	*La Donna Serpente, II. Serie*	48	[63] 4f	**d'Indy**	*Jour d'été à la Montagne*	79	7
Dvořák	*Slavonic Dances, No. 1—4*	72	181	**Inghelbrecht**	*Rapsodie de Printemps*	12	[6]
				Rogers	*Elegy*	6	[5]
Ferguson	*Partita for Orchestra*	36	2	**Rogers**	*Once Upon a Time, Five Fairy Tales*	11	[8]

STRINGS

Violin II

COMPOSER	WORK	PAGE	MEASURE	COMPOSER	WORK	PAGE	MEASURE
Albéniz–Arbós	El Puerto	35	[O] 1f	d'Indy	Jour d'été à la Montagne	47	[20]
				Mahler	Das Lied von der Erde	37	4b [47]

Violin I and II

Caja	2 Idilli Siracusani	4	9	Honegger	Le Chant de Nigamon	2	2b [7]

Viola

Coppola	Symphonie en La mineur	70	4b [9]	Stravinsky	Orpheus	16	[39]

Violoncello

Honegger	Horace Victorieux	2	3	Mahler	Das Lied von der Erde	80	[22] 7f
Honegger	Musique pour le "Phaedre" de G. D'Annunzio	27	2			92	[11] 2f
				Schönberg	Verklärte Nacht	28	1
				Sibelius	Symphony No. 6	25	7

Solo Violoncello

COMPOSER	WORK	PAGE	MEASURE
Schönberg	Pierrot Lunaire	52	[25] 6f

Soli Violoncello

Strauss, R.	Salomé's Dance	5	[F]

Bass

COMPOSER	WORK	PAGE	MEASURE	COMPOSER	WORK	PAGE	MEASURE
Britten	Sinfonietta	42	[16] 5f	Jolivet	Andante pour Orchestre à Cordes	9	[40]
Casella	La Donna Serpente, II. Serie	48	[63] 2f	Mahler	Symphony No. 9	3	4
Delannoy	Figures Sonores	38	3	Sibelius	Tapiola	20	3
d'Indy	Jour d'été à la Montagne	78	[38]	Villa-Lobos	Amazonas	9	[3]
James	Suite for String Orchestra	18	1				

Soli Bass

Kodály	Psalmus Hungaricus	43	[26]

Violin I and Viola

Mahler	Symphony No. 1	17	[12]

Violin II and Viola

Liszt	Hungarian Rhapsody No. 2	59	6

Viola and Violoncello

COMPOSER	WORK	PAGE	MEASURE	COMPOSER	WORK	PAGE	MEASURE
Schönberg	Verklärte Nacht	51	3	Strauss, R.	Salomé's Dance	38	[K] 8f
Strauss, R.	Eine Alpensinfonie	46	[42]	Villa-Lobos	Amazonas	3	1b [1]

NATURAL HARMONICS

Solo Viola and Violoncello

COMPOSER	WORK	PAGE	MEASURE
Berg	*Three Excerpts from "Wozzeck"*	**55**	[375]

Solo Violoncello and Bass

Charpentier	*Impressions d'Italie*	**125**	[32]

Violin I, II, Viola, and Violoncello

COMPOSER	WORK	PAGE	MEASURE	COMPOSER	WORK	PAGE	MEASURE
Mahler	*Symphony No. 3*	**133**	[19] 10f	**Mahler**	*Symphony No. 9*	**60**	20

Viola, Violoncello, and Bass

Sibelius	*Tapiola*	**32**	[K] 7f

Violin I, II, Viola, Violoncello, and Bass

Mahler	*Symphony No. 1*	**3**	1

(11)

Bass

Bloch	*Trois Poèmes Juifs*	**18**	4b [10]

(12)

Viola

Debussy–Ansermet	*Six Épigraphes Antiques*	**90**	[E]

(13)

Solo Violin I

Schönberg	*A Survivor from Warsaw*	**2**	6

Solo Violoncello

Schönberg	*Pierrot Lunaire*	**45**	[10] 1f

431

STRINGS

Bass

COMPOSER	WORK	PAGE	MEASURE	COMPOSER	WORK	PAGE	MEASURE
Debussy–Ansermet	Six Épigraphes Antiques	22	1	Stravinsky	Le Sacre du Printemps	77	[87]

Solo Bass

COMPOSER	WORK	PAGE	MEASURE
Miaskovsky	Symphony No. 8	127	[27] 1f

(14)

Harm.

Violin I

COMPOSER	WORK	PAGE	MEASURE	COMPOSER	WORK	PAGE	MEASURE
Charpentier	Impressions d'Italie	6	2	d'Indy	Jour d'été à la Montagne	38	[15]
						47	[20]

Soli Violin I

COMPOSER	WORK	PAGE	MEASURE
Albéniz–Arbós	Évocation	19	[H] 3f

Violin II

COMPOSER	WORK	PAGE	MEASURE
Inghelbrecht	Rapsodie de Printemps	6	[2]

Violin I and II

COMPOSER	WORK	PAGE	MEASURE
Roussel	Le Festin de l'Araignée	55	3

Viola

COMPOSER	WORK	PAGE	MEASURE	COMPOSER	WORK	PAGE	MEASURE
Debussy–Ansermet	Six Épigraphes Antiques	90	[E]	Mahler	Symphony No. 5	113	[33]
Honegger	Le Chant de Nigamon	2	2b [7]	Rabaud	La Procession Nocturne	30	3
				Roussel	Évocations, I	1	1

Solo Viola

COMPOSER	WORK	PAGE	MEASURE
Walton	Concerto for Violin and Orchestra	51	5

Bass

COMPOSER	WORK	PAGE	MEASURE	COMPOSER	WORK	PAGE	MEASURE
Rogers	Elegy	6	[5]	Villa-Lobos	Danses Africaines	93	[5]

(15)

o

Violin I

COMPOSER	WORK	PAGE	MEASURE	COMPOSER	WORK	PAGE	MEASURE
Inghelbrecht	Rapsodie de Printemps	40	6	Stravinsky	Scènes de Ballet	15	]25] 1f
Stravinsky	Fire-Bird Suite (1919)	11	[13] 1f				

NATURAL HARMONICS

Solo Violin

COMPOSER	WORK	PAGE	MEASURE
Schönberg	*Pierrot Lunaire*	18	1b [15]
			[15] 2f

Violin II

COMPOSER	WORK	PAGE	MEASURE	COMPOSER	WORK	PAGE	MEASURE
Berlioz	*Roméo et Juliette*	199	7	**Stravinsky**	*Petrouchka Suite*	70	[56]
Piston	*Symphony No. 2*	108	5				

Soli Violin II

Rozsa	*Concerto for String Orchestra*	31	[91]

Violin I and II

Villa–Lobos	*Amazonas*	12	4

Viola

Schönberg	*Verklärte Nacht*	51	3

Violoncello

COMPOSER	WORK	PAGE	MEASURE	COMPOSER	WORK	PAGE	MEASURE
Schönberg	*Verklärte Nacht*	27	9	**Stravinsky**	*Apollon Musagète*	20	[49] 4f

(16)

Violin II

COMPOSER	WORK	PAGE	MEASURE	COMPOSER	WORK	PAGE	MEASURE
d'Indy	*Jour d'été à la Montagne*	38	[15]	**Inghelbrecht**	*Rapsodie de Printemps*	6	[2]
		75	[37]				

Violin I and II

COMPOSER	WORK	PAGE	MEASURE	COMPOSER	WORK	PAGE	MEASURE
Milhaud	*Saudades do Brazil*	77	5	**Roussel**	*Le Festin de l'Araignée*	55	4

(17)

Violin I

Delius	*North Country Sketches*	24	[19] 2f

Violin II

Stravinsky	*Scènes de Ballet*	15	[25] 1f

STRINGS

Violin I and II

COMPOSER	WORK	PAGE	MEASURE
Villa-Lobos	*Amazonas*	**12**	[4]

Violoncello

Stravinsky	*Fire-Bird Suite* (1919)	**27**	[2]

Solo Violoncello

COMPOSER	WORK	PAGE	MEASURE	COMPOSER	WORK	PAGE	MEASURE
Britten	*Sinfonia da Requiem*	**57**	3	**Schönberg**	*A Survivor from Warsaw*	**2**	5

Soli Violoncello

Stravinsky	*Le Sacre du Printemps*	**80**	[91]

Bass

COMPOSER	WORK	PAGE	MEASURE	COMPOSER	WORK	PAGE	MEASURE
Bloch	*Trois Poèmes Juifs*	**16**	[8]	**Stravinsky**	*Fire-Bird Suite* (1919)	**22**	[12] 4f

(18)

Soli Violin I

Albéniz–Arbós	*Évocation*	**19**	[H] 3f

Violin I and II

Milhaud	*Saudades do Brazil*	**77**	6

Bass

COMPOSER	WORK	PAGE	MEASURE	COMPOSER	WORK	PAGE	MEASURE
Charpentier	*Impressions d'Italie*	**154**	[52] 41	**Villa-Lobos**	*Uirapurú*	**89**	[25]

Viola and Violoncello

Villa-Lobos	*Uirapurú*	**78**	[20]

(19)

Viola

Schönberg	*Verklärte Nacht*	**51**	3

Violoncello

COMPOSER	WORK	PAGE	MEASURE	COMPOSER	WORK	PAGE	MEASURE
Charpentier	*Impressions d'Italie*	**77**	3	**Schönberg**	*Verklärte Nacht*	**28**	1

NATURAL HARMONICS

(20)

Violin I

COMPOSER	WORK	PAGE	MEASURE
Villa-Lobos	*Amazonas*	9	[3]

Violin II

Fauré	*Pelléas et Mélisande*	42	I

(21)

Solo Violin

Schönberg	*Pierrot Lunaire*	5	[10]
		18	1b [15]
		45	[10]

Violin II

Villa-Lobos	*Amazonas*	9	[3]

Viola

Schönberg	*Kammersymphonie, Op. 9*	88	[77]

Solo Viola

Schönberg	*Pierrot Lunaire*	38	[29]

Solo Violoncello

Schönberg	*Pierrot Lunaire*	26	[10] 1f
		33	4b [20]

Violin II and Viola

Villa-Lobos	*Danses Africaines*	59	[8]

Violoncello and Soli Bass

Schönberg	*Fünf Orchesterstücke*	35	[5]

Violin II, Viola, and Soli Bass

Schönberg	*Fünf Orchesterstücke*	28	3b [11]

435

STRINGS

(22)

Violin I

COMPOSER	WORK	PAGE	MEASURE	COMPOSER	WORK	PAGE	MEASURE
Charpentier	*Impressions d'Italie*	45	9b [10]	**Villa-Lobos**	*Danses Africaines*	59	[8]
Villa-Lobos	*Amazonas*	9	[3]				
		23	4				

Violin I and II

COMPOSER	WORK	PAGE	MEASURE
Villa-Lobos	*Amazonas*	2	3

Violoncello

Schönberg	*Fünf Orchesterstücke*	35	[5]	**Schönberg**	*Kammersymphonie, Op. 9*	88	[77] 2f

Solo Violoncello

Schönberg	*Pierrot Lunaire*	38	[29]

Bass

Villa-Lobos	*Danses Africaines*	123	[17]

(23)

Violin I

Schönberg	*Fünf Orchesterstücke*	27	[10] 1f

Solo Violin

Schönberg	*Pierrot Lunaire*	33	4b [20]

Viola

Villa-Lobos	*Amazonas*	9	[3]

Violoncello

Villa-Lobos	*Uirapurú*	43	[9] 2f

Solo Violoncello

Schönberg	*Pierrot Lunaire*	26	[10] 1f

NATURAL HARMONICS

Violoncello and Soli Bass

COMPOSER	WORK	PAGE	MEASURE
Schönberg	*Fünf Orchesterstücke*	35	[5]

(24)

Violin I

Verdi	*Messa da Requiem*	160	147

(25)

Violin II

Villa-Lobos	*Amazonas*	23	4

Violin II and Viola

Villa-Lobos	*Amazonas*	9	[3]

(26) DOUBLE HARMONICS

English	Italian	French	German
Both tones as harmonics	Tutt'e due toni per armonici	Tous les deux tons en sons harmoniques	Beide Töne durch Flageolett

Violin I

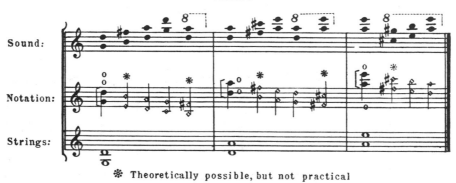

�֎ Theoretically possible, but not practical

COMPOSER	WORK	PAGE	MEASURE	COMPOSER	WORK	PAGE	MEASURE
Bartók	*Second Suite*	9	3b [8]	**Scarlatti–**	*Toccata, Bourrée, et*	7	5b [9]
Bartók	*Violin Concerto*	105	6b [349]	**Casella**	*Gigue*	21	9
Bloch	*America*	2	1	**Skilton**	*Suite Primeval, Part II*	6	6
Casella	*Paganiniana*	142	[21] 1f	**Villa-Lobos**	*Chôros No. 8*	24	[10] 2f
		167	3b [38]			99	[41]
Copland	*Billy the Kid Ballet Suite*	20	[14] 3f				

STRINGS

Solo Violin I

COMPOSER	WORK	PAGE	MEASURE
Bloch	*Concerto Grosso*	15	1b [20]

Violin II

COMPOSER	WORK	PAGE	MEASURE	COMPOSER	WORK	PAGE	MEASURE
Casella	*Paganiniana*	116	[3] 1f	**Inghelbrecht**	*Sinfonia Breve No. 1*	58	[34]
Inghelbrecht	*La Valse Retrouvée*	12	14	**Milhaud**	*La Création du Monde*	56	3b [54]
		24	3b [49]				

Violin I and II

COMPOSER	WORK	PAGE	MEASURE	COMPOSER	WORK	PAGE	MEASURE
Bloch	*America*	81	[47] 1f	**Guarnieri**	*Savage Dance*	24	3
Goossens	*Sinfonietta*	54	2				

Viola

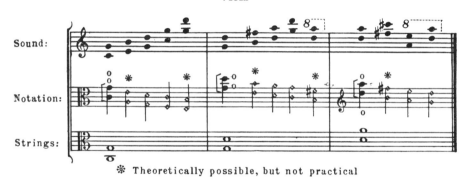

❋ Theoretically possible, but not practical

COMPOSER	WORK	PAGE	MEASURE	COMPOSER	WORK	PAGE	MEASURE
Ferroud	*Au Parc Monceau*	4	3	**Inghelbrecht**	*El Greco*	46	[41]

Violoncello

COMPOSER	WORK	PAGE	MEASURE	COMPOSER	WORK	PAGE	MEASURE
Bartók	*Concerto for Orchestra*	9	[149]	**Ibert**	*Escales*	40	[35]
Bartók	*Dance Suite*	41	66	**Inghelbrecht**	*La Métamorphose d'Ève*	5	4
Debussy	*Rondes de Printemps*	21	[12]	**Stravinsky**	*Pulcinella Suite*	10	[8]
Glazounov	*Violin Concerto in A minor*	67	[44] 1f				

NATURAL HARMONICS

Solo Violoncello

COMPOSER	WORK	PAGE	MEASURE
Stravinsky	*Pulcinella Suite*	**22**	[27]

Soli Violoncello

Casella	*Paganiniana*	**107**	1

Bass

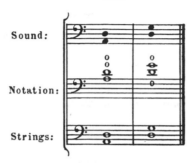

Bartók	*Divertimento for String Orchestra*	**19**	[25]	1f

Solo Bass

Stravinsky	*Concerto en Ré pour Orchestre à Cordes*	**17**	[60]	1f

Violin I and Viola

Scarlatti–Casella	*Toccata, Bourrée, et Gigue*	**26**	[19]	1f

Violin II and Viola

Debussy–Ansermet	*Six Épigraphes Antiques*	**37**	[A]

Violin I, II, and Viola

Bloch	*America*	**2**	1
		59	4
		150	[84]

Violin I and Violoncello

Kodály	*Galanta Dances*	**21**	[181]

STRINGS

Violin II and Violoncello

COMPOSER	WORK	PAGE	MEASURE	COMPOSER	WORK	PAGE	MEASURE
Bartók	*Second Suite*	5	[3] 8f	**Ravel**	*Alborada del Gracioso*	17	[12]

Violin I, II, and Violoncello

COMPOSER	WORK	PAGE	MEASURE
Bloch	*Schelomo*	8	[3]

Viola and Violoncello

COMPOSER	WORK	PAGE	MEASURE	COMPOSER	WORK	PAGE	MEASURE
Bartók	*Dance Suite*	59	22	**Debussy**	*Rondes de Printemps*	56	1
Bartók	*First Rhapsody for Violin and Orchestra*	4	[1]				

Violin I, Viola and Violoncello

COMPOSER	WORK	PAGE	MEASURE
Ferroud	*Au Parc Monceau*	23	[5] 7f

Violin II, Viola, and Violoncello

COMPOSER	WORK	PAGE	MEASURE
Bartók	*Dance Suite*	38	46

Chapter 57

ARTIFICIAL HARMONICS

(for terminology see Chapter 41, page 257)

(1) "HARMONICS"

Violin I

COMPOSER	WORK	PAGE	MEASURE	COMPOSER	WORK	PAGE	MEASURE
Debussy	*Jeux*	79	5	Rachmaninoff	*Rapsodie pour Piano et Orchestre*	21	[17]
Mahler	*Symphony No. 4*	149	347	Rudhyar	*Five Stanzas*	26	2

Solo Violin I

COMPOSER	WORK	PAGE	MEASURE
Rogers	*Characters from Hans Christian Andersen*	6	1

Soli Violin I

Kodály	*Psalmus Hungaricus*	51	3	Wagner, R.	*Prelude to Act I, "Lohengrin"*	1	2
Respighi	*The Birds*	43	[20] 5f				
Respighi	*Vetrate di Chiesa*	73	5				

Violin I and II

Ives	*Three Places in New England*	8	2b [D]	Wagner, R.	*Prelude to Act I, "Lohengrin"*	14	1

Soli Violin I and II

Herrmann	*Sinfonietta for String Orchestra*	11	1

Viola

Respighi	*Vetrate di Chiesa*	60	1

441

STRINGS

Soli Viola

COMPOSER	WORK	PAGE	MEASURE
Wagner, R.	*Forest Murmurs from "Siegfried"*	**20**	139

Violoncello

COMPOSER	WORK	PAGE	MEASURE	COMPOSER	WORK	PAGE	MEASURE
Rudhyar	*Sinfonietta*	**21**	3	**Wagner, R.**	*Forest Murmurs from "Siegfried"*	**23**	156
Stravinsky	*Concerto en Ré pour Orchestre à Cordes*	**13**	[44] 2f				

Solo Violoncelli

Kodály	*Psalmus Hungaricus*	**41**	[25]

Violin I and Viola

Rudhyar	*Five Stanzas*	**14**	[R] 5f

Violin I, II, and Viola

Mahler	*Symphony No. 6*	**130**	[92] 4f

(2)

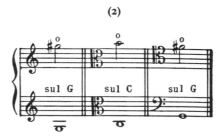

Violin I

Bax	*First Symphony*	88	2b [B]	**Pescara**	*Tibet*	2	6
Debussy	*Gigues*	1	5			39	[14]
Debussy	*Rondes de Printemps*	19	1	**Prokofieff**	*Ala et Lolly (Scythian Suite)*	27	2
de Falla	*El Amor Brujo*	37	[21] 2f			48	[27]
Gould	*Latin-American Symphonette*	8	[E] 6f	**Roussel**	*4me Symphonie*	39	[21] 9f
Ives	*Three Places in New England*	35	[H]	**Shostakovich**	*Symphony No. 1*	18	1b [30]
						25	1b [42]
McPhee	*Four Iroquois Dances*	15	3	**Stravinsky**	*Feuerwerk*	11	[10]
				Stravinsky	*Renard*	45	[28]

Solo Violin I

Kodály	*Summer Evening*	**52**	[330] 7f	**Stravinsky**	*Le Sacre du Printemps*	**75**	[83]

ARTIFICIAL HARMONICS

Soli Violin I

COMPOSER	WORK	PAGE	MEASURE	COMPOSER	WORK	PAGE	MEASURE
Ives	Three Places in New England	18	[I]	Rachmaninoff	The Bells	4	2b [3]
				Still	Bells	8	[6]

Violin II

COMPOSER	WORK	PAGE	MEASURE	COMPOSER	WORK	PAGE	MEASURE
Prokofieff	Romeo and Juliet, Suite No. 1	123	[78]	Tchaikovsky	Variations on a Rokoko Theme	21	171

Violin I and II

COMPOSER	WORK	PAGE	MEASURE	COMPOSER	WORK	PAGE	MEASURE
Barber	Medea	3	[2]	Stravinsky	Firebird Ballet Suite (1945)	40	[52] 3f
		67	I	Stravinsky	Scherzo Fantastique	16	[20]
		70	3				

Viola

COMPOSER	WORK	PAGE	MEASURE
Stravinsky	Petrouchka Suite	153	[129]

Violoncello

COMPOSER	WORK	PAGE	MEASURE	COMPOSER	WORK	PAGE	MEASURE
Debussy–Ansermet	Six Épigraphes Antiques	58	2	Riegger	Dichotomy	18	[6] 1f
Miaskovsky	Sinfonietta for String Orchestra	24	[17] 3f	Stravinsky	Concerto en Ré pour Orchestre à Cordes	30	[93] 2f
Respighi	Metamorphoseon, XII Modi	55	[29] 11f	Stravinsky	Firebird Ballet Suite (1945)	18	[20]

Bass

COMPOSER	WORK	PAGE	MEASURE
Debussy	Le Martyre de Saint Sébastien	15	[6]

Violin I and Violoncello

COMPOSER	WORK	PAGE	MEASURE	COMPOSER	WORK	PAGE	MEASURE
Stravinsky	Fire-Bird Suite (1919)	15	I	Stravinsky	Le Sacre du Printemps	74	[82] 1f

Viola and Violoncello

COMPOSER	WORK	PAGE	MEASURE	COMPOSER	WORK	PAGE	MEASURE
Honegger	Symphonie Liturgique	109	[17]	Strauss, R.	Eine Alpensinfonie	51	I

Violin I, Viola, and Violoncello

COMPOSER	WORK	PAGE	MEASURE
Stravinsky	Le Sacre du Printemps	73	[80] 2f

Violin I, II, Viola, and Violoncello

COMPOSER	WORK	PAGE	MEASURE
Thomson	The Seine at Night	25	5

443

STRINGS

Violin I, II, Viola, Violoncello, and Bass

COMPOSER	WORK	PAGE	MEASURE
Stravinsky	*Fire-Bird Suite* (1919)	**14**	[17]

(3) MINOR 3rd

Violoncello and Bass

Stravinsky	*Fire-Bird Suite* (1919)	**71**	[11]

(4) MAJOR 3rd

Violin I

Ravel	*Rapsodie Espagnole*	**28**	1

Violoncello

Stravinsky	*Feuerwerk*	**11**	1b [10]

(5) PERFECT 4th

Violin I

COMPOSER	WORK	PAGE	MEASURE	COMPOSER	WORK	PAGE	MEASURE
Barber	*Medea*	83	3	**Bloch**	*Evocations*	2	[2]
Bartók	*Concerto for Orchestra*	110	[259]			5	[5] 2f
Bartók	*Violin Concerto*	57	[32]			50	3

444

ARTIFICIAL HARMONICS

Violin I (contd.)

COMPOSER	WORK	PAGE	MEASURE	COMPOSER	WORK	PAGE	MEASURE
Borodin	*Symphony No. 1*	127	11	Milhaud	*Quatrième Symphonie*	14	[50]
Britten	*The Young Person's*					65	[190] 1f
	Guide to the			Milhaud	*Le Bal Martiniquais*	1	1
	Orchestra	49	5			11	2b [50]
Copland	*Dance Symphony*	33	[17] 1f	Milhaud	*Les Choéphores*	39	[H]
Copland	*Third Symphony*	41	1	Ravel	*Concerto pour la main*		
		90	1b [83]		*gauche*	55	1
Debussy	*Gigues*	33	[19] 2f	Ravel	*Daphnis et Chloé,*		
Debussy	*Iberia*	20	4		*Suite No. 2*	40	2
Debussy	*Jeux*	79	4	Ravel	*Rapsodie Espagnole*	39	1
Debussy	*La Mer*	108	1	Read	*Symphony No. I*	104	1
Debussy	*Le Martyre de Saint*			Respighi	*Trittico Botticelliano*	43	3
	Sébastien	39	3	Rosenthal	*Les Petits Métiers*	46	2
Debussy	*Première Rhapsodie*	37	3			72	[C]
Debussy	*Rondes de Printemps*	45	[23]	Roussel	*Évocations, II*	3	1b [1]
Delius	*North Country Sketches*	18	1			69	[31]
Diamond	*Timon of Athens*	14	90	Roussel	*Le Festin de l'Araignée*	33	3
Dukas	*La Péri*	77	1			60	[72]
		90	1	Roussel	*Suite en Fa*	89	[48]
Ferroud	*Au Parc Monceau*	2	1b [1]	Saint-Saëns	*Suite Algérienne*	21	4
Grofé	*Grand Canyon Suite*	91	[1] 2f	Siegmeister	*From my Window*	13	4b [15]
Honegger	*Le Roi David*	68	3	Stravinsky	*Feuerwerk*	11	1b [10]
Ibert	*Escales*	34	[29]	Szymanowski	*Symphonie Concertante*		
		46	[41]		*pour Piano et*		
Khachaturian	*Gayne Ballet Suite*				*Orchestre*	25	1
	No. 2	42	[4]	Taylor	*Ballet Music from*		
Milhaud	*IIᵉ Symphonie*	21	2		*"Casanova"*	22	[J]

Solo Violin I

COMPOSER	WORK	PAGE	MEASURE	COMPOSER	WORK	PAGE	MEASURE
Copland	*Third Symphony*	91	2	Ravel	*Ma Mère l'Oye*	7	[5]
Martinet	*Orphée*	19	5	Rimsky-			
Ravel	*Daphnis et Chloé,*			Korsakoff	*Capriccio Espagnol*	69	[S] 5f
	Suite No. 2	5	[156] 1f				

Soli Violin I

COMPOSER	WORK	PAGE	MEASURE	COMPOSER	WORK	PAGE	MEASURE
Casella	*Paganiniana*	91	1b [1]	Roussel	*Évocations, III*	1	1
Copland	*Third Symphony*	25	8	Roussel	*Suite en Fa*	7	[3]
Kodály	*Marosszék Dances*	55	2	Still	*Bells*	17	5
Rimsky-							
Korsakoff	*Russian Easter Overture*	32	4				

Violin II

COMPOSER	WORK	PAGE	MEASURE	COMPOSER	WORK	PAGE	MEASURE
Casella	*Paganiniana*	128	1	Dukas	*L'Apprenti Sorcier*	42	9
Copland	*Billy the Kid Ballet*			Honegger	*Horace Victorieux*	2	6
	Suite	52	[31] 2f	Mussorgsky-			
Copland	*Third Symphony*	19	4	Ravel	*Pictures at an Exhibition*	96	[78] 5f
		140	[121]	Pizzetti	*Concerto dell'Estate*	118	[50]
Debussy-	*Six Épigraphes*			Poot	*Symphonie*	9	2
Ansermet	*Antiques*	58	2	Ravel	*Alborada del Gracioso*	14	[9] 4f

STRINGS

Violin II (contd.)

COMPOSER	WORK	PAGE	MEASURE	COMPOSER	WORK	PAGE	MEASURE
Rivier	3 Pastorales	22	4	Siegmeister	Western Suite	51	[15] 1f
Sessions	Suite from "The Black			Still	Dismal Swamp	4	[3] 8f
	Maskers"	23	[24]	Stravinsky	Le Sacre du Printemps	91	[111]

Violin I and II

COMPOSER	WORK	PAGE	MEASURE	COMPOSER	WORK	PAGE	MEASURE
Barber	Medea	69	1b [51]	Pizzetti	Concerto dell'Estate	14	[6]
Bartók	Dance Suite	62	35	Poot	Symphonie	15	[7] 3f
Berlioz	Roméo et Juliette	199	7	Prokofieff	Ala et Lolly (Scythian	77	6
Bloch	Voice in the Wilderness	38	[31]		Suite)	100	[69]
Casella	La Donna Serpente,			Ravel	Rapsodie Espagnole	28	1
	I. Serie	25	[25] 3f	Read	Symphony No. I	40	6
Caturla	Trois Danses Cubaines	43	[19]	Rivier	Chant Funèbre	10	[4]
Copland	Third Symphony	149	[127] 1f	Rivier	Danse	27	8
Diamond	Music for Shakespeare's	13	[85] 3f	Schelling	A Victory Ball	5	1
	"Romeo and Juliet"	15	[95] 3f	Siegmeister	From my Window	33	4b [25]
Dukas	L'Apprenti Sorcier	44	9	Siegmeister	Ozark Set	8	[35] 1f
Gershwin	An American in Paris	22	4b [20]	Siegmeister	Sunday in Brooklyn	70	1b [45]
Grofé	Grand Canyon Suite	4	5	Siegmeister	Western Suite	4	3
Inghelbrecht	Rapsodie de Printemps	2	5			54	[45] 1f
Milhaud	2me Suite Symphonique	35	4	White	Five Miniatures	9	2
Milhaud	Ière Symphonie	5	2b [20]	Whithorne	The Dream Pedlar	65	4
Milhaud	Saudades do Brazil	34	5	Zimbalist	American Rhapsody	2	[1] 2f
Parodi	Preludio ad una					42	2b [32]
	Commedia	60	2				

Soli Violin I and II

COMPOSER	WORK	PAGE	MEASURE
Diamond	Music for Shakespeare's		
	"Romeo and Juliet"	39	[20] 3f

Viola

COMPOSER	WORK	PAGE	MEASURE	COMPOSER	WORK	PAGE	MEASURE
Alfvén	A Legend of the			de Falla	El Amor Brujo	40	1
	Skerries	17	1	Ferroud	Au Parc Monceau	44	[18]
Bloch	Trois Poèmes Juifs	17	[9] 4f	Harrison	Alleluia for Orchestra	20	[P] 3f
		28	2b [17]	Ibert	La Ballade de la Geôle	24	[15] 1f
		69	[6] 1f		de Reading	44	[30]
Casella	Paganiniana	6	[2]			62	[44] 2f
Debussy	Gigues	23	5	Mussorgsky-			
Debussy	Jeux	1	1	Ravel	Pictures at an Exhibition	58	[54]
Debussy	Le Martyre de Saint			Ravel	Ma Mère l'Oye	9	[9] 4f
	Sébastien	64	[28]	Read	Symphony No. I	38	2
Debussy	Première Rhapsodie	5	[2]	Scarlatti-	Toccata, Bourrée, et		
		23	5	Casella	Gigue	7	8b [9]
Diamond	Fourth Symphony	54	[30]	Stravinsky	Le Sacre du Printemps	105	[133]

446

ARTIFICIAL HARMONICS

Violoncello

COMPOSER	WORK	PAGE	MEASURE	COMPOSER	WORK	PAGE	MEASURE
Britten	Passacaglia from "Peter Grimes"	29	[12] 2f	Honegger	Suite d'Orchestre, "L'Impératrice aux	16	1
		30	2		Rochers"	20	[3] 1f
Debussy	Iberia	63	[43]	Ibert	Escales	1	1
Debussy	Jeux	24	4	Inghelbrecht	Rapsodie de Printemps	8	2
		114	[79]	Ravel	Daphnis et Chloé,		
Debussy	Le Martyre de Saint				Suite No. 2	44	[175] 3f
	Sébastien	15	[6]	Ravel	Le Tombeau de Couperin	38	[5]
Debussy	Rondes de Printemps	1	1	Rogers	Characters from Hans		
		19	1		Christian Andersen	6	2
Diamond	Fourth Symphony	96	2	Stravinsky	Fire-Bird Suite (1919)	23	[14] 1of
Honegger	Le Roi David	226	1	Turner	Gregorian Overture for		
					String Orchestra	19	233

Solo Violoncello

COMPOSER	WORK	PAGE	MEASURE
Stravinsky	Fire-Bird Suite (1919)	69	6

Soli Violoncello

Rosenthal	Les Petits Métiers	62	3

Bass

Rosenthal	Les Petits Métiers	109	1

Violin I and Viola

COMPOSER	WORK	PAGE	MEASURE	COMPOSER	WORK	PAGE	MEASURE
Bloch	Voice in the Wilderness	53	2	Moore	In Memoriam	12	[H]
Casella	Pupazzetti	37	[4]	Pizzetti	Concerto dell'Estate	103	2
Hindemith	Symphonic Meta-			Strauss, R.	Also Sprach		
	morphosis of Themes				Zarathustra	74	3
	by Weber	16	1	Turner	Gregorian Overture for		
Milhaud	Le Bal Martiniquais	5	[20]		String Orchestra	15	185

Violin II and Viola

COMPOSER	WORK	PAGE	MEASURE	COMPOSER	WORK	PAGE	MEASURE
Copland	Third Symphony	105	[95] 2f	Rivier	3 Pastorales	2	[2]
Dukas	Symphonie en Ut			Stravinsky	Petrouchka Suite	41	[30] 4f
	majeur	165	[L]	Stravinsky	Scherzo Fantastique	34	[50]
Honegger	Le Roi David	9	5				

Violin I, II, and Viola

COMPOSER	WORK	PAGE	MEASURE	COMPOSER	WORK	PAGE	MEASURE
Alfvén	A Legend of the			Casella	Pupazzetti	29	2b [6]
	Skerries	42	[16]	Debussy–	Six Épigraphes		
Bartók	Dance Suite	43	[31]	Ansermet	Antiques	29	[B]
Bloch	Voice in the Wilderness	87	1	Diamond	Timon of Athens	8	46

447

STRINGS

Violin I, II, and Viola (contd.)

COMPOSER	WORK	PAGE	MEASURE	COMPOSER	WORK	PAGE	MEASURE
Ibert	La Ballade de la Geôle de Reading	97	[73] 3f	Read	Sketches of the City	4	[1]
						10	3b [6]
Milhaud	Concerto pour Piano et Orchestre	19	1b [95]	Siegmeister	Ozark Set	80	[80]
				Tansman	Sonatine Trans-atlantique, III	20	3
Milhaud	Ière Symphonie	7	1b [25]				
Ravel	Concerto pour la main gauche	59	1	Taylor	Through the Looking Glass	43	5
				Thomson	Louisiana Story Suite	32	193

Soli Violin I, II, and Viola

COMPOSER	WORK	PAGE	MEASURE
de Falla	El Retablo de Maese Pedro	31	2

Violin I and Violoncello

COMPOSER	WORK	PAGE	MEASURE	COMPOSER	WORK	PAGE	MEASURE
Diamond	Music for Shakespeare's "Romeo and Juliet"	66	[120]	Saminsky	Litanies des Femmes	3	1

Soli Violin I and Violoncello

COMPOSER	WORK	PAGE	MEASURE	COMPOSER	WORK	PAGE	MEASURE
de Falla	El Retablo de Maese Pedro	1	3	Stravinsky	Le Sacre du Printemps	62	1b [72]

Violin I, II, and Violoncello

COMPOSER	WORK	PAGE	MEASURE	COMPOSER	WORK	PAGE	MEASURE
Diamond	Rounds for String Orchestra	29	[50] 3f	Honegger	Horace Victorieux	35	1
				Ravel	Alborada del Gracioso	17	[12]

Viola and Violoncello

COMPOSER	WORK	PAGE	MEASURE	COMPOSER	WORK	PAGE	MEASURE
Bartók	First Rhapsody for Violin and Orchestra	26	[10] 4f	Debussy	Rapsodie pour Orchestre et Saxophone	1	1
Bax	First Symphony	68	[E] 2f	Dukas	L'Apprenti Sorcier	1	1
Casella	La Donna Serpente, I. Serie	1	1	Ravel	Le Tombeau de Couperin	34	[18] 2f
Casella	La Donna Serpente, II. Serie	48	[63] 1f	Ravel	Tzigane	8	6
				Schönberg	Verklärte Nacht	27	8
Debussy	Le Martyre de Saint Sébastien	61	[27]	Slonimsky	My Toy Balloon	25	1

Soli Viola and Violoncello

COMPOSER	WORK	PAGE	MEASURE
Ibert	Féerique	1	1

Violin I, Viola, and Violoncello

COMPOSER	WORK	PAGE	MEASURE
Schmitt	Mirages pour Orchestre, No. 1	36	3

ARTIFICIAL HARMONICS

Violin II, Viola, and Violoncello

COMPOSER	WORK	PAGE	MEASURE
Diamond	*Rounds for String Orchestra*	20	2

Violin I, II, Viola, and Violoncello

COMPOSER	WORK	PAGE	MEASURE	COMPOSER	WORK	PAGE	MEASURE
Casella	*Elegia Eroica*	31	[43]	**Milhaud**	*2ᵐᵉ Suite Symphonique*	80	1
Diamond	*Fourth Symphony*	102	[230]	**Milhaud**	*Saudades do Brazil*	73	13
Dukas	*L'Apprenti Sorcier*	3	2b [3]	**Schmitt**	*Mirages pour Orchestre, No. 1*	29	[13]
Honegger	*Pacific 231*	1	1				
Ibert	*Escales*	36	[31] 2f				

Soli Violin I, II, Viola, and Violoncello

COMPOSER	WORK	PAGE	MEASURE
Casella	*Pupazzetti*	18	[5]

Violin I, II, Viola, and Bass

COMPOSER	WORK	PAGE	MEASURE
Diamond	*Rounds for String Orchestra*	3	[30] 1f

Violin I, Violoncello, and Bass

COMPOSER	WORK	PAGE	MEASURE
Rosenthal	*Les Petits Métiers*	59	[B]

(6) PERFECT 5th

Violin I

COMPOSER	WORK	PAGE	MEASURE	COMPOSER	WORK	PAGE	MEASURE
Bartók	*Dance Suite*	43	[31]	**Ferroud**	*Au Parc Monceau*	18	[4] 1of
Diamond	*Timon of Athens*	14	90	**Ravel**	*Rapsodie Espagnole*	28	1

Solo Violin I

COMPOSER	WORK	PAGE	MEASURE
Ravel	*Ma Mère l'Oye*	44	2

Violin II

COMPOSER	WORK	PAGE	MEASURE	COMPOSER	WORK	PAGE	MEASURE
Bartók	*Dance Suite*	62	36	**Copland**	*Dance Symphony*	33	[17] 1f

STRINGS

Viola

COMPOSER	WORK	PAGE	MEASURE	COMPOSER	WORK	PAGE	MEASURE
Ravel	*Vaises Nobles et Sentimentales*	**74**	[75] 10f	**Roussel**	*Symphonie en Sol mineur*	**38**	6

Violoncello

Ferroud	*Au Parc Monceau*	**4**	3	**Ravel**	*Rapsodie Espagnole*	**81**	2b [27]
		34	[9]				
		44	[18]				

Violin II and Violoncello

COMPOSER	WORK	PAGE	MEASURE
Bartók	*Dance Suite*	**31**	III

(7)

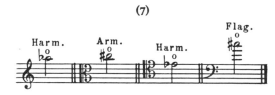

Soli Violin I

Kodály	*Psalmus Hungaricus*	**43**	[26]	**Pierné**	*Divertissements sur un Thème Pastorale*	**11**	1
Kodály	*Te Deum*	**76**	[430]				

Violin II

Coppola	*Symphonie en La mineur*	**70**	4b [9]	**James**	*Suite for String Orchestra*	**23**	[X]

Violin I and II

Berg	*Violin Concerto*	**77**	[125]	**Schönberg**	*Verklärte Nacht*	**51**	3
Coppola	*Suite Intima*	**31**	I				

Viola

Alfvén	*A Legend of the Skerries*	**11**	[3]	**Strauss, R.**	*Eine Alpensinfonie*	**80**	5b [74]

Violoncello

Debussy	*Le Martyre de Saint Sébastien*	**12**	I	**Sibelius**	*Tapiola*	**33**	334
Mahler	*Das Lied von der Erde*	**80**	[22] 7f	**Strauss, R.**	*Salomé's Dance*	**8**	1b [K]
Mahler	*Symphony No. 3*	**15**	[11] 4f	**Strauss, R.**	*Symphonia Domestica*	**67**	[84] 1f
Read	*Symphony No. 1*	**13**	[8] 2f	**Villa-Lobos**	*Amazonas*	**9**	[3]

ARTIFICIAL HARMONICS

Solo Violoncello

COMPOSER	WORK	PAGE	MEASURE
Poulenc	*Concerto pour deux Pianos et Orchestre*	**34**	[27] 2f

Violin I and Viola

Mahler	*Symphony No. 3*	**182**	2

Violin I, II, Viola, and Violoncello

Mahler	*Symphony No. 3*	**188**	4

Soli Violin I, II, Viola, and Violoncello

Mahler	*Symphony No. 8*	**207**	[199]

(8)

Violoncello

COMPOSER	WORK	PAGE	MEASURE	COMPOSER	WORK	PAGE	MEASURE
Debussy–Ansermet	*Six Épigraphes Antiques*	**21**	2	**Schönberg**	*A Survivor from Warsaw*	**12**	52

Solo Violoncello

Schönberg	*A Survivor from Warsaw*	**2**	5

(9)

Violin I

COMPOSER	WORK	PAGE	MEASURE	COMPOSER	WORK	PAGE	MEASURE
Albéniz–Arbós	*El Puerto*	**5**	1	**Inghelbrecht**	*Pour le jour de la première neige au vieux Japon*	**33**	[19]
		35	[O] 1f				
Albéniz–Arbós	*Évocation*	**22**	[J] 3f	**Mahler**	*Symphony No. 5*	**113**	[33]
Charpentier	*Impressions d'Italie*	**80**	5b [6]	**Rivier**	*Rapsodie pour Violoncelle et Orchestre*	**14**	8
Ferguson	*Partita for Orchestra*	**50**	1				
d'Indy	*Jour d'été à la Montagne*	**75**	[37]	**Roussel**	*Le Festin de l'Araignée*	**46**	3
		79	7	**Saint-Saëns**	*Suite Algérienne*	**51**	3

STRINGS

Solo Violin I

COMPOSER	WORK	PAGE	MEASURE
Milhaud	*IIe Symphonie*	**76**	[125] 2f

Violin II

COMPOSER	WORK	PAGE	MEASURE	COMPOSER	WORK	PAGE	MEASURE
Albéniz–Arbós	*Évocation*	**8**	4	**Honegger**	*Musique pour le "Phaedre" de G. D'Annunzio*	**18**	[3]
				Milhaud	*2me Suite Symphonique*	**90**	1b [46]

Violin I and II

Honegger	*Musique pour le "Phaedre" de G. D'Annunzio*	**27** **46**	2 1	**McKay**	*Sinfonietta No. 4*	**16**	[C]
				Schönberg	*Verklärte Nacht*	**51**	3
d'Indy	*Jour d'été à la Montagne*	**38**	[15]	**Villa-Lobos**	*Amazonas*	**2**	3
				White	*Idyl for Orchestra*	**12**	5

Viola

Debussy	*Première Rhapsodie*	**1**	2	**Strauss, R.**	*Also Sprach Zarathustra*	**99** **101**	1 2

Soli Viola

Walton	*Concerto for Violin and Orchestra*	**51**	5

Violoncello

Rabaud	*La Procession Nocturne*	**30**	3	**Roussel**	*Le Festin de l'Araignée*	**43**	[60]
Roussel	*Évocations, III*	**80**	1	**Sibelius**	*Tapiola*	**33**	333

Soli Violoncello

Strauss, R.	*Salomé's Dance*	**19**	1

Bass

Jolivet	*Andante pour Orchestre à Cordes*	**16**	1b [70]

Violin I and Viola

Honegger	*Le Chant de Nigamon*	**2**	2b [7]

ARTIFICIAL HARMONICS

Violin II and Viola

COMPOSER	WORK	PAGE	MEASURE
Respighi	*Vetrate di Chiesa*	**69**	[18]

Violin I, II, and Viola

COMPOSER	WORK	PAGE	MEASURE
Honegger	*Prélude pour "La Tempête"*	**10**	I

Viola and Violoncello

COMPOSER	WORK	PAGE	MEASURE	COMPOSER	WORK	PAGE	MEASURE
Debussy	*Gigues*	**2**	4b [1]	**Honegger**	*Horace Victorieux*	**2**	3

(10)

Violin I

COMPOSER	WORK	PAGE	MEASURE	COMPOSER	WORK	PAGE	MEASURE
Copland	*Appalachian Spring*	**56**	[46] 1f	**Ives**	*Three Places in New England*	**35**	2b [H]
Copland	*Music for the Theatre*	**71**	[59] 12f	**Rimsky-Korsakoff**	*Scheherazade*	**236**	588
Copland	*Third Symphony*	**82**	[73] 1f			**238**	593
Debussy–Ansermet	*Six Épigraphes Antiques*	**22**	I	**Stravinsky**	*Fire-Bird Suite* (1919)	**10**	I
Gershwin	*Concerto in F for Piano and Orchestra*	**63**	[7] 3f			**12**	1b [14]

Solo Violin I

COMPOSER	WORK	PAGE	MEASURE	COMPOSER	WORK	PAGE	MEASURE
Levant	*Nocturne*	**28**	114	**Schönberg**	*Pierrot Lunaire*	**52**	[25] 1f

Soli Violin I

COMPOSER	WORK	PAGE	MEASURE
Rozsa	*Concerto for String Orchestra*	**31**	[91]

Violin II

COMPOSER	WORK	PAGE	MEASURE	COMPOSER	WORK	PAGE	MEASURE
Copland	*Four Dance Episodes from "Rodeo"*	**25**	[25] 5f	**Respighi**	*Trittico Botticelliano*	**7**	[3]

Violin I and II

COMPOSER	WORK	PAGE	MEASURE	COMPOSER	WORK	PAGE	MEASURE
Moross	*Biguine*	**2**	I	**Schönberg**	*Verklärte Nacht*	**51**	3

Viola

COMPOSER	WORK	PAGE	MEASURE	COMPOSER	WORK	PAGE	MEASURE
Caturla	*Trois Danses Cubaines*	**43**	[19]	**Villa-Lobos**	*Amazonas*	**12**	[4]

STRINGS

Soli Viola

COMPOSER	WORK	PAGE	MEASURE
Schönberg	*A Survivor from Warsaw*	**13**	60

Violoncello

COMPOSER	WORK	PAGE	MEASURE	COMPOSER	WORK	PAGE	MEASURE
Debussy–Ansermet	*Six Épigraphes Antiques*	**90**	[E]	**Sibelius**	*Tapiola*	**33**	333

Violin I and Viola

Sibelius	*Pelleas and Melisande*	**29**	11

Violin II and Violoncello

Debussy–Ansermet	*Six Épigraphes Antiques*	**42**	[C]

Viola and Violoncello

Schönberg	*A Survivor from Warsaw*	**12**	52

(11)

Violin I

Debussy–Ansermet	*Six Épigraphes Antiques*	**21** **58**	2 2

(12)

Harm.

Soli Violin I

Schönberg	*Fünf Orchesterstücke*	**33**	[3]

Violin I and II

Mohaupt	*Town Piper Music*	**33**	[26]

Violin I, II, and Viola

Honegger	*Le Dit des Jeux du Monde*	**32**	[4] 5f

Chapter 58

MULTIPLE DIVISI

English	Italian	French	German
Divide(d)	Divisi	Divisé	Get(h)eilt
Div.	*Div.*	*Div.*	*get.*
All divided	Tutti divisi	Tous divisés	Alle geteilt

DIVISI a 2

English	Italian	French	German
Divide in two [2]	Divisi a due [2]	Divisé en deux [2]	Zweifach geteilt
Div. in 2	*Div. a 2; a due; a 2*	*Div. en 2*	*2-fach get.*
In 2	Divisi in due parti	En 2	Zu 2
All divided in 2 equal parts	Tutti a due parti uguali	Tous divisés en 2 parties égales	Alle in zwei gleichen Hälften geteilt
1st Half	I parte	La 1re moitié	Die erste [I.] Hälfte
2nd Half	II parte	La 2e moitié	Die zweite [II.] Hälfte
1st halves only	1ᵃ [I.] metà	1re moitié	1te Hälfte
			Die I. Spieler
2nd halves only	2ᵃ [II.] metà	2e moitié	2te Hälfte
			Die 2. Spieler
Half of section	La metà	La moitié	Die Hälfte
½ of desks			Nur die Hälfte
Only 1st half of desks	Solamente 1ᵃ metà di leggi Il I. di ogni leggio	Seulement 1re moitié des pupitres	Nur die erste Hälfte der Pulte
Other half	L'altra metà	L'autre moitié	Die andere Hälfte
Odd desks	Impari leggi	(Les) Pupitres impairs	Ungerade Pulte
Even desks	Pari leggi	(Les) Pupitres pairs	Gerade Pulte
One player at each desk	Iº di leggi	Les chefs des pupitres	Eine Spieler
1st player from each desk	All'ogni leggio soltanto il Iº sonatore	Les 1res (seules)	An jedem Pulte nur die erste Spieler
	1 della 1ᵃ metà	1re de chaque pupitre	
		Un [1] par pupitre	

UNISON

English	Italian	French	German
All	Non-divisi	Tous	Alle
Together	*non-div.*	Unies	Einfach
Unison	Unisoni		Nicht get(h)eilt
unis.	*unis.*		Zusammen
	Uniti		*zus.*
	Tutti		

(1) DIVISI a 3

English	Italian	French	German
Divide in three [3]	Divisi a tre [3]	Divisé en [par] 3	Dreifach get(h)eilt
Div. in 3	*Div. a 3; a 3*	*Div. en 3*	*3-fach get.*
In 3	Divisi in tre [3] parti	Divisés à 3 Parties	Geteilt in 3 Partieren
	Divisi 3 parti	En 3	Zu 3
	Divisi in III parti		
Divided in three equal parts	Divisi a tre parti uguali	Divisés en 3 parties égales	Zu 3 gleichen Theilen
All the remaining Vlns. [Vlas.; Vlc.; Bs.] div. in 3 equal parts	Tutti gli altri Vni. [Vle.; Vclli.; Cbi.] div. in 3 parti uguali	Tous les autres V^{ons} [Altos; V^{elles}.; C.B.] divisés en 3 parties égales	Sämtlich übrige Viol. [Br.; Vcll.; Kb.] in 3 gleich stark besetzten Partieren

455

STRINGS

Violin I

COMPOSER	WORK	PAGE	MEASURE	COMPOSER	WORK	PAGE	MEASURE
Bartók	Concerto for Orchestra	47	[10]	Mahler	Symphony No. 1	84	[10] 2f
Bartók	Concerto No. 3 for	36	[72]			138	2
	Piano and Orchestra	39	[79]	Mahler	Symphony No. 2	26	[13]
Bartók	Dance Suite	51	135			134	3
Bartók	Second Rhapsody for			Mahler	Symphony No. 3	55	[39] 1f
	Violin and Orchestra	42	[30]			154	[13] 4f
Bartók	Vier Orchesterstücke	8	[4] 1f	Mahler	Symphony No. 7	11	[6]
Bax	First Symphony	12	1	Martinet	Orphée	1	5
Bax	Fifth Symphony	26	1b [17]	Mason	Chanticleer—Festival		
Bloch	Evocations	67	1		Overture	30	[19]
Bloch	Schelomo	13	2	McKay	Sinfonietta No. 4	46	2
Bruckner	Symphony No. 8	6	[30] 1f	Miaskovsky	Sinfonietta for String	2	[5] 3f
Casella	Paganiniana	141	1		Orchestra	6	[18] 4f
		175	[44] 2f			9	[27] 2f
Copland	Concerto for Piano and			Miaskovsky	Symphony No. 6	155	[20]
	Orchestra	19	[14] 3f	Mussorgsky	Polonaise from "Boris		
Copland	El Salón México	23	5		Godunov"	26	2
Copland	First Symphony	16	2b [7]	Mussorgsky-			
Copland	Lincoln Portrait	44	[270]	Ravel	Pictures at an Exhibition	47	[39] 4f
Copland	Music for Radio	50	2	Pierné	Viennoise	31	[V]
Copland	Third Symphony	1	1	Poot	Symphonie	18	4
		35	1b [27]	Prokofieff	Piano Concerto No. 3	38	[30]
		153	[130]	Prokofieff	Romeo and Juliet,		
Cowell	Short Symphony (No. 4)	32	1		Suite No. 1	61	6
Debussy	Iberia	37	[23]	Prokofieff	Romeo and Juliet,	61	1
		48	[32]		Suite No. 2	84	2
		63	1	Prokofieff	Symphony No. 5	67	4b [38]
Debussy	Le Martyre de Saint					80	[46]
	Sébastien	39	3	Rabaud	La Procession Nocturne	9	5b [6]
Debussy-	Six Épigraphes	8	1	Rachmaninoff	2d Concerto pour Piano		
Ansermet	Antiques	14	[B]		et Orchestre	10	5
Diamond	Rounds for String			Ravel	Concerto pour Piano et		
	Orchestra	22	[20] 1f		Orchestre	52	2
Dukas	La Péri	40	1	Ravel	La Valse	80	[59]
		105	[15]	Ravel	Rapsodie Espagnole	28	1
Egge	Piano Concerto No. 2	25	2b [18]	Ravel	Tzigane	18	16
Gillis	Symphony No. 5½	52	[A]	Reger	Variations on a Theme	7	1
Glière	Russian Sailors' Dance	30	[196]		of Mozart	18	1
Grieg	Suite for Strings, "From					24	3
	Holberg's Time"	5	[B]			88	1
Grofé	Grand Canyon Suite	91	[1] 2f	Respighi	Antiche Danze ed Arie,		
Hindemith	Symphony in E-Flat	36	[19]		2ª Suite	40	1
Ibert	Escales	14	[9]	Respighi	The Fountains of Rome	1	1
		69	3			5	4
		73	3	Revueltas	Sensemayá	42	[39]
d'Indy	Jour d'été à la Montagne	108	[52] 7f	Rimsky-			
Inghelbrecht	El Greco	56	[47]	Korsakoff	Russian Easter Overture	7	[C] 1f
Khachaturian	Masquerade Suite	35	[8]	Sessions	Suite from "The Black		
Kodály	Marosszék Dances	29	1		Maskers"	93	1
Kodály	Summer Evening	5	[40]	Sessions	Symphony No. II	14	3
Mahler	Das Lied von der Erde	7	[4]			49	[Ff]
						134	[T]

Violin I (contd.)

COMPOSER	WORK	PAGE	MEASURE	COMPOSER	WORK	PAGE	MEASURE
Sibelius	*Symphony No. 2*	29	[O]	Vaughan Williams	*Norfolk Rhapsody, No. 1*	3	[A] 2f
Stillman-Kelley	*New England Symphony*	63	[L] 5f	Verdi	*Messa da Requiem*	158	130
Strauss, R.	*Also Sprach Zarathustra*	20	1	Villa-Lobos	*Uirapurú*	57	[13] 1f
		102	2	Wagner, R.	*Bacchanale from "Tannhäuser"*	51	1
Strauss, R.	*Don Quixote*	8	8	Wagner, R.	*Entrance of the Gods into Valhalla from "Das Rheingold"*	1	1
Strauss, R.	*Till Eulenspiegel's Merry Pranks*	59	18				
Stravinsky	*Chant du Rossignol*	15	[14]	Walton	*Concerto for Viola and Orchestra*	52	1b [46]
Stravinsky	*Fire-Bird Suite* (1919)	74	[16]			70	[62]
Stravinsky	*Firebird Ballet Suite (1945)*	30	[36]	Walton	*Concerto for Violin and Orchestra*	108	[54]
Stravinsky	*Le Sacre du Printemps*	76	1b [87]	Warlock	*Capriol Suite*	4	[B] 8f
		81	[93]	Whithorne	*The Dream Pedlar*	3	1
Stravinsky	*Petrouchka Suite*	153	4b [129]				
Stravinsky	*Symphony in Three Movements*	75	[130] 2f				

Violin II

COMPOSER	WORK	PAGE	MEASURE	COMPOSER	WORK	PAGE	MEASURE
Albéniz-Arbós	*Triana*	3	1	Kodály	*Summer Evening*	11	[80] 3f
Antheil	*Serenade for String Orchestra*	4	2b [9]	Liadov	*Kikimora*	5	1b [8]
Bartók	*Concerto for Orchestra*	23	462	Mahler	*Das Lied von der Erde*	13	[12] 2f
		39	189	Mahler	*Symphony No. 4*	164	[63]
		52	26	Mahler	*Symphony No. 5*	39	[15]
Bartók	*Dance Suite*	15	125			70	[12]
		88	[57] 1f			112	1
Bartók	*Violin Concerto*	32	213	Miaskovsky	*Symphony No. 6*	154	[19]
Bloch	*Evocations*	5	[5] 2f	Milhaud	*2me Suite Symphonique*	18	1
Casella	*La Donna Serpente, I. Serie*	11	2	Milhaud	*Quatrième Symphonie*	103	[125] 1f
Casella	*Paganiniana*	122	[7]	Mussorgsky	*Polonaise from "Boris Godunov"*	18	1
Charpentier	*Impressions d'Italie*	67	2b [15]	Mussorgsky-Ravel	*Pictures at an Exhibition*	48	1
Chávez	*Sinfonia de Antigona*	22	[33]	Prokofieff	*Alexander Nevsky*	127	[71]
Copland	*Third Symphony*	90	[83]	Prokofieff	*Piano Concerto No. 3*	63	[47]
Debussy	*Nuages*	4	4	Rachmaninoff	*Symphony No. 2*	12	4
Debussy	*Sirènes*	104	2			22	1
Debussy-Ansermet	*Six Épigraphes Antiques*	29	[B]	Respighi	*The Fountains of Rome*	60	[21] 2f
Delius	*North Country Sketches*	3	[1]	Roussel	*Suite en Fa*	44	1
Delius	*Summer Night on the River*	14	[8]	Sessions	*Suite from "The Black Maskers"*	23	[24]
Goldmark	*Overture, In Springtime*	7	[15]	Strauss, R.	*Also Sprach Zarathustra*	19	4
Ibert	*Escales*	1	1			70	1
		71	[63] 2f			108	1
Ibert	*La Ballade de la Geôle de Reading*	25	[16]	Strauss, R.	*Don Quixote*	19	1
Inghelbrecht	*El Greco*	25	2b [22]	Strauss, R.	*Eine Alpensinfonie*	58	3b [51]
Ives	*Third Symphony*	69	[5]	Stravinsky	*Fire-Bird Suite* (1919)	12	[14] 2f
						73	[15]
				Vaughan Williams	*Pastoral Symphony*	6	[B] 2f

STRINGS

Violin II (contd.)

COMPOSER	WORK	PAGE	MEASURE	COMPOSER	WORK	PAGE	MEASURE
Verdi	Messa da Requiem	148	63	Walton	Façade, Suite No. 1	48	8
Wagner, R.	Bacchanale from			Walton	Symphony	33	[19] 4f
	"Tannhäuser"	53	3	Whithorne	Fata Morgana	33	8b [29]

Violin I and II

COMPOSER	WORK	PAGE	MEASURE	COMPOSER	WORK	PAGE	MEASURE
Albéniz–Arbós	El Puerto	19	2	Dukelsky	Symphony No. 3	30	4
Antheil	Symphony No. 5	84	1b [9]	Egge	Piano Concerto No. 2	14	5b [10]
Aubert	Saisons	2	3b [1]	Elgar	In the South, Concert-Overture	54	7
Bartók	Concerto for Orchestra	34	87	Fitelberg	Nocturne for Orchestra	14	1
Bartók	Concerto No. 3 for Piano and Orchestra	85	[680] 9f	Fitelberg	Symphony No. 1	67	[120] 4f
Bartók	Dance Suite	41	71	Gillis	The Alamo	32	[K]
Bartók	Second Suite	21	7b [19]	Goldmark	Overture, In Springtime	14	[31]
		43	1	Goossens	Sinfonietta	70	[4]
		80	[4]	Griffes	The Pleasure Dome of Kubla Khan	36	2
Bax	Fifth Symphony	35	1	Hanson	Symphony No. 2, "Romantic"	83	1
		86	[11]	Harsanyi	Suite pour Orchestre	4	2b [15]
		136	[33] 2f	Hill	Lilacs	15	4
Bax	Sixth Symphony	25	[21]	Honegger	Symphonie Liturgique	109	[17] 4f
		53	[3]	Ibert	Féerique	1	1
Bax	The Garden of Fand	42	6	Inghelbrecht	Pour le jour de la première neige au vieux Japon	4	[2] 1f
Berlioz	Symphonie Fantastique	160	1			13	3
Bruckner	Symphony No. 9	77	507	Kodály	Marosszék Dances	20	1
Cadman	American Suite	27	8			33	1
Casella	Elegia Eroica	33	[50]	Kodály	Psalmus Hungaricus	16	3
Casella	La Donna Serpente, I. Serie	36	3	Kodály	Summer Evening	40	[240] 2f
Casella	La Donna Serpente, II. Serie	29	[37]	Khrennikov	Symphony No. 1	38	1b [210]
Copland	Concerto for Piano and Orchestra	61	3b [47]	Liadov	The Enchanted Lake	14	[7] 2f
				Maganini	South Wind	2	1
Copland	El Salón México	42	[39]			16	[O]
Copland	First Symphony	43	[30]	Maganini	Tuolumne	4	[B]
Copland	Third Symphony	25	4	Mahler	Symphony No. 2	143	[6]
		62	1b [48]	Mahler	Symphony No. 6	36	3
		79	[70]	Mahler	Symphony No. 8	25	[25] 2f
		103	2			122	[81]
		108	[98]	Martinet	Orphée	11	1
		148	3			66	[5]
Debussy	Fêtes	35	[6]	Miaskovsky	Symphony No. 22	54	2b [89]
Debussy	Jeux	67	1			69	[105] 5f
Debussy	La Mer	15	2	Milhaud	IIe Symphonie	25	[35] 1f
		58	[30]	Mussorgsky–Ravel	Pictures at an Exhibition	148	[119] 4f
		62	1	Poot	Symphonie	36	7
		85	1b [44]	Prokofieff	Cinderella Suite No. 1	147	[128]
Debussy	Le Martyre de Saint Sébastien	64	[28]	Rachmaninoff	The Bells	96	6b [100]
Debussy	Rhapsodie pour Orchestre et Saxophone	41	[G]	Ravel	Concerto pour la main gauche	13	[5]
						64	[35]
						81	[46]

458

MULTIPLE DIVISI

Violin I and II (contd.)

COMPOSER	WORK	PAGE	MEASURE	COMPOSER	WORK	PAGE	MEASURE
Ravel	*Daphnis et Chloé, Suite No. 1*	7	[77]	Strauss, R.	*Till Eulenspiegel's Merry Pranks*	17	4b [12]
Ravel	*Daphnis et Chloé, Suite No. 2*	63	[190] 4f	Stravinsky	*Chant du Rossignol*	10	[7]
Ravel	*Le Tombeau de Couperin*	32	[16]			31	[31]
Ravel	*Ma Mère l'Oye*	24	[14]	Stravinsky	*Concerto en Ré pour Orchestre à Cordes*	8	[27] 1f
Ravel	*Rapsodie Espagnole*	15	[5]			16	[55]
		51	[7]	Stravinsky	*Feuerwerk*	23	[23]
Ravel	*Shéhérazade*	4	[3]	Stravinsky	*Fire-Bird Suite* (1919)	10	1
		33	[16]			60	[33]
Ravel	*Valses Nobles et Sentimentales*	28	[27]			77	[19]
		51	[50]	Stravinsky	*Firebird Ballet Suite (1945)*	34	[43]
Reger	*Variations on a Theme of Mozart*	20	[4]	Stravinsky	*Jeu de Cartes*	16	[27] 2f
		91	2			25	[44] 1f
Respighi	*The Pines of Rome*	19	[5]			66	[128] 2f
		36	4			88	[175] 1f
Respighi	*Vetrate di Chiesa*	73	4	Stravinsky	*Le Sacre du Printemps*	72	[79] 1f
Roger-Ducasse	*Poème Symphonique sur le nom de Gabriel Fauré*	3	2			89	[109]
						92	1b [113]
						136	[192]
Ruggles	*Sun-Treader*	13	[52]	Stravinsky	*Ode*	22	2
Saint-Saëns	*Suite Algérienne*	21	4	Stravinsky	*Orpheus*	7	[13]
Schuman, W.	*Symphony for Strings*	12	94			13	[30]
Scriabin	*Le Divin Poème*	45	9			33	[87] 2f
		133	1			51	[134] 1f
Scriabin	*Le Poème de l'Extase*	23	1	Stravinsky	*Symphony in C*	34	1b [58]
		116	[23]	Stravinsky	*Symphony in Three Movements*	47	[84]
Scriabin	*Prométhée, Le Poème du Feu*	20	2b [13]			78	[140] 2f
		45	4b [30]			92	[158]
Sessions	*Suite from "The Black Maskers"*	53	[52] 2f			112	[186]
Sibelius	*Pohjola's Daughter*	38	2b [M]	Szymanowski	*Symphonie Concertante pour Piano et Orchestre*	48	1
Sibelius	*Symphony No. 5*	45	7b [H]	Vaughan Williams	*Symphony in D major (No. 5)*	70	1
Sibelius	*Tapiola*	19	[G]	Verdi	*Messa da Requiem*	206	1
		32	[K]	Wellesz	*Symphony in C*	44	[320] 4f
Still	*Bells*	2	[2]	Whithorne	*The Dream Pedlar*	22	[11]
Strauss, R.	*Eine Alpensinfonie*	107	[103] 9f			44	1
Strauss, R.	*Ein Heldenleben*	95	5				
		104	[54]				

Violin I, II, and III

COMPOSER	WORK	PAGE	MEASURE
Shostakovich	*Symphony No. 5*	85	[75]

Viola

COMPOSER	WORK	PAGE	MEASURE	COMPOSER	WORK	PAGE	MEASURE
Antheil	*Symphony No. 5*	77	8b [5]	Bartók	*Second Rhapsody for Violin and Orchestra*	30	[14]
Barber	*Music for a Scene from Shelley*	7	42				
		11	68	Bartók	*Second Suite*	59	4
Barber	*Second Symphony*	42	[29]	Bartók	*Violin Concerto*	104	[334]
		53	5	Bloch	*Schelomo*	8	[3]

STRINGS

Viola (contd.)

COMPOSER	WORK	PAGE	MEASURE	COMPOSER	WORK	PAGE	MEASURE
Bloch	*Trois Poèmes Juifs*	17	[9]	Rachmaninoff	*Die Toteninsel*	7	6
		24	[14]			53	[19] 4f
		28	2b [17]	Rachmaninoff	*2d Concerto pour Piano*		
		69	[6] 1f		*et Orchestre*	11	1
Bloch	*Voice in the Wilderness*	7	1			64	1b [26]
Brahms	*Ein deutsches Requiem*	28	2	Rachmaninoff	*Symphony No. 2*	9	[3] 11f
		49	146			21	13
Britten	*Serenade for Tenor,*					141	[53]
	Horn and Strings	34	1	Rachmaninoff	*The Bells*	32	[31]
Copland	*First Symphony*	30	5b [17]	Ravel	*Daphnis et Chloé,*		
Copland	*Four Dance Episodes*				*Suite No. 1*	10	[80]
	from "Rodeo"	57	2	Ravel	*Daphnis et Chloé,*	37	2
Debussy	*Iberia*	90	[57]		*Suite No. 2*	45	[176]
Debussy	*La Mer*	69	[35]	Read	*Symphony No. 1*	41	[17] 1f
Delius	*A Dance Rhapsody*			Reger	*Variations on a Theme*	2	7
	(No. 1)	27	1		*of Mozart*	9	[2]
Delius	*Sea Drift*	30	[9]	Respighi	*The Pines of Rome*	64	1
Dukas	*La Péri*	60	1	Schönberg	*Fünf Orchesterstücke*	40	[4]
		90	1	Schönberg	*Theme and Variations*	44	215
Grieg	*Norwegian Dances*	12	[D]	Schuman, W.	*Prayer in Time of War*	2	31
Griffes	*The Pleasure Dome of*			Sessions	*Symphony No. II*	47	[Ee] 1f
	Kubla Khan	33	[M] 3f			103	[B]
Honegger	*Mouvement*			Shostakovich	*Symphony No. 1*	73	[20]
	Symphonique No. 3	50	1b [17]			85	[36]
Honegger	*Symphonie pour Cordes*	32	[5]	Sibelius	*Symphony No. 6*	17	[I] 1f
Ibert	*Escales*	34	[29]	Siegmeister	*Western Suite*	3	1b [15]
Kodály	*Psalmus Hungaricus*	7	[4]	Still	*Poem for Orchestra*	21	2b [11]
Liadov	*The Enchanted Lake*	15	1b [8]	Stillman-	*Gulliver—His Voyage*		
Mahler	*Das Lied von der Erde*	74	[13]	Kelley	*to Lilliput*	77	1
		24	[27] 4f	Strauss, R.	*Also Sprach*		
		134	4b [57]		*Zarathustra*	137	4
Mahler	*Symphony No. 3*	5	[2] 7f	Strauss, R.	*Don Quixote*	106	1
		112	3	Strauss, R.	*Eine Alpensinfonie*	159	[142] 9f
Mahler	*Symphony No. 4*	117	56	Strauss, R.	*Ein Heldenleben*	34	5
Mahler	*Symphony No. 6*	152	1			46	5
Mahler	*Symphony No. 7*	14	[10]	Stravinsky	*Danses Concertantes*	80	[127] 2f
Mahler	*Symphony No. 8*	135	[99] 3f	Stravinsky	*Fire-Bird Suite (1919)*	72	[14]
		148	4b [117]	Stravinsky	*Le Sacre du Printemps*	20	5b [29]
McKay	*Sinfonietta No. 4*	91	[X]	Stravinsky	*Petrouchka Suite*	89	[76]
Miaskovsky	*Symphony No. 22*	11	[16] 5f			153	[129]
		32	[50] 5f	Stravinsky	*Scherzo Fantastique*	28	[42]
		46	[79] 6f	Vaughan			
Milhaud	*Quatrième Symphonie*	40	[90]	Williams	*A London Symphony*	72	1
Milhaud	*Two Marches*	24	[50]	Wagner, R.	*Forest Murmurs from*		
Pizzetti	*Concerto de'l'Estate*	15	[7]		*"Siegfried"*	7	74
		21	[9]	Walton	*Concerto for Violin and*		
Prokofieff	*Classical Symphony*	55	[44]		*Orchestra*	105	4
Prokofieff	*Romeo and Juliet,*			Walton	*Symphony*	37	[22] 8f
	Suite No. 2	68	[45]			113	1
Prokofieff	*Suite from the Ballet*			Wellesz	*Symphony in C*	47	[355]
	"Chout"	69	[93]				

MULTIPLE DIVISI

Violoncello

COMPOSER	WORK	PAGE	MEASURE	COMPOSER	WORK	PAGE	MEASURE
Antheil	Serenade for String Orchestra	6	[13]	Mahler	Symphony No. 6	149	2
Barber	Second Symphony	62	[8] 1f	Mahler	Symphony No. 9	12	10
Bartók	Violin Concerto	77	[59]			33	7b [12]
Bax	Third Symphony	36	[36] 4f	Miaskovsky	Sinfonietta for String Orchestra	15	[43] 3f
Bax	Fifth Symphony	141	[37]	Milhaud	IIe Symphonie	93	[100]
Bax	Sixth Symphony	54	3	Moross	Biguine	15	1
		74	[2]	Prokofieff	Lieutenant Kijé	38	2b [31]
Bloch	America	121	3	Prokofieff	Symphony No. 5	20	3b [11]
Bloch	Trois Poèmes Juifs	47	[4] 1f			51	25
		64	4	Rachmaninoff	Die Toteninsel	34	[13]
Brahms	Ein deutsches Requiem	5	1	Ravel	Daphnis et Chloé, Suite No. 2	1	[155] 1f
Bruckner	Symphony No. 5	131	[190] 6f	Ravel	La Valse	2	3
Casella	Paganiniana	162	[34]	Ravel	Ma Mère l'Oye	45	5
Casella	Pupazzetti	32	3	Respighi	Concerto Gregoriano per Violino e Orchestra	17	[8]
Creston	Two Choric Dances	28	[25] 1f				
Debussy	Iberia	55	1	Respighi	The Fountains of Rome	63	4
		58	[39] 2f	Respighi	The Pines of Rome	39	1
Debussy	La Mer	83	5	Rimsky-Korsakoff	Le Coq d'Or Suite	79	2
Debussy-Ansermet	Six Épigraphes Antiques	10	[F]	Rimsky-Korsakoff	Russian Easter Overture	11	[D]
Delius	Paris—Ein Nachtstück	3	5	Rimsky-Korsakoff	Symphony No. 2, "Antar"	74	[J]
Dukas	La Péri	34	[5]	Scriabin	Deuxième Symphonie	3	1
Egge	Symphony No. 1	83	4b [9]	Scriabin	Le Poème de l'Extase	100	1
Elgar	Falstaff	73	[73]			128	[27] 1f
de Falla	Nuits dans les Jardins d'Espagne	16	[9]			153	[32] 2f
Fitelberg	Nocturne for Orchestra	2	3b [12]	Schmitt	Mirages pour Orchestre, No. 1	8	[3]
		46	[270] 1f	Schönberg	A Survivor from Warsaw	4	16
Gershwin	An American in Paris	12	[10] 4f	Schuman, W.	Symphony for Strings	10	43
Gershwin	Concerto in F for Piano and Orchestra	55	6b [3]	Schuman, W.	Symphony No. III	62	279
		64	[9]	Sessions	Symphony No. II	65	6
Glazounov	Violin Concerto in A minor	17	[10]			99	1
						135	2
Grieg	Peer Gynt Suite No. 1	15	17	Sibelius	Symphony No. 1	64	4
Griffes	The Pleasure Dome of Kubla Khan	1	1	Sibelius	Symphony No. 3	37	1b [6]
		60	[Z] 4f	Sibelius	Symphony No. 4	5	[D] 5f
Gruenberg	The Enchanted Isle	1	1	Sibelius	Symphony No. 6	71	5
Halffter	Deux Esquisses Symphoniques	2	4	Sibelius	The Swan of Tuonela	9	3
Hindemith	Konzertmusik für Streichorchester und Blechbläser	20	6	Stillman-Kelley	Gulliver—His Voyage to Lilliput	107	2b [Z]
d'Indy	Deuxième Symphonie en Sib	73	[34]	Strauss, R.	Also Sprach Zarathustra	15	1
Liadov	Kikimora	20	[22]			72	1
Liszt	Eine Faust-Symphonie	7	[C]			165	4
Liszt	Tasso, Lamento e Trionfo	17	109	Strauss, R.	Don Quixote	70	4
Mahler	Symphony No. 1	22	5	Strauss, R.	Ein Heldenleben	79	1
Mahler	Symphony No. 4	102	246	Strauss, R.	Symphonia Domestica	25	[30] 4f
Mahler	Symphony No. 5	23	3				

STRINGS

Violoncello (contd.)

COMPOSER	WORK	PAGE	MEASURE	COMPOSER	WORK	PAGE	MEASURE
Strauss, R.	*Till Eulenspiegel's*	17	[11] 4f	Toch	*Hyperion*	22	[99]
	Merry Pranks	29	1b [21]	Vaughan			
Stravinsky	*Petrouchka Suite*	13	4	Williams	*A London Symphony*	20	[K]
		101	[88]	Vaughan	*Pastoral Symphony*	14	4
Stravinsky	*Symphonie de Psaumes*	19	[7] 1f	Williams		94	6
		29	7	Vaughan	*Symphony in D major*		
		36	4b [7]	Williams	*(No. 5)*	116	3b [18]
		57	[22]	Vaughan	*Symphony in E minor*		
Szymanowski	*Symphonie Concertante*			Williams	*(No. 6)*	79	5
	pour Piano et			Villa-Lobos	*Uirapurú*	6	1
	Orchestre	21	2	Wagner, R.	*Forest Murmurs from*		
Tansman	*Deux Moments*				*"Siegfried"*	3	28
	Symphoniques	20	[6] 7f				

Bass

COMPOSER	WORK	PAGE	MEASURE	COMPOSER	WORK	PAGE	MEASURE
Bloch	*Trois Poèmes Juifs*	62	1	Ravel	*Alborada del Gracioso*	14	[9] 4f
Delius	*Appalachia*	28	136	Ravel	*La Valse*	1	1
		48	215	Respighi	*Ballata delle Gnomidi*	30	[9] 3f
de Falla	*Nuits dans les Jardins*			Rieti	*L'Arca di Noè*	6	[5]
	d'Espagne	27	[20]	Rimsky-			
Fitelberg	*Symphony No. 1*	123	3b [371]	Korsakoff	*Le Coq d'Or Suite*	78	9
Inghelbrecht	*Pour le jour de la*			Schlein	*Dance Overture*	13	[F]
	première neige au	28	[16]	Schönberg	*Fünf Orchesterstücke*	9	5b [9]
	vieux Japon	42	3b [26]	Schuman, W.	*American Festival*		
Ives	*Three Places in New*				*Overture*	23	[285] 1f
	England	56	[Q]	Schuman, W.	*Symphony No. IV*	57	271
Mahler	*Das Lied von der Erde*	5	[2] 1f	Sessions	*Symphony No. II*	109	[E] 1f
		38	[49] 5f	Strauss, R.	*Don Quixote*	169	5
		65	[7] 2f	Strauss, R.	*Till Eulenspiegel's*		
Mahler	*Songs of a Wayfarer*	53	74		*Merry Pranks*	57	[39] 6f
Mahler	*Symphony No. 2*	112	[47]	Stravinsky	*Chant du Rossignol*	4	[1] 2f
Mahler	*Symphony No. 3*	188	1	Stravinsky	*Le Sacre du Printemps*	77	[87]
Malipiero	*Pause del Silenzio*	34	202	Vaughan	*Symphony in E minor*		
Prokofieff	*Suite from the Ballet*			Williams	*(No. 6)*	65	5
	"Chout"	52	1b [73]	Villa-Lobos	*Amazonas*	1	4

Violin I and Viola

COMPOSER	WORK	PAGE	MEASURE	COMPOSER	WORK	PAGE	MEASURE
Bartók	*Concerto No. 3 for*			Mahler	*Symphony No. 6*	55	2
	Piano and Orchestra	19	[112] 1f	Mussorgsky-			
Bartók	*Vier Orchesterstücke*	87	2	Ravel	*Pictures at an Exhibition*	142	115
Copland	*Four Dance Episodes*			Ravel	*Daphnis et Chloé,*		
	from "Rodeo"	51	1		*Suite No. 1*	57	[123]
Copland	*Statements*	45	[3]	Reger	*Variations on a Theme*		
Debussy-	*Six Épigraphes*				*of Mozart*	107	2
Ansermet	*Antiques*	43	2	Respighi	*Antiche Danze ed Arie,*		
Delius	*Three Orchestral Pieces*	10	[8] 4f		*2ª Suite*	43	2
Mahler	*Symphony No. 3*	100	[74]	Respighi	*The Pines of Rome*	67	8

MULTIPLE DIVISI

Violin I and Viola (contd.)

COMPOSER	WORK	PAGE	MEASURE	COMPOSER	WORK	PAGE	MEASURE
Schmitt	*Mirages pour Orchestre, No. 1*	10	[4]	Strauss, R.	*Ein Heldenleben*	60	[32]
Schönberg	*Fünf Orchesterstücke*	6	[6] 2f	Stravinsky	*Feuerwerk*	11	1b [10]
Scriabin	*Le Poème de l'Extase*	8	[1]	Stravinsky	*Petrouchka Suite*	92	1
		99	4	Walton	*Concerto for Violin and Orchestra*	114	4
Strauss, R.	*Also Sprach Zarathustra*	13	4				

Violin II and Viola

COMPOSER	WORK	PAGE	MEASURE	COMPOSER	WORK	PAGE	MEASURE
Bartók	*Deux Images*	46	[19] 14f	Prokofieff	*Piano Concerto No. 3*	2	[1]
Bax	*Third Symphony*	42	[43] 1f	Rachmaninoff	*The Bells*	38	2b [42]
Bernstein	*"Jeremiah" Symphony*	8	[9]	Ravel	*La Valse*	7	[6]
Bloch	*America*	180	2			79	[58]
Copland	*El Salón México*	7	[8]	Respighi	*Belfagor, Ouverture per Orchestra*	26	1
Copland	*Quiet City*	12	[13]	Scriabin	*Le Divin Poème*	157	1
Copland	*Third Symphony*	125	3	Scriabin	*Le Poème de l'Extase*	5	4
Debussy	*Nuages*	8	[4] 1f	Scriabin	*Prométhée, Le Poème du Feu*	11	[5]
Delius	*Paris—Ein Nachtstück*	4	10b [2]	Sessions	*Symphony No. II*	57	[Ll]
Dukas	*La Péri*	126	1	Shostakovich	*Symphony No. 7*	76	[65]
Elgar	*Symphony No. 1*	77	[66]	Strauss, R.	*Also Sprach Zarathustra*	128	5
Goossens	*Sinfonietta*	27	[12]			145	1
Kodály	*Psalmus Hungaricus*	41	[25]	Strauss, R.	*Ein Heldenleben*	198	[98] 7f
Kodály	*Summer Evening*	64	2b [420]	Stravinsky	*Chant du Rossignol*	42	[43]
Mahler	*Symphony No. 2*	138	[2]	Stravinsky	*Jeu de Cartes*	44	[84]
		161	1	Stravinsky	*Le Sacre du Printemps*	84	[101]
Mahler	*Symphony No. 6*	181	[120] 1f			112	[142]
Mahler	*Symphony No. 8*	130	[89]			123	1b [168]
Miaskovsky	*Symphony No. 8*	138	2				
		171	2				
Milhaud	*Quatrième Symphonie*	13	4				

Violin I, II, and Viola

COMPOSER	WORK	PAGE	MEASURE	COMPOSER	WORK	PAGE	MEASURE
Albéniz–Arbós	*Évocation*	19	[H]	Kabalevsky	*Suite from "Colas Breugnon"*	61	[62]
Barber	*Medea*	66	2b [49]	Kabalevsky	*Symphony No. 2*	93	[20]
		69	[51]	Kodály	*Galanta Dances*	61	[566]
Bartók	*Concerto for Orchestra*	43	[228]	Kodály	*Háry János Suite*	103	[2]
		99	[175]	Mahler	*Das Lied von der Erde*	7	[4]
Bartók	*Second Suite*	22	[20]	Mahler	*Symphony No. 6*	37	3
Bax	*The Garden of Fand*	6	1	Mahler	*Symphony No. 7*	83	1
Britten	*Serenade for Tenor, Horn and Strings*	35	[29]	Martinet	*Orphée*	26	[5]
		38	1	Miaskovsky	*Symphony No. 22*	24	[38]
Casella	*Pupazzetti*	15	[2]	Milhaud	*2me Suite Symphonique*	60	[33]
Converse	*American Sketches*	106	2	Milhaud	*Les Choéphores*	24	2
Copland	*Third Symphony*	121	[107] 1f	Poot	*Symphonie*	9	1
Debussy	*Rondes de Printemps*	13	[7] 2f	Prokofieff	*Ala et Lolly (Scythian Suite)*	11	3
Delius	*Paris—Ein Nachtstück*	29	[16]	Rabaud	*Divertissement sur des Chansons Russes*	9	[6]
de Falla	*Nuits dans les Jardins d'Espagne*	19	[13]			19	[12]
Hill	*Lilacs*	7	1b [3]	Ravel	*Daphnis et Chloé, Suite No. 1*	32	[103]
		47	7			59	[125]
Honegger	*Symphonie pour Cordes*	39	[13] 4f				

STRINGS

Violin I, II, and Viola (contd.)

COMPOSER	WORK	PAGE	MEASURE	COMPOSER	WORK	PAGE	MEASURE
Ravel	Daphnis et Chloé, Suite No. 2	65 76	[192] I	Scriabin	Prométhée, Le Poème du Feu	72	[53]
Ravel	Rapsodie Espagnole	48	3	Shostakovich	Symphony No. 1	18	1b [30]
Ravel	Valses Nobles et Sentimentales	66	[66]	Shostakovich	Symphony No. 5	21	[25] 1f
Respighi	The Fountains of Rome	50	[17]	Sibelius	Symphony No. 6	9	[D]
Rosenthal	Les Petits Métiers	94	[F] 2f	Strauss, R.	Ein Heldenleben	21	[10]
Satie–Debussy	Gymnopédies	3	[B]	Stravinsky	Feuerwerk	7	[7]
Schmitt	Mirages pour Orchestre, No. 1	27	[12]	Stravinsky	Fire-Bird Suite (1919)	5	[7]
Schmitt	Mirages pour Orchestre, No. 2	66	2	Szymanowski	Symphonie Concertante pour Piano et Orchestre	56	[6] 2f
Scriabin	Le Divin Poème	78	I	Wagner, R.	Prelude and Love Death from "Tristan und Isolde"	34	33

Violin I and Violoncello

COMPOSER	WORK	PAGE	MEASURE	COMPOSER	WORK	PAGE	MEASURE
Bloch	America	24	3	Mahler	Symphony No. 4	141	288
Copland	Dance Symphony	4	[2] 1f	McKay	Sinfonietta No. 4	52	I
Debussy	Iberia	69	3	Rachmaninoff	The Bells	13	[12]
Debussy–Ansermet	Six Épigraphes Antiques	21	2	Reger	Requiem	4	41
Mahler	Symphony No. 3	176	[31]	Villa-Lobos	Uirapurú	75	I

Violin II and Violoncello

COMPOSER	WORK	PAGE	MEASURE	COMPOSER	WORK	PAGE	MEASURE
Bartók	Deux Images	5	I	Scriabin	Le Poème de l'Extase	28 34	I [5]
Debussy	Iberia	51	[34] 4f	Wagner, R.	Prelude and Love Death from "Tristan und Isolde"	33	31
Mahler	Das Lied von der Erde	23	[25]				
Ravel	Alborada del Gracioso	39	[33]				
Ravel	La Valse	70 82	I [61]				

Violin I, II, and Violoncello

COMPOSER	WORK	PAGE	MEASURE	COMPOSER	WORK	PAGE	MEASURE
Barber	Music for a Scene from Shelley	14	82	Bax	Sixth Symphony	125	4b [39]
Bartók	Violin Concerto	103	[320]	Milhaud	IIe Symphonie	39	4b [135]
Bax	Second Symphony	9	5	Wagner, R.	Forest Murmurs from "Siegfried"	8	82

Violin I and Bass

COMPOSER	WORK	PAGE	MEASURE
Ravel	Concerto pour la main gauche	55	I

Violin I, II, and Bass

Luening	Two Symphonic Interludes	7	[25]

464

MULTIPLE DIVISI

Viola and Violoncello

COMPOSER	WORK	PAGE	MEASURE	COMPOSER	WORK	PAGE	MEASURE
Albéniz–				**Ravel**	*Shéhérazade*	34	2
Arbós	*Triana*	19	2	**Ravel**	*Tzigane*	8	6
Bartók	*Dance Suite*	54	157	**Schlein**	*Dance Overture*	4	1
Bloch	*Schelomo*	54	[32]	**Schmitt**	*Mirages pour Orchestre,*		
Bloch	*Trois Poèmes Juifs*	79	3		*No. 1*	18	2
Copland	*El Salón México*	8	5b [10]	**Scriabin**	*Deuxième Symphonie*	4	1
Copland	*Third Symphony*	92	[84] 3f	**Sibelius**	*Symphony No. 7*	64	8
Dukas	*La Péri*	37	2	**Strauss, R.**	*Ein Heldenleben*	219	4
		77	1	**Strauss, R.**	*Symphonia Domestica*	67	[84]
Elgar	*Symphony No. 2*	111	[116] 8f	**Stravinsky**	*Feuerwerk*	20	2b [20]
de Falla	*Nuits dans les Jardins*			**Stravinsky**	*Oedipus Rex*	96	[129]
	d'Espagne	47	[12]	**Stravinsky**	*Petrouchka Suite*	96	[83]
Gershwin	*An American in Paris*	84	4b [69]	**Stravinsky**	*Scherzo à la Russe*	6	[5]
Kodály	*Psalmus Hungaricus*	50	[30]	**Stravinsky**	*Symphony in C*	70	[145] 2f
Mahler	*Das Lied von der Erde*	139	[62] 1f	**Tansman**	*Deux Moments*		
Mahler	*Symphony No. 2*	198	[45]		*Symphoniques*	29	[9]
Mahler	*Symphony No. 4*	143	308	**Vaughan**			
Mahler	*Symphony No. 6*	119	5	**Williams**	*A London Symphony*	51	[GG]
Rachmaninoff	*Die Toteninsel*	8	2b [3]	**Vaughan**	*Symphony in E minor*	13	3
		18	[7]	**Williams**	*(No. 6)*	39	1
Rachmaninoff	*2d Concerto pour Piano*			**Walton**	*Concerto for Violin and*		
	et Orchestre	50	[18]		*Orchestra*	96	[49]

Viola and Bass

COMPOSER	WORK	PAGE	MEASURE
Respighi	*The Pines of Rome*	34	1

Violoncello and Bass

COMPOSER	WORK	PAGE	MEASURE	COMPOSER	WORK	PAGE	MEASURE
Bax	*November Woods*	26	2b [G]	**Rachmaninoff**	*The Bells*	41	[45]
Delius	*A Dance Rhapsody*			**Ravel**	*Valses Nobles et*		
	(No. 1)	3	1		*Sentimentales*	70	[71]
Inghelbrecht	*Rapsodie de Printemps*	13	2	**Schönberg**	*Fünf Orchesterstücke*	37	2
Mahler	*Symphony No. 1*	3	1	**Strauss, R.**	*Also Sprach*		
Mahler	*Symphony No. 2*	153	[13]		*Zarathustra*	61	9
Mahler	*Symphony No. 3*	79	[57]	**Strauss, R.**	*Ein Heldenleben*	211	[105]
Mahler	*Symphony No. 5*	30	[11]	**Whithorne**	*The Dream Pedlar*	53	[26] 1f

Violin I, Viola, and Violoncello

COMPOSER	WORK	PAGE	MEASURE	COMPOSER	WORK	PAGE	MEASURE
Debussy	*Jeux*	42	[29]	**Respighi**	*The Fountains of Rome*	54	1
Ravel	*Valses Nobles et*			**Strauss, R.**	*Also Sprach*		
	Sentimentales	18	[16]		*Zarathustra*	132	1

Violin II, Viola, and Violoncello

COMPOSER	WORK	PAGE	MEASURE	COMPOSER	WORK	PAGE	MEASURE
Elgar	*In the South, Concert-*			**Pescara**	*Tibet*	2	3
	Overture	55	3	**Reger**	*Requiem*	38	162
Ives	*"Washington's Birth-*			**Schmitt**	*Étude pour le "Palais*		
	day" from Symphony,				*Hanté" d'Edgar Poe*	51	[38]
	"Holidays"	3	[C]	**Sibelius**	*Symphony No. 7*	59	4

STRINGS

Violin II, Viola, and Violoncello (contd.)

COMPOSER	WORK	PAGE	MEASURE	COMPOSER	WORK	PAGE	MEASURE
Strauss, R.	*Ein Heldenleben*	70	[35]	Weinberger	*Polka and Fugue from*		
Stravinsky	*Le Sacre du Printemps*	117	[156]		*"Schwanda, the*		
Thomson	*The Seine at Night*	7	1b [4]		*Bagpiper"*	36	1b [110]
		11	6b [7]				

Violin I, II, Viola, and Violoncello

COMPOSER	WORK	PAGE	MEASURE	COMPOSER	WORK	PAGE	MEASURE
Albéniz–Arbós	*Fête-Dieu à Séville*	41	1ob [Q]	Rimsky-Korsakoff	*Le Coq d'Or Suite*	29	4
Bartók	*Dance Suite*	59	20	Scriabin	*Deuxième Symphonie*	93	[54]
Bartók	*Second Suite*	87	2	Scriabin	*Prométhée, Le Poème*		
Bax	*Second Symphony*	46	[25]		*du Feu*	65	2b [48]
Bax	*Third Symphony*	62	6	Stravinsky	*Feuerwerk*	25	[25]
Bax	*Fourth Symphony*	42	6b [30]	Thomson	*The Seine at Night*	25	2
Dukas	*Polyeucte, Ouverture*	36	[R]	Vaughan			
Elgar	*Symphony No. 2*	74	[79]	Williams	*Pastoral Symphony*	10	7
Gould	*Spirituals*	9	8			21	[L] 3f
Kodály	*Psalmus Hungaricus*	51	1			31	5
Mahler	*Symphony No. 6*	120	[81]	Wagenaar	*Sinfonietta for Small*		
Milhaud	*2me Suite Symphonique*	157	[72]		*Orchestra*	28	4b [1]

Violin I, Viola, and Bass

COMPOSER	WORK	PAGE	MEASURE
Mahler	*Symphony No. 8*	72	[89]

Violin I, II, Viola, and Bass

COMPOSER	WORK	PAGE	MEASURE	COMPOSER	WORK	PAGE	MEASURE
Inghelbrecht	*Rapsodie de Printemps*	2	3	Mahler	*Symphony No. 2*	183	[27]

Violin I, II, Violoncello, and Bass

COMPOSER	WORK	PAGE	MEASURE
Mahler	*Symphony No. 2*	141	4b [4]

Viola, Violoncello, and Bass

COMPOSER	WORK	PAGE	MEASURE	COMPOSER	WORK	PAGE	MEASURE
Mahler	*Symphony No. 4*	176	113	Schreker	*The Birthday of the*		
Milhaud	*IIe Symphonie*	27	[50] 1f		*Infanta, Suite*	19	3b [75]

Violin I, Viola, Violoncello, and Bass

COMPOSER	WORK	PAGE	MEASURE
Miaskovsky	*Symphony No. 21*	50	[49]

Violin II, Viola, Violoncello, and Bass

COMPOSER	WORK	PAGE	MEASURE	COMPOSER	WORK	PAGE	MEASURE
Schuman, W.	*Prayer in Time of War*	26	268	Schuman, W.	*Symphony for Strings*	15	95

MULTIPLE DIVISI

(2) DIVISI a 4

English	Italian	French	German
Divide in four [4]	Divisi a quatro [4]	Divisé en [par] 4	Vierfach get(h)eilt
Div. in 4	Div. a 4; a 4	Div. en 4	4-fach get.
In 4	Divisi in quatro [4] parti	Divisés à 4 Parties	Geteilt in 4 Partieren
	Divisi in IV parte	En 4	Zu 4

Violin I

COMPOSER	WORK	PAGE	MEASURE	COMPOSER	WORK	PAGE	MEASURE
Albéniz–Arbós	Évocation	8	8	Haydn	Symphony No. 45 in F♯ minor, "Farewell"	37	1
Albéniz–Arbós	Triana	10	3	Hindemith	Mathis der Maler	64	[15] 3f
		19	2	d'Indy	Istar, Variations		
Antheil	Serenade for String Orchestra	4	[8] 4f		Symphoniques	48	2
				d'Indy	Jour d'été à la Montagne	79	6
Balakirev–Casella	Islamey	36	[35]	Inghelbrecht	Sinfonia Breve No. 1	12	7
Bartók	Concerto for Orchestra	23	[456]	Kodály	Háry János Suite	10	[2]
Bartók	Deux Images	46	[19] 14f	Liadov	Eight Russian Popular Songs	34	[2] 6f
Bartók	Second Rhapsody for Violin and Orchestra	43	[32]	Mahler	Symphony No. 1	161	[55]
Bartók	Violin Concerto	86	[135]	Mahler	Symphony No. 2	16	6b [8]
Bax	First Symphony	11	1b [C]			187	[33]
Bloch	America	17	2b [9]	Mahler	Symphony No. 3	8	7
Charpentier	Impressions d'Italie	32	[8]			225	3b [26]
		114	[27]	Mahler	Symphony No. 4	149	336
Cowell	Short Symphony (No. 4)	23	1	Mahler	Symphony No. 5	193	8b [9]
Debussy	Iberia	6	[3] 4f	Mahler	Symphony No. 8	19	[18]
		10	8	Miaskovsky	Symphony No. 6	208	[103]
		25	[16]	Prokofieff	Symphony No. 5	20	3b [11]
		39	[24]	Ravel	Boléro	55	1
		52	[36]	Ravel	Daphnis et Chloé, Suite No. 1	8	[78]
		98	5	Ravel	Daphnis et Chloé, Suite No. 2	8	[157]
Debussy	Jeux	5	2	Ravel	Rapsodie Espagnole	24	1b [13]
		64	[43] 1f			67	[18[1f
Debussy	La Damoiselle Élue	45	[18]	Ravel	Valses Nobles et Sentimentales	55	2b [54]
Debussy	La Mer	8	1b [4]	Reger	Variations on a Theme of Mozart	9	[2]
		26	3	Respighi	Ballata delle Gnomidi	13	[3]
Debussy	Le Martyre de Saint Sébastien	69	5	Respighi	Belfagor, Ouverture per Orchestra	26	1
Debussy	Nuages	4	1	Respighi	Feste Romane	104	[31] 1f
		8	[4] 1f	Respighi	The Fountains of Rome	53	[18]
Debussy	Rondes de Printemps	4	[1] 1f	Revueltas	Sensemayá	40	[37]
Debussy	Sirènes	77	3	Rosenthal	Les Petits Métiers	75	1
		104	2	Roussel	Évocations, II	34	[15]
Delius	A Song Before Sunrise	9	6b [E]			69	[31]
Diamond	Rounds for String Orchestra	13	2b [190]	Saint-Saëns	3e Symphonie en Ut mineur	19	[G]
		42	2b [175]	Sibelius	En Saga	5	1
Dukas	La Péri	39	[6]	Sibelius	Symphony No. 6	29	[C]
		90	1			64	2
Goossens	Sinfonietta	5	[2] 4f				
		28	[13]				
		75	[6]				

STRINGS

Violin I (contd.)

COMPOSER	WORK	PAGE	MEASURE	COMPOSER	WORK	PAGE	MEASURE
Stillman-Kelley	*New England Symphony*	107	[P] 7f	Vaughan Williams	*Pastoral Symphony*	6	[B] 2f
Strauss, R.	*Also Sprach Zarathustra*	70	1	Villa-Lobos	*Amazonas*	5	1
		108	1			49	[20]
Strauss, R.	*Don Quixote*	68	4	Villa-Lobos	*Chôros No. 10*	27	2
Strauss, R.	*Ein Heldenleben*	219	6	Villa-Lobos	*Danses Africanes*	90	[3]
Stravinsky	*Fire-Bird Suite* (1919)	69	[6]	Walton	*Concerto for Viola and Orchestra*	31	4
Stravinsky	*Le Sacre du Printemps*	38	[49] 3f				

Violin II

COMPOSER	WORK	PAGE	MEASURE	COMPOSER	WORK	PAGE	MEASURE
Bax	*Fourth Symphony*	45	[34] 5f	Ravel	*Daphnis et Chloé, Suite No. 2*	10	[158]
Bloch	*Schelomo*	21	[9]			35	[168]
Bloch	*Trois Poèmes Juifs*	78	[13]			45	[176]
Britten	*Les Illuminations*	2	3	Ravel	*Rapsodie Espagnole*	66	[17]
Debussy	*Jeux*	42	[29]	Ravel	*Valses Nobles et Sentimentales*	54	[53] 2f
Debussy	*La Damoiselle Élue*	28	2	Rieti	*Sinfonia No. 5*	46	[53]
d'Indy	*Jour d'été à la Montagne*	108	[52] 7f	Scriabin	*Le Divin Poème*	202	1
Kodály	*Psalmus Hungaricus*	7	[4]			275	1
		50	[30]	Scriabin	*Le Poème de l'Extase*	163	1
Kodály	*Te Deum*	18	[105] 1f	Scriabin	*Prométhée, Le Poème du Feu*	75	1b [58]
		45	1b [256]	Sibelius	*Symphony No. 5*	99	1
Mahler	*Symphony No. 2*	134	3	Strauss, R.	*Also Sprach Zarathustra*	13	4
Mahler	*Symphony No. 3*	58	2b [42]			19	9
Mahler	*Symphony No. 4*	143	308	Strauss, R.	*Till Eulenspiegel's Merry Pranks*	59	18
Mahler	*Symphony No. 8*	183	[171]	Wagner, R.	*Forest Murmurs from "Siegfried"*	7	74
Mussorgsky-Ravel	*Pictures at an Exhibition*	47	[39]	Walton	*Concerto for Violin and Orchestra*	130	[65]
Poot	*Symphonie*	18	3				
Prokofieff	*Symphony No. 5*	146	3				
Ravel	*Daphnis et Chloé, Suite No. 1*	57	[123]				

Violin I and II

COMPOSER	WORK	PAGE	MEASURE	COMPOSER	WORK	PAGE	MEASURE
Balakirev-Casella	*Islamey*	13	2b [9]	Debussy	*Jeux*	115	[80] 1f
Bartók	*Dance Suite*	54	157	Debussy	*Le Martyre de Saint Sébastien*	65	2
Bartók	*Second Rhapsody for Violin and Orchestra*	30	[14]	Debussy	*Nuages*	3	4
Bax	*Third Symphony*	62	3			11	4
Bax	*Fourth Symphony*	62	3b [49]			14	2b [8]
Bax	*The Garden of Fand*	80	4	Debussy	*Rondes de Printemps*	17	3b [10]
Bax	*Tintagel*	16	[G]	Debussy	*Sirènes*	85	2
Bizet	*Roma*	66	2			110	3
Casella	*Elegia Eroica*	33	[50] 7f	Debussy-Ansermet	*Six Épigraphes Antiques*	58	2
Casella	*Pupazzetti*	27	4	Delius	*Appalachia*	80	330
Cesana	*Second American Symphony*	29	[22] 1f	Delius	*The Song of the High Hills*	14	[10]
Debussy	*Gigues*	13	5	Dohnányi	*Ruralia Hungarica*	85	10

Violin I and II (contd.)

COMPOSER	WORK	PAGE	MEASURE	COMPOSER	WORK	PAGE	MEASURE
Dukas	*La Péri*	1	1	**Roussel**	*Évocations, III*	12	1
Ibert	*La Ballade de la Geôle*			**Saint-Saëns**	*Suite Algérienne*	6	[A]
	de Reading	2	2b [2]			14	2
Inghelbrecht	*Pour le jour de la*			**Schönberg**	*Suite for String*		
	première neige au				*Orchestra*	14	231
	vieux Japon	42	3b [26]	**Scriabin**	*Le Divin Poème*	160	3
Inghelbrecht	*Rapsodie de Printemps*	12	[6]	**Scriabin**	*Le Poème*		
Ives	*Lincoln, The Great*				*de l'Extase*	100	1
	Commoner	14	2	**Sibelius**	*En Saga*	16	[C]
Mahler	*Symphony No. 2*	192	[38]	**Sibelius**	*Lemminkainen*		
Mahler	*Symphony No. 3*	108	[3]		*Journeys Homeward*	25	[F]
		172	1	**Sibelius**	*Symphony No. 5*	120	[I]
Mahler	*Symphony No. 6*	186	11	**Sibelius**	*Symphony No. 6*	17	[I] 1f
Malipiero	*Pause del Silenzio*	28	167	**Sibelius**	*Tapiola*	9	1b [C]
Miaskovsky	*Symphony No. 6*	117	2b [74]	**Sibelius**	*The Swan of Tuonela*	1	1
Poot	*Symphonie*	30	1	**Siegmeister**	*From my Window*	35	2
Prokofieff	*Ala et Lolly (Scythian*			**Siegmeister**	*Sunday in Brooklyn*	23	4
	Suite)	27	2	**Strauss, R.**	*Don Quixote*	166	11
Ravel	*Boléro*	41	[13] 2f	**Strauss, R.**	*Eine Alpensinfonie*	55	[47]
Ravel	*Concerto pour la main*			**Stravinsky**	*Chant du Rossignol*	73	[81] 2f
	gauche	62	[34] 1f	**Stravinsky**	*Petrouchka Suite*	96	[83]
Ravel	*Daphnis et Chloé,*			**Vaughan**			
	Suite No. 1	10	[80]	**Williams**	*A London Symphony*	193	3
Ravel	*Daphnis et Chloé,*			**Vaughan**			
	Suite No. 2	51	[180]	**Williams**	*Pastoral Symphony*	32	[T] 1f
Ravel	*La Valse*	86	5	**Villa-Lobos**	*Amazonas*	60	6
Ravel	*Rapsodie Espagnole*	3	[2] 6f	**Villa-Lobos**	*Chôros No. 8*	77	[29]
Ravel	*Shéhérazade*	2	2b [1]	**Wagner, R.**	*Tannhäuser Overture*	32	[D]
Read	*Sketches of the City*	17	[5]	**Wagner, R.**	*Prelude to Act I,*		
Reger	*Variations on a Theme*	93	1		*"Lohengrin"*	1	1
	of Mozart	101	1b [18]				

Viola

COMPOSER	WORK	PAGE	MEASURE	COMPOSER	WORK	PAGE	MEASURE
Alfvén	*A Legend of the*			**Mahler**	*Symphony No. 8*	20	1
	Skerries	11	[3]			76	2b [4]
Antheil	*Symphony No. 5*	85	[10] 6f	**Martinet**	*Orphée*	41	[13]
Barraine	*Deuxième Symphonie*	47	1	**Ravel**	*Daphnis et Chloé,*		
Bartók	*Second Suite*	4	[1]		*Suite No. 2*	1	2
Bloch	*Trois Poèmes Juifs*	85	[18] 1f	**Ravel**	*Rapsodie Espagnole*	29	1b [1]
Debussy-	*Six Épigraphes*			**Reger**	*Requiem*	3	21
Ansermet	*Antiques*	14	[B]	**Reger**	*Variations on a Theme*		
Delius	*The Song of the High*				*of Mozart*	14	1
	Hills	28	[24]	**Respighi**	*The Fountains of Rome*	56	19
Gershwin	*An American in Paris*	85	4	**Scriabin**	*Deuxième Symphonie*	5	4b [1]
Harsanyi	*Suite pour Orchestre*	4	2b [15]	**Scriabin**	*Le Divin Poème*	254	3
d'Indy	*Jour d'été à la Montagne*	47	[20]	**Schuman, W.**	*Symphony No. III*	62	282
Inghelbrecht	*Pour le jour de la*			**Shostakovich**	*Symphony No. 6*	30	[37]
	première neige au			**Sibelius**	*Symphony No. 6*	71	6
	vieux Japon	5	2	**Sibelius**	*Tapiola*	7	7
Kodály	*Psalmus Hungaricus*	3	1			11	4b [D]

STRINGS

Viola (contd.)

COMPOSER	WORK	PAGE	MEASURE	COMPOSER	WORK	PAGE	MEASURE
Sibelius	The Bard	3	5	Wagner, R.	Magic Fire Music from	48	1
Strauss, R.	Also Sprach				"Die Walküre"	50	2
	Zarathustra	105	2	Walton	Concerto for Violin and		
Villa-Lobos	Chôros No. 8	37	[16] 1f		Orchestra	105	5
				Wellesz	Symphony in C	47	[355] 2f

Violoncello

COMPOSER	WORK	PAGE	MEASURE	COMPOSER	WORK	PAGE	MEASURE
Barber	Music for a Scene from			Prokofieff	Symphony No. 5	143	[79]
	Shelley	1	17	Rachmaninoff	Symphony No. 2	27	7
Bax	November Woods	27	2			32	5
Bax	Sixth Symphony	25	2b [21]			141	2b [53]
Bloch	Trois Poèmes Juifs	12	7b [5]	Rachmaninoff	The Bells	96	6b [100]
Britten	Serenade for Tenor,	15	[11]	Ravel	Alborada del Gracioso	14	[9] 4f
	Horn and Strings	17	[13] 7f	Ravel	Rapsodie Espagnole	69	[19] 3f
Coppola	Symphonie en La			Respighi	Concerto Gregoriano		
	mineur	18	[11]		per Violino e	26	[14] 1f
Debussy	La Damoiselle Élue	37	[15]		Orchestra	48	[27]
Debussy	La Mer	19	2b [9]	Respighi	The Fountains of Rome	2	4
Debussy	Première Rhapsodie	31	2			10	[3] 5f
Delius	The Song of the High					50	[17]
	Hills	15	[11]			64	[23] 6f
Dohnányi	Ruralia Hungarica	8	[5] 1f	Respighi	The Pines of Rome	34	1
		21	[13] 3f			67	10
Dunn	Overture on Negro			Rimsky-			
	Themes	26	6b [L]	Korsakoff	Le Coq d'Or Suite	44	1
Egge	Piano Concerto No. 2	33	[24] 3f	Schönberg	Fünf Orchesterstücke	5	[5] 3f
Fitelberg	Symphony No. 1	70	[142]			7	1
Gershwin	Concerto in F for Piano					45	3
	and Orchestra	69	[13]	Shepherd	Horizons	97	1
d'Indy	Deuxième Symphonie	169	1b [80]	Sibelius	Symphony No. 7	49	2
	en Sib	173	3b [82]	Sibelius	Tapiola	12	5
d'Indy	Jour d'été à la Montagne	71	[35] 2f			32	[K]
d'Indy	Tableaux de Voyage	39	1	Sibelius	The Bard	2	4b [A]
Inghelbrecht	Pour le jour de la					6	[C]
	première neige au			Strauss, R.	Also Sprach	63	1
	vieux Japon	12	3b [6]		Zarathustra	168	1
Ives	"Washington's Birth-			Strauss, R.	Don Juan	17	7
	day" from Symphony,			Strauss, R.	Don Quixote	12	2
	"Holidays"	12	[R]			38	1
Liadov	Eight Russian Popular					70	2
	Songs	13	1			90	2
Mahler	Das Lied von der Erde	35	[44]			99	10
Mahler	Symphony No. 6	228	4b [147]			104	2
Mahler	Symphony No. 7	1	1			130	1
		77	[65] 4f			167	2
Mahler	Symphony No. 8	76	4b [6]	Strauss, R.	Ein Heldenleben	77	5
Martinet	Orphée	17	7			83	1b [44]
Miaskovsky	Sinfonietta for String					165	4
	Orchestra	24	[18] 5f			170	1
Moeran	Symphony in G minor	68	6b [36]			185	1

470

MULTIPLE DIVISI

Violoncello (contd.)

COMPOSER	WORK	PAGE	MEASURE	COMPOSER	WORK	PAGE	MEASURE
Stravinsky	*Oedipus Rex*	85	1b [117]	Villa-Lobos	*Amazonas*	9	[3]
Stravinsky	*Petrouchka Suite*	97	[84]	Wagner, R.	*Forest Murmurs from*		
Stravinsky	*Scènes de Ballet*	62	[102] 3f		*"Siegfried"*	6	70
Turina	*La Procesión del Rocío*	23	1	Wagner, R.	*Prelude and Love Death*		
Vaughan	*A London Symphony*	72	1		*from "Tristan und*		
Williams		92	[H]		*Isolde"*	21	112
Vaughan	*Symphony in E minor*						
Williams	*(No. 6)*	40	2				

Bass

COMPOSER	WORK	PAGE	MEASURE	COMPOSER	WORK	PAGE	MEASURE
Antheil	*McKonkey's Ferry*	29	[16]	Sibelius	*Symphony No. 4*	1	5
Bax	*November Woods*	52	1	Strauss, R.	*Also Sprach*		
Berlioz	*Symphonie Fantastique*	131	1		*Zarathustra*	18	1
Bloch	*Schelomo*	8	[3]	Strauss, R.	*Don Juan*	44	[L]
		59	2			51	[N]
Bloch	*Trois Poèmes Juifs*	18	[10]	Strauss, R.	*Don Quixote*	14	2
		74	1			26	1
Delius	*Appalachia*	84	352			36	8
Dvořák	*Symphony No. 5,*			Strauss, R.	*Till Eulenspiegel's*		
	"From the New				*Merry Pranks*	55	1b [38]
	World"	72	5	Stravinsky	*Fire-Bird Suite (1919)*	67	2b [2]
Honegger	*Symphonie Liturgique*	2	3	Stravinsky	*Petrouchka Suite*	86	75
Mahler	*Symphony No. 9*	31	[11]	Villa-Lobos	*Amazonas*	75	2
Rachmaninoff	*Die Toteninsel*	3	1				
		26	[10] 3f				
		70	[26]				

Violin I and Viola

COMPOSER	WORK	PAGE	MEASURE	COMPOSER	WORK	PAGE	MEASURE
Mahler	*Symphony No. 6*	183	9	Strauss, R.	*Also Sprach Zarathustra*	15	1

Violin II and Viola

COMPOSER	WORK	PAGE	MEASURE	COMPOSER	WORK	PAGE	MEASURE
Albéniz–				Prokofieff	*Ala et Lolly (Scythian*		
Arbós	*Navarra*	25	[L]		*Suite)*	76	7
Barraine	*Deuxième Symphonie*	55	5	Rimsky-	*Le Coq d'Or Suite*	31	[20] 7f
Bartók	*Second Suite*	111	5	Korsakoff		37	2
Mahler	*Symphony No. 3*	176	[31]	Strauss, R.	*Also Sprach Zarathustra*	66	3
Mahler	*Symphony No. 8*	96	[43] 5f	Strauss, R.	*Symphonia Domestica*	63	[81] 1f

Violin I, II, and Viola

COMPOSER	WORK	PAGE	MEASURE	COMPOSER	WORK	PAGE	MEASURE
Antheil	*Symphony No. 5*	102	[21]	Debussy	*La Mer*	10	1
Bartók	*Second Suite*	24	[21] 3f			27	[13]
		85	[5] 1f	Debussy	*Rondes de Printemps*	54	[28] 2f

STRINGS

Violin I, II, and Viola (contd.)

COMPOSER	WORK	PAGE	MEASURE	COMPOSER	WORK	PAGE	MEASURE
Delius	*The Song of the High Hills*	50	[49]	**Martinet**	*Orphée*	52	[18]
de Falla	*Three Dances from "The Three-Cornered Hat"*	91	5	**Ravel**	*La Valse*	51	1b [37]
				Ravel	*Ma Mère l'Oye*	45	5
d'Indy	*Istar, Variations Symphoniques*	3	[A]	**Ravel**	*Tzigane*	25	[25]
				Ravel	*Valses Nobles et Sentimentales*	70	[71]

Violin I and Violoncello

COMPOSER	WORK	PAGE	MEASURE	COMPOSER	WORK	PAGE	MEASURE
Albéniz-Arbós	*Fête-Dieu à Séville*	16	1	**Bartók**	*Second Suite*	71	5b [34]

Violin II and Violoncello

COMPOSER	WORK	PAGE	MEASURE	COMPOSER	WORK	PAGE	MEASURE
Debussy	*Iberia*	84	2	**Mahler**	*Symphony No. 2*	184	[28]

Violin I, II, and Violoncello

COMPOSER	WORK	PAGE	MEASURE
Bax	*Second Symphony*	10	2b [4]

Violin I and Bass

Villa-Lobos	*Amazonas*	27	[10]

Viola and Violoncello

COMPOSER	WORK	PAGE	MEASURE	COMPOSER	WORK	PAGE	MEASURE
Bizet	*Roma*	55	11	**Rimsky-Korsakoff**	*Le Coq d'Or Suite*	38	3
Dvořák	*Symphony No. 4*	7	2	**Sibelius**	*Symphony No. 7*	61	[V] 4f
Mahler	*Symphony No. 7*	44	[38]	**Strauss, R.**	*Also Sprach Zarathustra*	21	4
Mahler	*Symphony No. 8*	213	[211]				
Ravel	*Rapsodie Espagnole*	4	[3] 2f				

Viola and Bass

Inghelbrecht	*Rapsodie de Printemps*	7	2b [3]

Violoncello and Bass

COMPOSER	WORK	PAGE	MEASURE	COMPOSER	WORK	PAGE	MEASURE
Delius	*In a Summer Garden*	14	5b [12]	**Ravel**	*Rapsodie Espagnole*	11	[9] 7f
Mahler	*Symphony No. 7*	42	[35]	**Strauss, R.**	*Also Sprach Zarathustra*	62	1
Rachmaninoff	*The Bells*	102	[106]				

Violin I, Viola, and Violoncello

COMPOSER	WORK	PAGE	MEASURE	COMPOSER	WORK	PAGE	MEASURE
Albéniz-Arbós	*El Albaicín*	37	5b [Y]	**Honegger**	*Musique pour la "Phaedre" de G. D'Annunzio*	22	[6]

MULTIPLE DIVISI

Violin II, Viola, and Violoncello

COMPOSER	WORK	PAGE	MEASURE	COMPOSER	WORK	PAGE	MEASURE
Reger	*Requiem*	40	[175]	Vaughan Williams	*Symphony in E minor (No. 6)*	65	5

Violin I, II, Viola, and Violoncello

COMPOSER	WORK	PAGE	MEASURE	COMPOSER	WORK	PAGE	MEASURE
Debussy	*Jeux*	11	[8]	d'Indy	*Jour d'été à la Montagne*	14	[7] 1f
Debussy	*La Damoiselle Élue*	74	3	Mahler	*Symphony No. 3*	230	[31]
Debussy	*La Mer*	10	1	Mahler	*Symphony No. 8*	52	[59]
Debussy	*Rondes de Printemps*	38	4	Ravel	*Rapsodie Espagnole*	27	3
Delius	*The Song of the High Hills*	23	6b [18]	Vaughan Williams	*Pastoral Symphony*	12	1b [F]
Gruenberg	*The Enchanted Isle*	109	1b [530]				

Violin I, II, Violoncello, and Bass

COMPOSER	WORK	PAGE	MEASURE
Delius	*In a Summer Garden*	15	1

Violin I, II, Viola, Violoncello, and Bass

COMPOSER	WORK	PAGE	MEASURE	COMPOSER	WORK	PAGE	MEASURE
d'Indy	*Jour d'été à la Montagne*	110	[54]	Vaughan Williams	*Symphony in E minor (No. 6)*	149	2
Mahler	*Symphony No. 6*	122	[83]				
Strauss, R.	*Eine Alpensinfonie*	3	1				
		161	[145]				

(3) DIVISI a 5

Violin I

COMPOSER	WORK	PAGE	MEASURE	COMPOSER	WORK	PAGE	MEASURE
Bartók	*Second Suite*	16	6	Strauss, R.	*Don Quixote*	9	2
Casella	*Pupazzetti*	39	[6] 2f			145	1
Scriabin	*Le Divin Poème*	202	1	Strauss, R.	*Symphonia Domestica*	62	[79]
Strauss, R.	*Also Sprach Zarathustra*	135	4				

Violin II

COMPOSER	WORK	PAGE	MEASURE	COMPOSER	WORK	PAGE	MEASURE
Albéniz-Arbós	*El Albaicín*	37	5b [Y]	Strauss, R.	*Also Sprach Zarathustra*	15	1
Inghelbrecht	*Rapsodie de Printemps*	8	1			132	1
				Stravinsky	*Le Sacre du Printemps*	77	[87]

Violin I and II

COMPOSER	WORK	PAGE	MEASURE
Ives	*Lincoln, The Great Commoner*	13	1

Viola

COMPOSER	WORK	PAGE	MEASURE	COMPOSER	WORK	PAGE	MEASURE
Ravel	*Alborada del Gracioso*	14	[9] 4f	Strauss, R.	*Also Sprach Zarathustra*	110	2
Reger	*Variations on a Theme of Mozart*	4	[1] 3f			135	3
Scriabin	*Le Divin Poème*	298	1	Strauss, R.	*Don Quixote*	74	1

473

STRINGS

Violoncello

COMPOSER	WORK	PAGE	MEASURE	COMPOSER	WORK	PAGE	MEASURE
Ives	*Lincoln, The Great Commoner*	9	1	Stillman-Kelley	*Gulliver—His Voyage to Lilliput*	136	10b [K]
Mahler	*Symphony No. 8*	76	2b [4]	Strauss, R.	*Also Sprach Zarathustra*	62	6

Viola and Violoncello

COMPOSER	WORK	PAGE	MEASURE
Villa-Lobos	*Amazonas*	27	[10]

(4) DIVISI a 6

Violin I

COMPOSER	WORK	PAGE	MEASURE	COMPOSER	WORK	PAGE	MEASURE
Debussy	*Iberia*	56	[38]	Inghelbrecht	*Rapsodie de Printemps*	7	1b [3]
		61	[41]	Pick-Mangiagalli	*Piccola Suite*	23	1
Debussy	*Nuages*	2	[1]	Strauss, R.	*Also Sprach Zarathustra*	152	5
Debussy	*Sirènes*	76	2				
Debussy-Ansermet	*Six Épigraphes Antiques*	29	[B]	Stravinsky	*Le Sacre du Printemps*	84	[101]

Violin II

COMPOSER	WORK	PAGE	MEASURE	COMPOSER	WORK	PAGE	MEASURE
Bartók	*Vier Orchesterstücke*	87	2	Scriabin	*Le Divin Poème*	292	4

Violin I and II

COMPOSER	WORK	PAGE	MEASURE	COMPOSER	WORK	PAGE	MEASURE
Debussy	*Iberia*	94	[59] 1f	Ives	*"The Fourth of July" from Symphony, "Holidays"*	33	[X]
Debussy	*Nuages*	3	1	Ravel	*Alborada del Gracioso*	14	[9] 4f

Viola

COMPOSER	WORK	PAGE	MEASURE	COMPOSER	WORK	PAGE	MEASURE
Strauss, R.	*Also Sprach Zarathustra*	17	1	Strauss, R.	*Salomé's Dance*	10	[M]
		71	1	Stravinsky	*Le Sacre du Printemps*	80	[91]
		107	1				

Violoncello

COMPOSER	WORK	PAGE	MEASURE	COMPOSER	WORK	PAGE	MEASURE
Kodály	*Psalmus Hungaricus*	41	[25]	Strauss, R.	*Salomé's Dance*	19	1
Maganini	*Tuolumne*	3	8				

Violin II and Violoncello

COMPOSER	WORK	PAGE	MEASURE
Scriabin	*Le Divin Poème*	254	3

474

MULTIPLE DIVISI

(5) DIVISI a 7

Violin I

COMPOSER	WORK	PAGE	MEASURE	COMPOSER	WORK	PAGE	MEASURE
Scriabin	*Le Divin Poème*	298	1	Strauss, R.	*Also Sprach Zarathustra*	145	1
						154	5
						216	14

Violin II

COMPOSER	WORK	PAGE	MEASURE
Strauss, R.	*Also Sprach Zarathustra*	135	3

Violin I and II

Strauss, R.	*Also Sprach Zarathustra*	137	4

Violoncello

Strauss, R.	*Don Quixote*	110	5

Violin I, II, and Viola

Ives	*"The Fourth of July* *from Symphony,* *"Holidays"*	17 24	[M] 1f [R]

(6) DIVISI a 8

Violin I

Bax	*The Garden of Fand*	1 77	1 2

Viola

Stravinsky	*Chant du Rossignol*	14 51	[11] [53]

Bass

Villa-Lobos	*Amazonas*	9	[3]

(7) DIVISI a 9

Violin II

Strauss, R.	*Also Sprach Zarathustra*	140	2

Violoncello

Strauss, R.	*Also Sprach Zarathustra*	13	4

STRINGS

(8) DIVISI a 10

Violin I

COMPOSER	WORK	PAGE	MEASURE
Strauss, R.	*Also Sprach Zarathustra*	**138**	1

(9) DIVISI a 11

(no examples)

(10) DIVISI a 12

Viola

COMPOSER	WORK	PAGE	MEASURE
Strauss, R.	*Don Quixote*	**53**	2

Chapter 59

SOLO PARTS

English	Italian	French	German
One [1] Player	1. Solo	Un(e) Solo	(Nur) Ein [1] Spieler
(1) Solo Violin	(1) Solo Violino	(1) Violon Solo	(1) Solo Violine
(1) Solo Viola	(1) Solo Viola	(1) Alto Solo	(1) Solo Bratsche
(1) Solo Cello	(1) Solo Violoncello	(1) Violoncelle Solo	(1) Solo Violoncell
(1) Solo Bass	(1) Solo Contrabass	(1) Contrebasse Solo	(1) Solo Kontrabass
Violin solo	Violino solo	Violon solo	Violine solo
Viola solo	Viola solo	Alto solo	Bratsche solo
Cello solo	Violoncello solo	Violoncelle solo	Violoncell solo
Bass solo	Contrabasso solo	Contrebasse solo	Kontrabass solo
Only 1 (player)	1 solamente	1 seule	Nur 1
			Einer allein
Solo from 1st desk	Solo per il I° leggio	Solo du Ire pupitre	Solo vom 1. Pult

Violin (I or II)

COMPOSER	WORK	PAGE	MEASURE	COMPOSER	WORK	PAGE	MEASURE
Albéniz–				**Bloch**	Trois Poèmes Juifs	7	[2]
Arbós	Fête-Dieu à Séville	6	[B] 7f	**Bloch**	Voice in the Wilderness	9	3b [8]
Antheil	McKonkey's Ferry	38	[23]	**Brahms**	Symphony No. 1	70	90
Antheil	Over the Plains	51	1b [31]	**Britten**	Les Illuminations	4	1b [4]
Antheil	Serenade for String	12	[22]	**Bruckner**	Symphony No. 2	74	8b [200]
	Orchestra	17	[30]	**Casella**	La Donna Serpente,		
Antheil	Symphony No. 5	85	[10]		II. Serie	10	[15] 1f
		102	[21] 1f	**Chabrier**	Bourrée Fantastique	11	[4] 7f
Bach, C. P. E.	Concerto for Orchestra	7	[15]	**Converse**	American Sketches	71	1
Barber	Medea	13	[13] 6f	**Copland**	Appalachian Spring	2	[2]
Barraine	Deuxième Symphonie	57	3			64	1b [51]
Bartók	Deux Portraits	3	1	**Copland**	Billy the Kid Ballet		
		13	5		Suite	86	[49]
Bartók	Second Suite	71	[34] 4f	**Copland**	Dance Symphony	19	4
Bax	November Woods	85	1	**Copland**	First Symphony	60	1
Bax	Second Symphony	84	1b [5]	**Copland**	Music for Radio	23	[15] 4f
		149	1b [19]	**Copland**	Music for the Theatre	6	5
Bax	Third Symphony	113	1b [32]			18	4
Bax	Fourth Symphony	79	3b [4]			71	[59] 4f
		103	1b [19]	**Copland**	Third Symphony	91	2
Bax	The Garden of Fand	49	[M]	**Coppola**	Interlude Dramatique	31	[15] 16f
Beethoven	Leonore Overture No. 2	52	431	**Coppola**	Symphonie en La	50	4
Berg	Three Excerpts from	4	1b [320]		mineur	70	4b [9]
	"Wozzeck"	55	[375] 2f	**Cowell**	Short Symphony		
Bliss	Concerto for Piano and				(No. 4)	30	3b [F]
	Orchestra	47	[27]	**Cowell**	Symphonic Set	4	[25] 2f
Bloch	Hiver–Printemps	7	[2]	**Cras**	Journal de Bord	39	3
Bloch	Evocations	65	2	**Debussy**	Gigues	32	2

STRINGS

Violin (I or II) (contd.)

COMPOSER	WORK	PAGE	MEASURE	COMPOSER	WORK	PAGE	MEASURE
Debussy	Iberia	69	1	Holst	The Planets	35	7
		79	4			53	[III]
		97	[61]			68	12
Debussy	La Mer	13	[6]	Honegger	Musique pour le		
		46	[24]		"Phaedre" de	16	1
Debussy	Prélude à l'après-midi				G. D'Annunzio	46	2
	d'un Faune	20	4	Honegger	Quatrième Symphonie	3	3
Delius	A Dance Rhapsody,			Honegger	Symphonie Liturgique	111	4b [19]
	No. 2	25	[200] 1f	Ibert	Divertissement	8	2
Delius	Appalachia	88	[U] 1f	Ibert	Escales	51	[45] 1f
		128	559	Ibert	Féerique	21	1
Delius	A Song of Summer	5	[25] 3f	Ibert	La Ballade de la Geôle		
Delius	North Country				de Reading	24	[15]
	Sketches	51	[41] 1f	d'Indy	Deuxième Symphonie	113	[55]
Delius	Paris—Ein Nachtstück	29	[16] 2f		en Sib	174	[83] 2f
		47	2b [26]	d'Indy	Istar, Variations	10	1
Delius	Sea Drift	19	123		Symphoniques	86	[41] 1f
		44	248	d'Indy	Jour d'été à la Montagne	34	1
Delius	Three Orchestral Pieces	23	3			97	8
Dello Joio	Variations, Chaconne,			Jacobi	Concertino for Piano and		
	and Finale	26	1b [210]		String Orchestra	52	[30] 1f
Dukas	La Péri	135	[21]	James	Suite for String		
Dvořák	Symphony No. 4	70	[D]		Orchestra	15	[R] 2f
Dvořák	Carnival Overture	31	[K]	Janssen	New Year's Eve in		
Egge	Piano Concerto No. 2	28	[20]		New York	12	4
Elgar	Falstaff	76	[76] 2f	Jolivet	Andante pour Orchestre		
Elgar	Sea Pictures	31	2b [E]		à Cordes	14	[50]
Elgar	Symphony No. 1	77	[66] 3f	Khachaturian	Gayne Ballet Suite		
		98	[85]		No. 2	41	[3] 2f
Engel	The Creation	32	[17] 2f	Khachaturian	Masquerade Suite	31	[1]
Ferguson	Partita for Orchestra	56	6	Khrennikov	Symphony No. 1	93	1b [225]
Gershwin	An American in Paris	48	7b [43]	Knipper	Symphony No. 4	48	[38]
		65	[56] 3f	Kodály	Marosszék Dances	30	[140]
		82	[67]	Kodály	Summer Evening	52	[330] 7f
Gershwin	Concerto in F for Piano			Lambert	The Rio Grande	27	[12]
	and Orchestra	63	1b [7]	Liszt	Eine Faust-Symphonie	123	[B]
Gershwin	Rhapsody in Blue	31	[29]			157	17
Graener	Comedietta	26	128	Maganini	A Suite of Music by		
Griffes	The Pleasure Dome of				Royalty	17	[C]
	Kubla Khan	19	3	Maganini	At the Setting of the Sun	5	3
Griffes	The White Peacock	17	[E]	Mahler	Das Lied von der Erde	10	1b [8]
Harrison	Alleluia for Orchestra	12	[J]			20	3
Haydn	Symphony No. 1 in					85	[5]
	Eb major, "Drumroll"	24	1	Mahler	Songs of a Wayfarer	8	50
Herrmann	Sinfonietta for String					34	124
	Orchestra	7	7	Mahler	Symphony No. 2	27	7
Hill	Lilacs	44	4b [18]			97	8
Hindemith	Ballet Overture, Cupid					130	[3] 4f
	and Psyche	8	14	Mahler	Symphony No. 3	55	[39] 3f
Hindemith	Theme and Four Varia-					125	8
	tions, "The Four					153	[12]
	Temperaments"	15	1b [13]			189	[8]

478

Violin (I or II) (contd.)

COMPOSER	WORK	PAGE	MEASURE	COMPOSER	WORK	PAGE	MEASURE
Mahler	Symphony No. 4	19	[8] 1f	Rachmaninoff	Symphony No. 2	140	[52] 2f
		61	[21] 2f	Rachmaninoff	The Bells	35	[38] 1f
		73	6	Ravel	Ma Mère l'Oye	44	[6]
		122	101			47	[1] 4f
Mahler	Symphony No. 5	70	[12]	Respighi	Feste Romane	82	[25] 3f
Mahler	Symphony No. 6	123	[84] 2f	Respighi	Metamorphoseon, XII		
Mahler	Symphony No. 7	40	[33] 4f		Modi	41	1
		137	[146] 7f	Respighi	The Birds	18	2
Mahler	Symphony No. 8	21	2b [20]	Respighi	The Fountains of Rome	18	5
		113	1b [69]			56	[19]
		149	[118]			61	1
Mahler	Symphony No. 9	59	25	Respighi	Trittico Botticelliano	45	[18]
Malipiero	Pause del Silenzio	32	197	Riegger	Symphony No. 3	38	[200]
Malipiero	Seconda Sinfonia			Rimsky-	Capriccio Espagnol	9	1
	(Elegiaca)	49	[635] 1f	Korsakoff		26	[H]
Martinet	Orphée	6	2			30	[K]
		57	[21] 2f			38	2
Miaskovsky	Sinfonietta for String	2	[8]			67	[R]
	Orchestra	10	[30]	Rimsky-	Russian Easter Overture	2	1b [A]
		15	[44]	Korsakoff		8	1
		25	[19] 1f			42	2b [N]
Miaskovsky	Symphony No. 6	200	[5] 2f			73	3
Milhaud	Concerto pour Piano et	27	1b [45]	Rimsky-	Scheherazade	4	14
	Orchestre	40	[30] 1f	Korsakoff		15	[C]
Milhaud	Le Bal Martiniquais	28	2b [60]			31	[G]
		39	1b [125]			46	1
Milhaud	Ière Symphonie	13	[50] 3f			102	440
Milhaud	IIe Symphonie	9	[70]			135	142
		51	1b [35]			256	641
Milhaud	Opus Americanum No. 2	30	1b [190]			259	660
		59	1b [400]	Rivier	3 Pastorales	7	7
Milhaud	Two Marches	5	[15] 2f	Roger-	Poème Symphonique sur		
Moore	Village Music	5	1b [10]	Ducasse	le nom de Gabriel		
Morris	Prospice Symphony	61	1b [35]		Fauré	19	[7] 2f
Nicolai	Overture to "The Merry	11	50	Roussel	Le Festin de l'Araignée	37	1
	Wives of Windsor"	43	266	Roussel	Pour une Fête de		
Pescara	Tibet	32	1b [11]		Printemps	26	1b [10]
Poot	Symphonie	16	1	Roussel	Symphonie en Sol	48	[30] 1f
Poulenc	Concert Champêtre				mineur	67	2b [39]
	pour Clavecin et					118	2
	Orchestre	41	7	Rozsa	Concerto for String		
Prokofieff	Romeo and Juliet,				Orchestra	12	[122]
	Suite No. 1	42	1b [24]	Saint-Saëns	Danse Macabre	2	14
Prokofieff	Romeo and Juliet,			Scarlatti-	Toccata, Bourrée, et		
	Suite No. 2	86	[53]	Casella	Gigue	3	8b [3]
Prokofieff	Suite from the Ballet			Schelling	A Victory Ball	54	[14]
	"Chout"	135	[174]	Schlein	Dance Overture	17	[270]
Rabaud	La Procession Nocturne	7	[5] 2f	Schmitt	Mirages pour Orchestre,		
Rachmaninoff	Die Toteninsel	61	5		No. 1	20	1
Rachmaninoff	Piano Concerto No. 1	35	1b [24]	Schuman, W.	Symphony for Strings	12	83
Rachmaninoff	Rapsodie pour Piano et			Schumann, R.	Symphony No. 4	60	26
	Orchestre	60	[44] 4f				

STRINGS

Violin (I or II) (contd.)

COMPOSER	WORK	PAGE	MEASURE	COMPOSER	WORK	PAGE	MEASURE
Scriabin	*Le Divin Poème*	80	4	**Stravinsky**	*Danses Concertantes*	11	[17]
		157	4			88	[139] 2f
		188	5	**Stravinsky**	*Fire-Bird Suite* (1919)	17	6
		226	1	**Stravinsky**	*Firebird Ballet Suite*		
Scriabin	*Le Poème de l'Extase*	3	6		(1945)	28	[33] 1f
		18	3	**Stravinsky**	*Jeu de Cartes*	36	[71] 4f
		32	[4]			56	1b [103]
		40	[7]	**Stravinsky**	*Le Sacre du Printemps*	119	[161] 1f
		101	2	**Stravinsky**	*Orpheus*	4	[5]
		115	2			58	[146]
		165	2b [36]	**Stravinsky**	*Petrouchka Suite*	55	[42]
Scriabin	*Prométhée, Le Poème du*	11	10b [5]			120	[103]
	Feu	48	[32]			154	4
Sessions	*Symphony for Orchestra*			**Stravinsky**	*Scènes de Ballet*	41	[72]
	(No. 1)	40	[63] 1f			57	1b [94]
Sessions	*Symphony No. II*	47	[Ee]	**Stravinsky**	*Scherzo Fantastique*	34	[51]
		50	2			44	[63]
Shostakovich	*Symphony No.* 1	8	1b [14]	**Szymanowski**	*Symphonie Concertante*		
		20	1b [33]		*pour Piano et Orchestre*	50	1b [2]
		55	[16]	**Tansman**	*Sonatine Trans-*		
		73	[20]		*atlantique, I*	14	[5]
Shostakovich	*Symphony No.* 5	50	[45] 3f	**Taylor**	*Ballet Music from*		
		64	1b [57]		"Casanova"	38	3
Shostakovich	*Symphony No.* 6	116	[111]	**Taylor**	*Through the Looking*		
Shostakovich	*Symphony No.* 9	30	[22] 2f		*Glass*	107	[2]
Shostakovich	*The Golden Age,*			**Tchaikovsky**	*Manfred-Symphonie*	150	540
	Ballet Suite	29	[32]	**Tchaikovsky**	*Mozartiana*	44	162
Sibelius	*Symphony No.* 4	40	8	**Thomson**	*Louisiana Story Suite*	57	127
Skilton	*Suite Primeval, Part II*	3	7	**Toch**	*Fünf Stücke für*		
Strauss, R.	*Also Sprach*	170	1		*Kammerorchester*	18	2b [2]
	Zarathustra	217	10	**Toch**	*The Chinese Flute*	3	[3]
Strauss, R.	*Death and Transfigura-*					25	[18] 4f
	tion	11	1			53	[31] 1f
Strauss, R.	*Don Juan*	15	2	**Trapp**	*Symphonie No.* 4	71	[26]
		72	4b [V]	**Turina**	*La Procesión del Rocío*	8	[2]
Strauss, R.	*Don Quixote*	11	3	**Vaughan**	*A London Symphony*	146	[Y]
		16	2	**Williams**		191	[W] 6f
		130	2	**Vaughan**	*Job, A Masque for*		
		166	5	**Williams**	*Dancing*	81	1
Strauss, R.	*Ein Heldenleben*	45	[22]–[36]	**Vaughan**	*Overture to "The*		
		213	[106]	**Williams**	*Wasps"*	22	[H] 4f
		216	[108] 2f	**Vaughan**	*Pastoral Symphony*	4	3b [A]
Strauss, R.	*Rosenkavalier Waltzes*			**Williams**		55	[C]
	—*First Sequence*	11	[11] 12f			81	1b [W]
Strauss, R.	*Salomé's Dance*	25	[W] 5f			91	4
Strauss, R.	*Symphonia Domestica*	17	[20] 1f	**Vaughan**	*Symphony in D major*		
		29	[34]	**Williams**	(No. 5)	87	7
		90	[115] 6f	**Villa-Lobos**	*Chôros No.* 10	14	[G]
Strauss, R.	*Till Eulenspiegel's*	19	2b [14]	**Villa-Lobos**	*Uirapurú*	18	[1 bis]
	Merry Pranks	30	3b [22]			88	1b [24]
Stravinsky	*Apollon Musagète*	8	[20]	**Wagenaar**	*Sinfonietta for Small*		
Stravinsky	*Chant du Rossignol*	38	[38] 1f		*Orchestra*	30	[5] 1f

480

SOLO PARTS

Violin (I or II) (contd.)

COMPOSER	WORK	PAGE	MEASURE	COMPOSER	WORK	PAGE	MEASURE
Wagner, J.	*Symphony Number One*	5	[2] 2f	Walton	*Façade, Suite No. 1*	48	1
Wagner, R.	*Bacchanale from*			Weber	*Konzertstück für Klavier*		
	"Tannhäuser"	61	1		*und Orchester*	59	2
Wagner, R.	*Forest Murmurs from*			Whithorne	*The Dream Pedlar*	5	4
	"Siegfried"	7	1			26	5

Violin I and II

COMPOSER	WORK	PAGE	MEASURE	COMPOSER	WORK	PAGE	MEASURE
Borodin	*On the Steppes of*			Haydn	*Symphony No. 14 in*		
	Central Asia	1	1		*D major*	32	69
Diamond	*Music for Shakespeare's*			Hindemith	*Neues vom Tage*	5	[A]
	"Romeo and Juliet"	39	[20] 3f	Shepherd	*Horizons*	153	[R] 2f
				White	*Idyl for Orchestra*	1	3

Viola

COMPOSER	WORK	PAGE	MEASURE	COMPOSER	WORK	PAGE	MEASURE
Bach–	*Passacaglia and Fugue*			Egge	*Symphony No. 1*	105	[14]
Respighi	*in C minor*	2	[3]	Elgar	*In the South, Concert*		
Bartók	*Dance Suite*	89	[58]		*Overture*	64	3
Bax	*In the Faery Hills*	77	3	Elgar	*Variations, "Enigma"*	32	[21]
Bax	*Third Symphony*	60	6			59	[39]
Bax	*Fourth Symphony*	129	3b [15]	Gershwin	*An American in Paris*	70	[59]
Bax	*The Garden of Fand*	46	5	Golestan	*Concerto Roumain pour*		
Bloch	*America*	15	[8]		*Violon et Orchestre*	55	[S]
		61	[31] 2f	Gruenberg	*The Enchanted Isle*	72	[345] 3f
Bloch	*Schelomo*	59	3	Holst	*The Ballet from "The*	19	[14] 6f
Bloch	*Trois Poèmes Juifs*	4	1		*Perfect Fool"*	42	7b [32]
		11	3b [4]	Honegger	*Horace Victorieux*	3	6
		28	[17] 3f			35	4
Bloch	*Voice in the Wilderness*	11	[10]	Honegger	*Le Chant de Nigamon*	63	2
Britten	*Les Illuminations*	10	[4] 4f	Honegger	*Le Dit des Jeux du*		
		25	[2]		*Monde*	16	[1] 1f
Britten	*Passacaglia from "Peter*			Honegger	*Le Roi David*	29	6
	Grimes"	1	6			170	1
Britten	*Sinfonia da Requiem*	4	[3]	Honegger	*Musique pour la*		
Copland	*Dance Symphony*	16	[9]		*"Phaedre" de*		
		45	4		*G. D'Annunzio*	26	1b [8]
Copland	*First Symphony*	7	[8] 1f	Ibert	*Divertissement*	12	[2] 11f
Copland	*Music for the Theatre*	69	[57]	d'Indy	*Deuxième Symphonie*	86	[41]
Coppola	*Interlude Dramatique*	32	[16] 7f		*en Sib*	99	1
Coppola	*Suite Intima*	5	2	d'Indy	*Symphony on a French*		
		18	[7]		*Mountain Air*	56	5b [K]
Coppola	*Symphonie en La mineur*	56	1	Inghelbrecht	*La Métamorphose d'Ève*	18	[16] 4f
Debussy	*Iberia*	22	[14] 2f			35	1
Debussy	*Nuages*	10	[6]	Ippolitov-	*Caucasian Sketches*	40	2
Delius	*Appalachia*	127	550	Ivanov		51	6
Delius	*Summer Night on the*			James	*Suite for String*		
	River	14	[8] 1f		*Orchestra*	18	2
Dohnányi	*Ruralia Hungarica*	3	3	Jolivet	*Andante pour Orchestre*		
		11	[7] 3f		*à Cordes*	2	1
Dukas	*L'Apprenti Sorcier*	73	[56] 3f				

STRINGS

Viola (contd.)

COMPOSER	WORK	PAGE	MEASURE	COMPOSER	WORK	PAGE	MEASURE
Kabalevsky	Suite from "Colas Breugnon"	122	[3] 4f	Shepherd	Horizons	41	4
Kodály	Háry János Suite	35	1			68	[L] 1f
Kodály	Summer Evening	18	3	Sibelius	En Saga	26	[F] 1of
		38	[230]			44	1
Lekeu	Fantaisie sur Deux Airs					58	10
	Populaires Angevins	20	6	Sibelius	Symphony No. 4	45	1
Liszt	Eine Faust-Symphonie	35	[K] 2f	Sibelius	Violin Concerto	41	6
		90	2	Siegmeister	From my Window	12	[10]
		122	[A] 4f	Siegmeister	Ozark Set	49	[15]
Maganini	At the Setting of the Sun	2	[A]	Strauss, R.	Don Quixote	40	1
		20	[J] 3f			105	3
Mahler	Symphony No. 1	83	7b [9]	Strauss, R.	Ein Heldenleben	15	2
Mahler	Symphony No. 5	35	[13]			102	[53] 1f
		136	4			176	[89] 2f
Mahler	Symphony No. 8	119	3b [77]	Strauss, R.	Oboe Concerto	17	3
		150	6b [120]	Strauss, R.	Salomé's Dance	3	6b [C]
Mahler	Symphony No. 9	87	[23]	Strauss, R.	Till Eulenspiegel's Merry Pranks	47	[33]
		144	1ob [40]	Stravinsky	Concerto en Ré pour Orchestre à Cordes	1	1b [2]
Martinet	Orphée	10	[4]			17	[58] 1f
Milhaud	Concertino de Printemps	19	2b [120]	Stravinsky	Jeu de Cartes	37	[72] 2f
Milhaud	IIe Symphonie	81	[A]	Stravinsky	Symphony in C	15	[24] 2f
Milhaud	Opus Americanum No. 2	26	[165] 1f	Szymanowski	Symphonie Concertante pour Piano et Orchestre	75	[12]
Milhaud	Sérénade pour Orchestre	6	[3]	Turina	La Procesión del Rocío	7	4
Moeran	Symphony in G minor	31	5	Vaughan Williams	A London Symphony	50	[FF]
Porter	Music for Strings	6	[E]			80	[D]
Prokofieff	Symphony No. 6	9	[5] 3f			94	[L] 5f
		10	[6] 3f	Vaughan Williams	Norfolk Rhapsody, No. 1	3	1b [A]
Ravel	Ma Mère l'Oye	9	[9] 4f				
Respighi	Feste Romane	33	[9] 3f	Vaughan Williams	Pastoral Symphony	35	[B] 2f
Respighi	Metamorphoseon, XII Modi	41	2	Vaughan Williams	Symphony in D major (No. 5)	91	1b [1]
Rivier	3 Pastorales	10	[4] 1f	Wagenaar	Sinfonietta for Small Orchestra	35	[7] 2f
Rogers	Elegy	2	[1] 2f				
Rosenthal	Les Petits Métiers	58	2	Wagner, J.	Symphony Number One	50	5
Roussel	Évocations, I	60	1	Wagner, R.	Introduction to Act III, "Tristan und Isolde"	4	[1] 1of
Rozsa	Concerto for String Orchestra	20	1				
Saint-Saëns	Suite Algérienne	57	3	Walton	Façade, Suite No. 1	38	5
Sessions	Suite from "The Black Maskers"	13	2b [10]	Walton	Symphony	33	[19] 4f
		57	[56]	Zimbalist	American Rhapsody	8	2
Sessions	Symphony No. II	64	[Qq]				
Scriabin	Le Poème de l'Extase	6	2				

Violoncello

COMPOSER	WORK	PAGE	MEASURE	COMPOSER	WORK	PAGE	MEASURE
Antheil	Serenade for String Orchestra	10	[19]	Bax	Second Symphony	40	3b [22]
Bartók	Second Suite	3	5	Bax	Sixth Symphony	31	[28] 2f
Bax	First Symphony	22	6	Bax	November Woods	30	[J]
				Bax	The Garden of Fand	3	[A]

Violoncello (contd.)

COMPOSER	WORK	PAGE	MEASURE	COMPOSER	WORK	PAGE	MEASURE
Beethoven	Piano Concerto No. 4	18	123	de Falla	Nuits dans les Jardins		
		52	290		d'Espagne	51	[17]
		74	11	Glazounov	Violin Concerto in		
		91	170		A minor	58	1b [38]
		110	368	Grieg	Piano Concerto in		
Beethoven	Piano Concerto No. 5	30	158		A minor	37	6b [A]
		38	205	Griffes	The Pleasure Dome of		
		83	463		Kubla Khan	30	1
Berg	Violin Concerto	82	2b [150]	Harris	Third Symphony	1	2b [3]
Bliss	Concerto for Piano and			Harrison	Alleluia for Orchestra	14	[K] 5f
	Orchestra	159	[100] 1f	Haydn	Symphony No. 12 in		
Bloch	America	78	[45]		Bb major	26	1
Bloch	Evocations	1	3	Holst	The Ballet from "The		
Bloch	Trois Poèmes Juifs	12	[5]		Perfect Fool"	20	[15] 1f
		51	[6]	Holst	The Planets	39	1
		85	[18] 4f	Honegger	Concertino pour Piano	23	[14] 5f
Brahms	Ein deutsches Requiem	165	49		et Orchestre	44	1b [29]
Brahms	Piano Concerto No. 2	123	1	Honegger	Le Roi David	226	6
Britten	Les Illuminations	36	[4]	Honegger	Symphonie Liturgique	107	5
Britten	Serenade for Tenor,	34	1	Honegger	Symphonie pour Cordes	26	4b [7]
	Horn and Strings	36	[30] 3f	Ibert	Féerique	24	[16]
Bruckner	Symphony No. 1	40	[N] 2f	d'Indy	Deuxième Symphonie		
Copland	An Outdoor Overture	17	[105] 1f		en Sib	174	1
Copland	Dance Symphony	38	[22] 5f	d'Indy	Jour d'été à la Montagne	88	5
Copland	Music for Radio	50	2	Ives	A Set of Pieces	22	[C]
Copland	Music for the Theatre	5	[3]	Ives	Third Symphony	76	1
Coppola	Interlude Dramatique	33	2b [17]	Jacobi	Concertino for Piano		
Coppola	Suite Intima	82	8		and String Orchestra	29	[18] 3f
Cras	Âmes d'Enfants	35	[12]	Kay	Suite for Orchestra	55	[59]
Debussy	Gigues	23	6	Kerr	Symphony No. 1	9	[45] 3f
Debussy	Iberia	78	[51] 2f	Khachaturian	Gayne Ballet Suite		
Debussy	La Mer	8	[4]		No. 2	57	[14]
		28	2	Khrennikov	Symphony No. 1	94	[240]
Delius	Summer Night on the			Kodály	Háry János Suite	36	22
	River	10	[3]			43	52
Delius	Three Orchestral Pieces	18	1	Lekeu	Fantaisie sur Deux Aires		
Dello Joio	Variations, Chaconne,				Populaires Angevins	49	1
	and Finale	44	2b [110]	Liszt	Eine Faust-Symphonie	92	4
Dohnányi	Ruralia Hungarica	3	9			273	2
Dukelsky	Symphony No. 3	103	4	Liszt	Piano Concerto No. 2	32	1
Egge	Symphony No. 1	118	5b [29]	Liszt	Les Préludes	50	[K] 2f
Elgar	Cockaigne, Concert			Maganini	Tuolumne	15	1
	Overture	22	1b [14]	Mahler	Das Lied von der Erde	19	[20] 3f
Elgar	Falstaff	48	[49] 4f			28	[34] 3f
		136	[133] 3f			43	[9] 2f
Elgar	Sea Pictures	11	[A] 2f			105	[16] 1f
		29	[B] 2f			117	2
Elgar	Variations, "Enigma"	49	3	Mahler	Symphony No. 3	56	[40]
		82	[52]	Mahler	Symphony No. 7	48	1
		88	[56] 3f			168	[197]
				Mahler	Symphony No. 8	135	[98]
Engel	The Creation	21	[10] 4f	Mahler	Symphony No. 9	181	4

STRINGS

Violoncello (contd.)

COMPOSER	WORK	PAGE	MEASURE
Milhaud	Concerto pour Piano et	27	1b [40]
	Orchestre	31	1b [75]
Milhaud	Opus Americanum No. 2	49	1b [290]
Moeran	Symphony in G minor	70	3b [37]
		190	3b [124]
Moore	In Memoriam	23	[O]
Morris	Prospice Symphony	64	2
Piston	Concertino for Pianoforte		
	and Chamber		
	Orchestra	28	[195] 2f
Piston	Concerto for Orchestra	32	[4]
Pizzetti	Concerto dell'Estate	66	2b [24]
Poot	Symphonie	71	5b [33]
Poulenc	Aubade	60	2
Poulenc	Concerto pour deux		
	Pianos et Orchestre	34	[27] 2f
Prokofieff	Lieutenant Kijé	26	[17] 1f
Prokofieff	Romeo and Juliet,		
	Suite No. 2	30	[16] 5f
Prokofieff	Violin Concerto No. 2	43	2b [38]
Rabaud	La Procession Nocturne	29	[11] 3f
Rachmaninoff	The Bells	37	[40] 1f
Ravel	Alborada del Gracioso	36	[29] 4f
Read	Symphony No. I	73	[29] 1f
Respighi	Feste Romane	87	5
Respighi	Metamorphoseon, XII		
	Modi	40	[20] 1f
Respighi	The Fountains of Rome	7	1
		52	7
Respighi	The Pines of Rome	56	3
Respighi	Toccata per Pianoforte e		
	Orchestra	11	3
Riegger	Symphony No. 3	19	[95] 3f
Rimsky-			
Korsakoff	Capriccio Espagnol	52	1
Rimsky-	Russian Easter Overture	3	[A] 2f
Korsakoff		10	5
Rimsky-	Scheherazade	13	74
Korsakoff		29	155
		41	[M]
		53	85
		102	447
		256	639
Rogers	Once Upon a Time,		
	Five Fairy Tales	14	3b [11]
Schönberg	A Survivor from Warsaw	8	35
Schreker	The Birthday of the		
	Infanta, Suite	95	3b [485]
Schumann, R.	Manfred Overture	71	5
Scriabin	Le Poème de l'Extase	6	2
		100	1

COMPOSER	WORK	PAGE	MEASURE
Scriabin	Prométhée, Le Poème du		
	Feu	11	[5]
Shepherd	Horizons	25	5
Shostakovich	Symphony No. 1	10	[17] 2f
		47	[1]
		85	[36]
		85	[W] 24f
Sibelius	En Saga		
Sibelius	Pohjola's Daughter	3	2
Sibelius	Rakastava	7	12b [A]
		14	8b [D]
Sibelius	Symphony No. 1	55	3
Sibelius	Symphony No. 2	93	5
Sibelius	Symphony No. 4	1	6
		6	[E] 3f
		40	1
Sibelius	Symphony No. 7	63	[W]
Sibelius	The Swan of Tuonela	16	4
Sibelius	The Tempest,		
	Second Suite	23	4
Sibelius	Violin Concerto	39	6b [10]
		87	5
Siegmeister	From my Window	14	3b [20]
Siegmeister	Sunday in Brooklyn	9	1b [30]
Siegmeister	Western Suite	55	[55]
Skilton	Suite Primeval, Part I	2	5
Skilton	Suite Primeval, Part II	3	7
Strauss, R.	Also Sprach	47	1
	Zarathustra	74	4
		107	1
		170	5
Strauss, R.	Don Quixote	36	5
		41	9
		60	2
		76	2
		104	1
		154	1
		167	1
Strauss, R.	Eine Alpensinfonie	80	5b [74]
Strauss, R.	Ein Heldenleben	201	4
Strauss, R.	Oboe Concerto	47	[45]
Strauss, R.	Rosenkavalier Waltzes		
	—First Sequence	20	1b [21]
Strauss, R.	Symphonia Domestica	64	[82]
Stravinsky	"Dumbarton Oaks"		
	Concerto	23	[45] 2f
Stravinsky	Fire-Bird Suite (1919)	17	[1] 3f
		22	1
		41	[15]
		68	[3] 2f
Stravinsky	Jeu de Cartes	79	[155] 2f
Stravinsky	Le Sacre du Printemps	5	[7]
		80	[90] 3f

484

SOLO PARTS

Violoncello (contd.)

COMPOSER	WORK	PAGE	MEASURE	COMPOSER	WORK	PAGE	MEASURE
Stravinsky	*Oedipus Rex*	74	[100]	Vaughan Williams	*Symphony in D major (No. 5)*	74	[3]
Stravinsky	*Orpheus*	39	[101] 2f	Vaughan Williams	*Symphony in E minor (No. 6)*	148	[4] 1f
Stravinsky	*Petrouchka Suite*	9	2	Wagner, R.	*Bacchanale from "Tannhäuser"*	72	1
Stravinsky	*Quatre Études pour Orchestre*	18	2b [8]	Wagner, R.	*Eine Faust-Overture*	20	145
Stravinsky	*Symphonie de Psaumes*	4	3b [3]	Wagner, R.	*Introduction to Act III, "Tristan und Isolde"*	3	3
Szymanowski	*Symphonie Concertante pour Piano et Orchestre*	21	2	Walton	*Concerto for Viola and Orchestra*	1 / 46	[1] 1f / 3b [40]
Taylor	*Through the Looking Glass*	109	[3]	Walton	*Concerto for Violin and Orchestra*	156	1b [76]
Toch	*The Chinese Flute*	2	[2]	Walton	*Symphony*	37 / 119	[22] 8f / [89] 1f
Vaughan Williams	*A London Symphony*	83	6	Weber– Berlioz	*Invitation to the Dance*	1 / 51	1 / 408
Vaughan Williams	*Concerto Accademico for Violin and String Orchestra*	14	1	Wellesz	*Symphony in C*	46	[345] 2f
Vaughan Williams	*Job, A Masque for Dancing*	40	7	Zimbalist	*American Rhapsody*	15	1b [11]

Bass

COMPOSER	WORK	PAGE	MEASURE	COMPOSER	WORK	PAGE	MEASURE
Albéniz	*Catalonia, Suite No. 1*	38	[47]	Mahler	*Symphony No. 7*	140	[152]
Antheil	*Serenade for String Orchestra*	12	[22] 3f	Milhaud	*Opus Americanum No. 2*	74	4b [515]
Berg	*Violin Concerto*	4	[10] 1f	Moeran	*Sinfonietta*	30	3b [44]
Bloch	*Trois Poèmes Juifs*	86	[19]	Poulenc	*Concerto pour deux Pianos et Orchestre*	33	[26]
Copland	*Four Dance Episodes from "Rodeo"*	21	[20] 1f	Prokofieff	*Lieutenant Kijé*	25	[15] 2f
Diamond	*Music for Shakespeare's "Romeo and Juliet"*	53	[145] 2f	Prokofieff	*Suite from the Ballet "Chout"*	122	[156] 3f
Dukelsky	*Symphony No. 3*	135	[58] 4f	Prokofieff	*Violin Concerto No. 2*	56	123
Egge	*Symphony No. 1*	45	[46] 1f	Riegger	*Symphony No. 3*	107	1b [245]
Elgar	*Concerto for Violin and Orchestra*	84	1b [97]	Rimsky- Korsakoff	*Scheherazade*	29	157
de Falla	*Nuits dans les Jardins d'Espagne*	63	[30]	Rogers	*Characters from Hans Christian Andersen*	5	[4] 7f
Gold	*Allegorical Overture*	11	3	Rosenthal	*Les Petits Métiers*	95	2
Herrmann	*Sinfonietta for String Orchestra*	2	5	Schuman, W.	*Symphony No. IV*	1	1
Honegger	*Horace Victorieux*	35 / 61	1 / 1	Sessions	*Suite from "The Black Maskers"*	9	[6] 1f
Honegger	*Le Roi David*	178	3b [1]	Siegmeister	*From my Window*	8	2b [40]
James	*Suite for String Orchestra*	30	1	Siegmeister	*Western Suite*	65	4b [35]
Jolivet	*Andante pour Orchestre à Cordes*	15	[55]	Strauss, R.	*Rosenkavalier Waltzes —First Sequence*	16	[17]
Kodály	*Marosszék Dances*	31	6	Stravinsky	*Le Sacre du Printemps*	6	[8]
Loeffler	*Evocation*	10	[R] 2f	Stravinsky	*Oedipus Rex*	59	2b [86]
Mahler	*Symphony No. 1*	78	[1] 2f	Thomson	*Louisiana Story Suite*	41	86
Mahler	*Symphony No. 4*	11 / 165	72 / 67	Vaughan Williams	*Symphony in E minor (No. 6)*	20	[6]
				Villa-Lobos	*Chôros No. 10*	25	2
				Villa-Lobos	*Uirapurú*	6	1

485

Violin (I or II) and Viola

COMPOSER	WORK	PAGE	MEASURE	COMPOSER	WORK	PAGE	MEASURE
Barber	*Medea*	13	[12]	Milhaud	*Concerto pour Piano et Orchestre*	30	[60] 1f
Berg	*Three Excerpts from "Wozzeck"*	15	3b [375]	Milhaud	*Deuxième Concerto pour Violon et Orchestre*	64	1
		25	1b [20]	Ravel	*Daphnis et Chloé, Suite No. 2*	64	[191]
		59	2	Ravel	*Ma Mère l'Oye*	48	[2] 4f
Berg	*Violin Concerto*	39	[185] 1f	Rozsa	*Concerto for String Orchestra*	11	[117]
Bloch	*Trois Poèmes Juifs*	58	[12]	Schreker	*The Birthday of the Infanta, Suite*	41	1b [220]
Copland	*Concerto for Piano and Orchestra*	37	[26] 2f	Shepherd	*Horizons*	17	2
Coppola	*Scherzo Fantastique*	17	2b [9]			117	[C]
Debussy	*Danses Sacrée et Profane*	4	5	Strauss, R.	*Don Quixote*	62	3
Debussy	*Première Rhapsodie*	1	1			67	1
Delius	*Prelude to "Irmelin"*	42	2			106	1
Delius	*Summer Night on the River*	11	[5]	Strauss, R.	*Ein Heldenleben*	64	[33] 1f
		13	5	Strauss, R.	*Oboe Concerto*	20	[19]
Diamond	*Music for Shakespeare's "Romeo and Juliet"*	21	1	Strauss, R.	*Symphonia Domestica*	6	6
		29	[60] 1f	Stravinsky	*Four Norwegian Moods*	22	[30]
Gershwin	*An American in Paris*	2	[1] 4f	Stravinsky	*Orpheus*	6	[11] 1f
		49	3b [44]	Whithorne	*Fata Morgana*	4	[2] 3f
Gruenberg	*The Enchanted Isle*	11	1	Whithorne	*The Dream Pedlar*	6	[2]
Inghelbrecht	*El Greco*	25	[22]				
Jacobi	*Music Hall Overture*	29	[18]				
Mahler	*Symphony No. 4*	93	160				
Miaskovsky	*Sinfonietta for String Orchestra*	26	[21]				

Violin I, II, and Viola

COMPOSER	WORK	PAGE	MEASURE	COMPOSER	WORK	PAGE	MEASURE
Barraine	*Deuxième Symphonie*	57	7	Jacobi	*Concertino for Piano and String Orchestra*	4	[3]
Berlioz	*Harold en Italie*	195	4	Kodály	*Psalmus Hungaricus*	49	5
Bloch	*Hiver–Printemps*	20	4	Martinet	*Orphée*	88	1
Britten	*Les Illuminations*	39	[2]	Milhaud	*Concertino de Printemps*	19	[120] 3f
Britten	*Serenade for Tenor, Horn and Strings*	37	[31]	Milhaud	*Ière Symphonie*	18	3b [70]
Copland	*El Salón México*	22	6b [24]			67	3b [90]
Copland	*Music for the Theatre*	69	3b [57]	Milhaud	*Saudades do Brazil*	39	1
de Falla	*El Amor Brujo*	65	1			57	4
Harrison	*Alleluia for Orchestra*	20	[P] 2f	Prokofieff	*Romeo and Juliet, Suite No. 1*	81	[52]
Harrison	*Suite No. 2 for String Orchestra*	3	[4] 8f	Shepherd	*Horizons*	154	3
Hindemith	*Theme and Four Variations, "The Four Temperaments"*	47	2				

Violin (I or II) and Violoncello

COMPOSER	WORK	PAGE	MEASURE	COMPOSER	WORK	PAGE	MEASURE
Bax	*The Garden of Fand*	3	[A] 1f	Delius	*Summer Night on the River*	11	[4] 1f
Bloch	*Trois Poèmes Juifs*	70	1	Dello Joio	*Variations, Chaconne, and Finale*	44	[110] 2f
Copland	*Music for the Theatre*	43	2	Egge	*Piano Concerto No. 2*	33	[24] 3f
Debussy–Ansermet	*Six Épigraphes Antiques*	31	[C]	Elgar	*Symphony No. 1*	36	6
Delius	*Sea Drift*	10	[4]				

SOLO PARTS

Violin (I or II) and Violoncello (contd.)

COMPOSER	WORK	PAGE	MEASURE	COMPOSER	WORK	PAGE	MEASURE
de Falla	El Amor Brujo	84	[45]	Scriabin	Le Poème de l'Extase	37	2
Gould	Philharmonic Waltzes	29	[339] 2f	Sessions	Symphony No. II	17	[K]
Gruenberg	The Enchanted Isle	62	2b [275]	Shostakovich	Symphony No. 1	73	[20]
James	Suite for String Orchestra	1	2	Sibelius	Rakastava	11	4
Jolivet	Andante pour Orchestre			Sibelius	The Swan of Tuonela	12	3b [G]
	à Cordes	7	1b [30]	Strauss, R.	Also Sprach Zarathustra	48	2
Liszt	Eine Faust-Symphonie	158	3	Strauss, R.	Don Quixote	11	5
Martinet	Orphée	18	2			38	2
Miaskovsky	Sinfonietta for String					87	2
	Orchestra	19	7	Strauss, R.	Symphonia Domestica	46	4b [61]
Morris	Prospice Symphony	79	2b [90]	Stravinsky	Concerto en Ré pour		
Ravel	Ma Mère l'Oye	44	[6] 12f		Orchestre à Cordes	19	2b [65]
Read	Sketches of the City	20	[8]	Stravinsky	Orpheus	3	[4] 4f
Respighi	Ballata delle Gnomidi	58	1	Taylor	Through the Looking Glass	5	1
Respighi	The Fountains of Rome	56	[19] 2f	Toch	Fünf Stücke für		
Rozsa	Concerto for String				Kammerorchester	21	3b [6]
	Orchestra	28	[67]	Wagner, R.	Bacchanale from		
Satie–Debussy	Gymnopédies	3	[B]		"Tannhäuser"	70	3

Violin I, II, and Violoncello

COMPOSER	WORK	PAGE	MEASURE
Schönberg	Fünf Orchesterstücke	60	[15] 1f

Violin (I or II) and Bass

COMPOSER	WORK	PAGE	MEASURE	COMPOSER	WORK	PAGE	MEASURE
Bax	In the Faery Hills	59	4	Milhaud	Quatrième Symphonie	82	1b [35]
Copland	El Salón México	19	[19]				

Viola and Violoncello

COMPOSER	WORK	PAGE	MEASURE	COMPOSER	WORK	PAGE	MEASURE
Bloch	Evocations	1	[1]	Sibelius	The Swan of Tuonela	1	2b [A]
Bloch	Trois Poèmes Juifs	20	1b [12]			5	[C] 5f
Chabrier	Bourrée Fantastique	12	3	Strauss, R.	Don Quixote	42	4
Delius	Summer Night on the					65	3
	River	1c	[3] 6f			99	1
Dukelsky	Symphony No. 3	96	[40]			144	6
Elgar	In the South, Concert					163	1
	Overture	22	[13]	Stravinsky	Jeu de Cartes	38	4b [74]
Ferguson	Partita for Orchestra	52	2	Vaughan	A London Symphony	84	1
Honegger	Le Chant de Nigamon	1	3	Williams		145	[X] 5f
Kerr	Symphony No. 1	10	3b [55]	Vaughan	Job, A Masque for	10	[D] 1f
Miaskovsky	Sinfonietta for String			Williams	Dancing	41	3
	Orchestra	22	[12]	Vaughan			
Milhaud	Concertino de Printemps	25	[160] 3f	Williams	Pastoral Symphony	36	4b [C]
Milhaud	Saudades do Brazil	68	1	Vaughan	Symphony in D major	89	6
Poulenc	Aubade	24	2b [15]	Williams	(No. 5)	113	[15]
Scriabin	Le Poème de l'Extase	105	[21]	Walton	Symphony	116	[86] 4f

487

STRINGS

Viola and Bass

COMPOSER	WORK	PAGE	MEASURE	COMPOSER	WORK	PAGE	MEASURE
Prokofieff	Lieutenant Kijé	25	[15] 6f	Schönberg	Fünf Orchesterstücke	31	1
Rogers	Once Upon a Time,			Schönberg	Theme and Variations	27	106
	Five Fairy Tales	11	4b [8]	Tippett	Symphony No. 1	68	1b [4]

Violoncello and Bass

COMPOSER	WORK	PAGE	MEASURE	COMPOSER	WORK	PAGE	MEASURE
Barber	Second Symphony	25	4b [18]	Mendelssohn	A Midsummer Night's		
Beethoven	Leonore Overture No. 3	50	514		Dream Overture	26	276
Berg	Violin Concerto	15	[75] 2f	Milhaud	Opus Americanum		
		97	2		No. 2	55	1b [355]
Britten	Sinfonia da Requiem	57	2	Prokofieff	Lieutenant Kijé	34	4
Charpentier	Impressions d'Italie	114	[27] 2f	Schönberg	Fünf Orchesterstücke	43	[7]
Egge	Symphony No. 1	73	[72] 1f	Schuman, W.	Symphony for Strings	8	1
Elgar	Variations, "Enigma"	89	[57]	Stravinsky	Chant du Rossignol	15	[13]
de Falla	Nuits dans les Jardins					54	[58]
	d'Espagne	16	[9] 7f	Stravinsky	Concerto en Ré pour	24	[78] 2f
					Orchestre à Cordes	26	[81]
Maganini	Americanese	11	3	Stravinsky	Symphonie de Psaumes	37	4b [8]

Violin (I or II), Viola, and Violoncello

COMPOSER	WORK	PAGE	MEASURE	COMPOSER	WORK	PAGE	MEASURE
Antheil	Serenade for String			Mahler	Symphony No. 4	73	8
	Orchestra	11	[20] 3f			87	[5] 4f
Balakirev–				Miaskovsky	Sinfonietta for String	3	[10]
Casella	Islamey	23	1		Orchestra	11	[32]
Berg	Three Excerpts from					27	[22]
	"Wozzeck"	22	1	Ravel	Rapsodie Espagnole	9	[7]
Berg	Violin Concerto	98	1b [225]			24	[13]
Bloch	Evocations	73	3			66	[17]
		77	[53]	Scriabin	Le Poème de l'Extase	9	1
Casella	Italia	19	[13] 4f			102	2
Cowell	Symphonic Set	22	1	Strauss, R.	Dance Suite after		
Debussy	Iberia	49	2b [33]		François Couperin	70	10
Debussy	Nuages	13	3	Strauss, R.	Death and Transfigura-		
Delannoy	Figures Sonores	46	[21] 3f		tion	39	4
Dohnányi	Ruralia Hungarica	23	3	Stravinsky	Concerto en Ré pour	7	[21] 1f
Dvořák	Symphony No. 5,				Orchestre à Cordes	20	2b [68]
	"From the New			Stravinsky	Ode	6	[9]
	World"	70	6	Stravinsky	Orpheus	57	[143]
de Falla	Nuits dans les Jardins			Stravinsky	Symphony in Three	73	[130]
	d'Espagne	24	2		Movements	89	[154]
				Toch	The Chinese Flute	3	[3] 2f

Violin I, II, Viola, and Violoncello

COMPOSER	WORK	PAGE	MEASURE	COMPOSER	WORK	PAGE	MEASURE
Bartók	Second Suite	75	[1] 1f	Coppola	Interlude Dramatique	34	5b [18]
Bernstein	"Jeremiah" Symphony	59	[17]	Diamond	Rounds for String		
Bloch	America	72	12b [39]		Orchestra	22	[25]
		107	[62]	Dohnányi	Ruralia Hungarica	56	1
Britten	Sinfonia da Requiem	62	[43]	Dukelsky	Symphony No. 3	104	2b [43]

488

SOLO PARTS

Violin I, II, Viola, and Violoncello (contd.)

COMPOSER	WORK	PAGE	MEASURE	COMPOSER	WORK	PAGE	MEASURE
Geminiani	Concerto Grosso in G minor	1	1	Milhaud	Sérénade pour Orchestre	23	1
Gershwin	An American in Paris	54	2b [48]	Piston	Concertino for Piano— forte and Chamber Orchestra	31	[215]
Gershwin	Concerto in F for Piano and Orchestra	68	[12]	Piston	Concerto for Orchestra	15	[7]
Grieg	Suite for Strings, "From Holberg's Time"	17	8b [S]	Rivier	Danse	17	[16]
Harrison	Suite No. 2 for String Orchestra	2	4b [2]	Rozsa	Concerto for String Orchestra	38	[87] 3f
		8	4b [7]	Schuman, W.	Symphony for Strings	12	86
Hindemith	Theme and Four Variations, "The Four Temperaments"	8	9	Strauss, R.	Also Sprach Zarathustra	49	3
		58	1	Stravinsky	Apollon Musagète	16	[41]
Lambert	The Rio Grande	27	[13]			24	[59] 1f
Maganini	An Ornithological Suite	33	8b [A]	Stravinsky	Chant du Rossignol	72	5b [80]
Mahler	Symphony No. 5	187	14	Stravinsky	Symphony in C	42	[77] 1f
Mahler	Symphony No. 8	120	[78]	Thomson	Orchestra Suite from "The Plow that Broke the Plains"	15	[9] 1f
		207	[199]				
McDonald	Three Poems for Orchestra	9	[57]	Toch	The Chinese Flute	42	[25]
Milhaud	Concerto pour Piano et Orchestre	11	2b [45]	Turner	Gregorian Overture for String Orchestra	13	157
		15	1b [60]	Vaughan Williams	Fantasia on a Theme by Thomas Tallis	1	1
Milhaud	Introduction et Marche Funèbre	21	[100]				
Milhaud	Opus Americanum No. 2	50	[310] 3f				

Violin (I or II), Viola, and Bass

COMPOSER	WORK	PAGE	MEASURE
Strauss, R.	Don Quixote	63	3

Violin (I or II), Violoncello, and Bass

Copland	El Salón México	20	2b [20]	Delannoy	Figures Sonores	52	[23] 2f

Violin I, II, Violoncello, and Bass

Chávez	Sinfonia India	26	[33]

Viola, Violoncello, and Bass

Maganini	Symphony for Chamber Orchestra	9	[E]	Stravinsky	Concerto en Ré pour Violon et Orchestre	23	[51]

Violin (I or II), Viola, Violoncello, and Bass

Barber	Medea	34	1	Hindemith	Theme and Four Variations, "The Four Temperaments"	64	10
Berg	Violin Concerto	77	[125] 1f				

STRINGS

Violin I, II, Viola, Violoncello, and Bass

COMPOSER	WORK	PAGE	MEASURE	COMPOSER	WORK	PAGE	MEASURE
Bax	*First Symphony*	79	10	Milhaud	*Le Bal Martiniquais*	18	[85] 2f
Berg	*Three Excerpts from*			Milhaud	*Saudades do Brazil*	18	1
	"Wozzeck"	32	3b [55]	Milhaud	*Sérénade pour Orchestre*	20	7
Chávez	*Sinfonia India*	27	[35]	Mohaupt	*Town Piper Music*	18	8b [12]
Harrison	*Alleluia for Orchestra*	9	[G]	Skilton	*Suite Primeval, Part II*	6	4
Herrmann	*Sinfonietta for String*			Strauss, R.	*Dance Suite after*		
	Orchestra	5	[H] 4f		*François Couperin*	35	13
Hindemith	*Theme and Four Varia-*			Stravinsky	*Orpheus*	30	[77]
	tions, "The Four			Stravinsky	*Pulcinella Suite*	1	1
	Temperaments"	65	[45]	Vaughan			
Mahler	*Symphony No. 7*	162	[187]	Williams	*A London Symphony*	181	1

490

Chapter 60

SOLI PARTS

English	Italian	French	German
1st Desk [stand]	Primo [I°, 1°] Leggio	1 [1ᵉʳ] Pupitre	Erste [I] Pult
1 Desk [stand]			
1 desk only	1 leggio solamente	1 pupitre seulement	Nur ein [1] Pult
1st desk solo	I° leggio solo	1ᵉʳ pupitre solo	Erste Pult solo
Only two [2] Violins [Violas; Cellos; Basses]	Due [2] Violini [Viole; Violoncelli; Bassi] solamente	Seulement à 2 Violons [Altos; Violoncelles; Basses]	Nur zwei [2] Violinen [Bratschen; Violoncelle; Bässe]
2 (players) only	2 Soli	2 Soli	2 Spieler allein
2 Solo Violins [Violas; Cellos; Basses]	2 Soli Violini [Viole; Violoncelli; Bassi]	2 Soli Violons [Altos; Violoncelles; Basses]	2 Soli Violinen [Bratschen; Violoncelle; Bässe]
2 Violins (etc.) solo	2 Violini (etc.) soli	2 Violons (etc.) soli [seuls]	2 Violinen (etc.) soli [allein]
3 (1st Vlns., etc.) Solo	3 (Vln. I, etc.) Soli	3 (1ᵉʳᵉˢ Vons., etc.) Soli [seuls]	3 (1ᵗᵉ Viol., etc.) allein
Violin solo by 3 players	Violino solo a 3	Violon solo à 3	Violine Solo von Dreien
1st and 2nd desks	I° e 2° leggi	1ᵉʳ et 2ᵉ pupitres	Die erste u. zweite Pulte
1st two desks	2 Leggi solo	2 Pupitres solo	2 Pulte solo [einer allein] Die zwei [2] ersten Pulte
4 players	4 Soli	4 Soli	4 Soli [Spieler]
4 Solo Vlns. (etc.)	Soltanto 4		4 einzelne Viol. (etc.)
Only 2 desks	2 leggi solamente	2 pupitres seulement	Nur 2 Pulte
1st 3 [4; 5; 6, etc.] desks [stands]	I primi 3 [4; 5; 6, etc.] leggi	1. 2. 3. [4. 5. 6., etc.] pupitres	Die ersten 3 [4; 5; 6, etc.] Pulte I. II. III. (etc.) Pulte

Violin I or II

(1) 2★

COMPOSER	WORK	PAGE	MEASURE	COMPOSER	WORK	PAGE	MEASURE
Bartók	Vier Orchesterstücke	27	1	Copland	Four Dance Episodes from "Rodeo"	52	1b [1]
Bax	In the Faery Hills	40	1b [S]				
Bax	Second Symphony	41	2	Copland	Lincoln Portrait	13	[80] 1f
		104	[18] 2f	Copland	Third Symphony	82	[73]
Berg	Violin Concerto	29	3	Coppola	Suite Intima	45	1b [6]
		85	[170]	Debussy	Iberia	92	[58]
Bloch	Evocations	9	1	Debussy	Jeux	113	[78] 4f
Bloch	Schelomo	64	[39]	Debussy	Prélude à l'après-midi		
Borodin	On the Steppes of Central Asia	1	5		d'un Faune	27	[10] 1f
				Diamond	Timon of Athens	34	250
Brahms	Piano Concerto No. 1	40	3	Dukas	La Péri	39	[6]
		83	6	Egge	Symphony No. 1	91	4b [17]
Copland	Appalachian Spring	6	[7] 9f			105	[14] 4f

★ Figure refers to number of *soli* instruments.

491

STRINGS

Violin I or II (1) 2 (contd.)

COMPOSER	WORK	PAGE	MEASURE	COMPOSER	WORK	PAGE	MEASURE
Ferroud	Au Parc Monceau	17	2	Rimsky-Korsakoff	Symphony No. 2, "Antar"	39	7
Gershwin	An American in Paris	49	[44] 2f	Roger-Ducasse	Poème Symphonique sur le nom de Gabriel Fauré	25	[10] 2f
Goldmark	Overture, In Spring-time	14	[31]	Rogers	Characters from Hans Christian Andersen	4	[3] 1f
Harris	Third Symphony	22	4			6	1
		25	1	Rosenthal	Les Petits Métiers	99	2
Hindemith	Ballet Overture, Cupid and Psyche	9	[G]	Roussel	Suite en Fa	7	[3]
d'Indy	Jour d'été à la Montagne	13	1	Roussel	Symphonie en Sol mineur	36	6
Ives	Three Places in New England	18	[J]	Rozsa	Concerto for String Orchestra	6	[47]
Knipper	Symphony No. 4	77	[10]	Schönberg	Suite for String Orchestra	11	169
Kodály	Te Deum	76	[430]				
Levant	Nocturne	28	114	Schönberg	Theme and Variations	22	86
Liszt	Piano Concerto No. 1	9	58	Shepherd	Horizons	26	[J] 2f
Liszt	Piano Concerto No. 2	38	285	Sibelius	En Saga	59	1
Mahler	Symphony No. 1	85	5	Sibelius	Symphony No. 1	20	[L]
Mahler	Symphony No. 2	131	[4] 2f	Siegmeister	Sunday in Brooklyn	72	[50] 1f
Mahler	Symphony No. 9	38	7	Strauss, R.	Also Sprach Zarathustra	215	7
Martinet	Orphée	41	[13]	Stravinsky	Apollon Musagète	8	[21] 4f
Miaskovsky	Symphony No. 6	116	[73]	Stravinsky	Concerto en Ré pour Orchestre à Cordes	29	[88]
Milhaud	Concertino de Printemps	12	[75]	Stravinsky	Danses Concertantes	100	[161]
Milhaud	Concerto pour Piano et Orchestre	8	2b [30]	Stravinsky	"Dumbarton Oaks" Concerto	35	[70]
Milhaud	Deuxième Concerto pour Violon et Orchestre	51	[10]	Stravinsky	Four Norwegian Moods	40	[50]
Piston	Suite for Orchestra	43	[D] 6f	Stravinsky	Le Sacre du Printemps	17	2b [24]
Prokofieff	Ala et Lolly (Scythian Suite)	76	7	Stravinsky	Petrouchka Suite	52	[40] 3f
Ravel	Daphnis et Chloé, Suite No. 2	39	[171]			64	[49] 11f
Read	Symphony No. 1	4	[3]	Stringfield	A Negro Parade	30	[14]
Respighi	Ballata delle Gnomidi	30	2b [9]	Szymanowski	Symphonie Concertante pour Piano et Orchestre	25	1
Respighi	The Birds	43	[20] 5f				
Respighi	Vetrate di Chiesa	73	5	Toch	Hyperion	26	[128]
Rimsky-Korsakoff	Russian Easter Overture	3	[A] 1f	Verdi	Messa da Requiem	148	63
		32	4	Whithorne	The Dream Pedlar	61	[31]
Rimsky-Korsakoff	Scheherazade	257	245				

(2) 2 or 3

COMPOSER	WORK	PAGE	MEASURE
Beethoven	Leonore Overture No. 3	50	514

(3) 3

COMPOSER	WORK	PAGE	MEASURE	COMPOSER	WORK	PAGE	MEASURE
Albéniz–Arbós	Évocation	19	[H] 3f	Bloch	Voice in the Wilderness	33	[26]
Bartók	Dance Suite	42	76			84	[67]
Bax	November Woods	81	[X]	Britten	Serenade for Tenor, Horn and Strings	12	[9]
Bloch	Schelomo	6	1	Bruckner	Symphony No. 8	75	[D] 1f
Bloch	Trois Poèmes Juifs	28	1b [17]	Debussy	Rondes de Printemps	16	[9]

SOLI PARTS

Violin I or II (3) 3 (contd.)

COMPOSER	WORK	PAGE	MEASURE
Gould	Philharmonic Waltzes	29	[339] 14f
Hindemith	Ballet Overture, Cupid and Psyche	11	[I]
Hindemith	Nobilissima Visione	58	[39]
Hindemith	Theme and Four Varia-tions, "The Four Temperaments"	41	[31]
Kodály	Marosszék Dances	55	2
Levant	Nocturne	40	175
Maganini	South Wind	12	[L]
Mahler	Songs of a Wayfarer	9	2b [4]
Milhaud	Deuxième Concerto pour Violoncelle et Orchestre	49	[30] 3f
Milhaud	Ière Symphonie	63	1b [50]
Milhaud	IIe Symphonie	23	[20] 2f
Ravel	Daphnis et Chloé, Suite No. 2	5	[156] 1f
Ravel	Ma Mère l'Oye	7	[5]
Respighi	The Fountains of Rome	60	[21] 3f
Schmitt	Mirages pour Orchestre, No. 1	27	[12] 1f
Schönberg	Theme and Variations	13	51
Sessions	Suite from "The Black Maskers"	57	[56]
Siegmeister	Sunday in Brooklyn	19	[65] 2f
Strauss, R.	Eine Alpensinfonie	6	1b [5]
Strauss, R.	Ein Heldenleben	214	1
Strauss, R.	Don Quixote	47	5
Strauss, R.	Symphonia Domestica	68	85
Stravinsky	Danses Concertantes	62	1b [99]
Stravinsky	Firebird Ballet Suite (1945)	50	[64]
Stravinsky	Ode	4	[6]
Stravinsky	Petrouchka Suite	53	1b [41]
Stravinsky	Scènes de Ballet	34	[56]
Stravinsky	Scherzo à la Russe	10	[10]

(4) 4

COMPOSER	WORK	PAGE	MEASURE
Albéniz–Arbós	El Puerto	33	4
Albéniz–Arbós	Triana	14	1
Bartók	Concerto for Orchestra	23	[462]
Bartók	Dance Suite	14	[9]
		62	[43]
		88	[57]
Berg	Violin Concerto	91	1
Berlioz	Harold en Italie	8	10
Bloch	America	17	2b [9]
		61	[31]
Bloch	Evocations	2	[2]
Borodin	On the Steppes of Central Asia	24	270.
Casella	Pupazzetti	21	[7] 4f
Chabrier	Bourrée Fantastique	41	[14]
Charpentier	Impressions d'Italie	31	[7]
Copland	Concerto for Piano and Orchestra	40	[31]
Copland	Third Symphony	25	8
Debussy	Gigues	1	5
Debussy	Rondes de Printemps	10	[5] 2f
Diamond	Timon of Athens	23	141
Halffter	Deux Esquisses Symphoniques	8	2
Hindemith	Neues vom Tage	33	1
Kodály	Psalmus Hungaricus	51	2
Liszt	Eine Faust–Symphonie	132	[I]
		146	[T]
Mahler	Symphony No. 2	55	5
Mihalovici	Toccata pour Piano et Orchestre	140	2b [580]
Milhaud	Deuxième Concerto pour Violoncelle et Orchestre	44	1
		56	4b [65]
		115	[120]
Pizzetti	Concerto dell'Estate	77	3b [29]
Rachmaninoff	Die Toteninsel	17	[6]
Rachmaninoff	The Bells	11	2b [10]
Ravel	Rapsodie Espagnole	10	[8]
		64	[15] 4f
Roussel	Évocations, II	70	2b [32]
Roussel	Évocations, III	72	1
Roussel	Le Festin de l'Araignée	25	[28]
Schönberg	Suite for String Orchestra	20	364
Sibelius	Symphony No. 3	41	5
Strauss, R.	Don Quixote	7	9
Stravinsky	Chant du Rossignol	21	[22]
Stravinsky	Danses Concertantes	24	[34]
Stravinsky	Fire-Bird Suite (1919)	22	[12] 4f
Stravinsky	Le Sacre du Printemps	29	[39] 1f
		32	[42]
Szymanowski	Symphonie Concertante pour Piano et Orchestre	13	[7]
Thomson	Orchestra Suite from "The Plow that broke the Plains"	49	[46]
Wagner, R.	Prelude to Act I, "Lohengrin"	1	1
Walton	Concerto for Viola and Orchestra	18	1

(5) 5

COMPOSER	WORK	PAGE	MEASURE	COMPOSER	WORK	PAGE	MEASURE
Bartók	*Deux Portraits*	3	[1]	**Mahler**	*Symphony No. 8*	149	[118]
Bax	*Third Symphony*	30	2	**Strauss, R.**	*Till Eulenspiegel's*		
Maganini	*At the Setting of the Sun*	23	[M]		*Merry Pranks*	19	14

(6) 6

COMPOSER	WORK	PAGE	MEASURE	COMPOSER	WORK	PAGE	MEASURE
Bax	*The Garden of Fand*	80	1	**Hindemith**	*Symphonic Metamor-*		
Casella	*Paganiniana*	77	8		*phosis of Themes by*		
Copland	*First Symphony*	54	[39] 4f		*Weber*	16	1
Debussy	*Iberia*	20	1	**Holst**	*Beni Mora, Oriental*		
		83	[54]		*Suite*	23	[3]
Debussy	*Jeux*	48	[33]	**Liadov**	*Kikimora*	3	[5]
Debussy	*La Mer*	79	3	**Rachmaninoff**	*Die Toteninsel*	14	2
		80	[42] 7f	**Rachmaninoff**	*2d Concerto pour*	10	5
Debussy	*Le Martyre de Saint*				*Piano et Orchestre*	43	[15]
	Sébastien	32	4	**Read**	*Symphony No. I*	136	[48] 2f
Debussy–	*Six Épigraphes*			**Rimsky-**			
Ansermet	*Antiques*	2	[A] 1f	**Korsakoff**	*Scheherazade*	29	157
Gershwin	*Rhapsody in Blue*	21	[16]			40	[L]
Hindemith	*Konzertmusik für*			**Rogers**	*Once Upon a Time,*		
	Streichorchester und				*Five Fairy Tales*	1	[1]
	Blechbläser	47	3	**Roussel**	*Évocations, III*	55	[25]
Hindemith	*Neues vom Tage*	20	1	**Strauss, R.**	*Symphonia Domestica*	13	1b [14]

(7) 8

COMPOSER	WORK	PAGE	MEASURE	COMPOSER	WORK	PAGE	MEASURE
Copland	*Dance Symphony*	32	[16] 2f	**Pierné**	*Divertissements sur un*		
Debussy	*Gigues*	20	2		*Thème Pastorale*	11	1
Debussy	*Iberia*	25	[16]	**Pizzetti**	*Concerto dell'Estate*	35	5
Debussy	*La Mer*	106	5	**Roussel**	*Évocations, II*	36	[16]
Hill	*Lilacs*	3	1	**Roussel**	*Évocations, III*	1	1
				Weber	*Euryanthe Overture*	21	129

(8) 9

COMPOSER	WORK	PAGE	MEASURE
Scriabin	*Le Divin Poème*	188	6

(9) 10

Mahler	*Symphony No. 2*	192	[38] 8f

(10) 12

Rachmaninoff	*The Bells*	3	[2]	**Strauss, R.**	*Don Quixote*	8	8
						166	1

SOLI PARTS

Violin I and II

(1) 1–3★

COMPOSER	WORK	PAGE	MEASURE
Herrmann	Sinfonietta for String Orchestra	2	5b [B]

(2) 1–4

Wagner, R.	Forest Murmurs from "Siegfried"	7	74

(3) 2–2

COMPOSER	WORK	PAGE	MEASURE	COMPOSER	WORK	PAGE	MEASURE
Bartok	Dance Suite	62	35	Rogers	Once Upon a Time, Five Fairy Tales	38	1b [24]
Harris	Third Symphony	33	[27] 1f				
Pizzett²	Concerto dell'Estate	13	[5]	Still	Bells	17	5
						20	[22]

(4) 2–3

Bartók	Second Rhapsody for Violin and Orchestra	14	[8] 4f

(5) 3–2

Rozsa	Concerto for String Orchestra	31	[91]

(6) 3–3

Borodin	On the Steppes of Central Asia	2	16	Rimsky-Korsakoff	Symphony No. 2, "Antar"	149	[L] 2f
Dukas	L'Apprenti Sorcier	1	4	Strauss, R.	Salomé's Dance	7	[J]

(7) 3–4

Loeffler	Evocation	47	1b [52]

(8) 4–2

Bartók	Vier Orchesterstücke	60	1	Tansman	Sonatine Transatlantique, I	15	5

(9) 4–3

Bax	Sixth Symphony	29	[25] 5f

★ Figures refer to number of *soli* instruments ; i.e., 1 Vln. I — 3 Vln. II.

Violin I and II (contd.)

(10) 4-4

COMPOSER	WORK	PAGE	MEASURE	COMPOSER	WORK	PAGE	MEASURE
Bartók	Violin Concerto	94	[219]	Rachmaninoff	Die Toteninsel	38	1
Bax	November Woods	82	1	Rachmaninoff	Rapsodie pour Piano		
Borodin	On the Steppes of	2	28		et Orchestre	61	[45]
	Central Asia	24	279	Roussel	Évocations, II	53	3
Copland	Dance Symphony	33	[17] 1f	Shepherd	Horizons	59	5
Debussy	Jeux	114	1b [79]	Stillman-	Gulliver—His Voyage		
Dukelsky	Symphony No. 3	3	5	Kelley	to Lilliput	102	[V]
		133	1	Stillman-	New England	26	6
Hindemith	Symphony in E-Flat	79	[40]	Kelley	Symphony	46	[Z] 2f
Holst	The Planets	95	[X] 1f	Strauss, R.	Salomé's Dance	27	[Y] 1f
Poulenc	Concert Champêtre			Stravinsky	Scènes de Ballet	23	[42]
	pour Clavecin et						
	Orchestre	76	[3]				

(11) 4-8

COMPOSER	WORK	PAGE	MEASURE
Debussy	Jeux	30	[21]

(12) 6-4

COMPOSER	WORK	PAGE	MEASURE	COMPOSER	WORK	PAGE	MEASURE
Albéniz-				Debussy-	Six Épigraphes		
Arbós	Navarra	40	1b [R]	Ansermet	Antiques	54	3
Bartók	Concerto for Orchestra	10	[192]	Schreker	The Birthday of the		
Bartók	Dance Suite	90	[59]		Infanta, Suite	56	[350]

(13) 6-6

COMPOSER	WORK	PAGE	MEASURE	COMPOSER	WORK	PAGE	MEASURE
Bartók	Violin Concerto	116	[468]	Tansman	Deux Moments		
Ibert	Escales	2	[1] 1f		Symphoniques	1	1
Rimsky-	Scheherazade	28	[F]				
Korsakoff		43	226				
		255	[Z]				

(14) 6-8

COMPOSER	WORK	PAGE	MEASURE
Albéniz-Arbós	Fête-Dieu à Séville	31	1b [K]

(15) 8-4

COMPOSER	WORK	PAGE	MEASURE	COMPOSER	WORK	PAGE	MEASURE
Bartók	Concerto for Orchestra	23	[456]	Debussy	Le Martyre de Saint		
					Sébastien	61	[27]

(16) 8-8

COMPOSER	WORK	PAGE	MEASURE	COMPOSER	WORK	PAGE	MEASURE
Barber	Overture to "The			Vaughan	Overture to "The		
	School for Scandal"	3	3	Williams	Wasps"	49	329
Holst	The Planets	40	[V] 2f				

(17) 12-12

COMPOSER	WORK	PAGE	MEASURE	COMPOSER	WORK	PAGE	MEASURE
Debussy	Iberia	95	2	Debussy	Le Martyre de Saint		
					Sébastien	35	2b [15]

SOLI PARTS

Viola

(1) 2

COMPOSER	WORK	PAGE	MEASURE	COMPOSER	WORK	PAGE	MEASURE
Bax	*In the Faery Hills*	39	1b [R]	Inghelbrecht	*Pour le jour de la*		
Bax	*Sixth Symphony*	95	[20] 4f		*première neige au*		
Bloch	*Evocations*	6	[6]		*vieux Japon*	8	3
Bloch	*Trois Poèmes Juifs*	13	2b [6]	Mahler	*Das Lied von der Erde*	11	[9]
		55	1	Mahler	*Symphony No. 7*	102	1b [93]
Britten	*The Young Person's*			Milhaud	*Saudades do Brazil*	58	8
	Guide to the			Sessions	*Symphony for Orchestra*	45	[69]
	Orchestra	30	1		*(No. 1)*	73	[114] 1f
Casella	*La Donna Serpente,*			Siegmeister	*Sunday in Brooklyn*	46	[25] 1f
	I. Serie	2	[2]	Stillman-	*New England*		
Chávez	*Sinfonia India*	25	[29]	Kelley	*Symphony*	21	[I] 2f
		55	[75]	Strauss, R.	*Also Sprach*		
Copland	*Third Symphony*	81	5		*Zarathustra*	99	1
Elgar	*Symphony No. 1*	59	[52] 4f	Stravinsky	*Concerto en Ré pour*		
Engel	*The Creation*	56	[32]		*Orchestre à Cordes*	30	[91]
Holst	*Beni Mora, Oriental*			Stravinsky	*"Dumbarton Oaks"*		
	Suite	5	[2]		*Concerto*	36	[71]
Ibert	*La Ballade de la Geôle*			Stravinsky	*Le Sacre du Printemps*	81	[94] 2f
	de Reading	24	[15] 11f	Wagenaar	*Sinfonietta for Small*		
					Orchestra	38	3b [11]

(2) 3

COMPOSER	WORK	PAGE	MEASURE	COMPOSER	WORK	PAGE	MEASURE
Barraine	*Deuxième Symphonie*	25	[10]	Sessions	*Symphony for Orchestra*		
Milhaud	*Deuxième Concerto*				*(No. 1)*	63	[99]
	pour Violoncelle et			Stravinsky	*Le Sacre du Printemps*	72	[79] 4f
	Orchestre	65	1b [100]	Stravinsky	*Ode*	23	[41] 1f
Piston	*Concerto for Orchestra*	46	[10]	Stravinsky	*Petrouchka Suite*	96	[83]
Schönberg	*A Survivor from Warsaw*	9	43	Stravinsky	*Symphony in C*	43	1b [80]
				Walton	*Concerto for Viola and*		
					Orchestra	7	[7]

(3) 4

COMPOSER	WORK	PAGE	MEASURE	COMPOSER	WORK	PAGE	MEASURE
Bartók	*Concerto for Orchestra*	90	[96]	Inghelbrecht	*La Valse Retrouvée*	1	1
Debussy	*Iberia*	6	[3]	Rachmaninoff	*Die Toteninsel*	23	[9]
		91	3	Ravel	*Rapsodie Espagnole*	66	[17] 2f
Halffter	*Deux Esquisses*			Read	*Sketches of the City*	17	[5] 4f
	Symphoniques	10	2b [C]	Strauss, R.	*Don Quixote*	52	3
Hindemith	*Konzertmusik für*			Stravinsky	*Le Sacre du Printemps*	39	[50] 2f
	Streichorchester und			Stravinsky	*Scènes de Ballet*	6	[6]
	Blechbläser	48	4b [D]	Stravinsky	*Scherzo Fantastique*	34	[50] 1f

(4) 6

COMPOSER	WORK	PAGE	MEASURE	COMPOSER	WORK	PAGE	MEASURE
Albéniz– Arbós	*El Puerto*	32	[M]	Alfvén	*A Legend of the* *Skerries*	4	2b [1]

497

STRINGS

Viola (4) 6 (contd.)

COMPOSER	WORK	PAGE	MEASURE	COMPOSER	WORK	PAGE	MEASURE
Debussy	Jeux	13	[10]	Rachmaninoff	2d Concerto pour Piano et Orchestre	11	1
Hindemith	Konzertmusik für Streichorchester und Blechbläser	71	[O]	Strauss, R.	Also Sprach Zarathustra	101	2
Holst	Beni Mora, Oriental Suite	21	4b [1]	Strauss, R.	Don Quixote	10	4
Ibert	Féerique	1	1	Stravinsky	Le Sacre du Printemps	11	4b [13]

(5) 8

COMPOSER	WORK	PAGE	MEASURE
Bloch	Schelomo	77	[48]

Violoncello

(1) 2

COMPOSER	WORK	PAGE	MEASURE	COMPOSER	WORK	PAGE	MEASURE
Bach, J. C.	Sinfonia in Bb major	16	17	Liadov	The Enchanted Lake	1	1
Bax	The Garden of Fand	10	[C]	Liszt	Todtentanz für Piano und Orchester	34	270
Beethoven	Symphony No. 6, "Pastoral"	34	1	Mahler	Das Lied von der Erde	119	1
Casella	La Donna Serpente, I. Serie	1	4	Mahler	Symphony No. 7	48	3
						101	[92] 1f
Casella	Pupazzetti	14	2b [1]	Milhaud	Concerto pour Violoncelle et Orchestre	16	[55] 3f
Chávez	Sinfonia India	54	[73]	Milhaud	Deuxième Concerto pour Violon et Orchestre	74	[110]
Copland	An Outdoor Overture	20	[130]				
Debussy– Ansermet	Six Épigraphes Antiques	12	3b [A]	Milhaud	Opus Americanum No. 2	19	[125] 2f
Egge	Symphony No. 1	50	[53] 1f	Moeran	Symphony in G minor	30	3b [15]
		74	3b [1]	Parodi	Preludio ad una Commedia	12	[F]
Enesco	2e Rhapsodie Roumaine	1	1	Rimsky- Korsakoff	Symphony No. 2, "Antar"	131	[B] 1f
de Falla	Nuits dans les Jardins d'Espagne	64	[31]	Rogers	Characters from Hans Christian Andersen	16	1b [9]
de Falla	Three Dances from "The Three-Cornered Hat"	1	1	Rosenthal	Les Petits Métiers	62	2
Fitelberg	Nocturne for Orchestra	3	[18]	Roussel	Évocations, II	65	[29]
Gershwin	Concerto in F for Piano and Orchestra	63	[7] 7f	Schönberg	A Survivor from Warsaw	2	5
Grieg	Suite for Strings, "From Holberg's Time"	16	[R]	Schönberg	Theme and Variations	40	193
Hill	Lilacs	10	8	Scriabin	Le Divin Poème	70	2
Honegger	Concertino pour Piano et Orchestre	17	[10]	Sessions	Symphony for Orchestra (No. 1)	20	5b [29]
Honegger	Horace Victorieux	14	[5]	Shepherd	Horizons	43	3
		61	3			91	1b [J]
Honegger	Le Chant de Nigamon	52	[178]	Strauss, R.	Salomé's Dance	1	1
Honegger	Symphonie Liturgique	72	[18]	Stravinsky	Chant du Rossignol	18	[18] 1f
Ibert	Escales	1	1	Stravinsky	Concerto en Ré pour Orchestre à Cordes	22	[70]
Kodály	Summer Evening	5	1b [40]			32	[97]
Liadov	Eight Russian Popular Songs	34	[2]	Stravinsky	"Dumbarton Oaks" Concerto	37	4b [73]

498

SOLI PARTS

Violoncello (1) 2 (contd.)

COMPOSER	WORK	PAGE	MEASURE	COMPOSER	WORK	PAGE	MEASURE
Stravinsky	*Scènes de Ballet*	60	[96] 1f	Wagner, R.	*Eine Faust-Overture*	20	147
Szymanowski	*Symphonie Concertante pour Piano et*			Walton	*Façade, Suite No. 1*	40	4
						50	[G]
	Orchestre	54	[5]	Walton	*Symphony*	12	[7]
Tchaikovsky	*Piano Concerto No. 1 in Bb minor*	69	[S]				

(2) 2 or 4

COMPOSER	WORK	PAGE	MEASURE
Delius	*Appalachia*	61	261

(3) 3

COMPOSER	WORK	PAGE	MEASURE	COMPOSER	WORK	PAGE	MEASURE
Barber	*First Symphony*	69	1	Rimsky-			
Bax	*Fourth Symphony*	41	[28] 2f	Korsakoff	*Russian Easter Overture*	4	2
Borodin	*Symphony No. 3*	49	8			6	2
Halffter	*Deux Esquisses*	10	1b [C]	Schreker	*The Birthday of the*		
	Symphoniques	31	[D] 1f		*Infanta, Suite*	57	3
Kodály	*Psalmus Hungaricus*	41	[25]	Schuman, W.	*Symphony for Strings*	9	20
Liadov	*Kikimora*	5	[7]	Schuman, W.	*Symphony No. IV*	31	1
Liszt	*Eine Faust–Symphonie*	94	1	Strauss, R.	*Don Quixote*	51	1
Milhaud	*Deuxième Concerto*					56	1
	pour Violon et			Strauss, R.	*Salomé's Dance*	5	[F]
	Orchestre	73	[105] 2f	Strauss, R.	*Symphonia Domestica*	68	[85] 1f
Milhaud	*Quatrième Symphonie*	10	[35] 2f	Stravinsky	*Le Sacre du Printemps*	20	6b [29]
Piston	*Prelude and Fugue*	2	[A]			59	[67]
Ravel	*Concerto pour Piano et*					83	[100] 2f
	Orchestre	29	[22]	Stravinsky	*Symphony in C*	50	1b [96]
				Whithorne	*Fata Morgana*	4	[2]

(4) 4

COMPOSER	WORK	PAGE	MEASURE	COMPOSER	WORK	PAGE	MEASURE
Bartók	*Concerto for Orchestra*	58	2	Inghelbrecht	*La Valse Retrouvée*	2	10
Bax	*Fourth Symphony*	33	[22] 6f	Liadov	*Baba-Yaga*	39	5
		63	[50] 1f	Mahler	*Symphony No. 8*	152	[122]
Bizet	*L'Arlésienne Suite No. 2*	9	43	Martinet	*Orphée*	15	[7] 2f
		20	127	Milhaud	*Ière Symphonie*	64	[60] 1f
Bloch	*America*	80	3			71	[130] 2f
Bloch	*Schelomo*	60	[35]	Rachmaninoff	*Piano Concerto No. 3*	5	1
Bloch	*Trois Poèmes Juifs*	80	[14] 4f	Rachmaninoff	*Rapsodie pour Piano et*	44	9b [33]
Debussy	*Le Martyre de Saint*				*Orchestre*	92	[65]
	Sébastien	7	2b [3]	Saint-Saëns	*Danse Macabre*	23	[E]
Debussy-	*Six Épigraphes*			Schuman, W.	*Symphony for Strings*	12	76
Ansermet	*Antiques*	16	[C]	Shepherd	*Horizons*	71	8
Egge	*Symphony No. 1*	5	2	Siegmeister	*Sunday in Brooklyn*	61	2
		83	[10]	Strauss, R.	*Don Quixote*	61	7
Gershwin	*An American in Paris*	83	[68]			175	2
Grieg	*Suite for Strings, "From*			Strauss, R.	*Oboe Concerto*	39	[38]
	Holberg's Time"	5	2b [C]	Stravinsky	*Orpheus*	2	[2] 1f
Hindemith	*Ballet Overture, Cupid*			Stravinsky	*Petrouchka Suite*	1	[1]
	and Psyche	7	[E]	Wagner, R.	*Eine Faust-Overture*	20	149

STRINGS

Violoncello (contd.)

(5) 5

COMPOSER	WORK	PAGE	MEASURE
Rossini	*William Tell, Overture*	1	1

(6) 6

COMPOSER	WORK	PAGE	MEASURE	COMPOSER	WORK	PAGE	MEASURE
Copland	*Dance Symphony*	3	3b [1]	Read	*Sketches of the City*	6	1b [3]
Debussy	*Iberia*	54	[37]	Scriabin	*Le Poème de l'Extase*	108	1
Rachmaninoff	*2d Concerto pour Piano et Orchestre*	64	[26]	Shepherd	*Horizons*	89	[I]
Rachmaninoff	*The Bells*	23	[21]	Strauss, R.	*Ein Heldenleben*	175	2

(7) 8

COMPOSER	WORK	PAGE	MEASURE	COMPOSER	WORK	PAGE	MEASURE
Debussy	*Jeux*	24	4	Strauss, R.	*Don Quixote*	46	3

Bass

(1) 2

COMPOSER	WORK	PAGE	MEASURE	COMPOSER	WORK	PAGE	MEASURE
Britten	*The Young Person's Guide to the Orchestra*	34	5	Lambert	*The Rio Grande*	50	[26]
Chausson	*Symphonie en Si bémol majeur*	95	12	Malipiero	*Impressioni dal Vero, 3ª Parte*	20	1
Copland	*Dance Symphony*	4	[2] 1f	Parodi	*Preludio ad una Commedia*	18	3
Copland	*Third Symphony*	93	2	Pizzetti	*Concerto dell'Estate*	16	9
Diamond	*Timon of Athens*	17	107	Prokofieff	*Piano Concerto No. 3*	36	[28]
Elgar	*Concerto for Violoncello and Orchestra*	51	2b [40]	Prokofieff	*Romeo and Juliet, Suite No. 2*	60	[39]
Elgar	*Symphony No. 1*	117	[105] 1f	Ravel	*Le Tombeau de Couperin*	38	[4]
Glazounov	*Violin Concerto in A minor*	17	4b [11]	Respighi	*Vetrate di Chiesa*	69	[18] 2f
Griffes	*The Pleasure Dome of Kubla Khan*	18	[I] 2f	Rogers	*Once Upon a Time, Five Fairy Tales*	9	1
Halffter	*Deux Esquisses Symphoniques*	10	[C]	Schönberg	*A Survivor from Warsaw*	5	25
Honegger	*Chant de Joie*	12	1	Siegmeister	*Western Suite*	65	[35]
Honegger	*Suite d'Orchestre, "L'Impératrice aux Rochers"*	16	1	Stillman-Kelley	*Gulliver—His Voyage to Lilliput*	87	2
Honegger	*Symphonie No. IV*	65	[9]	Stillman-Kelley	*New England Symphony*	15	[D]
Ibert	*Escales*	46	[41] 2f	Strang	*Intermezzo*	13	82
Ibert	*La Ballade de la Geôle de Reading*	95	5b [71]	Stravinsky	*Fire-Bird Suite (1919)*	1	[1] 3f
Ibert	*Ouverture de Fête*	33	1	Vaughan Williams	*Job, A Masque for Dancing*	6	[B]
Khachaturian	*Concerto for Piano and Orchestra*	52	[390]			82	8
Knipper	*Symphony No. 4*	65	[19]	Wagner, R.	*Prelude and Love Death from "Tristan und Isolde"*	21	112
				Walton	*Concerto for Violin and Orchestra*	27	[15]
						89	[45] 3f

SOLI PARTS

Bass (contd.)

(2) 3

COMPOSER	WORK	PAGE	MEASURE	COMPOSER	WORK	PAGE	MEASURE
Kodály	*Te Deum*	75	[415]	**Poulenc**	*Concert Champêtre*		
Liadov	*The Enchanted Lake*	27	4		*pour Clavecin et*		
Mahler	*Symphony No. 3*	53	[37] 9f		*Orchestre*	9	5b [7]
Malipiero	*Impressioni dal Vero,*	4	[2]	**Schönberg**	*A Survivor from Warsaw*	4	16
	Iᵃ Parte	10	2				

(3) 4

COMPOSER	WORK	PAGE	MEASURE	COMPOSER	WORK	PAGE	MEASURE
Albéniz– Arbós	*Fête-Dieu à Séville*	41	1	**Hill**	*Lilacs*	15	4
Albéniz– Arbós	*Navarra*	2	[A]	**Honegger**	*Musique pour la "Phaedre" de G. D'Annunzio*	6	[4]
Aubert	*Saisons*	1	1	**Martinet**	*Orphée*	16	[8]
Bax	*Second Symphony*	129	2b [10]	**Respighi**	*The Fountains of Rome*	54	1
Berlioz	*Roméo et Juliette*	225	14	**Rimsky- Korsakoff**	*Le Coq d'Or Suite*	44	1
Bloch	*Evocations*	4	[4]	**Rimsky- Korsakoff**	*Scheherazade*	47	3
Bloch	*Schelomo*	67	[42] 1f	**Schelling**	*A Victory Ball*	69	4b [21]
Bloch	*Trois Poèmes Juifs*	40	1	**Schönberg**	*Fünf Orchesterstücke*	28	3b [11]
Debussy	*Iberia*	6	[3] 4f	**Schuman, W.**	*Symphony No. IV*	2	9
Debussy	*La Mer*	108	1	**Scriabin**	*Prométhée, Le Poème du Feu*	15	[8] 2f
Debussy	*Nuages*	16	[9]			73	[55] 2f
Debussy	*Première Rhapsodie*	2	4	**Wagner, R.**	*Funeral Music from "Götterdämmerung"*	6	27
Debussy	*Rondes de Printemps*	15	[8]				
Dukas	*La Péri*	60	1				
Gershwin	*An American in Paris*	29	[26]				

(4) 5

COMPOSER	WORK	PAGE	MEASURE
Hill	*Lilacs*	47	7

(5) 6

COMPOSER	WORK	PAGE	MEASURE	COMPOSER	WORK	PAGE	MEASURE
Rachmaninoff	*The Bells*	114	5b [119]	**Scriabin**	*Le Divin Poème*	151	3

Violin (I or II) and Viola

(1) 1–2*

COMPOSER	WORK	PAGE	MEASURE	COMPOSER	WORK	PAGE	MEASURE
Schönberg	*A Survivor from Warsaw*	4	18	**Strauss, R.**	*Also Sprach Zarathustra*	164	1

(2) 1–3

COMPOSER	WORK	PAGE	MEASURE	COMPOSER	WORK	PAGE	MEASURE
Milhaud	*IIᵉ Symphonie*	76	[125] 2f	**Strauss, R.**	*Eine Alpensinfonie*	103	[98] 4f

* Figures refer to number of *soli* instruments; i.e., 1 Vln. I (or II) — 2 Vla.

STRINGS

Violin (I or II) and Viola (contd.)

(3) 1-4

COMPOSER	WORK	PAGE	MEASURE
Dukelsky	*Symphony No. 3*	**13**	[6]

(4) 2-1

COMPOSER	WORK	PAGE	MEASURE	COMPOSER	WORK	PAGE	MEASURE
Allende	*3 Tonadas*	**10**	3	**Milhaud**	*Opus Americanum No. 2*	**21**	[135] 1f
Bloch	*Trois Poèmes Juifs*	**55**	6	**Moross**	*Paeans*	**10**	1
Chávez	*Sinfonia de Antigona*	**9**	[8] 7f	**Ravel**	*Rapsodie Espagnole*	**31**	[3]
Milhaud	*Concerto pour Piano et Orchestre*	**23**	[10] 2f	**Strauss, R.**	*Till Eulenspiegel's Merry Pranks*	**20**	7b [15]
Milhaud	*Deuxième Concerto pour Violoncelle et Orchestre*	**26**	[75]				

(5) 2-2

COMPOSER	WORK	PAGE	MEASURE	COMPOSER	WORK	PAGE	MEASURE
Barraine	*Deuxième Symphonie*	**48**	[1]	**Milhaud**	*Deuxième Concerto pour Violoncelle et Orchestre*	**54**	[55]
Debussy	*Iberia*	**72**	[48]				
Dvořák	*Die Waldtaube*	**52**	[20]				
Milhaud	*Deuxième Concerto pour Violon et Orchestre*	**63**	[65] 4f	**Milhaud**	*Le Bal Martiniquais*	**16**	2b [75]
				Rosenthal	*Les Petits Métiers*	**27**	2
				Strauss, R.	*Also Sprach Zarathustra*	**127**	5

(6) 2-3

Stravinsky	*Petrouchka Suite*	**45**	[34]

(7) 2-4

Walton	*Concerto for Violin and Orchestra*	**63**	[32] 3f

(8) 3-1

COMPOSER	WORK	PAGE	MEASURE	COMPOSER	WORK	PAGE	MEASURE
Albéniz- Arbós	*Triana*	**4**	3	**Respighi**	*Vetrate di Chiesa*	**88**	[25]
Respighi	*Metamorphoseon, XII Modi*	**42**	[21]	**Stravinsky**	*Scherzo à la Russe*	**10**	[9] 1f
				Whithorne	*Fata Morgana*	**23**	2

(9) 3-2

Bartók	*Second Rhapsody for Violin and Orchestra*	**9**	[5]

(10) 4-1

COMPOSER	WORK	PAGE	MEASURE	COMPOSER	WORK	PAGE	MEASURE
Sibelius	*En Saga*	**63**	[P]	**Strauss, R.**	*Symphonia Domestica*	**13**	1b [15]

SOLI PARTS

Violin (I or II) and Viola (contd.)

(11) 4–2

COMPOSER	WORK	PAGE	MEASURE	COMPOSER	WORK	PAGE	MEASURE
Bartók	*Concerto for Piano and Orchestra*	98	[12]	**Schönberg**	*Theme and Variations*	5	22
Bartók	*First Rhapsody for Violin and Orchestra*	21	[8]	**Stravinsky**	*Symphony in Three Movements*	70	[123] 3f

(12) 4–3

COMPOSER	WORK	PAGE	MEASURE
Whithorne	*Fata Morgana*	29	[24]

(13) 4–4

COMPOSER	WORK	PAGE	MEASURE	COMPOSER	WORK	PAGE	MEASURE
Casella	*Pupazzetti*	37	[4]	**Holst**	*Beni Mora, Oriental Suite*	25	[6]
Hanson	*Symphony No. 2, "Romantic"*	30	[K]	**Loeffler**	*A Pagan Poem*	47	[S] 1f

(14) 5–2

COMPOSER	WORK	PAGE	MEASURE
Bloch	*Evocations*	55	[40]

(15) 6–2

COMPOSER	WORK	PAGE	MEASURE
Stravinsky	*Le Sacre du Printemps*	81	1b [95]

(16) 6–3

COMPOSER	WORK	PAGE	MEASURE
Debussy	*Iberia*	68	[46] 1f

(17) 6–6

COMPOSER	WORK	PAGE	MEASURE
Debussy	*Iberia*	20	1

(18) 7–1

COMPOSER	WORK	PAGE	MEASURE
Bax	*Third Symphony*	30	8

(19) 8–2

COMPOSER	WORK	PAGE	MEASURE
Bizet	*L'Arlésienne Suite No. 1*	34	106

(20) 8–4

COMPOSER	WORK	PAGE	MEASURE	COMPOSER	WORK	PAGE	MEASURE
Copland	*Third Symphony*	123	[108] 3f	**Thomson**	*Orchestra Suite from "The Plow that Broke the Plains"*	49	[46] 1f

503

STRINGS

Violin (I or II) and Viola (contd.)

(21) 8–8

COMPOSER	WORK	PAGE	MEASURE
Debussy	*Jeux*	**1**	5

(22) 10–4

Bizet	*L'Arlésienne Suite No. 1*	**34**	105

Violin I, II, and Viola

(1) 1–4–4★

Loeffler	*Poem, La Bonne Chanson*	**23**	[P] 3f

(2) 2–1–1

Milhaud	*Ière Symphonie*	**12**	[45] 2f

(3) 2–2–1

COMPOSER	WORK	PAGE	MEASURE	COMPOSER	WORK	PAGE	MEASURE
Copland	*El Salón México*	**20**	[21] 7f	**Honegger**	*Symphonie pour Cordes*	**1**	5
Herrmann	*Sinfonietta for String Orchestra*	**2**	[A] 2f				

(4) 2–2–2

Albéniz–Arbós	*El Albaicín*	**11**	8	**Harsanyi**	*Suite pour Orchestre*	**39**	2b [70]
Elgar	*Symphony No. 1*	**143**	[129]	**Holst**	*The Planets*	**54**	11
				Moore	*In Memoriam*	**41**	[Aa]

(5) 2–2–4

Stillman-Kelley	*New England Symphony*	**49**	4b [A]

(6) 2–4–2

Liszt	*Eine Faust-Symphonie*	**139**	2

(7) 3–2–1

Albéniz–Arbós	*Fête-Dieu à Séville*	**43**	[R] 6f	**Sibelius**	*Violin Concerto*	**88**	[4]

★ i.e., 1 Vln. I — 4 Vln. II — 4 Vla.

504

SOLI PARTS

Violin I, II, and Viola (contd.)

(8) 4–2–2

COMPOSER	WORK	PAGE	MEASURE
Stillman-Kelley	New England Symphony	147	8b [X]

(9) 4–4–4

COMPOSER	WORK	PAGE	MEASURE	COMPOSER	WORK	PAGE	MEASURE
Bizet	L'Arlésienne Suite No. 1	48	61	Mihalovici	Toccata pour Piano et Orchestre	109	1b [420]
Gershwin	An American in Paris	12	[10] 4f	Pizzetti	Concerto dell'Estate	105	1
Hindemith	Konzert für Orchester	25	2b [60]	Stillman-Kelley	New England Symphony	125	14
		34	2	Stravinsky	Scènes de Ballet	64	[106]
Hindemith	Symphony in E-Flat	85	[44]				

(10) 6–4–2

COMPOSER	WORK	PAGE	MEASURE
Schreker	The Birthday of the Infanta, Suite	55	[345] 2f

(11) 6–4–8

COMPOSER	WORK	PAGE	MEASURE
Debussy	Jeux	114	[79]

(12) 8–4–4

COMPOSER	WORK	PAGE	MEASURE	COMPOSER	WORK	PAGE	MEASURE
Debussy	Le Martyre de Saint Sébastien	45	1	Hill	Lilacs	4	[2]
				Hindemith	Konzert für Orchester	15	[10] 1f

(13) 8–6–6

COMPOSER	WORK	PAGE	MEASURE
Debussy	Première Rhapsodie	9	2

(14) 8–8–4

COMPOSER	WORK	PAGE	MEASURE
Stillman-Kelley	New England Symphony	53	1b [C]

(15) 8–8–8

COMPOSER	WORK	PAGE	MEASURE	COMPOSER	WORK	PAGE	MEASURE
Bizet	L'Arlésienne Suite No. 1	48	72	Pizzetti	Concerto dell'Estate	13	[5] 12f

(16) 12–6–6

COMPOSER	WORK	PAGE	MEASURE
Debussy	Jeux	33	1

STRINGS

Violin (I or II) and Violoncello

(1) 1–2

COMPOSER	WORK	PAGE	MEASURE	COMPOSER	WORK	PAGE	MEASURE
Honegger	*Concertino pour Piano et Orchestre*	20	[12] 2f	**Strauss, R.**	*Dance Suite after François Couperin*	51	1
				Strauss, R.	*Don Quixote*	12	1

(2) 1–3

COMPOSER	WORK	PAGE	MEASURE
Berg	*Three Excerpts from "Wozzeck"*	14	[365] 2f

(3) 2–1

COMPOSER	WORK	PAGE	MEASURE	COMPOSER	WORK	PAGE	MEASURE
Albéniz–Arbós	*Évocation*	7	[B] 2f	**Liszt**	*Eine Faust-Symphonie*	297	3
Debussy	*Prélude à l'après-midi d'un Faune*	22	[J] 2f	**Mahler**	*Das Lied von der Erde*	20	[21]
		28	1	**Ravel**	*Shéhérazade*	36	[18]
Debussy–Ansermet	*Six Épigraphes Antiques*	15	2	**Strauss, R.**	*Also Sprach Zarathustra*	108	2
						216	1
Herrmann	*Sinfonietta for String Orchestra*	3	[C]	**Strauss, R.**	*Don Quixote*	61	2

(4) 2–2

COMPOSER	WORK	PAGE	MEASURE	COMPOSER	WORK	PAGE	MEASURE
Debussy	*Jeux*	48	4b [33]	**Shepherd**	*Horizons*	67	3
Malipiero	*Seconda Sinfonia (Elegiaca)*	18	4b [250]	**Vaughan Williams**	*A London Symphony*	43	[BB]
Martinet	*Orphée*	57	[21] 6f				

(5) 2–4

COMPOSER	WORK	PAGE	MEASURE
Strauss, R.	*Salomé's Dance*	19	1

(6) 3–1

COMPOSER	WORK	PAGE	MEASURE
Respighi	*Metamorphoseon, XII Modi*	9	5

(7) 3–3

COMPOSER	WORK	PAGE	MEASURE	COMPOSER	WORK	PAGE	MEASURE
Schönberg	*A Survivor from Warsaw*	5	24	**Schönberg**	*Theme and Variations*	13	51

(8) 4–1

COMPOSER	WORK	PAGE	MEASURE
Siegmeister	*From my Window*	46	2b [50]

506

SOLI PARTS

Violin (I or II) and Violoncello (contd.)

(9) 4–2

COMPOSER	WORK	PAGE	MEASURE	COMPOSER	WORK	PAGE	MEASURE
Debussy–Ansermet	*Six Épigraphes Antiques*	25	I	**Pizzetti**	*Concerto dell'Estate*	77	[29] 5f
				Whithorne	*Fata Morgana*	22	[19]

(10) 4–3

COMPOSER	WORK	PAGE	MEASURE
Liszt	*Eine Faust-Symphonie*	137	[M] 2f

(11) 4–4

COMPOSER	WORK	PAGE	MEASURE
Debussy	*Rondes de Printemps*	19	I

(12) 5–1

COMPOSER	WORK	PAGE	MEASURE
Berg	*Three Excerpts from: "Wozzeck"*	19	[395] 1f

(13) 6–1

COMPOSER	WORK	PAGE	MEASURE
Bloch	*Evocations*	7	[7]

(14) 6–6

COMPOSER	WORK	PAGE	MEASURE	COMPOSER	WORK	PAGE	MEASURE
Debussy	*Gigues*	35	[21] 3f	**Debussy**	*Jeux*	18	[13]

(15) 8–2

COMPOSER	WORK	PAGE	MEASURE
Copland	*Third Symphony*	122	1b [108]

(16) 8–8

COMPOSER	WORK	PAGE	MEASURE
Debussy	*Jeux*	54	2b [37]

(17) 9–3

COMPOSER	WORK	PAGE	MEASURE
Rogers	*Elegy*	7	4

(18) 12–6

COMPOSER	WORK	PAGE	MEASURE	COMPOSER	WORK	PAGE	MEASURE
Bizet	*L'Arlésienne Suite No. 1*	34	104	**Rachmaninoff**	*The Bells*	13	[12]
Debussy	*Iberia*	57	3				

(19) 14–6

COMPOSER	WORK	PAGE	MEASURE
Bizet	*L'Arlésienne Suite No. 1*	34	103

STRINGS

Violin (I or II) and Violoncello (contd.)

(20) 16–8

COMPOSER	WORK	PAGE	MEASURE
Bizet	*L'Arlésienne Suite No. 1*	**34**	102

(21) 18–10

Bizet	*L'Arlésienne Suite No. 1*	**34**	101

Violin I, II, and Violoncello

(1) 1–1–2

Elgar	*Symphony No. 2*	**30**	4b [34]

(2) 1–3–1

Martinet	*Orphée*	**19**	12

(3) 2–2–2

COMPOSER	WORK	PAGE	MEASURE	COMPOSER	WORK	PAGE	MEASURE
Holst	*Beni Mora, Oriental Suite*	**48**	[12] 9f	**Shepherd**	*Horizons*	**16**	2

(4) 3–2–3

Borodin	*Polovetzian Dances from "Prince Igor"*	**2**	14

(5) 4–4–1

Casella	*Pupazzetti*	**38**	[5]

(6) 4–4–2

Rachmaninoff	*Rapsodie pour Piano et Orchestre*	**62**	1

(7) 4–4–4

Mihalovici	*Toccata pour Piano et Orchestre*	**114**	3b [435]

(8) 12–12–8

Rachmaninoff	*The Bells*	**96**	6b [100]

508

SOLI PARTS

Violin (I or II) and Bass

(1) 2–1

COMPOSER	WORK	PAGE	MEASURE
Herrmann	*Sinfonietta for String Orchestra*	4	7b [F]

(2) 2–2

Malipiero	*Impressioni dal Vero, 3ª Parte*	21	[11]

(3) 2–3

Ravel	*Rapsodie Espagnole*	61	2

(4) 2–4

Revueltas	*Cuauhnahuac*	27	[41]

(5) 4–2

Diamond	*Timon of Athens*	23	147

(6) 8–2

Debussy	*Gigues*	33	[19] 2f

Violin I, II, and Bass

(1) 1–1–3

Schönberg	*A Survivor from Warsaw*	3	13

(2) 2–2–1

Villa-Lobos	*Uirapurú*	77	1

(3) 4–4–2

Pizzetti	*Concerto dell'Estate*	70	2

(4) 6–4–2

Rogers	*Elegy*	6	[5]

509

STRINGS

Viola and Violoncello

(1) 1–2

COMPOSER	WORK	PAGE	MEASURE	COMPOSER	WORK	PAGE	MEASURE
Casella	*Pupazzetti*	15	4b [2]	Schönberg	*Fünf Orchesterstücke*	21	[3]
Milhaud	*Deuxième Concerto pour*			Schuman, W.	*Undertow*	12	[140] 7f
	Violon et Orchestre	60	[45] 2f	Stravinsky	*Orpheus*	36	[94]

(2) 1–3

COMPOSER	WORK	PAGE	MEASURE
Milhaud	*IIe Symphonie*	56	[60] 1f

(3) 1–4

Albéniz-Arbós	*Navarra*	7	[C] 1f

(4) 2–1

COMPOSER	WORK	PAGE	MEASURE	COMPOSER	WORK	PAGE	MEASURE
Ravel	*La Valse*	62	1b [46]	Stravinsky	*Fire-Bird Suite* (1919)	52	[26]
Siegmeister	*Ozark Set*	51	4b [25]	Wagner, R.	*Forest Murmurs from*		
Strauss, R.	*Eine Alpensinfonie*	37	[34] 1f		*"Siegfried"*	20	139
Stravinsky	*Concerto en Ré pour*						
	Orchestre à Cordes	7	[24]				

(5) 2–2

COMPOSER	WORK	PAGE	MEASURE	COMPOSER	WORK	PAGE	MEASURE
Britten	*The Young Person's*			Schuman, W.	*Prayer in Time of War*	2	38
	Guide to the Orchestra	36	4	Szymanowski	*Symphonie Concertante*		
Coppola	*Suite Intima*	66	6		*pour Piano et*		
Elgar	*Symphony No. 2*	160	[153]		*Orchestre*	26	[14]
de Falla	*Three Dances from "The*			Turina	*La Procesión del Rocío*	21	7
	Three-Cornered Hat"	23	9	Vaughan			
Gould	*Spirituals*	7	8b [E]	Williams	*A London Symphony*	51	3b [GG]
Milhaud	*Ière Symphonie*	28	2b [105]	Vaughan	*Job, A Masque for*		
Schönberg	*Fünf Orchesterstücke*	29	1b [12]	Williams	*Dancing*	10	[D]

(6) 2–4

COMPOSER	WORK	PAGE	MEASURE	COMPOSER	WORK	PAGE	MEASURE
Stravinsky	*Le Sacre du Printemps*	77	[87]	Tchaikovsky	*Ouverture Solennelle,*		
					1812	1	1

(7) 3–2

COMPOSER	WORK	PAGE	MEASURE	COMPOSER	WORK	PAGE	MEASURE
Britten	*Passacaglia from "Peter*			Casella	*Pupazzetti*	16	|3|
	Grimes"	28	1				

510

SOLI PARTS

Viola and Violoncello (contd.)

(8) 3–3

COMPOSER	WORK	PAGE	MEASURE	COMPOSER	WORK	PAGE	MEASURE
Bartók	Violin Concerto	105	[349]	Rogers	Characters from Hans		
Read	Sketches of the City	5	[2]		Christian Andersen	17	4
				Schönberg	Theme and Variations	41	201

(9) 4–1

COMPOSER	WORK	PAGE	MEASURE
Bloch	Hiver–Printemps	30	[4] 8f

(10) 4–2

Albéniz–Arbós	Triana	19	2

(11) 4–3

Shostakovich	Symphony No. 1	59	[21]	Stravinsky	Le Sacre du Printemps	21	[30]

(12) 4–4

COMPOSER	WORK	PAGE	MEASURE	COMPOSER	WORK	PAGE	MEASURE
Debussy	Rondes de Printemps	12	1	Strauss, R.	Macbeth	79	[Dd] 3f
Rachmaninoff	Die Toteninsel	40	[15]	Vaughan	Concerto Accademico		
Read	Sketches of the City	3	1	Williams	for Violin and String		
Shepherd	Horizons	49	1		Orchestra	9	[Q]
		69	[M] 2f				

(13) 4–8

Rachmaninoff	Symphony No. 2	125	1
		141	[53]

(14) 5–5

Stravinsky	Concerto en Ré pour Orchestre à Cordes	13	[44]

(15) 6–6

Debussy	Gigues	2	4b [1]	Rachmaninoff	2d Concerto pour Piano et Orchestre	50	[18]

(16) 8–4

Whithorne	Fata Morgana	7	[8]

(17) 8–8

Debussy	Gigues	3	3

511

STRINGS

Viola and Bass

(1) 1–4

COMPOSER	WORK	PAGE	MEASURE
Debussy–Ansermet	*Six Épigraphes Antiques*	**19**	[E]

(2) 2–1

Bloch	*Evocations*	**52**	[38] 2f

(3) 2–2

COMPOSER	WORK	PAGE	MEASURE	COMPOSER	WORK	PAGE	MEASURE
Debussy–Ansermet	*Six Épigraphes Antiques*	**35**	I	**Schönberg**	*Theme and Variations*	**27**	II4

Violoncello and Bass

(1) 1–2

Fitelberg	*Nocturne for Orchestra*	**19**	[95] 6f	**Villa-Lobos**	*Uirapurú*	**90**	4

(2) 1–4

Stravinsky	*Concerto en Ré pour Orchestre à Cordes*	**17**	[60] If

(3) 1–6

Stravinsky	*Le Sacre du Printemps*	**7**	[10]

(4) 2–1

Bloch	*Hiver–Printemps*	**3**	I	**Debussy–Ansermet**	*Six Épigraphes Antiques*	**18**	[D]

(5) 2–2

Bax	*Fifth Symphony*	**63**	[40]	**Mahler**	*Symphony No. 2*	**15**	4
Casella	*Pupazzetti*	**15**	[2]	**Moeran**	*Symphony in G minor*	**173**	[117] If
Egge	*Symphony No. I*	**83**	[10] 4f	**Szymanowski**	*Symphonie Concertante pour Piano et*	**56**	[6] If
		92	5b [18]		*Orchestre*	**64**	[I]
Elgar	*Falstaff*	**145**	[145]				
Halffter	*Deux Esquisses Symphoniques*	**21**	Ib [A]	**Walton**	*Concerto for Violin and Orchestra*	**165**	[82]

(6) 2–3

Ravel	*Rapsodie Espagnole*	**59**	3

SOLI PARTS

Violoncello and Bass (contd.)

(7) 3–1

COMPOSER	WORK	PAGE	MEASURE	COMPOSER	WORK	PAGE	MEASURE
Debussy–Ansermet	*Six Épigraphes Antiques*	76	1	**Grieg**	*Suite for Strings, "From Holberg's Time"*	8	[F]

(8) 3–2

COMPOSER	WORK	PAGE	MEASURE
Shostakovich	*Symphony No. 1*	85	[36]

(9) 3–3

Barber	*Second Symphony*	53	1

(10) 3–4

Charpentier	*Impressions d'Italie*	127	3

(11) 4–1

COMPOSER	WORK	PAGE	MEASURE	COMPOSER	WORK	PAGE	MEASURE
Pierné	*Divertissements sur un Thème Pastorale*	35	1	**Stravinsky**	*Pulcinella Suite*	57	[97]

(12) 4–2

COMPOSER	WORK	PAGE	MEASURE	COMPOSER	WORK	PAGE	MEASURE
Casella	*Paganiniana*	90	1	**Stillman-Kelley**	*Gulliver—His Voyage to Lilliput*	77	[A]

(13) 4–4

COMPOSER	WORK	PAGE	MEASURE	COMPOSER	WORK	PAGE	MEASURE
d'Indy	*Jour d'été à la Montagne*	60	[29] 1f	**Schönberg**	*Fünf Orchesterstücke*	32	[1]
Pizzetti	*Concerto dell'Estate*	52	[20]	**Strauss, R.**	*Also Sprach Zarathustra*	61	1
Read	*Symphony No. 1*	137	5	**Walton**	*Concerto for Viola and Orchestra*	69	[61]
Rogers	*Once Upon a Time, Five Fairy Tales*	11	[8]				

(14) 5–1

Malipiero	*Pause del Silenzio*	30	183

(15) 6–2

Rimsky-Korsakoff	*Russian Easter Overture*	42	[M]

(16) 6–3

Bax	*Second Symphony*	82	[4]

513

STRINGS

Violoncello and Bass (contd.)

(17) 6–4

COMPOSER	WORK	PAGE	MEASURE	COMPOSER	WORK	PAGE	MEASURE
Debussy	*Iberia*	55	5	**Scriabin**	*Le Poème de l'Extase*	12	1
Mahler	*Symphony No. 9*	56	7			109	1

(18) 6–6

COMPOSER	WORK	PAGE	MEASURE
Rachmaninoff	*The Bells*	41	[45]

Violin (I or II), Viola, and Violoncello

(1) 1–1–2★

Bartók	First Rhapsody for Violin and Orchestra	26	[10] 4f	Vaughan Williams	Pastoral Symphony	8	1
Mahler	*Symphony No. 4*	102	242	**Villa-Lobos**	*Amazonas*	16	1

(2) 1–1–4

Ravel	*Rapsodie Espagnole*	68	1	**Szymanowski**	*Symphonie Concertante pour Piano et Orchestre*	51	2

(3) 1–2–1

de Falla	*El Retablo de Maese Pedro*	1	3	**Schönberg**	*Theme and Variations*	11	43

(4) 1–2–2

Bloch	*Trois Poèmes Juifs*	59	1b [13]	**Stravinsky**	*Chant du Rossignol*	74	2b [82]

(5) 1–2–3

Strauss, R.	*Also Sprach Zarathustra*	10	8

(6) 1–3–1

Mahler	*Symphony No. 7*	30	[24]

(7) 1–3–3

Mahler	*Symphony No. 8*	159	[133]	**Schönberg**	*A Survivor from Warsaw*	7	31

★ i.e., 1 Vln. I (or II) — 1 Vla. — 2 Vlc.

SOLI PARTS

Violin (I or II), Viola, and Violoncello (contd.)

(8) 1–4–5

COMPOSER	WORK	PAGE	MEASURE
Stravinsky	*Le Sacre du Printemps*	75	[83]

(9) 2–1–1

COMPOSER	WORK	PAGE	MEASURE	COMPOSER	WORK	PAGE	MEASURE
Bloch	*Trois Poèmes Juifs*	34	1	**Strauss, R.**	*Eine Alpensinfonie*	36	[32]
Milhaud	*Ière Symphonie*	14	[55]	**Villa-Lobos**	*Chôros No. 10*	5	[C] 2f

(10) 2–1–2

COMPOSER	WORK	PAGE	MEASURE
Enesco	*2e Rhapsodie Roumaine*	26	1

(11) 2–1–4

COMPOSER	WORK	PAGE	MEASURE
Shepherd	*Horizons*	61	[G]

(12) 2–2–2

COMPOSER	WORK	PAGE	MEASURE	COMPOSER	WORK	PAGE	MEASURE
Berg	*Three Excerpts from "Wozzeck"*	40	[300] 1f	**Elgar**	*Symphony No. 1*	104 / 121	1 / 1
Britten	*Les Illuminations*	15	6	**Strauss, R.**	*Rosenkavalier Waltzes —First Sequence*	9	[7] 3f
Casella	*Elegia Eroica*	21	[26]	**Toch**	*Fünf Stücke für Kammerorchester*	7	[7] 1f
Debussy	*Jeux*	38	[27] 2f				

(13) 2–2–3

COMPOSER	WORK	PAGE	MEASURE
Berg	*Three Excerpts from "Wozzeck"*	16	1b [380]

(14) 2–5–1

COMPOSER	WORK	PAGE	MEASURE
Bloch	*Trois Poèmes Juifs*	60	1

(15) 3–1–1

COMPOSER	WORK	PAGE	MEASURE	COMPOSER	WORK	PAGE	MEASURE
Bloch	*Evocations*	16	[14]	**Mahler**	*Symphony No. 7*	210	4b [251]
Herrmann	*Sinfonietta for String Orchestra*	9	4	**Respighi**	*Feste Romane*	37	1

(16) 3–1–2

COMPOSER	WORK	PAGE	MEASURE
Bloch	*America*	72	[39] 6f

STRINGS

Violin (I or II), Viola, and Violoncello (contd.)

(17) 3–2–1

COMPOSER	WORK	PAGE	MEASURE
Milhaud	*Quatrième Symphonie*	12	[45]

(18) 3–2–2

COMPOSER	WORK	PAGE	MEASURE
Schönberg	*A Survivor from Warsaw*	5	23

(19) 3–3–1

COMPOSER	WORK	PAGE	MEASURE
Rogers	*Once Upon a Time, Five Fairy Tales*	30	[19] 2f

(20) 3–8–5

COMPOSER	WORK	PAGE	MEASURE
Whithorne	*Fata Morgana*	7	[8] 4f

(21) 4–1–1

COMPOSER	WORK	PAGE	MEASURE
Bloch	*Concerto Grosso*	10	[13]

(22) 4–1–2

COMPOSER	WORK	PAGE	MEASURE
Elgar	*In the South, Concert Overture*	56	[34] 4f

(23) 4–2–1

COMPOSER	WORK	PAGE	MEASURE
Debussy	*Gigues*	9	[5]

(24) 4–2–2

COMPOSER	WORK	PAGE	MEASURE	COMPOSER	WORK	PAGE	MEASURE
Schönberg	*Suite for String Orchestra*	21	366	**Strauss, R.**	*Salomé's Dance*	38	[K] 8f

(25) 4–4–2

COMPOSER	WORK	PAGE	MEASURE
Dukas	*Symphonie en Ut majeur*	99	[G]

(26) 4–8–4

COMPOSER	WORK	PAGE	MEASURE
Whithorne	*Fata Morgana*	9	2b [10]

SOLI PARTS

Violin (I or II), Viola, and Violoncello (contd.)

(27) 5–2–2

COMPOSER	WORK	PAGE	MEASURE
Bloch	*Hiver–Printemps*	**41**	6

(28) 6–1–1

COMPOSER	WORK	PAGE	MEASURE
Bloch	*Trois Poèmes Juifs*	**56**	[10] 4f

(29) 6–4–4

COMPOSER	WORK	PAGE	MEASURE
Inghelbrecht	*La Valse Retrouvée*	**4**	[37]

(30) 6–6–1

COMPOSER	WORK	PAGE	MEASURE
Whithorne	*Fata Morgana*	**9**	[10]

(31) 7–1–3

COMPOSER	WORK	PAGE	MEASURE
Rogers	*Elegy*	**8**	[6]

(32) 7–6–6

COMPOSER	WORK	PAGE	MEASURE
Debussy	*Jeux*	**73**	[49] 1f

Violin I, II, Viola, and Violoncello

(1) 1–1–1–2★

COMPOSER	WORK	PAGE	MEASURE	COMPOSER	WORK	PAGE	MEASURE
de Falla	*Nuits dans les Jardins d'Espagne*	82	4	**Vaughan Williams**	*Symphony in E minor (No. 6)*	**157**	[10] 5f

(2) 1–1–1–3

COMPOSER	WORK	PAGE	MEASURE
Britten	*Les Illuminations*	**17**	4

(3) 1–1–2–2

COMPOSER	WORK	PAGE	MEASURE	COMPOSER	WORK	PAGE	MEASURE
Hanson	*Symphony No. 2, "Romantic"*	**127**	[P]	**Milhaud**	*Ière Symphonie*	**63**	2b [50]

(4) 1–2–1–1

COMPOSER	WORK	PAGE	MEASURE	COMPOSER	WORK	PAGE	MEASURE
Coppola	*Suite Intima*	**55**	1b [11]	**Milhaud**	*Ière Symphonie*	**7** / **24**	[25] / [90]

★ i.e., 1 Vln. I. — 1 Vln. II — 1 Vla. — 2 Vlc.

STRINGS

Violin I, II, Viola, and Violoncello (contd.)

(5) 1–6–6–1

COMPOSER	WORK	PAGE	MEASURE
Whithorne	*Fata Morgana*	**9**	[10] 1f

(6) 1–8–4–1

Loeffler	*Poem, La Bonne Chanson*	**24**	[Q]

(7) 2–1–1–1

COMPOSER	WORK	PAGE	MEASURE	COMPOSER	WORK	PAGE	MEASURE
Bloch	*Concerto Grosso*	**33**	[42] 3f	**Shepherd**	*Horizons*	**62**	[H] 2f
Delius	*Three Orchestral Pieces*	**26**	8				

(8) 2–1–2–1

Barber	*Music for a Scene from Shelley*	**16**	96

(9) 2–1–2–3

Bartók	*First Rhapsody for Violin and Orchestra*	**27**	[11] 3f

(10) 2–2–1–1

Respighi	*The Pines of Rome*	**54**	[14]

(11) 2–2–1–2

Bartók	*Concerto for Piano and Orchestra*	**23**	[27] 4f

(12) 2–2–1–3

de Falla	*Nuits dans les Jardins d'Espagne*	**46**	[10] 6f

(13) 2–2–2–1

de Falla	*El Retablo de Maese Pedro*	**59**	[62] 3f

(14) 2–2–2–2

Bach–Respighi	*Passacaglia and Fugue in C minor*	**21**	[14]	**Harris**	*Third Symphony*	**43**	[33] 1f
Debussy	*La Mer*	**50**	4	**Levant**	*Nocturne*	**16**	55
Debussy	*Le Martyre de Saint Sébastien*	**37**	[16] 2f	**Liszt**	*Eine Faust-Symphonie*	**124**	[C] 2f
				Rachmaninoff	*The Bells*	**117**	1b [122]
Diamond	*Timon of Athens*	**32**	221	**Vaughan Williams**	*A London Symphony*	**44**	1
Dukas	*La Péri*	**128**	[19 bis]	**Whithorne**	*Fata Morgana*	**30**	[25]
Elgar	*Symphony No. 1*	**55**	[48]				

SOLI PARTS

Violin I, II, Viola, and Violoncello (contd.)

(15) 2–2–2–3

COMPOSER	WORK	PAGE	MEASURE
Bartók	*Dance Suite*	61	29

(16) 2–2–4–4

Herrmann	*Sinfonietta for String Orchestra*	9	1 (IV)

(17) 2–4–8–7

Read	*Sketches of the City*	10	[6]

(18) 3–3–3–3

Bax	*Third Symphony*	67	1

(19) 3–4–4–4

Debussy	*Première Rhapsodie*	20	2b [6]

(20) 4–1–2–1

Strauss, R.	*Symphonia Domestica*	14	1

(21) 4–1–2–2

Schönberg	*Suite for String Orchestra*	39	577

(22) 4–2–1–1

Strauss, R.	*Eine Alpensinfonie*	46	[42]

(23) 4–2–4–4

Copland	*Appalachian Spring*	24	2

(24) 4–3–4–2

Shostakovich	*Symphony No. 1*	60	[22]

(25) 4–4–2–2

COMPOSER	WORK	PAGE	MEASURE	COMPOSER	WORK	PAGE	MEASURE
Debussy	*Le Martyre de Saint Sébastien*	61	[27] 4f	Moeran	*Sinfonietta*	32	8b [46]

(26) 4–4–4–4

COMPOSER	WORK	PAGE	MEASURE	COMPOSER	WORK	PAGE	MEASURE
Albéniz–Arbós	*El Albaicín*	34	6	Dvořák	*Symphony No. 5, "From the New World"*	69	[5]
Bizet	*L'Arlésienne Suite No. 1*	16	113	Holst	*The Planets*	122	[V]
Dukelsky	*Symphony No. 3*	134	1	Janssen	*New Year's Eve in New York*	39	[15]

STRINGS

Violin I, II, Viola, and Violoncello (contd.)

(27) 5–4–2–2

COMPOSER	WORK	PAGE	MEASURE
Coppola	*Suite Intima*	20	1

(28) 6–4–2–2

Debussy–Ansermet	*Six Épigraphes Antiques*	62	4

(29) 6–6–4–3

Mahler	*Symphony No. 2*	58	[3]

(30) 8–6–8–6

Debussy	*Jeux*	117	[81]

(31) 8–8–4–4

Vaughan Williams	*Overture to "The Wasps"*	29	212

(32) 8–8–6–6

Bizet	*L'Arlésienne Suite No. 1*	16	115

(33) 8–8–8–6

Rogers	*Once Upon a Time, Five Fairy Tales*	32	[20]

(34) 8–8–8–8

Hill	*Lilacs*	5	3

(35) 9–8–2–1

Whithorne	*The Dream Pedlar*	54	[27]

(36) 9–9–8–2

Martinet	*Orphée*	11	1

(37) 12–12–8–8

Bizet	*L'Arlésienne Suite No. 1*	16	117

(38) 12–12–12–3

Debussy	*Jeux*	75	2

520

SOLI PARTS

Violin (I or II), Viola, and Bass

(1) 1–1–2

COMPOSER	WORK	PAGE	MEASURE
Ravel	*Rapsodie Espagnole*	**69**	1

(2) 4–4–1

de Falla	*El Amor Brujo*	**93**	1

(3) 4–4–2

Stillman-Kelley	*Gulliver—His Voyage to Lilliput*	**81**	13

(4) 4–5–1

de Falla	*El Amor Brujo*	**85**	1

(5) 6–6–4

Debussy	*Iberia*	**77**	[50] 2f

Violin I, II, Viola, and Bass

(1) 2–1–1–1

Gould	*Philharmonic Waltzes*	**17**	6b [172]

(2) 2–2–2–2

Tchaikovsky	*Nutcracker Suite*	**116**	5

(3) 4–4–4–2

Holst	*The Planets*	**160**	[VIII]

Violin (I or II), Violoncello, and Bass

(1) 1–1–2

Coppola	*Symphonie en La mineur*	**7**	5

(2) 1–4–4

Szymanowski	*Symphonie Concertante pour Piano et Orchestre*	**86**	[20]

(3) 2–2–1

Strauss, R.	*Ein Heldenleben*	**172**	[87]

STRINGS

Violin (I or II), Violoncello, and Bass (contd.)

(4) 2–2–3

COMPOSER	WORK	PAGE	MEASURE
Bloch	*Evocations*	**49**	2

(5) 2–4–2

Debussy	*Jeux*	**64**	[43]

(6) 3–3–2

Dukas	*La Péri*	**90**	I

(7) 3–4–2

Antheil	*Symphony No. 5*	**71**	[54] 7f

(8) 4–2–2

Szymanowski	*Symphonie Concertante pour Piano et Orchestre*	**14**	4b [8]

(9) 4–3–5

Schönberg	*Fünf Orchesterstücke*	**35**	[5]

(10) 5–2–2

Read	*Symphony No. I*	**I**	I

(11) 10–4–2

Debussy	*Rondes de Printemps*	**22**	3

(12) 16–6–4

Debussy	*Iberia*	**56**	[38]

Violin I, II, Violoncello, and Bass

(1) 4–3–3–3

Kodály	*Psalmus Hungaricus*	**43**	[26]

(2) 6–4–1–2

Berlioz	*Three Pieces from "The Damnation of Faust"*	**34**	9

SOLI PARTS

Viola, Violoncello, and Bass

(1) 1–1–2

COMPOSER	WORK	PAGE	MEASURE
Maganini	*South Wind*	8	[G]

(2) 1–2–2

Loeffler	*A Pagan Poem*	3	1

(3) 1–4–4

Copland	*First Symphony*	7	[8] 7f

(4) 2–1–1

Stravinsky	*Fire-Bird Suite* (1919)	53	2b [27]

(5) 2–2–1

Sibelius	*Violin Concerto*	75	5
		86	[3]

(6) 2–2–2

COMPOSER	WORK	PAGE	MEASURE	COMPOSER	WORK	PAGE	MEASURE
Berg	*Violin Concerto*	45	[220] 2f	**Schönberg**	*A Survivor from Warsaw*	14	67
Ravel	*Rapsodie Espagnole*	60	6				

(7) 2–2–3

Bloch	*Trois Poèmes Juifs*	60	10

(8) 2–3–1

Herrmann	*Sinfonietta for String Orchestra*	10	16

(9) 2–6–1

Stillman-Kelley	*Gulliver—His Voyage to Lilliput*	138	[L]

(10) 3–2–4

Britten	*Passacaglia from "Peter Grimes"*	29	[12] 4f

(11) 4–2–4

Debussy	*Le Martyre de Saint Sébastien*	62	1

523

STRINGS

Viola, Violoncello, and Bass (contd.)

(12) 4–4–1

COMPOSER	WORK	PAGE	MEASURE
de Falla	*Nuits dans les Jardins d'Espagne*	**35**	1

(13) 4–4–4

COMPOSER	WORK	PAGE	MEASURE	COMPOSER	WORK	PAGE	MEASURE
Dukelsky	*Symphony No. 3*	**1**	1	**Strauss, R.**	*Ein Heldenleben*	**174**	[88]

(14) 6–2–2

Stravinsky	*Le Sacre du Printemps*	**80**	[91]

(15) 6–6–4

COMPOSER	WORK	PAGE	MEASURE	COMPOSER	WORK	PAGE	MEASURE
Casella	*Elegia Eroica*	**34**	[51]	**Rachmaninoff**	*The Bells*	**45**	[52] 6f

(16) 6–6–6

Debussy	*Le Martyre de Saint Sébastien*	**63**	3

(17) 8–4–2

Copland	*Concerto for Piano and Orchestra*	**59**	[44] 1f

Violin (I or II), Viola, Violoncello, and Bass

(1) 1–1–1–2★

Coppola	*Suite Intima*	**41**	4

(2) 1–4–4–2

Bax	*Second Symphony*	**100**	2b [16]

(3) 1–5–2–6

Stravinsky	*Le Sacre du Printemps*	**9**	[11]

(4) 1–6–6–4

Britten	*Les Illuminations*	**18**	1

★ i.e., 1 Vln. I (or II) — 1 Vla. — 1 Vlc. — 2 Bs.

SOLI PARTS

Violin (I or II), Viola, Violoncello, and Bass (contd.)

(5) 2–1–1–1

COMPOSER	WORK	PAGE	MEASURE
Prokofieff	Romeo and Juliet, Suite No. 2	65	[43]

(6) 2–1–2–1

COMPOSER	WORK	PAGE	MEASURE
Debussy–Ansermet	Six Épigraphes Antiques	75	I

(7) 2–1–3–1

COMPOSER	WORK	PAGE	MEASURE
Bartók	Dance Suite	31	III

(8) 2–2–1–1

COMPOSER	WORK	PAGE	MEASURE	COMPOSER	WORK	PAGE	MEASURE
Berg	Three Excerpts from "Wozzeck"	4	[320] 4f	de Falla	El Retablo de Maese Pedro	27	[30]

(9) 2–2–1–2

COMPOSER	WORK	PAGE	MEASURE
Rogers	Once Upon a Time, Five Fairy Tales	13	3

(10) 2–2–2–1

COMPOSER	WORK	PAGE	MEASURE	COMPOSER	WORK	PAGE	MEASURE
Sibelius	Violin Concerto	76	3	Walton	Concerto for Violin and Orchestra	97	7

(11) 2–3–2–1

COMPOSER	WORK	PAGE	MEASURE
Schönberg	A Survivor from Warsaw	13	60

(12) 3–1–6–2

COMPOSER	WORK	PAGE	MEASURE
Ravel	Concerto pour Piano et Orchestre	29	[23] 2f

(13) 3–2–4–1

COMPOSER	WORK	PAGE	MEASURE
Schönberg	Suite for String Orchestra	22	382

(14) 4–2–2–3

COMPOSER	WORK	PAGE	MEASURE
Bartók	Violin Concerto	98	[260]

(15) 4–6–4–2

COMPOSER	WORK	PAGE	MEASURE
Walton	Symphony	113	I

525

STRINGS

Violin (I or II), Viola, Violoncello, and Bass (contd.)

(16) 5–1–1–1

COMPOSER	WORK	PAGE	MEASURE
Diamond	*Rounds for String Orchestra*	20	1

(17) 5–2–3–4

COMPOSER	WORK	PAGE	MEASURE
Rogers	*Once Upon a Time, Five Fairy Tales*	12	2b [10]

(18) 5–4–4–2

COMPOSER	WORK	PAGE	MEASURE
Casella	*Paganiniana*	91	[I]

(19) 6–6–4–4

COMPOSER	WORK	PAGE	MEASURE
Albéniz–Arbós	*El Albaicín*	11	3

(20) 6–6–6–4

COMPOSER	WORK	PAGE	MEASURE
Debussy	*Iberia*	51	[34]

Violin I, II, Viola, Violoncello, and Bass

(1) 1–1–1–1–2★

COMPOSER	WORK	PAGE	MEASURE
Hindemith	*Symphonische Tänze*	10	4b [9]

(2) 1–1–1–2–1

COMPOSER	WORK	PAGE	MEASURE	COMPOSER	WORK	PAGE	MEASURE
de Falla	*El Amor Brujo*	79	1	Prokofieff	*Symphony No. 5*	206	[113]

(3) 1–1–1–2–2

COMPOSER	WORK	PAGE	MEASURE
Bizet	*Intermezzi from "Carmen"*	8	1

(4) 1–1–1–3–1

COMPOSER	WORK	PAGE	MEASURE
Herrmann	*Sinfonietta for String Orchestra*	11	11

(5) 1–1–1–3–2

COMPOSER	WORK	PAGE	MEASURE
Pierné	*Viennoise*	2	2

★ i.e., 1 Vln. I — 1 Vln. II — 1 Vla. — 1 Vlc. — 2 Bs.

SOLI PARTS

Violin I, II, Viola, Violoncello, and Bass (contd.)

(6) 1–1–1–5–2

COMPOSER	WORK	PAGE	MEASURE
Pierné	*Divertissements sur un Thème Pastorale*	**14**	2

(7) 1–1–1–6–2

Stravinsky	*Le Sacre du Printemps*	**62**	1b [72]

(8) 1–1–2–1–1

Milhaud	*Deuxième Concerto pour Violon et Orchestre*	**76**	[120]

(9) 1–1–2–2–1

Sessions	*Symphony for Orchestra (No. 1)*	**39**	3b [59]

(10) 1–2–1–2–2

Poulenc	*Concert Champêtre pour Clavecin et Orchestre*	**70**	[8] 1f

(11) 2–1–1–1–1

Strauss, R.	*Eine Alpensinfonie*	**38**	[36]

(12) 2–1–1–2–1

Gould	*Philharmonic Waltzes*	**17**	[172]

(13) 2–1–2–1–1

Rozsa	*Concerto for String Orchestra*	**39**	[97] 1f

(14) 2–2–1–5–4

Whithorne	*Fata Morgana*	**48**	[52]

(15) 2–2–2–1–1

de Falla	*El Retablo de Maese Pedro*	**71**	[72] 1f

527

STRINGS

Violin I, II, Viola, Violoncello, and Bass (contd.)

(16) 2–2–2–1–2

COMPOSER	WORK	PAGE	MEASURE
Lambert	The Rio Grande	51	[27]

(17) 2–2–2–2–1

COMPOSER	WORK	PAGE	MEASURE	COMPOSER	WORK	PAGE	MEASURE
de Falla	El Amor Brujo	9	[3] 1f	Miaskovsky	Symphony No. 8	127	[27]
		64	1	Sibelius	Violin Concerto	112	1
Herrmann	Sinfonietta for String Orchestra	10	1				

(18) 2–2–2–2–2

COMPOSER	WORK	PAGE	MEASURE	COMPOSER	WORK	PAGE	MEASURE
Busoni	Rondo Arlecchinesco	19	[18] 3f	Grofé	Grand Canyon Suite	68	[F]
Casella	Pupazzetti	18	[5]				

(19) 2–2–3–3–2

COMPOSER	WORK	PAGE	MEASURE
Rozsa	Concerto for String Orchestra	23	[28]

(20) 3–2–2–2–1

COMPOSER	WORK	PAGE	MEASURE
Dohnányi	Variations on a Nursery Song	102	2

(21) 3–2–2–4–6

COMPOSER	WORK	PAGE	MEASURE
Whithorne	Fata Morgana	34	[30]

(22) 3–2–3–3–3

COMPOSER	WORK	PAGE	MEASURE
Milhaud	IIᵉ Symphonie	46	[180] 1f

(23) 3–3–3–3–1

COMPOSER	WORK	PAGE	MEASURE
Milhaud	Les Choéphores	140	[B] 3f

(24) 3–3–3–3–2

COMPOSER	WORK	PAGE	MEASURE
Bax	Sixth Symphony	123	1

(25) 4–2–2–1–1

COMPOSER	WORK	PAGE	MEASURE
Ravel	Valses Nobles et Sentimentales	72	4b [73]

SOLI PARTS

Violin I, II, Viola, Violoncello, and Bass (contd.)

(26) 4–3–2–2–1

COMPOSER	WORK	PAGE	MEASURE
Strauss, R.	*Dance Suite after François Couperin*	**44**	1

(27) 4–3–4–6–2

COMPOSER	WORK	PAGE	MEASURE
Strauss, R.	*Also Sprach Zarathustra*	**11**	1

(28) 4–4–2–2–2

COMPOSER	WORK	PAGE	MEASURE
Vaughan Williams	*Concerto Accademico for Violin and String Orchestra*	**5**	6b [G]

(29) 4–4–2–4–1

COMPOSER	WORK	PAGE	MEASURE
Schönberg	*Suite for String Orchestra*	**23**	390

(30) 4–4–2–4–2

COMPOSER	WORK	PAGE	MEASURE
de Falla	*Nuits dans les Jardins d'Espagne*	**46**	[11]

(31) 4–4–3–3–3

COMPOSER	WORK	PAGE	MEASURE
Bartók	*Dance Suite*	**32**	[21]

(32) 4–4–4–1–1

COMPOSER	WORK	PAGE	MEASURE
Shostakovich	*Symphony No. 1*	**11**	[18]

(33) 4–4–4–2–2

COMPOSER	WORK	PAGE	MEASURE
Allende	*3 Tonadas*	**3**	[3]

(34) 4–4–4–4–2

COMPOSER	WORK	PAGE	MEASURE	COMPOSER	WORK	PAGE	MEASURE
McDonald	*Rhumba from 2nd Symphony*	**3**	[10] 2f	Tchaikovsky	*Nutcracker Suite*	**50**	1

(35) 4–4–4–4–4

COMPOSER	WORK	PAGE	MEASURE	COMPOSER	WORK	PAGE	MEASURE
Delius	*Three Orchestral Pieces*	**11**	1b [9]	Loeffler	*Evocation*	**20**	[12]
Dukelsky	*Symphony No. 3*	**6**	3	Schelling	*A Victory Ball*	**92**	[28a]
Grofé	*Grand Canyon Suite*	**68**	[F] 3f				

STRINGS

Violin I, II, Viola, Violoncello, and Bass (contd.)

(36) 5–4–4–5–2

COMPOSER	WORK	PAGE	MEASURE
Read	*Sketches of the City*	**20**	[8]

(37) 5–5–5–5–3

Strauss, R.	*Metamorphosen*	**3**	I

(38) 6–4–4–3–2

Mahler	*Symphony No. 5*	**169**	[30] 12f

(39) 6–6–4–4–2

de Falla	*Nuits dans les Jardins d'Espagne*	**37**	[3]

(40) 6–6–4–6–4

Ibert	*Escales*	**37**	I

(41) 6–6–6–4–4

Thomson	*Louisiana Story Suite*	**16**	85

(42) 6–8–8–8–4

Strauss, R.	*Also Sprach Zarathustra*	**12**	6

(43) 7–7–5–1–4

Debussy	*Première Rhapsodie*	**18**	3

(44) 8–8–5–4–2

Albéniz–Arbós	*El Puerto*	**34**	[N]

(45) 8–8–6–4–2

Vaughan Williams	*Concerto Accademico for Violin and String Orchestra*	**3**	[D]

(46) 8–8–6–4–4

COMPOSER	WORK	PAGE	MEASURE	COMPOSER	WORK	PAGE	MEASURE
Vaughan Williams	*Concerto Accademico for Violin and String Orchestra*	**1** **14** **21**	[A] 3f I [D] 1f	Vaughan Williams	*Pastoral Symphony*	**75**	I

SOLI PARTS

Violin I, II, Viola, Violoncello, and Bass (contd.)

(47) 8–8–8–8–8

COMPOSER	WORK	PAGE	MEASURE
Whithorne	*Fata Morgana*	47	[50]

(48) 10–10–6–6–4

Bartók	*Dance Suite*	43	[31]

Chapter 61

CHORD NOTATION

(1)

Violin I

COMPOSER	WORK	PAGE	MEASURE	COMPOSER	WORK	PAGE	MEASURE
Beethoven	*Leonore Overture No. 2*	1	1	**Mozart**	*Overture to*	4	23
Beethoven	*Piano Concerto No. 3*	2	24		*"Il Seraglio"*	14	109
		12	138	**Mozart**	*Symphony No. 40 in*		
Beethoven	*Piano Concerto No. 5*	89	491		*G minor*	17	192
Beethoven	*Symphony No. 6,*			**Mozart**	*Violin Concerto No. III*		
	"Pastoral"	74	203		*in G major*	19	160
Beethoven	*Symphony No. 7*	8	[A]	**Ravel**	*Daphnis et Chloé,*		
		10	40		*Suite No. 2*	115	2
Beethoven	*Symphony No. 8*	59	12	**Schumann, R.**	*Concerto for Violon-*	18	158
Brahms	*Violin Concerto in*				*cello and Orchestra*	68	550
	D major	17	[E]	**Schumann, R.**	*Symphony No. 1*	93	[G]
Grieg	*Piano Concerto in*			**Schumann, R.**	*Symphony No. 2*	36	239
	A minor	30	175	**Schumann, R.**	*Symphony No. 3*	1	1
Honegger	*Mouvement*					32	281
	Symphonique No. 3	8	2			61	562
Mahler	*Symphony No. 3*	33	[25]	**Scriabin**	*Piano Concerto in*		
Mendelssohn	*A Midsummer Night's*	11	120		*F♯ minor*	22	9
	Dream Overture	21	231	**Sibelius**	*Finlandia*	6	1
Mozart	*Ballet Music, "Les*			**Strauss, R.**	*Also Sprach*		
	Petits Riens"	1	1		*Zarathustra*	157	5
Mozart	*Horn Concerto No. II*	1	5	**Strauss, R.**	*Macbeth*	51	[S]
	in E♭ major	7	83	**Walton**	*Symphony*	187	[139] 1f
Mozart	*Overture to*						
	"Don Giovanni"	1	1				

Solo Violin I

COMPOSER	WORK	PAGE	MEASURE
Strauss, R.	*Also Sprach Zarathustra*	128	7

Violin II

COMPOSER	WORK	PAGE	MEASURE	COMPOSER	WORK	PAGE	MEASURE
Beethoven	*Symphony No. 7*	3	15	**Mozart**	*Piano Concerto (No. 23)*		
Mahler	*Das Lied von der Erde*	6	[3]		*in A major*	73	[E]
				Sibelius	*Symphony No. 5*	109	4

532

CHORD NOTATION

Violin I and II

COMPOSER	WORK	PAGE	MEASURE	COMPOSER	WORK	PAGE	MEASURE
Beethoven	*Consecration of the House, Overture*	55	200	Mozart	*Overture to "The Marriage of Figaro"*	24	292
Beethoven	*Piano Concerto No. 5*	6	19	Mozart	*Piano Concerto (No. 23)*	19	[G]
Beethoven	*Symphony No. 5*	43	149		*in A major*	59	3b [A]
		71	2	Mozart	*Symphony No. 39 in*	8	[B]
Beethoven	*The Ruins of Athens, Overture*	7	33		*Eb major*	42	1
		28	133	Mozart	*Symphony No. 41 in*		
Bloch	*America*	87	[51]		*C major, "Jupiter"*	84	420
Brahms	*Symphony No. 1*	7	41	Mozart	*Titus Overture*	1	1
Brahms	*Violin Concerto in*	21	348			8	4
	D major	32	525			22	7
Dunn	*Overture on Negro Themes*	3	1	Mozart	*Violin Concerto No. III in G major*	1	5
Flotow	*Alessandro Stradella*			Respighi	*Feste Romane*	132	[41]
	Overture	28	273	Respighi	*Vetrate di Chiesa*	55	1
d'Indy	*Deuxième Symphonie*			Rossini	*Semiramide, Overture*	5	37
	en Sib	68	1	Saint-Saëns	*Suite Algérienne*	81	13
Mahler	*Symphony No. 6*	73	[43]	Schumann, R.	*Symphony No. 1*	42	[C] 4f
Mendelssohn	*Symphony No. 3, "Scotch"*	135	226	Schumann, R.	*Symphony No. 4*	66	15
				Strauss, R.	*Also Sprach Zarathustra*	150	5
Mozart	*Concerto for 2 Pianos in Eb major*	16	147	Strauss, R.	*Oboe Concerto*	12	4
Mozart	*Overture to "The Impressario"*	16	14	Stravinsky	*Orpheus*	53	2b [137]

Viola

Beethoven	*Symphony No. 9*	233	637	Sibelius	*Symphony No. 1*	8	[D]
Mahler	*Symphony No. 9*	150	1				

Violoncello

Honegger	*Symphonie No. IV*	60	2	Shostakovich	*Symphony No. 7*	173	[207]

Violin I and Viola

COMPOSER	WORK	PAGE	MEASURE
Bloch	*Concerto Grosso*	1	1

Violin II and Viola

Mahler	*Symphony No. 5*	230	4b [29]	Smetana	*From Bohemia's Woods and Fields*	31	1

Violin I, II, and Viola

Beethoven	*Symphony No. 6, "Pastoral"*	33	507	Grieg	*Piano Concerto in A minor*	72	347
Borodin	*Symphony No. 2*	36	[L]	Jacobi	*Concertino for Piano*		
Brahms	*Ein deutsches Requiem*	205	201		*and String Orchestra*	3	[2]
Brahms	*Symphony No. 4*	168	310	Mahler	*Symphony No. 6*	245	[157] 4f
Chausson	*Symphonie en Si bémol*			Mahler	*Symphony No. 7*	186	2b [225]
	majeur	26	3	Mahler	*Symphony No. 8*	43	[48]

533

STRINGS

Violin I, II, and Viola (contd.)

COMPOSER	WORK	PAGE	MEASURE	COMPOSER	WORK	PAGE	MEASURE
Mahler	*Symphony No. 9*	III	[30]	Strauss, R.	*Symphonia Domestica*	123	[160] 8f
Mozart	*Overture to*			Stravinsky	*Le Sacre du Printemps*	130	[181]
	"Il Seraglio"	35	315	Stravinsky	*Symphony in Three*		
Respighi	*Toccata per Pianoforte*				*Movements*	120	[195] 2f
	e Orchestra	78	3	Vaughan			
Schönberg	*Theme and Variations*	58	276	Williams	*A London Symphony*	61	1
Shostakovich	*Piano Concerto*	27	[30]	Vaughan	*Overture to "The*		
Smetana	*Blanik*	75	2	Williams	*Wasps"*	66	455

Violin I, Viola, and Violoncello

COMPOSER	WORK	PAGE	MEASURE	COMPOSER	WORK	PAGE	MEASURE
Bach–	*Passacaglia and Fugue*			Mahler	*Symphony No. 9*	165	5
Respighi	*in C minor*	56	4	Tchaikovsky	*Symphony No. 2*	108	3

Violin I, II, Viola, and Violoncello

COMPOSER	WORK	PAGE	MEASURE	COMPOSER	WORK	PAGE	MEASURE
Bach–	*Prelude and Fugue in*			Respighi	*Antiche Danze ed Arie,*		
Respighi	*D major*	4	5		*2ª Suite*	17	6
Mahler	*Das Lied von der Erde*	21	[23]	Sibelius	*Pelleas and Melisande*	29	13
Mahler	*Symphony No. 5*	110	[32]	Walton	*Façade, Suite No. 2*	2	10
Mahler	*Symphony No. 7*	12	[7]				

(2)

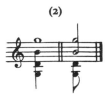

Violin I

COMPOSER	WORK	PAGE	MEASURE	COMPOSER	WORK	PAGE	MEASURE
Beethoven	*Piano Concerto No. 5*	1	1	Poulenc	*Deux Marches et un*		
Berlioz	*The Roman Carnival*				*Intermède*	20	6
	Overture	18	128	Rimsky-			
Dello Joio	*Variations, Chaconne,*			Korsakoff	*Scheherazade*	148	193
	and Finale	18	[150] 2f	Schumann, R.	*Symphony No. 2*	173	392
Mahler	*Symphony No. 4*	144	[12]	Strauss, R.	*Dance Suite after*		
Mahler	*Symphony No. 5*	230	4b [29]		*François Couperin*	119	3
				Wellesz	*Symphony in C*	60	[470] 1f

Violin II

COMPOSER	WORK	PAGE	MEASURE	COMPOSER	WORK	PAGE	MEASURE
Bach–	*Passacaglia and Fugue*			Schumann, R.	*Symphony No. 1*	118	5
Respighi	*in C minor*	56	4	Strauss, R.	*Dance Suite after*		
Mahler	*Symphony No. 6*	46	3b [29]		*François Couperin*	14	1
Rimsky-	*Capriccio Espagnol*	46	1	Strauss, R.	*Eine Alpensinfonie*	87	[85]
Korsakoff		59	[Q]	Stravinsky	*Le Sacre du Printemps*	56	[64]
		80	2				

CHORD NOTATION

Violin I and II

COMPOSER	WORK	PAGE	MEASURE	COMPOSER	WORK	PAGE	MEASURE
Berlioz	*Benvenuto Cellini Overture*	5	5	Mussorgsky	*Night on the Bald Mountain*	59	[R]
Brahms	*Violin Concerto in D major*	66	339	Rameau-Mottl	*Ballet Suite*	1	2
Britten	*The Young Person's Guide to the Orchestra*	26	5	Respighi	*Vetrate di Chiesa*	36	[11]
Elgar	*Symphony No. 1*	21	2	Rimsky-Korsakoff	*Capriccio Espagnol*	1	1
Kabalevsky	*The Comedians*	102	[88] 4f			89	2
Knipper	*Symphony No. 4*	98	[15]	Rimsky-Korsakoff	*Scheherazade*	8	[A]
		139	[45] 3f	Schumann, R.	*Symphony No. 2*	185	497
Kodály	*Marosszék Dances*	71	3b [330]	Schumann, R.	*Symphony No. 4*	124	232
Maganini	*A Suite of Music by Royalty*	12	7	Shostakovich	*Symphony No. 7*	104	[106] 1f
Mahler	*Symphony No. 8*	71	[88]			127	[142] 1f
Mozart	*Concerto for 2 Pianos in Eb major*	38	292	Stravinsky	*Le Sacre du Printemps*	46	[57] 4f
Mozart	*Overture to "The Marriage of Figaro"*	2	12	Stravinsky	*Oedipus Rex*	139	[197]
		12	150	Vaughan Williams	*A London Symphony*	25	[O] 1f

Viola

COMPOSER	WORK	PAGE	MEASURE
Britten	*The Young Person's Guide to the Orchestra*	5	4

Violoncello

COMPOSER	WORK	PAGE	MEASURE	COMPOSER	WORK	PAGE	MEASURE
Albéniz-Arbós	*Fête-Dieu à Séville*	27	1	Sibelius	*Symphony No. 2*	36	[S]
Copland	*Third Symphony*	94	[85] 1f	Strauss, R.	*Dance Suite after François Couperin*	9	3
Knipper	*Symphony No. 4*	13	[9] 4f	Strauss, R.	*Eine Alpensinfonie*	84	8b [82]

Violin I and Viola

COMPOSER	WORK	PAGE	MEASURE	COMPOSER	WORK	PAGE	MEASURE
Casella	*La Donna Serpente, II. Serie*	69	4	Respighi	*Antiche Danze ed Arie, 2ª Suite*	53	2b [15]
Ibert	*Divertissement*	62	[8] 8f				

Violin II and Viola

COMPOSER	WORK	PAGE	MEASURE	COMPOSER	WORK	PAGE	MEASURE
Borodin	*Symphony No. 3*	7	1	Brahms	*Symphony No. 1*	160	409

Violin I, II, and Viola

COMPOSER	WORK	PAGE	MEASURE	COMPOSER	WORK	PAGE	MEASURE
Bach-Respighi	*Prelude and Fugue in D major*	18	4	Honegger	*Mouvement Symphonique No. 3*	32	[11]
Beethoven	*Symphony No. 5*	99	151	Respighi	*The Birds*	2	7
Borodin	*Symphony No. 2*	20	[F] 1f			58	5
Borodin	*Symphony No. 3*	25	3	Tchaikovsky	*Mozartiana*	56	261
de Falla	*El Retablo de Maese Pedro*	24	8b [24]	Tchaikovsky	*Symphony No. 2*	70	5

STRINGS

Violin I, II, and Violoncello

COMPOSER	WORK	PAGE	MEASURE	COMPOSER	WORK	PAGE	MEASURE
Respighi	*Toccata per Pianoforte e Orchestra*	**77**	[34] 1f	**Tchaikovsky**	*Symphony No. 5*	**134**	[C]
						191	[Y]

Viola and Violoncello

COMPOSER	WORK	PAGE	MEASURE	COMPOSER	WORK	PAGE	MEASURE
Respighi	*Feste Romane*	**132**	[41]	**Tchaikovsky**	*Hamlet*	**1**	2

Violin I, II, Viola, and Violoncello

COMPOSER	WORK	PAGE	MEASURE	COMPOSER	WORK	PAGE	MEASURE
Mussorgsky– Ravel	*Pictures at an Exhibition*	**129**	[105]	**Respighi**	*Concerto Gregoriano per Violino e Orchestra*	**60**	[35] 3f
		151	[122]	**Tchaikovsky**	*Symphony No. 5*	**193**	469

Chapter 62

DOUBLE-STOPPED UNISONS

English	*Italian*	*French*	*German*
On two [2] strings	Sul due [2] corde	Sur deux [2] cordes	Auf zwei [2] Saiten

Violin I

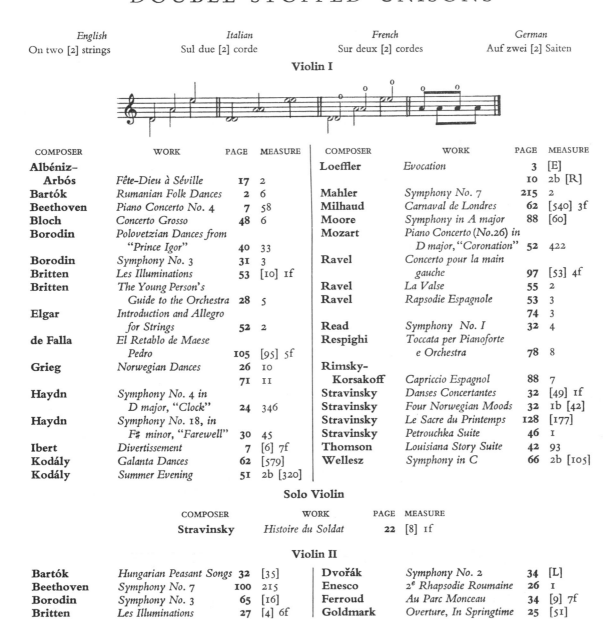

COMPOSER	WORK	PAGE	MEASURE	COMPOSER	WORK	PAGE	MEASURE
Albéniz-Arbós	*Fête-Dieu à Séville*	17	2	**Loeffler**	*Evocation*	3	[E]
						10	2b [R]
Bartók	*Rumanian Folk Dances*	2	6	**Mahler**	*Symphony No. 7*	215	2
Beethoven	*Piano Concerto No. 4*	7	58	**Milhaud**	*Carnaval de Londres*	62	[540] 3f
Bloch	*Concerto Grosso*	48	6	**Moore**	*Symphony in A major*	88	[60]
Borodin	*Polovetzian Dances from*			**Mozart**	*Piano Concerto (No.26) in*		
	"Prince Igor"	40	33		*D major, "Coronation"*	52	422
Borodin	*Symphony No. 3*	31	3	**Ravel**	*Concerto pour la main*		
Britten	*Les Illuminations*	53	[10] 1f		*gauche*	97	[53] 4f
Britten	*The Young Person's*			**Ravel**	*La Valse*	55	2
	Guide to the Orchestra	28	5	**Ravel**	*Rapsodie Espagnole*	53	3
Elgar	*Introduction and Allegro*					74	3
	for Strings	52	2	**Read**	*Symphony No. I*	32	4
de Falla	*El Retablo de Maese*			**Respighi**	*Toccata per Pianoforte*		
	Pedro	105	[95] 5f		*e Orchestra*	78	8
Grieg	*Norwegian Dances*	26	10	**Rimsky-**			
		71	11	**Korsakoff**	*Capriccio Espagnol*	88	7
Haydn	*Symphony No. 4 in*			**Stravinsky**	*Danses Concertantes*	32	[49] 1f
	D major, "Clock"	24	346	**Stravinsky**	*Four Norwegian Moods*	32	1b [42]
Haydn	*Symphony No. 18, in*			**Stravinsky**	*Le Sacre du Printemps*	128	[177]
	F♯ minor, "Farewell"	30	45	**Stravinsky**	*Petrouchka Suite*	46	1
Ibert	*Divertissement*	7	[6] 7f	**Thomson**	*Louisiana Story Suite*	42	93
Kodály	*Galanta Dances*	62	[579]	**Wellesz**	*Symphony in C*	66	2b [105]
Kodály	*Summer Evening*	51	2b [320]				

Solo Violin

COMPOSER	WORK	PAGE	MEASURE
Stravinsky	*Histoire du Soldat*	22	[8] 1f

Violin II

COMPOSER	WORK	PAGE	MEASURE	COMPOSER	WORK	PAGE	MEASURE
Bartók	*Hungarian Peasant Songs*	32	[35]	**Dvořák**	*Symphony No. 2*	34	[L]
Beethoven	*Symphony No. 7*	100	215	**Enesco**	*2e Rhapsodie Roumaine*	26	1
Borodin	*Symphony No. 3*	65	[16]	**Ferroud**	*Au Parc Monceau*	34	[9] 7f
Britten	*Les Illuminations*	27	[4] 6f	**Goldmark**	*Overture, In Springtime*	25	[51]

STRINGS

Violin II (contd.)

COMPOSER	WORK	PAGE	MEASURE	COMPOSER	WORK	PAGE	MEASURE
Guarnieri	*Brazilian Dance*	17	[75]	Respighi	*Feste Romane*	30	5
Mahler	*Das Lied von der Erde*	92	[11] 2f	Riisager	*Torgot Dance*	14	1b [70]
Mozart	*Symphony No. 35 in*	2	13	Rosenthal	*Les Petits Métiers*	6	2
	D major, "Haffner"	15	[F]	Ruggles	*Sun-Treader*	18	[85]
Mozart	*Violin Concerto No. III*					29	[139]
	in G major	2	17	Sibelius	*Symphony No. 6*	64	3
Parodi	*Preludio ad una*			Stravinsky	*Fire-Bird Suite (1919)*	10	1
	Commedia	1	3			36	[11] 1f
Prokofieff	*Classical Symphony*	68	[54]	Stravinsky	*Symphony in C*	30	[52]
Ravel	*La Valse*	20	[14] 2f	Tchaikovsky	*Symphony No. 6,*		
		69	[50] 2f		*"Pathétique"*	147	213
		112	5	Walton	*Symphony*	187	[139] 1f
Ravel	*Shéhérazade*	9	2				

Violin I and II

COMPOSER	WORK	PAGE	MEASURE	COMPOSER	WORK	PAGE	MEASURE
Bach, J. C.	*Sinfonia in D major*	1	1	Mozart	*Piano Concerto (No.26) in*		
		9	85		*D major, "Coronation"*	116	373
Bach–Respighi	*Prelude and Fugue in D major*	51	4	Mozart	*Symphony No. 35 in D major, "Haffner"*	1	1
Beethoven	*Symphony No. 2*	41	358			14	129
Berlioz	*The Roman Carnival*			Mozart	*Symphony No. 40 in*	2	16
	Overture	37	262		*G minor*	16	180
Bloch	*America*	87	[51] 5f			62	246
Borodin	*Polovetzian Dances from*			Mozart	*Violin Concerto No. III*		
	"Prince Igor"	84	[V]		*in G major*	11	90
Brahms	*Piano Concerto No. 1*	95	4	Rachmaninoff	*Symphony No. 2*	67	1
Brahms	*Symphony No. 4*	137	78	Ravel	*Concerto pour Piano et*	24	[18]
Brahms	*Tragic Overture*	51	3		*Orchestre*	71	6
Brahms	*Violin Concerto in*	34	571	Ravel	*Introduction et Allegro*	33	[25] 1f
	D major	66	347	Riegger	*Dichotomy*	23	[9]
Copland	*Four Dance Episodes*	77	[8]	Rimsky-Korsakoff	*Capriccio Espagnol*	2	6
	from "Rodeo"	96	6			6	5
Copland	*Statements*	8	5			8	3
Diamond	*Music for Shakespeare's*	4	1b [10]	Rossini	*Semiramide, Overture*	77	5
	"Romeo and Juliet"	13	[85] 2f	Rossini	*Tancredi, Overture*	38	5
Grofé	*Grand Canyon Suite*	122	[6]	Sessions	*Symphony for Orchestra*		
Loeffler	*Evocation*	12	[V] 1f		*(No. 1)*	45	1b [69]
Mahler	*Symphony No. 6*	52	[32]	Sibelius	*Symphony No. 3*	22	2
Milhaud	*Ière Symphonie*	86	2	Smetana	*Tabor*	69	399
		105	1b [145]	Stravinsky	*Le Sacre du Printemps*	16	1b [22]
Mozart	*Overture to "Il Seraglio"*	5	37	Stravinsky	*Petrouchka Suite*	120	[103]
				Vaughan Williams	*Job, A Masque for Dancing*	20	6

Viola

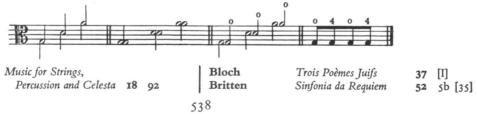

Bartók	*Music for Strings, Percussion and Celesta*	18	92	Bloch	*Trois Poèmes Juifs*	37	[I]
				Britten	*Sinfonia da Requiem*	52	5b [35]

DOUBLE-STOPPED UNISONS

Viola (contd.)

COMPOSER	WORK	PAGE	MEASURE	COMPOSER	WORK	PAGE	MEASURE
Casella	*La Donna Serpente, II. Serie*	5	[5]	Rimsky-Korsakoff	*Symphony No. 2, "Antar"*	104	[I]
Copland	*Two Pieces for String Orchestra*	13	[124]	Ruggles	*Sun-Treader*	13	[53]
Diamond	*Music for Shakespeare's "Romeo and Juliet"*	16	[100] 1f	Sessions	*Suite from "The Black Maskers"*	79	[77] 2f
Elgar	*Symphony No. 1*	21	5	Stillman-Kelley	*Gulliver—His Voyage to Lilliput*	90	[L]
de Falla	*El Retablo de Maese Pedro*	109	[98] 4f	Stravinsky	*"Dumbarton Oaks" Concerto*	28	[55] 1f
Grieg	*Norwegian Dances*	70	1	Stravinsky	*Le Sacre du Printemps*	130	[181]
Hindemith	*Kammermusik No. 4*	63	5	Stravinsky	*Symphony in Three Movements*	26	[37] 3f
Hindemith	*Konzert für Orchester*	35	[120]			119	1
Hindemith	*Mathis der Maler*	57	4	Szymanowski	*Symphonie Concertante pour Piano et Orchestre*		
Moore	*Symphony in A major*	68	4b [50]			6	[3]
		125	6	Turner	*Gregorian Overture for String Orchestra*	22	263
Prokofieff	*Classical Symphony*	35	1				
Ravel	*Boléro*	3	[1]	Vaughan Williams	*Symphony in F minor (No. 4)*	52	[10] 2f
		8	1				
		18	[8]				
Ravel	*Daphnis et Chloé, Suite No. 2*	45	[176]				
		52	2				
		94	1				

Violoncello

COMPOSER	WORK	PAGE	MEASURE	COMPOSER	WORK	PAGE	MEASURE
Bartók	*Music for Strings, Percussion and Celesta*	95	1	Prokofieff	*March and Scherzo from "The Love of the Three Oranges"*	3	1b [1]
Casella	*Italia*	9	[2] 1f	Ravel	*Concerto pour Piano et Orchestre*	95	6
Diamond	*Fourth Symphony*	32	1				
		92	3	Ravel	*La Valse*	49	[36]
		95	[210]	Ravel	*Valses Nobles et Sentimentales*	1	1
Diamond	*Music for Shakespeare's "Romeo and Juliet"*	18	[110] 1f	Respighi	*Feste Romane*	31	1
Egge	*Piano Concerto No. 2*	74	[17]	Respighi	*The Pines of Rome*	76	1
Harris	*Third Symphony*	22	3	Rogers	*Once Upon a Time, Five Fairy Tales*	32	[20] 8f
Kodály	*Summer Evening*	29	[170] 4f				
Mahler	*Das Lied von der Erde*	84	[3] 3f	Schelling	*A Victory Ball*	66	1
Mahler	*Symphony No. 5*	53	6	Sibelius	*En Saga*	57	[13]
Prokofieff	*Classical Symphony*	22	[18] 1f	Stravinsky	*Fire-Bird Suite (1919)*	24	1
		73	[84] 1f	Villa-Lobos	*Danses Africaines*	93	[5]

Bass

COMPOSER	WORK	PAGE	MEASURE	COMPOSER	WORK	PAGE	MEASURE
Bartók	*Second Rhapsody for Violin and Orchestra*	21	1	Harris	*When Johnny Comes Marching Home*	60	2b [330]

Bass (contd.)

COMPOSER	WORK	PAGE	MEASURE	COMPOSER	WORK	PAGE	MEASURE
Miaskovsky	*Sinfonietta for String Orchestra*	35	[8]	**Prokofieff**	*Romeo and Juliet, Suite No. 2*	24 / 33	[11] / [19]
				Read	*Symphony No. I*	60	7

Soli Bass

COMPOSER	WORK	PAGE	MEASURE
Rogers	*Once Upon a Time, Five Fairy Tales*	23	2

Violin I and Viola

COMPOSER	WORK	PAGE	MEASURE	COMPOSER	WORK	PAGE	MEASURE
Bach–Respighi	*Prelude and Fugue in D major*	12	1	**Stravinsky**	*Orpheus*	47	[125]

Violin II and Viola

COMPOSER	WORK	PAGE	MEASURE	COMPOSER	WORK	PAGE	MEASURE
Bartók	*Concerto for Orchestra*	76 / 82	[122] / [36]	**Mussorgsky**	*Night on the Bald Mountain*	59	2b [R]

Violin I, II, and Viola

COMPOSER	WORK	PAGE	MEASURE	COMPOSER	WORK	PAGE	MEASURE
Atterberg	*The Wise and the Foolish Virgins*	39	[M]	**Mozart**	*Overture to "Il Seraglio"*	35	315
Borodin	*Symphony No. 2*	50	4	**Mozart**	*Symphony No. 38 in D major, "Prague"*	1	1
Glinka	*March and Oriental Dances from "Russlan und Ludmila"*	501	7	**Mozart**	*Violin Concerto No.IV in D major*	7 / 27	57 / 212
Harris	*When Johnny Comes Marching Home*	25	[140]	**Schumann, R.**	*Symphony No. 4*	124	236
				Stravinsky	*Chant du Rossignol*	60	[61] 1f
Lalo	*Symphonie Espagnole*	40	3	**Vaughan Williams**	*Symphony in F minor (No. 4)*	41 / 62	3 / [19] 2f
Milhaud	*Deuxième Concerto pour Violoncelle et Orchestre*	82	1				

Violin I and Violoncello

COMPOSER	WORK	PAGE	MEASURE	COMPOSER	WORK	PAGE	MEASURE
Golestan	*Concerto Roumaine pour Violon et Orchestre*	43 / 104	7 / 6	**Rogers**	*Once Upon a Time, Five Fairy Tales*	13	3

Violin II and Violoncello

COMPOSER	WORK	PAGE	MEASURE
Rogers	*Elegy*	5	[4] 3f

Violin I, II, and Violoncello

COMPOSER	WORK	PAGE	MEASURE	COMPOSER	WORK	PAGE	MEASURE
Bloch	*Concerto Grosso*	1	1	**Lopatnikoff**	*Sinfonietta*	61	3
Harris	*When Johnny Comes Marching Home*	1	[10]	**Rimsky-Korsakoff**	*Russian Easter Overture*	105	5
Kabalevsky	*Suite from "Colas Breugnon"*	89	4b [14]	**Sibelius**	*The Tempest, First Suite*	17	4

DOUBLE-STOPPED UNISONS

Violin I, II, and Bass

COMPOSER	WORK	PAGE	MEASURE	COMPOSER	WORK	PAGE	MEASURE
Harris	Third Symphony	102	3b [69]	Harris	When Johnny Comes Marching Home	63	1

Viola and Violoncello

COMPOSER	WORK	PAGE	MEASURE	COMPOSER	WORK	PAGE	MEASURE
Dyson	Overture, "At the Tabard Inn"	64	6	Prokofieff	Suite from the Ballet "Chout"	133	[172]
Hindemith	Konzertmusik für Streichorchester und Blechbläser	25	2	Rimsky-Korsakoff	Symphony No. 2, "Antar"	112	1
Mahler	Symphony No. 7	206	[246] 1f	Sibelius	En Saga	75	1
Prokofieff	Romeo and Juliet, Suite No. 2	30	5b [16]	Sowerby	Concert Overture for Orchestra	60	1
				Stravinsky	Fire-Bird Suite (1919)	31	[4]

Violin I, II, Viola, and Violoncello

COMPOSER	WORK	PAGE	MEASURE	COMPOSER	WORK	PAGE	MEASURE
Copland	Two Pieces for String Orchestra	13	[124]	Stillman-Kelley	New England Symphony	130	[O]
Prokofieff	Suite from the Ballet "Chout"	123	[157]				

Violin I, Violoncello, and Bass

COMPOSER	WORK	PAGE	MEASURE
Stravinsky	Chant du Rossignol	82	3

Viola, Violoncello, and Bass

COMPOSER	WORK	PAGE	MEASURE	COMPOSER	WORK	PAGE	MEASURE
Harris	When Johnny Comes Marching Home	3	[20] 2f	Prokofieff	Classical Symphony	33	[28]

Violin I, II, Viola, Violoncello, and Bass

COMPOSER	WORK	PAGE	MEASURE	COMPOSER	WORK	PAGE	MEASURE
Harris	Third Symphony	57	5	Ravel	La Valse	52	[38]

Violin I

Copland	Third Symphony	11	4

Violin II

Albéniz–Arbós	Navarra	2	[A] 1f
		8	6
		32	4

Violin I and II

MacDowell	2nd Suite (Indian)	31	7
		119	9

541

Chapter 63

GLISSANDI AND PORTAMENTI

English	*Italian*	*French*	*German*
Chromatic glissando	Glissando cromatico	Chromatique glissando	Chromatisch Glissando
Glissando on one string	Glissando su una sola corda	Glissez sur une corde	Glissando auf einer Saite
Gliss. with same finger	Gliss. col uno dita	Glissez avec le même doigt	Gliss. mit einem Finger
Slide the finger	Strisciare il dita	En glissant le doigt	Mit dem Finger gleiten

(for further terminology see Chapter 8, page 68)

(1) ORDINARY GLISSANDO

Violin I

COMPOSER	WORK	PAGE	MEASURE	COMPOSER	WORK	PAGE	MEASURE
Bartók	Dance Suite	8	[6] 2f	Mahler	Symphony No. 5	48	2
Bartók	Divertimento for String					107	4b [31]
	Orchestra	32	4b [303]	Mahler	Symphony No. 8	91	1b [33]
Bartók	Second Suite	69	2			101	1b [51]
Bax	Fifth Symphony	40	[27]	Mahler	Symphony No. 9	8	5
Chasins	Rush Hour in Hong Kong	7	5	Moross	Paeans	2	[A]
Copland	Dance Symphony	46	[26] 11f	Prokofieff	Cinderella Suite No. 1	83	[63] 7f
Debussy	Iberia	56	[38]			94	6
		63	1	Prokofieff	Summer Day Suite	43	1
		75	3	Ravel	Concerto pour Piano		
Debussy	Jeux	36	5		et Orchestre	18	3
Debussy	Première Rhapsodie	27	2	Ravel	Rapsodie Espagnole	17	[7] 2f
Diamond	Rounds for String					75	[23]
	Orchestra	5	[70]	Ravel	Valses Nobles et		
Ferroud	Au Parc Monceau	8	1b [3]		Sentimentales	15	2b [12]
Gershwin	Concerto in F for Piano			Respighi	Feste Romane	85	3
	and Orchestra	102	[19] 1f	Rogers	Once Upon a Time,		
Hanson	"Merry Mount" Suite	29	5		Five Fairy Tales	50	[29] 4f
Ibert	Féerique	25	[17] 1f	Sessions	Suite from "The Black		
Jolivet	Andante pour Orchestre				Maskers"	101	1b [94]
	à Cordes	12	1	Sessions	Symphony No. II	32	[T]
Khachaturian	Gayne Ballet Suite			Strauss, R.	Till Eulenspiegel's		
	No. 2	29	[21] 4f		Merry Pranks	22	3
Mahler	Das Lied von der Erde	90	[9]	Stravinsky	Orpheus	20	[51]
		131	[52] 2f	Szymanowski	Symphonie Concertante		
Mahler	Symphony No. 2	189	[34] 6f		pour Piano et		
Mahler	Symphony No. 3	56	[40] 3f		Orchestre	7	[4]

GLISSANDI AND PORTAMENTI

Violin I (contd.)

COMPOSER	WORK	PAGE	MEASURE	COMPOSER	WORK	PAGE	MEASURE
Tchaikovsky	Capriccio Italien	34	5	Wagenaar	Sinfonietta for Small Orchestra	35	1b [7]
Villa-Lobos	Amazonas	34	4	Wellesz	Symphony in C	20	[135]
Villa-Lobos	Chôros No. 10	27	[2]				
Villa-Lobos	Uirapurú	45	1				

Solo Violin I

COMPOSER	WORK	PAGE	MEASURE	COMPOSER	WORK	PAGE	MEASURE
Bartók	Second Suite	71	[34] 4f	Strauss, R.	Till Eulenspiegel's Merry Pranks	20	3
Schönberg	Pierrot Lunaire	8	[35] 2f				
Shostakovich	Symphony No. 5	64	[57] 2f				

Soli Violin I

COMPOSER	WORK	PAGE	MEASURE	COMPOSER	WORK	PAGE	MEASURE
Loeffler	Evocation	47	[52] 4f	Stravinsky	Le Sacre du Printemps	29	[39] 1f

Violin II

COMPOSER	WORK	PAGE	MEASURE	COMPOSER	WORK	PAGE	MEASURE
Bartók	Concerto for Orchestra	34	[90]	Mahler	Symphony No. 7	38	1b [31]
Bartók	First Rhapsody for Violin and Orchestra	47	6	Ravel	Alborada del Gracioso	30	[24] 1f
Bartók	Music for Strings, Percussion and Celesta	69	[22]	Ravel	Concerto pour la main gauche	24	1b [11]
						97	[53] 4f
Honegger	Suite d'Orchestre, "L'Impératrice aux Rochers"	55	2	Ravel	Rapsodie Espagnole	42	[2] 2f
				Strauss, R.	Ein Heldenleben	159	3

Violin I and II

COMPOSER	WORK	PAGE	MEASURE	COMPOSER	WORK	PAGE	MEASURE
Barber	Medea	73	3	Mahler	Symphony No. 4	103	256
Bartók	Dance Suite	17	[11] 6f			142	300
Bloch	Trois Poèmes Juifs	26	1b [15]	Mahler	Symphony No. 5	76	[15] 1f
Cesana	Second American Symphony	29	[22] 1f	Mahler	Symphony No. 7	123	4b [120]
				Mahler	Symphony No. 8	144	[112] 2f
Copland	Dance Symphony	87	[52] 4f	Parodi	Preludio ad una Commedia	36	1b [R]
Copland	El Salón México	20	[21] 2f	Pizzetti	Concerto dell'Estate	13	[5]
Debussy	Gigues	30	5	Poot	Jazz-Music	3	[1] 2f
Elgar	Symphony No. 1	21	8	Prokofieff	Romeo and Juliet, Suite No. 1	91	3
Ferroud	Au Parc Monceau	37	2				
Gershwin	An American in Paris	6	[5]	Prokofieff	Suite from the Ballet "Chout"	99	[127] 2f
Ibert	Escales	5	[3]	Read	Symphony No. 1	9	4
		32	[27]			84	[32] 3f
Ives	Three Places in New England	86	1	Rogers	Characters from Hans Christian Andersen	19	3
Loeffler	Evocation	6	1b [J]				
Mahler	Das Lied von der Erde	25	[29] 7f	Schelling	A Victory Ball	58	[15] 1f
		56	3	Schönberg	Fünf Orchesterstücke	49	1b [3]
		112	[29]	Scriabin	Prométhée, Le Poème du Feu	45	3b [30]
Mahler	Symphony No. 2	28	1b [14]				
		48	[23] 3f	Sessions	Suite from "The Black Maskers"	76	[72]
		106	9				
		131	[4] 4f				

STRINGS

Violin I and II (contd.)

COMPOSER	WORK	PAGE	MEASURE	COMPOSER	WORK	PAGE	MEASURE
Sessions	*Symphony No. II*	43	3	**Strauss, R.**	*Eine Alpensinfonie*	46	[42]
		63	1b [Pp]			97	[93] 4f
Shostakovich	*Symphony No. 1*	84	6b [35]			162	13
Shostakovich	*Symphony No. 5*	81	5	**Strauss, R.**	*Rosenkavalier Waltzes*		
Shostakovich	*Symphony No. 9*	117	[89]		—*First Sequence*	29	4b [26]
Siegmeister	*Ozark Set*	61	[10]	**Stravinsky**	*Orpheus*	48	1b [130]
Slonimsky	*My Toy Balloon*	28	2	**Stravinsky**	*Petrouchka Suite*	133	7
				Walton	*Façade, Suite No. 1*	42	3

Soli Violin I and II

COMPOSER	WORK	PAGE	MEASURE
Mahler	*Symphony No. 8*	120	[78] 1f

Viola

COMPOSER	WORK	PAGE	MEASURE	COMPOSER	WORK	PAGE	MEASURE
Bartók	*Concerto for Orchestra*	61	[74]	**Jolivet**	*Andante pour Orchestre à Cordes*	3	[10] 4f
Bartók	*Divertimento for String Orchestra*	40	[513] 2f	**Pierné**	*Divertissements sur un Thème Pastorale*	9	1b [7]
Britten	*Les Illuminations*	31	2b [4]	**Prokofieff**	*Romeo and Juliet, Suite No. 2*	17	[7] 1f
Casella	*Paganiniana*	3	2				
Gould	*Latin-American Symphonette*	41	7b [4]	**Ravel**	*Daphnis et Chloé, Suite No. 1*	10	2b [80]
Gould	*Philharmonic Waltzes*	43	[500]	**Ravel**	*La Valse*	12	4
Ibert	*Escales*	54	6	**Strauss, R.**	*Eine Alpensinfonie*	61	[54] 1f
Ibert	*La Ballade de la Geôle de Reading*	25	[16] 1f	**Strauss, R.**	*Suite from "Le Bourgeois Gentilhomme"*	1	6
Janssen	*New Year's Eve in New York*	75	[31] 1f	**Walton**	*Façade, Suite No. 1*	14	3

Violoncello

COMPOSER	WORK	PAGE	MEASURE	COMPOSER	WORK	PAGE	MEASURE
Albéniz–Arbós	*Triana*	13	3	**Mahler**	*Symphony No. 2*	111	3
				Mahler	*Symphony No. 3*	11	[7]
Bartók	*Divertimento for String Orchestra*	37	1b [432]	**Mahler**	*Symphony No. 5*	57	[5] 9f
Bartók	*Vier Orchesterstücke*	38	4b [8]	**Mihalovici**	*Toccata pour Piano et Orchestre*	16	[45] 2f
Bloch	*Trois Poèmes Juifs*	73	[9]	**Milhaud**	*Ière Symphonie*	6	1
Britten	*Four Sea Interludes from "Peter Grimes"*	28	[4] 1f			22	[85] 1f
Copland	*Dance Symphony*	67	[40]	**Prokofieff**	*Suite from the Ballet "Chout"*	52	1b [73]
Dukelsky	*Symphony No. 3*	94	[39] 3f	**Prokofieff**	*Summer Day Suite*	48	1
Halffter	*Deux Esquisses Symphoniques*	2	4	**Ravel**	*La Valse*	77	[57]
				Rimsky-Korsakoff	*Scheherazade*	111	42
Herrmann	*Sinfonietta for String Orchestra*	2	2b [B]			138	159
				Rivier	*Ouverture pour un don Quichotte*	18	2
Ibert	*Escales*	21	[16]	**Rosenthal**	*Les Petits Métiers*	28	1
Mahler	*Das Lied von der Erde*	47	[17]	**Rudhyar**	*Sinfonietta*	21	1
Mahler	*Symphony No. 1*	21	4b [16]				

544

GLISSANDI AND PORTAMENTI

Violoncello (contd.)

COMPOSER	WORK	PAGE	MEASURE	COMPOSER	WORK	PAGE	MEASURE
Sessions	Symphony No. II	131	[R] 1f	Strauss, R.	Salomé's Dance	3	6b [C]
Skilton	Suite Primeval, Part II	26	1b [B]	Villa-Lobos	Chôros No. 8	72	1
Strauss, R.	Ein Heldenleben	66	2	Wagenaar	Sinfonietta for Small Orchestra	5	[3] 1f
Strauss, R.	Rosenkavalier Waltzes —First Sequence	18	[19] 7f	Walton	Façade, Suite No. 1	10	6

Solo Violoncello

COMPOSER	WORK	PAGE	MEASURE	COMPOSER	WORK	PAGE	MEASURE
Ravel	Ma Mère l'Oye	44	[6] 14f	Schönberg	Pierrot Lunaire	24	[15] 2f
Schönberg	Fünf Orchesterstücke	21	1b [4]			66	2

Soli Violoncello

COMPOSER	WORK	PAGE	MEASURE	COMPOSER	WORK	PAGE	MEASURE
Debussy–Ansermet	Six Épigraphes Antiques	16	[C]	Rogers	Characters from Hans Christian Andersen	9	[5]

Bass

COMPOSER	WORK	PAGE	MEASURE	COMPOSER	WORK	PAGE	MEASURE
Albéniz–Arbós	Évocation	14	[F]	Ives	"Washington's Birthday" from Symphony, "Holidays"	7	[J]
Bartók	Concerto for Orchestra	15	[271]				
		28	[513]	Janssen	New Year's Eve in New York	31	[12]
		135	[534]				
Bartók	First Rhapsody for Violin and Orchestra	28	[13] 3f	Lambert	The Rio Grande	6	2b [3]
Bartók	Music for Strings, Percussion and Celesta	25	167	Mahler	Symphony No. 7	138	[147] 5f
				Pizzetti	Concerto dell'Estate	1	1
Britten	Four Sea Interludes from "Peter Grimes"	24	1b [3]	Ravel	La Valse	6	5
						15	3
Britten	The Young Person's Guide to the Orchestra	32	12	Ravel	Ma Mère l'Oye	41	7
				Respighi	Feste Romane	18	1
Debussy–Ansermet	Six Épigraphes Antiques	63	[C]	Skilton	Suite Primeval, Part I	28	7
				Strauss, R.	Rosenkavalier Waltzes —First Sequence	22	[22] 2f
Gould	Latin-American Symphonette	36	2	Stravinsky	Chant du Rossignol	5	[2] 1f
				Szymanowski	Symphonie Concertante pour Piano et Orchestre	31	3

Violin I and Viola

COMPOSER	WORK	PAGE	MEASURE	COMPOSER	WORK	PAGE	MEASURE
Bartók	Concerto No. 3 for Piano and Orchestra	26	[154]	Mahler	Symphony No. 5	178	[3]
				Prokofieff	Violin Concerto No. 2	73	[67]
Ives	A Set of Pieces	19	1b [O]	Stravinsky	Le Sacre du Printemps	58	1b [66]
Ives	Three Places in New England	46	2	Stravinsky	Orpheus	25	2b [64]
				Whithorne	Fata Morgana	28	3

Violin I and Solo Viola

COMPOSER	WORK	PAGE	MEASURE
Prokofieff	Romeo and Juliet, Suite No. 2	67	1

STRINGS

Violin II and Viola

COMPOSER	WORK	PAGE	MEASURE	COMPOSER	WORK	PAGE	MEASURE
Barber	*Medea*	70	3	Mahler	*Symphony No. 4*	180	134
Casella	*Paganiniana*	64	[33]	Mahler	*Symphony No. 9*	31	1b [11]
Gould	*Spirituals*	20	6b [A]	Piston	*Concerto for Orchestra*	50	8
Griffes	*The Pleasure Dome of*			Prokofieff	*Summer Day Suite*	61	[29]
	Kubla Khan	7	2	Stravinsky	*Orpheus*	44	[121] 2f
Mahler	*Das Lied von der Erde*	22	1b [24]	Stravinsky	*Petrouchka Suite*	51	[39] 4f
Mahler	*Symphony No. 1*	41	2b [30]				

Violin I, II, and Viola

COMPOSER	WORK	PAGE	MEASURE	COMPOSER	WORK	PAGE	MEASURE
Bach–Respighi	*Prelude and Fugue in*			Mahler	*Symphony No. 9*	55	5
	D major	35	[12] 4f			90	7
Bartók	*Concerto for Orchestra*	74	[105]			171	3
Bartók	*Dance Suite*	24	[56]	Milhaud	*Opus Americanum No. 2*	79	[570] 11
Bax	*Second Symphony*	94	1	Mussorgsky–			
Britten	*Serenade for Tenor,*			Ravel	*Pictures at an Exhibition*	83	3
	Horn and Strings	22	1b [17]	Poot	*Symphonie*	45	[24] 1f
Copland	*Dance Symphony*	74	[45]	Prokofieff	*Romeo and Juliet,*		
Ferroud	*Au Parc Monceau*	21	3b [3]		*Suite No. 1*	117	[74] 1f
Gershwin	*An American in Paris*	21	4	Prokofieff	*Summer Day Suite*	15	[3] 4f
		65	[56] 1f	Prokofieff	*Symphony No. 6*	129	[95] 4f
		74	[62] 1f	Ravel	*Shéhérazade*	42	[3]
Gillis	*Symphony No. 5½*	72	1	Read	*Symphony No. 1*	18	2
Griffes	*The Pleasure Dome of*			Rivier	*Ouverture pour un don*		
	Kubla Khan	56	1		*Quichotte*	69	3b [32]
Herrmann	*Sinfonietta for String*			Rosenthal	*Les Petits Métiers*	8	1
	Orchestra	4	[F] 2f			52	2
Honegger	*Le Roi David*	184	1b [3]	Sessions	*Suite from "The Black*		
Ibert	*Féerique*	8	[5]		*Maskers"*	10	6b [7]
Ibert	*La Ballade de la Geôle*			Shostakovich	*Symphony No. 1*	70	[17]
	de Reading	87	[63] 1f			79	1b [29]
Khachaturian	*Gayne Ballet Suite*			Shostakovich	*Symphony No. 5*	51	[45] 4f
	No. 1	17	4	Stravinsky	*Ragtime*	3	3
Knipper	*Symphony No. 4*	93	[11]	Szymanowski	*Symphonie Concertante*		
Mahler	*Symphony No. 1*	65	16b [17]		*pour Piano et*		
					Orchestre	23	[13]

Violin I and Violoncello

COMPOSER	WORK	PAGE	MEASURE	COMPOSER	WORK	PAGE	MEASURE
Diamond	*Rounds for String*			Ravel	*Rapsodie Espagnole*	35	2b [8]
	Orchestra	27	[40]	Tchaikovsky	*Symphony No. 6,*		
Prokofieff	*Symphony No. 5*	116	2		*"Pathétique"*	88	102
Ravel	*Ma Mère l'Oye*	17	7				
		30	1b [19]				

Violin I and Soli Violoncello

COMPOSER	WORK	PAGE	MEASURE
Stravinsky	*Le Sacre du Printemps*	62	[72] 1f

GLISSANDI AND PORTAMENTI

Violin II and Violoncello

COMPOSER	WORK	PAGE	MEASURE	COMPOSER	WORK	PAGE	MEASURE
Bartók	Concerto for Orchestra	30	32	Ravel	Daphnis et Chloé, Suite No. 2	43	[174] 1f
Mahler	Symphony No. 4	17	[7]	Stravinsky	Le Sacre du Printemps	85	[103]

Violin I, II, and Violoncello

COMPOSER	WORK	PAGE	MEASURE	COMPOSER	WORK	PAGE	MEASURE
Britten	Sinfonia da Requiem	51	[34] 6f	Stravinsky	Le Sacre du Printemps	96	[117]
Mahler	Das Lied von der Erde	115	1				

Solo Violin I, II, and Violoncello

COMPOSER	WORK	PAGE	MEASURE
Milhaud	Saudades do Brazil	15	9

•

Viola and Violoncello

COMPOSER	WORK	PAGE	MEASURE	COMPOSER	WORK	PAGE	MEASURE
Bartók	Divertimento for String Orchestra	4	3b [42]	Mahler	Symphony No. 6	24	[14] 4f
Bartók	Violin Concerto	49	[364]	Milhaud	Saudades do Brazil	60	9
Benjamin	Overture to an Italian Comedy	16	[H]	Ravel	La Valse	66	[48]
						119	[93] 1f
Bloch	Trois Poèmes Juifs	81	[15]	Ravel	Valses Nobles et Sentimentales	57	[56] 3f
Elgar	Falstaff	83	4b [85]	Rudhyar	Five Stanzas	3	2b [A]
Ireland	Symphonic Rhapsody, "Mai-Dun"	15	6	Sessions	Symphony for Orchestra (No. 1)	45	2b [69]
Mahler	Symphony No. 4	68	323				

Solo Viola and Violoncello

COMPOSER	WORK	PAGE	MEASURE
Schönberg	Pierrot Lunaire	42	[20]

Violoncello and Bass

COMPOSER	WORK	PAGE	MEASURE	COMPOSER	WORK	PAGE	MEASURE
Benjamin	Overture to an Italian Comedy	7	3	Mahler	Symphony No. 3	48	4b [32]
Britten	Serenade for Tenor, Horn and Strings	18	[14] 2f	Mahler	Symphony No. 6	62	[38]
				Mahler	Symphony No. 8	31	[33] 6f
Copland	Concerto for Piano and Orchestra	18	[13]	Mihalovici	Toccata pour Piano et Orchestre	138	2b [565]
Debussy	Jeux	34	[24] 3f	Moross	Paeans	4	[C]
		98	[67]	Poot	Symphonie	50	[26]
Debussy	Le Martyre de Saint Sébastien	26	2	Ravel	La Valse	25	[17]
				Roussel	Suite en Fa	76	[38]
Debussy	Rondes de Printemps	49	[25]	Strauss, R.	Ein Heldenleben	48	4
Dukelsky	Symphony No. 3	139	2b [60]			211	[105]
Gould	Spirituals	9	3	Strauss, R.	Salomé's Dance	24	[V]
Griffes	The Pleasure Dome of Kubla Khan	61	3	Stravinsky	Fire-Bird Suite (1919)	39	[14]
				Stravinsky	Renard	110	1b [70]
Ives	"The Fourth of July" from Symphony, "Holidays"	34	1b [Y]			146	[90]
				Szymanowski	Symphonie Concertante pour Piano et Orchestre	78	[14] 2f
Ives	Three Places in New England	84	1	Weiss	American Life	4	3b [A]

STRINGS

Violin I, Viola, and Violoncello

COMPOSER	WORK	PAGE	MEASURE	COMPOSER	WORK	PAGE	MEASURE
Debussy	*Rondes de Printemps*	55	[29]	Rudhyar	*Five Stanzas*	16	[V] 1f
Honegger	*Concertino pour Piano et Orchestre*	19	1	Stravinsky	*Le Sacre du Printemps*	91	[III]
Ravel	*Rapsodie Espagnole*	61	[13] 1f	Villa-Lobos	*Uirapurú*	3	1
		89	[32]				

Violin II, Viola, and Violoncello

COMPOSER	WORK	PAGE	MEASURE	COMPOSER	WORK	PAGE	MEASURE
Albéniz–Arbós	*Navarra*	32	2	Bartók	*Hungarian Peasant Songs*	23	3b [24]
Bartók	*Concerto No. 3 for Piano and Orchestra*	53	1b [200]	Ibert	*La Ballade de la Geôle de Reading*	58	7

Violin I, II, Viola, and Violoncello

COMPOSER	WORK	PAGE	MEASURE	COMPOSER	WORK	PAGE	MEASURE
Bach–Respighi	*Passacaglia and Fugue in C minor*	4	[5]	Mahler	*Symphony No. 7*	100	1
Barber	*Medea*	77	3b [56]			135	[141] 1f
Bartók	*Dance Suite*	35	[31]	Mihalovici	*Toccata pour Piano et Orchestre*	7	[15]
		49	[121]			30	[80] 1f
		92	[149]	Mussorgsky–Ravel	*Pictures at an Exhibition*	106	1b [88]
Bartók	*Vier Orchesterstücke*	28	1			123	1b [101]
		58	[25] 2f	Pierné	*Viennoise*	22	1
Britten	*Sinfonia da Requiem*	21	1b [16]	Ravel	*Concerto pour Piano et Orchestre*	30	[24]
Britten	*The Young Person's Guide to the Orchestra*	48	2	Ravel	*Daphnis et Chloé, Suite No. 1*	16	1b [92]
Casella	*Elegia Eroica*	12	[8]	Ravel	*La Valse*	19	[13] 2f
Coppola	*Suite Intima*	57	1			42	[29]
		86	4	Rosenthal	*Les Petits Métiers*	68	[B]
Gould	*Latin-American Symphonette*	42	6			123	[A]
						145	2
Gould	*Spirituals*	23	[E] 1f	Saint-Saëns	*La Jeunesse d'Hercule*	38	1
Ibert	*Escales*	64	[60] 2f	Shostakovich	*Symphony No. 5*	66	6b [61]
Inghelbrecht	*Rapsodie de Printemps*	31	5	Strauss, R.	*Eine Alpensinfonie*	38	1b [37]
Mahler	*Symphony No. 2*	57	[2]			84	7b [82]
		77	5	Stravinsky	*Petrouchka Suite*	119	1
Mahler	*Symphony No. 6*	121	[82] 4f			124	1

Violin I, Violoncello, and Bass

COMPOSER	WORK	PAGE	MEASURE	COMPOSER	WORK	PAGE	MEASURE
Grofé	*Grand Canyon Suite*	53	1	Sessions	*Symphony No. II*	5	[C]
		88	[M]			60	2

Violin I, II, Violoncello, and Bass

COMPOSER	WORK	PAGE	MEASURE	COMPOSER	WORK	PAGE	MEASURE
Ravel	*Daphnis et Chloé, Suite No. 2*	123	3	Shostakovich	*Symphony No. 3*	76	[95]

GLISSANDI AND PORTAMENTI

Viola, Violoncello, and Bass

COMPOSER	WORK	PAGE	MEASURE	COMPOSER	WORK	PAGE	MEASURE
Alfvén	*A Legend of the Skerries*	6	3	Ravel	*Daphnis et Chloé, Suite No. 1*	3	[73]
Bartók	*Concerto for Piano and Orchestra*	101	[43]	Ravel	*Rapsodie Espagnole*	23	[12]
Mahler	*Symphony No. 4*	121	89	Ravel	*Valses Nobles et Sentimentales*	70	[71]
Mahler	*Symphony No. 5*	115	3	Walton	*Portsmouth Point Overture*	14	[11]
Mussorgsky–Ravel	*Pictures at an Exhibition*	15	[14]				

Violin II, Viola, Violoncello, and Bass

COMPOSER	WORK	PAGE	MEASURE
Ravel	*Alborada del Gracioso*	40	[34]

Soli Violin II, Viola, Violoncello, and Bass

Ravel	*Rapsodie Espagnole*	64	[15] 4f

Violin I, II, Viola, Violoncello, and Bass

COMPOSER	WORK	PAGE	MEASURE	COMPOSER	WORK	PAGE	MEASURE
Bartók	*Concerto No. 3 for Piano and Orchestra*	88	12	Gould	*Spirituals*	3	[A] 3f
Bartók	*Divertimento for String Orchestra*	25	1b [62]	Herrmann	*Sinfonietta for String Orchestra*	7	[L] 9f
Bartók	*Music for Strings, Percussion and Celesta*	14	[27]	Mahler	*Symphony No. 4*	133	210
				Mahler	*Symphony No. 7*	211	[252] 2f
Bartók	*Violin Concerto*	75	[44]	Poot	*Symphonie*	99	3b [43]
Cesana	*Second American Symphony*	155	[38] 1f	Ravel	*Daphnis et Chloé, Suite No. 2*	85	[203] 3f
						114	[216]
Copland	*Concerto for Piano and Orchestra*	56	[42]	Ravel	*La Valse*	111	[85]
		65	[49]	Revueltas	*Sensemayá*	37	[35]
				Villa-Lobos	*Amazonas*	75	2

(2) SLOW OR MEASURED GLISSANDO

English	Italian	French	German
Slow gliss.	Gliss. lento	Glissez lentement	Langsam Gliss.

Violin I and II

Grofé	*Grand Canyon Suite*	117	[4] 4f

Viola

Rudhyar	*Five Stanzas*	20	[C] 5f

Violin II and Viola

Villa-Lobos	*Chôros No. 8*	7	[3]

STRINGS

Violin I, II, and Viola

COMPOSER	WORK	PAGE	MEASURE
Hindemith	*Kammermusik No. 1*	**65**	[100] 1f

Violin II, Viola, Violoncello, and Bass

COMPOSER	WORK	PAGE	MEASURE
Gould	*Latin-American Symphonette*	**53**	4

English	Italian	French	German
Measured gliss. in quarter tones	Gliss. misurato in quarto di toni	Gliss. mesuré en quart de tons	Gemessener Gliss. in Vierteltöne

Violin I, II, and Viola

COMPOSER	WORK	PAGE	MEASURE
Riegger	*Dichotomy*	**50**	4

(3) IN HARMONICS

English	Italian	French	German
Glissando in harmonics	Glissando in armonici	Glissez des sons harmoniques En l'effleurant du doigt, les sons harmoniques notés se produiront alors automatiquement	Glissando auf den Flageolett

Violin I

COMPOSER	WORK	PAGE	MEASURE
Janssen	*New Year's Eve in New York*	**60**	1

Solo Violin I

COMPOSER	WORK	PAGE	MEASURE
Ravel	*Ma Mère l'Oye*	**7**	[5]

Violin I and II

COMPOSER	WORK	PAGE	MEASURE	COMPOSER	WORK	PAGE	MEASURE
Honegger	*Prélude pour "La Tempête"*	**26**	2	**Rogers**	*Once Upon a Time, Five Fairy Tales*	**41**	1
				Siegmeister	*Western Suite*	**8**	30

Viola

COMPOSER	WORK	PAGE	MEASURE	COMPOSER	WORK	PAGE	MEASURE
Bloch	*Trois Poèmes Juifs*	**17**	[9] 3f	**Stravinsky**	*Le Sacre du Printemps*	**9**	[11]
Siegmeister	*Western Suite*	**10**	35			**76**	[86] 6f

GLISSANDI AND PORTAMENTI

Violoncello

COMPOSER	WORK	PAGE	MEASURE
Villa-Lobos	*Amazonas*	20	[7]

Bass

Stravinsky	*Renard*	112	1b [72]

Violin II and Violoncello

Ravel	*Daphnis et Chloé,* *Suite No. 1*	8	[78]

Viola and Violoncello

COMPOSER	WORK	PAGE	MEASURE	COMPOSER	WORK	PAGE	MEASURE
Britten	*Les Illuminations*	4	[4]	**Ravel**	*Rapsodie Espagnole*	40	1b [1]
Ravel	*Concerto pour la main* *gauche*	55	1	**Respighi**	*Vetrate di Chiesa*	7	2

Violoncello and Bass

Villa-Lobos	*Chôros No. 10*	26	1

Violin I, II, Viola, and Violoncello

Stravinsky	*Chant du Rossignol*	73	[81]	**Stravinsky**	*Fire-Bird Suite (1919)*	3	[3] 1f

(4) TO A HARMONIC

Violin I

COMPOSER	WORK	PAGE	MEASURE	COMPOSER	WORK	PAGE	MEASURE
Britten	*Les Illuminations*	2	2	**Respighi**	*Ballata delle Gnomidi*	31	5
Diamond	*Rounds for String*	30	[60] 2f	**Rogers**	*Once Upon a Time,*		
	Orchestra	40	2b [160]		*Five Fairy Tales*	50	[29]
Gould	*Philharmonic Waltzes*	43	[500]	**Shostakovich**	*Piano Concerto*	8	1b [7]
Mahler	*Symphony No. 1*	13	3b [9]	**Shostakovich**	*The Golden Age, Ballet*		
Mahler	*Symphony No. 6*	140	[99]		*Suite*	15	4b [14]
Ravel	*Concerto pour la main*			**Strauss, R.**	*Also Sprach*		
	gauche	25	4		*Zarathustra*	147	3
Ravel	*Daphnis et Chloé,*			**Stravinsky**	*Le Sacre du Printemps*	116	3b [153]
	Suite No. 2	91	1b [206]	**Stravinsky**	*Quatre Études pour*		
Read	*Symphony No. I*	36	[15] 2f		*Orchestre*	16	2

Solo Violin I

Strauss, R.	*Don Quixote*	61	3	**Mahler**	*Symphony No. 1*	133	[19] 7

STRINGS

Violin I and II

COMPOSER	WORK	PAGE	MEASURE	COMPOSER	WORK	PAGE	MEASURE
Gould	Spirituals	26	5	Mihalovici	Toccata pour Piano et	58	[180]
Khachaturian	Masquerade Suite	65	6		Orchestre	107	1
		71	4	Parodi	Preludio ad una		
Mahler	Symphony No. 6	81	3b [49]		Commedia	15	[H]
				Shostakovich	Symphony No. 5	63	4

Viola

COMPOSER	WORK	PAGE	MEASURE
Stravinsky	Quatre Etudes pour Orchestre	13	2b [3]

Violoncello

COMPOSER	WORK	PAGE	MEASURE	COMPOSER	WORK	PAGE	MEASURE
Bartók	Hungarian Peasant Songs	23	4b [23]	Ravel	La Valse	40	5
Britten	Les Illuminations	35	[2] 7f	Ravel	Rapsodie Espagnole	81	2b [27]
Britten	Sinfonia da Requiem	63	6	Rosenthal	Les Petits Métiers	111	2
Debussy	Première Rhapsodie	39	3	Shostakovich	Symphony No. 5	66	[60]

Solo Violoncello

Ravel	Alborada del Gracioso	36	[29] 4f

Bass

Ravel	La Valse	12	5
		19	[13]

Solo Bass

Stravinsky	Histoire du Soldat	60	[4] 2f

Violin II and Viola

Ravel	Daphnis et Chloé, Suite No. 2	105	2b [212]

Violin I, II, and Viola

Britten	Sinfonia da Requiem	52	[35] 1f

Soli Violin I, II, and Viola

Strauss, R.	Also Sprach Zarathustra	127	8

Violin I and Violoncello

COMPOSER	WORK	PAGE	MEASURE	COMPOSER	WORK	PAGE	MEASURE
Casella	Paganiniana	64	[33]	Ravel	Ma Mère l'Oye	7	[5] 1f
Ravel	Daphnis et Chloé, Suite No. 2	103	1b [211]				

GLISSANDI AND PORTAMENTI

Viola and Violoncello

COMPOSER	WORK	PAGE	MEASURE	COMPOSER	WORK	PAGE	MEASURE
Respighi	*Concerto Gregoriano per Violino e Orchestra*	**46**	[26]	**Respighi**	*Vetrate di Chiesa*	**7**	I

Soli Violoncello and Bass

COMPOSER	WORK	PAGE	MEASURE
Ravel	*Rapsodie Espagnole*	**59**	2b [12]

Violin I, Viola, and Violoncello

Strauss, R.	*Symphonia Domestica*	**28**	[33]

Violin I, Soli Viola, and Violoncello

Strauss, R.	*Also Sprach Zarathustra*	**132**	3

Violin II, Viola, and Violoncello

Mussorgsky–Ravel	*Pictures at an Exhibition*	**10**	[9]

Violin I, II, Viola, and Violoncello

COMPOSER	WORK	PAGE	MEASURE	COMPOSER	WORK	PAGE	MEASURE
Bartók	*Music for Strings, Percussion and Celesta*	**55**	447	**Respighi**	*Ballata delle Gnomidi*	**33**	I

Viola, Violoncello, and Bass

Shostakovich	*Symphony No. 9*	**21**	[17]

Violin I, II, Viola, Violoncello, and Bass

Stravinsky	*Fire-Bird Suite* (1919)	**14**	[17]

(5) OTHER INDICATIONS

English	*Italian*	*French*	*German*
Gliss.—as high as possible; tear off!	Gliss.—anche alto che possible; strappate!	Gliss.—aussi haut que possible; arrachez!	Gliss.—so hoch wie möglich; reissen!

Violoncello and Bass

Toch	*The Chinese Flute*	**31**	3

English	*Italian*	*French*	*German*
Gliss. over entire fingerboard	Gliss. sopra tutta la tastiera	Gliss. sur toute la touche	Gliss. über das ganze Griffbrett

Violin I, II, Viola, and Violoncello

Hindemith	*Kammermusik No. 1*	**17**	I

553

Chapter 64

OFF-STAGE

(for terminology see Chapter 11, page 75)

Solo Viola

COMPOSER	WORK	PAGE	MEASURE	COMPOSER	WORK	PAGE	MEASURE
Charpentier	*Impressions d'Italie*	17	[15] 7f	**Inghelbrecht**	*Rapsodie de Printemps*	1	1

Soli Violin I, II, and Violoncello

COMPOSER	WORK	PAGE	MEASURE
Berlioz	*Harold en Italie*	195	4

Chapter 65

OPEN STRINGS

Violin I

COMPOSER	WORK	PAGE	MEASURE	COMPOSER	WORK	PAGE	MEASURE
Albéniz–Arbós	*Évocation*	23	[K]	Gould	*Spirituals*	4	[B] 6f
Albéniz–Arbós	*Triana*	4	4			18	9b [G]
		11	2	Loeffler	*Evocation*	10	2b [R]
		28	4	Mahler	*Das Lied von der Erde*	83	[2]
Bartók	*Deux Images*	20	1	Mahler	*Symphony No. 7*	129	[130]
Bartók	*Rumanian Folk Dances*	2	6	Pizzetti	*Concerto dell'Estate*	23	5
Bartók	*Violin Concerto*	23	[4]	Poot	*Symphonie*	12	[6]
Beethoven	*Symphony No. 8*	84	148			64	3
Berg	*Violin Concerto*	47	[235] 4f	Prokofieff	*Classical Symphony*	59	3
Bloch	*Evocations*	13	2	Ravel	*Rapsodie Espagnole*	36	1b [10]
Britten	*The Young Person's Guide to the Orchestra*	21	7	Respighi	*The Pines of Rome*	12	3
		23	4	Riisager	*Torgot Dance*	8	[35] 1f
Cras	*Journal de Bord*	11	1	Rimsky-Korsakoff	*Russian Easter Overture*	41	15
Diamond	*Rounds for String Orchestra*	6	3b [75]	Scriabin	*Le Poème de l'Extase*	28	4
		27	[40]	Sibelius	*En Saga*	11	1
Dukas	*Polyeucte, Ouverture*	15	1	Slonimsky	*My Toy Balloon*	25	1
Dvořák	*Violin Concerto in A minor*	87	289	Stillman-Kelley	*Gulliver—His Voyage to Lilliput*	56	1
Elgar	*Concerto for Violoncello and Orchestra*	13	[11]	Stravinsky	*Symphony in Three Movements*	85	2
Glinka	*March and Oriental Dances from "Russlan und Ludmila"*	500	7			100	[166] 1f
				Tchaikovsky	*Symphony No. 6, "Pathétique"*	11	71
						50	247
						103	10

Solo Violin I

COMPOSER	WORK	PAGE	MEASURE	COMPOSER	WORK	PAGE	MEASURE
Saint-Saëns	*Danse Macabre*	2	14	Wagenaar	*Sinfonietta for Small Orchestra*	30	[6] 1f
Stravinsky	*Histoire du Soldat*	12	[3]				

Violin II

COMPOSER	WORK	PAGE	MEASURE	COMPOSER	WORK	PAGE	MEASURE
Bartók	*Concerto for Orchestra*	99	[185]	Bloch	*Trois Poèmes Juifs*	49	[5]
Bartók	*Violin Concerto*	94	[219]			53	2b [8]
Beethoven	*Symphony No. 7*	100	216	Copland	*An Outdoor Overture*	12	[75] 1f

STRINGS

Violin II (contd.)

COMPOSER	WORK	PAGE	MEASURE	COMPOSER	WORK	PAGE	MEASURE
Diamond	Fourth Symphony	64	[75]	Ravel	Daphnis et Chloé,		
Ferroud	Au Parc Monceau	34	[9] 3f		Suite No. 1	21	[96]
Liszt	Les Préludes	36	157	Ravel	La Valse	20	[14] 2f
Loeffler	Evocation	8	[N]	Ravel	Rapsodie Espagnole	54	1
		32	1b [30]			75	1
Milhaud	La Création du Monde	56	[54] 5f	Read	Symphony No. 1	4	[3]
Pizzetti	Concerto dell'Estate	5	[2]	Respighi	Vetrate di Chiesa	11	1
Prokofieff	Classical Symphony	92	196	Rosenthal	Les Petits Métiers	81	[B] 2f

Soli Violin II

COMPOSER	WORK	PAGE	MEASURE
Rogers	Once Upon a Time, Five Fairy Tales	31	1

Violin I and II

COMPOSER	WORK	PAGE	MEASURE	COMPOSER	WORK	PAGE	MEASURE
Albéniz–Arbós	Fête-Dieu à Séville	9	7	Goldmark	Overture, In Spring-		
		24	[F]		time	23	[48] 5f
Albéniz–Arbós	Navarra	5	[B]	Grofé	Grand Canyon Suite	122	[6]
		35	[O]	Loeffler	Evocation	14	[Z]
Bartók	Concerto for Piano and			Loeffler	Poem, La Bonne		
	Orchestra	10	[11]		Chanson	47	[19]
Bartók	Dance Suite	37	42	Mahler	Songs of a Wayfarer	39	[20] 1f
		85	92	Mahler	Symphony No. 7	122	[118]
Bartók	Music for Strings,			Prokofieff	Piano Concerto No. 3	5	3
	Percussion and Celesta	59	473	Prokofieff	Romeo and Juliet,	115	[71] 6f
Brahms	Symphony No. 4	134	69		Suite No. 1	120	3
		137	78	Ravel	Daphnis et Chloé,		
Britten	Les Illuminations	29	1		Suite No. 1	33	[104]
Copland	Appalachian Spring	63	[50]	Read	Symphony No. 1	20	1b [10]
Diamond	Rounds for String			Rosenthal	Les Petits Métiers	138	2
	Orchestra	3	[25]	Skilton	Suite Primeval, Part I	15	4b [B]
Elgar	Introduction and Allegro			Stravinsky	Concerto en Ré pour		
	for Strings	23	[14] 1f		Violon et Orchestre	43	[90]
Enesco	Ière Rhapsodie Roumaine	48	[25]	Stravinsky	Jeu de Cartes	56	3b [103]
		58	[29]	Stravinsky	Petrouchka Suite	120	[103]

Viola

COMPOSER	WORK	PAGE	MEASURE	COMPOSER	WORK	PAGE	MEASURE
Berg	Three Excerpts from "Wozzeck"	36	[70]	Loeffler	Poem, La Bonne Chanson	37	[5] 1f
Bloch	Trois Poèmes Juifs	64	3b [3]	Milhaud	Cinq Symphonies pour		
Britten	Four Sea Interludes from "Peter Grimes"	16	3		Petit Orchestre	44	1b [30]
				Ravel	La Valse	79	1b [58]
Britten	Les Illuminations	37	1	Respighi	The Pines of Rome	19	[5] 5f
		49	1	Riisager	Torgot Dance	5	3b [15]

OPEN STRINGS

Viola (contd.)

COMPOSER	WORK	PAGE	MEASURE	COMPOSER	WORK	PAGE	MEASURE
Stillman-Kelley	Gulliver—His Voyage to Lilliput	58	[S] 2f	**Szymanowski**	Symphonie Concertante pour Piano et Orchestre	5	[2] 4f
Stravinsky	Danses Concertantes	29	[45]				

Violoncello

COMPOSER	WORK	PAGE	MEASURE	COMPOSER	WORK	PAGE	MEASURE
Albéniz-Arbós	Fête-Dieu à Séville	13	5	**Debussy**	Rondes de Printemps	6	[3] 1f
Bartók	Dance Suite	15	125	**Dukas**	La Péri	64	[9]
		27	75			85	3
		36	40	**Elgar**	Introduction and Allegro	25	1b [15]
		61	26		for Strings	51	1b [30]
		88	113	**Enesco**	2e Rhapsodie Roumaine	14	[9]
Bartók	First Rhapsody for Violin and Orchestra	33	[20] 2f	**Mahler**	Das Lied von der Erde	84	[3] 3f
				Mahler	Symphony No. 9	38	5
Berg	Violin Concerto	55	2	**Ravel**	La Valse	7	[6]
		66	[65] 5f	**Ravel**	Rapsodie Espagnole	27	4
Britten	Sinfonia da Requiem	21	5b [16]	**Sibelius**	Symphony No. 5	32	[A] 4f
Britten	The Young Person's Guide to the Orchestra	47	3	**Stillman-Kelley**	New England Symphony	100	[K] 1f
				Strauss, R.	Don Quixote	58	2
Debussy	Iberia	29	5	**Stravinsky**	Pulcinella Suite	69	[III] 3f

Soli Violoncello

COMPOSER	WORK	PAGE	MEASURE
Casella	Paganiniana	98	1

Bass

COMPOSER	WORK	PAGE	MEASURE	COMPOSER	WORK	PAGE	MEASURE
Bartók	Divertimento for String Orchestra	19	[25]	**Read**	Symphony No. I	1	1
				Stillman-Kelley	New England Symphony	69	[P] 2f
Enesco	2e Rhapsodie Roumaine	5	3				
Persichetti	The Hollow Men	3	[B] 6f				

Soli Violin I and Viola

COMPOSER	WORK	PAGE	MEASURE
Diamond	Music for Shakespeare's "Romeo and Juliet"	21	2b [10]

Violin II and Viola

COMPOSER	WORK	PAGE	MEASURE	COMPOSER	WORK	PAGE	MEASURE
Honegger	Le Chant de Nigamon	5	[16] 1f	**Ravel**	Rapsodie Espagnole	27	3
Prokofieff	Classical Symphony	95	[75] 1f				

557

STRINGS

Violin I, II, and Viola

COMPOSER	WORK	PAGE	MEASURE	COMPOSER	WORK	PAGE	MEASURE
Britten	*Sinfonia da Requiem*	21	5b [16]	**Riisager**	*Torgot Dance*	12	2b [60]
Copland	*Four Dance Episodes from "Rodeo"*	73	[5]	**Stillman-Kelley**	*New England Symphony*	100	[K] 1f
Elgar	*Introduction and Allegro for Strings*	51	1b [30]	**Vaughan Williams**	*Symphony in F minor (No. 4)*	98	4
Mahler	*Symphony No. 6*	150	4	**Villa-Lobos**	*Uirapurú*	71	[18]

Violin II and Violoncello

COMPOSER	WORK	PAGE	MEASURE
Strauss, R.	*Don Quixote*	59	1

Violin I, II, and Violoncello

COMPOSER	WORK	PAGE	MEASURE
Copland	*Two Pieces for String Orchestra*	13	3b [125]

Violin I, II, and Bass

COMPOSER	WORK	PAGE	MEASURE
Enesco	*2ᵉ Rhapsodie Roumaine*	7	4

Viola and Violoncello

COMPOSER	WORK	PAGE	MEASURE	COMPOSER	WORK	PAGE	MEASURE
Bartók	*Violin Concerto*	98	260	**Diamond**	*Rounds for String Orchestra*	37	[130] 6f
Berlioz	*Symphonie Fantastique*	26	5	**Enesco**	*Iᵉʳᵉ Rhapsodie Roumaine*	75	[36]

Violin I, II, Violoncello, and Bass

COMPOSER	WORK	PAGE	MEASURE
Stillman-Kelley	*New England Symphony*	11	[C]

Violin I, II, Viola, Violoncello, and Bass

COMPOSER	WORK	PAGE	MEASURE
Persichetti	*The Hollow Men*	10	1b [H]

Chapter 66

SPECIFIC STRINGS

(1)

English	Italian	French	German
A string	A corda	A [La] corde	A-Saite
A – – – – – – – –	Sul A' [La]	Sur (le) A [La]	Auf A
A ——————————⌐			Auf der A-Saite (zu spielen)
On the A string			

Violin I

English	Italian	French	German
II.	II. C. [corda]	II. corde	II.
2nd string	2ᵈ corda	2ᵉ corde	II-Saite
	Sul II	Sur la II. [2ᵉ] corde	
	Sulla IIᵃ		

COMPOSER	WORK	PAGE	MEASURE	COMPOSER	WORK	PAGE	MEASURE
Albéniz–				**Rachmaninoff**	*Rapsodie pour Piano et*	13	[10] 7f
Arbós	*Navarra*	38	2b [Q]		*Orchestre*	83	[59] 3f
Bartók	*Dance Suite*	37	42	**Ravel**	*La Valse*	68	[50]
Borodin	*Polovetzian Dances*			**Reger**	*Variations on a Theme*	2	3
	from "Prince Igor"	4	23		*of Mozart*	65	1
Britten	*Les Illuminations*	10	[4]			90	3
Britten	*Sinfonia da Requiem*	53	4b [36]	**Schelling**	*A Victory Ball*	31	3
Britten	*Sinfonietta*	25	7b [10]	**Sibelius**	*Symphony No. 1*	58	3
Elgar	*Cockaigne, Concert*			**Sibelius**	*Symphony No. 5*	32	[A] 2f
	Overture	21	[12] 2f	**Sibelius**	*Symphony No. 6*	81	10b [K]
Elgar	*Symphony No. 1*	7	[5] 5f	**Strauss, R.**	*Also Sprach*		
Elgar	*Variations, "Enigma"*	52	[33] 4f		*Zarathustra*	144	5
Glazounov	*Violin Concerto in*			**Stravinsky**	*Jeu de Cartes*	13	2b [24]
	A minor	44	[26] 4f			40	[78] 4f
Mahler	*Das Lied von der Erde*	131	1b [52]	**Stravinsky**	*Orpheus*	6	[10] 2f
Mahler	*Symphony No. 3*	214	[12]	**Stravinsky**	*Symphony in Three*		
Mahler	*Symphony No. 9*	9	4b [4]		*Movements*	75	1b [130]

Solo Violin

COMPOSER	WORK	PAGE	MEASURE
Schönberg	*Pierrot Lunaire*	6	[20] 1f

Violin II

COMPOSER	WORK	PAGE	MEASURE	COMPOSER	WORK	PAGE	MEASURE
Britten	*Sinfonia da Requiem*	59	[41] 1f	**Mahler**	*Symphony No. 1*	41	2b [30]
Glazounov	*Violin Concerto in*			**Ruggles**	*Sun-Treader*	46	219
	A minor	32	[19] 3f	**Schönberg**	*Kammersymphonie,*		
Jolivet	*Andante pour Orchestre*				*Op. 9*	77	[70]
	à Cordes	19	[80] 2f				

STRINGS

Violin I and II

COMPOSER	WORK	PAGE	MEASURE	COMPOSER	WORK	PAGE	MEASURE
Reger	Variations on a Theme of Mozart	18	1	Strauss, R.	Rosenkavalier Waltzes —First Sequence	22	[22] 1f
Strauss, R.	Ein Heldenleben	203	2b [102]	Stravinsky	Fire-Bird Suite (1919)	14	[17]

Viola

	English	Italian		French		German	
I.		1ª corda		1ère corde	I.		
Jolivet	Andante pour Orchestre à Cordes	4	[15]	Mussorgsky– Ravel	Pictures at an Exhibition	110	[91] 2f

Violoncello

	English	Italian		French		German	
I.		1ª corda		1ère corde	I.		
Bartók	Dance Suite	43	[31]	Rimsky– Korsakoff	Scheherazade	110	41
Britten	Sinfonia da Requiem	51	[34] 6f	Rogers	Elegy	7	7
Read	Symphony No. I	23	[11]	Shostakovich	Piano Concerto	6	6

Bass

	English	Italian		French		German	
III.		3ª corda		3e corde	III.		
Britten	Sinfonietta	42	[16] 5f	Stravinsky	Le Sacre du Printemps	80	[91]
Ravel	Le Tombeau de Couperin	4	[3] 6f				

Violin I, II, and Viola

COMPOSER	WORK	PAGE	MEASURE
Sessions	Suite from "The Black Maskers"	79	1b [77]

Violin I, II, and Violoncello

Mussorgsky– Ravel	Pictures at an Exhibition	110	[91]

Viola and Bass

Ravel	Le Tombeau de Couperin	25	6b [8]

SPECIFIC STRINGS

(2)

English	Italian	French	German
C string	C corda	C [Do; Ut] corde	C-Saite
On the C string	Sul C'	Sur (le) Ut	Auf C
			Auf der C-Saite

Viola

English	Italian	French	German
IV.	IV. C. [corda]	IV. corde	IV.
4th string	4ª corda	4ᵉ corde	IV–Saite
	Sul IV	Sur la IV. [4ᵉ] corde	
	Sulla IVᵃ		

COMPOSER	WORK	PAGE	MEASURE	COMPOSER	WORK	PAGE	MEASURE
Bach–	*Passacaglia and Fugue*			**Milhaud**	*Le Bal Martiniquais*	2	2
Respighi	*in C minor*	10	[8]	**Ravel**	*Daphnis et Chloé,*		
Bartók	*Dance Suite*	36	[25] 2f		*Suite No. 1*	10	[79]
Berg	*Three Excerpts from*			**Ravel**	*La Valse*	6	[5]
	"Wozzeck"	31	[45]			77	[57]
Bloch	*Schelomo*	56	[33]			103	[79]
Britten	*Les Illuminations*	14	[8] 2f	**Ravel**	*Le Tombeau de*		
Britten	*Passacaglia from "Peter*	1	6		*Couperin*	26	3b [9]
	Grimes"	28	1	**Ravel**	*Rapsodie Espagnole*	60	6
Britten	*Sinfonia da Requiem*	32	4b [23]	**Ravel**	*Tzigane*	16	9
Britten	*Sinfonietta*	43	10b [17]	**Riisager**	*Torgot Dance*	6	21
Harris	*When Johnny Comes*			**Schönberg**	*Verklärte Nacht*	24	[L] 1f
	Marching Home	44	[250] 1f	**Shostakovich**	*Symphony No. 5*	66	[60]
Herrmann	*Sinfonietta for String*			**Stravinsky**	*Le Sacre du Printemps*	9	[11]
	Orchestra	10	6	**Vaughan**	*Symphony in F minor*		
Mahler	*Symphony No. 9*	93	2	**Williams**	*(No. 4)*	106	[24]

Violoncello

English	Italian	French	German
IV.	4ª corda	4ᵉ corde	IV.

COMPOSER	WORK	PAGE	MEASURE	COMPOSER	WORK	PAGE	MEASURE
Bartók	*Concerto for Orchestra*	31	[52] 2f	**Mahler**	*Symphony No. 3*	11	[7]
Bartók	*Dance Suite*	43	[31] 2f	**Stravinsky**	*Quatre Études pour*		
Britten	*Serenade for Tenor,*				*Orchestre*	18	1b [8]
	Horn and Strings	35	[29] 6f	**Herrmann**	*Sinfonietta for String*		
Britten	*Sinfonia da Requiem*	57	[38] 2f		*Orchestra*	4	5b [E]
Britten	*Sinfonietta*	42	[16] 5f				

Solo Violoncello

COMPOSER	WORK	PAGE	MEASURE
Schönberg	*Pierrot Lunaire*	68	[35] 2f

Viola and Violoncello

COMPOSER	WORK	PAGE	MEASURE	COMPOSER	WORK	PAGE	MEASURE
Bach–	*Passacaglia and Fugue*			**Prokofieff**	*Suite from the Ballet*		
Respighi	*in C minor*	4	[5]		*"Chout"*	100	[128] 2f
Britten	*Les Illuminations*	4	[4]	**Ravel**	*Rapsodie Espagnole*	40	1b [1]

STRINGS

(3)

English	Italian	French	German
D string	D corda	D [Ré] corde	D-Saite
On the D string	Sul D′	Sur (le) Ré	Auf D
			Auf der D-Saite

Violin I

English	Italian	French	German
III.	III. C. [corda]	III. corde	III.
3rd string	3ª corda	3e corde	III-Saite
	Sul III	Sur la III. [3e] corde	
	Sulla IIIª		

COMPOSER	WORK	PAGE	MEASURE	COMPOSER	WORK	PAGE	MEASURE
Bach–Respighi	Passacaglia and Fugue in C minor	4	[5] 1f	Mahler	Symphony No. 9	9	4b [4]
						36	4b [13]
Berg	Three Excerpts from "Wozzeck"	31	1b [50]	Mussorgsky	Night on the Bald Mountain	21	[E] 1f
Britten	Sinfonia da Requiem	59	[40] 1f	Piston	Symphony No. 2	100	136
Copland	Third Symphony	55	1b [41]	Prokofieff	Romeo and Juliet, Suite No. 1	17	5
Delius	Three Orchestral Pieces	8	[5] 4f			118	4
Diamond	Music for Shakespeare's "Romeo and Juliet"	24	3b [30]	Rachmaninoff	Rapsodie pour Piano et Orchestre	48	5b [36]
		54	[5] 1f	Reger	Variations on a Theme of Mozart	2	1
Elgar	Cockaigne, Concert Overture	21	[12] 3f			70	[12]
Elgar	Symphony No. 1	7	[5] 4f	Schelling	A Victory Ball	31	3
		39	[32] 2f	Schönberg	Verklärte Nacht	33	[O]
Elgar	Symphony No. 2	64	[71]			44	7b [U]
Elgar	Variations, "Enigma"	52	[33]	Shepherd	Horizons	96	[M]
Ferroud	Au Parc Monceau	20	[2] 1f	Sibelius	Symphony No. 1	49	[A]
Glinka	Kamarinskaïa	13	131	Stravinsky	Orpheus	4	[5] 2f
Křenek	Symphonic Elegy	12	288	Stravinsky	Scènes de Ballet	23	1b [42]
Loeffler	Evocation	7	1b [L]	Vaughan Williams	A London Symphony	129	[P]
		34	[34]	Villa-Lobos	Uirapurú	3	1
Mahler	Das Lied von der Erde	131	[52] 1f			17	2
Mahler	Symphony No. 3	214	3b [12]			45	1
		221	[21] 3f				
Mahler	Symphony No. 5	126	2b [6]				

Solo Violin

COMPOSER	WORK	PAGE	MEASURE
Schönberg	Pierrot Lunaire	6	[15]
		49	1b [10]

Violin II

COMPOSER	WORK	PAGE	MEASURE	COMPOSER	WORK	PAGE	MEASURE
Bartók	Dance Suite	37	42	Schönberg	Verklärte Nacht	48	[W] 1f
Copland	Third Symphony	17	1b [12]	Thomson	The Seine at Night	1	5
Mahler	Symphony No. 8	102	1b [52]	Vaughan Williams	Symphony in E minor (No. 6)	47	[15] 2f
Moeran	Symphony in G minor	3	3			135	[39] 4f
Pizzetti	Concerto dell'Estate	77	[29] 6f	Walton	Symphony	115	[85] 4f
Reger	Variations on a Theme of Mozart	79	2				

SPECIFIC STRINGS

Violin I and II

COMPOSER	WORK	PAGE	MEASURE	COMPOSER	WORK	PAGE	MEASURE
Casella	*La Donna Serpente, I. Serie*	20	[21] 1f	**Scriabin**	*Piano Concerto in F♯ minor*	37	10b [3]
Coppola	*Suite Intima*	30	1	**Shostakovich**	*Symphony No. 7*	76	4b [68]
Mahler	*Symphony No. 9*	23	7	**Siegmeister**	*Western Suite*	4	3
Rimsky-Korsakoff	*Russian Easter Overture*	69	4	**Stravinsky**	*Fire-Bird Suite* (1919)	15	[18]
Schreker	*The Birthday of the Infanta, Suite*	28	[120] 2f	**Thomson**	*The Seine at Night*	5	3b [3]
				Vaughan Williams	*Symphony in F minor (No. 4)*	13	3b [9]

Viola

English		*Italian*		*French*		*German*	
II.		2ᵃ corda		2e corde		II.	
Jolivet	*Andante pour Orchestre à Cordes*		4 [15]	**Read**	*Symphony No. I*	53	[22]
Mussorgsky-Ravel	*Pictures at an Exhibition*	**110**	[91] 2f	**Thomson**	*Louisiana Story Suite*	14	74
				Vaughan Williams	*Symphony in E minor (No. 6)*	135	[40]

Violoncello

English		*Italian*		*French*		*German*	
II.		2ᵃ corda		2e corde		II.	
Bartók	*Dance Suite*	35	[24] 2f	**Ravel**	*Rapsodie Espagnole*	59	2b [12]
		43	[31] 1f	**Ravel**	*Tzigane*	16	1
		66	[50]	**Rimsky-Korsakoff**	*Scheherazade*	110	38
Britten	*Les Illuminations*	14	[8] 6f	**Rogers**	*Characters from Hans Christian Andersen*	9	[5]
Britten	*Sinfonia da Requiem*	63	6				
Herrmann	*Sinfonietta for String Orchestra*	10	18	**Rogers**	*Elegy*	7	4
Hindemith	*Kammermusik No. 4*	73	2	**Shostakovich**	*Piano Concerto*	6	5
Ravel	*Le Tombeau de Couperin*	44	2b [14]	**Sibelius**	*Symphony No. 3*	10	1
				Sibelius	*The Bard*	2	4b [A]

Bass

English		*Italian*		*French*		*German*	
II.		2ᵃ corda		2e corde		II.	
Bartók	*Dance Suite*	43	[31] 2f	**Ravel**	*Ma Mère l'Oye*	41	7
Ravel	*Le Tombeau de Couperin*	37	1b [3]	**Ravel**	*Tzigane*	5	[5] 4f
		43	[12]				

Violin I and Viola

COMPOSER	WORK	PAGE	MEASURE
Diamond	*Music for Shakespeare's "Romeo and Juliet"*	31	[10] 1f

Violin II and Viola

Sibelius	*Symphony No. 1*	27	[R] 1f

563

STRINGS

Violin I, II, and Viola

COMPOSER	WORK	PAGE	MEASURE	COMPOSER	WORK	PAGE	MEASURE
Grofé	*Grand Canyon Suite*	**111**	3	**Sibelius**	*Symphony No. 3*	**10**	11
Sessions	*Suite from "The Black Maskers"*	**79**	2b [77]				

Violin I and Violoncello

COMPOSER	WORK	PAGE	MEASURE
Sibelius	*Symphony No. 1*	**80**	[Q]

Violin I, II, and Violoncello

COMPOSER	WORK	PAGE	MEASURE	COMPOSER	WORK	PAGE	MEASURE
Mussorgsky–Ravel	*Pictures at an Exhibition*	**110**	[91]	**Rimsky-Korsakoff**	*Scheherazade*	**148**	193

Viola and Violoncello

COMPOSER	WORK	PAGE	MEASURE	COMPOSER	WORK	PAGE	MEASURE
Britten	*Les Illuminations*	**16**	3	**Stravinsky**	*Scènes de Ballet*	**16**	[27] 1f

Viola and Bass

COMPOSER	WORK	PAGE	MEASURE
Ravel	*Le Tombeau de Couperin*	**24**	[7] 1f

Violoncello and Bass

COMPOSER	WORK	PAGE	MEASURE
Piston	*Symphony No. 2*	**56**	1

Violin II, Viola, and Violoncello

COMPOSER	WORK	PAGE	MEASURE
Stravinsky	*Fire-Bird Suite (1919)*	**3**	[3] 1f

(4)

English	Italian	French	German
E string	E corda	E [Mi] corde	E-Saite
On the E string	Sul E′	Sur (le) Mi	Auf E
			Auf der E-Saite

Violin I

English	Italian	French	German
I.	I. C. [corda]	I. corde	I.
1st string	1ª corda	1ère corde	I-Saite
	Sul I	Sur la I. [1ère] corde	
	Sulla Iª		

COMPOSER	WORK	PAGE	MEASURE	COMPOSER	WORK	PAGE	MEASURE
Glazounov	*Violin Concerto in A minor*	**44**	[26] 4f	**Ravel**	*La Valse*	**68**	[50]
				Stravinsky	*Fire-Bird Suite (1919)*	**3**	[3] 1f

SPECIFIC STRINGS

Violin I and II

COMPOSER	WORK	PAGE	MEASURE
Thomson	*The Seine at Night*	**5**	2b [3]

Bass

English	*Italian*	*French*	*German*
IV.	4ª corda	4^e corde	IV.

COMPOSER	WORK	PAGE	MEASURE	COMPOSER	WORK	PAGE	MEASURE
Bartók	*Dance Suite*	**43**	[31] 1f	**Stravinsky**	*Le Sacre du Printemps*	**80**	[91]

(5)

English	*Italian*	*French*	*German*
G string	G corda	G [Sol] corde	G–Saite
On the G string	Sul G′	Sur (le) Sol	Auf G
			Auf der G–Saite

Violin I

English	*Italian*	*French*	*German*
IV.	IV. C. [corda]	IV. corde	IV.
4th string	4ª corda	4e corde	IV–Saite
	Sul IV	Sur la IV. [4e] corde	
	Sulla IV^a		

COMPOSER	WORK	PAGE	MEASURE	COMPOSER	WORK	PAGE	MEASURE
Albéniz–Arbós	*El Puerto*	**11**	[D] 2f	**Bruckner**	*Symphony No. 7*	**57**	4
						77	[Q]
Albéniz–Arbos	*Évocation*	**17**	6	**Bruckner**	*Symphony No. 8*	**69**	3
						77	[F]
						105	272
Albéniz–Arbós	*Navarra*	**32**	1	**Bruckner**	*Symphony No. 9*	**153**	1
Albéniz–Arbós	*Triana*	**7**	[B]	**Chávez**	*Sinfonia de Antigona*	**12**	[14]
				Chávez	*Sinfonia India*	**35**	[49]
Bach–Respighi	*Prelude and Fugue in D major*	**23**	1	**Debussy**	*Iberia*	**77**	[50] 2f
Barber	*First Symphony*	**17**	3	**Debussy**	*Printemps*	**22**	[11]
Bartók	*Dance Suite*	**65**	48			**64**	[31]
Berg	*Three Excerpts from "Wozzeck"*	**46**	[340] 3f	**Debussy–Ansermet**	*Six Épigraphes Antiques*	**14**	2b [B]
Bloch	*Evocations*	**18**	8	**Delius**	*Three Orchestral Pieces*	**5**	[3] 3f
		31	2b [25]	**Diamond**	*Fourth Symphony*	**35**	[25] 1f
Bloch	*Trois Poèmes Juifs*	**35**	[22] 2f	**Diamond**	*Music for Shakespeare's "Romeo and Juliet"*	**30**	3b [5]
Borodin	*Polovetzian Dances from "Prince Igor"*	**7**	39			**59**	[55]
		37	[H]	**Diamond**	*Rounds for String Orchestra*	**24**	1
Britten	*Four·Sea Interludes from "Peter Grimes"*	**54**	[I]			**37**	[135] 1f
				Dvořák	*Symphony No. 4*	**61**	5
Britten	*The Young Person's Guide to the Orchestra*	**42**	3	**Dvořák**	*Symphony No. 5, "From the New World"*	**63**	9
Bruckner	*Symphony No. 3*	**47**	[U]	**Elgar**	*Falstaff*	**5**	10
Bruckner	*Symphony No. 5*	**11**	109			**46**	[47]
		39	[P]			**145**	4b [145]
Bruckner	*Symphony No. 6*	**97**	[D] 4f	**Elgar**	*Symphony No. 1*	**39**	1b [32]

Violin I (contd.)

COMPOSER	WORK	PAGE	MEASURE	COMPOSER	WORK	PAGE	MEASURE
Elgar	Symphony No. 2	27	[30]	Milhaud	Deuxième Concerto		
		62	[68]		pour Violon et	45	2
Elgar	Variations, "Enigma"	2	1b [1]		Orchestre	78	2
		85	[54]	Milhaud	Opus Americanum		
de Falla	Three Dances from				No. 2	92	656
	"The Three-			Milhaud	IIe Symphonie	50	1b [30]
	Cornered Hat"	34	[9]	Milhaud	Quatrième Symphonie	99	[110] 4f
Fauré	Pénélope Prélude	1	1	Mussorgsky–			
Ferguson	Partita for Orchestra	59	[4] 1f	Ravel	Pictures at an Exhibition	49	[42]
		84	[15] 5f	Piston	First Symphony	7	1b [30]
Ferroud	Au Parc Monceau	2	[1]	Prokofieff	Ala et Lolly (Scythian		
Franck	Le Chasseur Maudit	77	354		Suite)	43	1b [24]
Grieg	Norwegian Dances	3	3	Prokofieff	Piano Concerto No. 3	100	[77]
		22	[G] 1f			164	[140]
		46	24	Prokofieff	Symphony No. 5	19	[10] 4f
Grieg	Suite for Strings,			Prokofieff	Violin Concerto No. 2	12	[10] 1f
	"From Holberg's			Rachmaninoff	Die Toteninsel	53	[19] 5f
	Time"	19	[V] 14f	Rachmaninoff	Rapsodie pour Piano		
Grofé	Grand Canyon Suite	62	2b [D]		et Orchestre	48	5b [36]
		106	3	Rachmaninoff	2d Concerto pour Piano		
Herrmann	Sinfonietta for String				et Orchestre	55	[21]
	Orchestra	2	5b [B]	Ravel	Daphnis et Chloé,	30	[166]
Hill	Sinfonietta for String				Suite No. 2	58	[185]
	Orchestra	10	1	Ravel	Introduction et Allegro	20	4b [14]
Hindemith	Nobilissima Visione	1	1	Ravel	La Valse	43	[30]
Honegger	Symphonie pour Cordes	3	[2] 8f			64	[47]
d'Indy	Jour d'été à la Montagne	86	[41]	Ravel	Valses Nobles et		
Ippolitov–					Sentimentales	6	[4]
Ivanov	Caucasian Sketches	21	2	Read	Symphony No. I	83	3
Kabalevsky	Symphony No. 2	29	[24] 1f	Revueltas	Cuauhnahuac	17	[24]
Křenek	Symphonic Elegy	12	285	Riisager	Torgot Dance	9	40
Lambert	The Rio Grande	28	[14]	Rimsky–			
Mahler	Das Lied von der Erde	26	[30] 4f	Korsakoff	Scheherazade	96	[P]
		125	[46] 5f	Ruggles	Sun-Treader	29	139
Mahler	Songs of a Wayfarer	12	[7] 3f	Schelling	A Victory Ball	30	2
Mahler	Symphony No. 1	93	[18]	Schönberg	Kammersymphonie,	87	[76]
Mahler	Symphony No. 3	6	[3] 4f		Op. 9	102	[89] 1f
		98	[73]	Schönberg	Verklärte Nacht	22	[J] 10f
		138	[4]			32	5
Mahler	Symphony No. 5	37	[14] 3f			48	3b [W]
		167	11b [29]	Schreker	The Birthday of the		
Mahler	Symphony No. 8	82	[18]		Infanta, Suite	60	[365] 2f
Mahler	Symphony No. 9	10	5	Shostakovich	Piano Concerto	32	[41]
		32	8	Shostakovich	Symphony No. 7	24	[34] 5f
		85	9			37	3b [41]
		127	3			158	[179] 2f
Malipiero	Pause del Silenzio	16	[C]	Sibelius	Karelia–Suite	17	[C]
Malipiero	Seconda Sinfonia			Sibelius	Symphony No. 3	62	[14] 1f
	(Elegiaca)	50	645	Siegmeister	Sunday in Brooklyn	66	1
McPhee	Four Iroquois Dances	22	[1]	Still	Poem for Orchestra	6	[2]
Miaskovsky	Sinfonietta	39	[17]			14	[8]

SPECIFIC STRINGS

Violin I (contd.)

COMPOSER	WORK	PAGE	MEASURE	COMPOSER	WORK	PAGE	MEASURE
Strauss, R.	Ein Heldenleben	35	[17]	Vaughan	A London Symphony	8	4
		77	4	Williams		152	2
		146	1	Vaughan	Symphony in D major		
Stravinsky	Le Sacre du Printemps	17	[24] 2f	Williams	(No. 5)	93	9
Stravinsky	Orpheus	4	[5]	Vaughan	Symphony in E minor	47	[15] 2f
Tchaikovsky	Symphony No. 5	86	1b [G]	Williams	(No. 6)	135	[39] 1f
Tchaikovsky	Symphony No. 6,			Wagner, R.	Introduction to Act III,		
	"Pathétique"	30	170		"Tristan und Isolde"	5	2
Turner	Gregorian Overture for			Walton	Façade, Suite No. 1	19	[E]
	String Orchestra	4	49	Walton	Symphony	27	6
						121	1b [91]

Solo Violin

COMPOSER	WORK	PAGE	MEASURE
Schönberg	Pierrot Lunaire	6	[15] 1f
		49	4b [10]

Violin II

COMPOSER	WORK	PAGE	MEASURE	COMPOSER	WORK	PAGE	MEASURE
Albéniz–Arbós	El Albaicín	4	2	Mahler	Das Lied von der Erde	46	[14] 1f
				Mahler	Symphony No. 1	106	[8]
Albéniz–Arbós	El Puerto	3	2	Mahler	Symphony No. 2	22	[11] 1f
						63	1b [6]
Albéniz–Arbós	Fête-Dieu à Séville	28	[H] 2f	Mahler	Symphony No. 3	39	3
Barber	First Symphony	8	[3] 1f	Mahler	Symphony No. 5	60	[7] 2f
Barber	Music for a Scene from			Mahler	Symphony No. 8	67	[83] 2f
	Shelley	11	1			91	1b [33]
Bartók	First Rhapsody for			Mahler	Symphony No. 9	75	4
	Violin and Orchestra	47	6	Mussorgsky–Ravel	Pictures at an Exhibition	133	[108]
Bartók	Music for Strings,			Ravel	La Valse	103	[79]
	Percussion and Celesta	143	2b [280]	Read	Symphony No. I	55	3
Debussy	Printemps	29	1b [14]	Ruggles	Sun-Treader	51	238
Diamond	Music for Shakespeare's			Schönberg	Kammersymphonie,	71	[67]
	"Romeo and Juliet"	54	[5] 1f		Op. 9	91	1b [80]
Elgar	In the South, Concert			Sessions	Suite from "The Black		
	Overture	34	[20]		Maskers"	43	5
Elgar	Symphony No. 1	5	[3] 2f	Shepherd	Horizons	35	1
de Falla	Three Dances from			Strauss, R.	Rosenkavalier Waltzes		
	"The Three-Cornered Hat"	28	[4] 1f		—First Sequence	35	1b [31]
Herrmann	Sinfonietta for String			Strauss, R.	Also Sprach		
	Orchestra	3	1		Zarathustra	168	3
Kodály	Galanta Dances	19	167	Wagner, R.	Prelude and Love		
Loeffler	Evocation	2	1b [B]		Death from "Tristan		
					und Isolde"	6	43

Violin I and II

COMPOSER	WORK	PAGE	MEASURE	COMPOSER	WORK	PAGE	MEASURE
Albéniz–Arbós	El Albaicín	18	[I] 7f	Albéniz–Arbós	El Puerto	21	2b [H]
						30	4b [L]

STRINGS

Violin I and II (contd.)

COMPOSER	WORK	PAGE	MEASURE	COMPOSER	WORK	PAGE	MEASURE
Bach–	*Passacaglia and Fugue*	4	[5]	Elgar	*Symphony No. 1*	85	[73]
Respighi	*in C minor*	29	[18]	Elgar	*Symphony No. 2*	51	[57] 1f
		55	4			93	[93]
Barber	*First Symphony*	92	1b [48]			170	1
Barber	*Medea*	61	3b [46]	Elgar	*Variations, "Enigma"*	24	[15]
Bartók	*Concerto for Orchestra*	6	[86] 4f	Fauré	*Pénélope Prélude*	17	[9] 3f
		56	[45]	Ferroud	*Au Parc Monceau*	20	[2]
		88	4b [81]	Glinka	*Kamarinskaïa*	5	39
Bartók	*Dance Suite*	48	2b [35]			15	161
Bartók	*Deux Images*	13	[6] 1f	Grieg	*Norwegian Dances*	32	5
Bartók	*Hungarian Peasant Songs*	10	1			56	[F]
Bartók	*Music for Strings,*	20	2	Grieg	*Piano Concerto in*		
	Percussion and Celesta	48	1		*A minor*	37	18b [A]
		65	1b [520]	Grofé	*Grand Canyon Suite*	94	[2]
Berg	*Three Excerpts from*					110	[1]
	"Wozzeck"	31	[45]	Harris	*Third Symphony*	57	4
Bloch	*Evocations*	22	[17]	Herrmann	*Sinfonietta for String*		
Bloch	*Schelomo*	27	1		*Orchestra*	10	13
		38	[22] 3f	Hindemith	*Kammermusik No. 1*	7	1
		56	[33]	Holst	*The Planets*	86	[VI]
Bloch	*Trois Poèmes Juifs*	48	1	Honegger	*Pacific 231*	47	207
Borodin	*On the Steppes of*			Honegger	*Symphonie Liturgique*	3	[1]
	Central Asia	16	193	Ibert	*Escales*	39	[34]
Britten	*Sinfonia da Requiem*	33	[24]			48	[42]
		51	[34] 6f	d'Indy	*Istar, Variations*	10	8
Britten	*The Young Person's*				*Symphoniques*	41	5b [5]
	Guide to the Orchestra	27	8	d'Indy	*Jour d'été à la Montagne*	74	4
Bruckner	*Symphony No. 5*	55	[B]	Ireland	*A London Overture*	44	2b [28]
Bruckner	*Symphony No. 6*	64	1	Janssen	*New Year's Eve in*		
Bruckner	*Symphony No. 8*	60	[B] 2f		*New York*	71	1
		128	301	Kalinnikov	*Symphony No. 1*	86	[G]
Bruckner	*Symphony No. 9*	10	[D]	Kodály	*Marosszék Dances*	4	2
		159	[C]	Lalo	*Le Roi d'Ys Ouverture*	5	5
Carse	*A Romantic Legend*	17	4			22	[G]
Casella	*La Donna Serpente,*			Mahler	*Das Lied von der Erde*	35	[44] 4f
	I. Serie	20	[21]	Mahler	*Songs of a Wayfarer*	40	20
Chabrier	*España, Rhapsodie*	17	8	Mahler	*Symphony No. 1*	115	[13]
Copland	*An Outdoor Overture*	8	55	Mahler	*Symphony No. 2*	31	[15]
Copland	*Billy the Kid Ballet*					157	[15] 6f
	Suite	17	1b [12]	Mahler	*Symphony No. 3*	3	6
Copland	*First Symphony*	49	13b [36]			41	3
Debussy	*Printemps*	75	1			213	[10]
Diamond	*Fourth Symphony*	37	[40] 2f	Mahler	*Symphony No. 5*	12	3
Diamond	*Music for Shakespeare's*					31	9
	"Romeo and Juliet"	10	1b [70]			75	3
Diamond	*Timon of Athens*	1	1			133	7
		16	2b [105]	Mahler	*Symphony No. 9*	34	4
Dukas	*La Péri*	66	2			57	1
Elgar	*Cockaigne, Concert-*					166	1
	Overture	20	1b [18]	Malipiero	*Pause del Silenzio*	34	201
Elgar	*Introduction and Allegro*			Miaskovsky	*Sinfonietta*	4	[13] 4f
	for Strings	52	6	Miaskovsky	*Symphony No. 21*	34	[34]

568

SPECIFIC STRINGS

Violin I and II (contd.)

COMPOSER	WORK	PAGE	MEASURE	COMPOSER	WORK	PAGE	MEASURE
Milhaud	Deuxième Concerto pour Violoncelle et Orchestre	84	1	Sibelius	Symphony No. 6	65	3
				Siegmeister	Ozark Set	26	3
Milhaud	Deuxième Concerto pour Violon et	84	2	Siegmeister	Sunday in Brooklyn	46	[25] 1
	Orchestre	139	1b [205]	Siegmeister	Western Suite	35	39
Mussorgsky	Night on the Bald			Stravinsky	Quatre Études pour Orchestre	2	4b [1]
	Mountain	39	204	Stringfield	A Negro Parade	34	3
Mussorgsky-Ravel	Pictures at an Exhibition	65	[56]	Taylor	Ballet Music from "Casanova"	27	[L]
Piston	First Symphony	62	[120] 2f	Taylor	Through the Looking Glass	43	1
Poot	Jazz-Music	3	[1]	Thomson	Louisiana Story Suite	14	74
Poot	Symphonie	13	6	Thomson	The Seine at Night	1	1
		54	4	Tchaikovsky	Hamlet	III	2
Rachmaninoff	2d Concerto pour Piano et Orchestre	5	6	Tchaikovsky	Suite from the Ballet, "The Sleeping Beauty"	76	5
Rachmaninoff	Symphony No. 2	40	2	Tchaikovsky	Symphony No. 6,	III	51
Ravel	Daphnis et Chloé, Suite No. 2	70	[195]		"Pathétique"	123	96
Ravel	La Valse	44	[31]			206	147
		113	[86]	Vaughan Williams	A London Symphony	33	5
Respighi	The Pines of Rome	19	[5] 4f			178	[P] 2f
Revueltas	Cuauhnahuac	4	[5]	Vaughan Williams	Job, A Masque for Dancing	91	[Yy]
Schreker	The Birthday of the Infanta, Suite	28	[120] 1f	Vaughan Williams	Overture to "The Wasps"	2	7b [A]
		68	1b [390]	Vaughan Williams	Symphony in F minor	11	[8] 1f
Schuman, W.	Symphony for Strings	1	1		(No. 4)	44	[4] 3f
Schuman, W.	Symphony No. IV	57	270			80	[5]
Schuman, W.	Undertow	32	2	Wagner, R.	Entrance of the Guests from "Tannhäuser"	14	[B]
Scriabin	Piano Concerto in F♯ minor	36	9	Wagner, R.	Prelude and Love Death from "Tristan und Isolde"	3	22
Sessions	Suite from "The Black Maskers"	72	[69] 2f	Wagner, R.	Preludes to Act I and III, "Lohengrin"	13	63
Shostakovich	Symphony No. 7	76	3b [68]	Walton	Concerto for Violin and Orchestre	58	[30]
Shostakovich	Symphony No. 9	44	[35]				
Sibelius	Symphony No. 1	118	8	Walton	Symphony	33	7b [20]
Sibelius	Symphony No. 3	63	[15] 1f			84	[60] 3f
Sibelius	Symphony No. 5	59	7				
		81	[E] 1f				

Viola

English		Italian			French		German		
III.		3ª corda			3e corde		III.		

Bartók	Concerto for Orchestra	88	4b [81]	Milhaud	Deuxième Concerto pour Violon et Orchestre	81	4
Bartók	Dance Suite	35	[24] 2f				
Berg	Three Excerpts from "Wozzeck"	31	1b [50]	Milhaud	Le Bal Martiniquais	2	1
Britten	Sinfonia da Requiem	32	2b [23]	Piston	Concerto for Orchestra	60	[5]
Jolivet	Andante pour Orchestre à Cordes	3	[10] 4f	Piston	Prelude and Fugue	1	4
Mahler	Symphony No. 1	65	14b [17]	Ravel	Le Tombeau de Couperin	26	4b [9]

STRINGS

Viola (contd.)

COMPOSER	WORK	PAGE	MEASURE	COMPOSER	WORK	PAGE	MEASURE
Read	Symphony No. I	24	3	Vaughan Williams	Symphony in F minor (No. 4)	26	[17] 1f
Schönberg	Verklärte Nacht	44	7b [U]	Ruggles	Sun-Treader	27	130
Stravinsky	Fire-Bird Suite (1919)	14	[17]				
Thomson	The Seine at Night	1	5				

Violoncello

	English	Italian		French		German	
III.		3ª corda		3ᵉ corde		III.	

Bartók	Concerto for Orchestra	127	[441] 5f	Hindemith	Kammermusik No. 4	72	1
Bartók	Dance Suite	24	1b [16]	Ravel	Le Tombeau de Couperin	6	4b [5]
		43	[31] 1f			21	[3] 3f
Britten	Passacaglia from "Peter Grimes"	28	1	Shostakovich	Piano Concerto	6	4
Herrmann	Sinfonietta for String Orchestra	4	6b [E]	Shostakovich	Symphony No. 5	66	[60] 1f

Bass

	English	Italian		French		German	
I.		1ª corda		1ère corde		I.	

Bartók	Dance Suite	43	[31]	Ravel	Le Tombeau de Couperin	36	[2] 3f
						38	[4]

Violin I and Viola

d'Indy	Istar, Variations Symphoniques	20	[I]	Ruggles	Sun-Treader	40	191
Mahler	Symphony No. 2	122	3	Sessions	Suite from "The Black Maskers"	105	1
Piston	Suite for Orchestra	21	4				

Violin I, II, and Viola

Bartók	Dance Suite	24	4b [16]	Piston	Suite for Orchestra	52	1
Britten	Sinfonia da Requiem	22	7	Piston	Symphony No. 2	31	151
		52	[35] 1f	Sessions	Suite from "The Black Maskers"	78	[76]
Chabrier	España, Rhapsodie	44	7	Sibelius	Pohjola's Daughter	46	2b [R]
Elgar	Cockaigne, Concert Overture	10	1b [4]	Sibelius	Symphony No. 2	105	2b [B]
Elgar	Symphony No. 2	141	[139]	Sibelius	Symphony No. 3	19	5b [11]
d'Indy	Istar, Variations Symphoniques	22	[J]	Strauss, R.	Also Sprach Zarathustra	206	5
Kalinnikov	Symphony No. I	177	[B]	Vaughan Williams	Job, A Masque for Dancing	58	[Ff]
Piston	Concertino for Pianoforte and Chamber Orchestra	11	1b [65]			92	11
		49	4	Vaughan Williams	Symphony in F minor (No. 4)	41	2
Piston	Concerto for Orchestra	17	[10]	Wagner, J.	Symphony Number One	22	[3] 1f

SPECIFIC STRINGS

Violin I and Violoncello

COMPOSER	WORK	PAGE	MEASURE
Sibelius	*Symphony No.* 1	**122**	1b [H]

Violin I, II, and Violoncello I

Schönberg	*Verklärte Nacht*	23	[K] 13f

Viola and Violoncello

COMPOSER	WORK	PAGE	MEASURE	COMPOSER	WORK	PAGE	MEASURE
Britten	*Les Illuminations*	16	3	**Piston**	*Symphony No.* 2	I	3

Violin I, II, Viola, and Violoncello

Mahler	*Symphony No.* 9	**60**	20

Chapter 67

REVERSE ARPEGGIO

English	*Italian*	*French*	*German*
Downward [reverse] arpeggio	Arpeggio discendente	Arpège descendant	Fallendes Arpeggio
Hold(ing) the instrument backwards	Tenendo l'instrumento al rovescio	En tenant l'instrument renversé	Das Instrument rückwärts haltend
With the bow held backwards	Col'arco al rovescio	Avec l'archet renversée	Den Bogen rückwärts halten

Violoncello

COMPOSER	WORK	PAGE	MEASURE	COMPOSER	WORK	PAGE	MEASURE
Bartók	*Divertimento for String Orchestra*	33	[342]	**Debussy**	*Iberia*	88	[56]
Bartók	*Second Rhapsody for Violin and Orchestra*	6	[2]	**Piston**	*Suite for Orchestra*	19	[H]

Violin I, II, and Viola

COMPOSER	WORK	PAGE	MEASURE
Schmitt	*Mirages pour Orchestre, No. 1*	32	3b [15]

Violoncello and Bass

COMPOSER	WORK	PAGE	MEASURE
Mozart	*Violin Concerto No. V in A major*	66	165

Chapter 68

SCORDATURA (UNUSUAL TUNING)

English	Italian	French	German
Lower A (string) to G♯	Accordate A in G♯	Descendez le La un demi-ton plus bas	A nach Gis herunterstimmen
Lower C (string) to B	Accordate C in B / Abbassa la IV. corda al Si	Baissent la corde Do au Si	Mit auf H herabgestimmen C-Saite
Lower G (string) to G♭	Accordate G in G♭	Baissez la corde Sol au Sol♭	G nach Ges herunterstimmen
Lower G to F♯	Accordate G in F♯	Baissez la corde Sol au Fa♯ / Baissez le Sol d'un demi-ton	Die G-Saite werden auf Fis hinabgestimmt
Raise G (string) to G♯	Accordate G in G♯	Accordez Sol au Sol♯	
Retune 4th string	Rimette la IV. corda	Réaccordez la IV. corde	Stimmen die G-Saite wie vorher
Tune 1st string (E) to D	Muta I*a* corda (E) in D	La I. corde (Mi) accordée en Ré	Stimmen die G-Saite auf Gis
Tune 3rd string (G) to A	Muta III*a* corda (G) in A	La III. corde (Sol) accordée en La	Gestimmt E in D / Gestimmt G in A
Tune G string normally	Accordate il G corda come di solito	Accordez le Sol comme d'ordinaire	G-Saite wieder normale Stimmung

(1) VIOLIN I or II [SOLO VIOLIN]

COMPOSER	WORK	PAGE	MEASURE		COMPOSER	WORK	PAGE	MEASURE
Mahler	Symphony No. 4	73	1		Bax	First Symphony	80	[K]
					Hindemith	Symphonische Tänze	68	1
					Strauss, R.★	Ein Heldenleben	79	[40] 3f
							83	5
Saint-Saëns	Danse Macabre	1	1					
Stravinsky	Fire-Bird Suite (1919)	3	[3] 1f		Bax	First Symphony	57	1

(2) VIOLA [SOLO VIOLA]

COMPOSER	WORK	PAGE	MEASURE		COMPOSER	WORK	PAGE	MEASURE
Inghelbrecht	La Valse Retrouvée	1	1		Albéniz-Arbós	El Albaicín	40	[BB] 1f
					Bax	First Symphony	57	1
							80	[K]
					Strauss, R.	Don Quixote	61	5

★ *N.B.* The low F♯ in Vln. I, II of Strauss' *Symphonia Domestica*, p. 57 [73] 1f, is not an example of scordatura, but is an intentional "error" in notation.

573

(3) VIOLONCELLO [SOLO VIOLONCELLO]

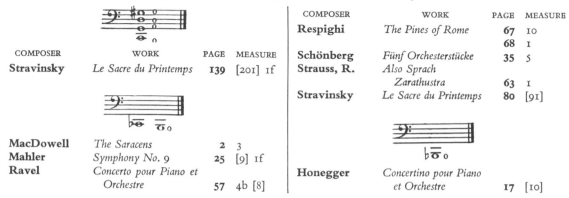

COMPOSER	WORK	PAGE	MEASURE
Stravinsky	*Le Sacre du Printemps*	**139**	[201] 1f

COMPOSER	WORK	PAGE	MEASURE
Respighi	*The Pines of Rome*	**67**	10
		68	1
Schönberg	*Fünf Orchesterstücke*	**35**	5
Strauss, R.	*Also Sprach Zarathustra*	**63**	1
Stravinsky	*Le Sacre du Printemps*	**80**	[91]

COMPOSER	WORK	PAGE	MEASURE
MacDowell	*The Saracens*	**2**	3
Mahler	*Symphony No. 9*	**25**	[9] 1f
Ravel	*Concerto pour Piano et Orchestre*	**57**	4b [8]

COMPOSER	WORK	PAGE	MEASURE
Honegger	*Concertino pour Piano et Orchestre*	**17**	[10]

(4) BASS—Classical and Early Romantic Orchestra

Beethoven	*Coriolanus Overture*
Beethoven	*Leonore Overture No. 2*
Beethoven	*Leonore Overture No. 3*
Beethoven	*Piano Concerto No. 2*
Beethoven	*Piano Concerto No. 4*
Beethoven	*Piano Concerto No. 5*
Beethoven	*Symphony No. 3, "Eroica"*
Beethoven	*Symphony No. 4*
Beethoven	*Symphony No. 5*
Beethoven	*Symphony No. 6, "Pastoral"*
Beethoven	*Symphony No. 7*
Beethoven	*Symphony No. 9*
Haydn	*Symphony No. 1 in Eb major, "Drumroll"*
Haydn	*Symphony No. 3 in Eb major*
Haydn	*Symphony No. 7 in C major, "Le Midi"*
Haydn	*Symphony No. 11 in G major, "Military"*
Haydn	*Symphony No. 12 in Bb major*
Haydn	*Symphony No. 15 in Bb major, "La Reine"*
Mendelssohn	*Ruy Blas Overture*
Mendelssohn	*Symphony No. 3, "Scotch"*
Mendelssohn	*Three Pieces from "A Midsummer Night's Dream"*
Mozart	*Symphony No. 39 in Eb major*
Mozart	*Symphony No. 40 in G minor*
Mozart	*Symphony No. 41 in C major, "Jupiter"*
Mozart	*Violin Concerto No. I in Bb major*
Schubert	*Symphony No. 2*

Schubert	*Symphony No. 4, "Tragic"*
Schubert	*Symphony No. 5*
Schubert	*Symphony No. 6*
Schubert	*Symphony No. 7*
Schubert	*Symphony No. 8, "Unfinished"*
Schumann, R.	*Symphony No. 1*
Schumann, R.	*Symphony No. 2*
Schumann, R.	*Symphony No. 3*

Beethoven	*Coriolanus Overture*
Beethoven	*Piano Concerto No. 4*
Beethoven	*Symphony No. 4*
Beethoven	*Symphony No. 5*
Beethoven	*Symphony No. 6, "Pastoral"*
Beethoven	*Symphony No. 7*
Beethoven	*Symphony No. 9*
Cherubini	*Anakreon Overture*
Handel	*Music for the Royal Fireworks*
Handel	*Water Music in F*
Haydn	*Symphony No. 2 in D major, "London"*
Haydn	*Symphony No. 3 in Eb major*
Haydn	*Symphony No. 4 in D major, "Clock"*
Haydn	*Symphony No. 5 in D major*
Haydn	*Symphony No. 6 in G major, "Surprise"*
Haydn	*Symphony No. 7 in C major, "Le Midi"*
Haydn	*Symphony No. 11 in G major, "Military"*

SCORDATURA (UNUSUAL TUNING)

(4) BASS—Classical and Early Romantic Orchestra (contd.)

COMPOSER	WORK
Haydn	Symphony No. 13 in G major
Haydn	Symphony No. 14 in D major
Haydn	Symphony No. 17 in C major, "L'Ours"
Haydn	Symphony No. 18 in F♯ minor, "Farewell"
Mendelssohn	Calm Sea and a Prosperous Voyage, Overture
Mendelssohn	Fingal's Cave Overture
Mendelssohn	Ruy Blas Overture
Mendelssohn	Symphony No. 3, "Scotch"
Mendelssohn	Symphony No. 4, "Italian"
Mendelssohn	Three Pieces from "A Midsummer Night's Dream"
Mozart	Piano Concerto (No.26) in D major, "Coronation"
Mozart	Symphony No. 39 in E♭ major
Mozart	Symphony No. 40 in G minor
Mozart	Symphony No. 41 in C major, "Jupiter"
Rossini	La Gazza Ladra, Overture
Schubert	Symphony No. 2
Schubert	Symphony No. 5
Schubert	Symphony No. 7
Schubert	Symphony No. 8, "Unfinished"
Schumann, R.	Symphony No. 1
Schumann, R.	Symphony No. 2

COMPOSER	WORK
Beethoven	Symphony No. 6, "Pastoral"
Beethoven	Symphony No. 7
Beethoven	Symphony No. 9
Haydn	Symphony No. 1 in E♭ major, "Drumroll"
Mozart	Symphony No. 39 in E♭ major

COMPOSER	WORK
Mozart	Symphony No. 41 in C major, "Jupiter"
Schubert	Rosamunde Overture
Schubert	Symphony No. 2
Schubert	Symphony No. 8, "Unfinished"
Schumann, R.	Symphony No. 2

COMPOSER	WORK
Beethoven	Leonore Overture No. 2
Beethoven	Symphony No. 1
Beethoven	Symphony No. 4
Beethoven	Symphony No. 5
Beethoven	Symphony No. 6, "Pastoral"
Beethoven	Symphony No. 7
Beethoven	Symphony No. 8
Beethoven	Symphony No. 9
Cherubini	Anakreon Overture
Handel	Water Music in F
Haydn	Symphony No. 1 in E♭ major, "Drumroll"
Haydn	Symphony No. 6 in G major, "Surprise"
Haydn	Symphony No. 7 in C major, "Le Midi"
Haydn	Symphony No. 17 in C major, "L'Ours"
Mendelssohn	Ruy Blas Overture
Mendelssohn	Symphony No. 3, "Scotch"
Mozart	Symphony No. 40 in G minor
Mozart	Symphony No. 41 in C major, "Jupiter"
Schubert	Symphony No. 2
Schubert	Symphony No. 4, "Tragic"
Schubert	Symphony No. 8, "Unfinished"
Schumann, R.	Symphony No. 2

(5) BASS—Modern Orchestra

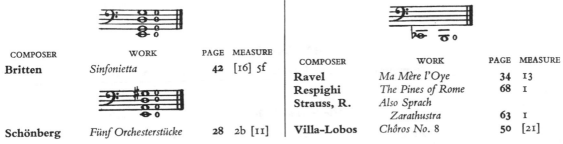

COMPOSER	WORK	PAGE	MEASURE
Britten	Sinfonietta	42	[16] 5f
Schönberg	Fünf Orchesterstücke	28	2b [11]

COMPOSER	WORK	PAGE	MEASURE
Ravel	Ma Mère l'Oye	34	13
Respighi	The Pines of Rome	68	1
Strauss, R.	Also Sprach Zarathustra	63	1
Villa-Lobos	Chôros No. 8	50	[21]

Chapter 69

SENZA VIBRATO

English	*Italian*	*French*	*German*
No vibrato	Non-vibrato	Non-vibrant	Nicht vibrierend
Without vibrato	Senza vibrato	Sans vibrer	

Solo Violin I

COMPOSER	WORK	PAGE	MEASURE	COMPOSER	WORK	PAGE	MEASURE
Ferguson	*Partita for Orchestra*	**56**	6	**Stravinsky**	*Firebird Ballet Suite*		
Stravinsky	*Chant du Rossignol*	**75**	[83]		(1945)	**28**	[33] 1f

Soli Violin I

COMPOSER	WORK	PAGE	MEASURE
Stravinsky	*Scènes de Ballet*	**34**	[56]

Violin II

Copland	*Statements*	**45**	[3] 2f

Violin I and II

Berg	*Violin Concerto*	**62**	3	**Maganini**	*South Wind*	**2**	1

Viola

Berg	*Violin Concerto*	**80**	[135]

Violoncello

Copland	*Statements*	**49**	[7] 1f	**Fitelberg**	*Nocturne for Orchestra*	**2**	3b [12]

Soli Violoncello

Stravinsky	*Scènes de Ballet*	**60**	[96] 1f

Violin II and Viola

Berg	*Violin Concerto*	**6**	2b [30]

576

SENZA VIBRATO

Violin I, II, and Viola

COMPOSER	WORK	PAGE	MEASURE
Harrison	*Alleluia for Orchestra*	14	[K]

Viola and Violoncello

COMPOSER	WORK	PAGE	MEASURE
Strauss, R.	*Ein Heldenleben*	81	3b [42]

Violin I, II, Viola, and Violoncello

COMPOSER	WORK	PAGE	MEASURE	COMPOSER	WORK	PAGE	MEASURE
Berg	*Violin Concerto*	33	1	Harrison	*Alleluia for Orchestra*	20	[P]

Violin I, II, Viola, Violoncello, and Bass

COMPOSER	WORK	PAGE	MEASURE
Moore	*In Memoriam*	23	[O] 3f

Chapter 70

MISCELLANEOUS EFFECTS

Violin I

English	*Italian*	*French*	*German*
Pizz. and arco **at** the same time	Pizz. ed arco simultaneamente	Pizz. et l'archet au même temps	Pizz. u. Bogen im gleichen Zeit

COMPOSER	WORK	PAGE	MEASURE
Villa-Lobos	*Amazonas*	41	4

English	*Italian*	*French*	*German*
At the point, like col legno	Punta d'arco, quasi col legno	A la pointe, comme col legno	Spitze des Bogens, wie col legno

Walton	*Concerto for Violin and Orchestra*	19	[11]

Solo Violin I

English	*Italian*	*French*	*German*
Slow vibrato	Vibrato lento	Vibrez lentement	Langsam vibrierend

Rogers	*Characters from Hans Christian Andersen*	6	1

Violin I and II

English	*Italian*	*French*	*German*
Country-fiddle style	—	Comme un crincrin	Wie eine Fiedel

Siegmeister	*Ozark Set*	58	3

English	*Italian*	*French*	*German*
Pluck open string (D) and then stop E vigorously at once without further plucking	Pizz. la corda aperta (D) e poi pressate l'E vigorosamente subito senza pizz. di più	Arrachez la corde ouverte (Ré) et puis pressez Mi vigoureusement, tout à coup sans plus arracher	Die öffene Saite (D) reissen und dann E kräftig angreifen ohne wieder reissen

Villa-Lobos	*Uirapurú*	71	[18]

MISCELLANEOUS EFFECTS

Violin I and II (contd.)

English	Italian	French	German
Start on the point (of bow)	Incominciate alla punta (d'arco)	Commencez au bout (de l'archet)	Am Spitze (des Bogens) beginnen

COMPOSER	WORK	PAGE	MEASURE
Chávez	*Sinfonia India*	47	3b [63]

Solo Violoncello

Doppelgriff es [E♭] u.h. [B]

Schönberg	*Pierrot Lunaire*	45	[10] 1f

Bass

English	Italian	French	German
Quarter tones	Quarto di toni	Quart de tons	Vierteltöne

Moross	*Paeans*	5	1b [E]

English	Italian	French	German
Trill: broken rumble	Trillo: interrotto sordo barbugliato	Trille: roulement brisé	Triller: gebrochenes Drähnen

Ives	*Three Places in New England*	57	[R]

Violin I and Viola

English	Italian	French	German
Near the bridge, like trumpets	Poco sul pont., quasi trombe	A peu près du chevalet, comme trompettes	Nahe zum Steg, wie Trompetten

Britten	*Les Illuminations*	2	3

Violin I, II, and Viola

English	Italian	French	German
Tap with bow on back (of instrument)	Percuotete col arco al dorso (del instrumento)	Frappez légèrement avec l'archet au dos (de l'instrument)	Mit dem Bogen auf die Rückseite (des Instrumentes) leicht klopfen

Fernandez	*Batuque*	9	[8] 1f

Solo Viola and Violoncello

English	Italian	French	German
Nasal tone	Tono nasale	Ton nasillard	Nasaler Ton

Villa-Lobos	*Chôros No. 8*	33	[14]

STRINGS

Violoncello and Bass

English	Italian	French	German
With the bow—like pizz.	Arco—quasi pizz.	Archet—comme pizz.	Bogen—wie Pizz.

COMPOSER	WORK	PAGE	MEASURE
Stravinsky	*Quatre Études pour Orchestre*	17	[6]

Violin I, II, Viola, and Violoncello

English	Italian	French	German
Like an accordion	Quasi fisarmonica	Comme un accordéon	Wie eine Handharmonika

Rosenthal	*Les Petits Métiers*	17	7b [E]

English	Italian	French	German
Tap on the belly (of instrument) with finger	Percuotete sul lato superiore (del'instrumente) col una dita	Frappez légèrement sur le côté supérieur (de l'instrument) avec un doigt	Mit Finger auf der Oberseite (des Instrumentes) leise klopfen

Fuleihan	*Mediterranean*	27	[E]

Violin I, Viola, Violoncello, and Bass

English	Italian	French	German
Quarter tones sharp	Quarto di toni acuti	Quart de tons aigus	Vierteltöne hoch

Moross	*Paeans*	1	4

Violin I, II, Viola, Violoncello, and Bass

English	Italian	French	German
Spiccato on the nut	Spiccato al talone	Spiccato au talon	Spiccato am Frosch

Schelling	*A Victory Ball*	79	1

Outside: upper bowing
Inside: lower bowing

COMPOSER	WORK	PAGE	MEASURE	COMPOSER	WORK	PAGE	MEASURE
Persichetti	*The Hollow Men*	6	[E]	**Schuman, W.**	*Undertow*	44	5
Schuman, W.	*Symphony No. IV*	60	4b [290]	**Sibelius**	*Symphony No. 7*	29	1

Chapter 71

STRING TERMINOLOGY

English	Italian	French	German
All desks muted	Tutt'i leggi con sord.	Sourds. à tous les pup.	Alle Pulte mit Dämpfer
All the basses except the 1st player	Tutti i bassi salvo il I°	Toutes Contrebasses sauf la 1ère	Alle die Bässe mit Ausnahme von dem ersten Spieler
All the 1st [2nd] Vlns. put on mutes except the 1st desk	Tutti Vln. I [II] mettete i sordini salvo il I° leggio	Tous les 1ers [2ds] V°ns mettent la sourd. excepté le 1er pupitre	Alle ersten [zweiten] Viol. mit Ausnahme des ersten Pultes gedämpft
All the others	Tutti gli altri Tutti le altre	Tous les autres	Alle die Andere
Avoid the open A [C; D; E; G] string	Evitare la corda aperta La [Do; Re; Mi; Sol]	Évitez la corde ouverte La [Ut; Ré; Mi; Sol]	Nicht das leere A [C; D; E; G] nehmen
Different tone for each desk	Tono differente per ogni leggio	Un ton different pour chaque pupitre	Je ein Ton von einem Pult
Divisi by desks	Divisi al leggi	Divisés par pupitres	Pultweise geteilt
Double-stop	Doppia corda	Double corde	Doppelgriff
5-string Bass	Contrabasso con quintupolo corde	Contrebasse à cinq cordes	Fünfsaitiger Kontrabass
Join the other Vlns. [Vlas., etc.]	Col gli altri Vni. [altre Vle., etc.]	Avec les autres V°ns [Altos, etc.]	Mit den andern Viol. [Br., etc.]
Last desk only	Solamente l'ultimo leggio	Seulement le dernier pupitre	Nur letztes Pult
Let the bow undulate	Lasciate ondeggiare l'arco	En laissant flotter l'archet	Den Bogen auf- und abwallen lassen
Lightly touching the string	Toccante leggiermente la corda	En effleurant la corde	Die Saite leicht berühren
Only those Basses with low C-string	Soltanto i Bassi colla C-bassa corda	Seulement les C.B. avec la C-basse corde	Nur die mit Kontra-C versehenen Bässe
On one string	Sul una corda	Sur une corde	Auf einer Saite
On the same string	Alla stessa corda	Sur la même corde	An der gleichen Saite
Pizz.—tearing the string	Pizz.—strappando la corda	Pizz.—en arrachant la corde	Pizz.—anreissen
Stay in 1st [2nd; 3rd; 4th, 5th; 6th; 7th; 8th; 9th, etc.] position	Rimanete in 1ª [IIª; IIIª; IVª; Vª; VIª; VIIª; VIIIª; IXª, etc.] posizione	Restez I [II; III; IV; V; VI; VII; VIII; IX, etc.] position	Im 1 [2; 3; 4; 5; 6; 7; 8; 9, etc.] Positur bleiben
Stay in position	Rimanete in posizione	Rester Restez	In Positur bleiben
Still muted	Sempre con sord.	Toujours avec sourd.	Immer noch mit Dämpfer
The others	Gli altri Tutti	Tous	Die übrigen
The other desks	Gli altri leggi	Les autres pupitres	Die andere Pulte
Violin solo with 1st Vlns.	Violino solo col Vni. primo [I°]	Le Solo V°n avec les autres	Violine Solo mit den andern 1ten Viol.

LIST OF PUBLISHERS

No.	PUBLISHER	U.S.A. AGENTS	BRITISH AGENTS
1	Affiliated Music Corp., New York	Edition Musicus—New York, Inc.	
2	Arrow Music Press, Inc., New York	American Music Center, Inc., New York	Boosey & Hawkes, Ltd., London
3	Associated Music Publishers, Inc., New York		
4	Augener, Ltd., London	Broude Brothers, New York	
5	Axelrod Publications, Inc., Providence, R.I.		
6	M. Baron Co., New York		
7	Édition M.P. Belaieff, Paris	Associated Music Publishers, Inc., New York	Boosey & Hawkes, Ltd., London
8	W. Bessel and Cie., Paris	Boosey & Hawkes, Inc., New York	Boosey & Hawkes, Ltd., London
9	C. C. Birchard & Co., Boston, Mass.		
10	Bomart Music Publications, Long Island City, N.Y.		
11	Boosey & Hawkes, Inc., Lynbrook, L.I., N.Y.		Boosey & Hawkes, Ltd., London
12	Ed. Bote & G. Bock, Berlin	Associated Music Publishers, Inc., New York	Novello & Co., Ltd., London
13	Breitkopf & Härtel, Leipzig	Associated Music Publishers, Inc., New York	British & Continental Music Agencies, Ltd., London
14	British & Continental Music Agencies, Ltd., London	Associated Music Publishers, Inc., New York	
15	Broadcast Music, Inc., New York	Associated Music Publishers, Inc., New York	
16	Broude Brothers, New York		
17	Brucknerverlag, Wiesbaden, G.M.B.H.	C. F. Peters Corporation, New York	
18	Chappell & Co., Inc., New York		Chappell & Co., Ltd., London
19	Charling Music Corp., New York	Mayfair Music Corp., New York	
20	J. & W. Chester, Ltd., London	E. B. Marks Music Corp., New York	
21	Composers Press, Inc., New York		
22	Cos Cob Press, Inc., New York	American Music Center, Inc., New York	
23	J. Curwen and Sons, Ltd., London	G. Schirmer, Inc., New York	
24	R. Deiss, Paris (now Éditions Salabert, Paris)	Salabert, Inc., New York	J. & W. Chester, Ltd., London

No.	PUBLISHER	U.S.A. AGENTS	BRITISH AGENTS
25	Durand et Cie., Paris	Elkan-Vogel Co., Inc., Philadelphia	
26	Edition Musicus-New York, Inc., New York		
27	Édition Russe de Musique, Paris (now Boosey & Hawkes, Inc., New York)	Boosey & Hawkes, Inc., New York	Boosey & Hawkes, Ltd., London
28	Éditions Sociales Internationales, Paris	Elkan-Vogel Co., Inc., Philadelphia	
29	Elkan-Vogel Co., Inc., Philadelphia, Pa.		
30	Enoch et Cie., Paris	Southern Music Publishing Company, Inc., New York	
31	Max Eschig Éditions, Paris	Associated Music Publishers, Inc., New York	
32	Ernst Eulenburg, London	C. F. Peters Corporation, New York	
33	Carl Fischer, Inc., New York		
34	J. Fischer & Bro., New York		
35	Charles Foley, New York		
36	Foetisch Frères S.A., Éditeurs, Paris	E. C. Schirmer Co., Boston, Mass.	J. & W. Chester, Ltd., London
37	Adolf Fürstner, Berlin	Boosey & Hawkes, Inc., New York	Boosey & Hawkes, Ltd., London
38	G. & C. Music Corp., New York	Chappell & Co., Inc., New York	
39	Carl Gehrmans Musikforlag, Stockholm	Southern Music Publishing Company, Inc., New York	
40	A. Gutheil, Paris (now Boosey & Hawkes, Inc., New York)	Boosey & Hawkes, Inc., New York	Boosey & Hawkes, Ltd., London
41	J. Hamelle, Paris		J. & W. Chester, Ltd., London
42	Wilhelm Hansen, Copenhagen	G. Schirmer, Inc., New York	Novello & Co., Ltd., London; and J. & W. Chester, Ltd., London
43	Harms, Inc., New York		
44	Heugel et Cie, Paris	Mercury Music Corp., New York	
45	International Music Co., New York		
46	Jean Jobert, Paris	Elkan-Vogel Co., Inc., Philadelphia	J. & W. Chester, Ltd., London
47	P. Jurgenson, Leipzig		
48	C. F. Kahnt-Nachfolger, Leipzig		Novello & Co., Ltd., London
49	Edwin F. Kalmus, New York		
50	Le Chant du Monde, Paris	Elkan-Vogel Co., Inc., Philadelphia	
51	Leduc et Cie., Paris	M. Baron Co., New York	J. & W. Chester, Ltd., London
52	Leeds Music Corporation, New York		
53	F. E. C. Leuckart, Leipzig	Associated Music Publishers, Inc., New York	Novello & Co., Ltd., London
54	Harald Lyche and Co., Musickforlag, Oslo	C. F. Peters Corporation, New York	

LIST OF PUBLISHERS

No.	Publisher	U.S.A. Agents	British Agents
55	Edward B. Marks Music Corp., New York		
56	Mercury Music Corporation, New York		
57	Mills Music, Inc., New York		
58	Murdoch, Murdoch & Co., London	Chappell & Co., Inc., New York	
59	Music Press, Inc., New York	Mercury Music Corp., New York	
60	New Music Edition, New York	American Music Center, Inc., New York	
61	Novello & Co., Ltd., London	The H. W. Gray Co., Inc., New York	
62	Oxford University Press, Inc., New York		Oxford University Press, London
63	C. F. Peters Corporation, New York		
64	Pro Art Publications, New York		
65	G. Ricordi & C., Milan	G. Ricordi & Co., New York	
66	Robbins Music Corporation, New York		
67	Rouart-Lerolle et Cie, Paris (now Éditions Salabert, Paris)	Salabert, Inc., New York	J. & W. Chester, Ltd., London
68	Rózsavölgyi és Társa, Budapest		J. & W. Chester, Ltd., London
69	Rozsanyai, Budapest		J. & W. Chester, Ltd., London
70	Salabert, Inc., New York		J. & W. Chester, Ltd., London
71	G. Schirmer, Inc., New York		Chappell & Co., Ltd., London
72	B. Schott's Söhne, Mainz	Associated Music Publishers, Inc., New York	
73	Éditions Maurice Senart, Paris (now Éditions Salabert, Paris)	Salabert, Inc., New York	J. & W. Chester, Ltd., London
74	C. F. W. Siegel, Leipzig		Novello & Co., Ltd., London
75	N. Simrock, G.M.B.H., Leipzig	Associated Music Publishers, Inc., New York	
76	Southern Music Publishing Company, Inc., New York		
77	Stainer & Bell, Ltd., London	Galaxy Music Corp., New York	
78	Universal Edition, A.G., Vienna	Associated Music Publishers, Inc. New York	
79	University of Washington Press, Seattle, Wash.	E. F. Kalmus, New York	
80	Weintraub Music Co., New York		
81	Wiener Philharmonischer Verlag (Universal Ed.), Vienna	Associated Music Publishers, Inc., New York	

LIST OF COMPOSERS AND WORKS[1]

ALBÉNIZ, Isaac
  Catalonia, Suite No. 1 (25)
ALBÉNIZ–ARBÓS
  El Albaicín
  El Puerto
  Évocation   (31); [72]
  Fête-Dieu à Séville
  Triana
  Navarra (31)
ALFVÉN, Hugo
  A Legend of the Skerries (39)
  Midsommarvaka (42)
ALLENDE, Pedro Humberto
  3 Tonadas (70); [73]
ANTHEIL, George
  McKonkey's Ferry
  Over the Plains   (80)
  Serenade for String Orchestra
  Symphony No. 5 (52)
ARNELL, Richard
  Sinfonia (3)
ATTERBERG, Kurt M.
  Ballade und Passacaglia (32)
  The Wise and the Foolish Virgins (39)
AUBERT, Louis
  Saisons (25)
BACH, Carl Philip Emanuel–STEINBERG
  Concerto for Orchestra in D major (16); [27]
BACH, Johann Christian
  Sinfonia in B♭ major   (63); [32]
  Sinfonia in D major
BACH, Johann Sebastian–RESPIGHI
  Passacaglia and Fugue in C minor   (65)
  Prelude and Fugue in D major
BACH–STOKOWSKI
  Chorale-Prelude, "Wir Glauben All' An Einem Gott"
  Fugue in G minor—The Shorter   (16)
  Komm Süsser Tod
BALAKIREV, Mili–CASELLA
  Islamey (47)
BALOGH, Erno
  Portrait of a City (29)

BARBER, Samuel
  Essay for Orchestra
  First Symphony
  Medea
  Music for a Scene from Shelley   (71)
  Overture to "The School for Scandal"
  Second Essay for Orchestra
  Second Symphony
BARRAINE, Elsa
  Deuxième Symphonie (50)
BARTÓK, Béla
  Concerto for Orchestra (11)
  Concerto for Piano and Orchestra (No. 1) (78)
  Concerto No. 3 for Piano and Orchestra (11)
  Dance Suite (78); [11, 81]
  Deux Images (68); [11]
  Deux Portraits (69); [11]
  Divertimento for String Orchestra (11)
  First Rhapsody for Violin and Orchestra   (11); [78]
  Hungarian Peasant Songs
  Music for Strings, Percussion and Celesta (81); [11]
  Rumanian Folk Dances (11)
  Second Rhapsody for Violin and Orchestra (11); [78]
  Second Suite (11); [81]
  Vier Orchesterstücke (78)
  Violin Concerto (11)
BAX, Sir Arnold
  First Symphony
  Second Symphony
  Third Symphony
  Fourth Symphony   (18)
  Fifth Symphony
  Sixth Symphony
  In the Faery Hills
  Mediterranean   (58)
  November Woods
  The Garden of Fand (18)
  Tintagel (58)
BECKER, John J.
  Concerto Arabesque for Piano and Orchestra
  Concerto for Horn and Orchestra   (60)
  Soundpiece No. 2

[1] In recent years some publishers of miniature scores have sold out their catalogues to other firms. In such cases it has been thought desirable to include the numbers of both the former and the present firms of publishers, since libraries and similar collections might possess only the older issues.

BEETHOVEN, Ludwig van
Consecration of the House, Overture (32); [13]
Coriolanus Overture (32); [11, 13, 44, 49, 64, 65, 81]
Egmont Overture (32); [11, 44, 49, 64, 65, 72, 81]
Fidelio Overture (32); [11, 13, 64]
Leonore Overture No. 2 (32); [13]
Leonore Overture No. 3 (32); [6, 11, 13, 44, 49, 64, 65, 81]
Overture to Prometheus (32); [11, 13, 49, 64, 81]
Piano Concerto No. 1 (49); [11, 13, 32, 63, 64]
Piano Concerto No. 2
Piano Concerto No. 3 } (49); [11, 13, 32, 63]
Piano Concerto No. 4 (49); [11, 13, 32, 63, 64. 81]
Piano Concerto No. 5 (49); [11, 13, 16, 32, 63, 64]
Symphony No. 1 (32); [6, 11, 13, 25, 49, 64, 65, 81]
Symphony No. 2 (32); [11, 13, 16, 25, 49, 64, 65, 81]
Symphony No. 3, "Eroica" (32); [6, 11, 13, 25, 44, 49, 64, 65, 81]
Symphony No. 4 (32); [11, 13, 16, 25, 49, 64, 65, 81]
Symphony No. 5 (81); [6, 11, 13, 25, 32, 44, 49, 64, 65]
Symphony No. 6, "Pastoral"
Symphony No. 7 } (32); [6, 11, 13, 25, 44, 49, 64, 65, 81]
Symphony No. 8
Symphony No. 9 (32); [11, 13, 16, 25, 49, 64, 65, 81]
The Ruins of Athens, Overture (32); [13, 81]
Violin Concerto in D major (6); [11, 13, 16, 32, 44, 49, 63, 65, 81]

BENJAMIN, Arthur
From San Domingo
Jamaican Rhumba } (11)
Overture to an Italian Comedy

BERG, Alban
Three Excerpts from "Wozzeck"
Violin Concerto } (81)

BERGSMA, William
Music on a Quiet Theme (2)

BERLIOZ, Hector
Benvenuto Cellini Overture (32)
Harold en Italie (32); [13, 45]
Roméo et Juliette (32); [13]
Symphonie Fantastique (32); [13, 49]
The Roman Carnival Overture (32); [11, 13, 44, 49, 81]
Three Pieces from "The Damnation of Faust" (32); [13, 44, 49]

BERNSTEIN, Leonard
"Jeremiah" Symphony (43)

BIZET, Georges
Intermezzi from "Carmen" (49)
L'Arlésienne Suite No. 1
L'Arlésienne Suite No. 2 } (32); [13, 49]
Prelude to "Carmen" (49)
Roma (32)
Symphony No. 1 (78); [81]

BLANCAFORT, Manuel
Mati de Festa a Puig-Gracios (70); [73]

BLISS, Arthur
Concerto for Piano and Orchestra (61)

BLOCH, Ernest
America
Concerto Grosso } (9)
Evocations
Hiver–Printemps
Schelomo } (71)
Trois Poèmes Juifs
Voice in the Wilderness

BORODIN, Alexander
On the Steppes of Central Asia (7); [32, 49, 65]
Polovetzian Dances from "Prince Igor" (7); [11, 32, 49, 81]
Symphony No. 1 (8); [11, 32, 81]
Symphony No. 2 (32); [8, 11, 49, 81]
Symphony No. 3 (7); [32, 52]

BOSMANS, Arthur
La Vie en bleu (70); [73]

BRAHMS, Johannes
Academic Festival Overture (32); [11, 49, 75]
Concerto for Violin and Violoncello in A minor (32); [45, 75]
Ein deutsches Requiem (32); [16, 45, 49, 81]
Piano Concerto No. 1 (49); [11, 32, 45, 63]
Piano Concerto No. 2 (49); [6, 11, 32, 65, 75]
Song of the Fates (81); [49]
Symphony No. 1 (49); [6, 11, 32, 64, 65, 75, 81]
Symphony No. 2 (49); [6, 11, 32, 44, 64, 65, 75, 81]
Symphony No. 3 (49); [6, 11, 32, 64, 65, 75, 81]
Symphony No. 4 (49); [6, 11, 32, 44, 64, 65, 75, 81]
Tragic Overture (32); [11, 49, 64, 75]
Variations on a Theme by Haydn (49); [6, 11, 32, 75, 81]
Violin Concerto in D major (6); [11, 32, 44, 49, 64, 65, 75]

BRITTEN, Benjamin
Four Sea Interludes from "Peter Grimes"
Les Illuminations
Passacaglia from "Peter Grimes"
Serenade for Tenor, Horn and Strings } (11)
Sinfonia da Requiem
Sinfonietta
The Young Person's Guide to the Orchestra

BRUCH, Max
Violin Concerto in G minor (32); [49]

BRUCKNER, Anton
Symphony No. 1
Symphony No. 2 } (17); [78]
Symphony No. 3 (17); [81]
Symphony No. 4 (17); [49, 78, 81]
Symphony No. 5 (17); [78]
Symphony No. 6 (81); [17]
Symphony No. 7 (81); [17, 32, 49]
Symphony No. 8 (81); [17]
Symphony No. 9 (81); [17, 32, 78]

LIST OF COMPOSERS AND WORKS

Busoni, Ferruccio
Rondo Arlecchinesco (13); [14, 81]

Cadman, Charles Wakefield
American Suite (21)
Dark Dancers of the Mardi Gras (26)

Caja, Alfonso
2 Idilli Siracusani (70); [73]

Carpenter, John Alden
Sea Drift (71)

Carse, Adam
A Romantic Legend (4)

Carter, Eliott
Holiday Overture (2)

Casella, Alfredo
Elegia Eroica (78)
Italia (78); [81]
La Donna Serpente, I. Serie ⎫
La Donna Serpente, II. Serie ⎭ (65)
Paganiniana (81)
Pupazzetti (81); [20, 72]

Caturla, Alejandro García
Trois Danses Cubaines (70); [73]

Cesana, Otto
Second American Symphony (1)

Chabrier, Emmanuel
Bourrée Fantastique (30)
España, Rhapsodie (30); [32, 49]
Joyeuse Marche ⎫
Ouverture de "Gwendoline" ⎬ (30)
Suite Pastorale ⎭

Charpentier, Gustave
Impressions d'Italie (44)

Chasins, Abram
Rush Hour in Hong Kong (34)

Chausson, Ernest
Symphonie en Si bémol majeur (70); [45, 49, 67]

Chávez, Carlos
Sinfonia de Antigona ⎫
Sinfonia India ⎭ (71)

Cherubini, Luigi
Anakreon Overture (32); [13]

Chopin, Frederic
Piano Concerto No. 1 (49); [13]

Cimarosa, Domenico
Overture to "The Secret Marriage" (32)

Converse, Frederick S.
American Sketches (49)

Copland, Aaron
An Outdoor Overture ⎫
Appalachian Spring ⎬ (11)
Billy the Kid Ballet Suite ⎭
Concerto for Piano and Orchestra ⎫
Dance Symphony ⎬ (22)
El Salón México (11)
First Symphony (22)
Four Dance Episodes from "Rodeo" ⎫
Lincoln Portrait ⎬ (11)
Music for Radio ⎭
Music for the Theatre (22)
Quiet City ⎫
Statements ⎬ (11)
Third Symphony ⎭
Two Pieces for String Orchestra (2)

Coppola, Piero
Interlude Dramatique (70); [73]
Scherzo Fantasque ⎫
Suite Intima ⎬ (31)
Symphonie en La mineur (70); [73]

Cowell, Henry
Short Symphony (No. 4) (3)
Symphonic Set (2)

Cras, Jean
Âmes d'enfants ⎫
Journal de Bord ⎭ (70); [73]

Creston, Paul
Two Choric Dances (71)

Daniels, Mabel
Deep Forest (34)

Davidson, Harold
Auto Accident (60)

Debussy, Claude Achille
Danses Sacrée et Profane (25)
Fêtes (from Three Nocturnes) (25); [11, 45, 46, 49]
Gigues ⎫
Iberia ⎪
Jeux ⎬ (25)
La Damoiselle Élue ⎪
La Mer ⎪
Le Martyre de Saint Sébastien ⎭
Nuages (from Three Nocturnes) (25); [11, 45, 46, 49]
Prélude à l'après-midi d'un Faune (25); [6, 11, 32, 45, 46, 49]
Première Rhapsodie ⎫
Printemps ⎪
Rapsodie pour Orchestre et Saxophone ⎬ (25)
Rondes de Printemps ⎭
Sirènes (from Three Nocturnes) (25); [11, 45, 46, 49]

Debussy–Ansermet
Six Épigraphes Antiques (25)

589

DEBUSSY–BUSSER
  Petite Suite (25)

DELANNOY, Marcel
  Figures Sonores (31)

DELIUS, Frederick
  A Dance Rhapsody (No. 1) (53); [81]
  A Dance Rhapsody, No. 2 (4)
  Appalachia (11); [81]
  A Song Before Sunrise (4)
  A Song of Summer (11)
  Brigg Fair (81)
  Eventyr, Once Upon a Time (4)
  In a Summer Garden (53)
  North Country Sketches (4)
  Paris—Ein Nachtstück (78)
  Prelude to "Irmelin" (11)
  Sea-Drift (81)
  Summer Night on the River (62); [49]
  The Song of the High Hills (78)
  Three Orchestral Pieces (11)

DELLO JOIO, Norman
  Variations, Chaconne, and Finale (33)

DIAMOND, David
  Elegy in Memory of Maurice Ravel (76)
  Fourth Symphony (71)
  Music for Shakespeare's "Romeo and Juliet" (11)
  Rounds for String Orchestra (29)
  Timon of Athens (52)

DOHNÁNYI, Ernst von
  Ruralia Hungarica (68)
  Variations on a Nursery Song (75); [32]

DUKAS, Paul
  La Péri (25)
  L'Apprenti Sorcier (25); [45, 49]
  Polyeucte, Ouverture (25)
  Symphonie en Ut majeur (70); [67]

DUKELSKY, Vladimir
  Symphony No. 3 (33)

DUNN, James P.
  Overture on Negro Themes (34)

DVOŘÁK, Antonin
  Carnival Overture (32); [11, 49, 75]
  Concerto for Violin in A minor (32); [75]
  Concerto for Violoncello and Orchestra (32); [45, 75, 81]
  Die Waldtaube ⎫ (75); [81]
  Der Wassermann ⎭
  Serenade for Strings (49); [12]
  Slavonic Dances, Nos. 1–4 (6); [75, 81]
  Symphony No. 2 (75); [81]
  Symphony No. 4 (61); [32, 49]
  Symphony No. 5, "From the New World" (32); [6, 11, 49, 64, 75, 81]

DYSON, George
  Overture, "At the Tabard Inn" (62)

EGGE, Klaus
  Piano Concerto No. 2 ⎫ (54)
  Symphony No. 1 ⎭

ELGAR, Sir Edward
  Cockaigne, Concert Overture (11)
  Concerto for Violin and Orchestra ⎫ (61)
  Concerto for Violoncello and Orchestra ⎭
  Falstaff (61); [32]
  In the South, Concert Overture (61)
  Introduction and Allegro for Strings (61); [32]
  Sea Pictures (11)
  Symphony No. 1 ⎫ (61)
  Symphony No. 2 ⎭
  Variations, "Enigma" (61); [11, 32, 49]

ENESCO, Georges
  Ière Rhapsodie Roumaine (30); [6, 49]
  2e Rhapsodie Roumaine (30); [49]

ENGEL, Lehman
  The Creation (3)

de FALLA, Manuel
  El Amor Brujo ⎫ (20); [31, 72]
  El Retablo de Maese Pedro ⎭
  Nuits dans les Jardins d'Espagne (31); [72]
  Three Dances from "The Three-Cornered Hat" (20); [31, 72]

FAURÉ, Gabriel
  Pelléas et Mélisande (41)
  Pénélope, Prélude (44)

FERGUSON, Howard
  Partita for Orchestra (11)

FERNANDEZ, Oscar Lorenzo
  Batuque (60)

FERROUD, Pierre O.
  Au Parc Monceau (70); [67]

FITELBERG, Jerzy
  Nocturne for Orchestra (3)
  Symphony No. 1 (55)

FLOTOW, Friedrich von
  Alessandro Stradella Overture (81); [32]

FRANCK, César
  Le Chasseur Maudit (32)
  Les Éolides (30); [32]
  Symphony in D minor (32); [6, 11, 49, 64]
  Variations Symphoniques (32); [11, 30, 49]

FULEIHAN, Anis
  Mediterranean (71)

GEMINIANI, Francesco
  Concerto Grosso in G minor (32)

GERSHWIN, George
An American in Paris
Concerto in F for Piano and Orchestra } (43)
Rhapsody in Blue

GILLIS, Don
Symphony No. 5½ (11)
The Alamo (18)

GLAZOUNOV, Alexander
Violin Concerto in A minor (32); [7, 11]

GLIÈRE, Reinhold
Russian Sailors' Dance (49)

GLINKA, Michael
Kamarinskaïa (32); [7]
March and Oriental Dances from "Russlan und Ludmila" (26); [47]
Russlan und Ludmila, Overture (32); [49, 72]

GLUCK, Christoph W.
Overture to "Alceste" (32); [13]
Overture to "Iphigénie en Aulide" (32); [13, 49]

GOLD, Ernest
Allegorical Overture (3)

GOLDMARK, Carl
Overture, In Springtime (6); [72]

GOLESTAN, Stan
Concerto Roumain pour Violon et Orchestre (70)

GOOSSENS, Eugene
Sinfonietta (20)

GOULD, Morton
American Salute
Latin-American Symphonette } (57)
Philharmonic Waltzes (38)
Spirituals (57)

GRAENER, Paul
Comedietta (32)

GREEN, RAY
Three Inventories of Casey Jones (60)

GRETCHANINOFF, Alexander
Troisième Symphonie (7)

GRÉTRY, André–MOTTL
Ballet Suite, Céphale et Procris (16); [49, 63]

GRIEG, Edvard
Norwegian Dances
Peer Gynt Suite No. 1 } (49); [63]
Piano Concerto No. 2 in A minor (6); [11, 16, 32, 49, 63, 64, 81]
Suite for Strings, "From Holberg's Time"
The Last Spring } (49); [63]

GRIFFES, Charles T.
The Pleasure Dome of Kubla Khan
The White Peacock } (71)

GROFÉ, Ferde
Grand Canyon Suite (66)

GRUENBERG, Louis
The Enchanted Isle (9)

GUARNIERI, Camargo
Brazilian Dance
Negro Dance } (3)
Savage Dance

HALFFTER, Ernesto
Deux Esquisses Symphoniques (31); [72]

HANDEL, George Frederick
Music for the Royal Fireworks (64); [11, 13]
Water Music in F (64); [11, 13, 44]

HANSON, Howard
"Merry Mount" Suite (43)
Symphony No. 1, "Nordic"
Symphony No. 2, "Romantic" } (33); [9]

HARRIS, Roy
Third Symphony
When Johnny Comes Marching Home } (71)

HARRISON, Lou
Alleluia for Orchestra (60)
Suite No. 2 for String Orchestra (56)

HARSANYI, Tibor
Ouverture Symphonique (70); [73]
Suite pour Orchestre (70)

HAYDN, Franz Joseph
Concerto in D major for Piano and Orchestra (32); [45, 49]
Symphony No. 1 [103] in E♭ major, "Drumroll" (49); [11, 13, 32, 63, 64, 65, 81]
Symphony No. 2 [104] in D major, "London" (49); [11, 13, 32, 64, 65, 81]
Symphony No. 3 [99] in E♭ major (32); [6, 13, 65]
Symphony No. 4 [101] in D major, "Clock" (81); [11, 13, 32, 44, 49, 64, 65]
Symphony No. 5 [93] in D major (32); [13]
Symphony No. 6 [94] in G major, "Surprise" (49); [6, 11, 13, 32, 44, 64, 65, 81]
Symphony No. 7 in C major, "Le Midi" (32); [11, 13, 64, 65, 81]
Symphony No. 7 [97] in C major (32); [65, 81]
Symphony No. 11 [100] in G major, "Military" (49); [11, 13, 32, 44, 64, 65, 81]
Symphony No. 12 [102] in B♭ major (32); [13, 49]
Symphony No. 13 [88] in G major (32); [13]
Symphony No. 14 [96] in D major, "Miracle" (32); [13]
Symphony No. 15 [85] in B♭ major, "La Reine" (32); [11, 13, 64, 65, 81]
Symphony No. 16 [92] in G major, "Oxford" (32); [11, 13, 44, 64, 65, 81]
Symphony No. 17 [82] in C major, "L'Ours" (32); [13, 65, 81]
Symphony No. 18 [45] in F♯ minor, "Farewell" (32); [13, 45, 65, 81]
Violoncello Concerto (32); [13, 16, 49, 63]

LIST OF COMPOSERS AND WORKS

HERRMANN, Bernard
  Sinfonietta for String Orchestra (60)

HILL, Edward Burlingame
  Lilacs (22)
  Sinfonietta for String Orchestra (2)

HINDEMITH, Paul
  Ballet Overture, Cupid and Psyche (3)
  Kammermusik No. 1 (Op. 24, No. 1)
  Kammermusik No. 4 (Op. 36, No. 3)
  Konzert für Orchester
  *Konzertmusik für Streichorchester und
    Blechbläser* } (72); [31]
  Mathis der Maler
  Neues vom Tage
  Nobilissima Visione (72)
  Symphonic Metamorphosis of Themes by Weber (3); [72]
  Symphonische Tänze } (72)
  Symphony in E-flat
  Theme and Four Variations, "The Four Temperaments" (3)

HOLST, Gustav
  A Somerset Rhapsody (11)
  Beni Mora, Oriental Suite (23)
  The Ballet from "The Perfect Fool" (61)
  The Planets (11); [23]

HONEGGER, Arthur
  Chant de Joie
  Concertino pour Piano et Orchestre
  Horace Victorieux } (70); [73]
  Le Chant de Nigamon
  Le Dit des Jeux du Monde
  Le Roi David (36)
  Mouvement Symphonique No. 3
  Musique pour la "Phaedre" de G. D'Annunzio } (70); [73]
  Pacific 231 (70); [73, 81]
  Prélude, Fugue, Postlude (70)
  Prélude pour "La Tempête"
  Rugby } (70); [73]
  Suite d'Orchestre, "L'Impératrice aux Rochers"
  Symphonie Liturgique
  Symphonie No. IV } (70)
  Symphonie pour Cordes
  Symphonie pour Orchestre (70); [73]

HOWE, Mary
  Stars (21); [26]

IBERT, Jacques
  Divertissement (25)
  Escales
  Féerique } (51)
  La Ballade de la Geôle de Reading
  Ouverture de Fête

D'INDY, Vincent
  Deuxième Symphonie en Sib (25)
  Istar, Variations Symphoniques (25); [49]
  Jour d'été à la Montagne (25)
  Symphony on a French Mountain Air (45); [49]
  Tableaux de Voyage (51)

INGHELBRECHT, Désiré Emile
  El Greco (70)
  La Métamorphose d'Ève
  La Valse Retrouvée } (70); [73]
  Pour le jour de la première neige au vieux Japon (70)
  Rapsodie de Printemps (70); [73]
  Sinfonia Breve No. 1 (70)

IPPOLITOV-IVANOV, Michailovich
  Caucasian Sketches (49); [45, 47]

IRELAND, John
  A London Overture (11)
  Symphonic Rhapsody, "Mai-Dun" (4)

IVES, Charles E.
  A Set of Pieces
  Lincoln, The Great Commoner
  "The Fourth of July" from Symphony, "Holidays" } (60)
  Third Symphony (2)
  Three Places in New England (9); [56]
  "Washington's Birthday" from Symphony, "Holidays" (60)

JACOBI, Frederick
  Concertino for Piano and String Orchestra (29)
  Music Hall Overture (52)

JAMES, Philip
  Suite for String Orchestra (16); [49]

JANÁČEK, Leos
  Sinfonietta (78)

JANSSEN, Werner
  New Year's Eve in New York (9)

JOHNSON, Horace
  Imagery (34)

JOLIVET, André
  Andante pour Orchestre à Cordes (44)

KABALEVSKY, Dmitri
  Suite from "Colas Breugnon"
  Symphony No. 2 } (52)
  The Comedians

KALINNIKOV, Basile
  Symphony No. 1 (49); [47]

KAY, Ulysses
  Suite for Orchestra (15)

KERR, Harrison
  Symphony No. 1 (2)

LIST OF COMPOSERS AND WORKS

KHACHATURIAN, Aram
Concerto for Piano and Orchestra
Gayne Ballet Suite No. 1
Gayne Ballet Suite No. 1-A   (52)
Gayne Ballet Suite No. 2
Masquerade Suite

KHRENNIKOV, Tikhon
Symphony No. 1 (52)

KNIPPER, Lev
Symphony No. 4 (52)

KODÁLY, Zoltan
Galanta Dances
Háry János Suite   (11); [81]
Marosszék Dances
Psalmus Hungaricus (78)
Summer Evening   (11); [78]
Te Deum

KŘENEK, Ernst
Symphonic Elegy (29)

LALO, Edouard
Le Roi d'Ys Ouverture (44); [32]
Symphonie Espagnole (32); [25, 49]

LAMBERT, Constant
The Rio Grande (62)

LA VIOLETTE, Wesley
Largo Lyrico (52)

LEKEU, Guillaume
Fantaisie sur Deux Airs Populaires Angevins (70)

LEVANT, Oscar
Nocturne (60)

LIADOV, Anatole
Baba-Yaga (7); [11, 32, 45, 49]
Eight Russian Popular Songs (32); [7, 11, 16, 45, 49]
Kikimora   (32); [7, 11, 45, 49]
The Enchanted Lake

LISZT, Franz
Eine Faust-Symphonie (32); [13]
Hungarian Rhapsody No. 2 (49)
Les Préludes (49); [11, 13, 32, 44, 64, 81]
Piano Concerto No. 1 (32); [11, 16, 49]
Piano Concerto No. 2 (32); [13]
Tasso, Lamento e Trionfo (81); [13, 49]
Todtentanz für Piano und Orchester (74)

LOEFFLER, Charles Martin
A Pagan Poem (71)
Evocation (9)
Poem, La Bonne Chanson (71)

LOPATNIKOFF, Nikolai
Sinfonietta (3)

LUENING, Otto
Two Symphonic Interludes (1)

MACDOWELL, Edward
2nd Suite (Indian)   (13)
The Saracens

MAGANINI, Quinto
Americanese   (26)
An Ancient Greek Melody
An Ornithological Suite (26); [34]
A Suite of Music by Royalty
At the Setting of the Sun
South Wind   (26)
Symphony for Chamber Orchestra
Tuolumne (1); [26]

MAHLER, Gustav
Das Lied von der Erde (78); [11]
Songs of a Wayfarer (81)
Symphony No. 1 (11); [78]
Symphony No. 2 (78); [11, 49]
Symphony No. 3 (11); [78]
Symphony No. 4 (45); [11, 81]
Symphony No. 5 (63)
Symphony No. 6 (48)
Symphony No. 7 (12)
Symphony No. 8   (11); [78]
Symphony No. 9

MALIPIERO, G. Francesco
Impressioni dal Vero, I Parte (70); [73, 81]
Impressioni dal Vero, 3ª Parte (78); [81]
Pause del Silenzio (81)
Seconda Sinfonia (Elegiaca) (65)

MARTINET, Jean-Louis
Orphée (44)

MASON, Daniel Gregory
Chanticleer—Festival Overture (9)

MCDONALD, Harl
Bataan
Rhumba from 2nd Symphony   (29)
Three Poems for Orchestra

MCKAY, George Frederick
Sinfonietta No. 4 (79)

MCPHEE, Colin
Four Iroquois Dances (60)

MENDELSSOHN, Felix
A Midsummer Night's Dream Overture (49); [11, 13, 32, 63, 64, 81]
Calm Sea and Prosperous Voyage, Overture (32); [13, 63]
Fingal's Cave Overture (49); [11, 13, 32, 44, 63, 65, 81]
Ruy Blas Overture (32); [13]
Symphony No. 3, "Scotch" (49); [11, 13, 32, 63, 64, 65, 81]
Symphony No. 4, "Italian" (32); [11, 13, 44, 49, 64, 65, 81]
Three Pieces from "A Midsummer Night's Dream" (49); [13, 32]

593

MIASKOVSKY, Nikolai
Fragment Lyrique (60)
Sinfonietta for String Orchestra (52); [78]
Symphony No. 6
VIII. Symphonie } (78)
Symphony No. 21
Symphony No. 22 } (52)

MIHALOVICI, Marcel
Divertissement pour Petit Orchestre (31)
Toccata pour Piano et Orchestre (44)

MILHAUD, Darius
Cinq Études pour Piano et Orchestre
Cinq Symphonies pour Petit Orchestre } (78)
Concerto pour Piano et Orchestre
Concertino de Printemps } (70); [24]
Concerto pour Violoncelle et Orchestre
Deuxième Concerto pour Violon et
Orchestre
Deuxième Concerto pour Violoncelle } (3)
et Orchestre
2me Suite Symphonique ("Protée") (25)
Four Sketches (56)
Introduction et Marche Funèbre (28)
La Création du Monde (31)
La Mort d'un Tyran (28)
Le Bal Martiniquais (52)
Le Carnaval de Londres (70)
Les Choéphores (44)
Opus Americanum No. 2 ("Moses") (29)
Ière Symphonie (44)
IIe Symphonie (44)
Quatrième Symphonie (70)
Saudades do Brazil (31)
Sérénade pour Orchestre (78)
Suite Française (52)
Suite Provençale (70); [24]
Two Marches (71)

MOERAN, Ernest J.
Sinfonietta
Symphony in G minor } (61)

MOHAUPT, Richard
Town Piper Music (3)

MOORE, Douglas
In Memoriam (29)
Symphony in A major (71)
Village Music (59)

MOROSS, Jerome
Biguine
Paeans } (60)

MORRIS, Harold
Prospice Symphony (1)

MOZART, Wolfgang Amadeus
Balletmusic, "Les Petits Riens," K.10 (32); [13]
Bassoon Concerto in Bb major, K.191 (32); [49]
Clarinet Concerto in A major, K.622 (32); [13, 49]
Concerto for 2 Pianos in Eb major, K.365 (32); [13, 45, 49]
Horn Concerto No. II in Eb major, K. 417 (32); [13, 49]
Overture to "Cosi fan Tutte," K.588 (64); [6, 11, 13, 32, 49, 81]
Overture to "Don Giovanni," K.527 (64); [11, 13, 32, 44, 49, 65, 81]
Overture to "Il Seraglio," K.384 (64); [11, 13, 32, 81]
Overture to "The Impresario," K.486 (49); [13, 16, 32, 81]
Overture to "The Magic Flute," K.620 (49); [11, 13, 32, 44, 64, 65, 81]
Overture to "The Marriage of Figaro," K.492 (49); [6, 11, 13, 32, 44, 64, 65, 81]
Piano Concerto (No. 23) in A major, K.488 (64); [11, 13, 16, 32, 44, 49, 65, 81]
Piano Concerto (No. 26) in D major, "Coronation," K.537 (64); [11, 13, 16, 32, 49]
Symphony No. 28 in C major, K.200 (49); [13, 16, 32, 81]
Symphony No. 35 in D major, "Haffner," K.385 (49); [11, 13, 16, 32, 44, 64, 65, 81]
Symphony No. 36 in C major, "Linz," K.425 (64); [11, 13, 16, 32, 49, 65, 81]
Symphony No. 38 in D major, "Prague," K.504 (64); [11, 13, 16, 32, 44, 65, 81]
Symphony No. 39 in Eb major, K.543 (49); [6, 11, 13, 16, 32, 44, 64, 65, 81]
Symphony No. 40 in G minor, K.550 (81); [6, 11, 13, 16, 32, 44, 49, 64 65,]
Symphony No. 41 in C major, "Jupiter," K.551 (49); [6, 11, 13, 16, 32, 44, 64, 65, 81]
Titus Overture, K.621 (32); [13, 49]
Violin Concerto No. I in Bb major, K.207 (32)
Violin Concerto No. III in G major, K.216 (32); [11, 13, 49, 65]
Violin Concerto No. IV in D major, K.218 (32); [11, 13, 16, 44, 49, 65]
Violin Concerto No. V in A major, K.219 (32); [11, 13, 16, 49, 65]

MUSSORGSKY, Modeste
Introduction to "Khovanchtchina" (32); [11, 45, 49]
Night on the Bald Mountain (32); [11, 45, 81]
Polonaise from "Boris Godunov" (49); [8, 26]

MUSSORGSKY–RAVEL
Pictures at an Exhibition (11); [27]

NICOLAI, Otto
Overture to "The Merry Wives of Windsor" (49); [11, 12, 13, 32, 81]

NYSTEDT, Knut
The Land of Suspense (54)

594

LIST OF COMPOSERS AND WORKS

PARODI, Renato
  Preludio ad una Commedia (70)
PERSICHETTI, Vincent
  The Hollow Men (29)
PESCARA, Aurelio
  Tibet, Symphonic Sketch (3)
PICK–MANGIAGALLI, Riccardo
  Notturno e Rondo Fantastico }
  Piccola Suite   } (65)
PIERNÉ, Gabriel
  Divertissements sur un Thème Pastoral }
  Viennoise   } (70)
PIKET, Frederick
  Curtain Raiser to an American Play (3)
PISTON, Walter
  Concertino for Pianoforte and Chamber Orchestra (2)
  Concerto for Orchestra (22)
  First Symphony (71)
  Prelude and Allegro for Organ and Strings (2)
  Prelude and Fugue   }
  Suite for Orchestra } (22)
  Suite from the Ballet, "The Incredible Flutist" }
  Symphony No. 2   } (2)
PIZZETTI, Ildebrando
  Concerto dell'Estate   }
  Introduzione all' "Agamennone" di Eschilo } (65)
POOT, Marcel
  Jazz–Music }
  Symphonie   } (31)
PORTER, Quincy
  Music for Strings (59)
POULENC, Francis
  Aubade   }
  Concert Champêtre pour Clavecin et Orchestre }
  Concerto pour deux Pianos et Orchestre   } (70)
  Deux Marches et un Intermède   }
PROKOFIEFF, Serge
  Ala et Lolly (Scythian Suite) (11); [40]
  Alexander Nevsky   }
  Cinderella Suite No. 1 } (52)
  Classical Symphony (6); [11, 16, 40, 49]
  Lieutenant Kijé (11); [16, 49]
  March and Scherzo from "The Love of the Three Oranges"
    (11); [27]
  Peter and the Wolf (52); [11, 64]
  Piano Concerto No. 3 (11); [40]
  Romeo and Juliet, Suite No. 1 }
  Romeo and Juliet, Suite No. 2 } (52)
  Suite from the Ballet "Chout" (11); [40]
  Summer Day Suite (52)
  Symphony No. 5 (52); [49]
  Symphony No. 6 (52)
  Violin Concerto No. 2 (6)

RABAUD, Henri
  Divertissement sur des Chansons Russes (30)
  La Procession Nocturne (25)
RACHMANINOFF, Sergei
  Die Toteninsel (13); [11, 40, 45]
  Piano Concerto No. 1 (11); [40]
  2d Concerto pour Piano et Orchestre (40); [11, 16, 49, 64]
  Piano Concerto No. 3 (11); [40]
  Rapsodie pour Piano et Orchestre (35); [31]
  Symphony No. 2 (49); [40]
  The Bells (40); [11]
RAMEAU, Jean Philippe–MOTTL
  Ballet Suite (16); [49, 63]
RAVEL, Maurice
  Alborada del Gracioso (31)
  Boléro   }
  Concerto pour la main gauche   }
  Concerto pour Piano et Orchestre   }
  Daphnis et Chloé, Suite No. 1   }
  Daphnis et Chloé, Suite No. 2   } (25)
  Introduction et Allegro   }
  La Valse   }
  Le Tombeau de Couperin   }
  Ma Mère l'Oye   }
  Menuet Antique (30)
  Rapsodie Espagnole   }
  Shéhérazade   }
  Tzigane   } (25)
  Valses Nobles et Sentimentales }
READ, Gardner
  First Overture (21)
  Prelude and Toccata }
  Sketches of the City } (49)
  Symphony No. I (1)
REGER, Max
  Requiem (81); [75]
  Variations on a Theme of Mozart (32); [12]
RESPIGHI, Ottorino
  Antiche Danze ed Arie, 2ª Suite }
  Ballata delle Gnomidi   } (65)
  Belfagor, Ouverture per Orchestra }
  Concerto Gregoriano per Violino e Orchestra (78)
  Feste Romane   }
  Metamorphoseon, XII Modi   }
  The Birds   }
  The Fountains of Rome   }
  The Pines of Rome   } (65)
  Toccata per Pianoforte e Orchestra }
  Trittico Botticelliano   }
  Vetrate di Chiesa   }
REVUELTAS, Silvestre
  Cuauhnahuac }
  Sensemayá   } (71)

LIST OF COMPOSERS AND WORKS

RIEGGER, Wallingford
 Dichotomy (60)
 Symphony No. 3 (3)

RIETI, Vittorio
 L'Arca di Noè (78)
 Serenata (70)
 Sinfonia No. 5 }
 Sinfonia Tripartita } (3)

RIISAGER, Knudage
 Torgot Dance (54)

RIMSKY-KORSAKOFF, Nicolas
 Capriccio Espagnol (49); [7, 11, 32, 64]
 Dance of the Buffoons (49); [8]
 Le Coq d'Or Suite (49); [47, 81]
 Russian Easter Overture }
 Scheherazade } (49); [7, 11, 32]
 Symphony No. 2, "Antar" (49); [8, 11, 32, 81]

RIVIER, Jean
 Chant Funèbre
 Danse
 Ouverture pour un don Quichotte } (70); [73]
 Rapsodie pour Violoncelle et Orchestre
 3 Pastorales

ROGER-DUCASSE, Jean Jules
 Le Joli Jeu de Furet
 Poème Symphonique sur le nom de Gabriel Fauré } (25)
 Sarabande

ROGERS, Bernard
 Characters from Hans Christian Andersen }
 Elegy } (29)
 Once Upon a Time, Five Fairy Tales (49)

ROPARTZ, J. Guy
 Soir sur les Chaumes (25)

ROSENTHAL, Manuel
 Les Petits Métiers (46)

ROSSINI, Giacomo
 La Gazza Ladra, Overture (32); [13, 81]
 La Scala di Seta, Overture (32); [13, 49]
 L'Italiani in Algeri, Overture (32)
 Semiramide, Overture }
 Tancredi, Overture } (32); [13]
 The Barber of Seville, Overture (32); [13, 16, 49, 65, 81]
 William Tell, Overture (49); [13, 32]

ROUSSEL, Albert
 Évocations, I
 Évocations, II
 Évocations, III
 Le Festin de l'Araignée
 Pour une Fête de Printemps } (25)
 4me Symphonie
 Rapsodie Flamande
 Suite en Fa
 Symphonie en Sol mineur

ROZSA, Miklos
 Concerto for String Orchestra (52)

RUDHYAR, Dane
 Five Stanzas }
 Sinfonietta } (60)

RUGGLES, Carl
 Sun-Treader (60)

RUSSELL, William
 Fugue for Eight Percussion Instruments }
 Three Dance Movements } (60)

SAINT-SAËNS, Camile
 Danse Macabre (25); [11, 49]
 La Jeunesse d'Hercule }
 Le Carnaval des Animaux } (25)
 Omphale's Spinning Wheel (25); [11, 49]
 Suite Algérienne }
 3e Symphonie en Ut mineur } (25)

SAMINSKY, Lazare
 Litanies des Femmes (70)

SATIE, Erik–DEBUSSY
 Gymnopédies (67); [49, 70]

SCARLATTI, Domenico–CASELLA
 Toccata, Bourrée, et Gigue (70); [73]

SCHELLING, Ernest
 A Victory Ball (53)

SCHLEIN, Irving
 Dance Overture (3)

SCHMITT, Florent
 Étude pour le "Palais Hanté" d'Edgar Poe }
 La Tragédie de Salomé
 Mirages pour Orchestre } (25)
 Rapsodie Viennoise
 Ronde burlesque (44)

SCHÖNBERG, Arnold
 A Survivor from Warsaw (10)
 Fünf Orchesterstücke (63)
 Kammersymphonie, Op. 9 }
 Pierrot Lunaire } (81)
 Suite for String Orchestra }
 Theme and Variations } (71)
 Verklärte Nacht (32); [45]

SCHREKER, Franz
 The Birthday of the Infanta, Suite (81)

SCHUBERT, Franz
 Rosamunde Overture (49); [11, 13, 32, 81]
 Symphony No. 2 (32); [13]
 Symphony No. 4, "Tragic" (32); [11, 13, 64]
 Symphony No. 5 (49); [11, 13, 32, 81]
 Symphony No. 6 (32); [13]
 Symphony No. 7 (6); [11, 13, 32, 49, 63, 64, 81]
 Symphony No. 8, "Unfinished" (81); [6, 11, 13, 32, 44, 49, 63, 64, 65]

596

LIST OF COMPOSERS AND WORKS

SCHUMAN, William
  American Festival Overture
  Prayer in Time of War
  Symphony for Strings   (71)
  Symphony No. III
  Symphony No. IV
  Undertow

SCHUMANN, Robert
  Concerto for Violoncello and Orchestra (32); [13, 45]
  Manfred Overture (32); [13]
  Piano Concerto in A minor (6); [11, 13, 16, 32, 44, 49]
  Symphony No. 1 (49); [11, 13, 32, 44, 63, 81]
  Symphony No. 2 (81); [11, 13, 32, 49, 63]
  Symphony No. 3 (64); [11, 13, 32, 44, 49, 63, 81]
  Symphony No. 4 (81); [11, 13, 32, 44, 49, 63, 65]

SCRIABIN, Alexandre
  Deuxième Symphonie   (7)
  Le Divin Poème
  Le Poème de l'Extase (32); [7, 11]
  Piano Concerto in F♯ minor (16); [7]
  Prométhée, Le Poème du Feu (27)

SESSIONS, Roger
  Suite from "The Black Maskers"   (22)
  Symphony for Orchestra (No. 1)
  Symphony No. II (71)

SHEPHERD, Arthur
  Horizons (9)

SHOSTAKOVICH, Dimitri
  Piano Concerto (16); [49]
  Symphony No. 1 (49); [11, 26, 52]
  Symphony No. 3 (52)
  Symphony No. 5 (11); [26, 49, 52]
  Symphony No. 6
  Symphony No. 7   (52)
  Symphony No. 9
  The Golden Age, Ballet Suite (49)

SHOSTAKOVICH–STOKOWSKI
  Prelude in E-flat minor (16)

SIBELIUS, Jean
  Die Okeaniden (13)
  En Saga (14); [13]
  Finlandia (13); [11, 14, 49]
  Karelia-Suite (13); [14]
  Lemminkainen Journeys Homeward (49); [13, 14]
  Pelleas and Melisande   (49)
  Pohjola's Daughter
  Rakastava
  Symphony No. 1   (13); [14]
  Symphony No. 2
  Symphony No. 3 (49); [32]

Symphony No. 4 (13); [14]
Symphony No. 5 (42); [13, 14]
Symphony No. 6 (42); [49]
Symphony No. 7 (42); [13, 14]
Tapiola   (13); [14]
The Bard
The Swan of Tuonela (49); [11, 13, 14, 64]
The Tempest, Prelude
The Tempest, First Suite   (42)
The Tempest, Second Suite
Violin Concerto (32); [16, 45]

SIEGMEISTER, Elie
  From my Window (18)
  Ozark Set   (55)
  Sunday in Brooklyn
  Western Suite (3)
  Wilderness Road (52)

SKILTON, Charles Sandford
  Suite Primeval, Part I   (33)
  Suite Primeval, Part II

SLONIMSKY, Nicolas
  My Toy Balloon (5)

SMETANA, Bedrich
  Blaník
  From Bohemia's Woods and Fields   (32)
  Libuša Overture
  Overture to "The Bartered Bride" (32); [6, 11, 12, 81]
  Tábor (32)
  The Moldau (Vltava) (32); [11, 65]
  Šárka (32); [49]
  Vyšehrad (32)

SOWERBY, Leo
  Concert Overture for Orchestra (59)
  From the Northland (71)
  Prairie (9)

STAROKADOMSKY, Michael
  Concerto for Orchestra (52)

STILL, William Grant
  Bells (52)
  Dismal Swamp (60)
  In Memoriam   (52)
  Poem for Orchestra

STILLMAN-KELLEY, Edgar
  Gulliver—His Voyage to Lilliput   (1)
  New England Symphony

STRANG, Gerald
  Intermezzo   (60)
  Percussion Music

STRAUSS, Richard
  Also Sprach Zarathustra (32); [81]
  Dance Suite after François Couperin (37); [81]
  Death and Transfiguration (49); [11, 32, 61, 81]
  Don Juan (49); [11, 32, 61, 63, 81]
  Don Quixote (81); [32, 49, 61]
  Eine Alpensinfonie (53); [32]
  Ein Heldenleben (32); [3, 53]
  Macbeth (78); [32, 63, 81]
  Metamorphosen } (11)
  Oboe Concerto }
  Rosenkavalier Waltzes—First Sequence (11); [37]
  Salomé's Dance (37); [11]
  Suite from "Le Bourgeois Gentilhomme" (32); [37, 81]
  Symphonia Domestica (12); [3, 32]
  Till Eulenspeigel's Merry Pranks (49); [11, 32, 61, 81]

STRAVINSKY, Igor
  Apollon Musagète } (11); [27]
  Chant du Rossignol }
  Concerto en Ré pour Orchestre à Cordes (11)
  Concerto en Ré pour Violon et Orchestre (72)
  Danses Concertantes (3); [72]
  "Dumbarton Oaks" Concerto (72)
  Ebony Concerto (19)
  Fire-Bird Suite (1919) (47); [11, 20, 49, 72]
  Firebird Ballet Suite (1945) (52)
  Feuerwerk (Fireworks) (72); [31, 45]
  Four Norwegian Moods (3); [72]
  Histoire du Soldat (81); [20, 72]
  Jeu de Cartes (72); [31]
  Le Sacre du Printemps (27); [11, 49]
  Les Noces (20); [81]
  Mass (11)
  Ode (72)
  Oedipus Rex (11); [27]
  Orpheus (11)
  Petrouchka Suite (27); [11, 49, 64]
  Pulcinella Suite (11); [20, 27]
  Quatre Études pour Orchestre (11); [27]
  Ragtime (20); [72, 81]
  Renard (81); [20]
  Scènes de Ballet (3)
  Scherzo à la Russe (18): [3]
  Scherzo fantastique (72); [31, 47]
  Suite No. 1 for Small Orchestra (20); [72, 81]
  Symphonie de Psaumes (11); [27]
  Symphony in C (72)
  Symphony in Three Movements (3); [72]

STRINGFIELD, Lamar
  A Negro Parade (34)

SZYMANOWSKI, Karol
  Symphonie Concertante pour Piano et Orchestre (31)

TANSMAN, Alexandre
  Deux Moments Symphoniques (31)
  Short Suite (52)
  Sonatine Transatlantique (51)

TAYLOR, Deems
  Ballet Music from "Casanova" } (34)
  Through the Looking Glass }

TCHAIKOVSKY, Peter Ilyitch
  Capriccio Italien (49); [11, 32, 64]
  Francesca da Rimini (32); [12, 45, 49]
  Hamlet (11); [32]
  Manfred-Symphonie (32); [47]
  March Slav (49); [32, 47]
  Mozartiana (32); [47]
  Nutcracker Suite (No. 1) (32); [6, 11, 64]
  Ouverture Solennelle, 1812 (49); [11, 32, 64]
  Piano Concerto No. 1 in B♭ minor (6); [11, 32, 64]
  Romeo and Juliet (49); [6, 11, 12, 32, 64]
  Serenade for Strings (49); [32]
  Suite from the Ballet, "The Sleeping Beauty" (49); [47]
  Symphony No. 2 (7); [49]
  Symphony No. 3 (17); [47]
  Symphony No. 4 (49); [11, 32, 64, 81]
  Symphony No. 5 (81); [6, 11, 32, 49, 64]
  Symphony No. 6, "Pathétique" (32); [6, 11, 49, 64, 81]
  Variations on a Rokoko Theme (32)

THOMAS, Ambroise
  Mignon Overture (49); [44]

THOMSON, Virgil
  Louisiana Story Suite (71)
  Orchestra Suite from "The Plow that Broke the Plains" (59)
  Tango Lullaby (56)
  The Seine at Night (71)

TIPPETT, Michael
  Symphony No. 1 (72)

TOCH, Ernst
  Fünf Stücke für Kammerorchester (72)
  Hyperion (52)
  Pinocchio (3)
  The Chinese Flute (72)

TRAPP, Max
  Symphonie No. 4 (32)

TURINA, Joaquín
  La Procesión del Rocío (70); [67]

TURNER, Godfrey
  Fanfare, Chorale and Finale (2)
  Gregorian Overture for String Orchestra (3)

VARÈSE, Edgar
  Hyperprism } (23)
  Intégrales }
  Ionisation (60)

LIST OF COMPOSERS AND WORKS

VAUGHAN WILLIAMS, Ralph
A London Symphony (77)
Concerto Accademico for Violin and String Orchestra (62)
Fantasia on a Theme by Thomas Tallis (11); [23]
Job, a Masque for Dancing ⎫
Norfolk Rhapsody No. 1 ⎭ (62)
Overture to "The Wasps" (23); [11, 72]
Pastoral Symphony (11); [23]
Symphony in F minor (No. 4) ⎫
Symphony in D major (No. 5) ⎪
Symphony in E minor (No. 6) ⎬ (62)
The Lark Ascending ⎭

VERDI, Giusseppe
I Vespri Siciliani Overture (32); [65]
Messa da Requiem (32); [16, 45, 49, 81]
Overture to "La Forza del Destino" (32); [65]

VILLA-LOBOS, Heitor
Amazonas ⎫
Chôros No. 8 ⎪
Chôros No. 10 ⎬ (31)
Danses Africaines ⎪
Uirapurú (3) ⎭

WAGENAAR, Bernard
Sinfonietta for Small Orchestra (22)

WAGNER, Joseph
Symphony Number One (1)

WAGNER, Richard
Bacchanale from "Tannhäuser" (49); [25, 32]
Eine Faust-Overture (32); [13]
Entrance of the Gods into Valhalla from "Das Rheingold" (49); [72]
Entrance of the Guests from "Tannhäuser" (49); [13]
Forest Murmurs from "Siegfried" (32); [72]
Funeral Music from "Götterdämmerung" (81); [32, 72]
Good Friday Spell from "Parsifal" (81); [72]
Introduction to Act III, "Tristan und Isolde" (49); [13]
Magic Fire Music from "Die Walküre" (49); [32, 72]
Prelude and Love Death from "Tristan und Isolde" (49); [11, 13, 32, 44, 64, 65, 81]
Preludes to Act I and III, "Lohengrin" (49); [11, 13, 25, 32, 44, 64, 81]
Prelude to "Die Meistersinger von Nürnberg" (32); [11, 44, 64, 65, 72, 81]
Rienzi Overture (81); [13, 32]

Siegfried's Rhine Journey from "Die Götterdämmerung" (49); [72]
Tannhäuser Overture (49); [11, 13, 25, 32, 44, 64, 65, 81]
The Flying Dutchman Overture (81); [11, 25, 32, 64]
The Ride of the Valkyries from "Die Walküre" (49); [11, 13, 32, 64, 65, 81]

WALTON, William
Concerto for Viola and Orchestra ⎫
Concerto for Violin and Orchestra ⎪
Façade, Suite No. 1 ⎪
Façade, Suite No. 2 ⎬ (62)
Portsmouth Point Overture ⎪
Symphony ⎭

WARD, Robert
Jubilation—An Overture (3)

WARLOCK, Peter
Capriol Suite (11)

WEBER, Carl Maria von
Der Freischütz Overture (49); [6, 11, 13, 32, 44, 81]
Euryanthe Overture (49); [11, 13, 32, 81]
Konzertstück für Klavier und Orchester (32); [13, 16]
Oberon Overture (49); [11, 13, 32, 44, 81]

WEBER-BERLIOZ
Invitation to the Dance (32); [13, 65]

WEINBERGER, Jaromir
Polka and Fugue from "Schwanda, the Bagpiper" (81); [78]

WEINGARTNER, Felix
Lustige Ouvertüre (13)

WEISS, Adolph
American Life (60)

WELLESZ, Egon
Symphony in C (72)

WHITE, Paul
Five Miniatures ⎫
Idyl for Orchestra ⎬ (29)

WHITHORNE, Emerson
Fata Morgana ⎫
The Dream Pedlar ⎬ (22)

WOLF, Hugo
Der Feuerreiter (81)

ZIMBALIST, Efrem
American Rhapsody (71)

INDEX OF ABBREVIATIONS

A., *see* Alto & Harp
Ahb., *see* English Horn
Al pontic., *see* Sul ponticello
Alt., *see* Alto & Viola
Altfl. [Alto fl.], *see* Alto Flute
am Griff., *see* Sul tasto
Ant. Cymbs. [Zimb.], *see* Antique Cymbals
arm., *see* Harmonics
Arp., *see* Harp
a.s., *see* Sul ponticello
avec sourd., *see* Mutes

B., *see* Bass(es)
Bar., *see* Baritone
Bass Cl. [Clar.], *see* Bass Clarinet
Bassfl., *see* Bass Flute
Bassklar., *see* Bass Clarinet
Bassp., *see* Bass Trombone
Basstrp., *see* Bass Trumpet
Bck., *see* Cymbals
B. Clt., *see* Bass Clarinet
B.D. [B.Dr.], *see* Bass Drum
Beck., *see* Cymbals
B.-Kl., *see* Bass Clarinet
Bn. [Bns.], *see* Bassoon
Bons, *see* Bassoon
B.-Pos., *see* Bass Trombone
Br., *see* Viola
Bs., *see* Bass(es)
Bs. Cl. [Clar.], *see* Bass Clarinet
Bs. Dr., *see* Bass Drum
Bs. Fl., *see* Bass Flute
Bsns., *see* Bassoon
Bs. Ob., *see* Bass Oboe
B'ss'n. [Bssns.], *see* Bassoon
Bs. Tb., *see* Bass Tuba
Bs. Tbn. [Trbn.], *see* Bass Trombone
Bs. Trpt., *see* Bass Trumpet
BT. [Btb.], *see* Bass Tuba
B. Trb., *see* Bass Trombone

C., *see* Contralto & Violoncello
Ca., *see* Bass Drum
Caisse R., *see* Tenor Drum
Camp. [Cample.], *see* Chimes
Camptta., *see* Glockenspiel
C. An. [Angl.], *see* English Horn
C. à p., *see* Cornet
Car., *see* Glockenspiel
Cast(s)., *see* Castanets
C.B. [Cb.], *see* Bass(es)
C.-bassi, *see* Bass(es)

Cbi., *see* Bass(es)
C. Bn. [Cbn.], *see* Contrabassoon
C. *Bon*, *see* Contrabassoon
C.-Bsn. [C.B'ss'n.; Cbssn.], *see* Contrabassoon
C. B'ssoon., *see* Contrabassoon
C. cl. [*Clre*], *see* Snare Drum
Cel. [Celes.], *see* Celesta
Cemb., *see* Harpsichord
C. F. [C.-Fag.], *see* Contrabassoon
C. Fg. [Cfg.], *see* Contrabassoon
Cg. [C. I.], *see* English Horn
Cimb. ant., *see* Antique Cymbals
Cin., *see* Cymbals
C. Ing. [C. ingl.], *see* English Horn
Clar. B. [basse; basso], *see* Bass Clarinet
Clar(s). [Clarts.], *see* Clarinet
Clav., *see* Harpsichord
Cl. b. [b'o.], *see* Bass Clarinet
Cl. p. [pc.; picc.], *see* D [Eb] Clarinet
Cl(s). [Clts.], *see* Clarinet
Cmplli., *see* Glockenspiel
Cnti. [Cnts.], *see* Cornet
Con. Bs., *see* Bass(es)
Con. Bssn., *see* Contrabassoon
con sord., *see* Muffled & Mutes
Cont., *see* Alto
Cont. F., *see* Contrabassoon
Cor. A. [Ang.], *see* English Horn
Cor. à p., *see* Cornet
Cor. igl. [ingl.], *see* English Horn
Cor(s)., *see* Cornet & Horn
Cr., *see* Horn
C. r., *see* Tenor Drum
Crot., *see* Antique Cymbals
c.s., *see* Mutes & Sons étouffés
Cse. roul., *see* Tenor Drum
Csse cl., *see* Snare Drum
Ctb. [Ctrb.], *see* Bass(es)
Ctre Bon, *see* Contrabassoon
Cy. [Cym.], *see* Cymbals
Cymb. Ant., *see* Antique Cymbals
Cymb(s)., *see* Cymbals
Cymb. s., *see* Suspended Cymbal

D . . ., *see* Flutter-tonguing
D.-B. [Db.], *see* Bass(es)
D. Bn. [Dbn.; D. Bssn.], *see* Contrabassoon
D Cl., *see* D Clarinet
Div., *see* Divisi
D-Klar., *see* D Clarinet

Eb Cl., *see* Eb Clarinet
E. H. [Hrn.], *see* English Horn
Eng. Hn., *see* English Horn
Engl. H. [Englh.], *see* English Horn
Engl. Hr. [Horn], *see* English Horn
Es-Kl., *see* Eb Clarinet

Fag. [Fg.], *see* Bassoon
Fing. cymbs., *see* Antique Cymbals
Flag., *see* Harmonics
Fl. Alto, *see* Alto Flute
Flatterz., *see* Flutter-tonguing
flaut., *see* Sul tasto
Fl. b. [basse; basso], *see* Bass Flute
Fl. c'alto., *see* Alto Flute
Fl. en [in] Sol, *see* Alto Flute
Fl. in G., *see* Alto Flute
Fl. p. [picc.], *see* Piccolo
Fl(s)., *see* Flute
Fltne., *see* Alto Flute

G., *see* Gong
G. A., *see* Gli altri
G. C., *see* Bass Drum
Gdes Fl., *see* Flute
ged., *see* Muffled & Mutes & Sons étouffés
Geig. I [II], *see* Violin
gest., *see* Stopped Tones
get., *see* Divisi
gew. [gewöhn.], *see* Muffle off & Natural position & Open tones
G Fl., *see* Alto Flute
Gl., *see* Glissando & Glockenspiel
gliss., *see* Glissando
Glock., *see* Chimes & Glockenspiel
Glockengl., *see* Chimes
Glocksp. [Glsp.], *see* Glockenspiel
Gr. C. [*Cse*.], *see* Bass Drum
gr. Fl., *see* Flute
Griffbr., *see* Sul tasto
G. [gr.] Tr., *see* Bass Drum

H., *see* Horn
Harm., *see* Harmonics & Harmonium
harm(s)., *see* Harmonics
Hautb. [Hb.], *see* Oboe
Heck. [Heckelph.], *see* Bass Oboe
Hfe., *see* Harp
Hn(s)., *see* Horn
Hob., *see* Oboe
Hp(s)., *see* Harp
Hpsichd., *see* Harpsichord

INDEX OF ABBREVIATIONS

Hr., *see* Horn
Hrf., *see* Harp
Hrn(s)., *see* Horn
Hrp(s)., *see* Harp
Hs., *see* Horn
H^{tb}, *see* Oboe

J. de T., *see* Glockenspiel
jeu ord., *see* Normal bowing

Kast., *see* Castanets
K.-B. [Kb.; Kbass.], *see* Bass(es)
K. D. [Drs.; Drum], *see* Timpani
K.-Fag. [Kfg.], *see* Contrabassoon
Kielfl., *see* Harpsichord
Kl. [Klar.], *see* Clarinet
Klav., *see* Piano
Kl. Fl., *see* Piccolo
Kl. in D [Es], *see* D [E♭] Clarinet
Kl. Mtr. [Tr.], *see* Snare Drum
Kontrab., *see* Bass(es)
Kontrafag., *see* Contrabassoon
Ktb., *see* Bass(es)

L. H. [l.h.], *see* Left-hand pizzicato
l. v., *see* Vibrato

maj. tr., *see* Trills
m. D., *see* Left-hand pizzicato & Mutes
m. [mit] Dmpf. [Sord.], *see* Mutes
m. Dpf., *see* Mutes
m. g., *see* Left-hand pizzicato
Mil. dr., *see* Snare Drum
min. tr., *see* Trills
modo ord., *see* Muffle off & Natural position & Open tones
m. s., *see* Left-hand pizzicato
M.-Sop., *see* Alto

nat. [nat. pos.], *see* Muffle off & Natural position & Normal bowing & Open tones
nicht trem., *see* Measured Tremolo & Non-tremolo
non-arpegg., *see* Non-arpeggiato
non-div., *see* Unison
non-trem., *see* Measured Tremolo & Non-tremolo

Ob. c'alto., *see* English Horn
Ob(s)., *see* Oboe
o. D. [Dpf], *see* Mutes off
ohne Dmpf., *see* Mutes off
ord. [ord. pos.], *see* Mutes off & Natural position & Normal bowing
Org., *see* Organ
Ott. [Otta.], *see* Piccolo
ouv., *see* Open Tones

P. [Pi.], *see* Cymbals & Piano
Par. dr., *see* Tenor Drum

Pauke., *see* Timpani
Pav^{on} en l'air, *see* Bells Up
P. F., *see* Piccolo
Pf. [Pfte.], *see* Piano
Piat., *see* Cymbals
Pic. [Picc.], *see* Piccolo
Pist., *see* Cornet
pizz., *see* Pizzicato
Pk., *see* Timpani
Pn. [P.-no.; Pno.], *see* Piano
p. n., *see* Normal bowing
Pns., *see* Cornet
port., *see* Glissando
Pos., *see* Trombone
pos. nat., *see* Natural position & Normal bowing
pos. ord. [Pos^{on} ord^{re}], *see* Natural position & Normal bowing
P^{te} Cl., *see* D [E♭] Clarinet
P^{te} c^{sse} cl., *see* Small Side Drum
P^{te} Fl., *see* Piccolo
P^{te} tamb., *see* Small Side Drum
Ptti., *see* Cymbals

(R), *see* At [on] the rim
rrr, *see* Flutter-tonguing
R. Tr., *see* Tenor Drum

S., *see* Soprano
sans sourd., *see* Muffle off & Mutes off
Sarr., *see* Sarrusophone
Sassaf. [Sax.], *see* Saxophone
S. C. [Cymb.], *see* Suspended Cymbal
Schtr., *see* Tambourine
S. D., *see* Snare Drum
senza sord., *see* Muffle off & Mutes off
Sf., *see* Xylophone
Sm. Fl., *see* Piccolo
Sn. dr., *see* Snare Drum
Sop. [Sopr.], *see* Soprano
sord., *see* Mutes
Sord. ab!, *see* Mutes off
Sourd., *see* Muffled & Mutes
Spd. Cym., *see* Suspended Cymbal
spring. Bog., *see* Saltando
sul pont., *see* Sul ponticello
sul tast., *see* Sul tasto

T., *see* Tenor
Tab., *see* Tabor
Tam. [Tam-t.; Tamt.], *see* Tam-tam
Tamb., *see* Snare Drum & Tabor & Tambourine & Tenor Drum
Tamb. B. [de B(asq).], *see* Tambourine
Tamb. gr., *see* Bass Drum
Tamb. P., *see* Tabor
Tamb. picc., *see* Small Side Drum
Tamb. r., *see* Tenor Drum
tast., *see* Sul tasto
Tb., *see* Trumpet & Tuba

T. b., *see* Tambourine
Tba., *see* Trumpet & Tuba
Tb. B., *see* Bass Tuba
Tbe., *see* Trombone & Trumpet
Tbles., *see* Timpani
Tbnes. [Tbni.], *see* Trombone
T.-bones, *see* Trombone
Tbr. b., *see* Tambourine
Tbres., *see* Glockenspiel
Tb. ten., *see* Tenor Tuba
T'buro mil., *see* Snare Drum
T. D., *see* Tenor Drum
T. de B., *see* Tambourine
T. de P., *see* Tabor
Ten., *see* Tenor & Tenuto
Ten. dr., *see* Tenor Drum
Tenp., *see* Trombone
Ten. Tb. [Tentb.], *see* Tenor Tuba
Timb. [Timp.], *see* Timpani
tkt., *see* Triple-Tonguing
T. M. [Tmb.], *see* Snare Drum
Tmb. gr., *see* Bass Drum
Tmboni., *see* Trombone
Tmb. r., *see* Tenor Drum
Tmbrno., *see* Tambourine
T.-ni., *see* Trombone
T. p., *see* Tabor
Tp., *see* Timpani
T.-Pos., *see* Trombone
Tps. [Tpt(s).; Tpttes.], *see* Trumpet
tr., *see* Trills
Tr. [Trb.], *see* Trombone & Trumpet
Tr. b. [Trb. b(assa)], *see* Bass Trumpet
Tr. Basse, *see* Bass Trumpet
Trbn. [Trbni.], *see* Trombone
Trbn. b., *see* Bass Trombone
Trbns., *see* Trombone
trem., *see* Flutter-tonguing & Tremolando & Tremolo
Trg. [Trgl.; Triang.], *see* Triangle
tr. mag. [maj.], *see* Trills
tr. min., *see* Trills
Trmp., *see* Trumpet
Trni., *see* Trombone
Tromb(s)., *see* Trombone
Tromp., *see* Trumpet
Trp. [Trpt(s).], *see* Trumpet
T. T. [T.-t.], *see* Tam-tam
T. Trb., *see* Trombone
Tymp., *see* Timpani

unis., *see* Unison

V. I. [II], *see* Violin
Va(s)., *see* Viola
Vc., *see* Violoncello
Vcell. [V.-Celli.; Vcello(s).], *see* Violoncello
Vcl(l). [Vcllo.; Vclli.], *see* Violoncello
V^{elles}, *see* Violoncello
vib., *see* Flutter-tonguing & Vibrato

INDEX OF ABBREVIATIONS

Vibraf. [Vibrahp.; Vibraph.], *see* Vibraphone

Viol. [Vl.] (I; II), *see* Violin

Violonc., *see* Violoncello

Vla(s)., *see* Viola

Vlc., *see* Violoncello

Vle., *see* Viola

Vln(s)., *see* Violin

Vlos., *see* Violoncello

Vl(s)., *see* Violin

Vni. [Vns.], *see* Violin

Xf. [Xil.], *see* Xylophone

Xyl. [Xylph.], *see* Xylophone

Zilf., *see* Xylophone

zus., *see* Unison

Zymb., *see* Cymbal

INDEX OF NOTATION

: *see* Arpeggiato

(●) : *see* At pitch

(R) : *see* At the rim

: *see* Back of the bridge

: *see* Back of the bridge; Clash

: *see* Chord Notation

: *see* Chords (pizzicati)

: *see* Chords (pizzicati); Double-stopped Unisons; L.h. pizzicato

⊢ : *see* Clash

: *see* Clash (Cymbal, Gong, etc.)

+ : *see* Clash; L.h. pizzicato; Stopped (tones); Woodwind harmonics

: *see* Dampened

: *see* Dampen full

: *see* Dampen half-way

: *see* Double Harmonics

: *see* Double-stopped Unisons

: *see* Double-stopped Unisons; With 2 sticks

: *see* Double-tonguing

⊓ : *see* Down-bow

: *see* Finger Tremolo

: *see* Flutter-tonguing

605

〜 : *see* Flutter-tonguing; "Growl"; "Wah-wah"; "Wow"

 : *see* L.h. pizzicato

⌇ : *see* Flutter-tonguing; Tremolando; Tremolo

⌒ : *see* Legato bowing; Vibrato

} : *see* Glissando

> − ∧ } : *see* Marcato bowing

♪ ⅜♪ ♩̂♪. : *see* Measured Tremolo

} : *see* Miscellaneous Effects (Harp)

〜 : *see* Glissando; "Wah-wah"

o : *see* Nail pizzicato

} : *see* Glissando to a harmonic

([} : *see* Non-arpeggiato; Pizzicato with 2 fingers

↑ : *see* Hand in bell

o − + : *see* Open—Stopped

} : *see* Harmonics

: *see* Piano Harmonics

(: *see* Portamento; "Rip"

o : *see* Harmonics; Natural notes; Open; Open Strings; With the fist

⋮ : *see* Quadruple Harmonics

♭½♮ } : *see* Quarter tones

 : *see* Reverse Arpeggio

v ⊓ v ⊓ : *see* Reverse Bowing

a2 ~~~~ : *see* Rubbed together

 : *see* Saltando

 : *see* Separate Bowings

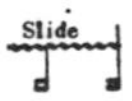 : *see* Slide (Wire-brush on Cymbal, etc.)

~ : *see* "Smear"

 : *see* "Snap" pizzicato

. . . . : *see* Spiccato bowing

 : *see* Staccato bowing

+ - o : *see* Stopped—Open

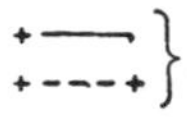 : *see* Stopped (tones)

⊓ ⊓ ⊓ ⊓ : *see* Successive Down-bows

v v v v : *see* Successive Up-bows

 : *see* Timpani Chords

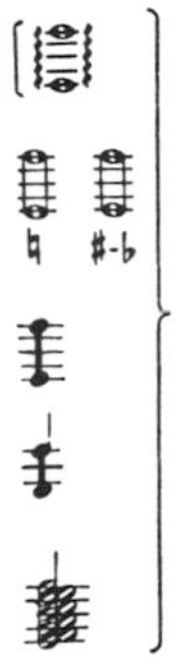 : *see* Tone-clusters

 : *see* Tremolando; Trills

 : *see* Tremolando; Trills

 : *see* Tremolando; Tremolo; Trills; 2-Timpani Roll

 : *see* Tremolando; Tremolo; 2-Timpani Roll

 : *see* Tremolando; Tremolo; Trills

 : *see* Tremolo glissando

△ △ : *see* Triangle

tr~~~~ : *see* Trills; 2-Timpani Roll

 : *see* Triple Harmonics

 : *see* Triple-tonguing

v : *see* Up-bow

INDEX OF NUMERALS

½ bouché [chiuso; gestopft], 120
½ [half] muted—½ [half] open, 403
½ of desks, 455
½ arco—½ pizz., 337

1ᵃ corda, 560, 564, 570
1 Alto flute, 32, 33
(1) Alto Solo, 477
1ᵃ metà, 455
1ᵃ metà con sord . . . , 403
1 Bass clarinet, 31–4
1 Bass oboe, 33
1 Bassoon, 29
1 Bass trumpet, 31–3
1 Bass tuba, 33
1 Contrabassoon, 30–4
1 Contrabass trombone, 31–2
1 Contrabass tuba, 31
(1) Contrebasse Solo, 477
1 Cornet, 144
1 Cymbale frappée . . . , 232
1 Cymbale roulée . . . , 232
1 della 1ᵃ metà, 455
1 Desk [stand], 491
1 desk only, 491
1 D Trumpet, 33
1 English horn, 31–4
1ᵉʳᵉ corde, 560, 564, 570
1ᵉʳᵉ moitié avec sourd . . . , 403
1ᵉʳᵉˢ archet—2ᵐᵉˢ pizz., 337
1ᵉʳ et 2ᵉ pupitres, 491
1ᵉʳ Pupitre, 491
1ᵉʳ pupitre solo, 491
1ᵉʳˢ Violon(s), 10
1 Flute, 29
1 Geigen, 10
1 Hälfte mit Dämpfer . . . , 403
1 Heckelphone, 33
1 Horn, 144–5
1 Large cymbal, 34
1 leggio solamente, 491
1º arco—2º pizz., 337
1º e 2º leggi, 491
1º Leggio, 491
1 Piccolo, 30–4
1 Player, 161–2, 171, 477
1 Posthorn, 145
1 [1ᵉʳ] Pupitre, 491
1 pupitre seulement, 491
1ʳᵉ de chaque pupitre, 455
1ʳᵉ moitié, 455
1 (un) par pupitre, 455
1 Small cymbal, 34

1 Small Timpani, 33
1 solamente, 477
1. Solo, 477
(1) Solo Violin [Viola; Cello; Bass], 477
(1) Solo Violine [Bratsche; Violoncell; Kontrabass], 477
(1) Solo Violino [Viola; Violoncello; Contrabasso], 477
1. Spieler, 477
1st and 2nd desks, 491
1st and 2nd Horns muted, 152
1st Desk [stand], 491
1st desk solo, 491
1st Half, 455
1st halves only, 455
1st Horn take mute, 152
1st player from each desk, 455
1st string, 564
1st 3 [4; 5; 6, etc.] desks [stands], 491
1st two desks, 491
1st Violin(s), 10
1ᵗᵉ Hälfte, 455
1 Tenor tuba, 33
1 Trombone (off-stage), 144
1 Trumpet (off-stage), 33, 144–5
1 Tuba, 30–4
(1) Violoncelle Solo, 477
(1) Violon Solo, 477
1. 2. 3. [4. 5. 6., etc.] pupitres, 491

I. 560, 564, 570
I.C. [corda], 564
I. corde, 564
I mit Bog.—II Pizz., 337
Iº di leggi, 455
Iº Leggio, 491
Iº leggio solo, 491
I parte, 455
I Piatto rullo . . . , 232
I Piatto uniti alla (gran) cassa, 182
I Pult, 491
I-Saite, 564
Ist Orchestra, 405
I [1.] Violine(n), 10
I. II. III. (etc.) Pulte . . . , 491

2ᵃ corda, 559, 563
2ᵃ metà, 455
2 Bassoons, 29–31, 33–4
2 Bass tubas, 31
2 Becken mit Teller(n), 181
2 Clarinets, 29–34
2 Clarini, 29

2 Cornets, 30, 32
2 Cornetti, 29
2 [two] cymbals clashed [free], 181
2 Cymbals (free), 181
2ᵈˢ Violon(s), 10
2ᵉ corde, 559, 563
2 [Two] 8-Part Choruses, 29, 32
2ᵉ moitié, 455
2 English horns, 32
2. esecutori [suonatori], 172, 211
2 [deux] exécutants, 172, 211
2-fach get., 455
2 Flicorni [Roman Horns], 145
2 Flutes, 29–34
2-fold, 83
2. Geigen, 10
2 Harps, 30, 32–4
2 Horns, 29, 30
2 leggi solamente [solo], 491
2nd Fl. takes Picc., 83
2nd Half, 455
2nd halves only, 455
2nd Ob. takes Eng. Hn., 83
2nd string, 559
2 Oboes, 29–34
2 Organs, 29
2 [due] Piatti, 181
2 [due] Piatti al [nel] modo ord., 181
2-[two] plate clash [crash], 181
2 [two] plates together, 183
2 [two] players, 162, 171–2, 211
2 (players) only, 491
2. prende Cor. ing., 83
2. Pulte solo [einer allein], 491
2 Roman Horns [Flicorni], 145
2 [zwei] Schläger, 211
2 Soli, 491
2 Soli Violinen [Bratschen; Violoncelle; Bässe], 491
2 Soli (Violini) [Viole, etc.], 491
2 Solo Violins [Violas; Cellos; Basses], 491
2 Soli Violons [Altos; Violoncelles; Basses], 491
2 [zwei] Spieler, 172
2 Spieler allein, 491
2 [two] sticks, 158, 172
2 Tenor tubas, 31
2 Timpani, 29–31, 34
2-[two] Timpani roll, xvi, 158, 171–2
2 Trombones (off-stage), 33, 145
2 Trumpets, 29–31, 33–4, 144–5

2 Tubas, 30, 33
2 Violinen (etc.) soli [allein], 491
2 [due] Violini [Viole; Violoncelli; Bassi] solamente, 491
2 Violini (etc.) soli, 491
2 Violins (etc.) solo, 491
2 Violons (etc.) soli [seuls], 491

II. 559, 563
II.C. [corda], 559
II. corde, 559
II [2nd] Ob. to E. H., 83
IInd Orchestra, 405
II parte, 455
II-Saite, 559
II [2.] Violine(n), 10

3ª corda, 560, 562, 569–70
3 Bassoons, 31–3
3 Buccine [Roman Trumpets], 145
3 Caisses [Casse], 212
3 Clarinets, 31–4
3 Drums, 212
3ᵉ corde, 560, 562, 569–70
3 (1ᵗᵉ Viol., etc.) allein, 491
3-fach get., 455
3 (1st Vlns., etc.) Solo, 491
3 Flutes, 30–1, 34
3 4-Part Male Choruses, 32
3 Oboes, 29, 31–3
3 Players, 162, 172
3 (1ᵉʳᵉˢ Vᵒⁿˢ, etc.) Soli [seuls], 491
3rd Cl. change to B. Cl., 83
3rd Cl. in B♭ change to E♭ Cl., 83
3rd Fl. alternates with Picc., 83
3rd string, 562
3 Roman Trumpets [Buccine], 145

3 Timpani, 31–4
3 Trombones, 29–34, 145
3 Trommeln, 212
3 Trumpets, 29–34, 144
3 (Vln. I, etc.) Soli, 491

III., 560, 562, 569–70
III.C. [corda], 562
III. corde, 562
III-Saite, 562

4ª corda, 561, 565
4 Bassoons, 30, 32
4 Bayreuth tubas, 32
4ᵉ corde, 561, 565
4 einzelne Viol. (etc.), 491
4-fach get., 467
4 Flutes, 29, 32
4-Händig, 225, 241
4 Hands, 225, 241
4 Harps, 32
4 Horns, 30–4
4 Horns muted, 152
4 Piccolos, 32
4 players, 163, 491
4 Soli [Spieler], 491
4 Solo Vlns. (etc.), 491
4 Tenor tubas, 33
4th string, 561, 565
4 Timpani, 30–33
4 Trombones, 33
4 Trumpets, 32–3, 144–5
4 Tubas, 31, 33
4 Violins, 29

IV., 561, 565
IV.C. [corda], 561, 565
IV. corde, 561, 565
IV-Saite, 561, 565

5 Solo voices, 32
5-string Bass, 281, 581
5 Timpani, 34

6 Harps, 31
6-Part Female Chorus, 33
6 Roman Trumpets, 33
6 Timpani, 32–3
6 Trombones, 32
6 Trumpets, 32

8 Basses, 31
8 Horns, 31–3
8-Part Chorus, 32
8 Solo Voices, 32
8 Trumpets, 29
8 Violas, 29

9 Basses, 30

10 Horns, 32, 33
10 Violas, 30

11 Violoncellos, 30

12 Horns, 33, 145
12 Violas, 31
12 Violoncellos, 31

13 Solo voices, 31

15 Violin I, II, 30

16 Violon I, II, 31

INDEX OF NOMENCLATURE AND TERMINOLOGY

A — — — — — — — —, 559
A——————|, 559
A and B-Flat clarinet, 15
Abbassa la IV. corda al Si, 573
Abdämpfen, 165, 268
Abgestossen, 294
A calotta, 75
Accented (bows), 291
Accordate A in G♯, 573
Accordate C in B, 573
Accordate G in F♯ [G♭; G♯], 573
Accordate il G corda come di solito, 573
Accordate la corda la più bassa in Si♭, 271
Accordato in alto, 212
Accordé en haut, 212
Accordez en Fa♯ mineur, 273
Accordez la corde la plus basse en Si♭, 271
Accordez le Sol comme d'ordinaire, 573
Accordez Sol au Sol♯, 573
Accrochez la Cymb. au pied, 182
A corda [La corde], 559
Actual pitch [sound], 273, 409
Add mute(s), 104
A deux [2], 83
A due [2], 83, 181, 455
Agitare, 215
Agitées l'une contre l'autre, 183
Agité(ez), 215
A la corde, 288, 372
A la guitarra, 266, 325
A la jante, 197
A la pointe, 307
A la pointe, comme col legno, 578
Al banjo, 325
All, 455
Alla chitarra [clavecin], 266
Alla corda, 283
Alla maniera stridente, 149
Alla stessa corda, 581
All desks muted, 581
All divided, 455
All divided in 2 equal parts, 455
Alle, 455
Alle die Andere, 581
Alle die Bässe mit Ausnahme . . . , 581
Alle ersten [zweiten] Viol. mit Ausnahme . . . , 581

Alle geteilt, 455
Alle in den Bläsern . . . . , 63
Alle in zwei gleichen Hälften geteilt, 455
Alle Pulte mit Dämpfer, 581
All'estremità, 180, 197
All'estremità (della membrana), 163
Allmählich die Dämpfer aufsetzen, 405
Allmählich öffnen, 111
Allmählich Sordinen ab [an], 405, 406
All'ogni leggio soltanto il Iº sonatore, 455
Allow to vibrate, 233
All the basses except the 1st player, 581
All the 1st [2nd] Vlns. put on mutes . . . , 581
All the others, 581
All the remaining Vlns. . . . , 455
A l'octave réelle, 273, 409
A l'ordinaire, 181, 372
Al ordinario, 72
Al ponticello, 381
Al punto, 307
Al solito, 372
Al tallone, 305
Alt(e), 10
Altflöte, 6
Althoboe, 6
Alto Flute, 6, 13, 32–4, 57, 61, 65–7
Alto(i), 10
Alto(s), 10
Alto solo, 477
Alzate sordino(i), 104
Amboss, 9
A metà arco, 311
Am Frosch, 305
Am Griffbrett, 394
Am Metallrand um Fell schlagen, 164
Am Rand (des Felles), 163, 180, 196–7, 214
Am Spitze (des Bogens) beginnen, 579
Am Steg, 381
A nach E tief, 233
A nach Gis herunterstimmen, 573
Anche nasale che possibile, 81
Anderes Becken nehmen, 232
An der gleichen Saite, 581

An der Seite des Kessels schlagen, 164
An der Spitze des Bogens, 307
An der Spitze gestrichen, 307
An jedem Pulte nur die erste Spieler, 455
Antike Zimbeln, 8
Antique Cymbals, 8, 32–3, 158, 226
Anvil [Steel Bar, Pipe], 9, 223, 228
A peine frôlé, 181, 197
Aperta(e) [aperto(i)], 104, 112
Aperto(i)—Chiuso(i), 125
A peu près du chevalet . . . , 579
A pied(e), 201
Appena toccata, 181, 197
Appuyer une baguette sur la peau . . . , 198
Après avoir frappé les cymbales . . . , 194
Apri poco a poco, 111
A punta d'arco, 307
a 4, 467
A 4 mains (mani), 225, 241
Archet, 322
Archet—comme pizz., 580
Archi [Strumenti a corde], 10
Arco, 322
Arco per arco, 283
Arco—quasi pizz, 580
Armonica, 9
Armonici: come è scritto, 273
Armonici: non un'ottava più alta, 273
Armonici: suono, 273
Armonico(i), 41, 74, 225, 242, 257, 273
Armonico sul A [C; D; E; G] corda, 408
Arpa(e), 9
Arpégé, 322
Arpège descendant, 572
Arpégez le pizzicato, 322
Arpeggiate, 322
Arpeggiated, 279
Arpeggiato, xviii, 279, 322–5
Arpeggio discendente, 572
Arrachez la corde ouverte (Ré) . . . , 578
Artificial Harmonics, xviii, 280, 441–54
A-Saite, 559
As if muted, 80

As nasal as possible, 81
Assordate a mezza, e tutta, 195
Assordate col il dita, 194
Assordate i toni . . . , 220
Assordate le corde colla palma . . . , 242
A string, 559
A [au] talon, 305
At heel (of bow), 305
A to low E, 233
At pitch, 273, 409
a 3, 455
Attach the cymb. to the foot-beater, 182
At (the) edge [rim], 180
At (the) edge of (the) head, 163, 196
At the end of the bow, 307
At (the) frog, 305
At [on] the nut, 305
At the point, like col legno, 578
At the point [tip] (of the bow), 307
At (the) rim (of head), 163, 180, 197
At the tip [point] (of the bow), 307
Au bord, 180
Au bord (de la membrane [peau]), 163, 196
Au centre, 164
Au chevalet, 381
Auf A, 559
Auf beiden Fellen, 198
Auf C, 561
Auf D, 562
Auf das Fell, 199, 215
Auf das Fell mit dünnen Ruten, 232
Auf dem Holzrand (den Trommel), 199, 221
Auf dem Holzstäbchen, 199
Auf dem Knie gestreichen, 214
Auf dem Rand, 180
Auf dem Steg, 381
Auf dem Theater, 75
Auf den Boden werfen, 220
Auf den hölzernen Rahmen, 199
Auf den Saiten, 232
Auf den Schellen, 214
Auf den vier Saiten . . . , 381
Auf der A–Saite (zu spielen), 559
Auf der Bühne, 75
Auf der C–Saite (zu spielen), 561
Auf der D–Saite (zu spielen), 562
Auf der E–Saite (zu spielen), 564
Auf der G–Saite (zu spielen), 565
Auf der kleinen Trommel, 220
Auf der mitte des Bogens, 311
Auf die Kuppel, 183
Auf die Seite gedreht, 198
Auf E, 564
Auf einer Saite, 581
Auf G, 565
Auf Holz geschlägen, 199
Auf zwei [2] Saiten, 537

Au milieu, 183
Au milieu de la membrane [peau], 164, 198, 221
Au [du] milieu de l'archet, 311
Au naturel, 372
Aus der Ferne, 75
Ausklingen lassen, 233
Aussi nasillard que possible, 81
Aus vollen Hals, 149
Au [à] talon, xviii, 279, 305–7
Auto [Taxi] Horn, 9, 228
Autohorn, 9
Avanzare il suono, 151
Avec baguette(s), 232
Avec corde(s), 210
Avec deux [2] baguettes, 172
Avec deux [2] baguettes sur une cymbale, 232
Avec la main, 109, 120, 184, 215
Avec la pointe (de l'archet), 307
Avec l'archet, 322
Avec l'archet renversée, 572
Avec le bois, 372
Avec le dos de l'archet, 372
Avec le genou, 214
Avec le manche de la mailloche, 184, 222
Avec le pouce, 213, 333
Avec les autres Vons [Altos, etc.], 581
Avec les cordes lâches [relâchées], 209
Avec les doigts, 215
Avec les jointures, 216
Avec les ongles, 164
Avec les pointes des doigts, 200
Avec le talon, 305
Avec l'extrémité grosse . . . , 184
Avec l'extrémité mince . . . , 184
Avec l'ongle, 330
Avec médiateur, 272
Avec plateaux, 181
Avec sourdine — +, 119
Avec sourdine—cuivré, 118
Avec sourdine—cuivré — +, 120
Avec sourdine, imitant le cornet antique, 150
Avec sourdine, non-cuivrer, 111
Avec sourdine(s), 79, 104
Avec sourdine(s)—Ouvert(s), 122
Avec timbre(s), 210
Avec toute la longueur de l'archet, 310
Avec un morceau mince de feutre . . . , 212
Avec verges, 232
Avoid the open A [C; D; E; G] string, 581

Bacchetta a due capi, 167
Bacchetta di giunco con la testa di capoc, 166
Bacchetta di Piatto, 166

Bacchetta di Triangolo, 167
Bacchetta(e) a bambagia, 166
Bacchetta(e) d'acciaio, 167
Bacchetta(e) di canna, 166
Bacchetta(e) di capoc, 167
Bacchetta(e) di cotone, 166
Bacchetta(e) di feltro [feltro duro; feltro medio-duro; feltro medio-molle; feltro molle], 166
Bacchetta(e) di ferro, 166
Bacchetta(e) di gommaelastica [gommaelastica dura; gomma-elastica mezza-dura; gomma-elastica quarta-dura], 166
Bacchetta(e) di Gran cassa, 166
Bacchetta(e) di lana, 167
Bacchetta(e) di legno, 167
Bacchetta(e) di metallo, 166
Bacchetta(e) di pelle [pelle cruda; pelle dure; pelle medio-duro], 166
Bacchetta(e) di spugna, 167
Bacchetta(e) di Tamburo militare, 166
Bacchetta(e) di Timpano(i) [Timpani a feltro; Timpani a legno; Timpani a pelle cruda; Timpani a spugna; Timpani grosse; Timpani molle; Timpani molle a feltro; Timpani molto dure; Timpani molto molle], 166, 167
Bacchetta(e) di Zilafono, 167
Bacchetta(e) dure [molle], 166
Bacchetta(e) felpate, 166
Bacchetta(e) grosse, 167
Bacchetta(e) leggiere, 166
Bacchetta(e) media-dura, 166
Bacchetta(e) molle [dure], 166
Bacchetta(e) molto dure [molle], 167
Bacchetta(e) ordinaria, 166
Bacchetta(e) sottile, 167
Bacchette soli, 233
Back of (the) bridge, xviii, 381
Baguette de Cymbale, 166
Baguette de Triangle, 167
Baguette en jonc à tête de capoc, 166
Baguette mince à petite tête en éponge, 167
Baguette mince en bois, 167
Baguette(s) assez dur(es) [dur(es); très dures], 166, 167
Baguette(s) d'acier, 167
Baguette(s) de [en] bois, 167
Baguette(s) de Caisse claire, 166
Baguette(s) de caoutchouc dur [semi-dur], 166
Baguette(s) de coton, 166
Baguette(s) de cuir dur, 166
Baguette(s) de [en] métal, 166
Baguette(s) de peluche, 166
Baguette(s) d'éponge [en éponge], 167

Baguette(s) de Timbale(s) [Timbale(s) douce(s); Timbale(s) en bois; Timbale(s) en éponge; Timbale(s) en feutre; Timbale(s) en feutre douce(s); Timbale(s) en peau; Timbale(s) épaisse(s); Timbale(s) très douce(s); Timbale(s) très dure(s)], 166, 167
Baguette(s) de Xylophone, 167
Baguette(s) douce(s) [très douce(s)], 166, 167
Baguette(s) dur(es), 166
Baguette(s) en [de] bois, 167
Baguette(s) en canne, 166
Baguette(s) en caoutchouc [caoutchouc quart-dur], 166
Baguette(s) en capoc, 167
Baguette(s) en cuir [cuir assez dur(es); cuir brut], 166
Baguette(s) en [d'] éponge, 167
Baguette(s) en fer, 166
Baguette(s) en feutre [feutre assez dur(es); feutre assez molle(s); feutre douce(s); feutre dur], 166
Baguette(s) en laine, 167
Baguette(s) en [de] métal, 166
Baguette(s) en peau, 166
Baguette(s) en rotin, 166
Baguette(s) épaisse(s), 167
Baguette(s) légère(s), 166
Baguette(s) mince(s), 167
Baguette(s) normale(s) [ordinaire(s)], 166
Baguette(s) ouateuse(s), 166
Baguettes solos, 233
Baguette(s) très douce(s), 167
Baguette(s) très dur(es), 167
Baguette [mailloche] sur Cymbale, 232
Baissent la corde Do au Si, 573
Baissez la corde Sol au Fa♯ [Sol♭], 573
Baissez la corde Sol au Sol♭, 573
Baissez le Sol d'un demi-ton, 573
Baissez les touches sans sonner, 242
Baissez Ut♯ à Ut♮, 233
Balai métallique, 167
Balayez un balai métallique . . . , 164
Balzato, 300
Barely touched, 181, 197
Baritone(s), 10
Baritono(i), 10
Baryton(e), 10
Bass (Bässe), 10
Bass Clarinet, xv, 6, 16, 31–4, 40, 50–1, 57, 59, 62, 65–71, 83
Bass Drum, xvii, 7, 30–4, 158, 196–211
Bass drum alone (with Cymb. detached), 201
Bass drum stick(s), 166, 184, 216
Basse(s), 10

Bass(es), 10, 28–34, 279–581
Bassflöte, 6
Bass Flute, 6
Bassk[c]larinette, 6
Bass Oboe, 6, 33
Basso continuo, 29
Basso(i), 10
Basson(s), 6
Bassoon(s), xv, 6, 17, 29–34, 40, 51–4, 57–62, 66–7, 69–71, 77–9, 81–3
Bassposaune, 7
Bass solo, 477
Bass Trombone, 7, 21
Basstrompete, 7
Bass Trumpet, 7, 31–3
(Bass) Tuba, 7, 31, 33, 90, 101–3
(Bass)tuba, 7
Bâton mince d'acier, 167
Batteria [Percussione; Strumenti a percossa], 7
Batterie, 7
Battery, 7
Battuta di Timpano, 167
Battuta(e) metale, 166
Battuto coll'arco, 304
Baumwollschlägel, 166
Bayreuth tubas, 32
Beater(s) [Hammer(s); Mallet(s); Stick(s); Striker(s)], 166
Beat with maracas, 172
Becken, 8
Becken allein, 182
Becken am Rand halten . . . , 194
Becken am Riemen hängend, 232
Becken an der grosse Trommel befestigt . . . , 182
Becken angebunden . . . , 182
Becken (frei), 8
Becken freihängend, 8
Becken frei mit Schlägel, 232
Becken freischwingend, 8
Becken gewöhnlich, 181
Becken nach Anschlag . . . , 194
Beckenschlägel, 166
Bedeckt, 165
Behind [below] the bridge, 381
Behind the scene [stage], 75
Beide Schalen, 181
Beide Töne durch Flag., 437
Bells, xvi, 8, 23, 31–3, 158, 173–9
Bell(s) down, 72
Bell(s) in the air, 72, 91
Bells Up—Brasses, xvi, 91, 141–3
Woodwinds, xv, 40, 72–3
Below [behind] the bridge, 381
Ben accordato, 232
Ben arpeggiando gli accordi, 322
B-Flat and A Clarinet, 6, 15
B♭ Trumpet, 20
Bien accordé, 232
Bien enveloppé de toile . . . , 220

Bisb[p]igliando, 269
Biting, 150
Bläser [Blasinstrumente], 6
Blechbläser [Blechinstrumente], 7
Blechern, 112
Blechinstrumente [Blechbläser], 7
Bloc de métal, 9
Blocs à papier de verre, 9
Blocs chinois, 9
Blocs de bois [Wood-blocs], 9
Blousée [Blouser(ez)], 163, 180
Blousée[er; ez] avec baguette(s), 180
Blouser(ez) [Blousée], 163, 180
Bogen, 322
Bogenmitte, 311
Bogen—wie Pizz, 580
Bois, 6
Boîte à clous [Maracas], 9
Bongos, 9, 222, 224
Both tones as harmonics, 437
Bottle, 225
Bouché(ez), 112
Bouché(ez) et cuivré(ez), 112
Bouché(s)—Ouvert(s), 122
Bouchez—Ouvert, 122
Bounce the bow, 300
Bouncing bow, 300
Bouteillophone, 228
Bow, 322
Bow and Finger Tremoli combined, xviii, 279, 363–4
Bow-Finger tremolo, xviii, 279, 354–7
Bowing, xviii, 278–9, 283–321
Bow on string, 283
Bow tremolo, ix–x, xviii, 279, 347–9
Box filled with sand, 228
Boys' Choir, 32
Brass(es), ix, xvi, 7, 19–21, 29–34, 85–152, 158, 278
Brass mutes, 91, 104–9
Brass notation, 112, 115, 120–2, 125, 133, 146–9, 605–7
Brass Terminology, xiv, 91, 152
Brassy, 91, 112
Brassy—Open, 122
Brassy sounds [tones], 91, 112–21
Bratsche(n), 10
Bratsche solo, 477
Break bottle !, 225
Breit ausstreichen [gezogen], 310
Bridge, 381
Brisez la bouteille !, 225
Brosse en fil de métal, 167
Broussez avec la baguette, 181
Broussez avec une pièce d'argent, 181
Brummeisen, 9
Brushed with a silver coin, 181
Brushed with stick, 181
Brush(es) [Wire-brush], 167
Brush the head [skin] with the thumb, 213

Brush [flick] the jingles, 214
Bubbolo, 9
Buccine [Roman Trumpets], 33, 145
By means of the l.h., 328

Caisse claire, 7
Caisse roulante, 8
Cambia A in E bassa, 233
Cambia C♯ in C♮, 233
Cambia in Fl. gr. [Ob., etc.], 83
Cambia in Ob., 83
Campana in aria [alto; su], 72
Campane, 8
Campane in alto [aria; su], 72
Campanelle di vacca, 9
Campanelle(i), 8
Campane nell'aria, 72
Campanetta, 8
Cane stick(s), 166
Cane stick with fibre head, 166, 202, 217
Cannon shot(s), 211
Cappello sopra campana, 110
Cardboard mute(s), 104–5
Carillon, 8
Cassa di metallo, 9
Cassa rullante, 8
Casse di legno [Legno], 9
Castagnette(s), 8
Castanets, 8, 32, 223
Catene, 9
C corda, 561
C [Do; Ut] corde, 561
Celesta, xvii, 9, 24, 32–3, 237–41
Celeste, 9
'Cello(i), 10
Cello(s), 10
Cello solo, 477
Cembalo [Clavicembalo], 10, 29, 226
Cembalon [Cimbalom], 9, 226
Center of bow, 311
Center of (the) head, 198
Ceppi chinosi, 9
Ceppi di carta vetro, 9
Cfg. muta in Fag. 3 [Fg. III], 83
Chaînes, 9
Chains, 9, 228
Change C♯ to C♮, 233
Change en Gᵈᵉ Fl., 83
Change Eng. Hn. to 2nd Ob [Ob II], 83
Change to A [B♭, F, etc.], 83, 152
Change to Fl., 83
Change(z) en Fa [La, Mi, Si♭, etc.], 83, 152
Changez le Mi aigu en Do, 233
Changez l'Ut♯ au Fa♯ haut, 233
Changez Sol♯ en Si, 233
Changez Ut♯ en Ut♮, 233
Chapeau sur le pavillon, 110
Chevalet, 381

Chime-Bells, 8
Chimes (tubular), 8, 23, 174
Chinese Blocks [Drums], 9, 228
Chinese Cymbal, 8
Chinesische Blocke, 9
Chinesische Zimbel, 8
Chitarra [Guitarre], 9
Chiuse, 112
Chiuse, imitando il Corno, 121
Chiuso — +, 117
Chiuso(i), 112
Chiuso(i)—Aperto(i), 122
Chocalho, 228
Chœur, 10
Choke(d), 163
Chor, 10
Chord Notation, xviii, 281, 532–6
Chord—one hand, xvii, 254–5
Chords (glissandi), 250, 254–6
Chords—Harp, xvii, 250, 254–6
    Strings, xviii, 279, 281, 325–6, 532–6
    Timpani, xvi, 158, 161–3
Chords (pizzicati), xviii, 279, 325–6
Chord—two hands, xvii, 255
Chorus, 10, 29–30, 32–3
Chromatic glissando, 542
Chromatique glissando, 542
Chromatisch Glissando, 542
Cigolio, 194
Cimbali antichi, 8
Cimbalom [Cembalon], 9, 221–3, 225–6
Cinellen, 8
Cinelli, 8
Cinglant, 195
Cis in Fis hoch, 233
Cis nach C umstimmen (zurück-stimmen), 233
Cithare, 9
Clarinet(s), xv, 6, 15, 29–34, 40, 50, 57–62, 64–73, 76–8, 80–3
Clarinette basse, 6
C[K]larinette in Es [D], 6
C[K]larinette(n), 6
Clarinette(s), 6
Clarinetto basso, 6
Clarinetto(i), 6
Clarinetto piccolo in Mi♭ [Re], 6
Clarini, 29
Clarino, 7
Clarone, 6
Clash(ed), 158, 181
Clavecin, 10
Claves [Cuban Sticks], 9, 228
Clavicembalo [Cembalo], 10, 226
Claxon, 228
Cloches, 8
Clochettes, 8
Closed (tones), 91, 112
Close to (the) bridge, 381
Close to (the) rim, 163

Cl. 3º in B♭ muta in Cl. Picc. in E♭, 83
Cl. 3 mutano in Cl. basso, 83
C nach Cis umstimmen, 233
Coarsely (blown), 80, 149
Coconut Shells, 229
Col altre [col gli altri], 581
Col'arco al rovescio, 572
Col ginocchio, 214
Col gli altri [col altre], 581
Col gli altri Vni. [altre Vle., etc.], 581
Col il dita, 215
Colla(e) punta(e) (dell'arco), 307
Colla(e) unghia(e), 272, 330
Colla mano, 109, 120, 184, 215
Colla mazza, 232
Colla nocce, 216
Coll'arco slanciato e saltante, 300
Col Legno [ligno], ix–x, xviii, 279–80, 372–80
Col legno & Modo ordinario (arco) combined, xviii, 379–80
Col legno & Pizzicato combined, xviii, 378–9
Col legno & Sul ponticello combined, xviii, 280, 393
Col legno battuto [tratto], 372–3
Col legno gestrichen, 372
Col legno glissando, xviii, 280, 372
Col legno non-tremolo, xviii, 280, 373–8
Col legno on harmonics, xviii, 280, 372
Col legno tratto [battuto], 372–3
Col legno tremolo, xviii, 280, 373
Colle sordine, 104
Coll'estremità di legno della bacchetta, 184
Coll'estremità grossa . . . , 184
Coll'estremità sottile . . . , 184
Colle unghie, 164
Col ligno [legno], 372–80
Colli verghi, 232
Coll'punto, 307
Col mancio della mazza, 184, 200, 222
Color Organ, 226
Colpete, 215
Colpete al ordinario, 163
Colpete colle marache, 172
Colpete col rovescio . . . , 195
Colpete con legno, 184
Colpete le corde con magli . . . , 243
Colpete sul orlo . . . , 164
Colpete sul timballo di rame, 164
Colpo, 215
Colpo col mano . . . , 331
Colpo con triangolo, 183
Colpo(i) di cannone, 211
Colpo(i) di lingua, 63
Col pollice, 333
Col pollice (sulla membrana), 213

Colpo sul ginocchio, 214
Col pugno, 214
Col punto del arco, 307
Col tallone, 305
Combinations, 250, 256, 260
Combinations—two hands, 260
Come campana, 149
Come è scritto, 273, 409
Come guitarra, 266
Come richiamo, 80
Come tromba(e), 80–1
Come un eco, 76, 109
Comme avec sourdine, 80
Comme de cris perçants, 149
Comme guitare, 81
Commencez au bout (de l'archet), 579
Comme pizzicato, 81, 151
Comme staccato—haletant, 151
Comme un accordéon, 580
Comme un canon, 211
Comme un crincrin, 578
Comme une cloche, 149
Comme une harpe, 242
Comme une trompette, 80–1
Comme une voix d'oiseau, 80
Comparative Table of Ranges, xv, 4, 11–28
Con bacchetta(e), 232
Con corda(e), 210
Con due [2] bacchette, 172
Con due [2] bacchette a piatto, 232
Con la bacchetta, 372
Con l'arco, 322
Con l'arco in tutta la sua lunghezza, 310
Con larga arcata, 310
Con mediatore, 272
Con molto arco, 310
Con sordina(e) [sordino(i)], 79, 90, 104, 165, 194, 268, 280
Con sordini poco a poco, 405
Con sordino — +, 119
Con sordino—chiuso — +, 120
Con sordino, imitando il cornetto antico, 150
Con sordino—Naturale, 122
Con sordino, non-chiuso, 111
Con sord. leggio a leggio, 405
Con timbro, 210
Continuo, 29
C[K]ontrabass(bässe), 10
Contra Bass(es), 10
Contrabasso con quintupolo corde, 581
Contrabasso(i), 10
Contrabassoon, xv, 7, 17, 30–4, 40, 54–5, 69–70, 83
Contrabassoon change to 3rd Bssn., 83
Contrabasso solo, 477

Contrabass trombone, 31–2
Contrabass tuba, 31
C[K]ontrafagott, 7
Contrafagotto, 7
Contrebasse à cinq cordes, 581
Contrebasse(s), 10
Contrebasse solo, 477
Contrebasson, 7
Contralto(es), 10
Contre le pupitre, 110, 199
Contro il leggio, 110
Con tutta la lunghezza dell'arco, 310
Con un minuto frammento . . . , 212
Coperto con un cappello, 110
Coperto con un pezzo di tela, 174
Coperto(i), 112, 165
Coprire la membrana . . . , 211–12
Coprire le lamine . . . , 174
Cor Anglais, 6
Cor d'auto, 9
Corde del Tamburo lasciare, 209
Cordes [Instruments à cordes], 10
Cor. ing. muta in Ob.2 [Ob. II], 83
Cornet(s) 7, 29–30, 32, 106, 128–9, 132, 135–6, 140, 144
Cornet(s)-à-pistons, 7
Cornett(e), 7
Cornetto(i) a pistoni, 7
Corni [Tbe.; Trbni.] con sord., 152
Corni I e II colle sordine, 152
Corni I–IV con sordini, 152
Corno(i), 7
Corno di automobile, 9
Corno di vacca, 9
Corno inglese, 6
Corno I mette il sordino, 152
Coro, 10
Cor(s), 7
Cotton stick(s), 166
Country-fiddle style, 578
Coup avec le bois d'une baguette, 184
Couvrez les plaques . . . , 174
Cover the metal with a silk cloth, 174
Cowbells, 9, 33, 222, 227
Cowhorn, 9
Crash Cymbal, 8
Crash(ed), 181
Crécelle, 9
Crotales, 8
C♯ in F♯ alta, 233
C-Saite, 561
C string, 561
C♯ to high F♯, 233
C Trumpet, 20
Cuban Drums, 222
Cuban Sticks [Claves], 9, 228
Cuckoo, 229
Cuica [String Drum], 230
Cuivré, 112
Cuivré — +, 117
Cuivré, imitant un Cor, 121

Cuivres, 7
Cuivré(s)—Ouvert(s), 122
Cuivrez (le son), 112
Cuivrez—Ouvert, 122
Cup mute(s), 90, 104, 105
Cymbal alone, 182
Cymbale blousée, 180
Cymbale Chinoise, 8
Cymbale contre Cymbale, 181
Cymbale fixée à la Grosse caisse, 182
Cymbale libre avec baguette, 232
Cymbales à main, 181
Cymbales Antiques, 8
Cymbale seul, 182
Cymbales (libres), 8
Cymbales plateaux, 181
Cymbale (suspendue), 8
Cymbal, fixed, 182
Cymbal, free, 8
Cymbal hung by its strap, 232
Cymbal—pair, 181
Cymbal(s), xvii, 8, 30–4, 158, 180–95, 232
Cymbal stick, 166, 217
Cymbal (struck) attached to bass drum, 182
Cymbal struck with drumstick, 232
Cytharra, 9, 227

Dalle due parti, 198
Damp(en), 163, 268
Dampened by holding with fingers, 194
Dampened — Harp, 250, 268
  Percussion, xvi, xvii, 158, 163, 174, 180, 194, 196, 213
Dampened with one hand . . . , 174
Dampen [stop] half-way, and full, 195
Dämpfen, 163
Dämpfer, 104–5
Dämpfer ab ! [absetzen], 104
Dämpfer allmählich ab, 406
Dämpfer ansetzen, 104
Dämpfer auf !, 104
Dämpfer aufsetzen [ansetzen; nehmen; vorbereiten], 104
Dämpfer nach und nach abnehmen, 406
Dämpfer nehmen, 104
Dämpfer weg, 104
Dämpfung ab, 165
Damp [muffle] instantly, 163
Dans la coulisse, 75
Dans les quatres cordes . . . , 381
Dans le style jazz, 150
Dans le style "Pianola," 243
Dans un chapeau, 110
Dark tone, 150
Das Fell mit dem Daumen streifen, 213

Das Instrument rückwärts haltend, 572
D [E♭] Clarinet, 6, 15, 32–4
D corda, 562
D [Ré] corde, 562
Definitive Ranges, 11–28
De la pointe (de l'archet), 307
Demi-sourdine, 111
Den Bogen auf- und abwallen lassen, 581
Den Bogen rückwärts halten, 572
Den Schlägel beiseite legen, 232
Den Ton forcieren, 151
De pleine gorge, 149
Derrière la scène, 75
Descendez le La un demi-ton plus bas, 573
Descendre le Ut♯ au Ut♮, 233
Détaché (à la corde), 42, 278, 283, 354
Détaché bowing, x, xviii, 283–7
Detached (on the string), 283, 354
Détaché trill or interval, xviii, 279, 354
Détimbrée(s), 209
Deux [2] exécutants, 172, 211
Deux pédales, 243
Deux, si nécessaire (ad lib.), 179
Deux [2] Violons (etc.) seuls, 491
Dicker Paukenschlägel, 167
Dicker Schlägel, 167
Die andere Hälfte, 455
Die andere Pulte, 581
Die Becken an der grossen Trommel anzuhängend, 182
Die dritte Fl. wechselt . . . , 83
Die dritte Kl. in B nimmt Es-Klar., 83
Die erste [I.] Hälfte, 455
Die erste [1] Hälfte mit Dämpfer . . . , 403
Die I. Spieler, 455
Die ersten 3 [4; 5; 6, etc.] Pulte, 491
Die erste u. zweite Pulte, 491
Die G-Saite werden auf Fis hinab-gestimmt, 573
Die Hälfte, 455
Die öffene Saite (D) reissen und dann E . . . , 578
Die Saite kneipen, 271
Die Saite leicht berühren, 581
Die Saiten mit Hammern . . . , 243
Die Saite schnappen lassen, 332
Dietro il ponticello, 381
Dietro la scena, 75
Die übrigen, 581
Die zwei [2] ersten Pulte, 491
Die 2 Fl. nehmen kl. Fl., 83
Die zweite [II.] Hälfte, 455
Die 2. Spieler, 455
Different tone for each desk, 581
Div. a 2; [a due], 455
Div. a 3, 455

Div. en 2, 455
Div. en 3, 455
Div.—½ arco—½ pizz., 337
Div.—I mit Bog.—II Pizz., 337
Divide(d), 455
Divided in three equal parts, 455
Divide in four [4], 467
Divide in three [3], 455
Divide in two [2], 455
Div. in 2, 455
Div. in 3, 455
Divisé, 455
Divisé en deux [2], 455
Divisé en [par] 4, 467
Divisé en [par] 3, 455
Divisés à 4 Parties, 467
Divisés à 3 Parties, 455
Divisés en 3 parties égales, 455
Divisés par pupitres, 581
Divisi, 280, 455
Divisi a 5, xviii, 473–4
Divisi a 10, xviii, 476
Divisi a 12, xviii, 476
Divisi a due [2], 455
Divisi al leggi, 581
Divisi a 9, xviii, 475
Divisi a 8, xviii, 475
Divisi a quatro [4], xviii, 467–73
Divisi a 6, xviii, 474
Divisi a 7, xviii, 475
Divisi a tre [3], xviii, 455–66
Divisi a tre parti uguali, 455
Divisi a 11, xviii, 476
Divisi by desks, 581
Divisi in due parti, 455
Divisi in IV parte, 467
Divisi in quatro [4] parti, 467
Divisi in III parti, 455
Divisi in tre [3] parti, 455
Divisi 3 parti, 455
Div.—1ères archet—2mes pizz., 337
Div.—1o arco—2o pizz., 337
Do [C; Ut] corde, 561
Donnermaschine, 9
Do not roll, 264
Don't damp(en), 233
Doppelgriff, 581
Doppeltdämpfer, 104
Doppia corda, 581
Doppio sordino, 104
Double-bass(es), 10
Double Bassoon, 7
Double corde, 581
Double harmonics—Harp, xvii, 250, 259
    Strings, 437–40
Double mailloche, 167
Double mute(s), 104–5
Double sourdine, 104
Double stick, 167, 172
Double-stop, 581

Double-stopped unisons, xviii, 281, 537–41
Double-tonguing—Brasses, xvi, 91
    Woodwinds, xv, 40, 56–9
Down bow(s), 279, 313–17
Downward [reverse] arpeggio, 572
Drag with wire-brush, 200
Drahtbürste, 167
Draw a bow across sharp edge . . . , 179
Drawn [or tapped] with the bow stick, 372
Dreifach get(h)eilt, 455
Drums, xvii, 7–9, 158, 196–212, 232
Drumstick(s), 166, 175, 185, 202, 229
Dry, 82, 163, 264
D-Saite, 562
D string, 562
D Trumpet, 33
Du bout de l'archet, 307
Due, anche se necessario (ad lib), 179
Due [2] esecutori [suonatori], 172, 211
Due pedali, 243
Due [2] Piatti, 181
Due [2] piatti al [nel] modo ordinario, 181
Due [2] suonatori [esecutori], 172, 211
Due [2] Violini [Viole, etc.] solamente, 491
Dulcimer, 9
Du [au] milieu de l'archet, 311
Dumpf, 165
Dunkler Ton, 150
Dünner Metallschlägel, 167
Dünne Ruten, 167
Durch Reibung an der Kante . . . , 219
Du talon, 305

Écho [Echo], 76, 109
Echo Sounds, xvi, 91, 109
Echoton, 76, 109
Echotonartig, 109
Echo-tone(s), xv, 41, 76, 109
Eco, 76, 109
E corda, 564
E [Mi] corde, 564
Écrasez avec un maillet . . . , 226
Effet, 273, 409
Effleurez [glissez] avec un balai métallique, 200
Effleurez [tintez] les cliquetis, 214
E♭ [D] Clarinet, 6, 15, 32–4
Ein Becken mit dem Holzschaft . . . , 184
Ein Beckenteller mit Paukenschlägel, 232
Eine Drahtbürste . . . halten, 194
Einer allein, 477
Eine [1] Spieler, 455

Einfach, 455
Ein Schlägel um Fell . . . , 198
Ein Stück Papier . . . , 271
Einzelne gestopfte Töne . . . , 112
Eisenschlägel, 166
Employez une planche longue . . . , 243
En arrière du chevalet, 381
Enclume, 9
En cuivrant, 112
En 2, 455
End of (the) bow, 307
En écho, 109
En effleurant la corde, 581
En frappant la table . . . , 331
Engl. Hn. nimmt Ob. 2 [Ob. II], 83
Englisch(es) Horn, 6
English Horn, ix, xv, 6, 14, 30–4, 40, 48–9, 58–9, 61–2, 64, 66–71, 73–5, 82–3
English horn harmonics, 40, 74
En glissant, 68, 251
En glissant le doigt, 542
Enharmonics, xvii, 250, 262–3, 281
En harmonique en se servant . . . , 74
En harmoniques, 41, 257
En jetant l'archet, 300
En l'air, 183
En laissant flotter l'archet, 581
En l'effleurant du doigt . . . , 550
Enlevez la (les) sourdine(s), 104
En 4, 467
En Ré majeur, 273
En tenant l'instrument renversé, 572
En 3, 455
"Eolian tremolo," 250
Eoliphone [Machine à vent], 9, 32
Erste [I] Pult, 491
Erste Pult solo, 491
Erste Violine(n), 10
E-Saite, 564
Esecutato sulla cassa . . . , 232
E string, 564
Étouffé(s) [étouffez], 163, 268
Étouffez à demi, et tout à fait, 195
Étouffez avec les doigts, 194
Étouffez les cordes avec la paume . . . , 242
Étouffez (le son), 163
Étouffez les tons . . . , 220
Even desks, 455
Evitare la corda aperta La [Do, etc.], 581
Évitez la corde La . . . , 581
Evolution of the Modern Symphony Orchestra, xv, 4, 29–34
Exécuté avec une archet . . . , 179
Extreme or Extended Ranges—
   Brasses, xvi, 90, 92–103
   Timpani, xiv, 158–61
   Woodwinds, xv, 40, 43–55

Fagott(e), 6
Fagotto(i), 6
Faire vibrer le son, 77, 147, 334
Faites claquer la corde, 332
Faites doucement vibrer, 273
Faites vibrer en frottant au bord, 219
Fallendes Arpeggio, 572
Fa risaltare il suono, 334
Fast gleitend zwichen den Noten, 150
Fast trem., 347
Fate scappiero la corda, 332
Fa vibrare il suono, 77
Felt [or soft] hat(s) over bell(s), 110
Felt stick(s), 166–7, 185, 202, 222
Felt timpani stick(s), 166, 203
Female chorus, 33
Ferro del Triangolo, 167
Fest in Stoff gewickelt . . . , 220
F Horn, 19
Fiberdämpfer, 104
Fibre mute(s), 90, 104, 106
Field drum, 8
Filz Paukenschlägel, 166
Filzschlägel, 166
Fingerboard, 394
Finger Cymbals, 8
Finger tremolo, xviii, 279, 354–6
First [1st] halves (only), 455
Fist, 214
Flageolett, 41, 74, 225, 242, 257, 273
Flageolett auf der A-[C; D; E; G] Saite, 408
Flageolett: Klang, 273
Flageolett: Klingt wie angegeben [notieren], 273
Flageolett: Nicht eine Oktave höher, 273
"Flam" stroke, 198
"Flare," xvi, 91, 146
Flasche zerbrechen!, 225
Flatterzunge, 63
Flautando [Flautato], 394
Flauto basso, 6
Flauto contralto, 6
Flauto(i), 6
Flauto in Sol, 6
Flautone, 6
Flauto piccolo, 6
Fl. II° muta in Picc., 83
Fl. 2 riprenda l'Ottavino, 83
Flexatone, 227
Flick [brush] the jingles, 214
Flicorni, 145
Fl. 2 [II] take Picc., 83
Flûte Alto, 6
Flûte Basse, 6
Flûte en Sol, 6
Flute harmonics, 40, 74
Flute in G, 6
Flute-like, 394

Flute(s), xv, 6, 13, 29–34, 40, 44–6, 56–71, 74–5, 77, 80, 82–3
Flutter [Flutter-tongue], 63
Flutter-tonguing—Brasses, ix, xvi, 91, 130–2
   Woodwinds, xv, 40, 42, 63–7
"Flux," 250
Fouet, 9
Fracassate con uno maglio . . . , 226
Fracassate la bottiglia!, 225
Frappé avec l'archet, 304
Frappée à l'ordinaire, 181
Frappée avec la triangle, 183
Frappée avec le bois, 184, 200
Frappée(s) [Frapper(ez)], 215
Frappées, comme à l'ordinaire, 163
Frappez à la manière ordinaire, 163
Frappez avec l'envers . . . , 195
Frappez avec les maracas, 172
Frappez en laissant vibrer, 233
Frappez légèrement avec l'archet . . . , 579
Frappez légèrement sur le côté supérieur . . . , 580
Frappez les cordes avec des baguettes . . . , 243
Frappez sur la timbale de cuivre, 164
Frappez sur le cercle . . . , 164
Frappez sur le genou, 214
Fregate con uno guanto . . . , 211
Fregato in circola . . . , 164
Frog (of bow), 305
Frôlé, 181, 197
Frôlée(s) [Frôlez], 183
Frôlées [frottées] l'une contre l'autre, 183
Frôlez dans un arc . . . , 164
Frôlez la membrane . . . , 213
Frottée(s) [Frottez], 183
Frottez avec un gant . . . , 211
Frulato, 63
Frusta, 9
Full bow on each note, 310
Full bow(s), xviii, 279, 310
Full length of bow, 310
Full organ, 237, 241
Full-throated, 149
Fünfsaitiger Kontrabass, 581

Ganze Bogen(länge), 310
Ganzton Triller, 133
G corda, 565
G [Sol] corde, 565
Gedämpft, 104, 165, 194, 268
Gedämpft, ein antikes Cornett nachahmend, 150
Gedämpft mit einem Seidentuch überdeckt, 174
Gedämpft—Offen, 122
Gegen das Pult, 110
Gekratzt und geschlagen, 221

Gemessener Gliss. . . . , 550
Gently vibrate (the string), 273
Gerade Pulte, 455
Gestimmt E in D, 573
Gestimmt G in A, 573
Gestopft, 112
Gestopft — +, 117
Gestopft, ein Horn nachahmend, 121
Gestopfter Ton, 112
Gestopft—Offen, 122
Gestossen, 354
Gestrichen, 283
Geteilt in 3 Partieren, 455
Geteilt in 4 Partieren, 467
Get(h)eilt, 455
Gettando l'arco, 300
Gettato, 300
Gewöhnlich, 72, 165, 181, 199, 257, 266, 372, 381, 394
Gewöhnlicher Klöpper [Schlägel], 166
Gewöhnlicher schlagen, 163
Gezogen, 288
Ginger-ale bottle, 224
Gis nach H stimmen, 233
Gitarre, 9
Glass Plates, 226
(Glass) smashed with a mallet . . . , 226
Gleich [Schnell] abdämpfen, 163
Gleitend über die Holzkasten, 225
Gli altri, 581
Gli altri leggi, 581
Glide (the) full bow, 310
Gliss.—anche alto che possible; strappate!, 553
Glissando across the resonators, 158, 179
Glissando across (wood) blocks, 225
Glissando—A moll, 273
Glissando auf den Flageolett, 550
Glissando auf den Saiten, 241
Glissando auf den schwarzen [weissen] Tastatur, 238
Glissando auf der Saite mit dem Nagel . . . , 225
Glissando auf einer Saite, 542
Glissando avec le levier, 165, 271
Glissando—C dur, 273
Glissando, chord—one hand [two hands], xvii, 254–5
Glissando colla pedale, 165, 271
Glissando (col legno), xviii, 280–1, 372
Glissando combinations, xvi, 256
Glissando con una bacchetta . . . , 271
Glissando cromatico, 542
Glissando—gamme de Do majeur, 273
Glissando—gamme de La mineur, 273

Glissando(i)—Brasses, xvi, 91, 137–40
Harp, ix, xvii, 250–6, 273
Keyboard Instruments, xvi, 237–9
Percussion, xiv, 158, 165, 173–4, 179
Strings, x, xviii, 279–81, 542–53
Woodwinds, xv, 40, 68–71
Glissando in armonici, 550
Glissando—in Do maggiore, 273
Glissando in harmonics, xviii, 281, 550–1
Glissando—in La minore, 273
Glissando in one hand, xvii, 250–3
Glissando in two hands, xvii, 250, 253–4
Glissando mit einem . . . Holzschlägel . . . , 271
Glissando mit Pedal, 165, 271
Glissando on one string, 542
Glissando on string with nail . . . , 225
Glissando on (the) black [or white] keys, 238
Glissando on the strings, 241
Glissando over the entire keyboard, 238
Glissando (pizzicati), xviii, 279, 281, 327–8
Glissando pour la Timbale à levier, 165
Glissando rapido circolando . . . , 220
Glissando—scale of A minor, 273
Glissando—scale of C major, 273
Glissando sopra tutte i taste, 238
Glissando sui legni, 225
Glissando sui risonatori, 179
Glissando sulla corda colla unghie . . . , 225
Glissando sulle corde, 241
Glissando sulle taste bianche [nere], 238
Glissando (sul ponticello), xviii, 280–1, 381–2
Glissando (sul tasto), xviii, 280–1, 394–5
Glissando su una sola corda, 542
Glissando to a harmonic, xviii, 281, 551–3
Glissando (tremoli), xviii, 279, 281, 356–7
Glissando über das ganze Griffbrett, 553
Glissando über die ganze Klaviatur, 238
Glissando über die Resonatoren, 179
Glissando with . . . stick, 271
Gliss.—as high as possible; tear off!, 553
Gliss.—aussi haut que possible; arrachez!, 553
Gliss. col uno dita, 542
Glissé(ez), 68, 251

Glisser tout le long de l'archet, 310
Glissez avec la même doigt, 542
Glissez [effleurez] avec un balai métallique, 200
Glissez avec une baguette . . . , 271
Glissez des sons harmoniques, 550
Glissez des touches blanches [noires], 238
Glissez en effleurant la corde . . . , 381
Glissez en La min., 273
Glissez en Ut maj., 273
Glissez lentement, 549
Glissez rapidement avec la baguette . . . , 220
Glissez sur la corde avec l'ongle . . . , 225
Glissez sur les blocs, 225
Glissez sur les cordes, 241
Glissez sur les résonateurs, 179
Glissez sur toutes les touches, 238
Glissez sur une corde, 542
Gliss. lento, 549
Gliss. mesuré . . . , 550
Gliss. misurato . . . , 550
Gliss. mit einem Finger, 542
Gliss. . . . near the bridge, 381
Gliss.—other indications, xviii, 553
Gliss. over entire fingerboard, 553
Gliss.—passando . . . al ponticello, 381
Gliss.—so hoch wie möglich; reissen!, 553
Gliss. sopra tutta la tastiera, 553
Gliss. sur toute la touche, 553
Gliss. über die Saite . . . , 381
Gliss. with same finger, 542
Glocken, 8
Glockengeläute, 8
Glockenspiel, xvi, 8, 22, 32–4, 158, 173–9
Glockenspiel à clavier, 9
G nach Ges herunterstimmen, 573
Gong, xvii, 8, 31–4, 158, 213–20
Gourds [Shakers], 229
Gradually remove mutes, 406
Gramophone Record, 33, 227
Gran arco, 310
Gran cassa, 7
Grande arcata, 310
Grande(s) Flûte(s), 6
Gran ripieno, 241
Grattate le corde . . . , 243
Grattez les cordes . . . , 243
Gr. C. seule (avec Cymb. décrochée), 201
Grelots, 9
Grob (geblasen), 80, 149–50
Grosse Caisse, 7
Grosse caisse à pied avec cymbale, 182
Grosse Flöte(n), 6
Grosse Flöte vorbereiten, 83

Grosse Strich, 310
Grosse Trommel, 7
Grosse Trommelschlägel, 166
Grosse Trommel Stock, 166
Grossier, 150
"Growl," xvi, 91, 146
G-Saite, 565
G-Saite wieder normale Stimmung, 573
G string, 565
Guáchara, 229
Guimbarde, 9
Güiro, 9, 33, 229
Guitar, 9, 158, 225, 227
Guitare, 9
Guitar-like tone, 250
Guitarre [Chitarra], 9
Gummischlägel, 166
Gut stimmen, 232

Halb gedämpft, 111
Halbharte Gummischlägel, 166
Halbton Triller, 133
Halb und ganz dämpfen, 195
Half-hard [or hard] rubber stick(s), 166, 175
Half-mute(d), 111
Half [½] muted—half [½] open, 403
Half of section, 455
Half-stopped, xvi, 120
Hammer(s); [Beater(s); Mallet(s); Stick(s); Striker(s)], 166, 186, 193, 217
Hand drum, 8, 221
Hand im Schalltrichter, 109, 120
Hand in [over] bell, xvi, 109, 120
Hand notes, 120
Hand over [in] bell, 91, 109
Hand-stopped, 91, 120
Hanging cymbal, 8
Hard felt stick(s), 166, 168, 203
Hard leather stick(s), 166, 168
Hard [or half-hard] rubber stick(s), 166, 175
Hard rubber xylophone mallets, 186
Hard stick(s), 166–8, 175, 185–6, 203, 217, 223
Harfe(n), 9
Harmonica [Mouth organ], 9, 227
Harmonic on A[C; D; E; G] string, 408
Harmonics: Actual pitch [sound], 273, 409
Harmonics—Artificial, 280, 441–54
Harmonics: At [real] pitch, 273, 409
Harmonics—Brasses, 149
    Harp, xvii, 250, 257–61, 273
    Keyboard Instruments, 237, 242
    Percussion, 225
    Strings, xviii, 280–1, 408–54
    Woodwinds, xv, 40, 74

Harmonics — combinations — two hands, xvii, 250, 260–1
Harmonics: double—Harp, xvii, 250, 259
    Strings, 437–40
Harmonics (keys pressed down without sounding), 242
Harmonics: major 6th, 427–9
Harmonics: major 3rd, 419–21, 444
Harmonics: minor 3rd, 418, 444
Harmonics—Natural, 280, 408–40
Harmonics: octave, 429–31
Harmonics: perfect 5th, 424–7, 449–50
Harmonics: perfect 4th, 421–4, 444–9
Harmonics: Real [at] pitch, 273
Harmonics: Sound [Sounding where written], 273
Harmonics: Written sounds, 273
Harmonika [Mundharmonika], 9
Harmonique à La [Mi; Ré; Sol; Ut], 407
Harmonique(s), 41, 74, 242, 257, 273
Harmoniques: à l'octave [hauteur] réelle, 273
Harmoniques: Effet, 273
Harmoniques: Sons écrits [réels], 273
Harmonium, 10, 32, 222, 226
Harmon mute(s), 90, 104, 106
Harpeggiert, 322
Harpe(s), 9
Harp notation, 251, 253–7, 259–60, 262, 264, 269, 272, 605–7
Harp(s), ix, xvii, 9, 25, 30–4, 244–73, 278
Harpsichord, 10
Harp terminology, xviⁱ, 250, 273
Hartgummischlägel, 166
Hartkautschukschlägel, 166
Hartlederschlägel, 166
Hat mute(s), 104
Hat(s) over bell(s), xvi, 91, 110
Hautbois, 6
Hautbois d'amour, 6
Hauteur réelle, 273, 409
Heavy mallet [wooden hammer], 166, 186, 223
Heckelphon(e), 6, 33
Heel of bow, 305
Heerdenglocken, 9
Held like a guitar, 325
High trumpets (Clarini), 29
Hinaufziehn, 68
Hinter dem Orchester, 75
Hinter dem Steg (spielen), 221, 381
Hinter der Bühne [Scene], 75
Hinunterziehn, 68
Hissing, 194
(Hit) in center (of head), 164
Hit in middle, 164
Hit [strike] with (the) bow, 304

Hit with triangle, 183
Hoboe(n), 6
[H]Oboe nehmen, 83
Hoch E nach C umstimmen, 233
Hoch gestimmt, 212
Hohl klingend, tonlos, 81
Hold a wire-brush against vibrating cymbal, 194
Hold cymbals together after striking, 194
Hold [press] down keys silently, 242
Hold high, 72
Holding the instrument backwards, 572
Hollow sounding, cracked, without tone (color), 81
Holzbläser, 6
Holzhammer, 166
Holzharmonika, 8
Holzkasten [Holzton, Holztrommel], 9
Holz-Paukenschlägel, 167
Holzschlägel, 167
Holzton [Holzkasten; Holztrommel], 9
Homonyms, xvii, 250, 262–3
Homonyms in one hand, 262
Homonyms in two hands, 262–3
Hörner 1, 2 mit Dämpfer, 152
Hörner 1–4 gedämpft, 152
Horn 1 nimmt Dämpfer, 152
Hörner [Tromp.; Pos.] m.D., 152
Horn (Hörner), 7
Horn(s), xvi, 7, 19, 29–34, 90–5, 106–7, 109–37, 139–45, 147, 149, 152
Horns [Trpts.; Trbns.] muted, 152
Horse-hooves, 229
Hung cymbal, 8
Hung cymbal rolled with timpani sticks, 232
Hut über den Schalltrichter, 110

I 2 Fl. muta in Picc., 83
Il corde col arco naturale, 372
Il I. di ogni leggio, 455
Il sordino "Jazz," 104
Il 3 Fl. alterna con un Picc., 83
Im 1 . . . Positur bleiben, 581
Im Fis moll vorbereiten, 273
Im Jazzstil, 150
Immer noch mit Dämpfer, 581
Immer ungebrochen, 264
Impari leggi, 455
Im Pianolastil, 243
In aria, 183
Incominciate alla punta (d'arco), 579
Incudine, 9
In der Entfernung [Ferne], 75
In der Luft, 183
In der Mitte, 183
In der Mitte des Felles, 164, 198, 221

Indian drum, 231
In distanza, 75
In D major, 273
In ein Hut, 110
In Entfernung aufgesteilt, 75
In F ändern, 152
In felt [or soft] hat(s), 110
In 4, 467
In harmonics, 41, 257, 281, 550–1
In hat(s), 110
In lontananza ed invisibili, 75
In margine, 180, 197
In modo grossolano, 150
(In) modo ordinario, 72, 104, 372
In one hand—Harp glissandi, xvii, 251–3
    Harp homonyms, xvii, 262–3
In Positur bleiben, 581
In soft [or felt] hat(s), 110
In stand, xvi, 91, 110
In stilo jazz, 150
In stilo "Pianola," 243
Instruments à clavier, 9
Instruments à cordes [Cordes], 10
Instruments à vent, 6
Instruments of the Orchestra, 1–34
Interna, 75
Intervals [Chords],xvi,xviii,158,161–3
In the air, 183
In the center [middle], 198
In the distance, 75
In the jazz style, 150
In the middle [center], 198
In 3, 455
In 2, 455
In two hands—Harp glissandi, xvii, 253–4
    Harp homonyms, xvii, 262–3
In uno cappello, 110
In usual manner, 72
Involguto strettamente in tela . . . , 220
In weiter Entfernung, 75
I primi 3 [4; 5; 6, etc.] leggi, 491
Iron stick(s), 166, 186, 217
Isoliert postiert, 75

"Jazz"-dämpfer, 104
Jazz Effects, xvi, 41, 91, 146–8
Jazz mute(s), 104, 106
Je ein Ton von einem Pult, 581
Jeté, 300
Jeu de Timbres, 8
Jeu ordinaire, 372, 381, 394
Jew's Harp, 9. 227
Jingles, 9, 229
Join the other Vlns. [Vlas., etc.], 581
Joué délicatement avec les doigts . . . , 211
Joué sur le cadre . . . , 232
Jouez en arrière du chevalet, 221

Kartondämpfer, 104
Kastagnetten, 8
Keine Dämpfer, 104
Kept in vibration . . . , 219
Ketten, 9
Kettle Drums, 7
Keyboard Instruments, xvii, 9–10, 235–43, 278
Keyboard notation, 238–40, 242, 605–7
Kielflügel, 10
Klang, 273, 409
Klapper [Knarre; Ratsche], 9
K[C]larinette in D[Es], 6
K[C]larinette(n), 6
Klavier, 10
Kl. 3 nimmt B.-Kl., 83
Kleine Flöte, 6
Kleine Fl. vorbereiten, 83
Kleine Militärtrommel, 7
Kleiner Holzschlägel, 166
Kleiner Schlägel, 166
Kleines Stäbchen mit kleinem Schwammkopf, 167
Kleine Trommel, 7
Kleine Trommel Stock, 166
Klimpernd, 333
Klingen lassen, 233
Klingt wie angegeben [notiert], 273, 409
Klöpper, 166
Knarre [Klapper; Ratsche], 9
Knife-blade, 166
K[C]ontrabass(bässe), 10
Kontrabass solo, 477
Kontrafag. nimmt ein drittes Fagott, 83
K[C]ontrafagott, 7
Kurz (gestrichen), 163, 294

La au Mi bas [grave], 233
L'accent (>) indique le coup . . . , 214
La corde [A corda], 559
La 2ᵉ moitié, 455
La 2ᵉ prend la Pᵗᵉ [le Cor Ang.], 83
Laid horizontal—without resonance, 219
Laid on side, 198
Laisser mourir le son, 233
Laissez la baguette, 232
Laissez vibrer, 233, 334
Laissez vibrer doucement . . . , 232
L'Alto [le Violon] sous le bras . . . , 325
L'altra metà, 455
Lama di coltello, 166
La main dans le pavillon, 109, 120
La mano nella campana, 109, 120
Lame d'un canif, 166
La metà, 455
La moitié, 455
Lange Bogen, 310

Lang gestrichen, 288
Lang gezogen, 310
Langsam Gliss., 549
Langsam vibrierend, 179, 578
La Pᵗᵉ Fl. reprend la Gᵈᵉ Fl., 83
La I. corde (Mi) accordée en Ré, 573
La Iᵉʳᵉ Cor met la sourdine, 152
La 1ʳᵉ moitié, 455
La première [Iᵉʳᵉ] moitié avec sourd . . . , 403
La prima [1ᵃ] metà con sord. . . . , 403
L'archet bien à la corde, 288
L'archet de [en] toute sa longueur, 310
Large bottle filled with marbles, 229
Large Gourds, 228
Lasciare la bacchetta, 232
Lasciar estinguere, 233
Lasciare vibrare, 233
Lascia svanire, 233
Lasciate cadre sul palco, 220
Lasciate ondeggiare l'arco, 581
Lasciate vibrare leggieramente . . 232
Lasci spegnere, 233
La sourdine "Jazz," 104
Last desk only, 581
La 3ᵉ change avec la Pᵗᵉ, 83
La 3ᵉ change en Cl. basse, 83
La 3ᵉ Cl. en Si♭ prend . . . , 83
La III. corde (Sol) accordée en La, 573
"Laughing," 148
La Ut♯ au Ut♮, 233
L'autre moitié, 455
Lay 1 stick on head of drum . . . , 198
Leather stick(s), 166, 186, 223
Le Cᵇᵒⁿ prend le 3 Bᵒⁿ, 83
Le Cor Ang. prendra le 2ᵈ Hᵗᵇ, 83
Le coup frappé avec le genou, 214
Lederschlägel, 166
Left-hand pizzicato, xviii, 279, 328–9
Legato [Ligato], 288
Legato bowing, xviii, 278, 288
Legno [Casse di legno], 9
Leicht berühren, 181, 197, 232
Leichter Schlägel, 166
Leicht vibrieren lassen . . . , 232
Les autres pupitres, 581
Les chefs des pupitres, 455
Les deux [2] cymbales [plateaux], 181
Les 2 Gᵈᵉˢ Fls. prennent la Pᵗᵉ Fl., 83
Les 2 plateaux [cymbales], 181
Le signe + indique le pizz . . . , 328
Le signe + veut dire pizz. . . . , 328
Les notes marquées + pizz. . . . , 328
Les notes marquées + seront jouées . . . , 328
Le Solo Vᵒⁿ avec les autres, 581
Les pavillons en l'air, 72
Les portamenti indiquées par . . . , 68
Les 1ʳᵉˢ (seules), 455
(Les) Pupitres impairs [pairs], 455

Les 4 Cors avec sourdines, 152
Les V^ons . . . enlèveront leurs sourds. . . . , 406
Let drop on the floor, 220
Le trille (tr.) indique le pouce, 213
Let ring [sound; vibrate], 233
Let sound [tone] die away, 233
Let string snap, 332
Let string strike fingerboard, 332
Let the bow undulate, 581
Let tone [sound] die away, 233
Let vibrate [ring; sound], 233, 334
Let vibrate gently . . . , 232
Levano successivamente i sordini, 406
Levare la sordina [sourdine], 104
Levato, 72
Le Violon [l'Alto] sous le bras . . . , 325
L.h. near soundingboard . . . , 271
L.H. Resonanztisch . . . , 271
Ligato [legato], 288
Lightly rubbed, 181, 197
Lightly touching the string, 581
Light stick(s), 166, 176
Like a bell, 149
Like a bird-call, 80
Like a cannon, 211
Like a guitar, 81, 266
Like a harp, 242
Like an accordion, 580
Like a trumpet, 80, 81
Like pizzicato, 81, 151
Like screaming, 149
Like staccato—panting, 151
Linke Hand, 328
L'instrument en guitare, 325
Lion roar [String Drum], 9, 230
"Lip slur," xvi, 146
Loco, 72, 112, 372
Lointain, 75
Long bow(s), 310
Long Drum, 8
Lontano, 75
Loosen snares, 209
Löwengebrüll, 9
Lower A (string) to G♯, 573
Lower C♯ to C♮, 233
Lower C (string) to B, 573
Lower G (string) to G♭, 573
Lower G to F♯, 573
Lower the bell(s), 72
Low on strings, 250, 266
Low (slow vibrato), 179
L'Ut monte au Ut♯, 233

Macchina a venti, 9
Macchina di tuono, 9
Machine à tonnerre, 9
Machine à vent [Eoliphone], 9
Maglio, 166

Mailloche de Grosse Caisse, 166
Mailloche(s) [Tampon(s)], 166
Mailloche [baguette] sur Cymbale, 232
Main gauche [m.g.], 328
Major 6th (Harmonics), 427–9
Major 3rd (Harmonics)), 419–21, 444
Major [or minor] trill, 133
Mal accordé, 211
Male chorus, 30, 32
Mallet(s) [Beater(s); Hammer(s); Stick(s); Striker(s)], 166
Mandoline, 9, 32, 227
Mandolino, 9
Mano sinistra [m.s.], 328
Mantenuto in vibrazione . . . , 219
Maracas [Boite à clous], 9, 158, 229
Marache, 9
Marcato, 291
Marcato bowing, xviii, 278, 291–4
Marimba, xvi, 9, 158, 173–9
Marked, 291
Markiert (gestrichen), 291
Marteau, 166
Martelé bowing, xviii, 278, 291–4
Martelé(er), 278, 291
Martellato, 291
Martello, 291
Mazza della Gran cassa, 166
Mazza(e), 166
Mazzetta(e), 166
Measured glissando, xviii, 281, 549–50
Measured gliss. in quarter tones, 550
Measured tremolo, xviii, 279, 357–60
Medium hard felt [or leather] stick(s), 166, 203
Medium hard stick(s), 166, 168
Medium soft felt stick(s), 166, 168
Messerklinge, 166
Metal Block, 9
Metalldämpfer, 104
Metallkasten, 9
Metallschlägel, 166
Metallstäbchen, 167
Metal mute(s), 104, 106
Metal stick(s), 166, 176, 186
Methods of Playing or Striking—
  Drums, xvii, 158, 196–201
  Cymbals, xvii, 158, 180–4
  Gong, Tambourine & Triangle, xvii, 158, 213–16
  Other Percussion, xvii, 158, 221–2
  Timpani, xvi, 158, 163–4
Mette il [la] sordino[a], 104
Mettent la sourdine, 104
Mettere sordino, 104
Mettere sulla tamburo militare, 220
Mettete i sordini, 104
Mettete le sordine uno dopo l'altro, 405

Mettete una bacchetta sulla membrana . . . , 198
Mettete un frammento di carto . . . , 271
Mettez la (les) sourdine(s), 104
Mettez les sourdines une à une, 405
Mettez progressivement les sourdines, 405
Mettez sur la caisse claire, 220
Mettez un mouchoir sur la peau, 211
Mettez un papier . . . , 271
Mettez un papier sur la peau, 212
Mettono le sordine, 104
Mettre sourdine(s), 104
Mezzo-soprano(i), 10
Mezzo-sordino, 111
M.g. près de la table . . . , 271
Mi[E] corde, 564
Middle of (the) bow, xviii, 279, 311
Military Drum, 7
Minor 3rd (Harmonics), 418, 444
Minor [or major] trill, 133
Miscellaneous effects—Brasses, xvi, 91, 149–51
  Harp, xvii, 250, 271–2
  Strings, xix, 282, 578–80
  Woodwinds, xv, 41, 80–2
Miscellaneous terminology, 41, 83, 91, 152, 158, 232–3, 237, 273, 282, 581
Mit aufgehobenem Schalltrichter, 72
Mit (aufgeworfenem) springendem Bogen, 300
Mit auf H herabgestimmen C-Saite, 573
Mit aufwärts gerichteten Schalltrichter, 72
Mit Bogen, 322
Mit breitem Strich, 310
Mit Dämpfer [Sordinen], 79, 104
Mit Dämpfer — +, 119
Mit Dämpfer—Gestopft, 118
Mit Dämpfer—Gestopft — +, 120
Mit Dämpfer, nicht gestopft, 111
Mit dem Bogen auf der scharfen Kante . . . , 179
Mit dem Bogen auf die Rückseite . . . , 579
Mit dem Bogen geschlagen, 304
Mit dem Daumen, 333
Mit dem Daumen (über das Fell), 213
Mit dem dicken Ende . . . , 184
Mit dem dünnen Ende . . . , 184
Mit dem Finger gleiten, 542
Mit dem Fuss, 201
Mit dem Hand schlagen . . . , 331
Mit dem Holz zu Streichen, 372
Mit dem Knie, 214
Mit dem Knöcheln, 216
Mit dem Nagel, 164, 272, 330
Mit dem Nagel Pizzicato, 242

Mit dem Rücken einer Säge . . . , 195
Mit dem Stiel des Klöppels, 184, 200, 222
Mit dem Triangel geschlagen, 183
Mit den andern Viol. [Br.], etc.], 581
Mit den Fingern, 215
Mit den Fingern gedämpft, 194
Mit den Fingern Pizzicato, 221
Mit (den) Teller(n), 181
Mit der Faust, 214
Mit der ganzen länge des Bogens, 310
Mit der hand, 109, 120, 184, 215
Mit (der) Schlägel, 232
Mit der unteren Note trillern, 133
Mit Drahtbürste nah dem Rand . . . , 164
Mit dünnen Filzstück . . . , 212
Mit einem Drahtbürste gleiten, 200
Mit einem harzigen Handschuh . . . , 211
Mit einem Holzstäbchen . . . , 232
Mit einem Papier . . . , 212
Mit einem Seidentuch . . . , 174
Mit einem Stock (leicht) berühren, 181, 233
Mit einem Taschentuch . . . , 211
Mit einer Drahtbürste . . . , 164
Mit einer Nadel stecken, 226
Mit einer Silbermünze . . . , 181
Mit Finger auf der Oberseite . . . , 580
Mit Fingerspitzen, 200
Mit Flageolett, 41, 257
Mit Hammer zerschlagen . . . , 226
Mit Holz geschlagen, 184
Mit liegendem Bogen, 288
Mit Maracas schlagen, 172
Mit Mediator, 272
Mit Münzen trillern, 164
Mit Ruten, 232
Mit Schnarrseite, 210
Mit Sordinen [Dämpfer], 79, 104
Mit Teller(n), 181
Mit weichen Schlägel . . . , 232
Mit Zuhilfenahme der linken Hand, 328
Mit zwei [2] Schlägel, 172
Mit zwei [2] Schlägel auf Becken, 232
Modo ordinario, 104, 112, 165, 181, 199, 266, 381, 394
Modo ordinario and Sul ponticello combined, 393
Möglichst nasal, 81
Monter(ez) l'Ut au Ut♯, 233
Morceau de fil de fer, 166
Mordace, 150
Mordant, 150
Mouth organ [Harmonica], 9
M.s. sulla tavola . . . , 271
Muffled, xvi, xvii, 158, 165, 194, 201, 216, 222, 250, 268
Muffled with a piece of cloth, 174

Muffle [damp] instantly, 163
Muffle notes by holding l.h. against triangle, 220
Muffle off [on], 165
Muffle the strings with the l.h. palm . . . , 242
Multiple Divisi, xviii, 280, 455–76
Mundharmonika [Harmonika], 9
Musical Tumblers, 227
Muta C♯ in C♮, 233
Muta E alta in C, 233
Muta G♯ in B, 233
Muta [mutano] in A [B♭; F, etc.], 83, 152
Muta [mutano] in Clar. [Fl.; Picc., etc.], 83
Muta in F♯ minore, 273
Muta in Re maggiore, 273
Mutano C in C♯, 233
Mutano [muta] in A [B♭; F, etc.], 83, 152
Mutano [muta] in Fl. [Cl.; Picc., etc.], 83
Muta Iᵃ corda (E) in D, 573
Muta IIIᵃ corda (G) in A, 573
Muted, xv–xviii, 41, 79, 104, 158, 194, 216, 222, 280, 403–7
Muted— – +, xvi, 119
Muted [Stopped] and Open combined, xvi, xviii, 121, 403–5
Muted—brassy, xvi, 118
Muted—brassy – +, 120
Muted effects, 91, 109–11
Muted, in imitation of an antique cornet, 150
Muted: one player grasps tubes . . . , 174
Muted—Open, 122
Muted, without stopping, 111
Mute in stand, 110
Mutes—Brasses, xvi, 90–1, 104–11
Percussion, xvii, 165, 194, 201, 216, 222
Strings, xviii, 280, 403–7
Woodwinds, xv, 79
Mute(s) off [out], 104
Mutes off gradually, xviii, 406–7
Mutes off one by one, 280, 406
Mute(s) on, 104
Mutes on gradually, xviii, 405
Mutes on one by one, 280, 405
Mute(s) out [off], 104
Mute Types, xvi, 90–1, 104–9
Mute with felt crown, 105, 109
Mute with hand, 109
Mute with rubber bushing, 105, 109
Muting, 90–1, 158, 280, 403–7

Nach C (um)stimmen, 233
Nahe zum Steg, wie Trompetten, 579
N'arpéger pas, 264

Nail pizzicato, xviii, 279, 330
Nasaler Ton, 579
Nasal tone, 579
Natural(e), 112, 165
Naturale—Con sordino, 125
Natural Harmonics—Horn, 91, 149
Strings, xviii, 280, 408–40
Naturally, 372
Natural notes, 149
Natural (position), 72, 372, 381, 394
Natural (sounds; tones), 112, 257, 266
Naturel(s), 72, 112, 165, 372
Naturleder Paukenschlägel [Schlägel], 166
Natürlich, 72, 112, 372
Natur Noten (ohne Ventil), 149
Naturtöne, 149
Nearly sliding between the notes, 150
Near soundingboard, 266
Near [on] the bridge, 381
Near the bridge, like trumpets, 579
Near (the) center [middle], 198, 221
Near (the) frog, 305
Near (the) rim, 158, 163
Near the sound-board, 250, 266
Nehmen [nimmt] Dämpfer, 104
Nehmen Klar. in A [B], 83
Nehmen nach und nach die Dämpfer ab, 406
Ne jamais arpéger les accords, 264
Nella scena lontano, 75
Nel mezzo della membrana, 164, 198, 221
Nicht abdämpfen, 233
Nicht arpeggieren [harpeggiert], 264
Nicht brechen [gebrochen], 241, 264
Nicht das leere A [C; D; E; G] nehmen, 581
Nicht eine Oktave höher, 273
Nicht gebrochen [brechen], 264
Nicht get(h)eilt, 455
Nicht glissando, 151
Nicht harpeggiert [arpeggieren], 264
Nicht mit Dämpfer, 104
Nicht sordinirt, 104
Nicht tremolierend, 357, 373
Nicht vibrierend, 80–1, 150, 576
Nimmt (auch) Dämpfer, 104
Nimmt grosse Fl. [kl. Flöte], 83
No glissando, 151
Nomenclature of Instruments, xv, 4, 6–10
No mute(s), 104
Non-armonici, 257
Non arpégé, 241, 264
Non-arpeggiando [arpeggiato; arpeggio], 241, 264
Non-arpeggiato [arpeggiando]—Harp, xvii, 250, 264–5
Keyboard Instruments, 241
Non col legno, 372

Non-divisi, 455
Non-glissando, 151
Non-glissant, 151
Non-legato, 278, 354
Non-marcato, 288
Non-pizzicato(i), 337
Non sordina(e), sordino(i), 104
Non-spiccato, 283, 288
Non-staccato, 283, 288
Non sul pont., 381
Non sul tasto, 394
Non-transposing mute(s), 104, 106
Non-tremolo (col legno),xviii,280,373
Non-tremolo(i), 82
Non-tremolo (sul ponticello), xviii, 280, 389–92
Non-tremolo (sul tasto), xviii, 280, 398–401
Non un'ottava più alta, 273
Non-vibrant, 80, 150, 576
Non-vibrato, 80–1, 150, 576
Normal, 72, 112, 181
Normal bowing, 372
No snares, 209
Not arpeggiated, 241, 264
Note aperte [naturale], 149
Notes naturelles, 149
Not muted, 104
No vibrato, 80, 150, 576
Nur die erste Hälfte der Pulte, 455
Nur die Hälfte, 455
Nur die mit Kontra-C versehenen Bässe, 581
Nur 1, 477
Nur ein [1] Pult, 491
(Nur) Ein [1] Spieler, 477
Nur letztes Pult, 581
Nur mit Schlägel, 233
Nur 2 Pulte, 491
Nur zwei [2] Violinen [Bratschen, etc.], 491

Oboe contralto, 6
Oboe d'amore, 6
Oboe harmonics, 40, 74
Oboe(i), 6
Oboe(n), 6
O[Ho]boe nehmen, 83
Oboe(s), xv, 6, 14, 29–34, 40, 46–8, 57–9, 61–2, 64–75, 78–80, 82–3
Octave (Harmonics), 429–31
Odd desks, 455
Off, 163
Offen, 104, 112
Offen—Gedämpf [Gestopft], 125
Off mutes, 104
Off-Stage—Brasses, xvi, 91, 144–5
   Percussion, xvii, 158, 174, 202, 216, 222
   Strings, xviii, 281, 554
   Woodwinds, xv, 41, 75

Ohne Brechung, 264
Ohne Dämpfer [Sordinen], 104
Ohne Dämpfer − +, 119
Ohne Dämpfer—Gestopft, 119
Ohne Dämpfer—Gestopft − +, 120
Ohne Pedal; Keine Resonanz, 179
Ohne Resonanz—horizontal gelegt, 219
Ohne Schellen, 220
Ohne Schnarrseite, 209
Ohne Sordinen [Dämpfer], 104
On both sides [skins], 198
One [1] player, 158, 161–2, 171, 477
One player at each desk, 455
On harmonics—Col legno, xviii, 280, 372
   Sul ponticello, xviii, 280, 382–3
   Pizzicato, xviii, 279, 330–1
   Sul tasto, xviii, 280, 395
   Tremolo, xviii, 279, 361–3
Only 1st half of desks, 455
Only 1 (player), 477
Only those Basses with low C-string, 581
Only two [2] desks, 491
Only two [2] Violins [Violas, etc.], 491
On one string, 581
On the A [C; D; E; G] string, 559
On the bell [body], 199
On [near] the bridge, 381
On (the) center [dome], 183
On the C string, 561
On the D string, 562
On (the) edge, 180
On [at] (the) edge of (the) skin, 163
On the E string, 564
On [over] the fingerboard, 394
On the four strings . . . , 381
On the frame [hoop], 199, 221
On the G string, 565
On (the) head [skin], 199
On the hoop [frame], 199, 221
On the jingles, 214
On (the) knee, 214
On [at] the nut, 305
On (the) rim (of the drum), 197, 214
On the same string, 581
On (the) shell [wood], 197, 199
On (the) side, 199
On the skin [head], 199, 215
On the skin with thin sticks, 232
On the snares, 232
On the wood [shell], 197, 199
On two [2] strings, 537
Open, 104, 112
Open − +, xvi, 119
Open—Brassy, xvi, 119, 125
Open—brassy − +, 120
Open little by little, 111
Open—Muted, 125

Open—Stopped, xvi, 91, 125–7
Open strings, xix, 279, 281, 555–8
Open tones, 112
Ordinaire(ment), 72
Ordinario, 72, 104, 181
Ordinary, 72
Ordinary [Regular; Usual] beater(s) [hammer(s); mallet(s); stick(s); striker(s)], 166, 168, 186–7, 204, 223
Ordinary glissando, xviii, 281, 542–9
Ordinary Method of Striking, 163
Ordinary mute(s), 105, 107
Ordinary position, 372
Organ, xvii, 10, 29, 32, 237–9, 241
Organo, 10
Orgel, 10
Orgue, 10
Orizzontalmente — senza risonanza, 219
Ôtent la sourd., 104
Ôter[ez] la (les) sourdine(s), 104
Ôtez les sourdines petit à petit, 406
Ôtez les sourdines une à une, 406
Ôtez progressivement les sourdines, 406
Other Effects–Keyboard Instruments, xvii, 241–3
   Percussion, xvi–xvii, 158, 172, 194–5, 211–12, 219–20, 225–6
Other half, 455
Other indications—Brasses, xvi, 111, 120–1
   Strings, xviii, 553
Other Keyed Percussion Instruments, xviii, 226
Other Percussion Instruments, xvii, 158, 221–6
Other Pitched Percussion Instruments, xvii, 158, 226–8
Other Unpitched Percussion Instruments, xvii, 158, 228–31
Ottavino, 6
Ottoni, 7
"Oua-oua," 148
Out of tune . . . , 211
Ouvert—Bouchez, 125
Ouvert—Cuivrez, 125
Ouvert(s), 104, 112
Ouvert(s)—Avec sourdine(s), 125
Ouvert(s)—Bouché(s), 125
Ouvert(s)—Cuivré(s), 125
Ouvrez, 104
Ouvrez peu à peu, 111
Overblown, 40, 91, 112
Over [on] the fingerboard, 394
Overtones, 237

Padded stick(s), 166, 168, 187, 217
Parade Drum, 8
Pari leggi, 455

Partition, 6

Partitur(a), 6

Passate uno scovolo di fil di ferro . . . , 164

Pauken, 7

Paukenschlägel, 167

Paviglione(i) in alto [su], 72

Pavillon en l'air, 72

Pavillon(s) en haut, 72

Pedal glissando(i), xvi, 158, 165, 271

Pedal note [tone], 100

Pedal off; no resonance, 179

Pedal Timpani—glissando, 165

Pedalton, 100

Pedal tone [note], 100

Peitsche, 9

Peitschend, 195

Percuotete col arco al dorso . . . , 579

Percuotete sul lato superiore . . . , 580

Percussion, ix, xvi–xvii, 7–9, 22–4, 29–34, 90, 153–233, 237, 250, 278

Percussione [Batteria; Strumenti a percossa], 7

Percussion notation, 161, 163, 165, 171–3, 178, 181, 183, 214, 605–7

Percussion Terminology, xvii, 158, 232–3

Perfect 5th (Harmonics), 424–7, 449–50

Perfect 4th (Harmonics), 421–4, 444–9

Petite baguette (en bois), 166

Petite caisse claire, 8

Petite Clarinette en Mi♭ [Ré], 6

Petite Flûte, 6

Petite Mailloche [baguette], 166

Petit tambour, 8

Piano(forte), xvii, 10, 32–4, 237–43

Piano harmonics, 242

Piatti a due [2], 181

Piatti (a due; a 2), 8

Piatti ausklingen, 181

Piatto chinoso, 8

Piatto (colpo) colla mazza, 232

Piatto con [contro] piatto, 181

Piatto fissato alla (gran) cassa, 182

Piatto oscillante, 8

Piatto solo, 182

Piatto (sospeso), 8

Piatto sospeso dalla sua lascia, 232

Piatto sospeso (rullo) con bacchetta, 232

Picc. cambia in Fl. gr., 83

Picc. change en 2e Fl., 83

Picc. muta in Fl. 2 [Fl. II], 83

Picc. nehmen gr. Fl., 83

Picc. nimmt zweite Fl., 83

Piccola bacchetta, 166

Piccola bacchetta con la testa di spugna, 167

Piccola bacchetta di legno [metallo], 166–7

Piccolo, xv, 6, 12, 30–4, 40, 43–4, 56–63, 65–7, 69–72, 74, 82–3

Piccolo harmonics, 40, 74

Piccolo takes Fl., 83

Picc. takes 2nd Fl. [Fl. II], 83

Pincer la corde, 271

Pinch the string, 271

Pipe [Anvil; Steel Bar], 9

Piquez avec une épingle, 226

Piston(s), 7

Pitched Percussion Instruments, xvii, 158, 173–9

Pizz. allowing the string to slap the fingerboard, 332

Pizz. and arco at the same time, 578

Pizz.—anreissen, 581

Pizz. auf den Saiten mit einer Gabel—Gliss., 242

Pizz. auf den Saiten mit Fingerspitzen, 242

Pizz. auf einer Saite, 327

Pizz. auf Flageolett, 330

Pizz. avec deux [2] doigts, 336

Pizz. avec les doigts, 221

Pizz. avec l'ongle, 242, 330

Pizz. col due [2] dita, 336

Pizz. colla unghia, 242, 330

Pizz. con il dita, 221

Pizz. ed arco simultaneamente, 578

Pizz.—en arrachant la corde, 581

Pizz. en glissant le doigt, 327

Pizz. et l'archet au même temps, 578

Pizzicando, 333

Pizzicati & Non-Pizzicati combined, xviii, 279, 337–46

Pizzicato glissando, 279, 327–8

Pizzicato(i), ix–x, xviii, 279, 322–46

Pizzicato on the strings with a fork—gliss., 242

Pizzicato—Sul ponticello, xviii, 280, 383–4

Sul tasto, xviii, 280, 395

Pizz. la corda, 271

Pizz. la corda aperta . . . , 578

Pizz. mit dem Nagel, 330

Pizz. mit zwei [2] Fingern, 336

Pizz. on harmonics, xviii, 279, 330

Pizz. on one string, 327

Pizz. on the strings with the fingertips, 242

Pizz.—strappando la corda, 581

Pizz. strisciando il dita, 327

Pizz. sull'armonici, 330

Pizz. sulle corde colla forchetta—gliss., 242

Pizz. sulle corde e sulle punte delle dita, 242

Pizz. sul una corda, 327

Pizz. sur les cordes avec les pointes des doigts, 242

Pizz. sur les cordes avec une fourchette—gliss., 242

Pizz. sur les sons harmoniques, 330

Pizz. sur une corde, 327

Pizz.—tearing the string, 581

Pizz. tremolando, xviii, 333

Pizz. u. Bogen im gleichen Zeit, 578

Pizz. u. mit dem Finger gleiten, 327

Pizz. vibrato, xviii, 334–6

Pizz. with back of fingernail, 242

Pizz. with the fingernail . . . , 330

Pizz. with two [2] fingers, xviii, 279, 336

Place a handkerchief over drum head, 211

Place a piece of paper between the strings, 271

Place a piece of paper on the drum head, 212

Placé à plat, 198

Placé à plat—sans résonance, 219

Placed on snare drum, 220

Place fingers or palm of l.h. on strings, 242

Place mute(s), 104

Played behind the bridge, 221

Played delicately with the fingers . . . , 211

Played on the shell (of the drum) . . . , 232

Pleine orgue, 241

Plucked and stopped, 268

Plucked with the fingertips, 221

Pluck open string (D) . . . , 578

Plunger mute(s), 105, 107

Plüschlägel, 166

Plush stick(s), 166, 187

Poco sul pont., quasi trombe, 579

Pointe (de l'archet), 307

Point (of the bow), 307

Pop bottles, 223, 229

Portamento(i), xviii, 40, 68–71, 281, 551–3

Portando, 68

Portare, 68

Posaune(n), 7

Position naturelle [normale; ordinaire], 72, 199, 372

Posizione ordinaria, 72, 372

Pos. [Hörner; Tromp.] m.D., 152

Posthorn, 145

Pour l'oreille, 409

Poussez le son, 151

Prende il Picc., 83

Prendero Clar. in A [B♭], 83

Prendete l'altro piatto, 232

Prendono Picc., 83

Prenez la baguette [mailloche], 232

Prenez la Clar. in La [Si♭], 83

Prenez la G^de Fl., 83
Prenez la (les) sourdine(s), 104
Prenez la mailloche [baguette], 232
Prenez la P^te Fl., 83
Prenez l'autre Cymbale, 232
Prenez le doigté ½ ton . . . , 109
Prenez le H^tb, 83
Preparare la sordina, 104
Prepare mute(s), 104
Préparez la (les) sourdine(s), 104
Préparez Ut♮, 233
"Près de la table," xvii, 250, 266-7
Près du chevalet, 381
Presque glissant entre les notes, 150
Press [hold] down keys silently, 242
Presso la tavola, 266
Pricked with a pin, 226
Primo [I°; 1°] leggio, 491
Pultweise geteilt, 581
Punta d'arco, xviii, 279, 307-10
Punta d'arco, quasi col legno, 578
Punta dell'arco, 307
Punturato con uno spillo, 226
Pupitres impairs [pairs], 455
Push the sound, 151
Put in F♯ minor, 273
Put on mute(s), 104
Put on mutes gradually [one by one], 405
Put stick aside, 232

Quadruple harmonics, xvii, 250, 260
Quart de tons, 151, 579
Quart de tons aigus, 580
Quarter-hard rubber stick(s), 166, 176
Quarter-tones, 151, 282, 579
Quarter tones sharp, 580
Quarto di toni, 151, 579
Quarto di toni acuti, 580
Quasi arpa, 242, 322
Quasi cannone, 211
Quasi chitarra [guitaro; guitarra], 266, 325
Quasi con sordino, 80
Quasi fisarmonica, 580
Quasi glissando, 150
Quasi guitarra [chitarra], 81, 266, 325
Quasi pizzicato, 81, 151
Quasi staccato—palpitando, 151
Quasi trombe, 80

Raganella [Sistrum], 9
Raise C to C♯, 233
Raise G (string) to G♯, 573
Raise the bell(s), 72
R. and L. pedals, 243
Rand mit Holz geschlagen, 197
Ranges, xv, 4, 11-28, 40, 43-55, 90, 92-103, 158-61
Ranz de [à] vaches, 9
Râpe, 9

Râpé et frappé, 221
Rapid gliss. with triangle stick . . . , 220
Raspato e battuto, 221
Raspe, 9
Rasped and beaten, 221
Raspel, 9
Rasper [Güiro], 9, 221, 229
Ratchet [Rattle], 9, 230
Ratsche [Klapper; Knarre], 9
Rattan stick(s), 166, 176
Rattle [Ratchet], 9, 33
Rawhide (timpani) stick(s), 166, 187, 204
"Ray Robison" mute(s), 105, 108
Réaccordez la IV. corde, 573
Real pitch [sound], 273, 409
Rebounding (bow), 300
Ré[D]corde, 562
Reco-Reco, 221, 229
Regular [Ordinary; Usual] beater(s) [hammer(s); mallet(s); stick(s); striker(s)], 166, 186-7, 204, 223
Regular mute(s), 105, 107
Remettez [remettre] les sourdines, 104
Remove muffle, 165
Remove mute(s), 104
Remove [take off] mutes gradually [one by one], 406
Removes mutes imperceptibly, 406
Reprendre [reprenez] la Grande Flûte, 83
Reprendre l'archet, 322
Reprenez [reprendre] la Grande Flûte, 83
Resonanz(tisch), 266
Rester(ez), 581
Restez I . . . position, 581
Retain hold of edge . . . , 194
Retenez au bord . . . , 194
Retire la (les) sourdine(s), 104
Retune 4th string, 573
Reverse [downward] arpeggio, xix, 281, 572
Reverse bowing, xviii, 279, 311-13
"Riant," 148
Ricochet, 300
"Ridente," 148
"Ride" solo, 212
Rim [R], 197
Rim shot, 200
Rimanete in posizione, 581
Rimanete in I^a . . . posizione, 581
Rimette la IV. corda, 573
"Rip," xvi, 147
Riprende la sordina, 104
Riprendere l'arco, 322
Risonante di piena gola, 149
Rod [Switch], 167, 206
Rohrschlägel, 166

Rohrstäbchen mit Kopf aus Kapok, 166
Roll [tremolo], 158, 322
Roll at center [in middle] (of head), 164
Roll—beginning at center . . . , 212
Roll—beginning at the rim . . . , 212
Roll(ed) with the fingers, 200, 222
Roll(ed) with two [2] sticks, 232
Roll in middle [at center] (of head), 164
Roll on one side with soft sticks, 232
Roll on suspended cymbal with sticks, 232
Roll with sponge sticks, 232
Roman Horns [Flicorni], 145
Roman Trumpets [Buccine], 33, 145
Roulé avec les doigts, 200, 222
Roulée avec des baguettes éponges, 232
Roulée avec deux [2] baguettes, 232
Roulée sur une seul côté . . . , 232
Roulement sur une cymbale . . . , 232
Roulez—commençant au bord . . . , 212
Roulez—commençant au milieu . . . , 212
Roulez en balançant une planche . . . , 243
Rub a rosined glove . . . , 211
Rubbed in a circle with wire-brush, 164
Rubbed together, 183
Rubber (covered) stick(s), 166, 176, 217, 223
Rub head [skin] with thumb, 213
Rugghio di leone, 9
Rührtrommel, 8
Rullato, 63
Rullo col il dita, 200, 222
Rullo colle bacchette di spugna, 232
Rullo con due [2] bacchette, 232
Rullo—dall'orlo . . . , 212
Rullo—dal medio . . . , 212
Rullo sopra uno lato . . . , 232
Rute (Ruthe), 9, 167

Saiteninstrumente [Streicher], 10
Saiten mit der linken Handfläche dämpfen . . . , 242
Saiten mit einer Münze . . . kratzen, 243
Saltando [Saltato], xviii, 279, 300-4
Saltante, 300
Saltarello, 300
Saltato [Saltando], 300
Saltellato, 300
Sämtliche übrige Viol . . . , 455
Sandpaper (blocks), 9, 230
Sandpapierblocke, 9
Sans arpéger, 264

Sans baguette(s), 181
Sans corde(s), 209
Sans pédale; non résonnant, 179
Sans sourdine — +, 119
Sans sourdine—cuivré, 119
Sans sourdine—cuivré — +, 120
Sans sourdine(s), 104, 165
Sans timbre(s), 209
Sans tintements, 220
Sans vibrer, 80-1, 150, 576
Sarrusofone, 7
Sarrusophon(e), 7
Sassofone(i), 6
Sautillé, 300
Saxophon(e), 6
Saxophone(s), 6, 18, 65-7, 69, 71-3,
    77-8, 81
Scacciapensieri, 9
Schalltrichter auf! [hoch], 72
Schalltrichter in die Höhe, 72
Scharf, 150
Scharf abreissen, 268
Scharf gestossen, 294
Schelle, 9
Schellentrommel, 8
Schlägel, 166
Schlägel auf den Becken, 232
Schlägel mit hartem Filz, 166
Schlägel mit Kopf aus Kapok, 167
Schlägel mit viertelhartem Gummi,
    166
Schlägel mit ziemlich hartem Filz
    [Leder], 166
Schlägel mit ziemlich weichen Filz,
    166
Schlagen, 215
Schlaginstrumente [Schlagzeug], 7
Schmetternd, 112
Schnell [gleich] abdämpfen, 163, 268
Schnelles Glissando mit Triangel-
    schlägel . . . , 220
Schnelles Trem., 347
Schriller, scharfer Ton, 80
Schütteln, 215
Schwamm-Paukenschlägel, 167
Schwammschlägel, 167
Schwerer Schlägel, 166
Scordata, 211
Scordatura, xix, 281, 573-5
Score, 6
Scovolo di fil di ferro, 167
Scratch strings lengthwise with a
    coin . . . , 243
Sec(co)—Harp, 264, 268
    Percussion, 163
    Woodwinds, 82
Secoué(er), 215
Secouez, 215
Segno (◌) indica uno pizz. forte . . . ,
    332
Segno per il pizz. . . . , 328

Segno per il suono chiuso, 112
Sehr schwerer Paukenschlägel, 167
Sehr schwerer Schlägel, 167
Sehr weicher Paukenschlägel, 167
Sehr weicher Schlägel, 167
Sempre con sord., 581
Senza arpeggiare, 264
Senza corda(e), 209
Senza pedale; non risonanza, 179
Senza sordina(e) [sordino(i)], 104, 165,
    280
Senza sordini poco a poco, 406
Senza sordino — +, 119
Senza sordino—chiuso, 119
Senza sordino—chiuso — +, 120
Senza sord. leggio a leggio, 406
Senza timbro, 209
Senza tintinnie, 220
Senza vibrato—Brasses, 150
    Strings, xix, 282, 576-7
    Woodwinds, 80
Separate bows, 283
Setz den Dämpfer ab, 104
Seulement à 2 Violons [Altos, etc.],
    491
Seulement le dernier pupitre, 581
Seulement les C. B. avec la C-basse
    corde, 581
Seulement 1ʳᵉ moitié des pupitres,
    455
Shake (hoop), 215
Shakers [Gourds], 229
Short, 163
Short (bows), 294
Short [small] stick(s), 166, 188, 204
Shot, 200
Shrill, pinched tone, 80
Side Drum, 7
Side [snare] drum stick(s), 166
Sifflement, 194
Sign (◌) indicates a strong pizz. . . . ,
    332
Signe (◌) indique un ferme . . . , 332
Signe (◌) indique un pizz. . . . , 332
Signe (◌) = pizz. fort . . . , 332
Signe pour les sons bouchés, 112
Sign for stopped tones, 112
Si lasci vibrare, 233
Si levano i sordini, 104
Silofono, 8
Sine sordino(i), 104
Single harmonics—in either hand,
    xvii, 257-9
Siren, 9, 230
Sirena, 9
Sirène, 9
Sistrum [Raganella], 9
Slack(ened) snares, 209
Slap (a la jazz), 331
"Slap" pizzicato, xviii, 279, 331
Slapstick [Whip], 9, 230

Slap-tongue, xv, 41, 78
Sleighbells, 9, 227
Slide, 68, 251
Slide the finger, 327, 542
Slide [swish] with brush, 200
Slow glissando, xviii, 281, 549-50
Slow vibrato, 578
Small cymbal, 33-4
Small dinner bell, 230
Small Drum(s), 222
Small Flute, 6
Small Hammer, 223
Small Side Drum, 8, 210, 224
Small [short] stick(s), 166, 204
Small wood(en) stick, 166, 168
"Smear," xvi, 91, 147
Smooth (bows), 288
Smorzate, 163
"Snap" pizzicato, xviii, 279, 332-3
Snare Drum, xvii, 7, 31-4, 158, 196-
    212
Snare [side] drum stick(s), 166, 168,
    188, 204, 218, 224
Snare drum sticks, wrapped with
    felt, 204
Snares loose(ned) [slack(ened)], 209
Snares muffled [off], 209
Snares on, 210
Snares slack(ened) [loose(ned)], 209
Soffocato (subito), 163
Soft cardboard mute(s), 105, 108
Soft felt (timpani) stick(s), 166, 167,
    177, 189, 205
Soft [felt] hat(s) over bell(s), 110
Soft (timpani) stick(s), 166-7, 169,
    176-7, 188-9, 205, 218
Soft Wood Hammer, 224
Solamente l'ultimo leggio, 581
Solamente 1ᵃ metà di leggi, 455
Sol [G] corde, 565
Soli Parts, xviii, 280, 491-531
Solo du 1ʳᵉ pupitre, 477
Solo from 1st desk, 477
Solo Parts, xviii, 280, 477-90
Solo per il Iᵒ leggio, 477
Solo Quartet (strings), 299, 316, 416
Solo Quartet (voices), 30
Solo Quintet (string), 346
Solo tone mute(s), 105, 108
Solo voices, 30-2
Solo vom 1. Pult, 477
Soltanto i Bassi colla C-bassa corda,
    581
Soltanto 4, 491
Sonagli, 9
Sonato dietro il ponticello, 221
Son normal, 372
Sonorité aigre, pincée, 80
Sonorité creuse, fêlée, sans timbre, 81
Sonorité grossière, 80, 149
Sons bouchés [cuivrés], 112

Sons d'écho, 109
Sons d'ongles, 272
Son(s) écrits [réels], 273, 409
"Sons étouffés," xvii, 250, 268
Sons harmoniques, 41, 225, 257
Son(s) naturel(s), 104, 112, 257, 266
Son(s) ordinaire(s) [ouvert(s)], 104, 112
Son(s) réels [écrits], 273. 409
Son(s) voilé(s), 109, 165
Sopra, 72
Sopran(e), 10
Soprano(i), 10
Soprano(s), 10
Sordina(e) [sordino(i)], 104–5
Sordinen, 104–5
Sordinen ab! [auf; weg], 104
Sordino di capoc, 104
Sordino di cartone (molle), 104–5
Sordino di metallo, 104
Sordino levare, 104
Sordino mettere, 104
Sostenete le taste tacitamente, 242
Sound, 273
Sounding where written, 273, 409
Sourdine de capoc, 104
Sourdine de métal, 104
Sourdine en carton (doux), 104–5
Sourdine en cuivre, 104
Sourdine oua-oua [Woo-Woo], 105
Sourdine(s), 104–5, 165, 194
Sourdines aux 1ère et 2e Cors, 152
Sourdines aux 3 Trombones [Cors; Tromp.], 152
Sourdine Woo-Woo [oua-oua], 105
Sourds. à tous les pup., 581
Sourds. aux 4 Cors [Tpttes.; Tbnes.], 152
Specific Strings, xix, 281, 559–71
Spiccato, 278, 294–300
Spiccato al talone, 580
Spiccato am Frosch, 580
Spiccato au talon, 580
Spiccato bowing, xviii, 294–300
Spiccato on the nut, 580
Spitze (des Bogens), 307
Spitze des Bogens, wie col legno, 578
Spitzig, 150
Sponge stick(s), 167, 169, 189–90, 205, 218, 224
Sponge timpani stick(s), 167, 205
Springbogen, 300
Springender Bogen, 300
Staccato—Harp, 268
Strings, xviii, 278, 294–300
Staccato bowing, xviii
Stahlschlägel, 167
Stark anblasen, 112
Starkes Portamento, 68
Start on the point (of bow), 579
Stay in 1st . . . position, 581

Stay in position, 581
Steel Bar [Anvil; Pipe; Plate], 9, 223–4, 228
Steel stick(s), 167, 177
Stick on cymbal, 232
Stick(s) with fibre head [knob], 167, 190, 206
Stick(s) [Beater(s); Hammer(s); Mallet(s); Striker(s)], 166, 228
Stick Types xvi-vii, 158, 166–71, 175–7, 184–93, 202–9, 216–19, 222–5
Stierhorn, 9
Still muted, 581
Stimmen die G-Saite auf Gis, 573
Stimmen die G-Saite wie vorher, 573
Stimmt die tiefste Saite nach B, 271
"Stomp the beat," 194
Stop [dampen] half-way, and full, 195
Stop(ped), 268
Stopped — +, xvi, 117
Stopped and Open combined, xvi, 121
Stopped, imitating a horn, 121
Stopped—Open, xvi, 91, 122–4
Stopped or Brassy Tones, xvi, 112–21
Stopped (tones), xvi, 91, 112
Stopped with hand, 120
Stop (quickly), 163
Straight mute(s), 105, 107
Streicher [Saiteninstrumente], 10
Strich für Strich, 283
Strike [struck], 215
Strike in usual manner, 163
Strike on copper kettle (of timpani), 164
Strike on knee, 214
Strike on metal rim around head, 164
Striker(s) [Beater(s); Hammer(s); Mallet(s); Stick(s)], 166
Strike (the) rim, 197
Strike the strings with hard rubber mallets, 243
Strike with back of a saw-blade on cymbal . . . , 195
Strike [hit; struck] with bow, xviii, 279, 304
Strike with the hand, 331
String Drum [Lion roar], 9, 230
String mutes, 280, 403–7
String notation, 283, 288, 291, 294, 300, 311, 313, 318, 322, 325, 327–8, 330, 332–4, 336–7, 347, 350, 354, 356–7, 361, 363, 365, 372, 378–9, 381, 393, 402, 408–9, 411–13, 417–29, 431–9, 441–2, 444, 449–51, 453–4, 532, 534, 537–9, 541–2, 550–1, 555–7, 572–5, 578–80, 605–7
Strings, ix–x, xviii–ix, 10, 26–34, 90, 275–581
String Terminology, xix, 581

Strisciando, 68, 251
Strisciare il dita, 542
Striscia(ta), 68, 251
Strisciate con scovolo di fil di ferro, 200
Stroke(d), 213
Strosciando, 195
Struck [strike], 215
Struck near rim, 163
Struck together, 181
Struck [strike] with bow, 304
Struck with the wood, 184, 200
Strumenti a corde [Archi], 10
Strumenti a fiato [Strumenti di ventro], 6
Strumenti a percossa [Batteria; Percussione], 7
Strumenti di legno, 6
Strumenti di metallo, 7
Strumenti di tasto, 9
Strumenti di ventro [Strumenti a fiato], 6
Strumenti d'ottone, 7
Strum(ming), 333
Stürze hoch [in die Höhe], 72
Sub ponticello, 381
Successive Down-bows, xviii, 313–17
Successive Up-bows, xviii, 318–21
Sul A', 408–9, 411–13, 420–9, 559
Sul bordo, 180, 197
Sul bordo (della membrana), 163, 196
Sul C', 408, 411–13, 418–20, 422–3, 425–6, 428–9, 442, 561
Sul D', 408–9, 411–12, 417–28, 562
Sul due [2] corde, 537
Sul E', 408–9, 413, 420–1, 423–4, 426–9, 564
Sul G', 281, 409, 411–12, 417–29, 442, 565
Sul La [A'], 559
Sulla cassa, 199, 221
Sulla membrana, 199, 215
Sulla cupola, 183
Sulla membrana con bacchette sottile, 232
Sulla Ia [IIa; IIIa; IVa], 559, 561–2, 564–5
Sulla tastiera, 394
Sulla tavola, 266
Sul lato, 198
Sulle corde, 232
Sulle punte delle dita, 200
Sulle quattro corde . . . , 381
Sulle tintinnie, 214
Sull'orlo, 180, 214
Sul mezzo, 183
Sul pont. glissando, xviii, 280, 381–2
Sul Ponticello, ix–x, xviii, 279–80, 381–93
Sul Ponticello & Modo Ordinario combined, xviii, 280, 393

Sul Ponticello—back of the bridge, xviii, 381
Sul pont. non-trem., xviii, 280, 389–92
Sul pont. on harmonics, xviii, 280, 382–3
Sul pont. pizzicato, xviii, 280, 383–4
Sul pont. tremolo, xviii, 384–9
Sul I [II; III; IV], 559, 561–2, 564–5
Sul punta (d'arco), 307
Sul punto del arco, 307
Sul talone, 305
Sul Tasto, x, xviii, 279–80, 394–402
Sul Tasto & Sul Ponticello combined, xviii, 402
Sul tasto glissando, xviii, 280, 394–5
Sul tasto non-tremolo, xviii, 280, 398–401
Sul tasto on harmonics, xviii, 280, 395
Sul tasto pizzicato, xviii, 280, 395
Sul tasto tremolo, xviii, 280, 395–8
Sul una corda, 581
Suonare col arco sul taglio . . . , 179
Suonare ruvido, 80, 149
Suonate tutte le taste . . . , 243
Suono, 273, 409
Suono(i) chiuso(i), 112
Suono(i) flautato(i), 41, 257, 394
Suono tenebroso, 150
Sur deux [2] cordes, 537
Surdinen weg, 104
Sur la caisse, 199, 221
Sur la II [2e] corde, 559
Sur la même corde, 581
Sur la peau, 199, 215
Sur la peau avec des baguettes minces, 232
Sur la 1ère [2e, 3e, 4e] corde, 559, 564
Sur la I. [1ère] corde, 564
Sur la protubérance, 183
Sur la IV. [4e] corde, 561, 565
Sur [vers] la touche, 394
Sur la III. [3e] corde, 562
Sur (le) A [La], 559
Sur le bois, 372
Sur le bois (du Tambour), 197
Sur (le) bord [rebord], 180, 197, 214
Sur le bord (de la membrane [peau]), 163
Sur le cadre, 199
Sur le cercle, 197
Sur [vers] le chevalet, 381
Sur (le) La [A], 559
Sur (le) Mi, 564
Sur (le) Ré, 562
Sur le rebord [bord], 180, 197, 214
Sur (le) Sol, 565
Sur le(s) timbre(s), 232
Sur les tintements, 214
Sur (le) Ut, 561
Sur membrane, 199
Sur tous les deux côtés, 198

Sur une corde, 581
Suspended Cymbal, xvii, 8, 158
Suspended cymbal with stick, 232
Sweep wire-brush across head near rim, 164
Swishing, 195
Swish [slide] with brush, 200
Switch [rod], 167, 206
Switches, 9, 230

Table, 266
Table of Ranges, xv, 4, 11–28
Tabor, 8, 224
Take A [Bb] Clar., 83
Take drumstick, 232
Take Fl. [Oboe; Picc.], 83
Take mute(s), 104
Take off mute(s), 104
Take off [remove] mutes gradually [one by one], 406
Take Picc. [Fl.; Ob.], 83
Take the other cymbal, 232
Talon (de l'archet), 305
Talone, 305
Tambour à corde, 9
Tambour de Basque, 8
Tambourin (de Provence), 8
Tambourine, xvii, 8, 31–4, 158, 213–20
Tambourin Provençal, 8
Tambour (militaire), 7
Tamburello Basco, 8
Tamburin, 8
Tamburino, 8
Tamburo, 7, 8
Tamburo Basco, 8
Tamburo grande, 7
Tamburo grosso, 7
Tamburo (militare), 7
Tamburo piccolo, 8
Tamburo rullante, 8
Tampon de la Grosse Caisse, 166
Tampon(s) [Mailloche(s)], 166
Tam-tam, 8
Tap on the belly (of instrument) with finger, 580
Tapotant, 333
Tapped [or drawn] with (the) bow stick, 372
Tap with bow on back (of instrument), 579
Tarolle, 8, 210, 224
Tastaturlanges Brett . . . , 243
Tasteninstrumente, 9
Tasten stumm niederdrücken, 242
Taxi [Auto] horn, 9, 228
Tbe. [Corni; Trbni.] con sord., 152
Teller mit Schlägel, 232
Tenendo l'instrumento al rovescio, 572
Temple Bells, 228

Temple Blocks, 9, 231
Teneramente, coi quintupolo dita . . . , 211
Tenete i piatti insieme . . . , 194
Tenete l'orlo . . . , 194
Tenete uno scovolo di fil di ferro . . . , 194
Tenez un balai métallique . . . , 194
Tenir (le Tamb. de B.) tout bas au sol . . . , 220
Tenor Drum, ix, xvii, 8, 31–2, 158, 196–212
Tenore(i), 10
Ténor(es), 10
(Tenor)posaune(n), 7
Tenor(s), 10
Tenor (Tenöre), 10
(Tenor) Trombone, 7, 20
Tenortuba, 7
Tenor Tuba, 7, 31, 33
Tenuto, 334
The other desks, 581
The others, 581
The sign + indicates pizz. . . . , 328
The 2 Fls. change to Piccs., 83
Thick stick(s), 167
Thick timpani stick(s), 167, 206
Thin metal [or wood] stick(s), 167, 218
Thin stick(s), 167, 218
Thin stick with sponge head, 167, 206
Thin wood [or metal] stick(s), 167, 218
Thumb pizzicato, xviii, 279, 333
Thumb (trill), 213
Thunder-machine, 9, 33, 231
Thunder-sheet, 9
Tight(en) snares, 210
Timbales, 7
Timbres, 8, 9
Timbre sombre, 150
Timpani [Timpany; Tympany], xvi, 7, 22 29–34, 158–72, 233
Timpani chords, 161–3
Timpanic sounds, 250
Timpani stick(s), 167, 169, 190–2, 206–8, 219, 224
Tinkling "Pianola" style, 243
Tintez [effleurez] les cliquetis, 214
Tip of (the) bow, 307
t k t t k t, 60
To a harmonic, 281, 551–3
To be played on natural harmonics, 149
Toccante leggiermente la corda, 581
Toccata colla bacchetta, 181
Toccata colla moneta d'argenta, 181
Toccato con una bacchetta, 233
Together, 83, 181, 455
Toglie la sordina, 104

Togliere sordino(i), 104
Togliere successivamente le sordine, 406
Tolgono le sordine, 104
Tom-Tom, 158, 221, 223–5, 231
Ton de pédale, 100
Tone-clusters, xvii, 237, 239
Töne durch linke Hand . . . , 220
Tongued, 82
Ton nasillard, 579
Tono cavernoso, senza colore, 81
Tono differente per ogni leggio, 581
Tono di pedale, 100
Tono nasale, 579
Tono squillante e pizzicotto, 80
Touche, 394
Touched with stick, 233
Touchée avec une baguette, 233
Toujours avec sourd., 581
Tous, 455, 581
Tous divisés, 455
Tous divisés en 2 parties égales, 455
Tous les autres, 581
Tous les autres V^{ons} . . . , 455
Tous les deux tons en sons harmoniques, 437
Tous les 1ers [2^{ds}] V^{ons} mettent la sourd. . . . , 581
Toute l'archet sur chaque note, 310
Toutes Contrebasses sauf la 1ère, 581
Toy balloons, 226
Traînez, 68
Trap drum, 8
Tratto, 372
Trbni. [Corni; Tbe.] con sord., 152
Trbns. [Horns; Trpts.] muted, 152
Trem. auf Flageolett, 361
Tremolando(i)—Harp, xvii, 250, 269
  Keyboard Instruments, xvii, 237, 240–1
  Percussion, xvi, 158, 178
  Pizzicati, xviii, 333
  Strings, xviii, 279, 333
Tremoli & Non-tremoli combined, xviii, 279, 365–71
Tremolo auf einem Beckenteller . . . , 195
Trémolo avec la langue, 63
Tremolo (bow), ix–x, xviii, 279, 347–9
Tremolo (bow and finger combined), xviii, 279, 363–4
Tremolo (bow-finger), xviii, 279, 354–6
Tremolo by rocking a board . . . , 243
Tremolo—Col legno, xviii, 280–1, 373
  Sul ponticello, xviii, 280, 384–9
  Sul tasto, xviii, 280, 395–8
Tremolo dendolando un'asse . . . , 243
Trémolo dental, 63
Tremolo durch Holzbrett . . . , 243
Trémolo en roulant la langue, 63
Tremolo (finger), 279, 350–3

Tremolo glissando, xviii, 279, 356–7
Tremolo(i)—Brasses, xvi, 91, 133
  Harp, xvii, 269–70
  Keyboard Instruments, xvii, 237, 240–1
  Percussion, xvi, 158
  Strings, xviii, 279, 347–71, 384–9
  Woodwinds, 63
Tremolo (measured), 279, 357–60
Tremolo misurato, 279, 357
Tremolo on cymbal with a 'cello bow, 195
Tremolo on harmonics, xviii, 279, 361–3
Trémolo roulé, 63
Tremolo sulla piatto . . . , 195
Trémolo sur une cymbale . . . , 195
Trémolo très régulier, 357
Trem. rapido, 347
Trém. serré, 347
Trem. sull'armonici, 361
Trém. sur les sons harmoniques, 361
Très à la corde, 288
Très sec, 163, 268
Très timbrée, 210
Triangel, 8
Triangelschlägel, 167
Triangle, xvii, 8, 30–4, 158, 213–20
Triangle stick, 167, 169, 177, 192, 208, 219, 224
Triangolo, 8
Trill a 2, 183
Trillare al nota di sotto, 133
Trill: broken rumble, 579
Trille, 133, 269
Trill(ed), 133, 183
Trille majeur [mineur], 133
Triller, 133, 269
Triller: gebrochenes Drähnen, 579
Trille: roulement brisé, 579
Triller (zu 2), 183
Trillez avec des pièces d'argent, 164
Trillez avec la note en bas, 133
Trillo, 133, 215, 269
Trillo (a 2), 183
Trillo colle monete, 164
Trillo: interrotto sordo barbugliato, 579
Trillo maggiore [minore], 133
Trill(s)—Brasses, xvi, 91, 133–6
  Harp, xvii, 250, 269
  Percussion, 183
  Strings, xviii, 354
Trill with note below, 133
Trill with pennies [coins], 164
Trill with tongue while playing, 63
Tringle du Triangle, 167
Triple harmonics, xvii, 250, 259
Triple-tonguing—Brasses, xvi, 91, 128–9
  Woodwinds, xv, 40, 60–2

Trocken, 82
Tromba bassa, 7
Tromba(e), 7
Trombe [Cni; Trbni.] con sord, 152
Trombone Basse, 7
Trombone basso, 7
Tromboni [Cni; Tbe.] con sord., 152
Trombone(i) tenore(i), 7
Trombone(s), xvi, 7, 20–1, 29–34, 90–1, 99–101, 105–11, 115, 124, 127, 129, 131–2, 135–6, 138–40, 142–8, 150–2
Trommelstock, 166
Trompete(n), 7
Trompette Basse, 7
Trompette(s), 7
Tromp. [Hörner; Pos.] m.D., 152
Trpts. [Horns; Trbns.] muted, 152
Trumpet(s), xvi, 7, 20, 29–34, 90–1, 95–8, 105–11, 114–15, 117–21, 123–4, 127–32, 134–7, 139–40, 142–48, 150, 152
Tuba, xvi, 7, 21, 30–4, 90, 101–3, 107, 131–2, 135, 139–40, 143, 151
Tuba (bassa; [Basse]), 7
Tuba tenore, 7
Tubes, 8
(Tubular) Chimes, 8
Tuned high, 212
Tune 1st string (E) to D, 573
Tune G♯ to B, 233
Tune G string normally, 573
Tune high E to C, 233
Tune lowest string to B♭, 271
Tune 3rd string (G) to A, 573
Turkish crash, 8
Tutt'e due toni per armonici, 437
Tutti, 455, 581
Tutti a due parti uguali, 455
Tutti divisi, 455
Tutti gli altri [l'altri], 581
Tutti gli altri Vni . . . , 455
Tutti i bassi salvo il 1º, 581
Tutt'i leggi con sord., 581
Tutti l'altri [gli altri], 581
Tutti le altre, 581
Tutti Vln. I [II] mettete i sordini . . . , 581
Tutto l'arco, 310
Two [2] cymbals clashed, 181
Two [2] cymbals (free), 181
Two hands (Harp), 250, 253–5, 260–3
Two-headed stick, 167, 192, 208
Two, if necessary (ad lib.), 179
Two–[2] plate clash [crash], 181
Two [2] plates together, 183
Two [2] players, 30, 33, 158, 162, 171, 211
Two–[2] Timpani roll, 158, 171–2
Two players (on same part), 172
Tympany [Timpani; Timpany], 7

Unbroken, 264
Une cymbale suspendue par sa courroie, 232
Une paire, 181
Une [uno] solo, 477
Ungerade Pulte, 455
Unies, 455
Unison, 83, 455
Unisono(i), 455
Uniti, 455
Unmuted, 104, 280
Uno [une] solo, 477
Un [1] par pupitre, 455
Un ton différent pour chaque pupitre, 581
Unusual tuning, xix, 573
Un voile sur la peau de la timbale, 165
Up bow(s), 279, 318–21
Use a 4 ft. board to play all the keys, 243
Usual [Ordinary; Regular] beater(s) [hammer(s); mallet(s); stick(s); striker(s)], 166, 186–7, 204, 223
Ut♯ change en Ut♮, 233
Ut [C; Do] corde, 561
Ut♮ de Ut♯, 232

Velato, 165
Verges, 9, 167
Verghe(i), 9, 167
Verklingen lassen, 233
Vers la pointe, 307
Vers [sur] la touche, 394
Vers [sur] le chevalet, 381
Verstimmt, 211
Very hard leather sticks, 224
Very hard [or soft] stick(s), 167, 169
Very hard timpani stick(s), 167
Very soft [or hard] sticks, 167
Very soft (timpani) stick(s), 167, 192
Via sordina(e) [sordino(i)], 104
Vibrafono, 9
Vibraharp [Vibraphone], 9, 24, 158, 173–9
Vibrando, 63, 77, 334
Vibrant, 77
Vibraphon(e) [Vibraharp], xvi, 9
Vibrate (the sound), 77, 334
Vibrato—Brasses, xvi, 147
     Percussion, 233
     Strings, xviii, 279, 334–6
     Woodwinds, xv, 41, 77
Vibrato dolce, 273
Vibrato lento, 179, 578
Vibrato linguale, 63
Vibrato (pizzicato) xviii, 334
Vibrer(ez), 77, 334
Vibrez lentement, 179, 578
Vibrierend, 77, 147
Vibrieren lassen, 334

Viel Bogenwechsel, 310
Viel Bogen (wechseln), 310
Vierfach get(h)eilt, 467
Vierteltöne, 151, 579
Vierteltöne hoch, 580
Viola(e), 10
Viola(s), 10, 27, 29–34, 279–581
Viola solo, 477
Violine solo, 477
Violine Solo mit den andern 1ten Viol., 581
Violine Solo von Dreien, 491
Violino(i) I [II], 10
Violinophone, 228
Violin(o) solo, 477
Violino solo a 3, 491
Violino solo col Vni. primo [Io], 581
Violin solo by 3 players, 491
Violin solo with 1st Vlns., 581
Violin(s) I and/or II, 10, 26, 29–34, 279–581
Violoncell(e), 10
Violoncelle(o) solo, 477
Violoncelle(s), 10
Violoncello(i), 10
Violoncello(s), 10, 27, 29–34, 279–581
Violoncell solo, 477
Violone, 10
Violon solo, 477
Violon solo à 3, 491
Voices, 10, 29–33
Voilée avec une pièce de toile, 174
Voilée(s), 165
Voilé(s), 109
Volles Werke, 241

"Wah-wah," xvi, 148
Wah-wah mute(s), 105, 108
Wattierterschlägel, 166
"Wau-wau," 148
Wa-wa [Wah-wah; Wha-wha] mute(s), 90, 105, 108
Wechseln in A [B; F, etc.], 83, 152
Wechseln in D dur, 273
Wechseln in E [A; B, etc.], 152
Weichenfilz Paukenschlägel, 166
Weichenfilzschlägel, 166
Weicher Kartondämpfer, 105
Weicher Paukenschlägel, 166
Weicher Schlägel, 166
Weich vibrierend, 273
Well-tuned, 232
Wha-wha [wa-wa; wah-wah] mute(s), 105, 108
Whip [Slapstick], 9, 230
"Whip," 41, 81
"White" tone, 81
Whole bow(s), 310
Wie eine Fiedel, 578
Wie eine Gitarre, 81, 325
Wie eine Glocke, 149

Wie eine Handharmonika, 580
Wie eine Harfe, 242
Wie eine Kanone, 211
Wie eine Trompete, 80–1
Wie eine Vogelstimme, 80
Wie ein Naturlaut, 149
Wie gedämpft, 80
"Wie Gelächter," 148
Wie pizzicato, 81, 151
Wie schreiend, 149
Wie staccato—keuchend, 151
Wind instruments [Winds], 6–7
Wind-machine, 9, 33, 158, 231
Windmaschine, 9
Winds [Wind instruments], 6–7, 90
Wirbel auf den Beckenteller mit Schlägel, 232
Wirbel mit den Fingern, 200, 222
Wirbel mit den Schwammschlägel, 232
Wirbel mit zwei [2] Schlägel, 232
Wirbel—vom Rand . . . , 212
Wirbel—von der Mitte . . . , 212
Wire-brush [Brush(es)], 167, 169, 192, 208
Wirklicher Ton [Töne], 409
With a thin piece of felt on middle of drum head, 212
With foot-beater [foot-pedal], 201
With full bow, 310
With hair and stick at point . . . , 372
With mute(s), 104
Without jingles, 220
Without mute(s), 104
Without snares, xvii, 209
Without stick, 181
Without vibrato, 80, 150, 576
With plates, 181
With plectrum, 250, 272
With snares, 210
With snares loose(ned) [slack(ened)], 209
With stick(s), 232
With sticks only, 233
With switches, 232
With (the) back of (the) bow, 372
With (the) bow, 322
With the bow held backwards, 572
With the bow—like pizz., 580
With the fingernail(s)—Harp, 250, 272
     Percussion, 164
     Strings, 330
With the fingers [fingertips], 200, 215
With (the) fist, 214
With (the) hand, 109, 184, 215
With (the) handle of (the) stick, 184, 222
With the knee, 214
With (the) knuckles, 216
With (the) nail, 330

With (the) thumb, 213, 333
With thick end of (the) stick, 184
With thin end of (the) stick, 184
With two [2] fingers, xviii, 336
With two [2] sticks, xvi, 158, 172
With two [2] sticks on cymbal, 232
With wooden end of (the) stick, 184
Wood Blocks, 9, 158, 222, 224, 231
Wood-blocs [Blocs de bois], 9
Wooden hammer [heavy mallet], 166, 224
Wooden hammer on a plank, 231
Wood(en) stick(s), 167, 170, 177, 193, 209, 219, 224
Wood(en) timpani stick(s), 167, 171, 193, 209
Wood stick with rubber bands . . . , 193
Woodwind harmonics, 40, 74
Woodwind mutes, 41, 79
Woodwind notation, 56, 60, 63, 68, 74, 605–7
Woodwinds, xv, 6–7, 12–18, 29–83, 90–1, 278

Woodwind Terminology, xv, 41, 83
Wollschlägel, 167
Wool stick(s), 167
"Woo-woo," 148
"Wow," xvi, 148
Wrapped tightly in a cloth . . . , 220
Written sounds, 273

Xocalho, 228
Xy[i]lofono, 8
Xylophon(e), xvi, 8, 23, 32–4, 158, 173–9
Xylophone stick(s), 167, 193
Xylophonschlägel, 167

Zart mit den Fingern gespielt . . . , 211
Zeichen (⌀) bezeichnet ein Pizz. . . . , 332
Zeichen (⌀) = ein starkes Pizz., 332
Zeichen für ein Pizz. . . . , 328

Zeichen für einzelne gestopfte Töne, 112
Ziemlichschwerer Schlägel, 166
Zilafono, 8
Zischend, 194
Zither, 9, 227
Zu 3, 455
Zu 3 gleichen Theilen, 455
Zum Steg, 381
Zungenstosse, 82
Zusammen, 83, 455
Zu 4, 467
Zu 4 Händen, 225, 241
Zu 2, 83, 455
Zwei [2] Becken mit Teller(n), 181
Zweifach geteilt, 455
Zweiköpfige Schlägel, 167
Zwei Pedale, 243
Zwei [2] Schläger, 211
Zwei [2] Spieler, 172
Zweite Ob. nimmt Engl. Hn., 83
Zweite Violine(n), 10
Zwei, wenn nötig (ad lib.), 179
Zymbel, 8

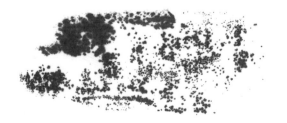